Shojo Beat

Skip·Beat!

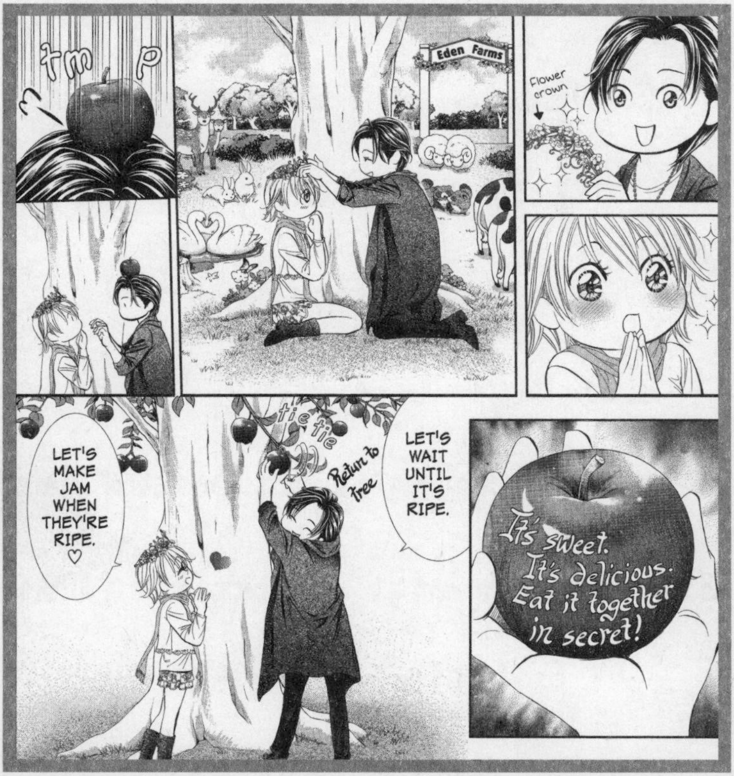
Flower crown
Eden Farms
tmp
It's sweet. It's delicious. Eat it together in secret!
LET'S WAIT UNTIL IT'S RIPE.
tie tie
Return to tree
LET'S MAKE JAM WHEN THEY'RE RIPE. ♡

46

Story & Art by Yoshiki Nakamura

Skip·Beat!
Volume 46

CONTENTS

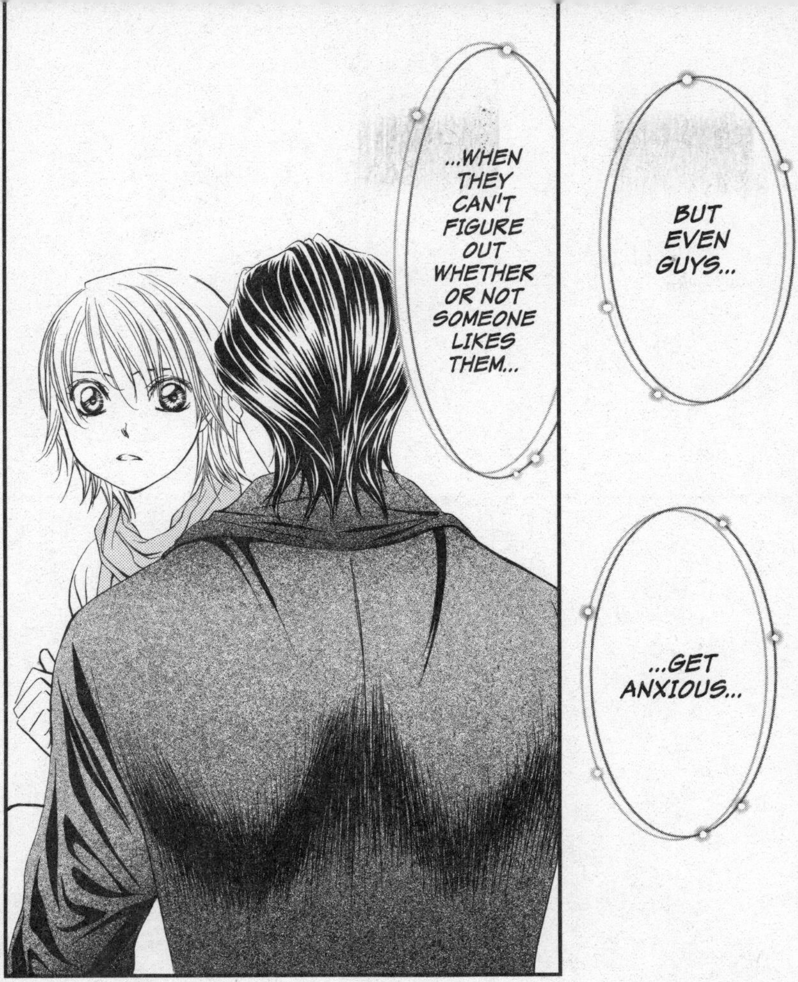
BUT EVEN GUYS...
...WHEN THEY CAN'T FIGURE OUT WHETHER OR NOT SOMEONE LIKES THEM...
...GET ANXIOUS...

Skip·Beat!

Act 280: Calamity's Fierce Assault—Barging onto Noah's Ark

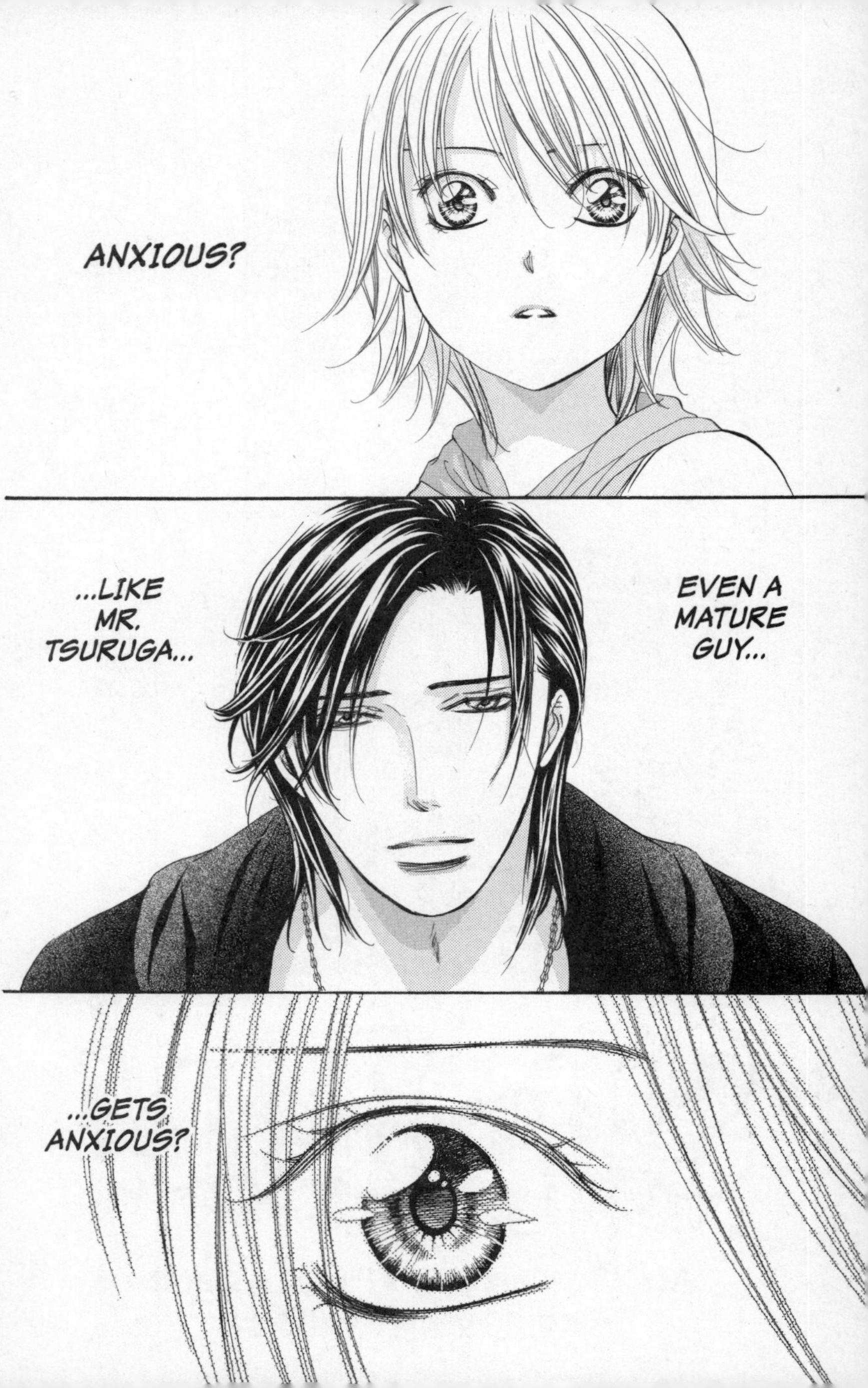
ANXIOUS?
EVEN A MATURE GUY...
...LIKE MR. TSURUGA...
...GETS ANXIOUS?

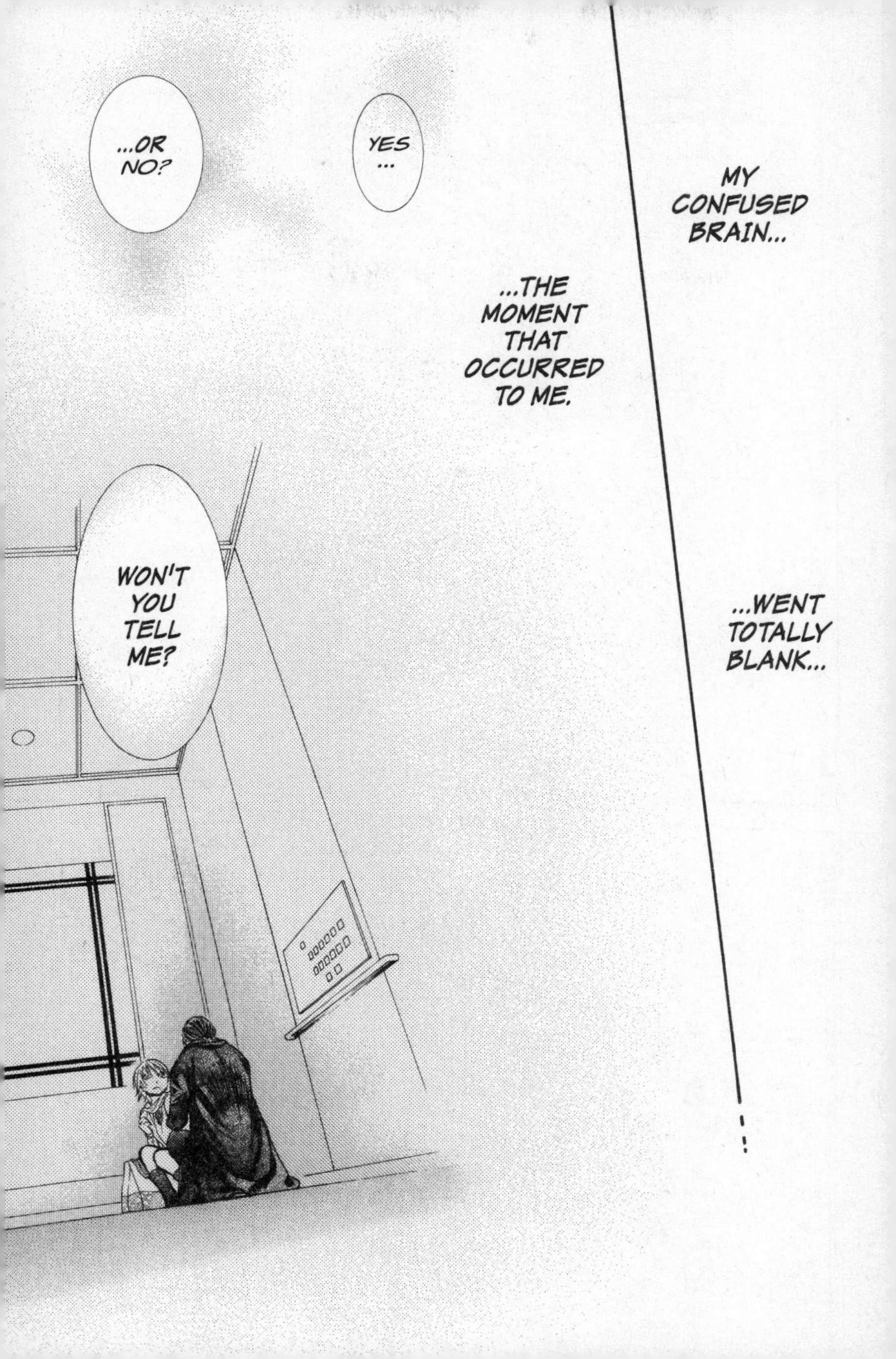
MY CONFUSED BRAIN...
...WENT TOTALLY BLANK...
YES ...
...OR NO?
...THE MOMENT THAT OCCURRED TO ME.
WON'T YOU TELL ME?

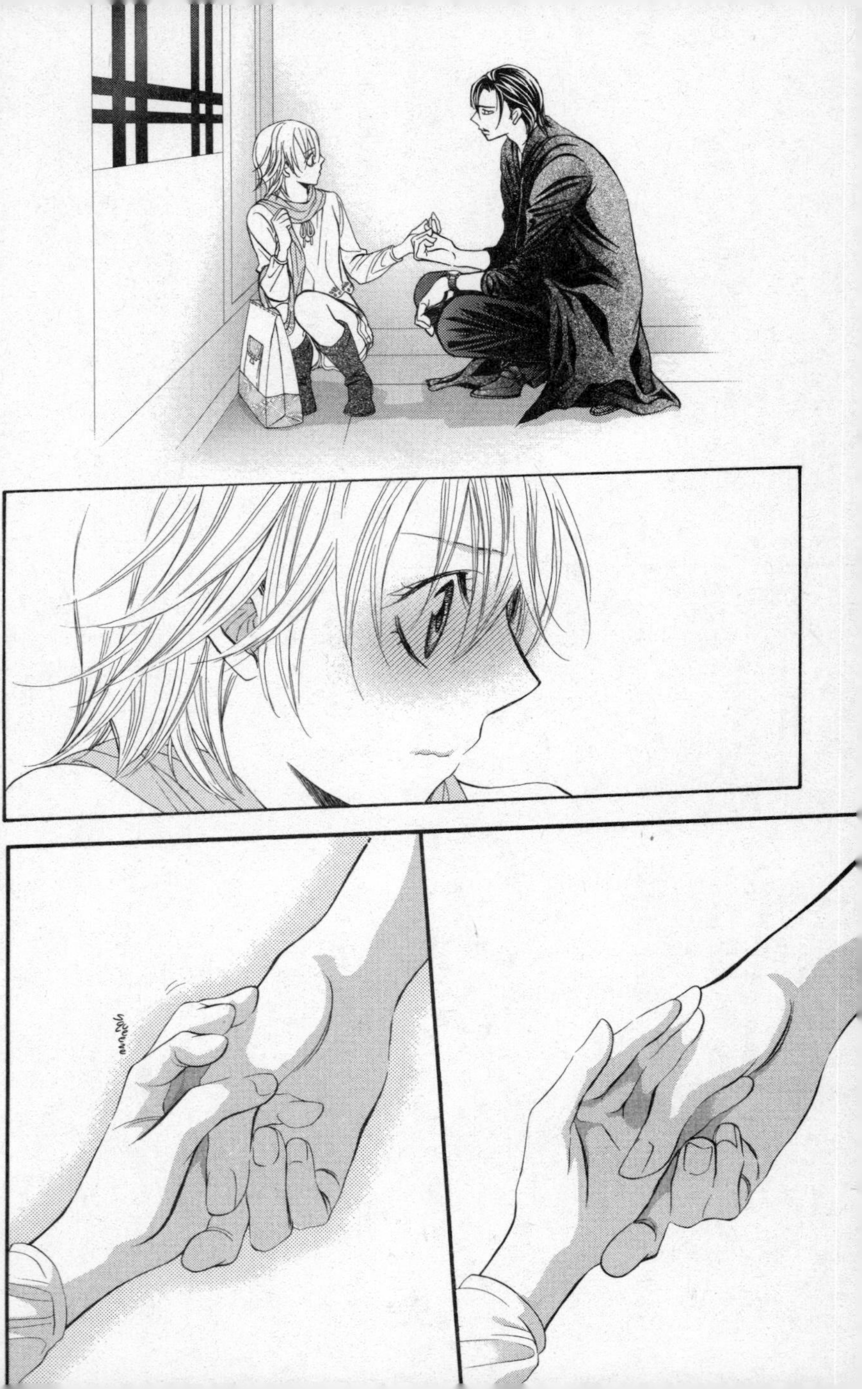
squeeze

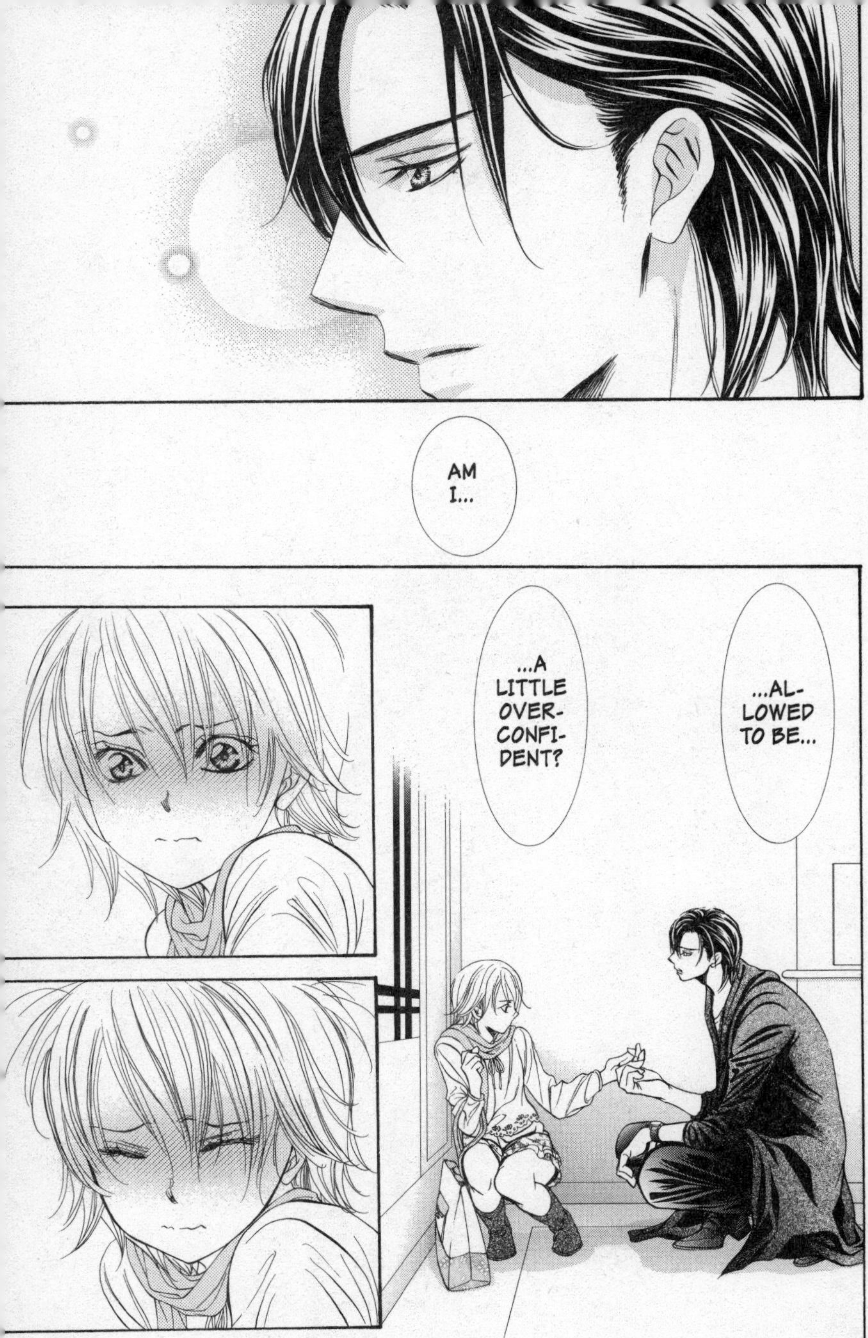
AM I...
...AL-LOWED TO BE...
...A LITTLE OVER-CONFI-DENT?

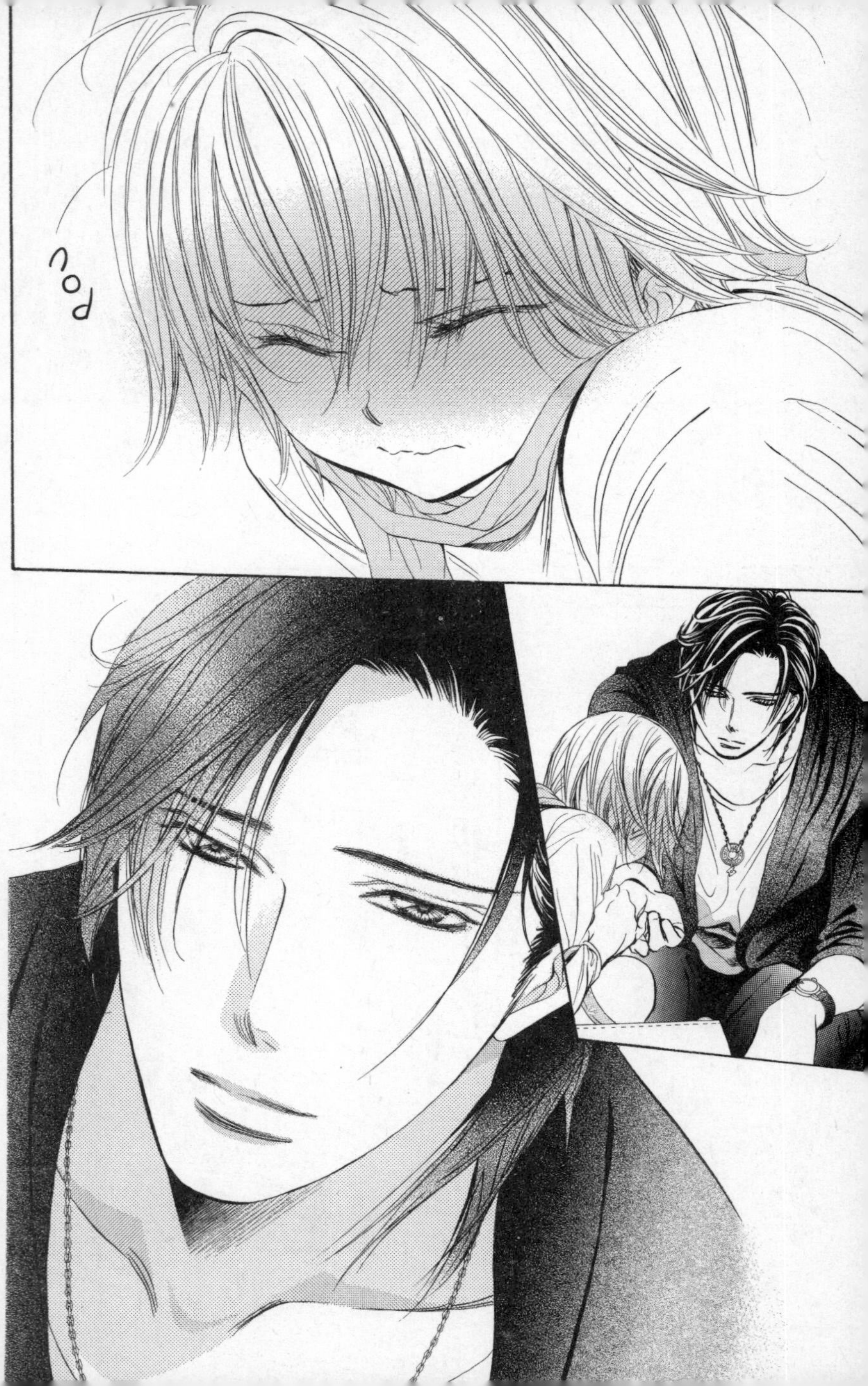
pou

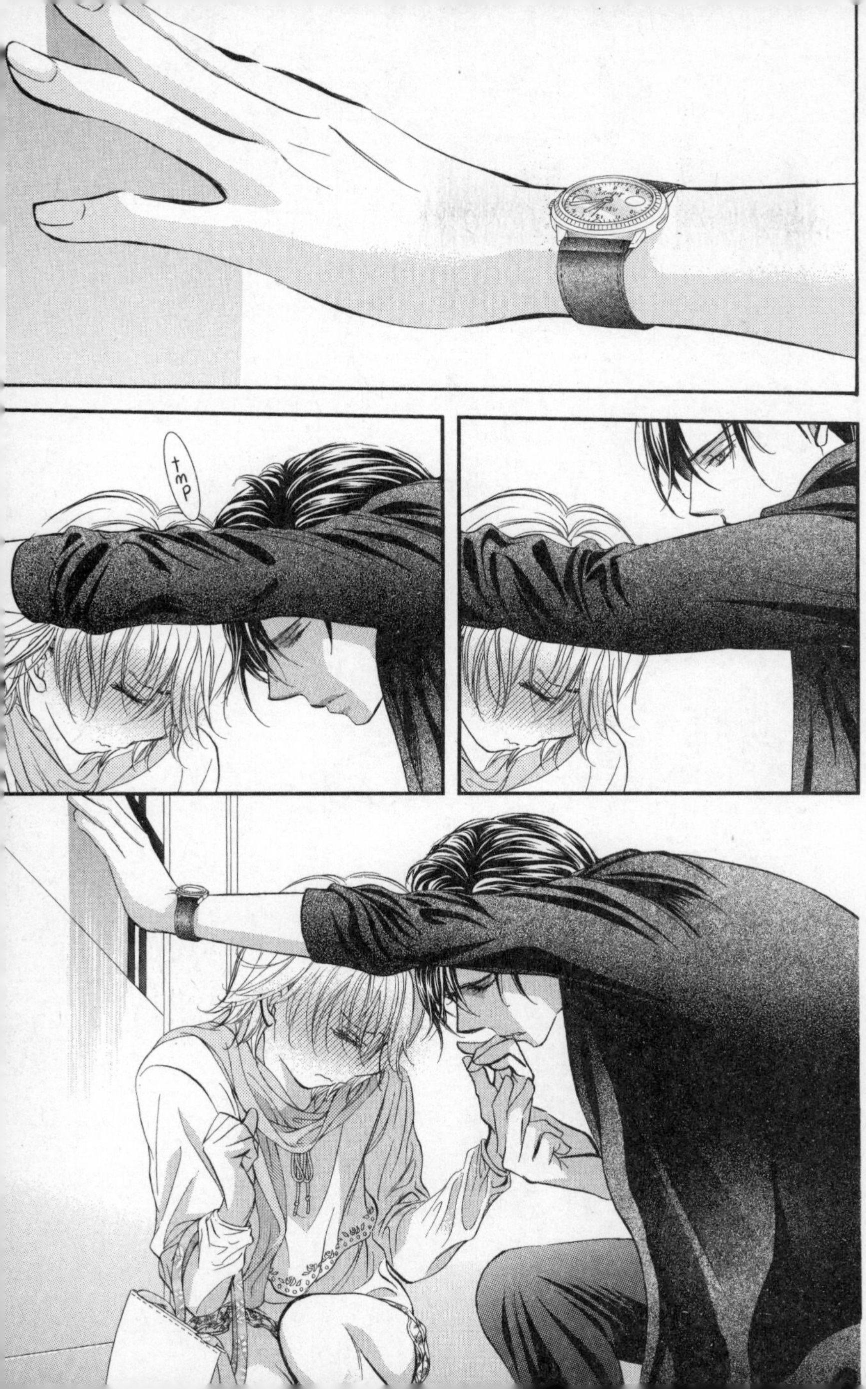
tmp

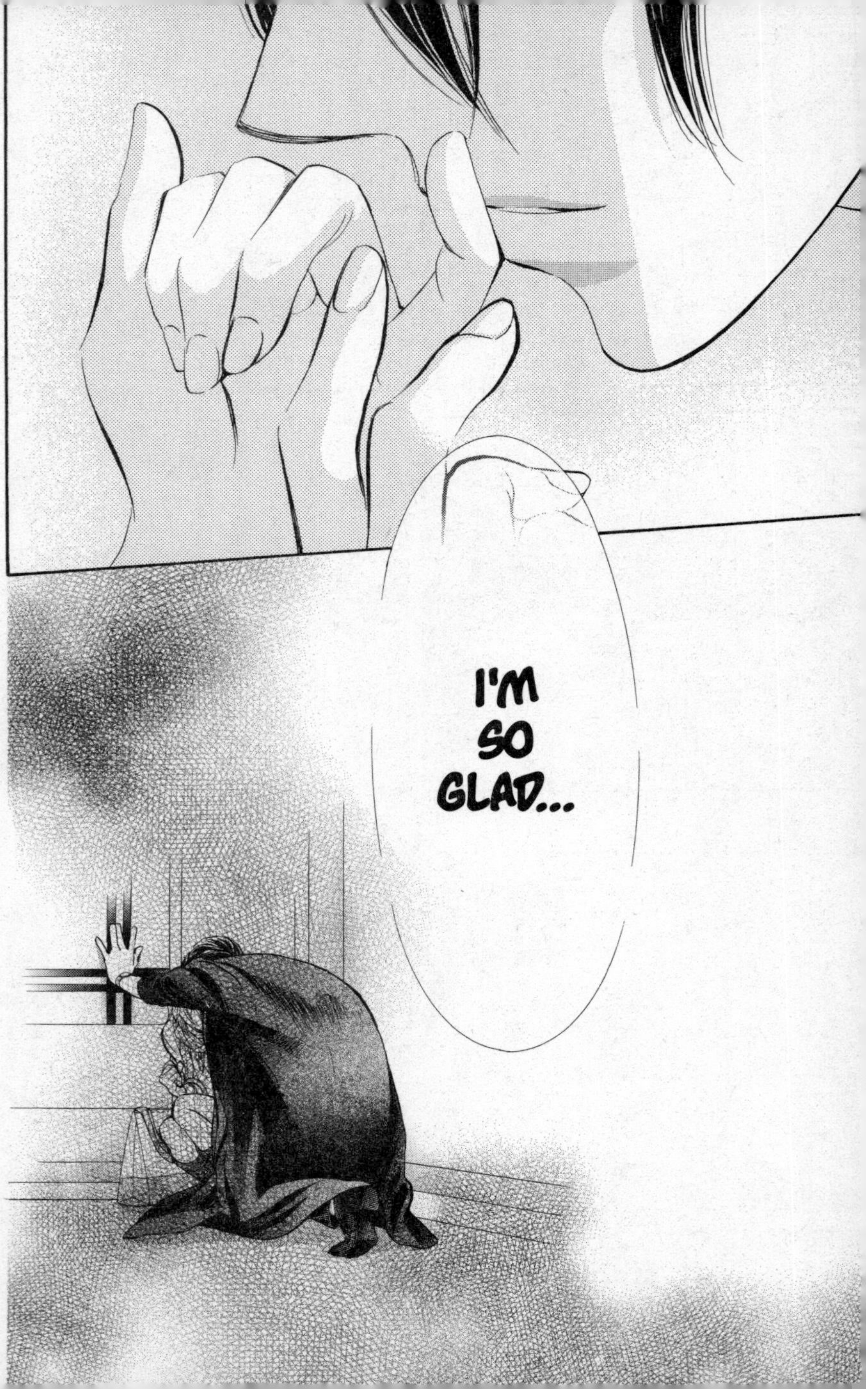
I'M SO GLAD...

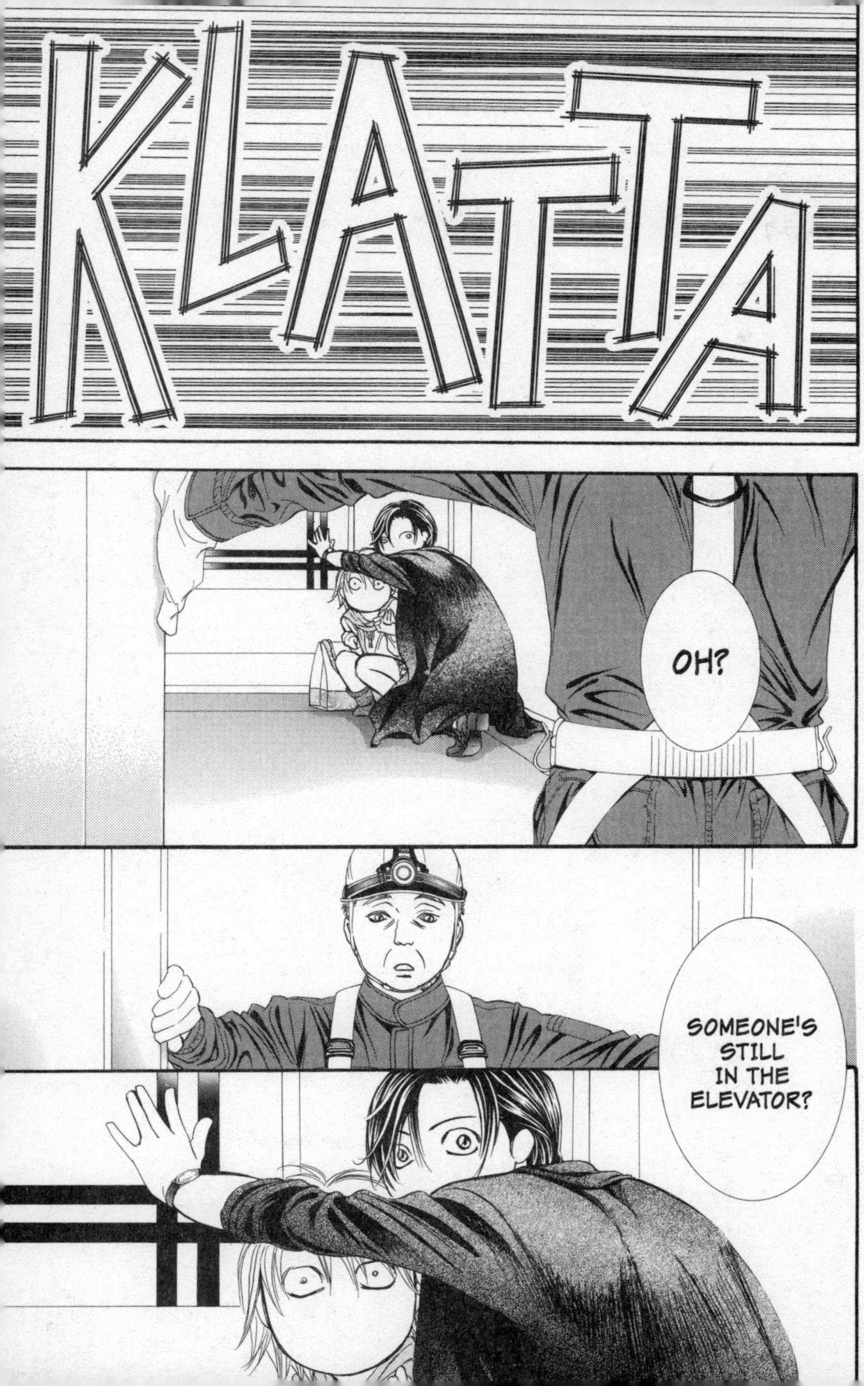
KLATTA
OH?
SOMEONE'S STILL IN THE ELEVATOR?

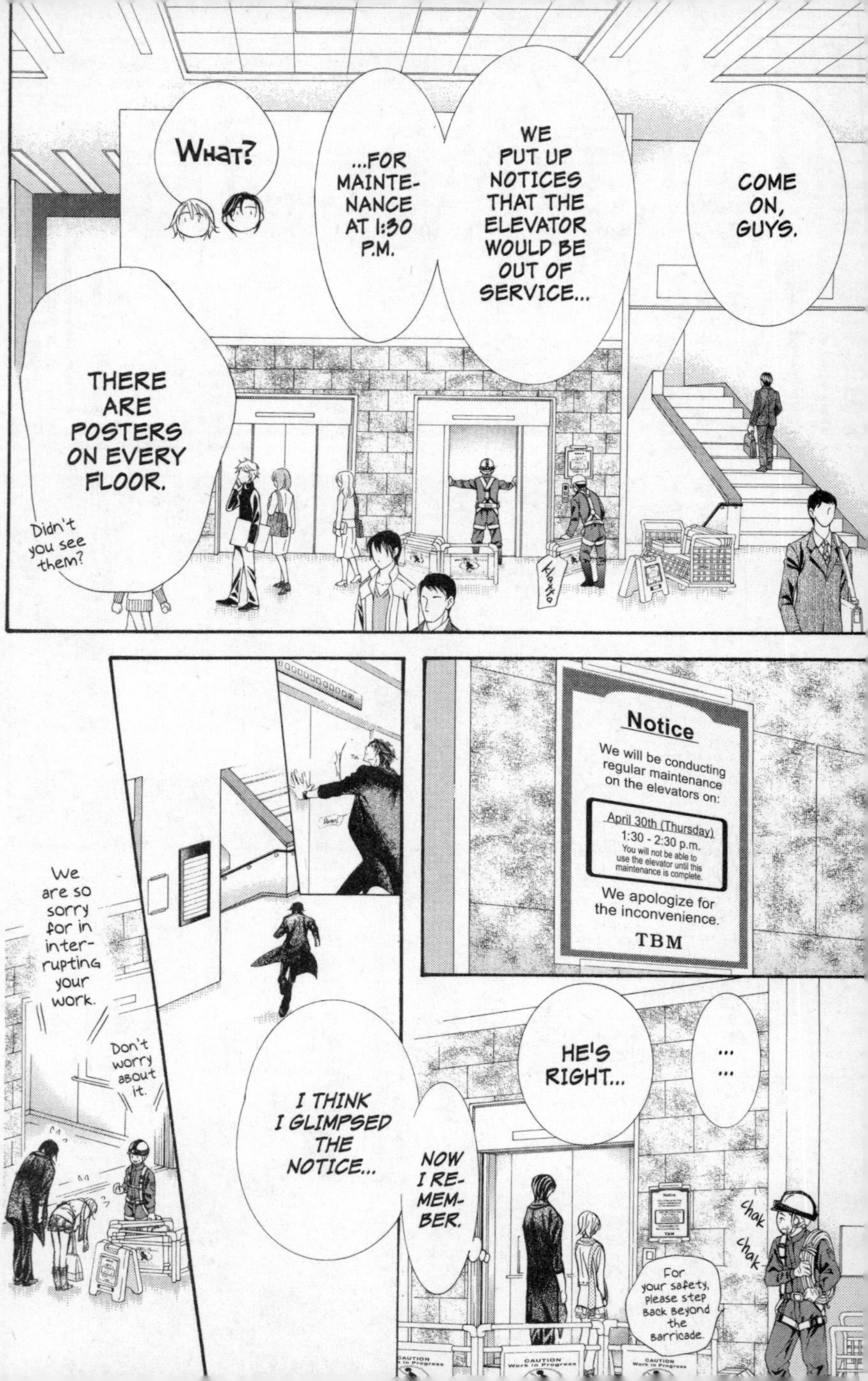
COME ON, GUYS.
WE PUT UP NOTICES THAT THE ELEVATOR WOULD BE OUT OF SERVICE...
...FOR MAINTENANCE AT 1:30 P.M.
WHAT?
THERE ARE POSTERS ON EVERY FLOOR.
Didn't you see them?
Notice
We will be conducting regular maintenance on the elevators on:
April 30th (Thursday)
1:30 - 2:30 p.m.
You will not be able to use the elevator until this maintenance is complete.
We apologize for the inconvenience.
TBM
......
HE'S RIGHT...
chak chak
For your safety, please step back beyond the barricade.
I THINK I GLIMPSED THE NOTICE...
NOW I REMEMBER.
We are so sorry for interrupting your work.
Don't worry about it.

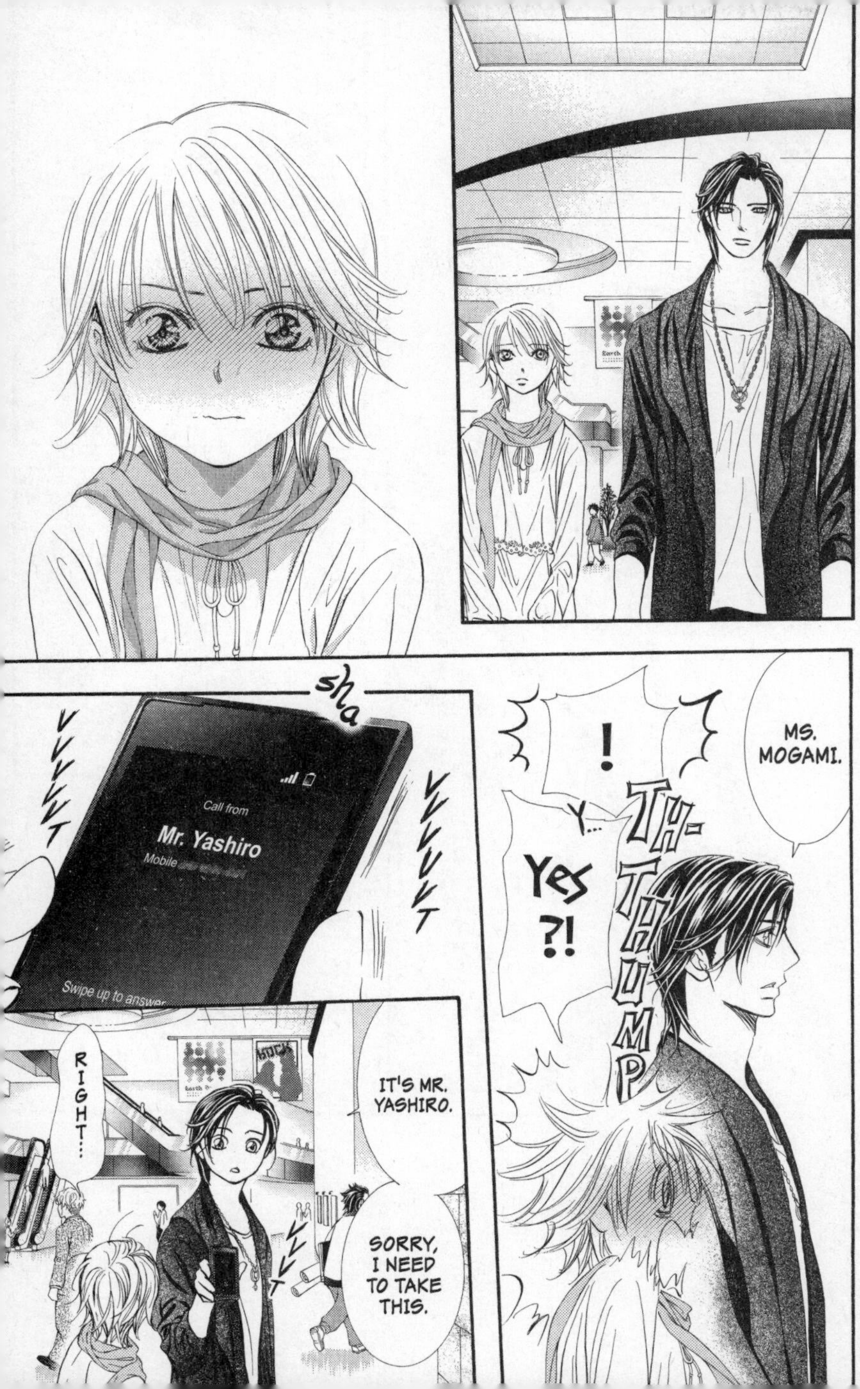
MS. MOGAMI.
!
Y...
Yes?!
TH-THUMP
sha
VVVVVT
VVVVVT
Call from
Mr. Yashiro
Mobile
Swipe up to answe
IT'S MR. YASHIRO.
SORRY, I NEED TO TAKE THIS.
RIGHT...
VVVT

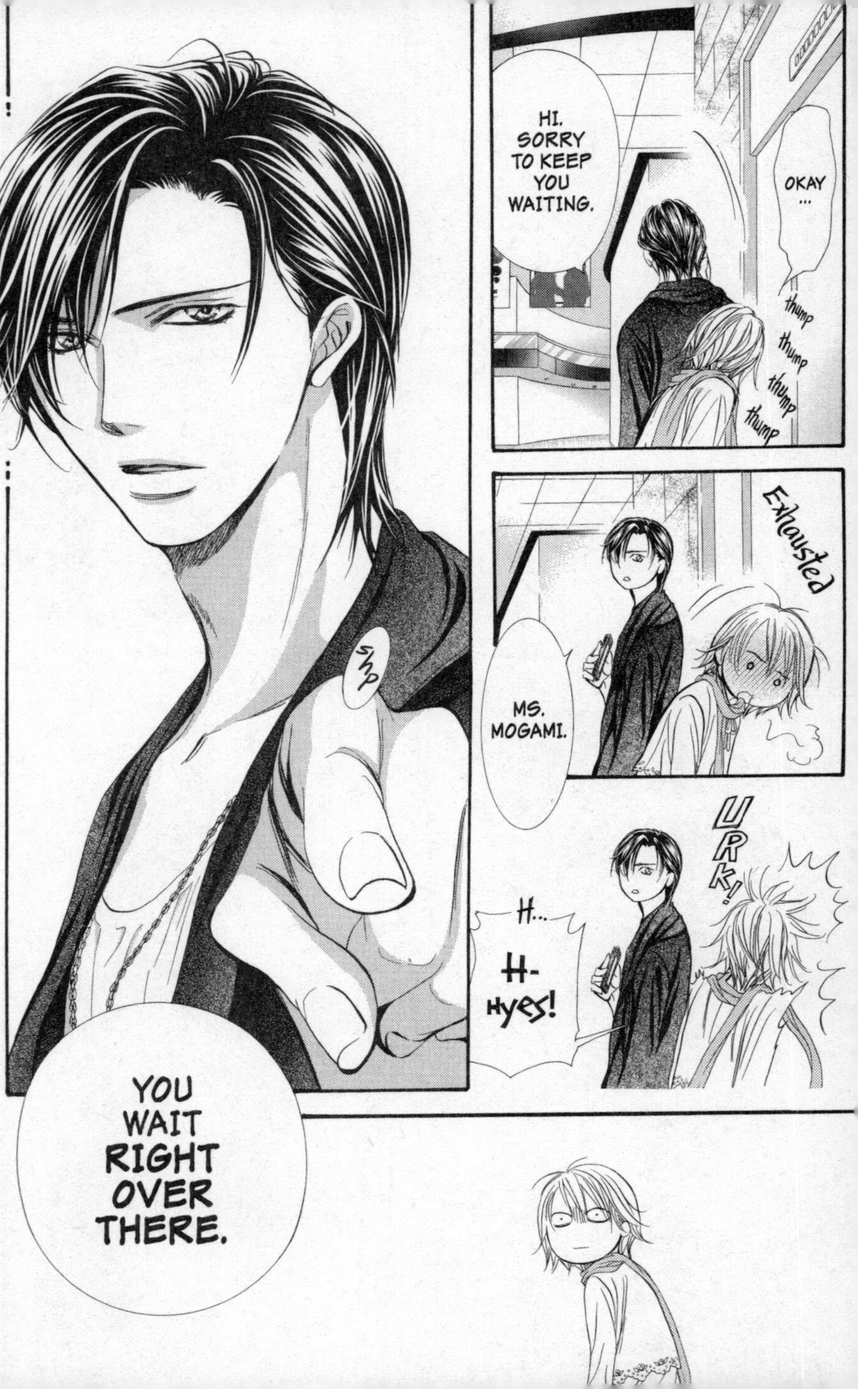
OKAY ...
thump thump thump thump
HI. SORRY TO KEEP YOU WAITING.
Exhausted
MS. MOGAMI.
URK!
H...
H-HYES!
shp
YOU WAIT RIGHT OVER THERE.

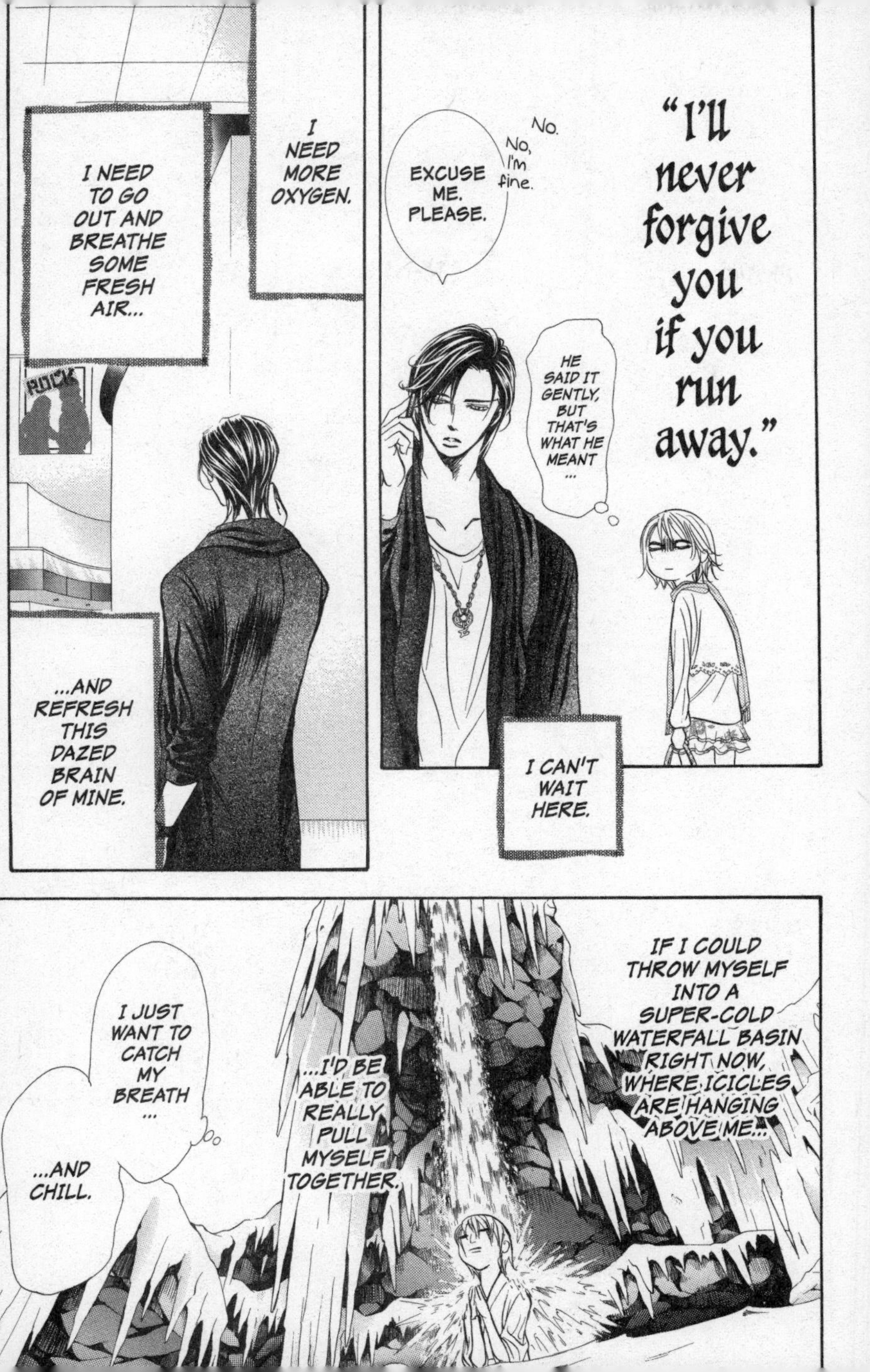
"I'll never forgive you if you run away."
No. No, I'm fine.
EXCUSE ME. PLEASE.
HE SAID IT GENTLY, BUT THAT'S WHAT HE MEANT...
I CAN'T WAIT HERE.
I NEED MORE OXYGEN.
I NEED TO GO OUT AND BREATHE SOME FRESH AIR...
...AND REFRESH THIS DAZED BRAIN OF MINE.
IF I COULD THROW MYSELF INTO A SUPER-COLD WATERFALL BASIN RIGHT NOW, WHERE ICICLES ARE HANGING ABOVE ME...
...I'D BE ABLE TO REALLY PULL MYSELF TOGETHER.
I JUST WANT TO CATCH MY BREATH...
...AND CHILL.

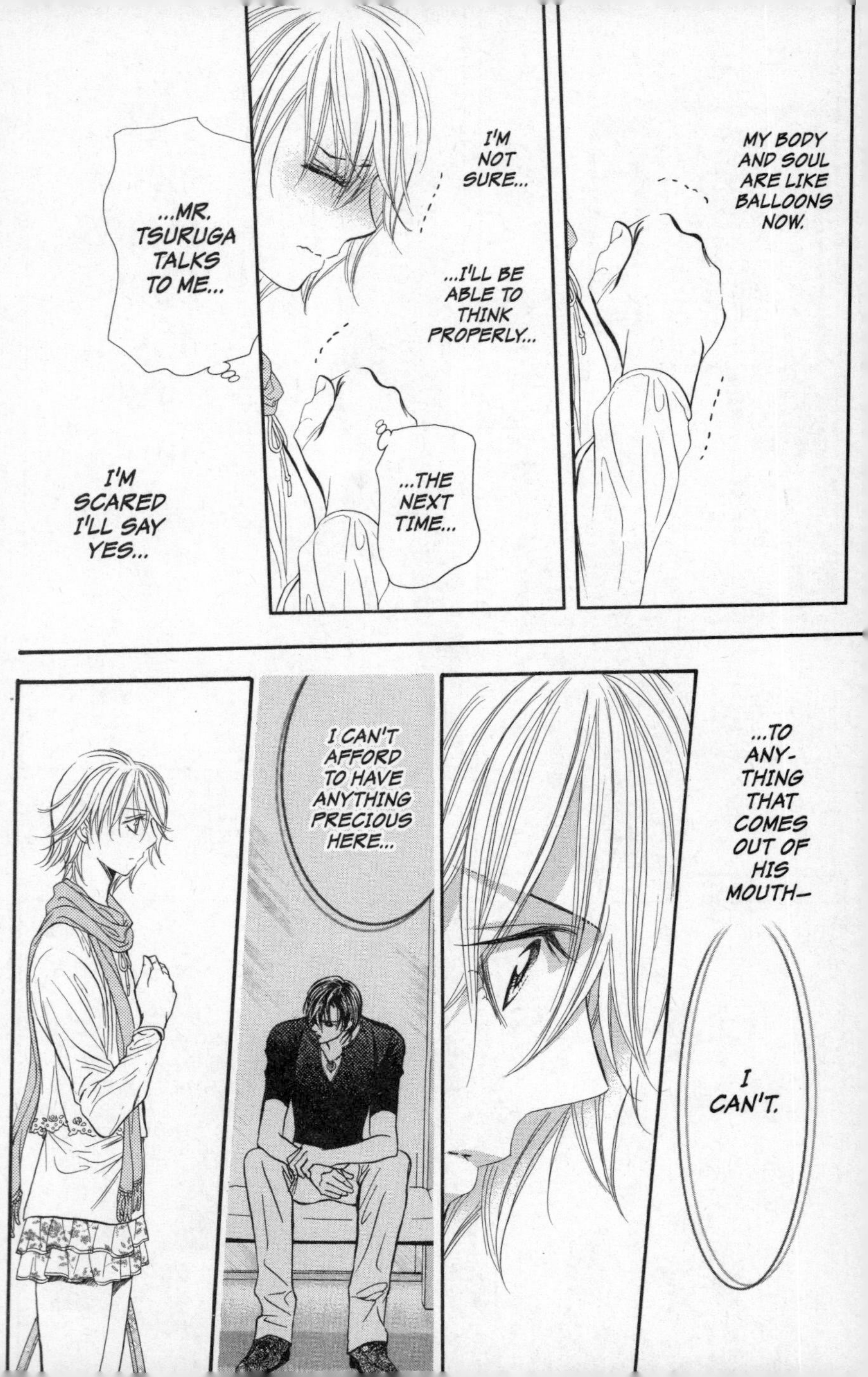
MY BODY AND SOUL ARE LIKE BALLOONS NOW.
I'M NOT SURE...
...I'LL BE ABLE TO THINK PROPERLY...
...THE NEXT TIME...
...MR. TSURUGA TALKS TO ME...
I'M SCARED I'LL SAY YES...
...TO ANY-THING THAT COMES OUT OF HIS MOUTH—
I CAN'T.
I CAN'T AFFORD TO HAVE ANYTHING PRECIOUS HERE...

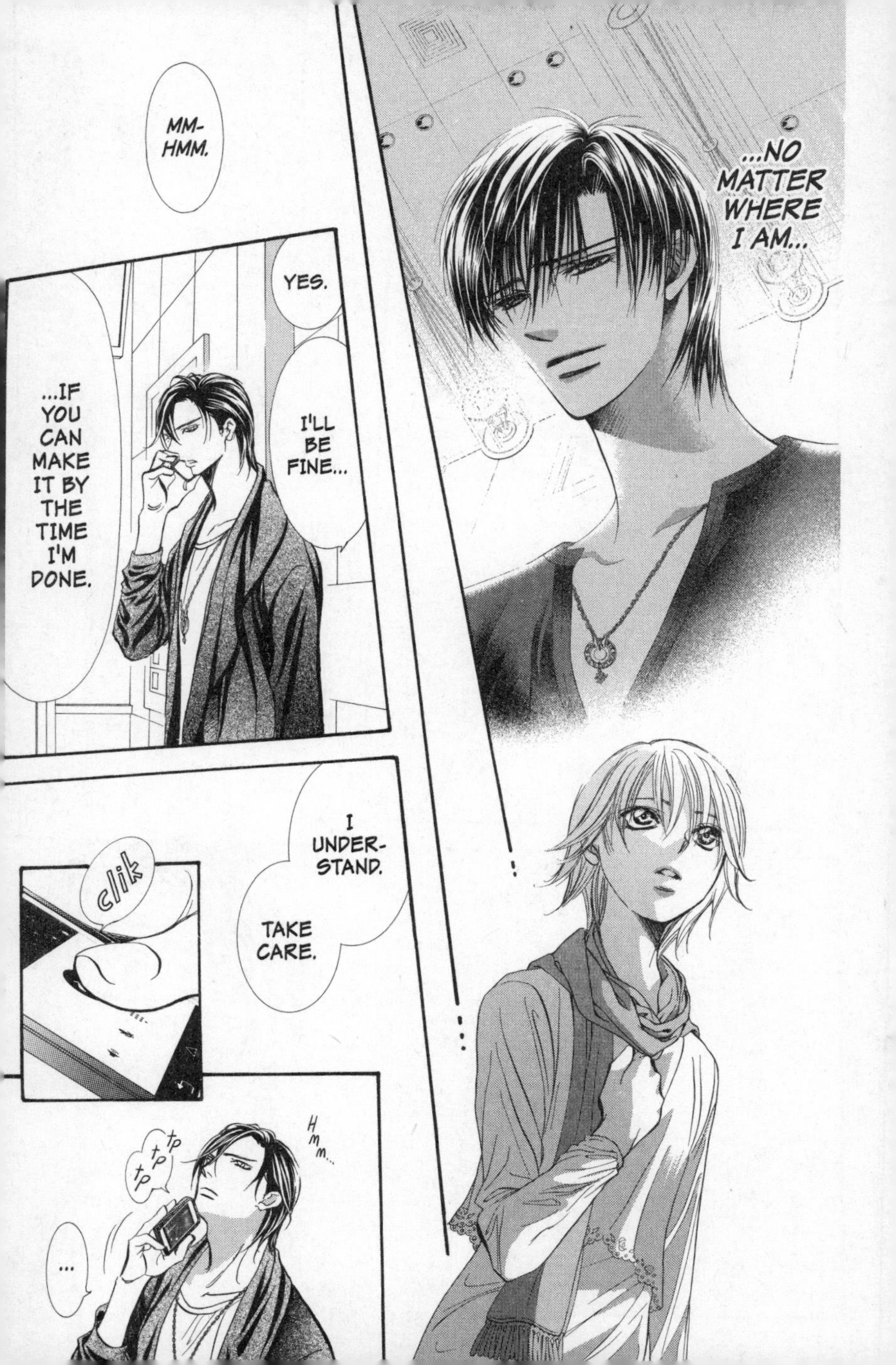
...NO MATTER WHERE I AM...
MM-HMM.
YES.
I'LL BE FINE...
...IF YOU CAN MAKE IT BY THE TIME I'M DONE.
!
...
I UNDERSTAND.
TAKE CARE.
clik
HMM...
tp tp tp
...

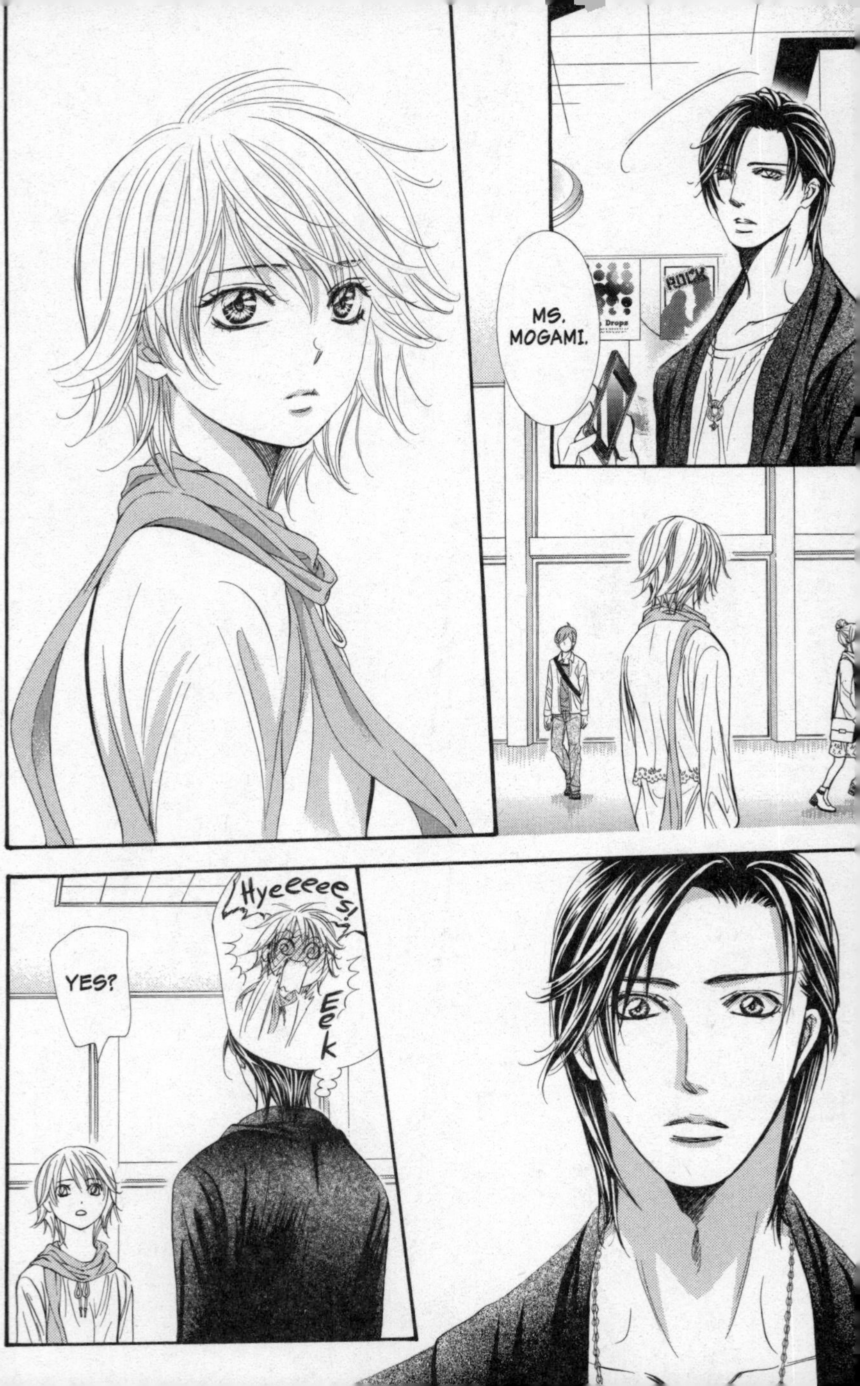
MS. MOGAMI.
Drops
ROCK
YES?
Hyeeeees!
Eek

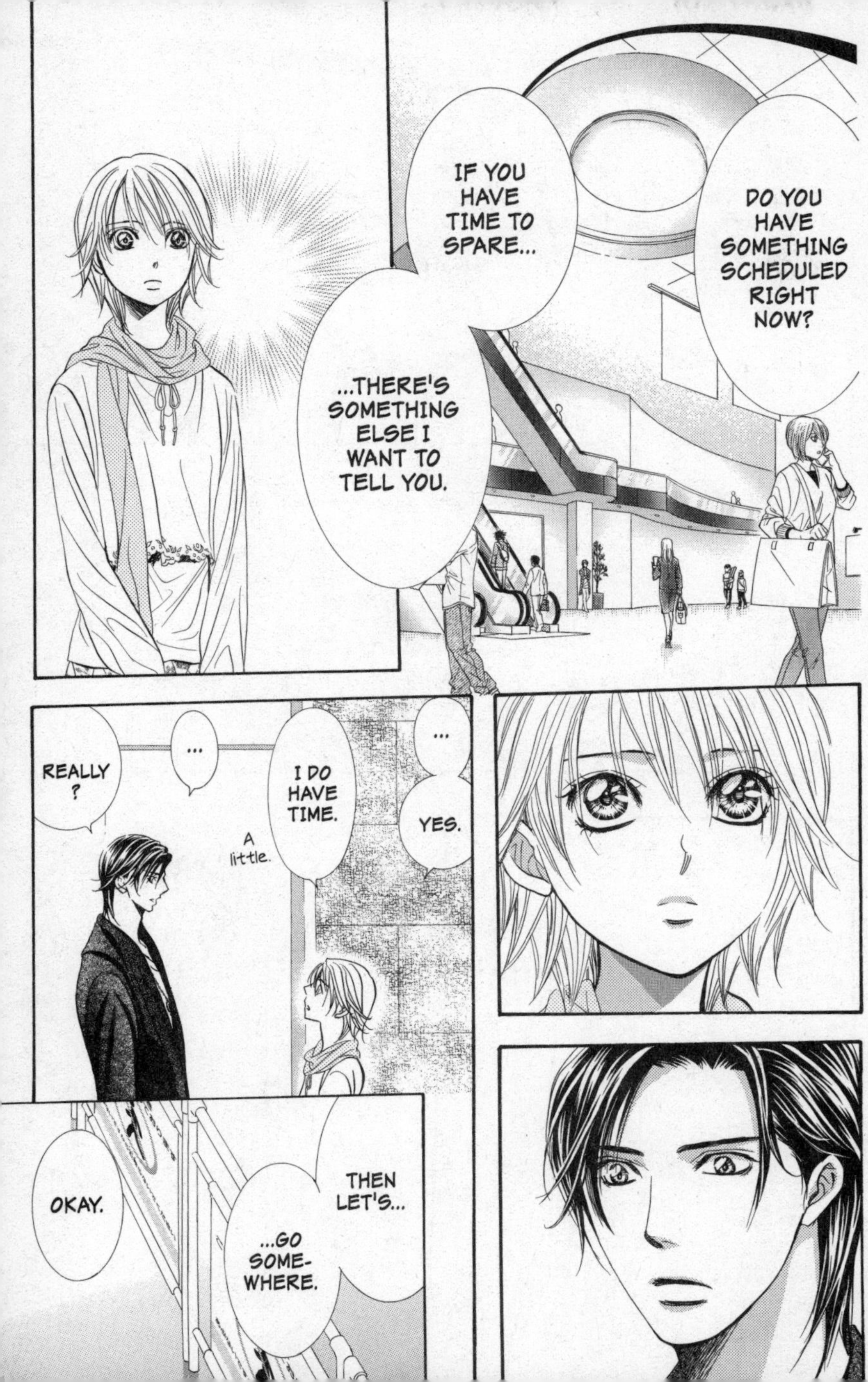
DO YOU HAVE SOMETHING SCHEDULED RIGHT NOW?
IF YOU HAVE TIME TO SPARE...
...THERE'S SOMETHING ELSE I WANT TO TELL YOU.
...
YES.
I DO HAVE TIME.
A little.
...
REALLY?
THEN LET'S...
...GO SOMEWHERE.
OKAY.

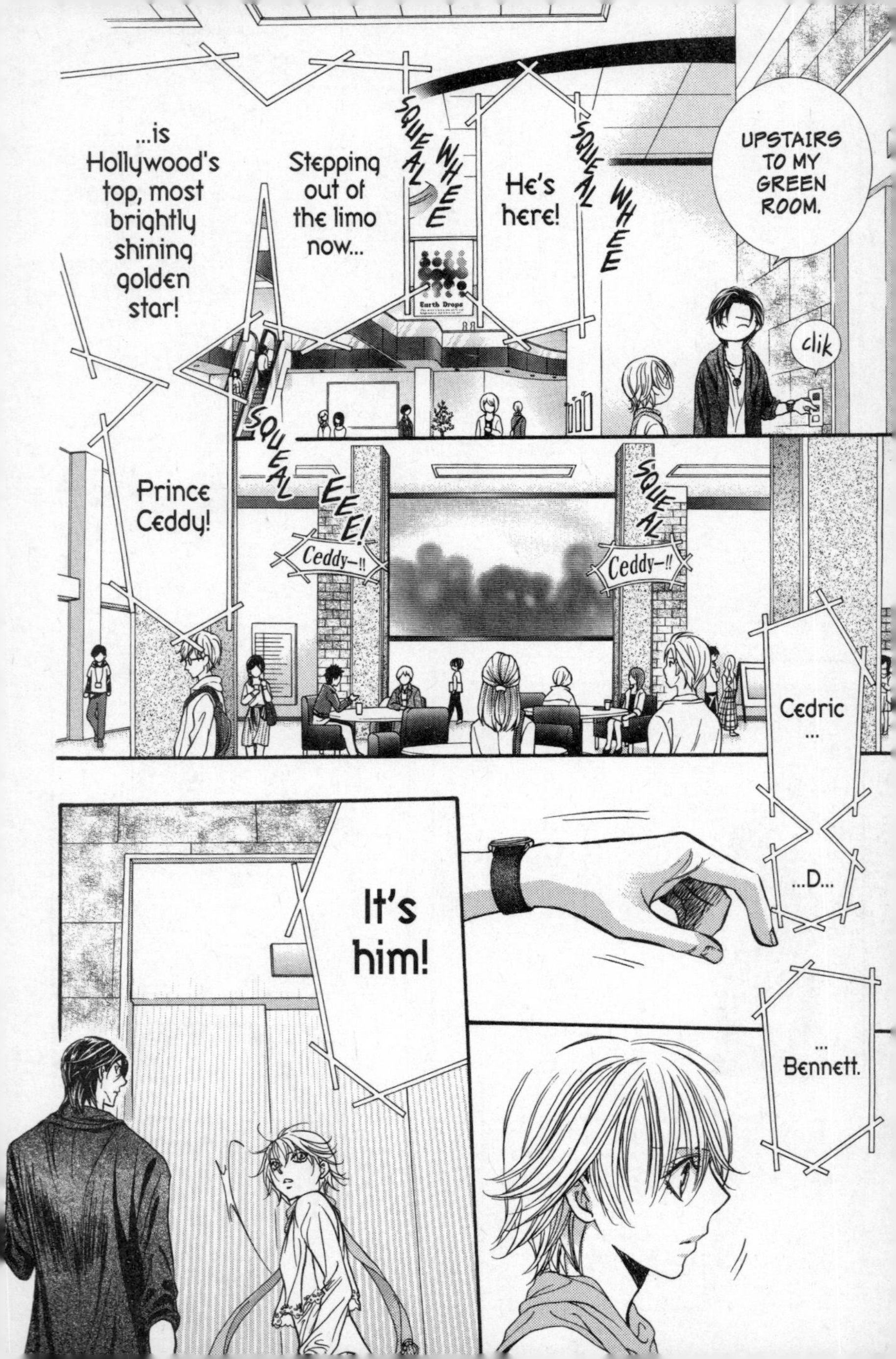
UPSTAIRS TO MY GREEN ROOM.
clik
SQUEAL
WHEE
He's here!
SQUEAL
WHEE
Stepping out of the limo now...
...is Hollywood's top, most brightly shining golden star!
SQUEAL
Ceddy—!!
EEEE!
Ceddy—!!
SQUEAL
Prince Ceddy!
Cedric ...
...D...
... Bennett.
It's him!

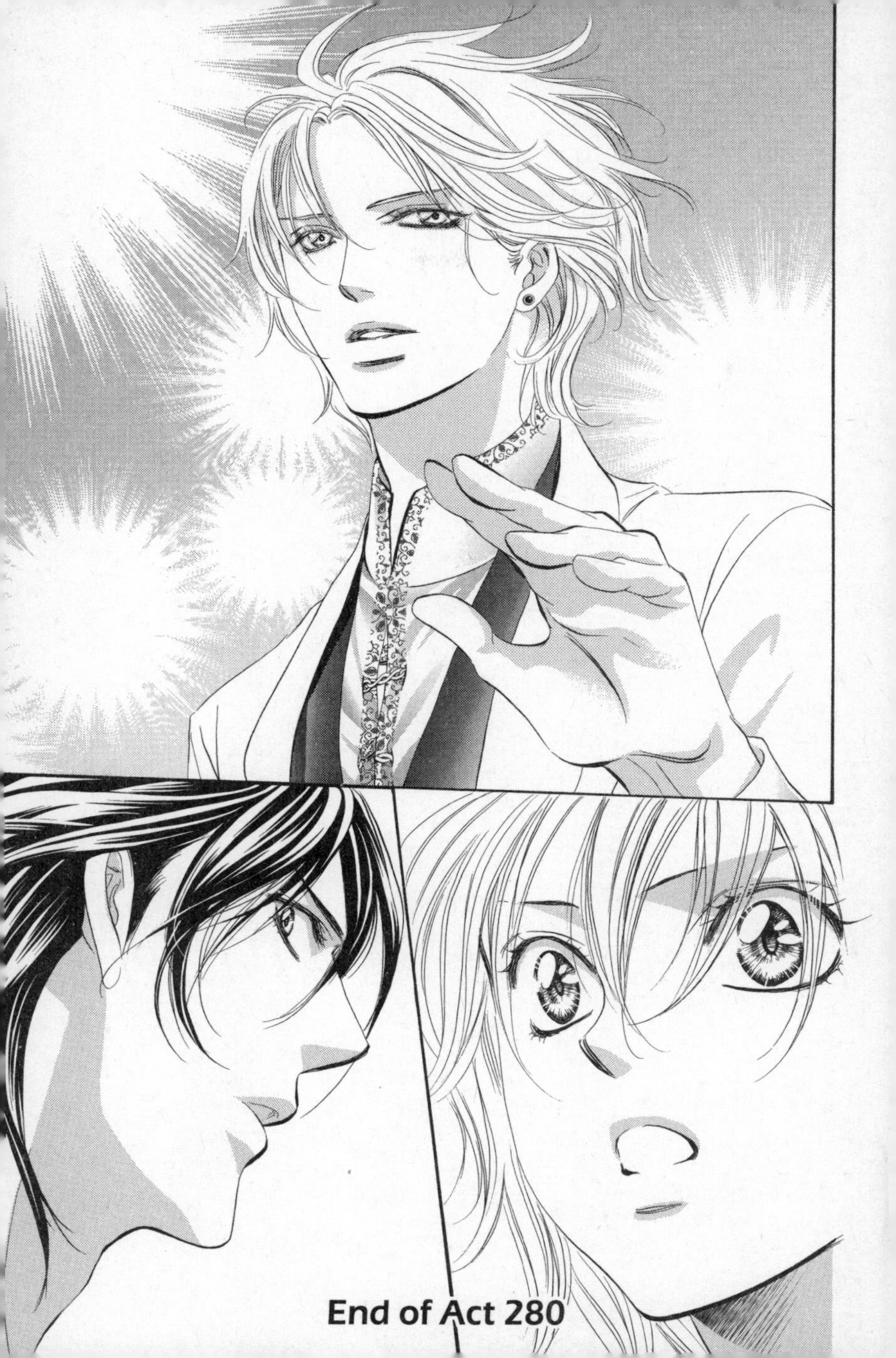
End of Act 280

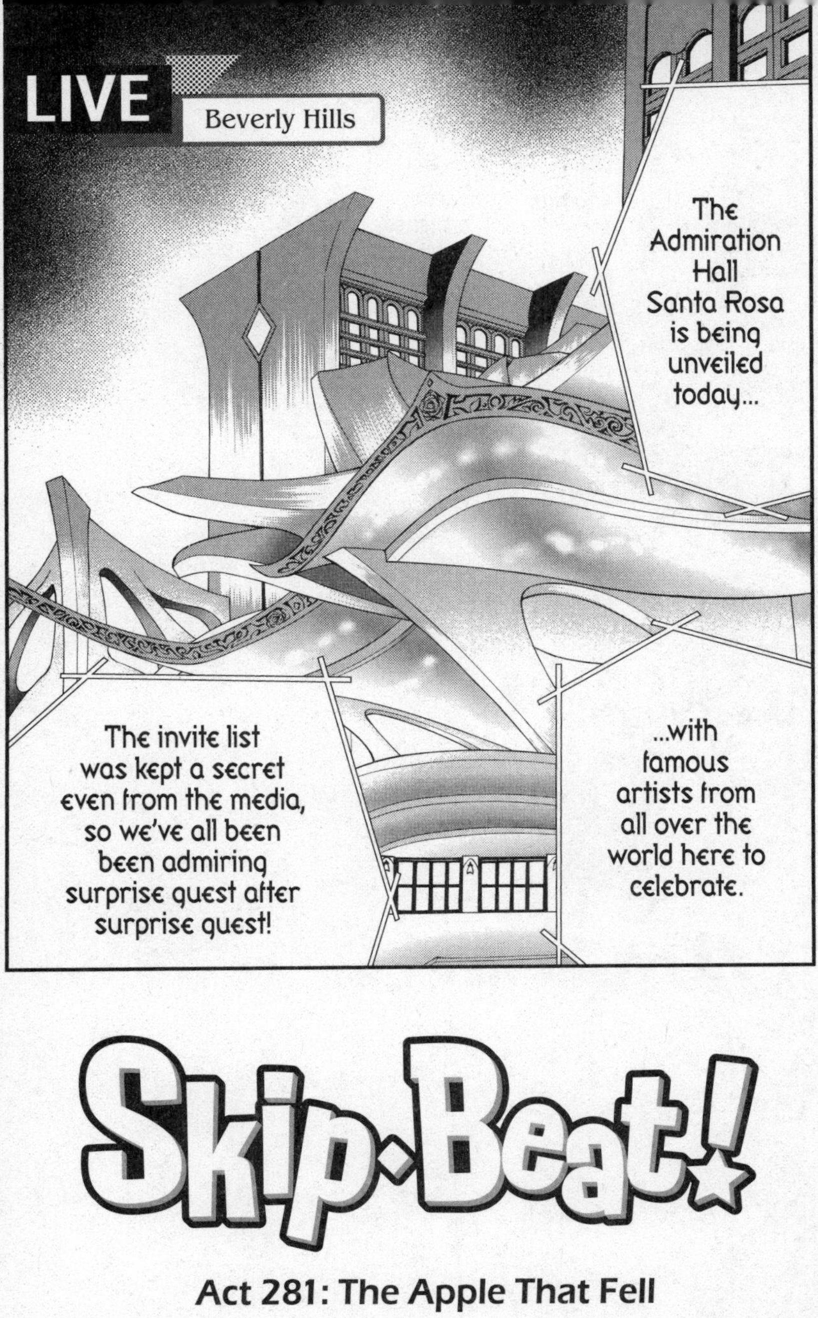
LIVE
Beverly Hills
The Admiration Hall Santa Rosa is being unveiled today...
...with famous artists from all over the world here to celebrate.
The invite list was kept a secret even from the media, so we've all been been admiring surprise guest after surprise guest!

Skip·Beat!

Act 281: The Apple That Fell

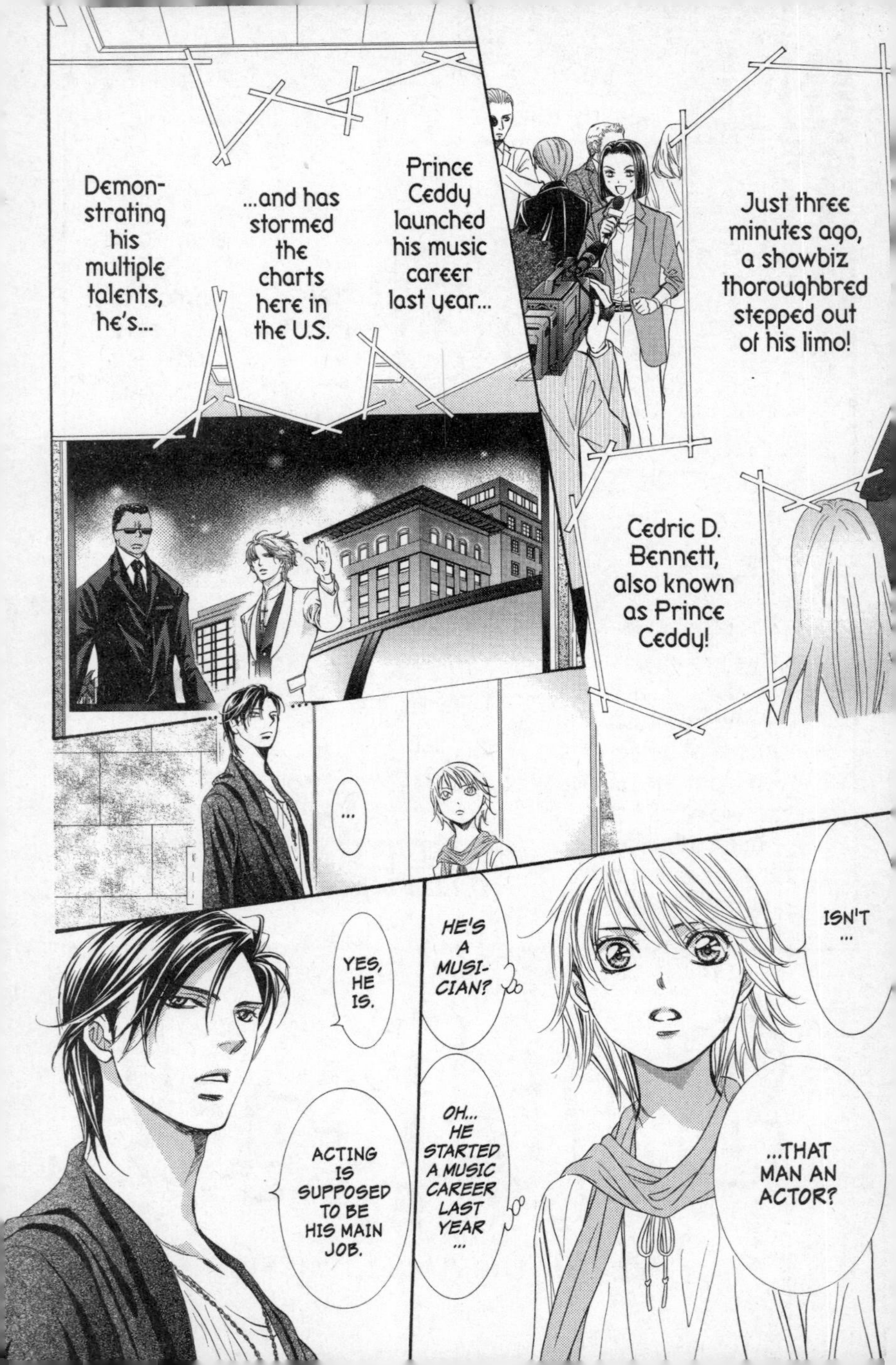
Just three minutes ago, a showbiz thoroughbred stepped out of his limo!
Prince Ceddy launched his music career last year...
...and has stormed the charts here in the U.S.
Demonstrating his multiple talents, he's...
Cedric D. Bennett, also known as Prince Ceddy!
...
ISN'T ...
...THAT MAN AN ACTOR?
HE'S A MUSICIAN?
OH... HE STARTED A MUSIC CAREER LAST YEAR ...
YES, HE IS.
ACTING IS SUPPOSED TO BE HIS MAIN JOB.

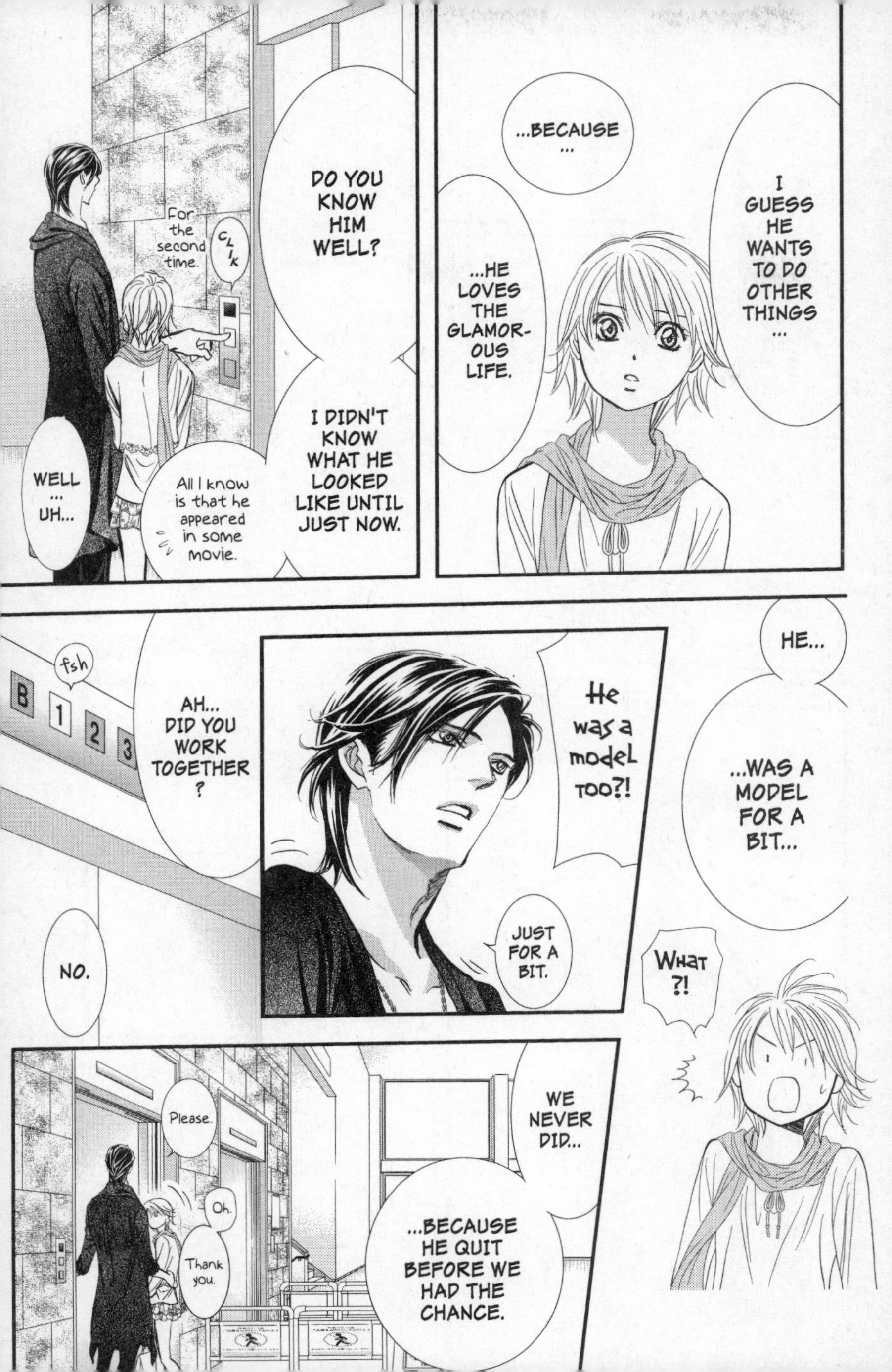
I GUESS HE WANTS TO DO OTHER THINGS ...
...BECAUSE ...
...HE LOVES THE GLAMOROUS LIFE.
DO YOU KNOW HIM WELL?
For the second time.
CLIK
I DIDN'T KNOW WHAT HE LOOKED LIKE UNTIL JUST NOW.
All I know is that he appeared in some movie.
WELL ... UH...
HE...
...WAS A MODEL FOR A BIT...
WHAT ?!
He was a model too?!
JUST FOR A BIT.
fsh
AH... DID YOU WORK TOGETHER ?
NO.
WE NEVER DID...
...BECAUSE HE QUIT BEFORE WE HAD THE CHANCE.
Please.
Oh.
Thank you.

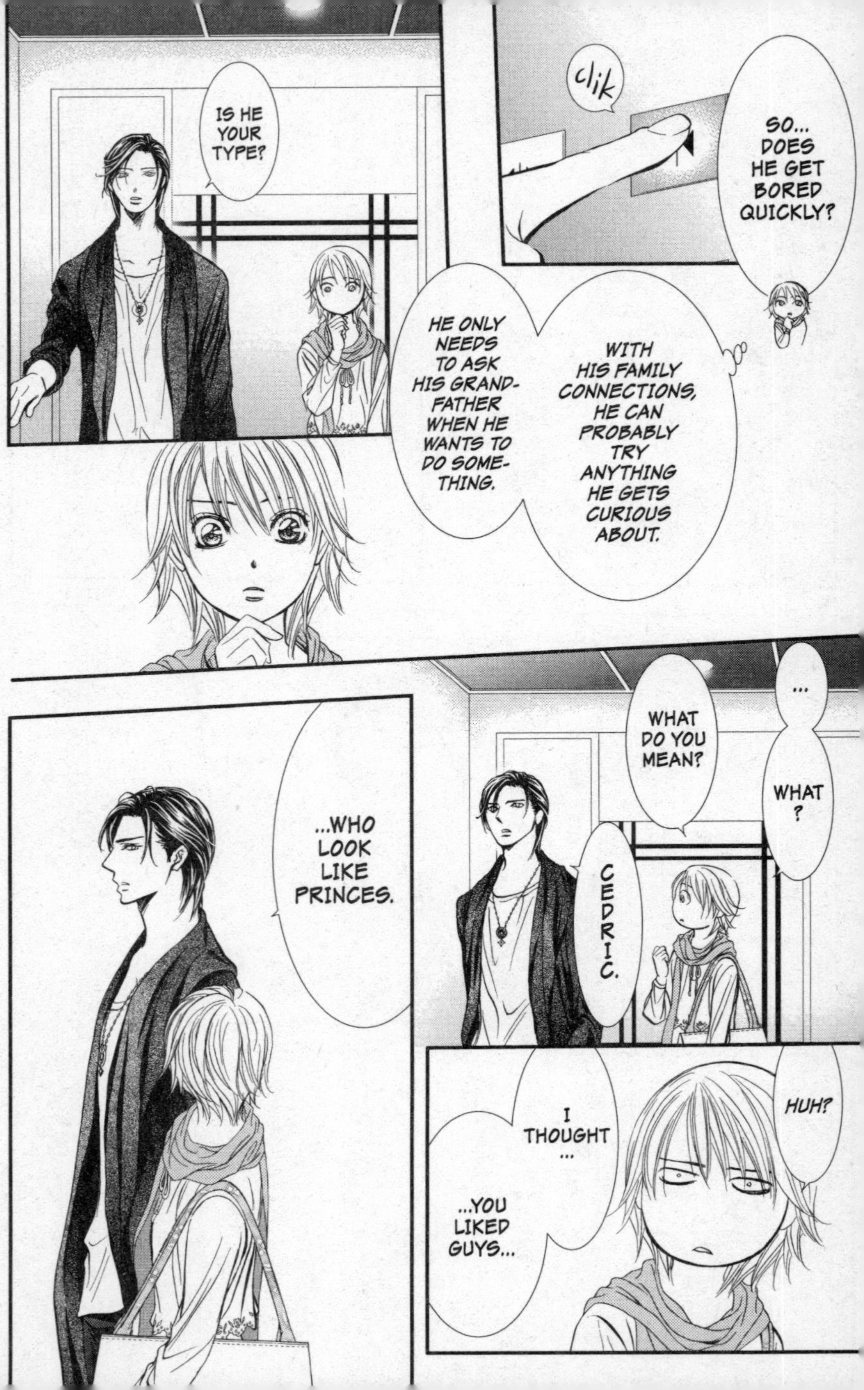
SO... DOES HE GET BORED QUICKLY?
clik
IS HE YOUR TYPE?
WITH HIS FAMILY CONNECTIONS, HE CAN PROBABLY TRY ANYTHING HE GETS CURIOUS ABOUT.
HE ONLY NEEDS TO ASK HIS GRAND-FATHER WHEN HE WANTS TO DO SOME-THING.
...
WHAT?
WHAT DO YOU MEAN?
CEDRIC.
HUH?
I THOUGHT...
...YOU LIKED GUYS...
...WHO LOOK LIKE PRINCES.

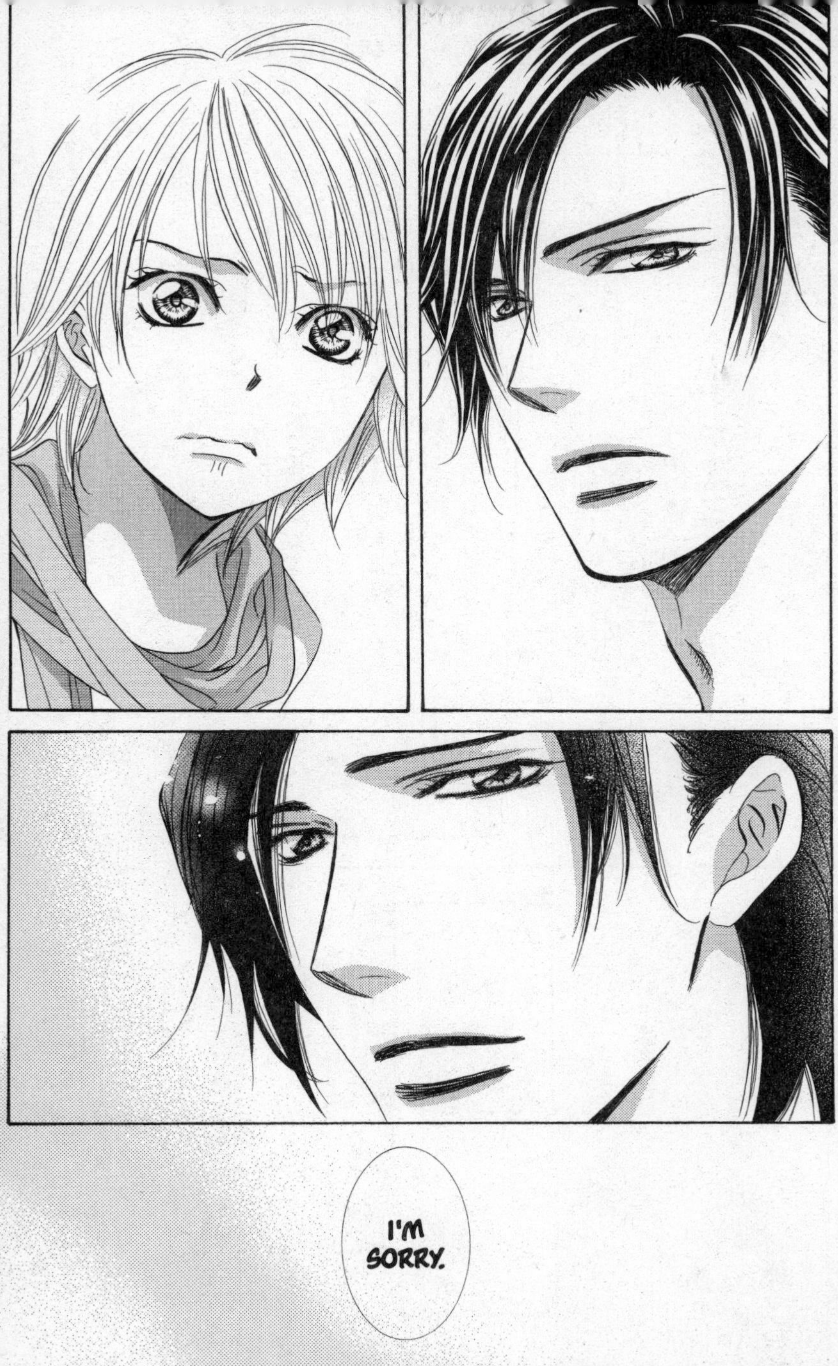
I'M
SORRY.

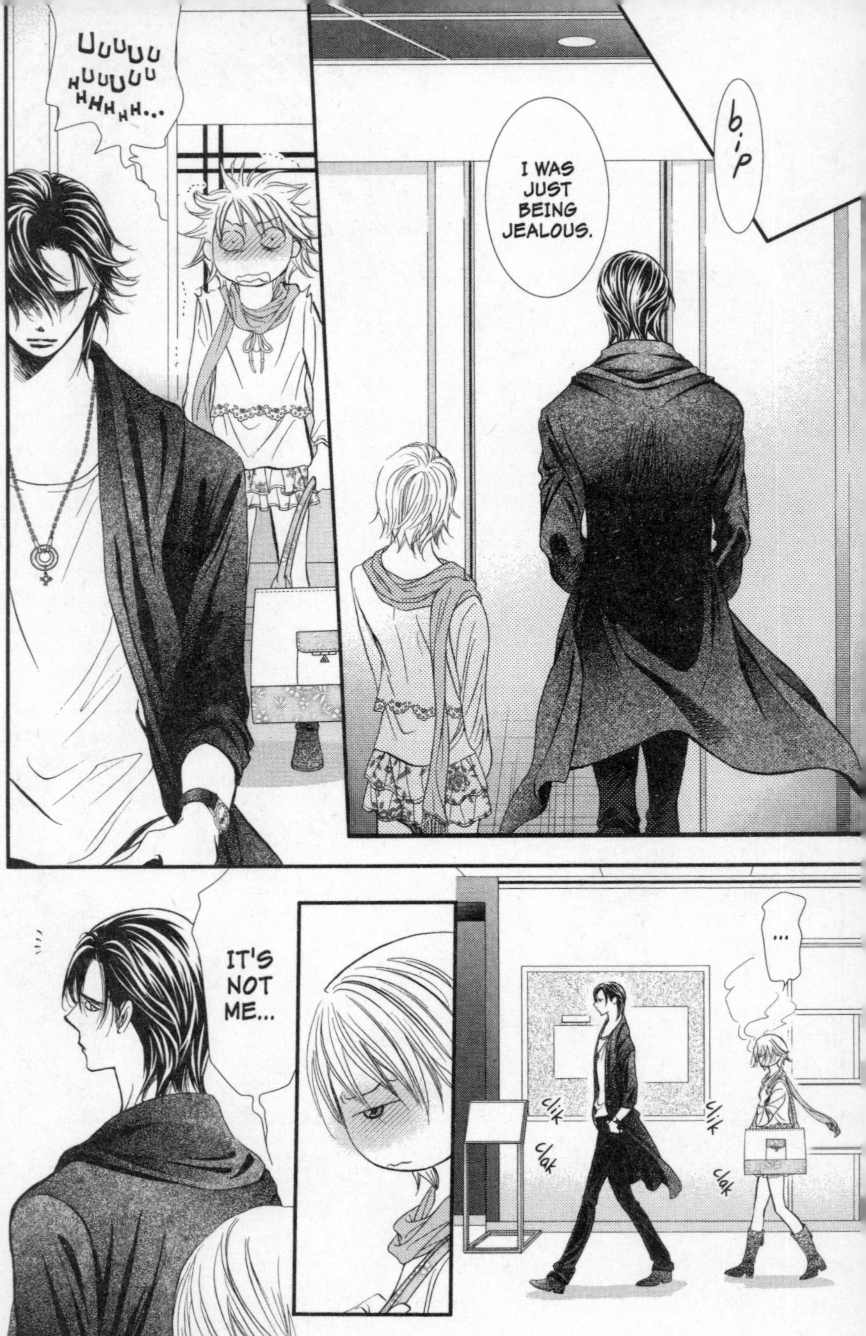
bip
I WAS JUST BEING JEALOUS.
UUUUU HUUUUU HHHHH...
...
clik
clak
clik
clak
IT'S NOT ME...

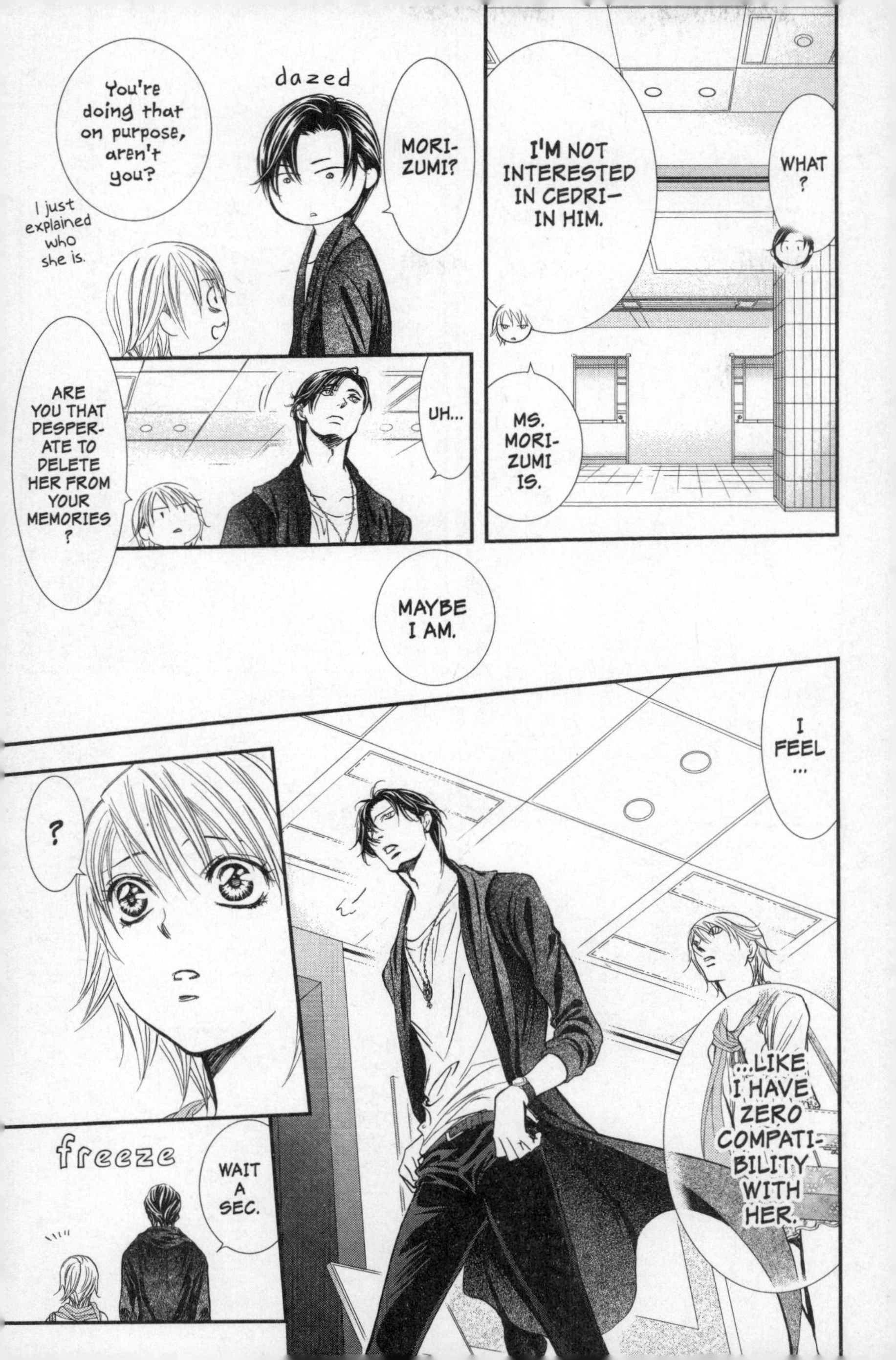
WHAT?
I'M NOT INTERESTED IN CEDRI— IN HIM.
MS. MORIZUMI IS.
dazed
MORIZUMI?
You're doing that on purpose, aren't you?
I just explained who she is.
UH...
ARE YOU THAT DESPERATE TO DELETE HER FROM YOUR MEMORIES?
MAYBE I AM.
I FEEL...
...LIKE I HAVE ZERO COMPATIBILITY WITH HER.
?
freeze
WAIT A SEC.

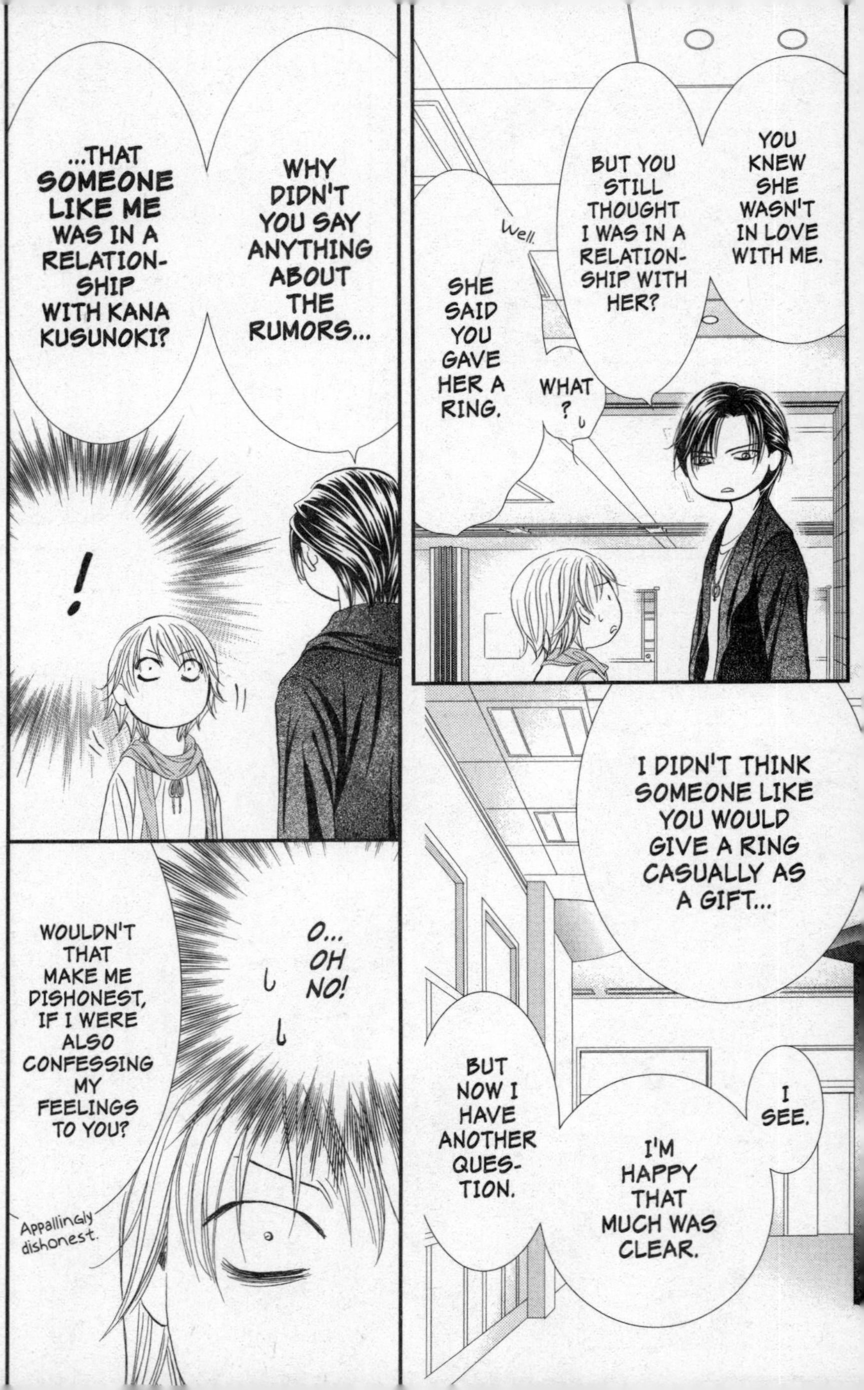
YOU KNEW SHE WASN'T IN LOVE WITH ME.
BUT YOU STILL THOUGHT I WAS IN A RELATION-SHIP WITH HER?
WHAT?
Well.
SHE SAID YOU GAVE HER A RING.
I DIDN'T THINK SOMEONE LIKE YOU WOULD GIVE A RING CASUALLY AS A GIFT...
I SEE.
I'M HAPPY THAT MUCH WAS CLEAR.
BUT NOW I HAVE ANOTHER QUES-TION.
WHY DIDN'T YOU SAY ANYTHING ABOUT THE RUMORS...
...THAT SOMEONE LIKE ME WAS IN A RELATION-SHIP WITH KANA KUSUNOKI?
!
O... OH NO!
WOULDN'T THAT MAKE ME DISHONEST, IF I WERE ALSO CONFESSING MY FEELINGS TO YOU?
Appallingly dishonest.

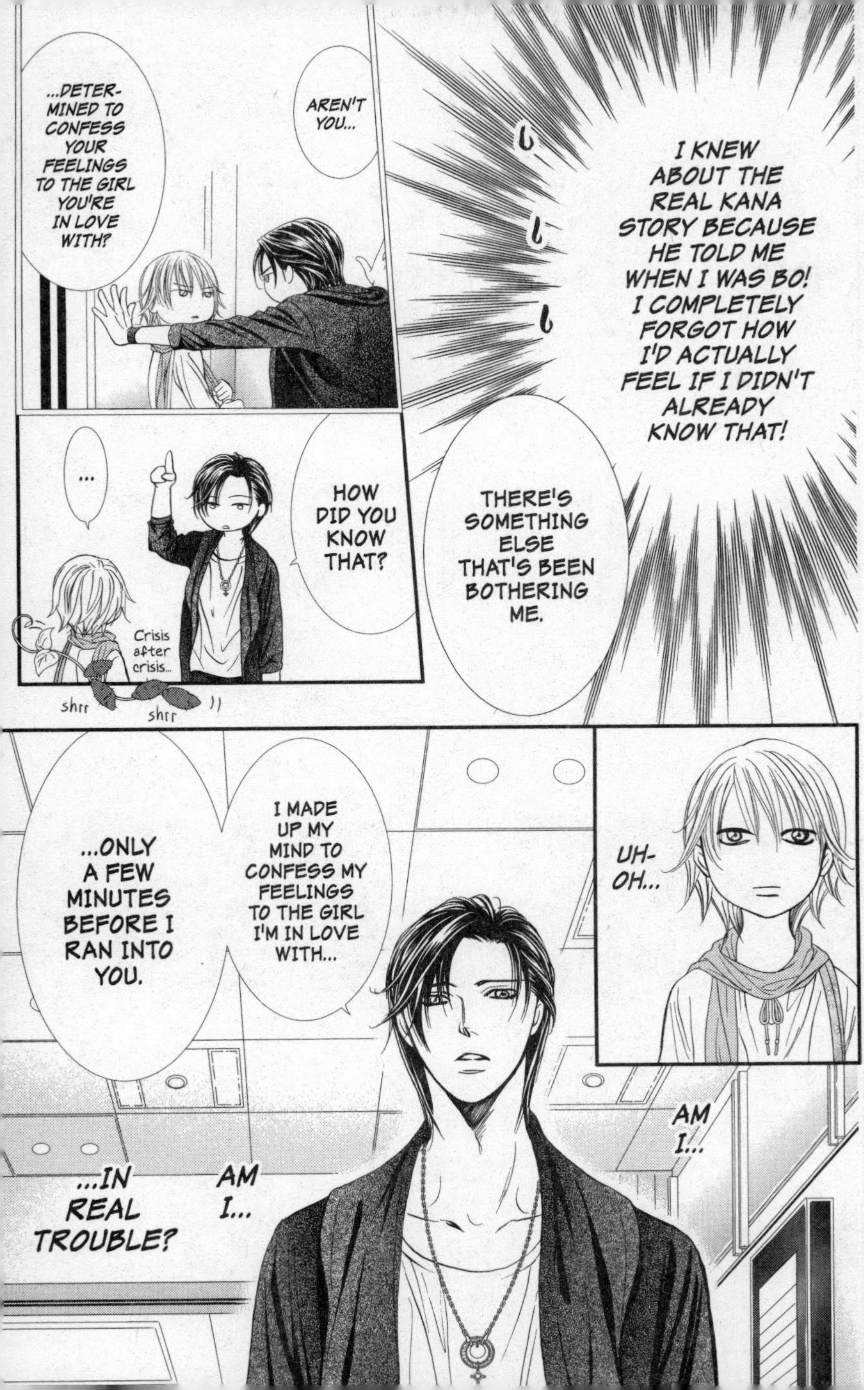
I KNEW ABOUT THE REAL KANA STORY BECAUSE HE TOLD ME WHEN I WAS BO! I COMPLETELY FORGOT HOW I'D ACTUALLY FEEL IF I DIDN'T ALREADY KNOW THAT!
THERE'S SOMETHING ELSE THAT'S BEEN BOTHERING ME.
AREN'T YOU...
...DETERMINED TO CONFESS YOUR FEELINGS TO THE GIRL YOU'RE IN LOVE WITH?
HOW DID YOU KNOW THAT?
...
Crisis after crisis...
shrr
shrr
UH-OH...
I MADE UP MY MIND TO CONFESS MY FEELINGS TO THE GIRL I'M IN LOVE WITH...
...ONLY A FEW MINUTES BEFORE I RAN INTO YOU.
AM I...
AM I...
...IN REAL TROUBLE?

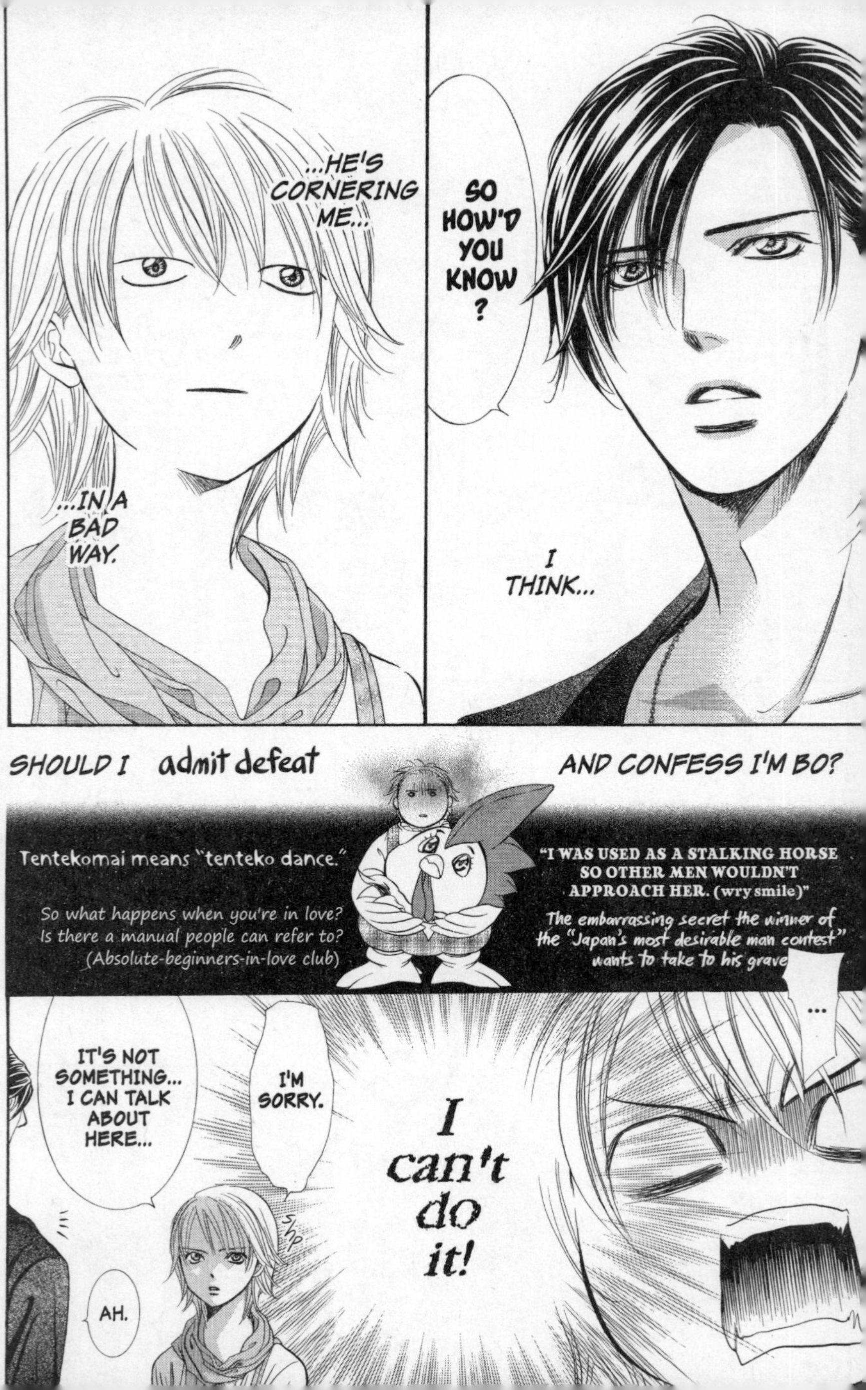
SO HOW'D YOU KNOW?
I THINK...
...HE'S CORNERING ME...
...IN A BAD WAY.
SHOULD I admit defeat AND CONFESS I'M BO?
"I WAS USED AS A STALKING HORSE SO OTHER MEN WOULDN'T APPROACH HER. (wry smile)"
The embarrassing secret the winner of the "Japan's most desirable man contest" wants to take to his grave
Tentekomai means "tenteko dance."
So what happens when you're in love? Is there a manual people can refer to? (Absolute-beginners-in-love club)
...
I can't do it!
I'M SORRY.
IT'S NOT SOMETHING... I CAN TALK ABOUT HERE...
SHP
AH.

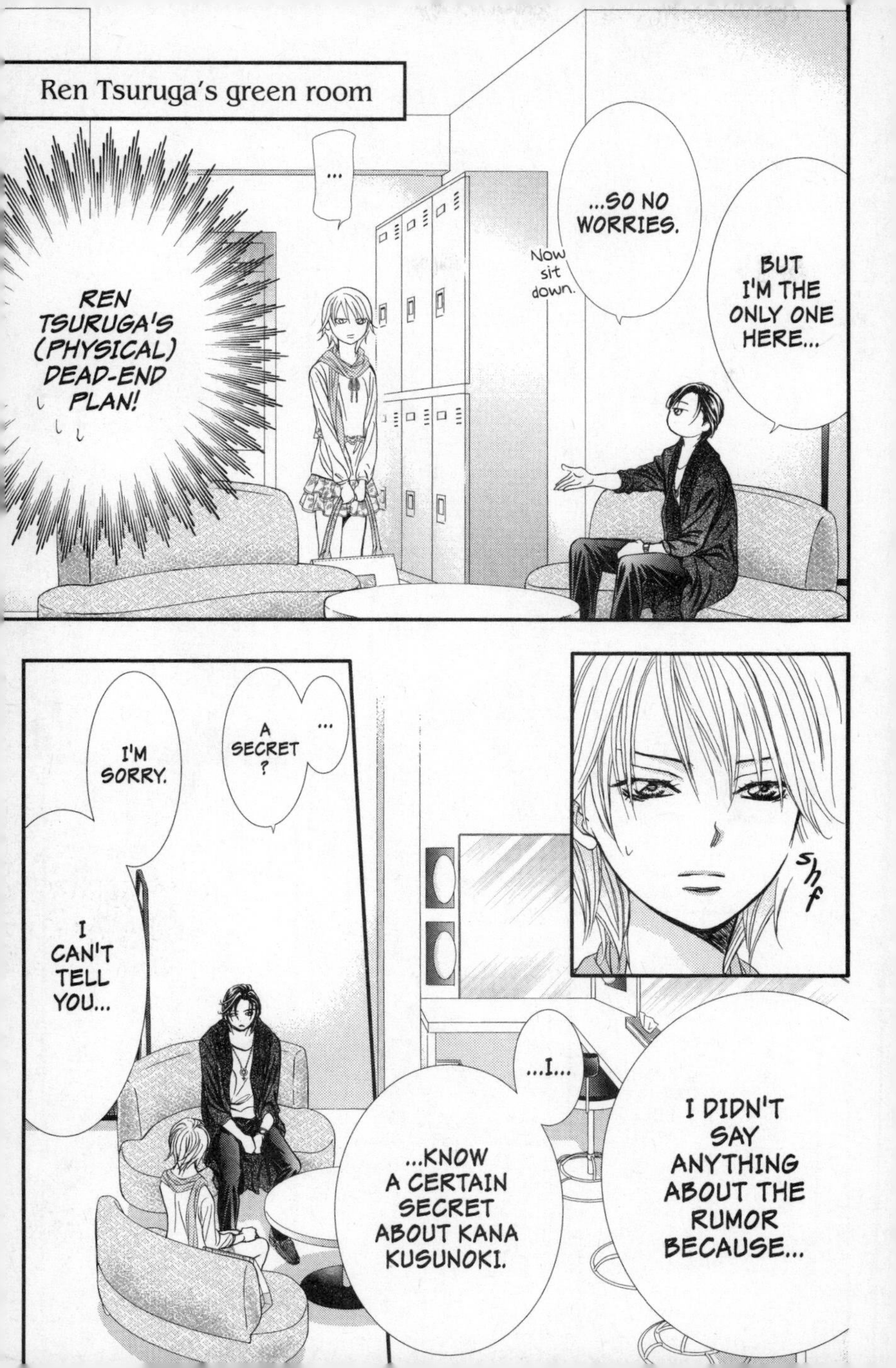
Ren Tsuruga's green room
BUT I'M THE ONLY ONE HERE...
...SO NO WORRIES.
Now sit down.
...
REN TSURUGA'S (PHYSICAL) DEAD-END PLAN!
shf
I DIDN'T SAY ANYTHING ABOUT THE RUMOR BECAUSE...
...I...
...KNOW A CERTAIN SECRET ABOUT KANA KUSUNOKI.
...
A SECRET?
I'M SORRY.
I CAN'T TELL YOU...

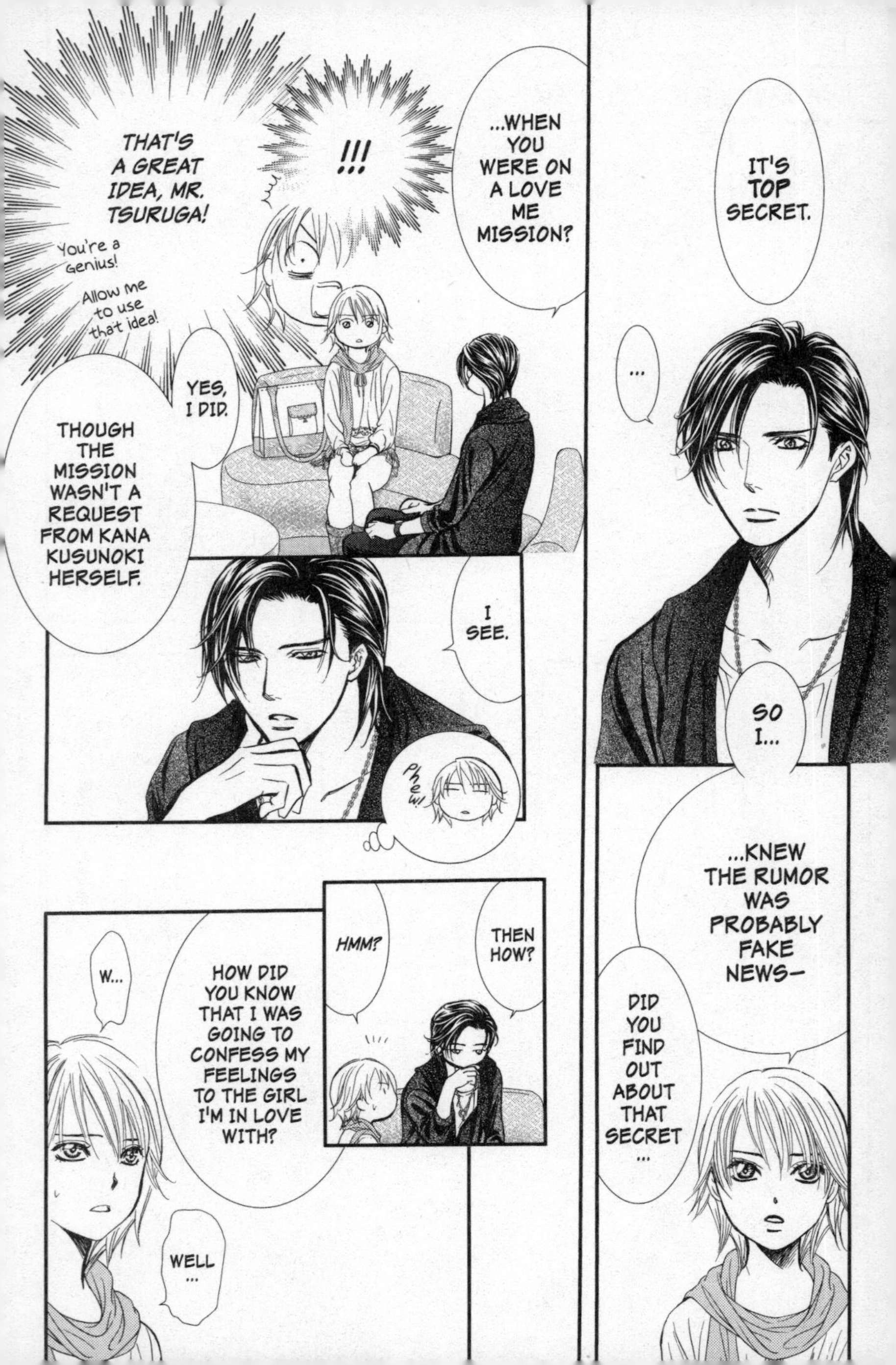
...WHEN YOU WERE ON A LOVE ME MISSION?
!!!
THAT'S A GREAT IDEA, MR. TSURUGA!
You're a Genius!
Allow me to use that idea!
YES, I DID.
THOUGH THE MISSION WASN'T A REQUEST FROM KANA KUSUNOKI HERSELF.
I SEE.
Phew!
THEN HOW?
HMM?
HOW DID YOU KNOW THAT I WAS GOING TO CONFESS MY FEELINGS TO THE GIRL I'M IN LOVE WITH?
W...
WELL...
IT'S TOP SECRET.
...
SO I...
...KNEW THE RUMOR WAS PROBABLY FAKE NEWS—
DID YOU FIND OUT ABOUT THAT SECRET...

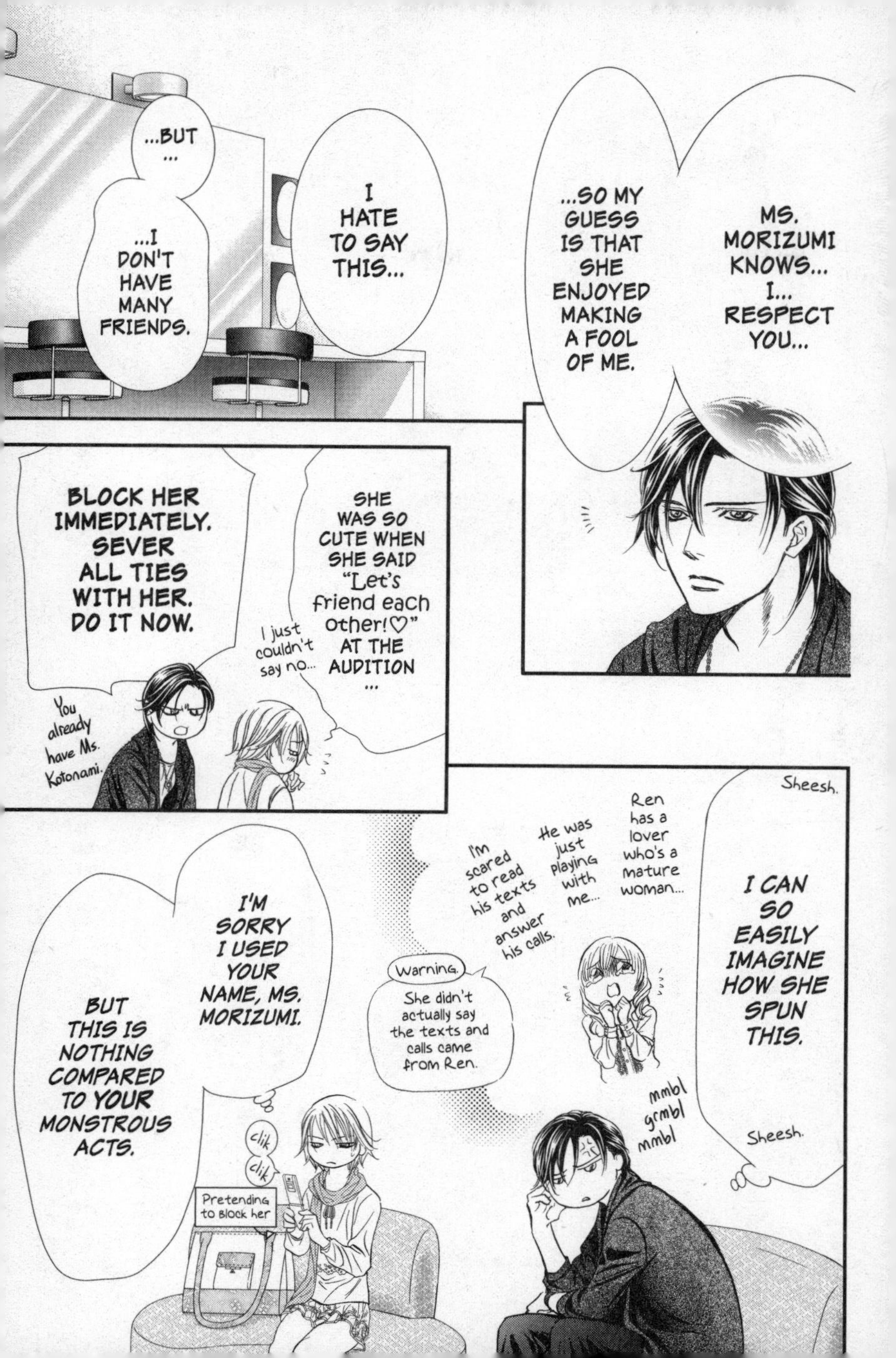
MS. MORIZUMI KNOWS... I... RESPECT YOU...
...SO MY GUESS IS THAT SHE ENJOYED MAKING A FOOL OF ME.
I HATE TO SAY THIS...
...BUT ...
...I DON'T HAVE MANY FRIENDS.
SHE WAS SO CUTE WHEN SHE SAID "Let's friend each other!♡" AT THE AUDITION ...
I just couldn't say no...
BLOCK HER IMMEDIATELY. SEVER ALL TIES WITH HER. DO IT NOW.
You already have Ms. Kotonami.
Sheesh.
I CAN SO EASILY IMAGINE HOW SHE SPUN THIS.
Sheesh.
Ren has a lover who's a mature woman...
He was just playing with me...
I'm scared to read his texts and answer his calls.
mmbl grmbl mmbl
Warning.
She didn't actually say the texts and calls came from Ren.
I'M SORRY I USED YOUR NAME, MS. MORIZUMI.
BUT THIS IS NOTHING COMPARED TO YOUR MONSTROUS ACTS.
clik
clik
Pretending to block her

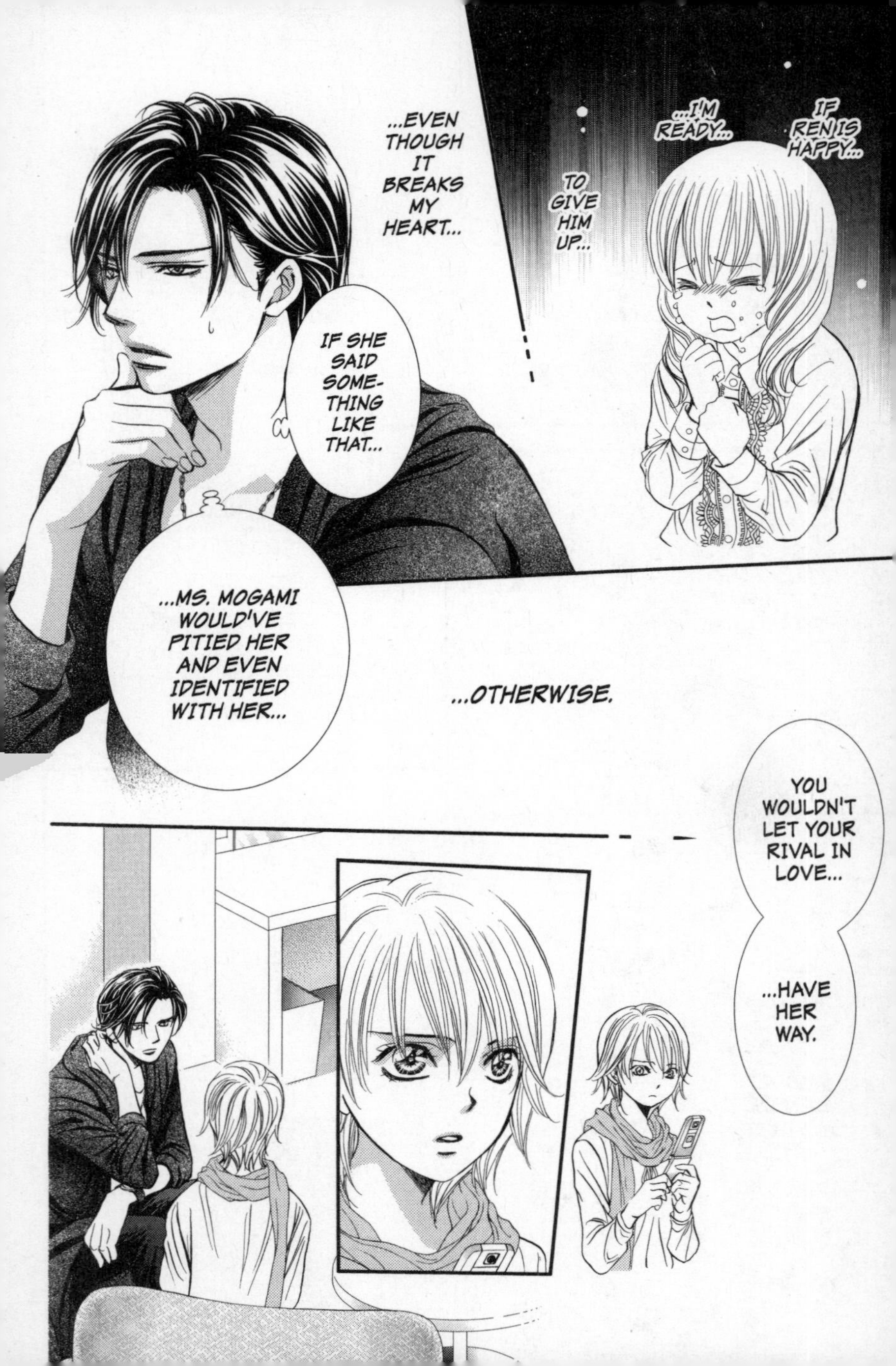
IF REN IS HAPPY...
...I'M READY...
TO GIVE HIM UP...
...EVEN THOUGH IT BREAKS MY HEART...
IF SHE SAID SOME-THING LIKE THAT...
...MS. MOGAMI WOULD'VE PITIED HER AND EVEN IDENTIFIED WITH HER...
...OTHERWISE.
YOU WOULDN'T LET YOUR RIVAL IN LOVE...
...HAVE HER WAY.

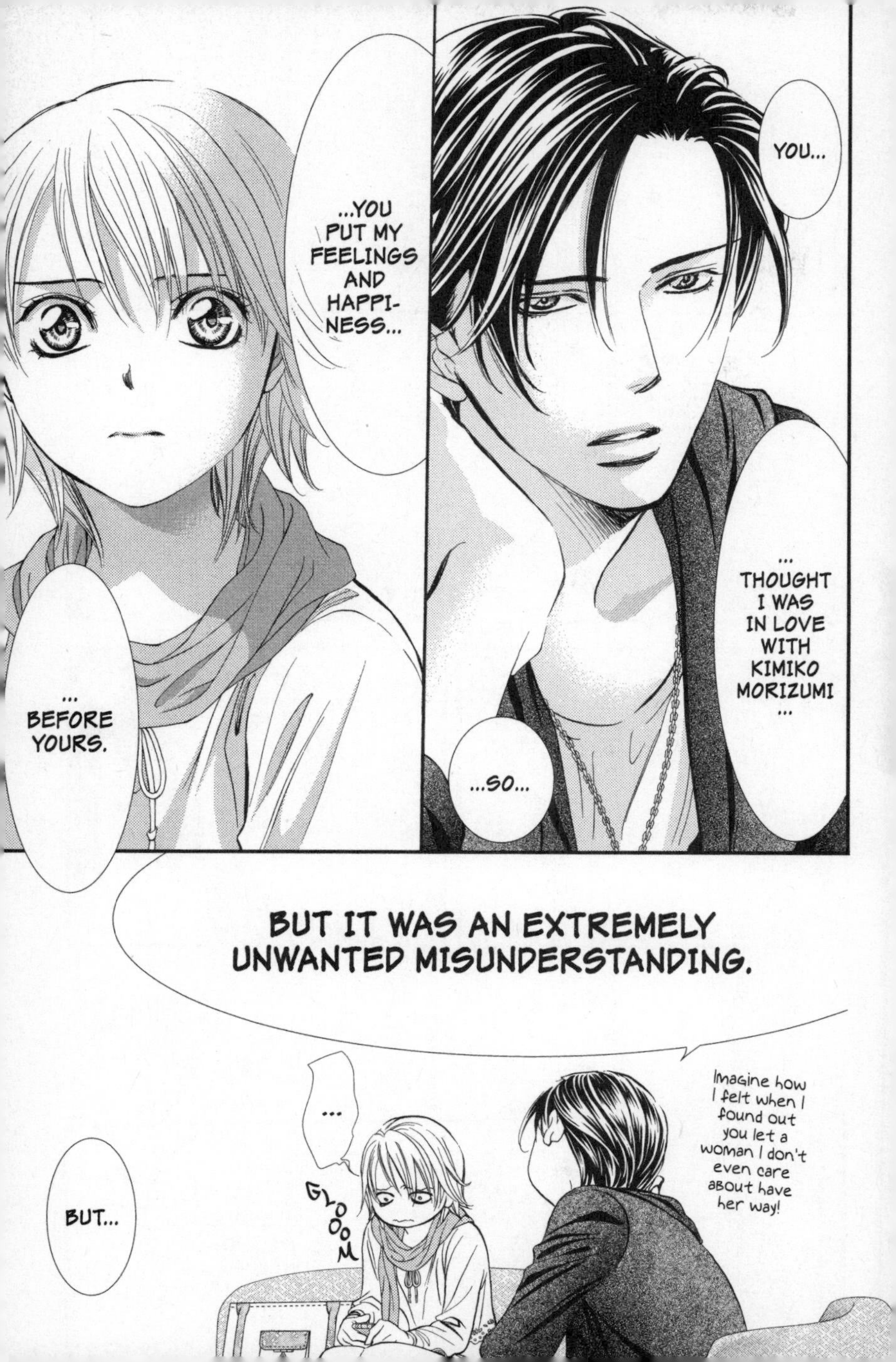
YOU...
...THOUGHT I WAS IN LOVE WITH KIMIKO MORIZUMI...
...SO...
...YOU PUT MY FEELINGS AND HAPPINESS...
...BEFORE YOURS.
BUT IT WAS AN EXTREMELY UNWANTED MISUNDERSTANDING.
Imagine how I felt when I found out you let a woman I don't even care about have her way!
...
GLOOOM
BUT...

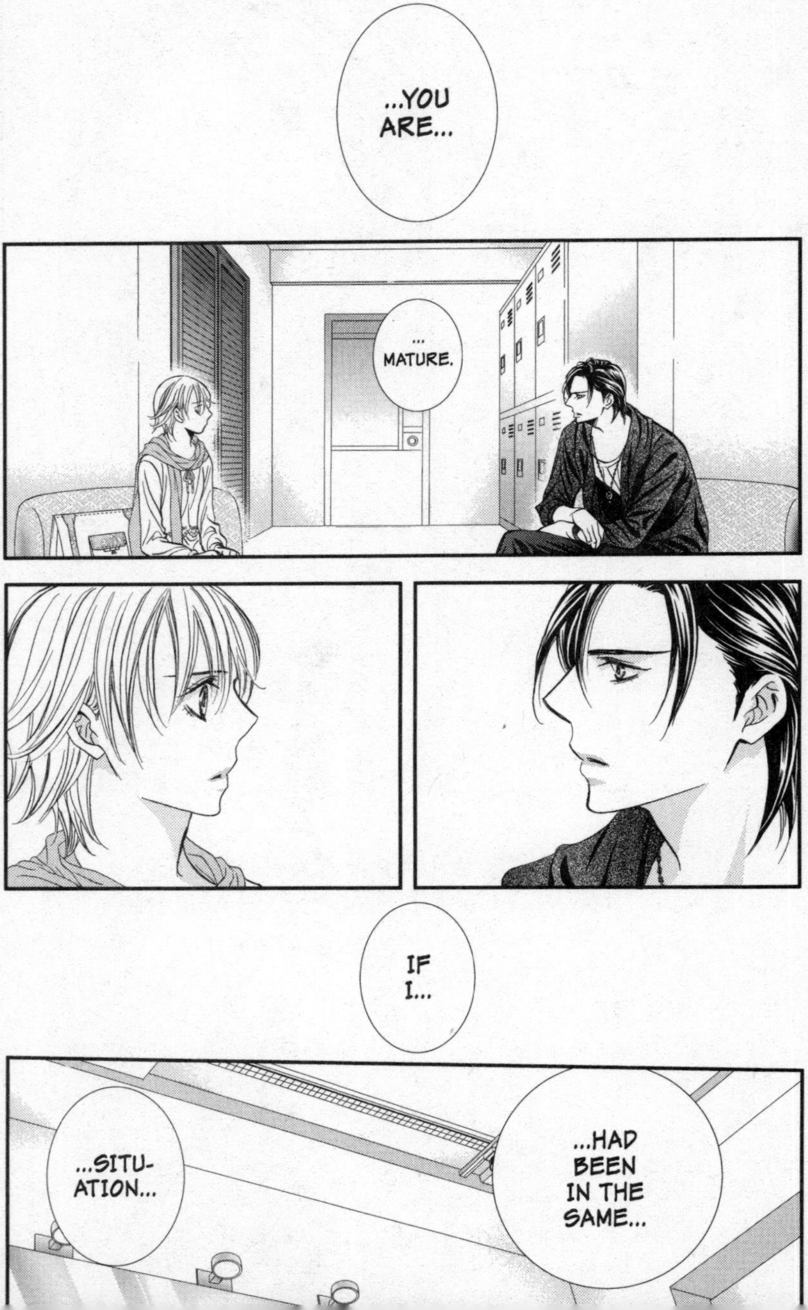
...YOU ARE...
... MATURE.
IF I...
...HAD BEEN IN THE SAME...
...SITU-ATION...

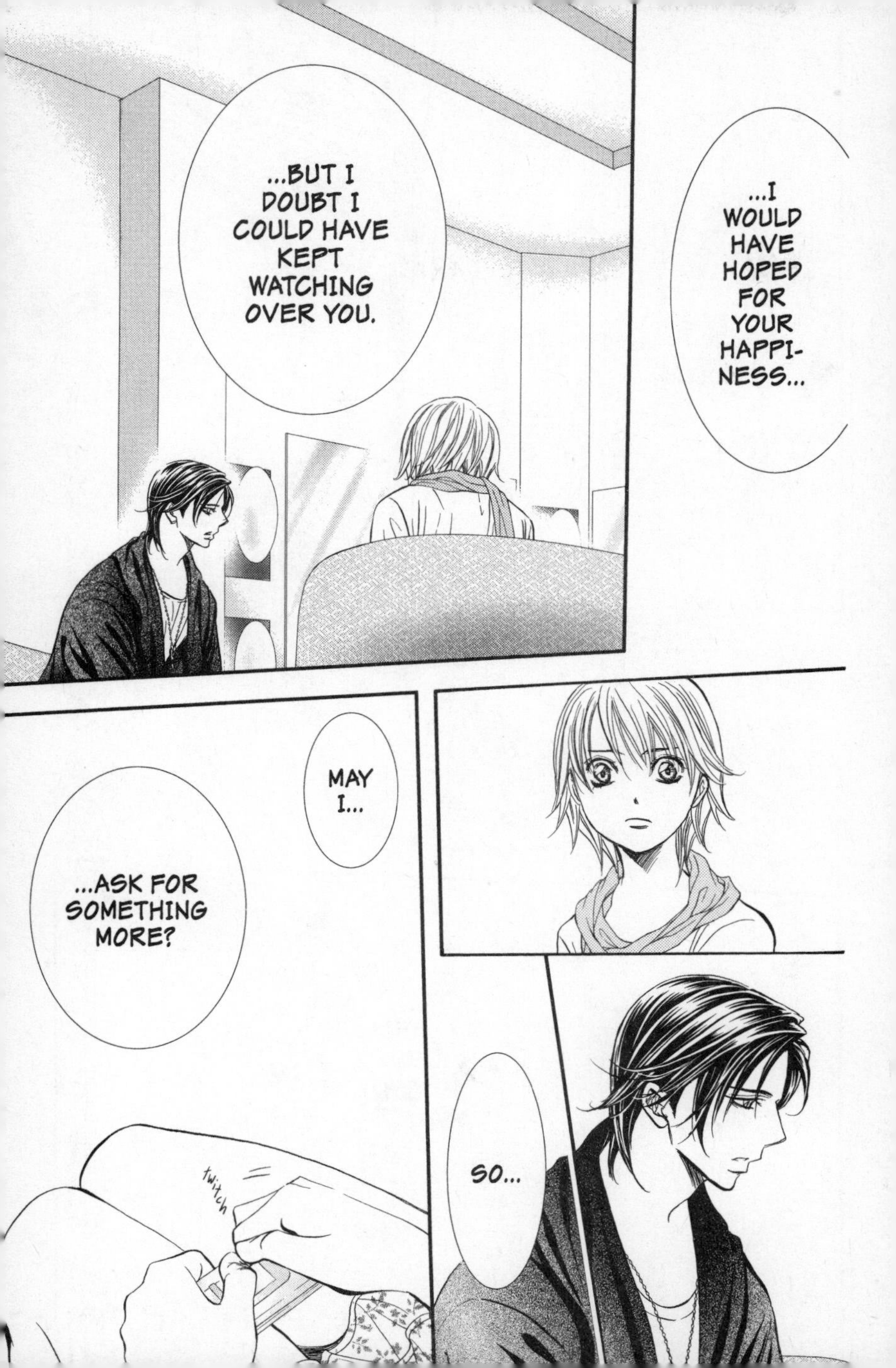
...I WOULD HAVE HOPED FOR YOUR HAPPINESS...
...BUT I DOUBT I COULD HAVE KEPT WATCHING OVER YOU.
SO...
MAY I...
...ASK FOR SOMETHING MORE?
twitch

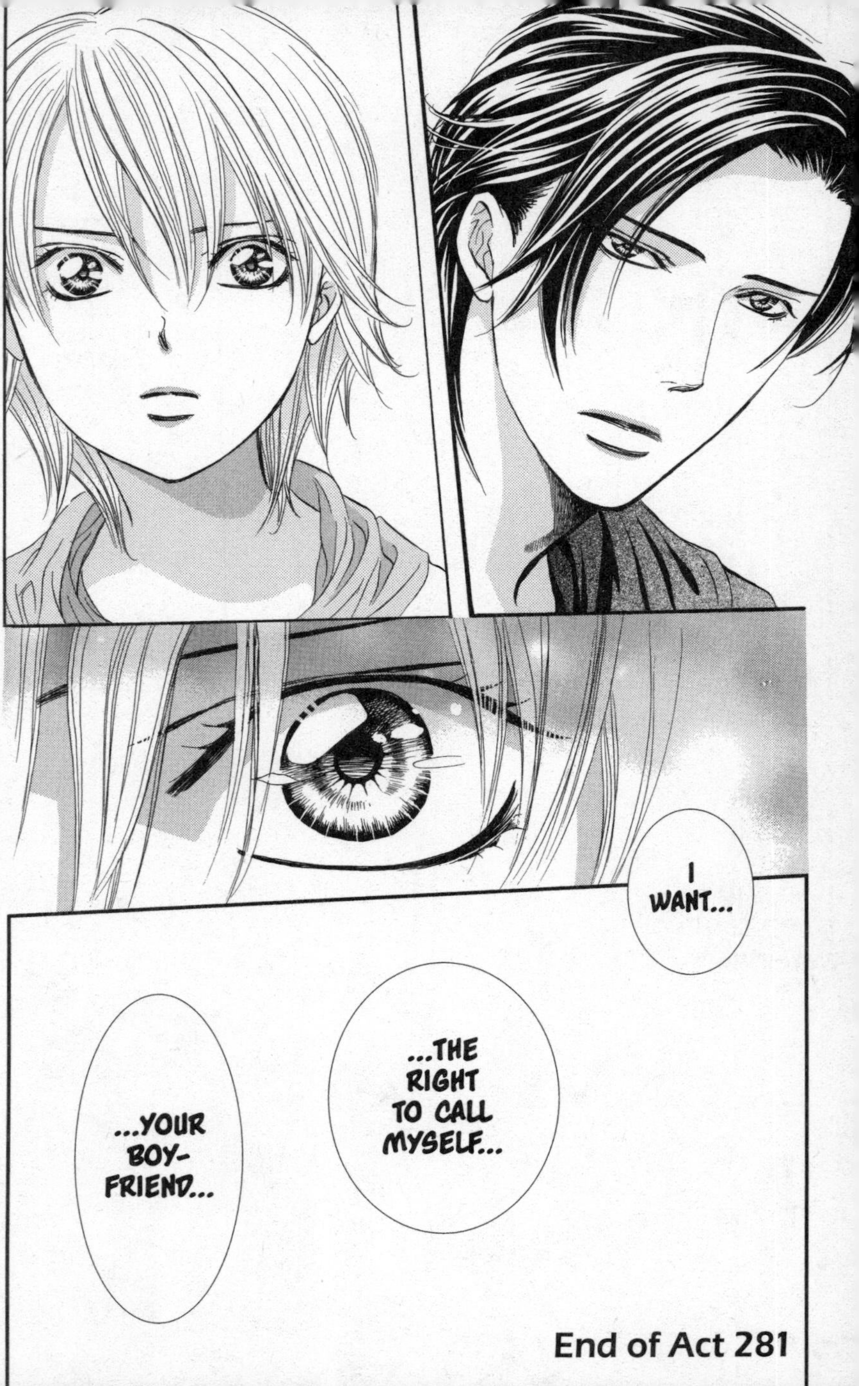
I WANT...
...THE RIGHT TO CALL MYSELF...
...YOUR BOY-FRIEND...
End of Act 281

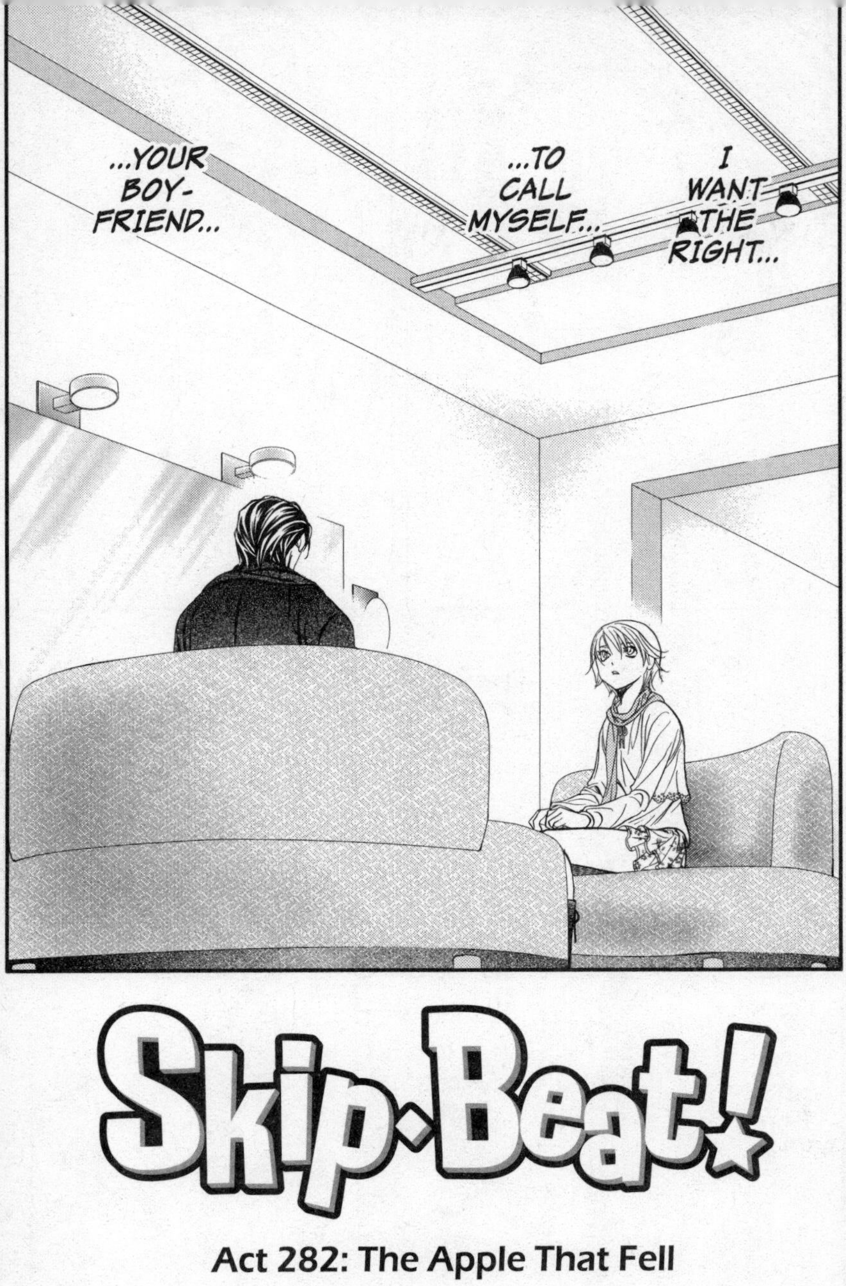
I WANT THE RIGHT...
...TO CALL MYSELF...
...YOUR BOY-FRIEND...

Skip·Beat!

Act 282: The Apple That Fell

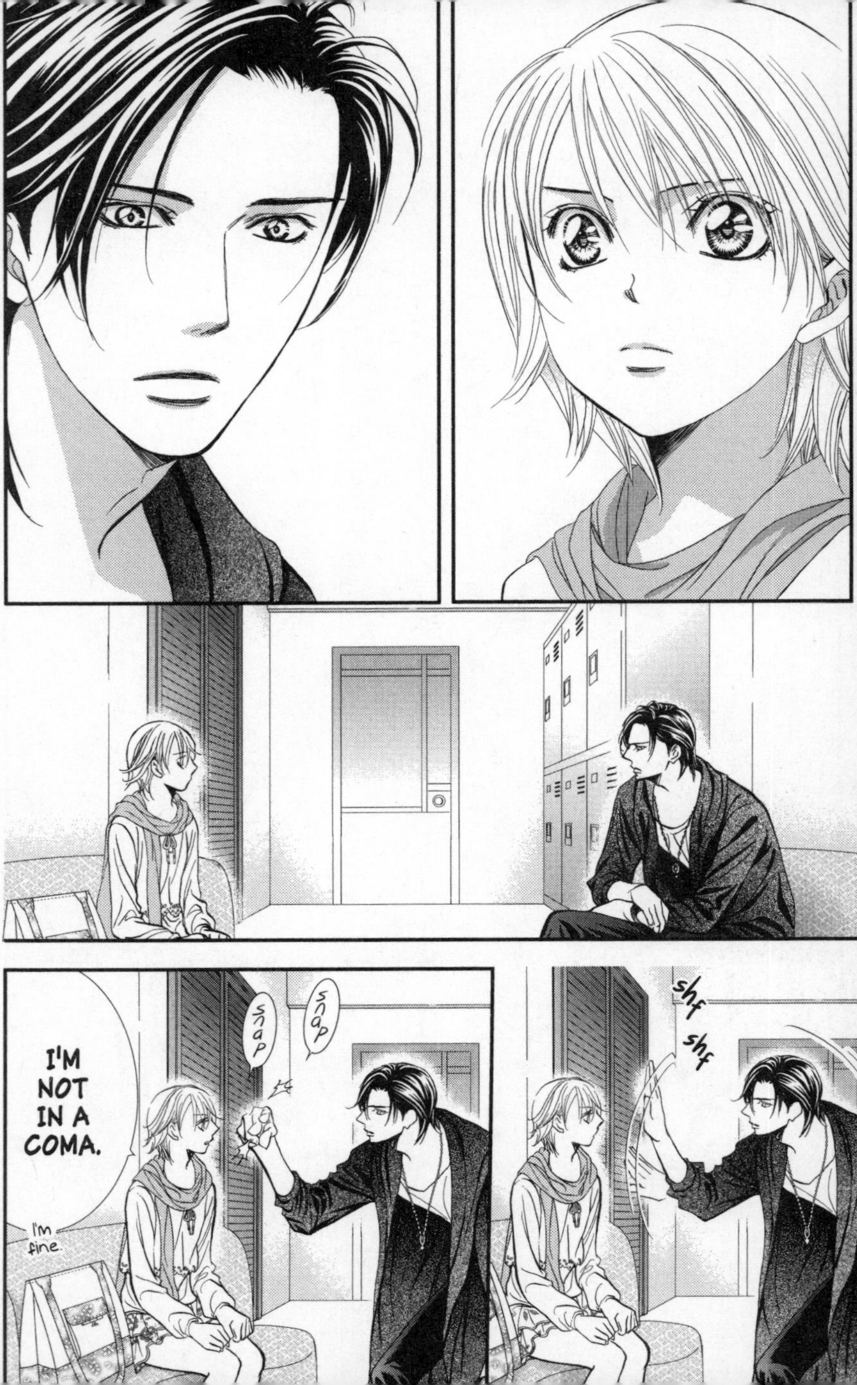
shf
shf
snap
snap
I'M NOT IN A COMA.
I'm fine.

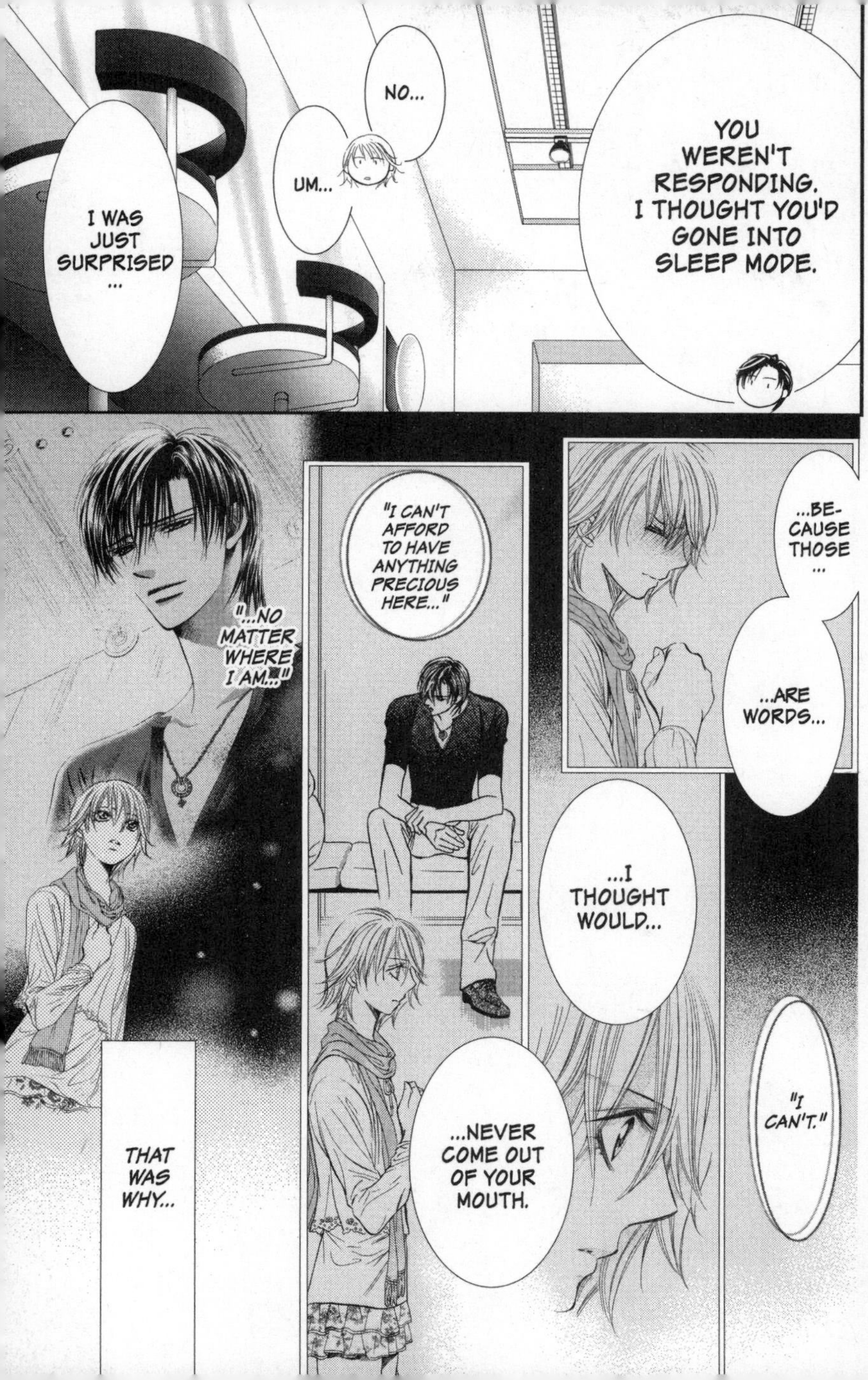
YOU WEREN'T RESPONDING. I THOUGHT YOU'D GONE INTO SLEEP MODE.
NO...
UM...
I WAS JUST SURPRISED...
...BE-CAUSE THOSE...
...ARE WORDS...
...I THOUGHT WOULD...
"I CAN'T."
...NEVER COME OUT OF YOUR MOUTH.
"I CAN'T AFFORD TO HAVE ANYTHING PRECIOUS HERE..."
"...NO MATTER WHERE I AM..."
THAT WAS WHY...

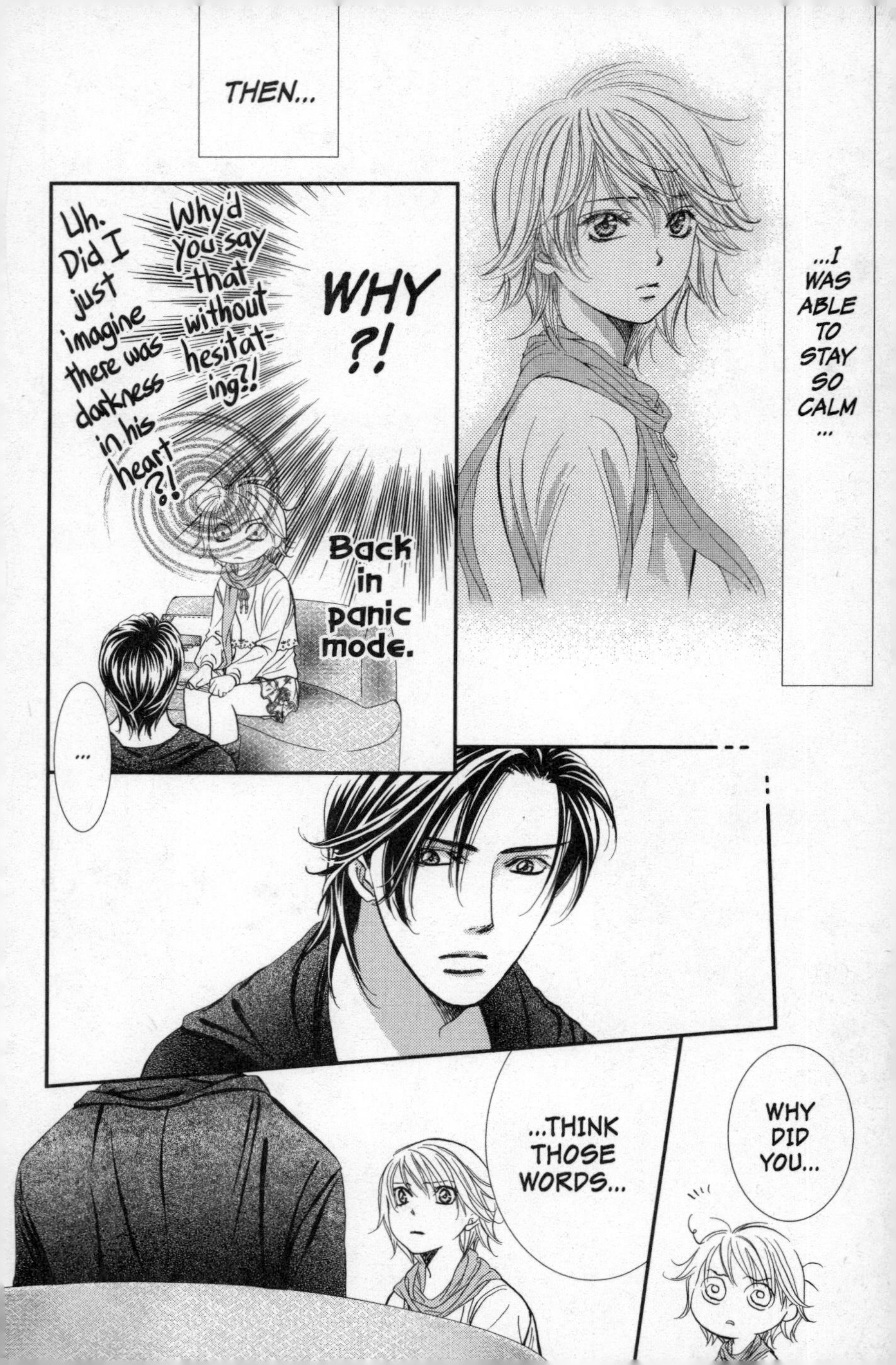

...I WAS ABLE TO STAY SO CALM...
THEN...
WHY ?!
Why'd you say that without hesitating?!
Uh. Did I just imagine there was darkness in his heart ?!
Back in panic mode.
...
WHY DID YOU...
...THINK THOSE WORDS...

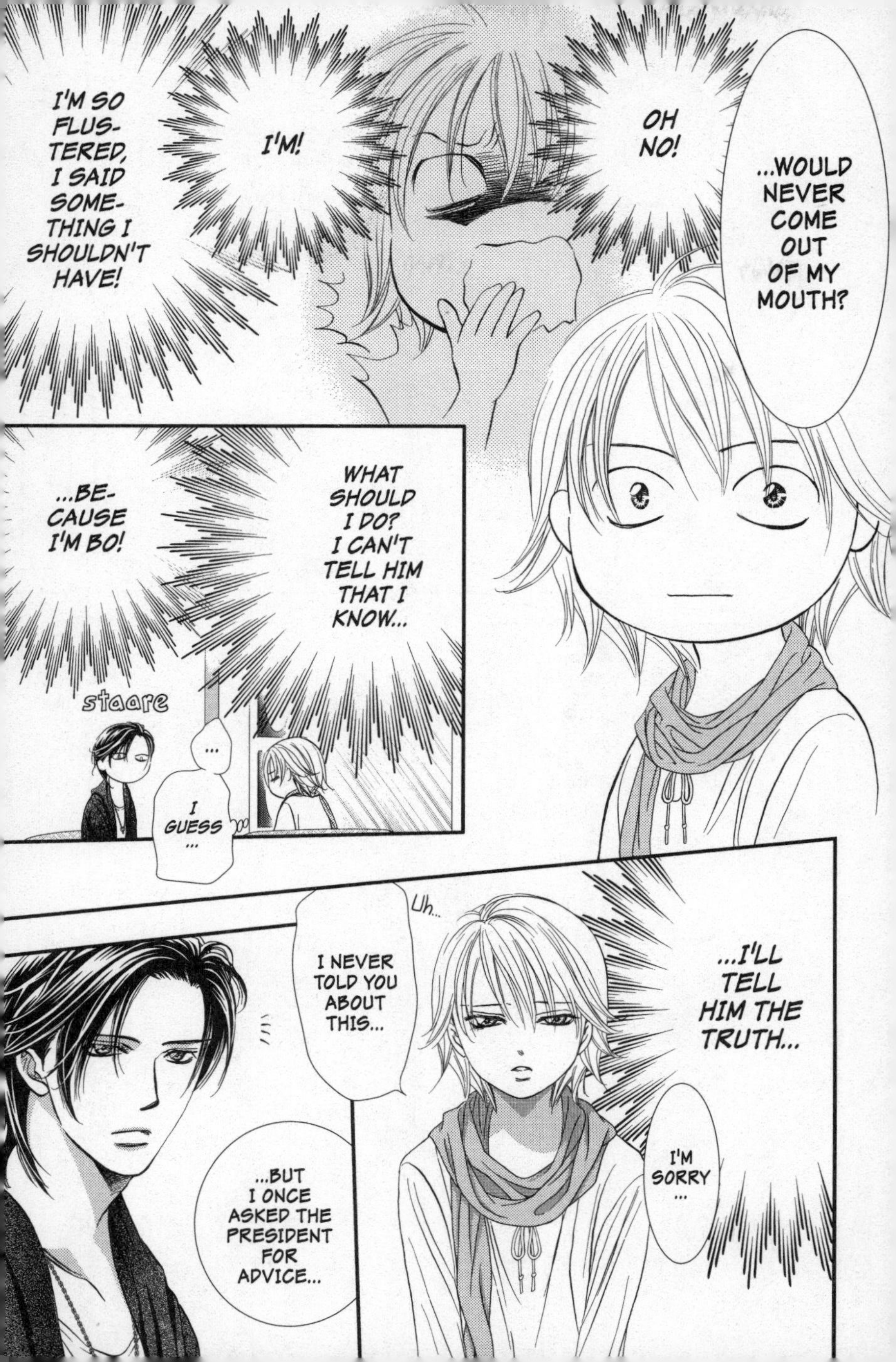
...WOULD NEVER COME OUT OF MY MOUTH?
OH NO!
I'M!
I'M SO FLUSTERED, I SAID SOMETHING I SHOULDN'T HAVE!
WHAT SHOULD I DO? I CAN'T TELL HIM THAT I KNOW...
...BECAUSE I'M BO!
staare
...
I GUESS...
...I'LL TELL HIM THE TRUTH...
I'M SORRY...
Uh...
I NEVER TOLD YOU ABOUT THIS...
...BUT I ONCE ASKED THE PRESIDENT FOR ADVICE...

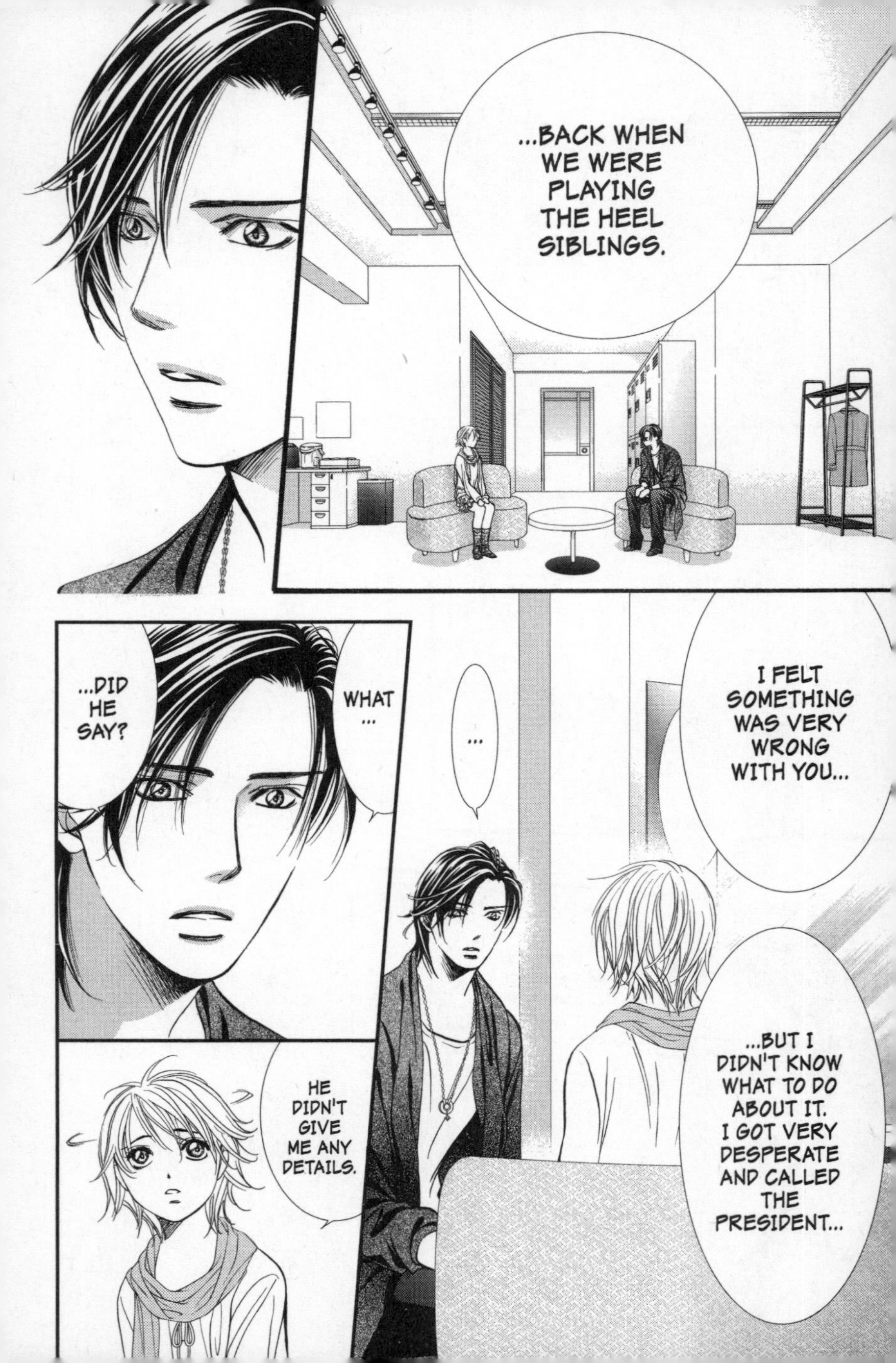
...BACK WHEN WE WERE PLAYING THE HEEL SIBLINGS.
I FELT SOMETHING WAS VERY WRONG WITH YOU...
...
...BUT I DIDN'T KNOW WHAT TO DO ABOUT IT. I GOT VERY DESPERATE AND CALLED THE PRESIDENT...
WHAT...
...DID HE SAY?
HE DIDN'T GIVE ME ANY DETAILS.

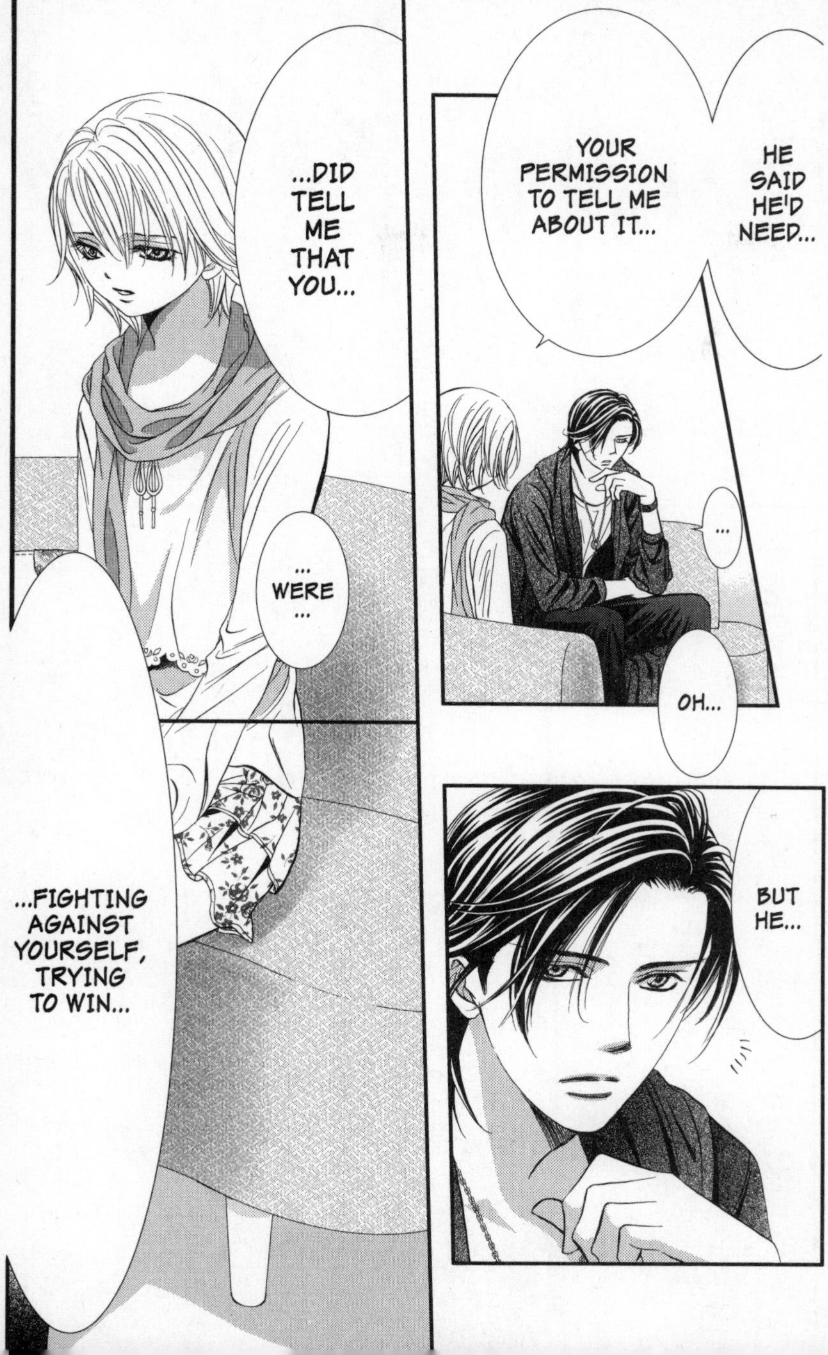
HE SAID HE'D NEED...
YOUR PERMISSION TO TELL ME ABOUT IT...
...
OH...
BUT HE...
...DID TELL ME THAT YOU...
...WERE...
...FIGHTING AGAINST YOURSELF, TRYING TO WIN...

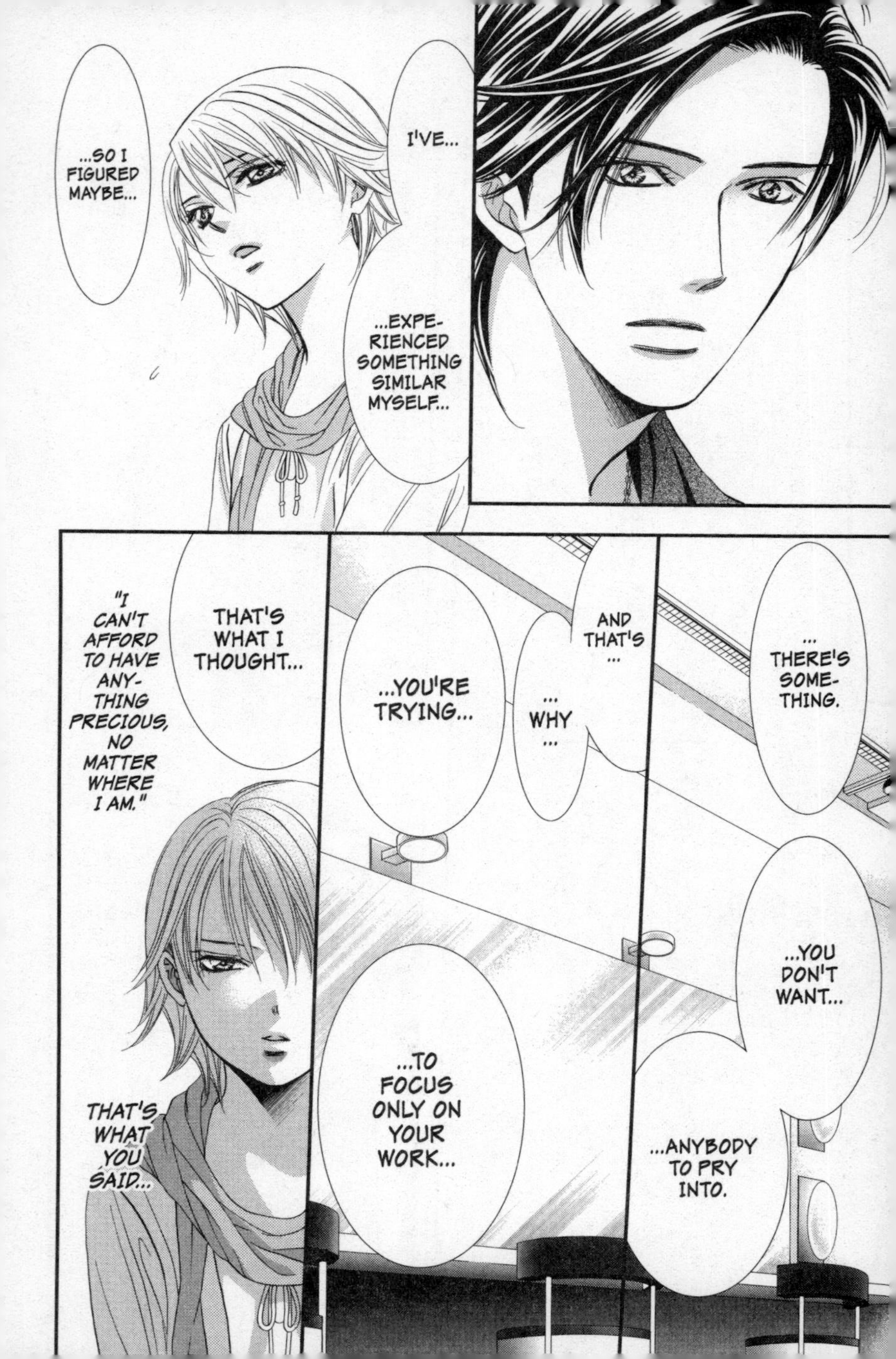
I'VE...
...EXPERIENCED SOMETHING SIMILAR MYSELF...
...SO I FIGURED MAYBE...
... THERE'S SOMETHING.
...YOU DON'T WANT...
...ANYBODY TO PRY INTO.
AND THAT'S ...
... WHY ...
...YOU'RE TRYING...
...TO FOCUS ONLY ON YOUR WORK...
THAT'S WHAT I THOUGHT...
"I CAN'T AFFORD TO HAVE ANYTHING PRECIOUS, NO MATTER WHERE I AM."
THAT'S WHAT YOU SAID...

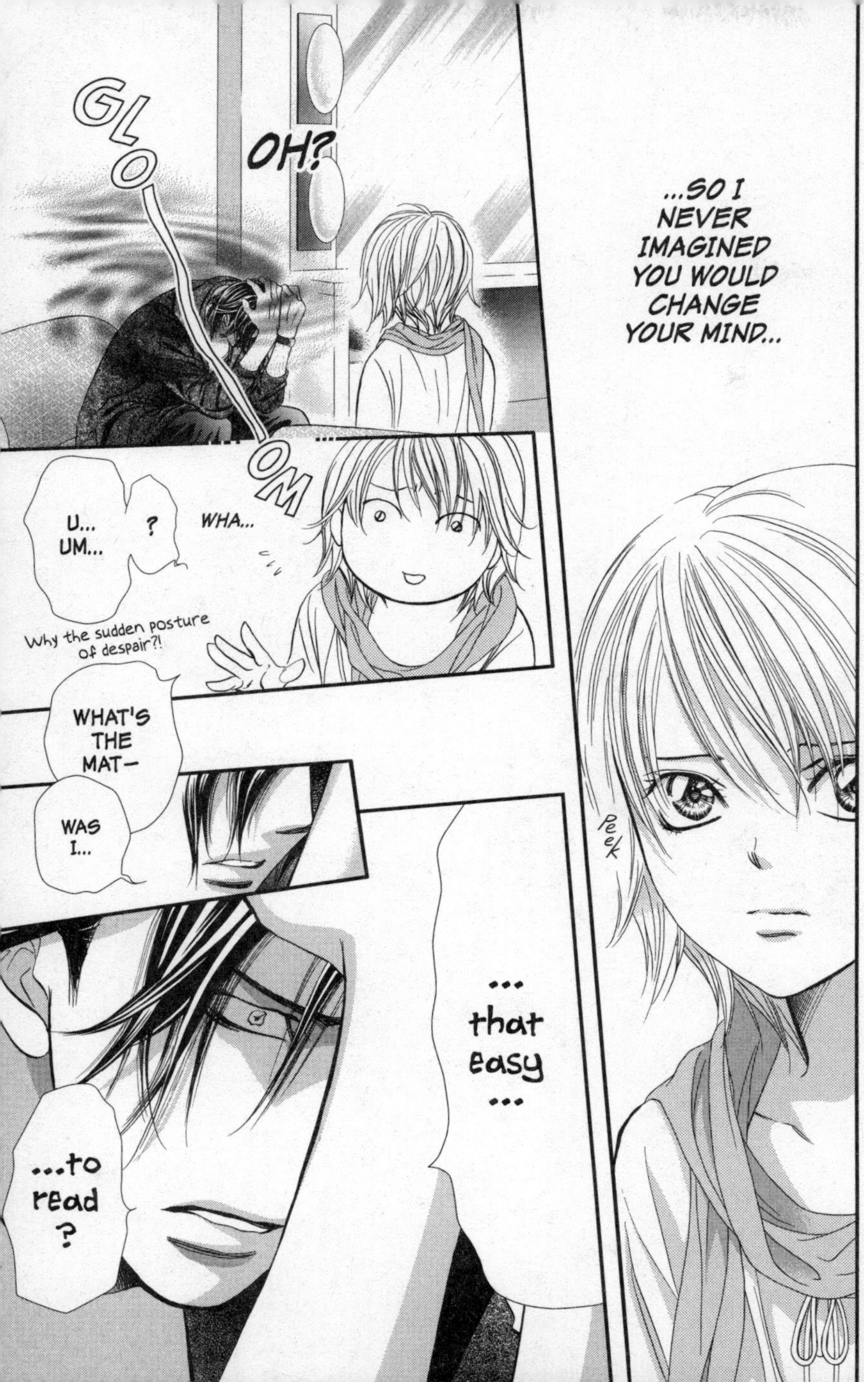
...SO I NEVER IMAGINED YOU WOULD CHANGE YOUR MIND...
Peek
OH?
GLOOM
WHA...
?
U... UM...
Why the sudden posture of despair?!
WHAT'S THE MAT—
WAS I...
...that easy...
...to read?

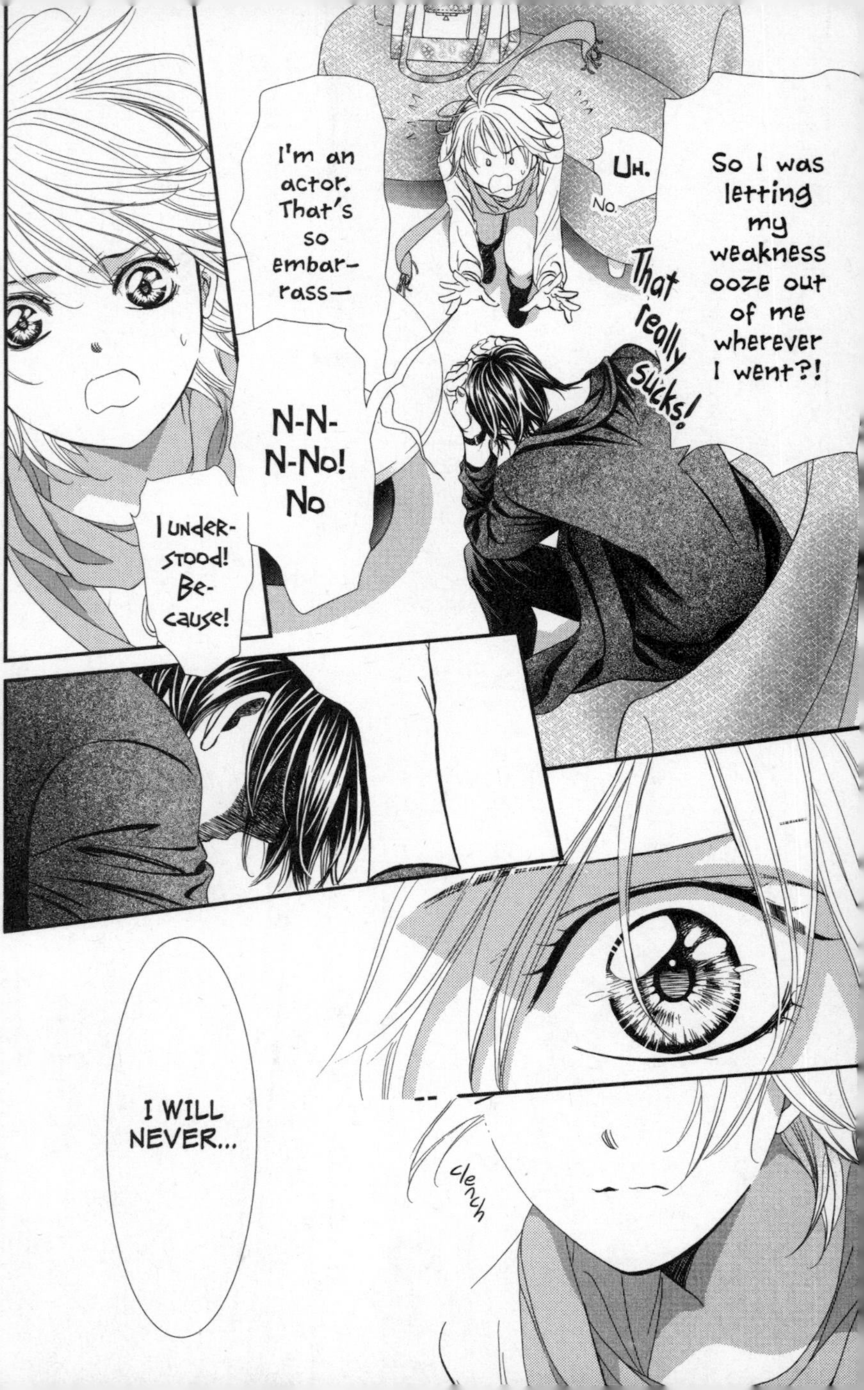
So I was letting my weakness ooze out of me wherever I went?!
That really sucks!
Uh.
No.
I'm an actor. That's so embarrass—
N-N-N-No! No
I under-stood! Be-cause!
clench
I WILL NEVER...

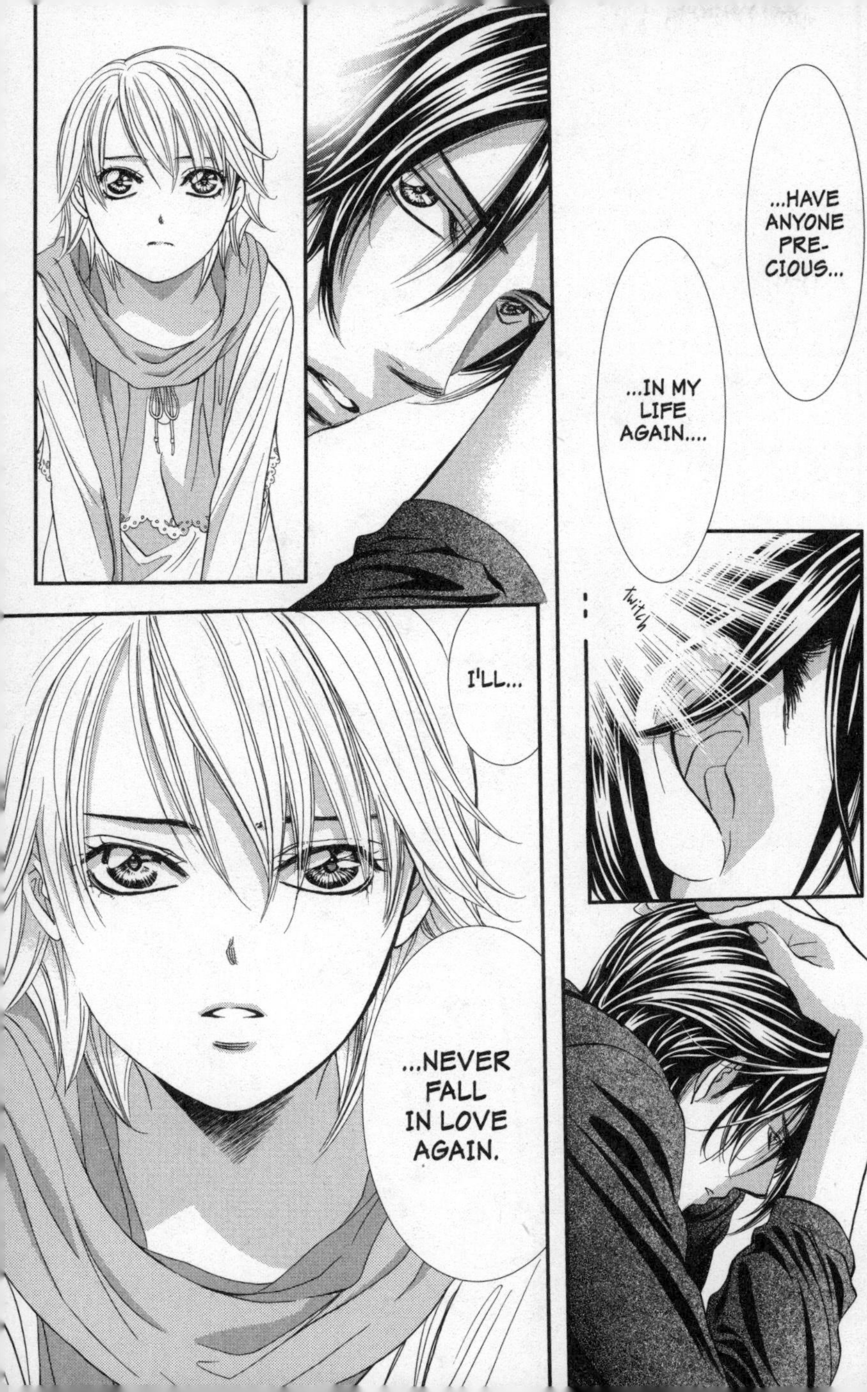
...HAVE ANYONE PRE- CIOUS...
...IN MY LIFE AGAIN....
twitch
:
I'LL...
...NEVER FALL IN LOVE AGAIN.

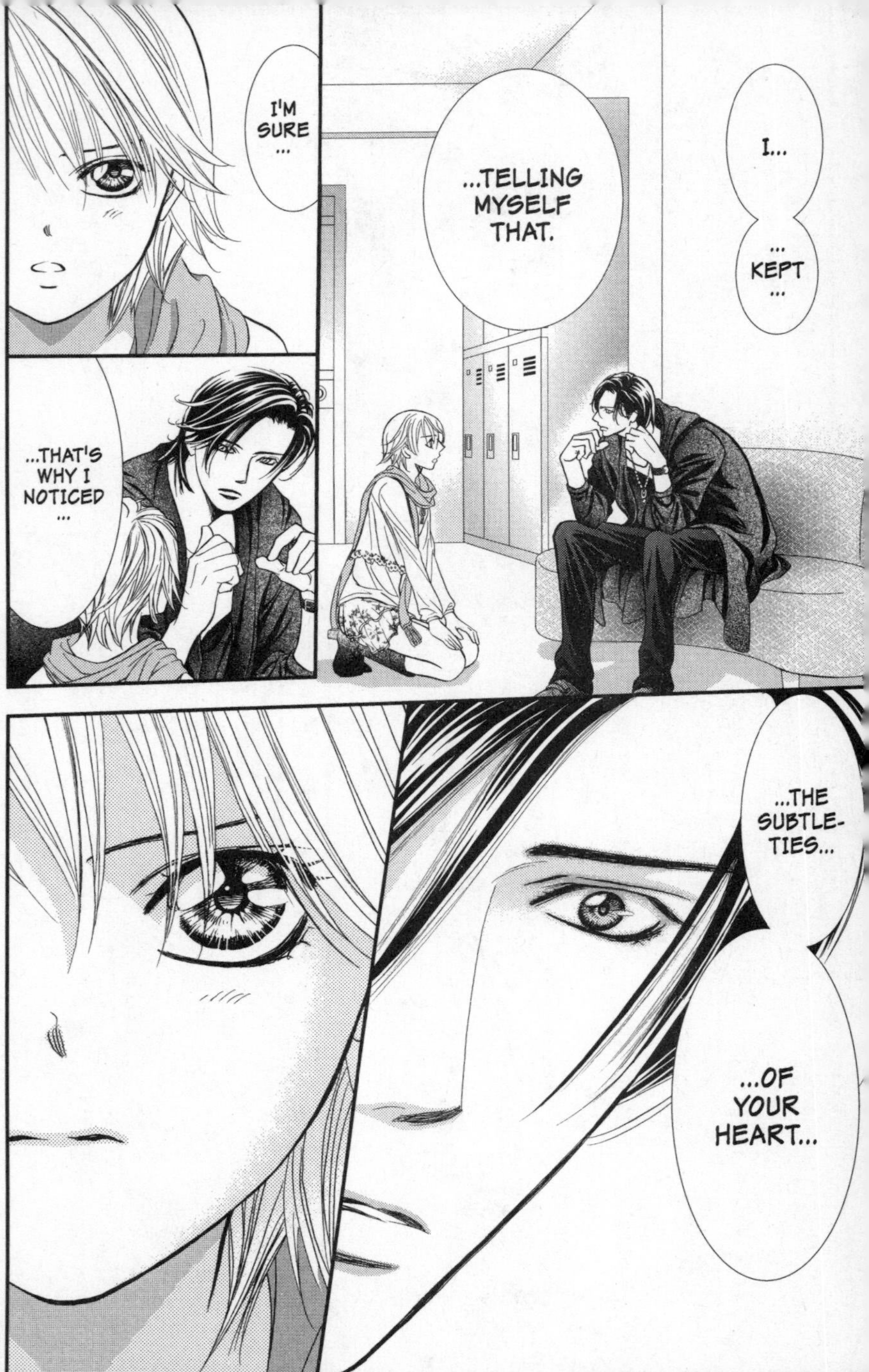
I...
...KEPT...
...TELLING MYSELF THAT.
I'M SURE...
...THAT'S WHY I NOTICED...
...THE SUBTLE-TIES...
...OF YOUR HEART...

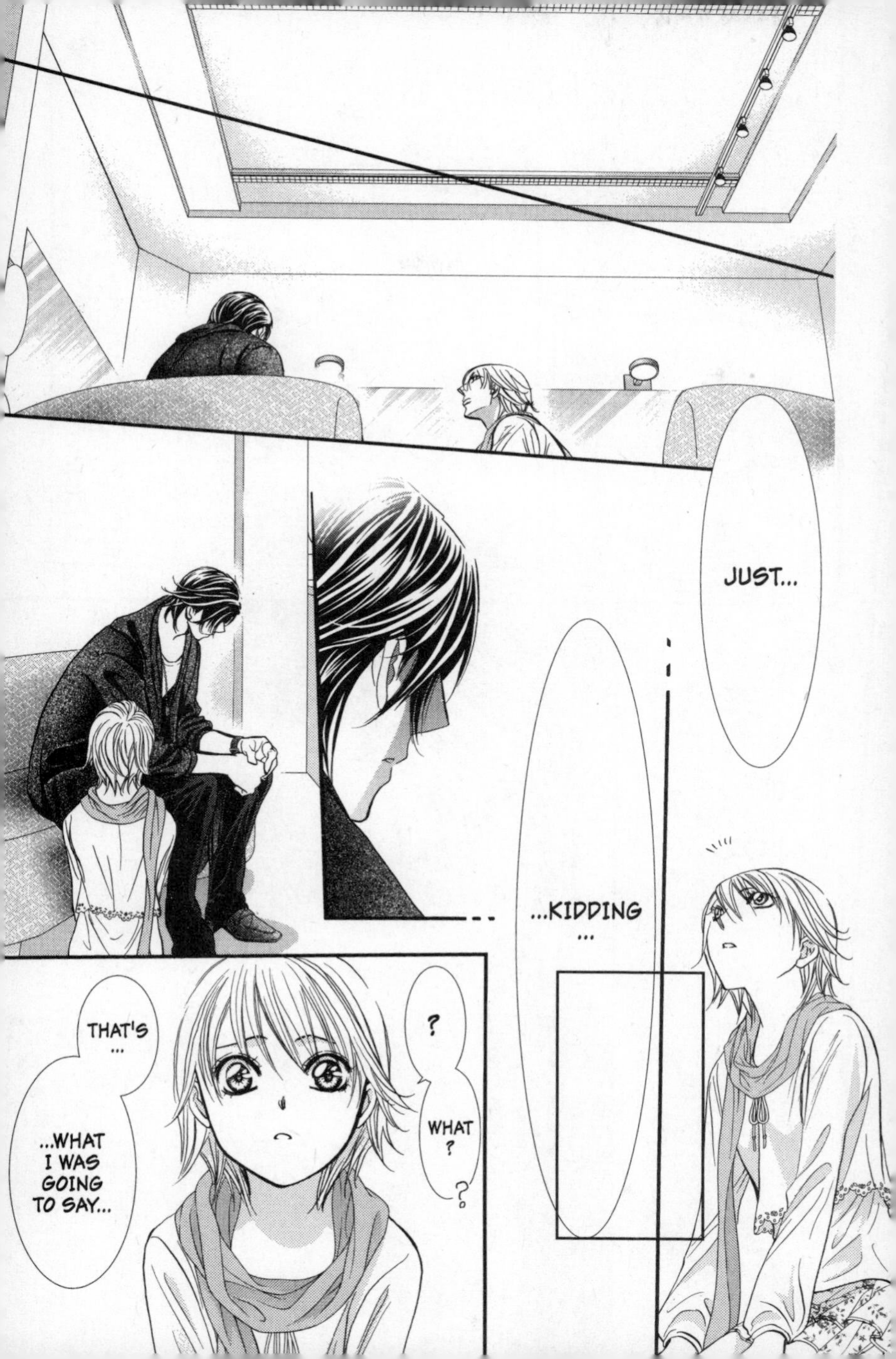
JUST...
...KIDDING...
? WHAT? ?
THAT'S...
...WHAT I WAS GOING TO SAY...

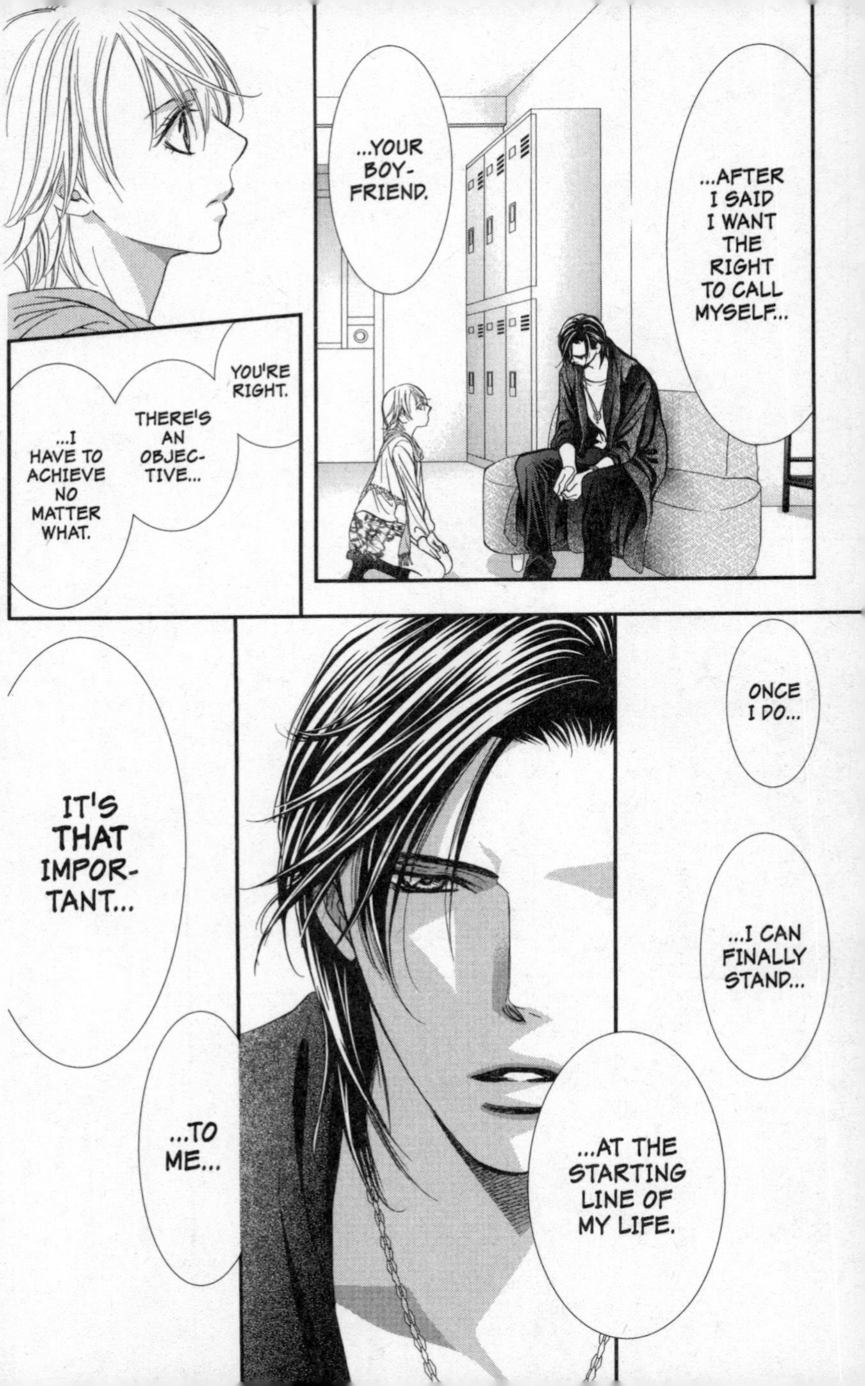
...AFTER I SAID I WANT THE RIGHT TO CALL MYSELF...
...YOUR BOY-FRIEND.
YOU'RE RIGHT.
THERE'S AN OBJEC-TIVE...
...I HAVE TO ACHIEVE NO MATTER WHAT.
ONCE I DO...
...I CAN FINALLY STAND...
...AT THE STARTING LINE OF MY LIFE.
IT'S THAT IMPOR-TANT...
...TO ME...

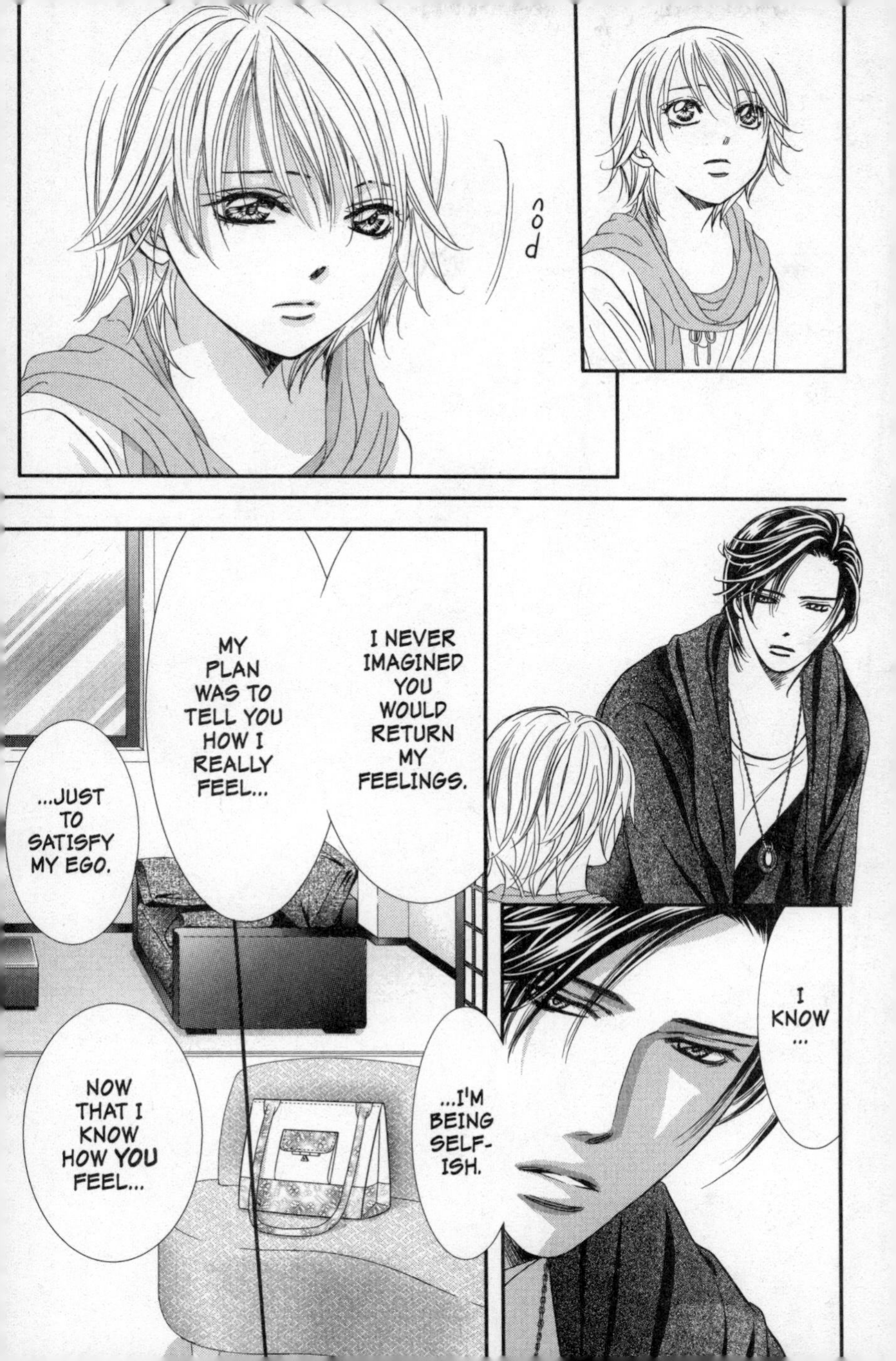
nod
I NEVER IMAGINED YOU WOULD RETURN MY FEELINGS.
MY PLAN WAS TO TELL YOU HOW I REALLY FEEL...
...JUST TO SATISFY MY EGO.
NOW THAT I KNOW HOW YOU FEEL...
I KNOW...
...I'M BEING SELF-ISH.

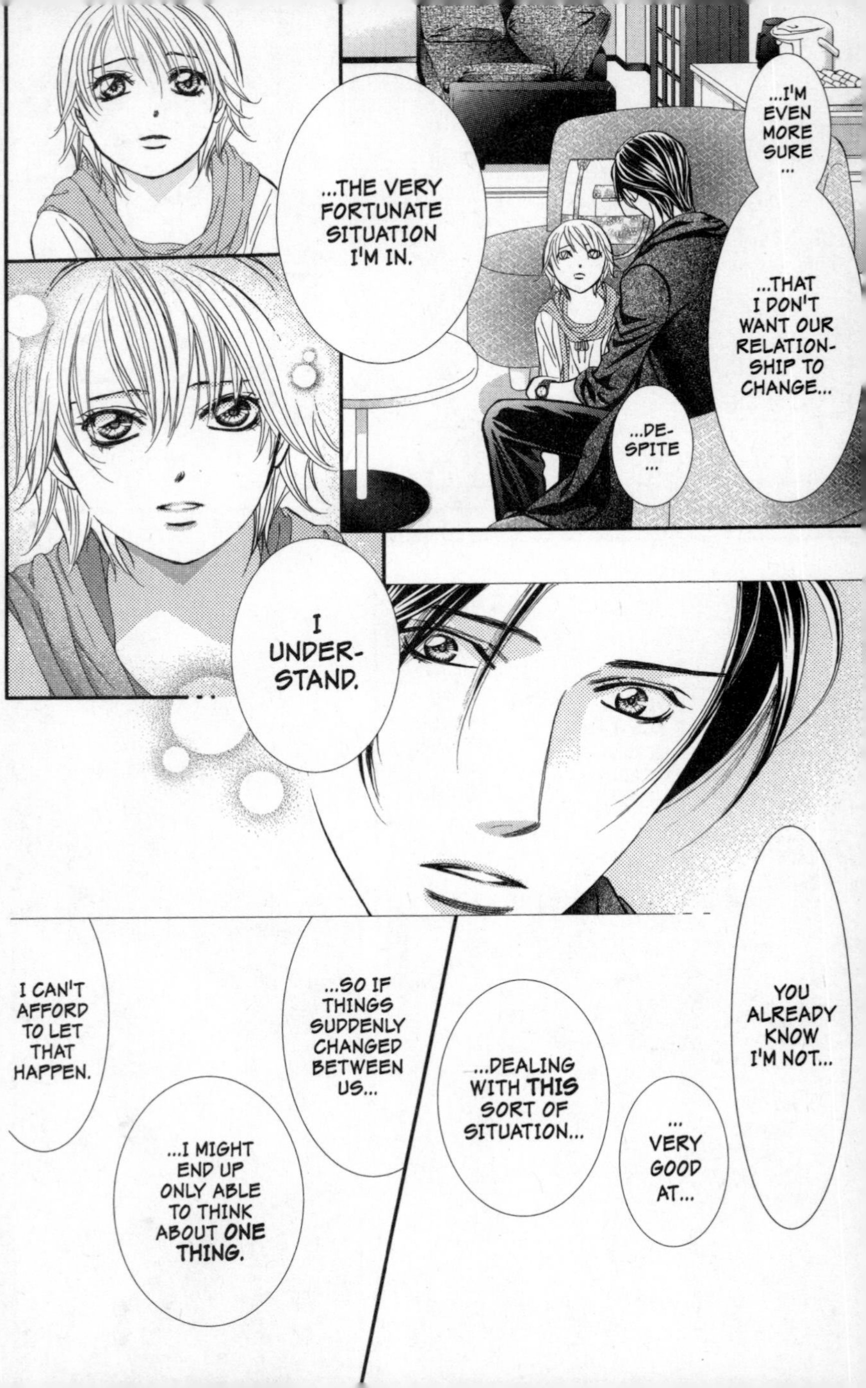
...I'M EVEN MORE SURE ...
...THAT I DON'T WANT OUR RELATION-SHIP TO CHANGE...
...DE-SPITE ...
...THE VERY FORTUNATE SITUATION I'M IN.
I UNDER-STAND.
YOU ALREADY KNOW I'M NOT...
... VERY GOOD AT...
...DEALING WITH THIS SORT OF SITUATION...
...SO IF THINGS SUDDENLY CHANGED BETWEEN US...
...I MIGHT END UP ONLY ABLE TO THINK ABOUT ONE THING.
I CAN'T AFFORD TO LET THAT HAPPEN.

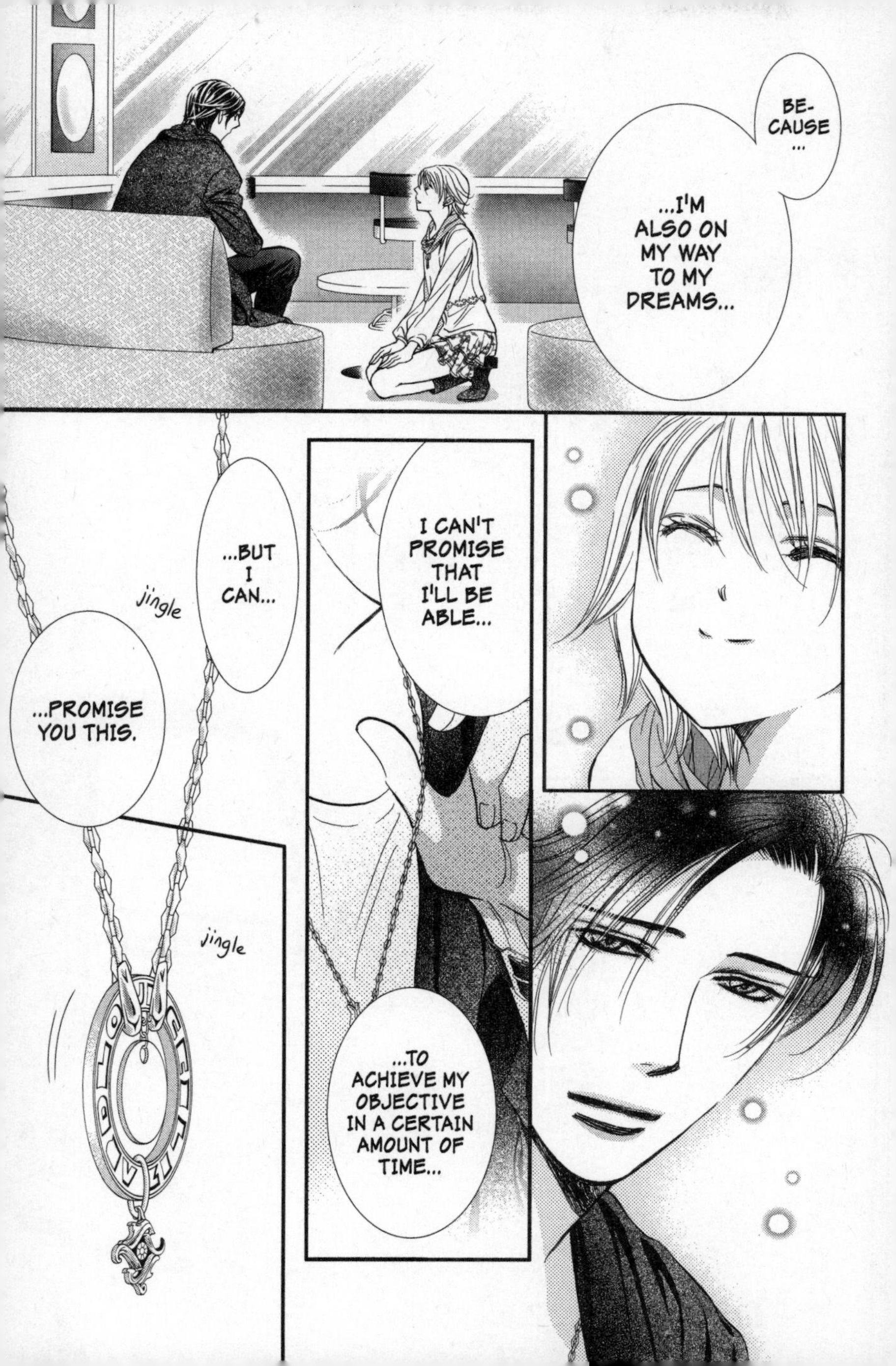
BE-CAUSE...
...I'M ALSO ON MY WAY TO MY DREAMS...
I CAN'T PROMISE THAT I'LL BE ABLE...
...TO ACHIEVE MY OBJECTIVE IN A CERTAIN AMOUNT OF TIME...
...BUT I CAN...
jingle
...PROMISE YOU THIS.
jingle

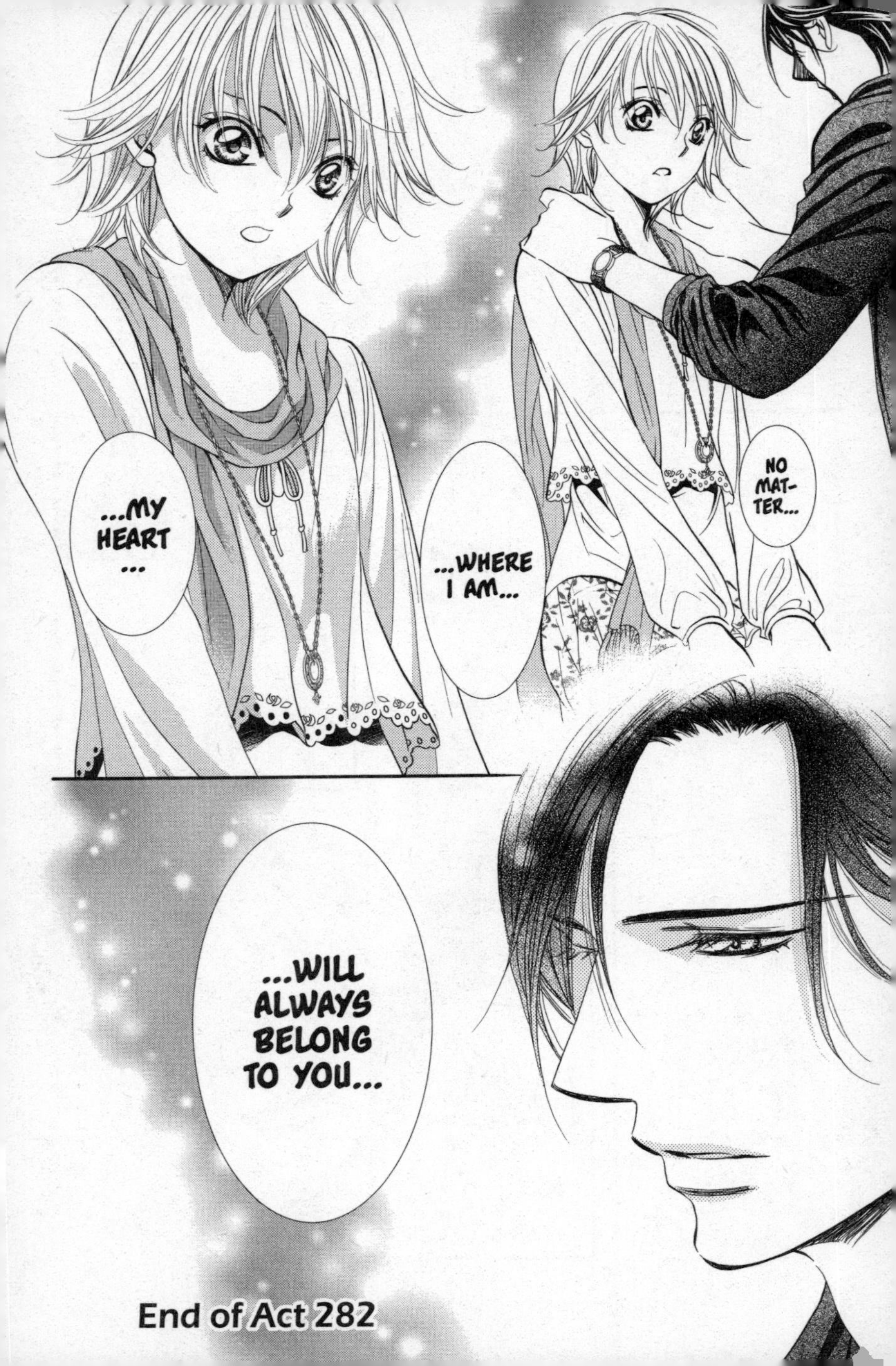
NO MATTER...
...WHERE I AM...
...MY HEART...
...WILL ALWAYS BELONG TO YOU...

End of Act 282

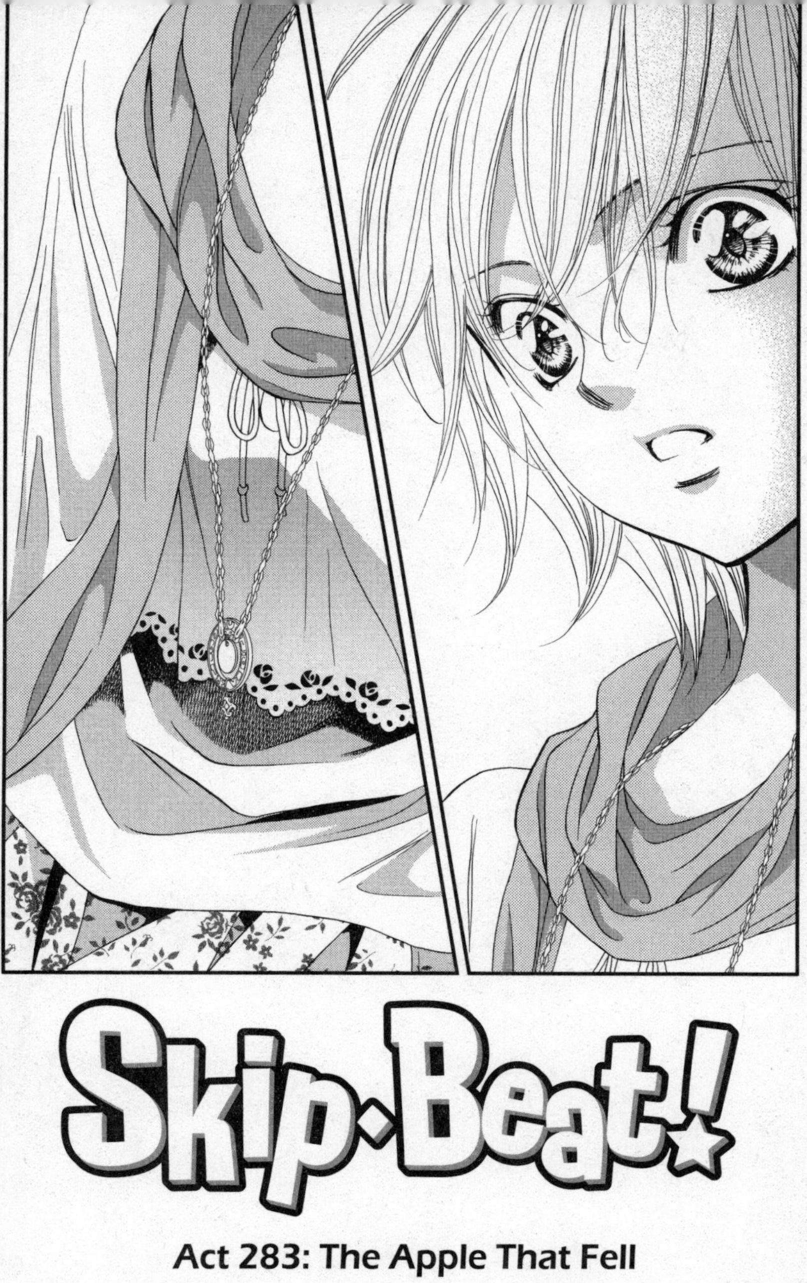

Skip·Beat!

Act 283: The Apple That Fell

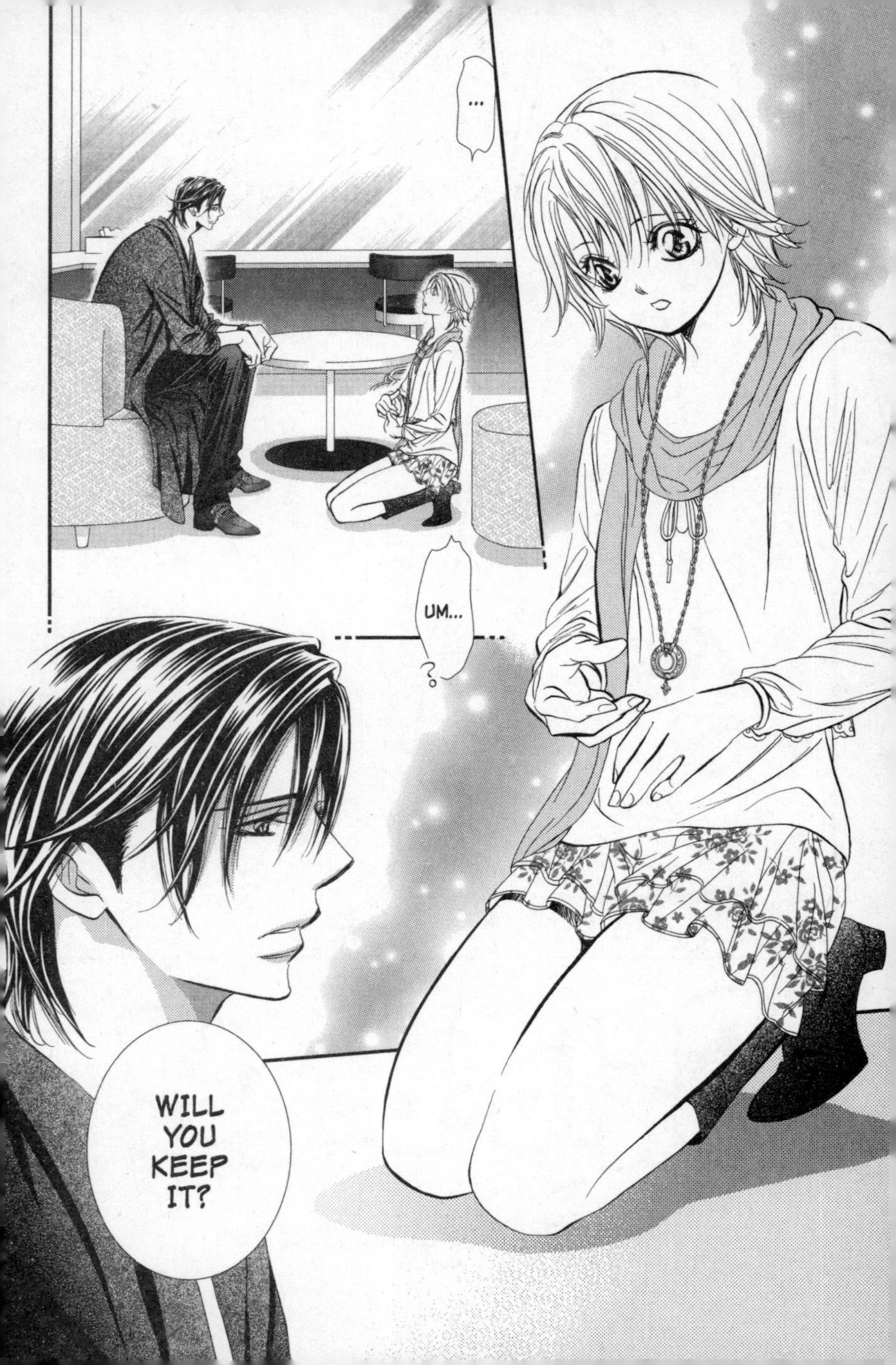
...
UM...?
WILL YOU KEEP IT?

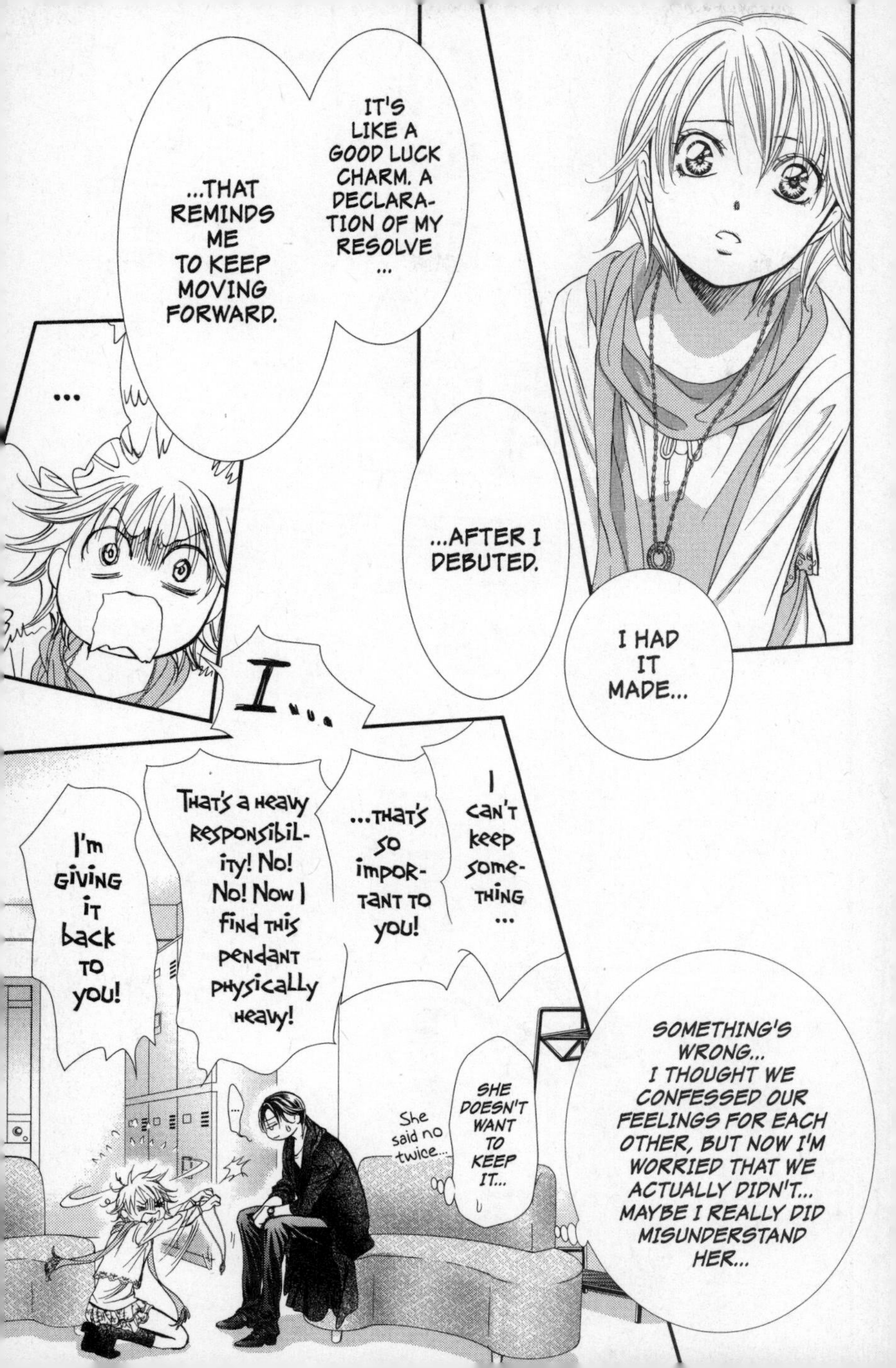
I HAD IT MADE...
...AFTER I DEBUTED.
IT'S LIKE A GOOD LUCK CHARM. A DECLARATION OF MY RESOLVE...
...THAT REMINDS ME TO KEEP MOVING FORWARD.
...
I...
I can't keep something...
...that's so important to you!
That's a heavy responsibil-ity! No! No! Now I find this pendant physically heavy!
I'm giving it back to you!
SOMETHING'S WRONG... I THOUGHT WE CONFESSED OUR FEELINGS FOR EACH OTHER, BUT NOW I'M WORRIED THAT WE ACTUALLY DIDN'T... MAYBE I REALLY DID MISUNDERSTAND HER...
SHE DOESN'T WANT TO KEEP IT...
She said no twice...
...

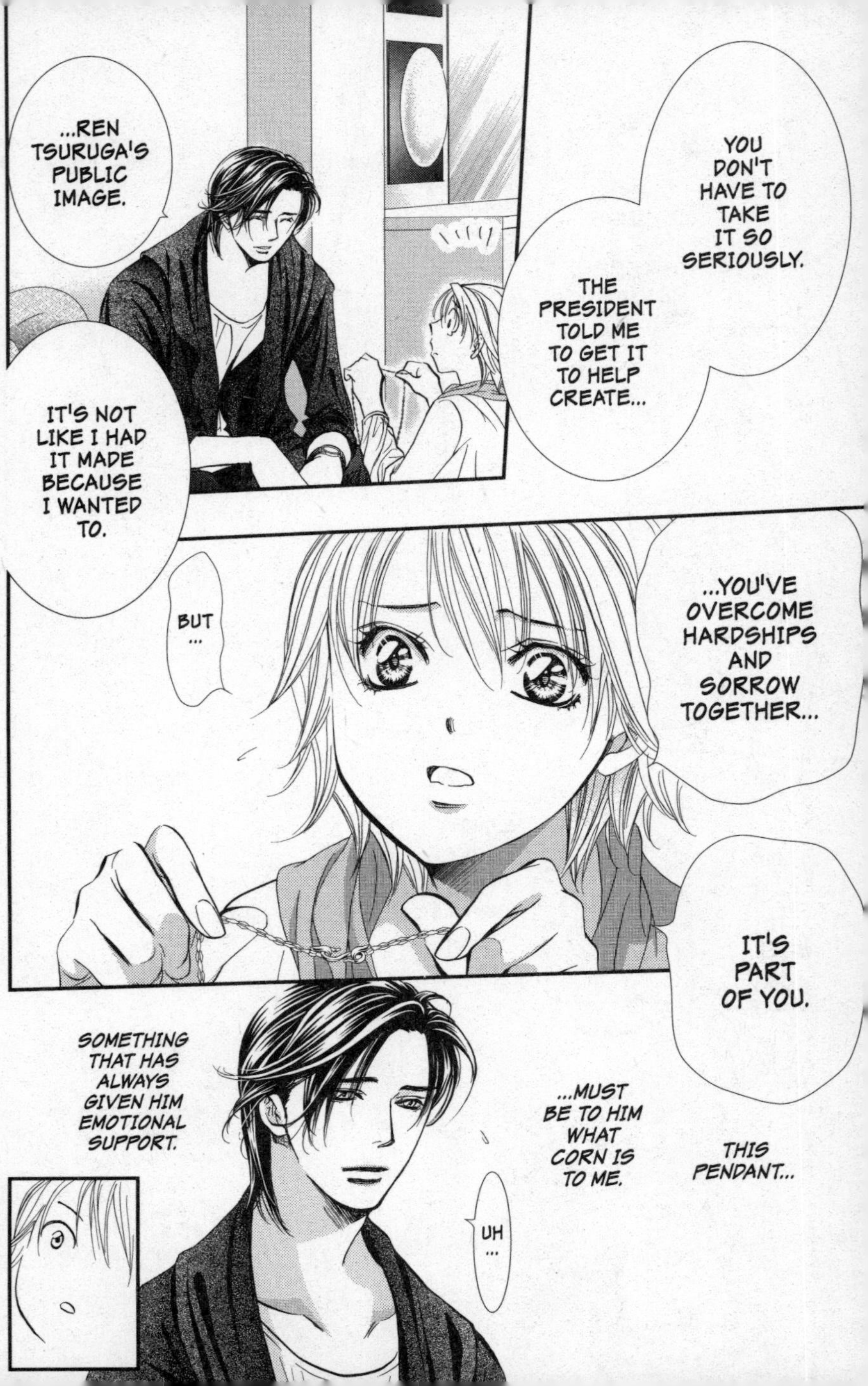
YOU DON'T HAVE TO TAKE IT SO SERIOUSLY.
THE PRESIDENT TOLD ME TO GET IT TO HELP CREATE...
...REN TSURUGA'S PUBLIC IMAGE.
IT'S NOT LIKE I HAD IT MADE BECAUSE I WANTED TO.
...YOU'VE OVERCOME HARDSHIPS AND SORROW TOGETHER...
BUT ...
IT'S PART OF YOU.
THIS PENDANT...
...MUST BE TO HIM WHAT CORN IS TO ME.
SOMETHING THAT HAS ALWAYS GIVEN HIM EMOTIONAL SUPPORT.
UH ...

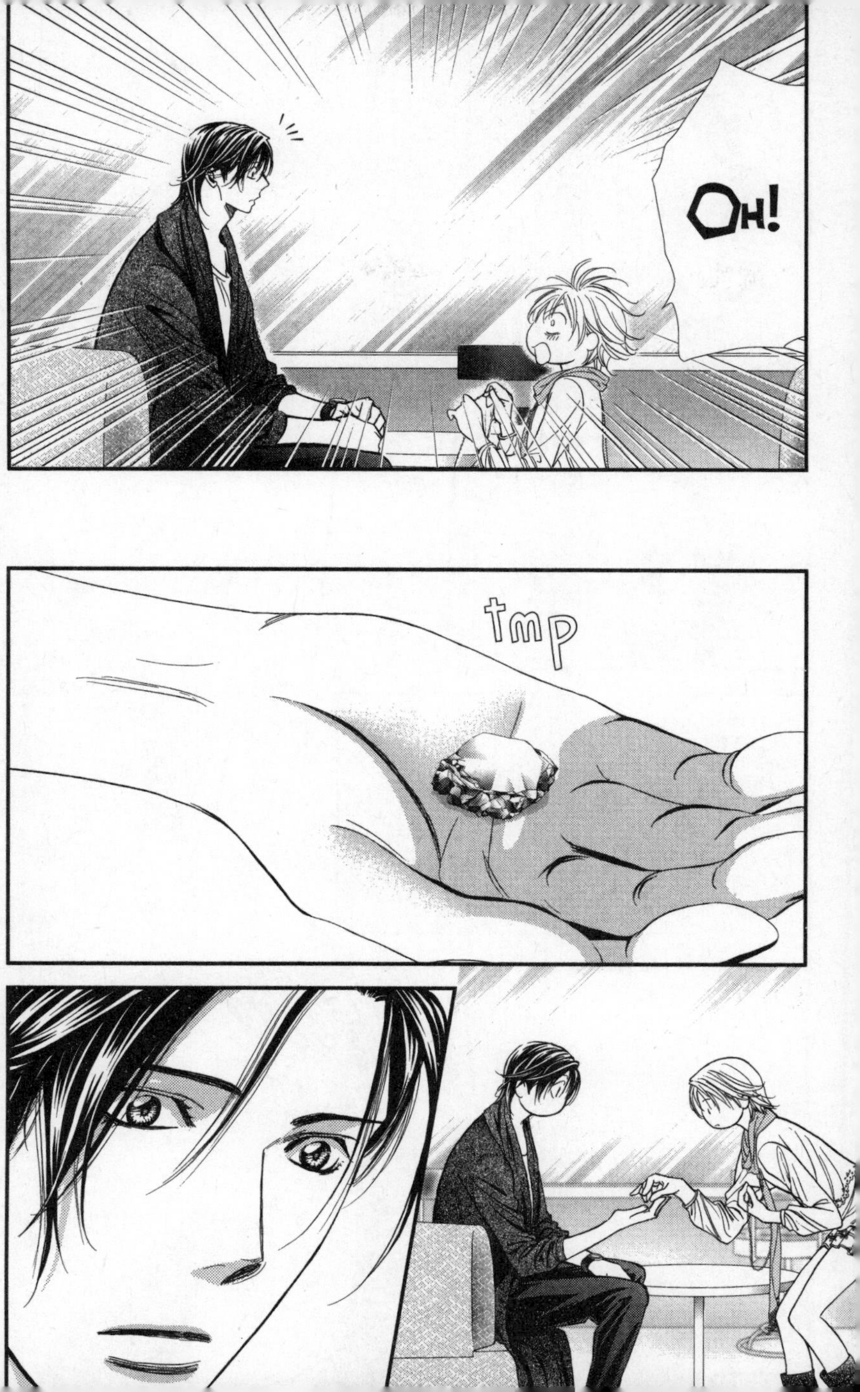
OH!
tmp

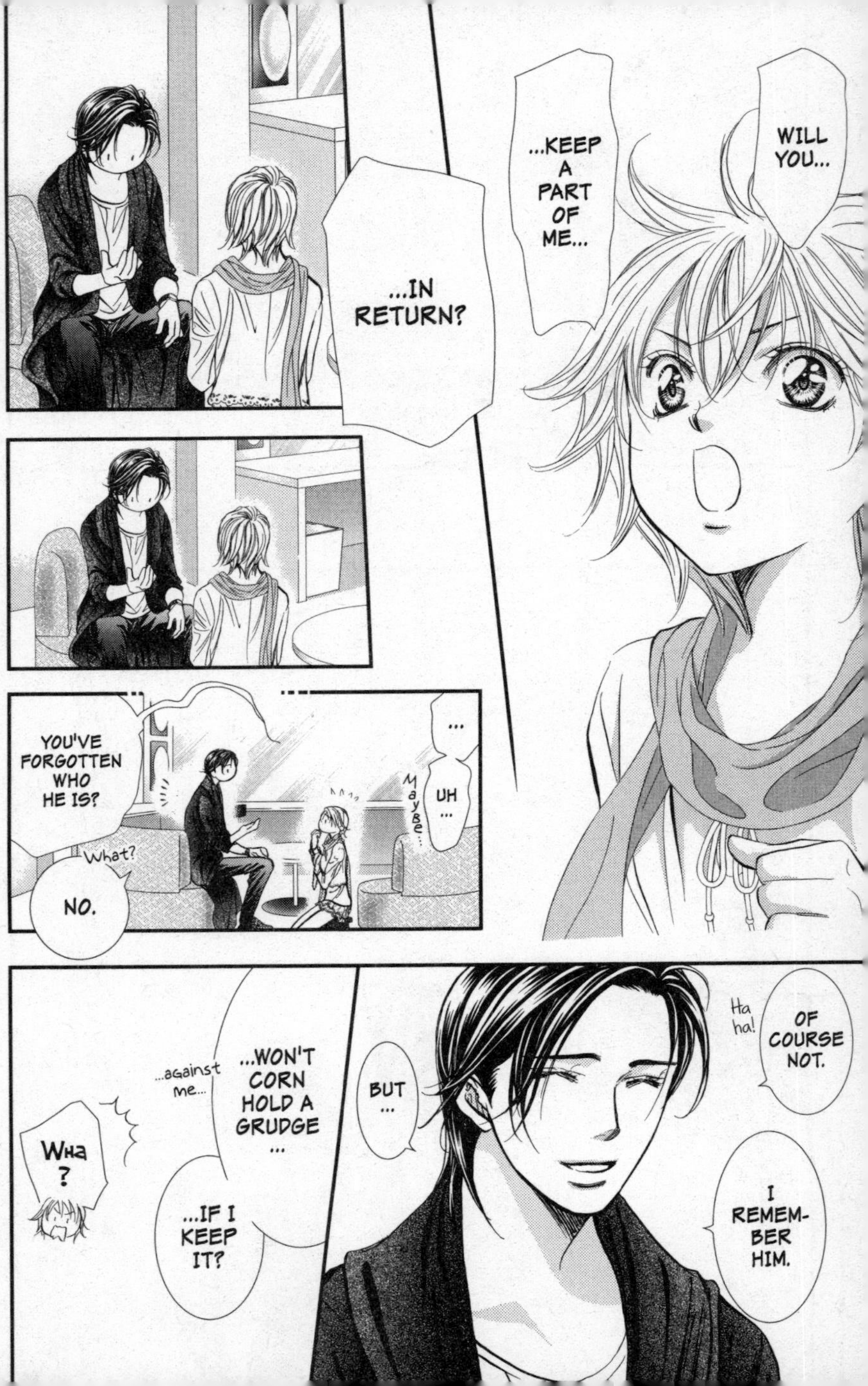
WILL YOU...
...KEEP A PART OF ME...
...IN RETURN?
...
UH ...
Maybe...
YOU'VE FORGOTTEN WHO HE IS?
What?
NO.
Ha ha!
OF COURSE NOT.
I REMEM-BER HIM.
BUT ...
...WON'T CORN HOLD A GRUDGE ...
...against me...
...IF I KEEP IT?
Wha ?

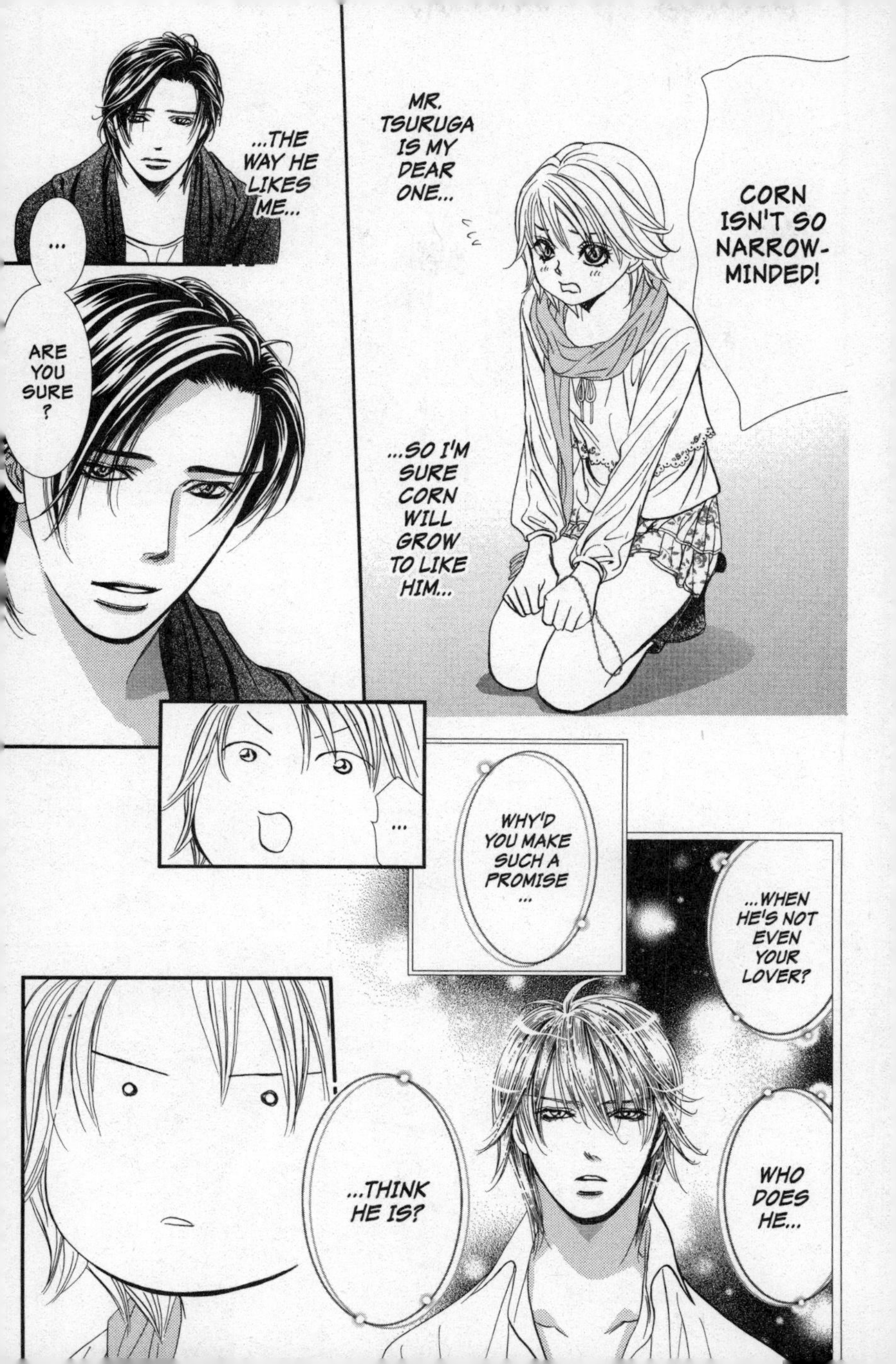
CORN ISN'T SO NARROW-MINDED!
MR. TSURUGA IS MY DEAR ONE...
...SO I'M SURE CORN WILL GROW TO LIKE HIM...
...THE WAY HE LIKES ME...
...
ARE YOU SURE?
...
WHY'D YOU MAKE SUCH A PROMISE...
...WHEN HE'S NOT EVEN YOUR LOVER?
WHO DOES HE...
...THINK HE IS?

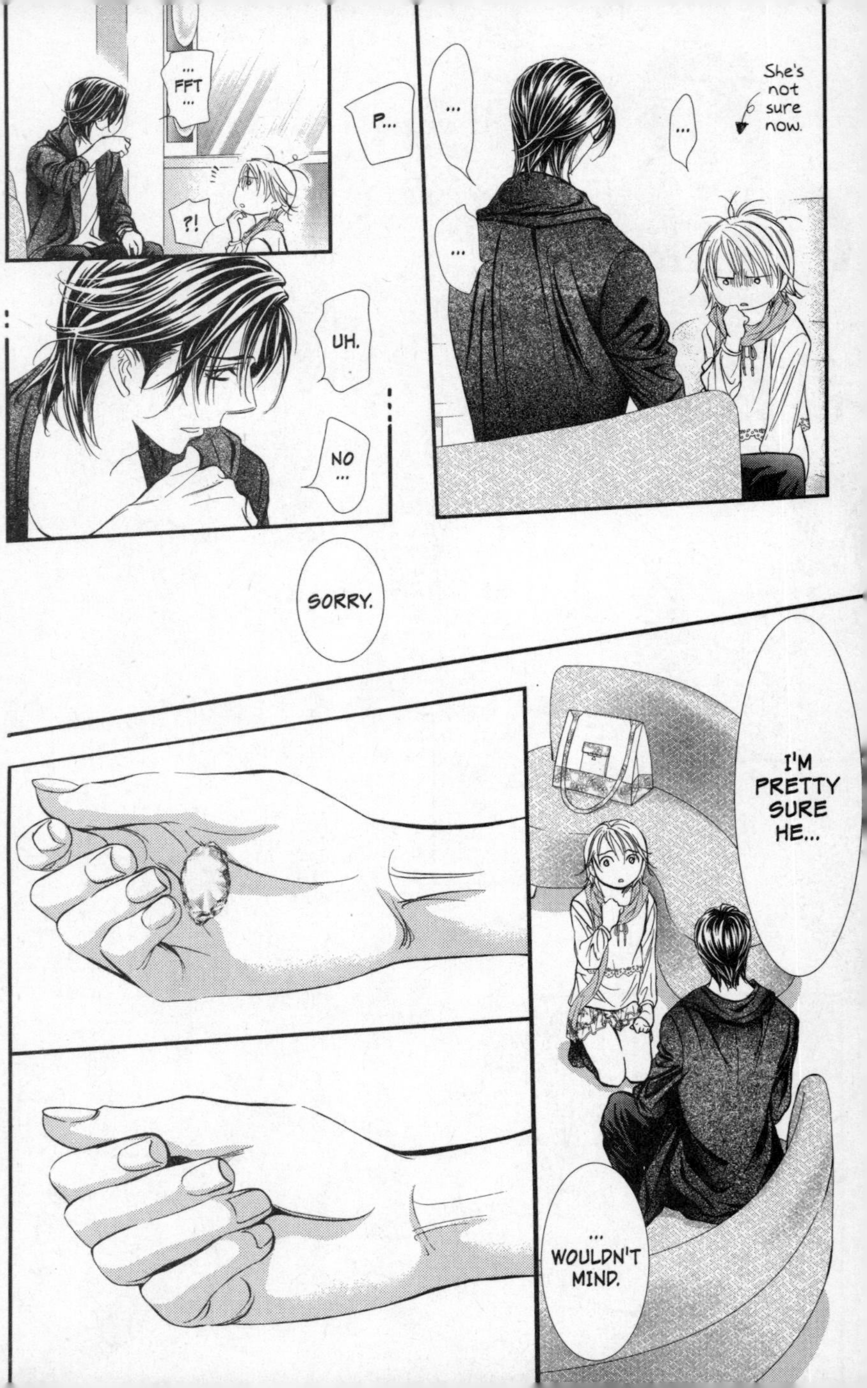
She's not sure now.
...
...
...
... FFT ...
P...
?!
UH.
NO ...
SORRY.
I'M PRETTY SURE HE...
... WOULDN'T MIND.

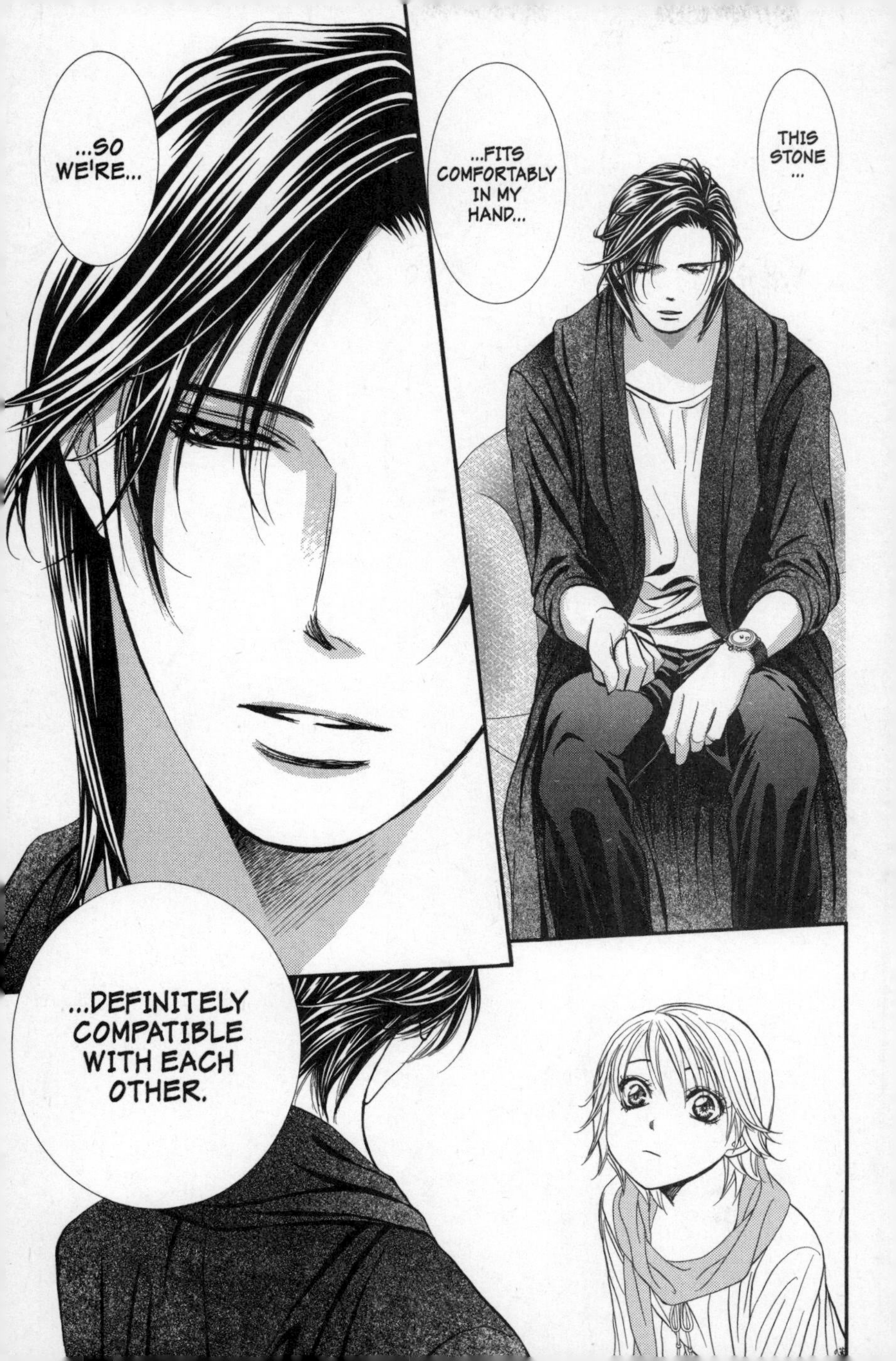
THIS STONE ...
...FITS COMFORTABLY IN MY HAND...
...SO WE'RE...
...DEFINITELY COMPATIBLE WITH EACH OTHER.

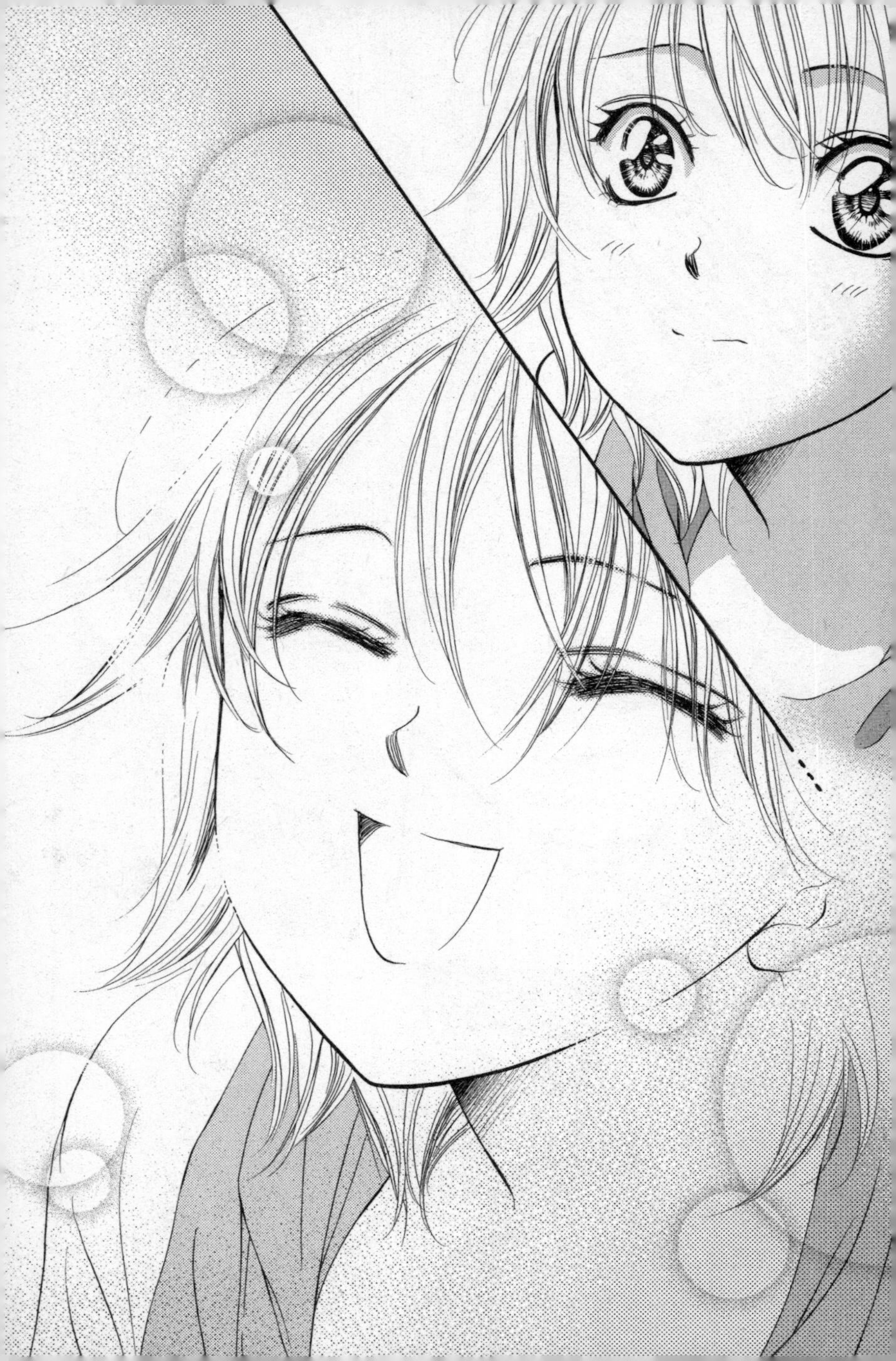

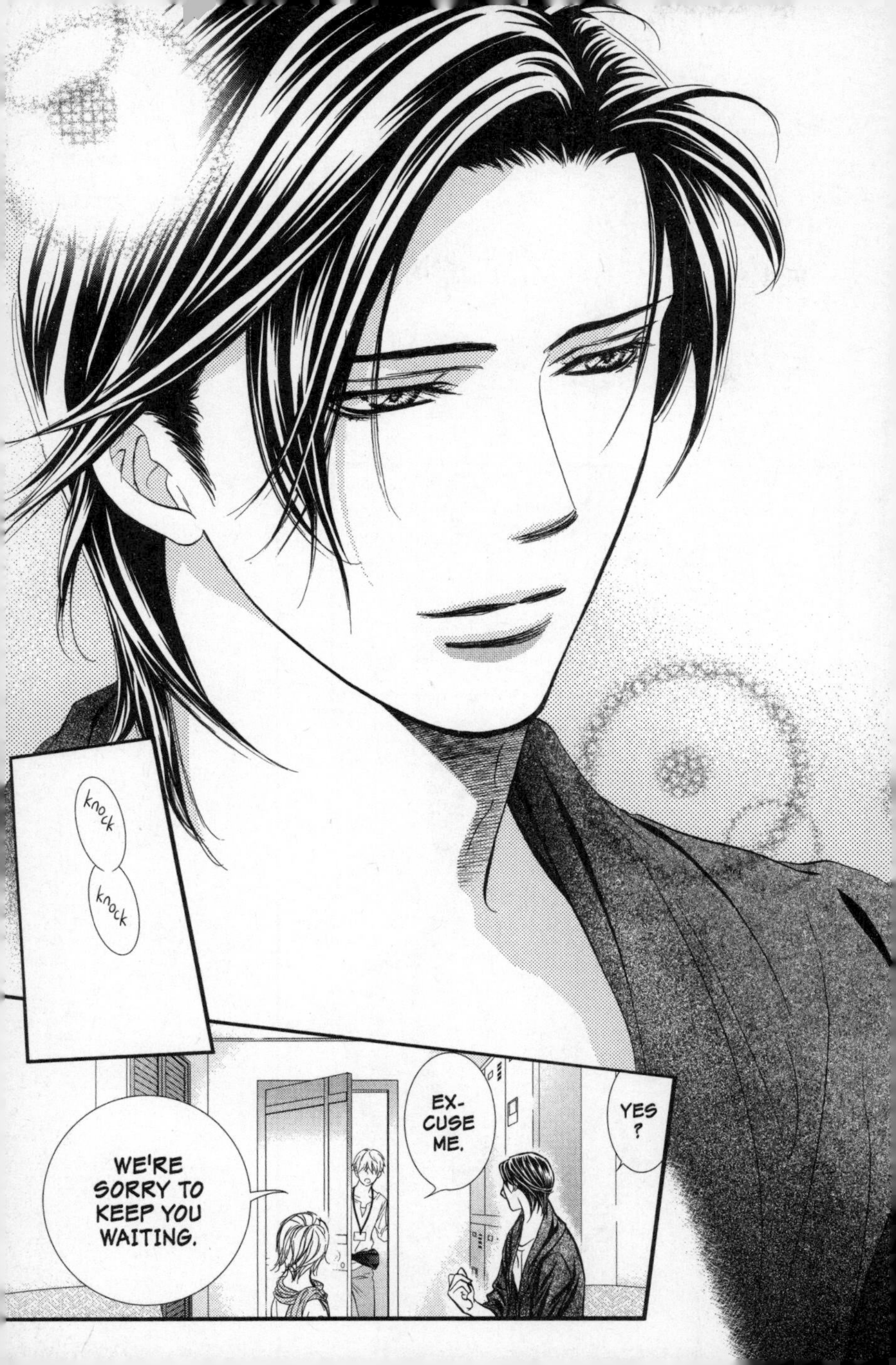
knock
knock
YES?
EX-CUSE ME.
WE'RE SORRY TO KEEP YOU WAITING.

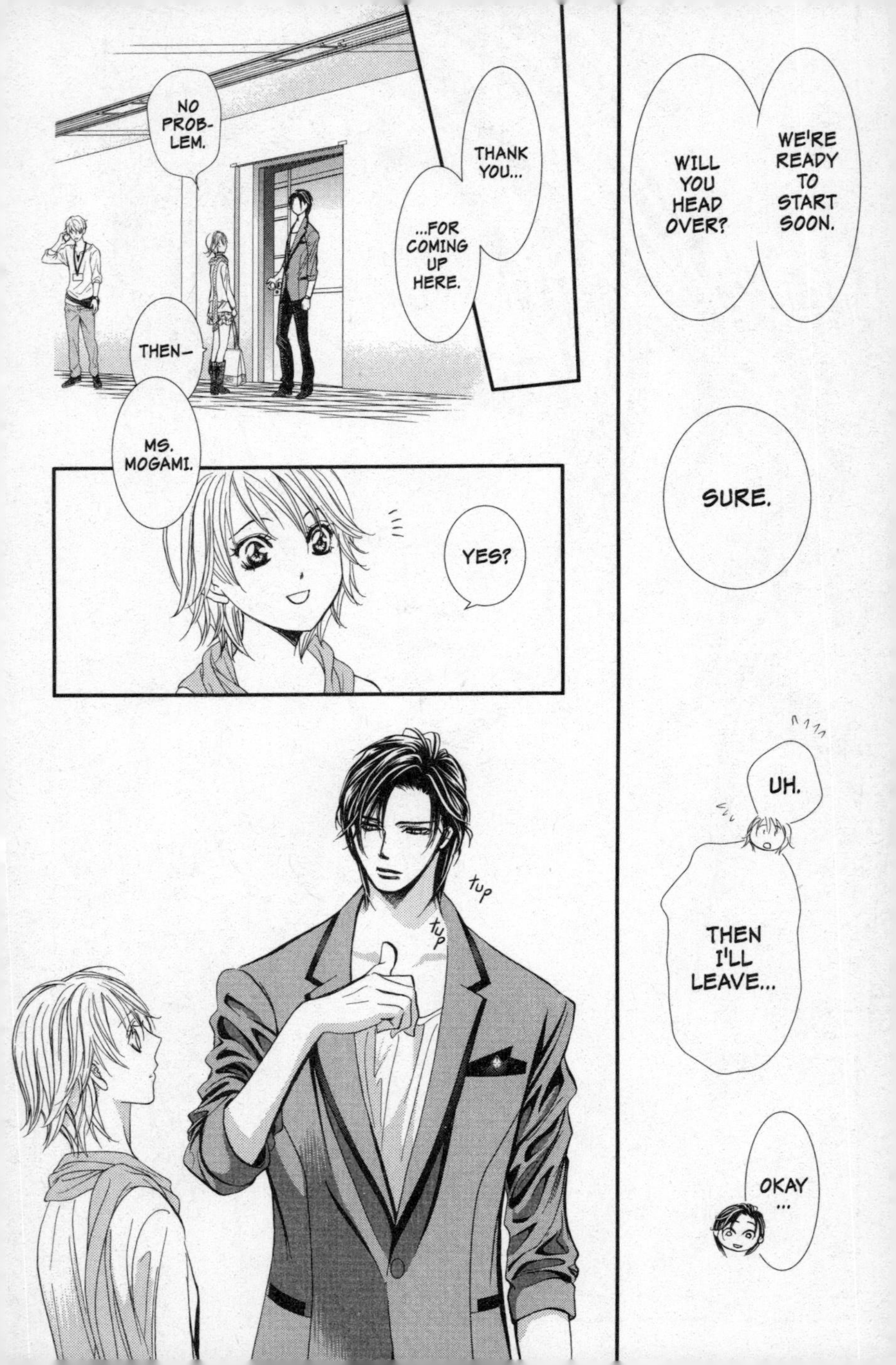
WE'RE READY TO START SOON.
WILL YOU HEAD OVER?
SURE.
UH.
THEN I'LL LEAVE...
OKAY ...
THANK YOU...
...FOR COMING UP HERE.
NO PROB-LEM.
THEN—
MS. MOGAMI.
YES?
tup
tup

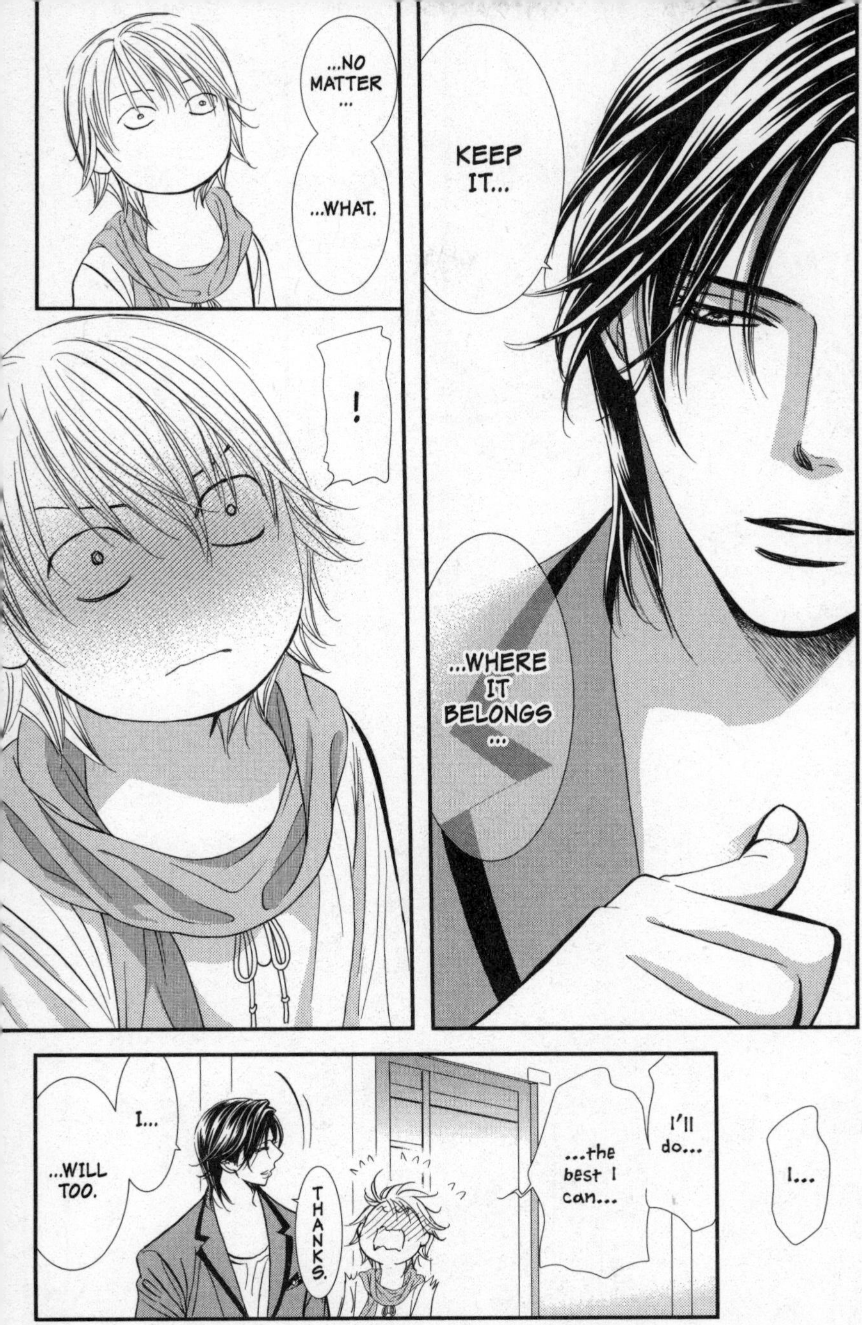
KEEP IT...
...WHERE IT BELONGS...
...NO MATTER...
...WHAT.
!
I...
I'll do...
...the best I can...
THANKS.
I...
...WILL TOO.

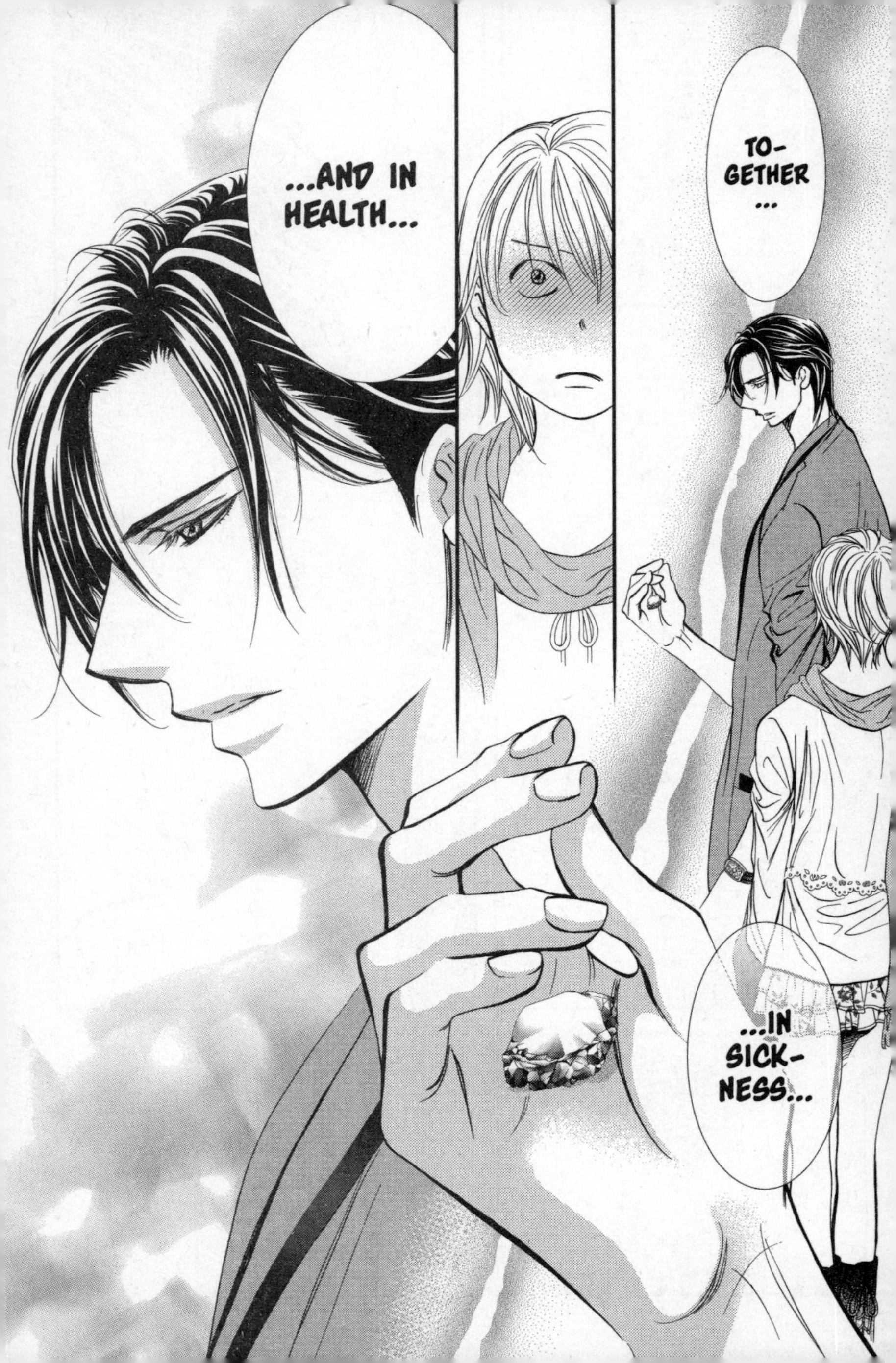
TO-GETHER...
...IN SICK-NESS...
...AND IN HEALTH...

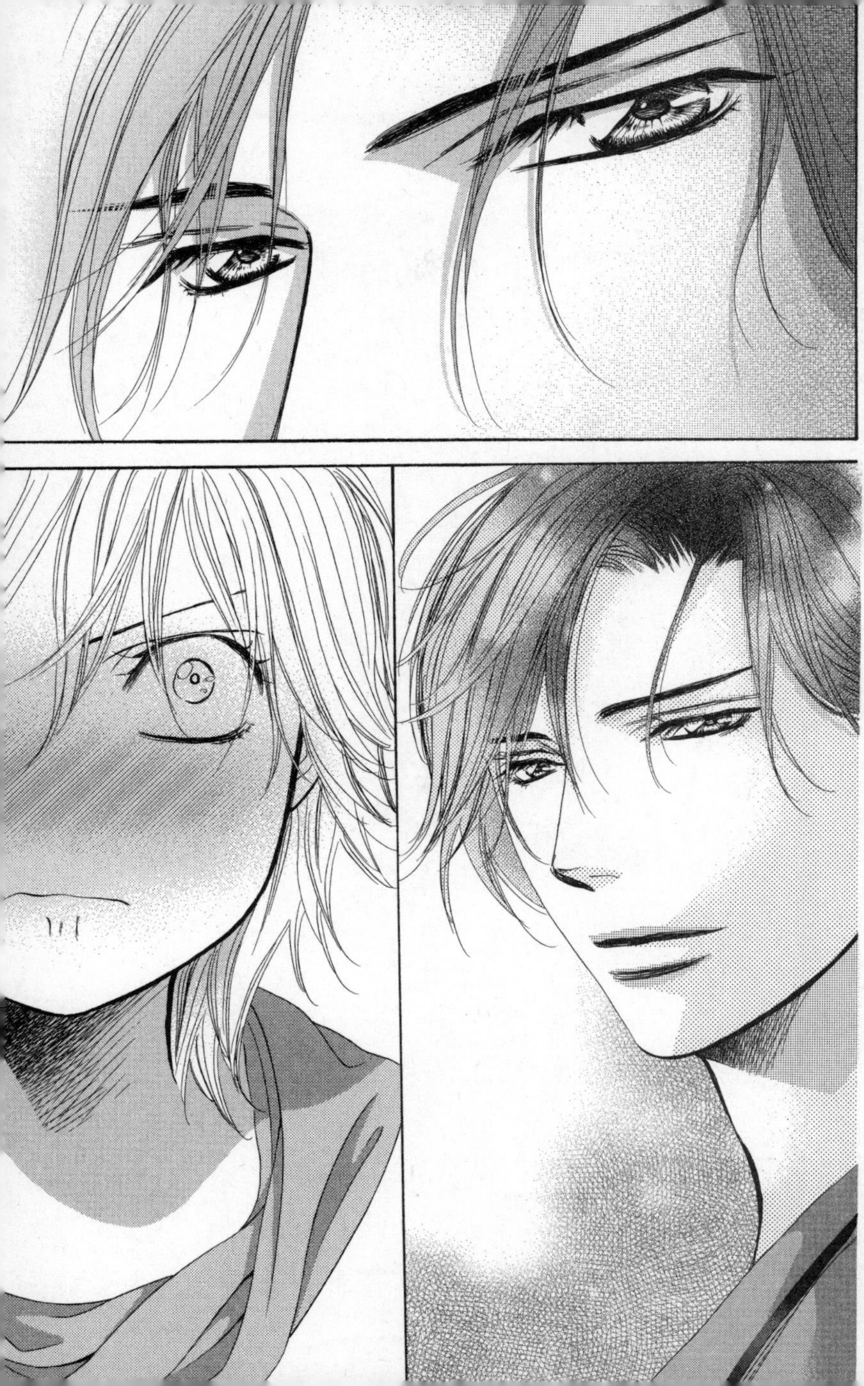

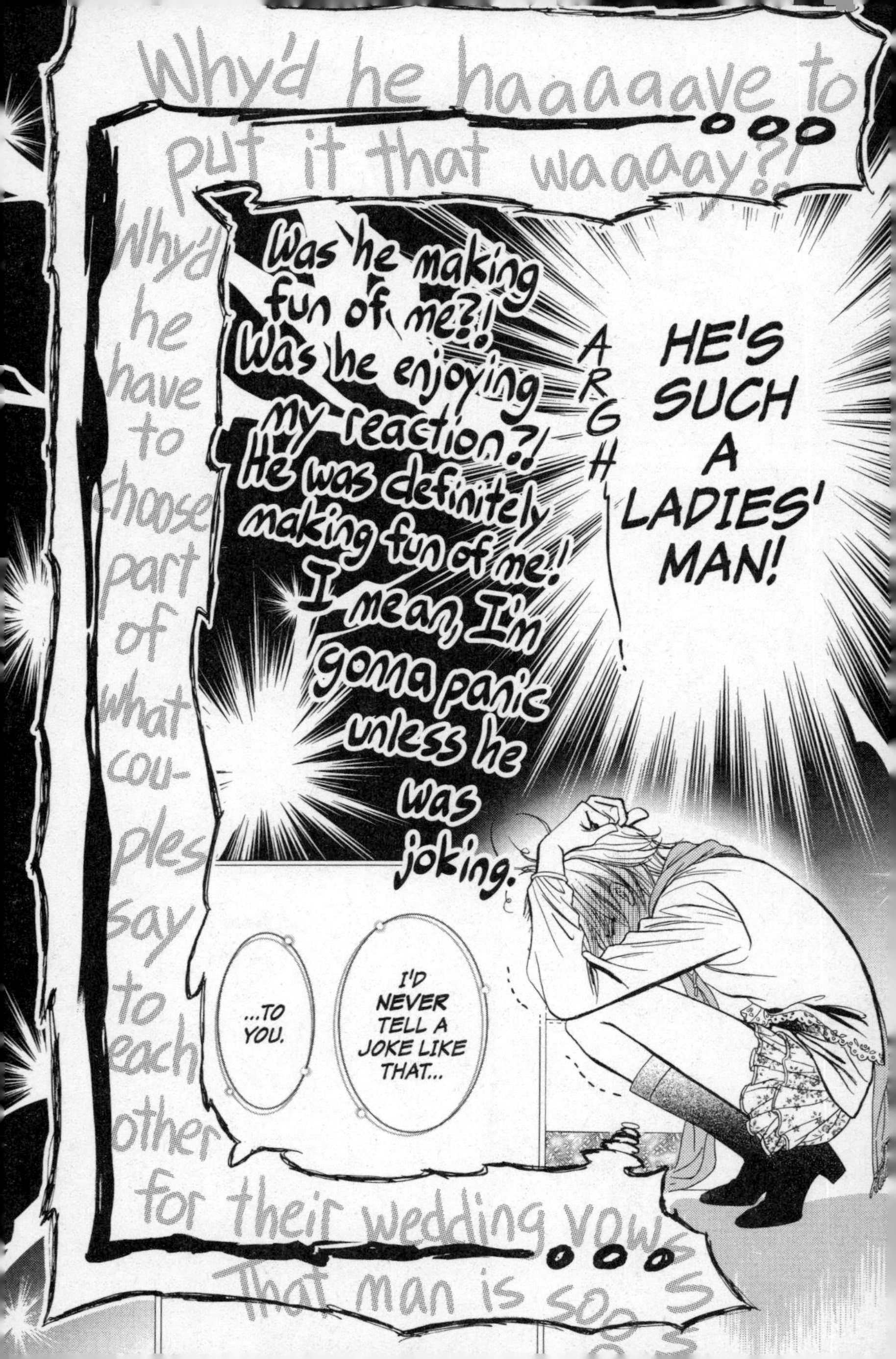
Why'd he haaaaave to put it that waaaay?!
HE'S SUCH A LADIES' MAN!
ARGH!
Was he making fun of me?! Was he enjoying my reaction?! He was definitely making fun of me! I mean, I'm gonna panic unless he was joking.
Why'd he have to choose part of what couples say to each other for their wedding vows...
That man is so
I'D NEVER TELL A JOKE LIKE THAT...
...TO YOU.

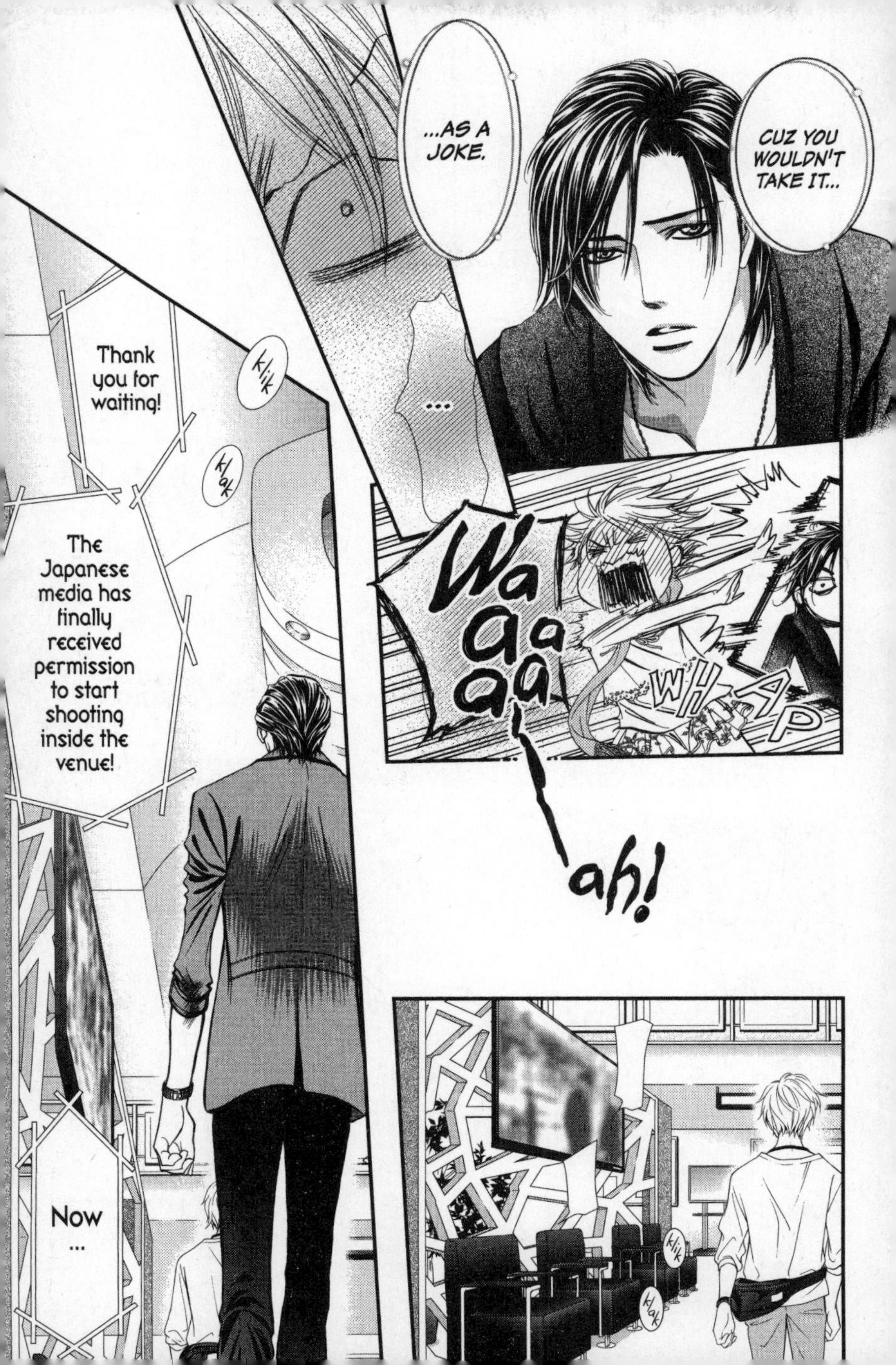
CUZ YOU WOULDN'T TAKE IT...
...AS A JOKE.
...
Waaaaa
WHAP
ah!
klik
klak
Thank you for waiting!
klik
klak
The Japanese media has finally received permission to start shooting inside the venue!
Now ...

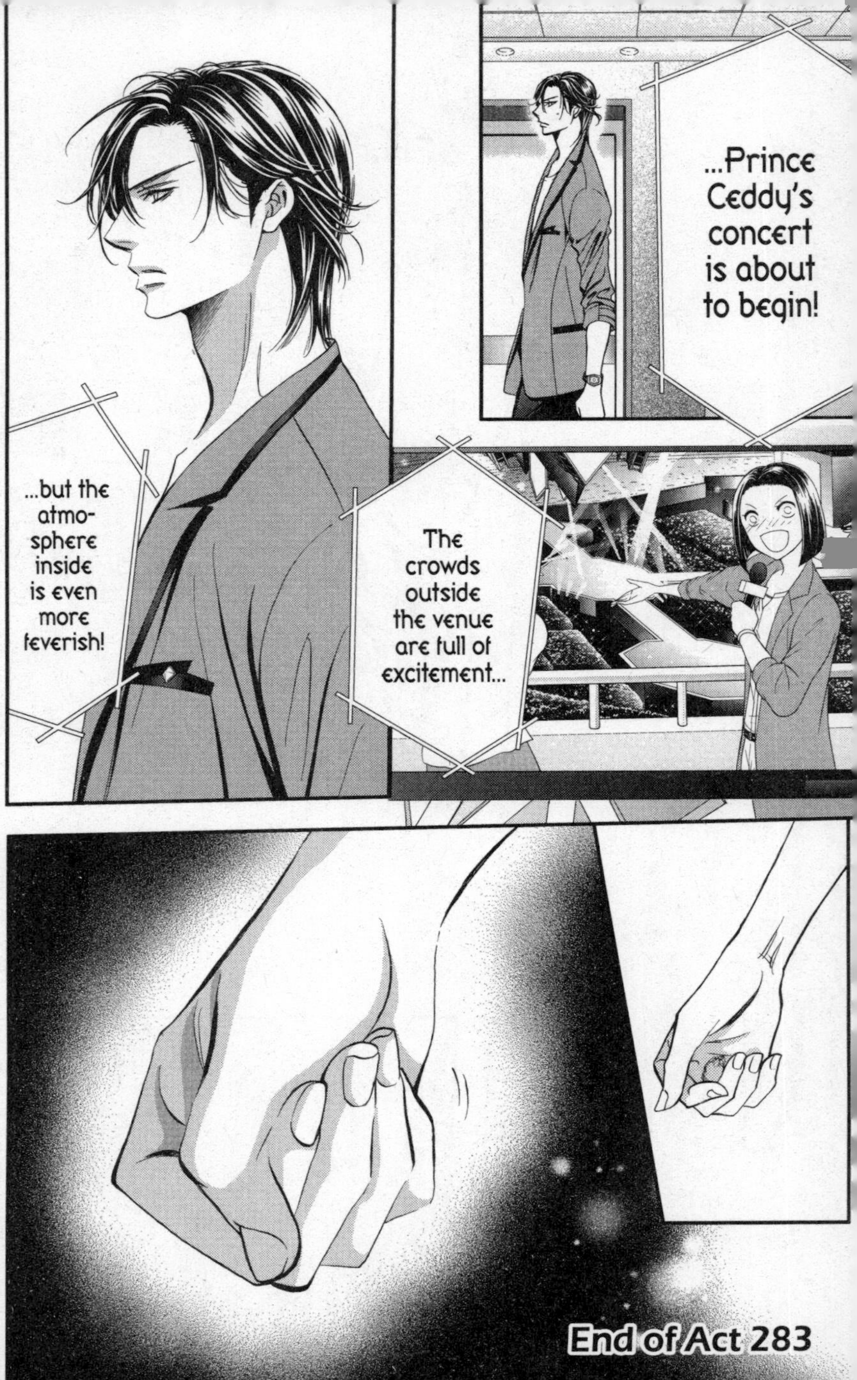
The crowds outside the venue are full of excitement...
...but the atmosphere inside is even more feverish!
...Prince Ceddy's concert is about to begin!
End of Act 283

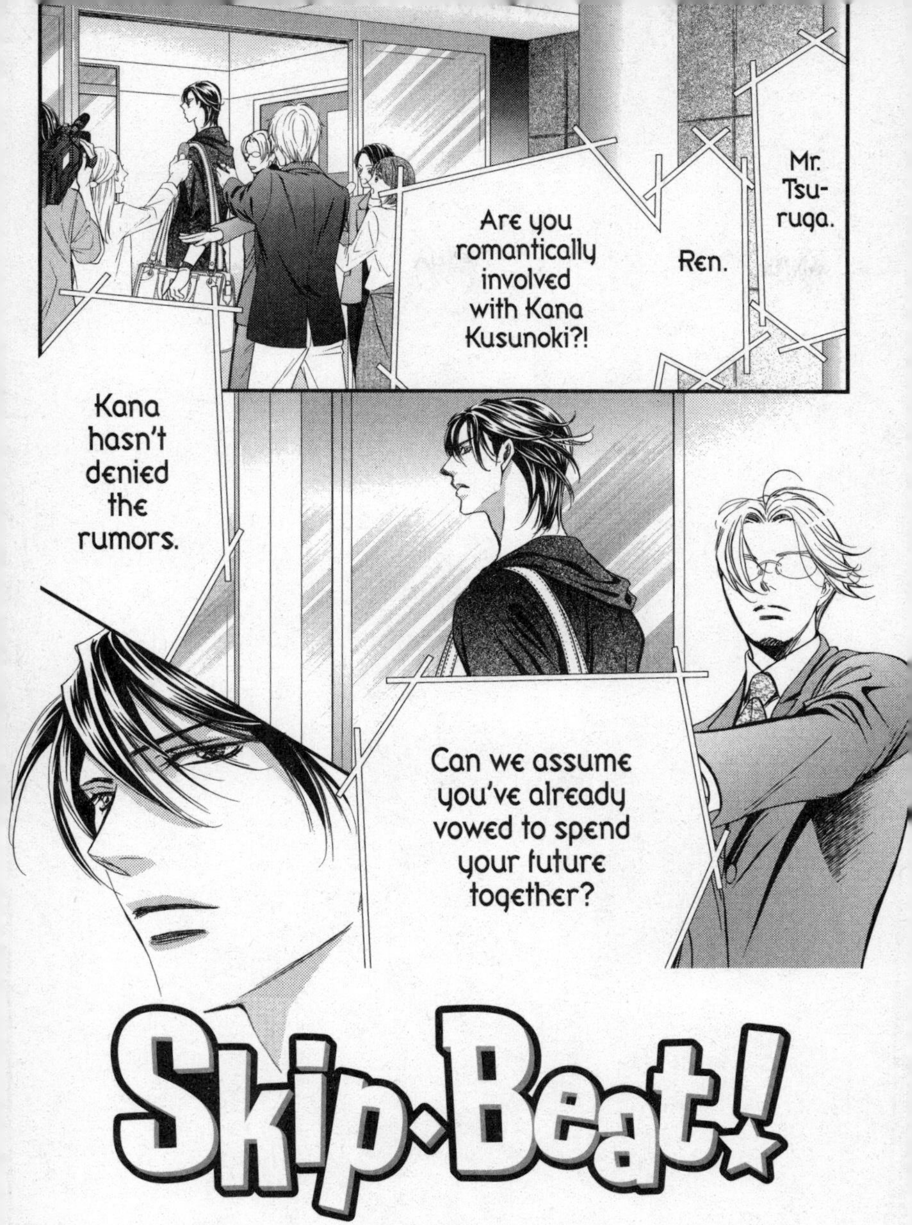
Mr. Tsuruga.
Ren.
Are you romantically involved with Kana Kusunoki?!
Kana hasn't denied the rumors.
Can we assume you've already vowed to spend your future together?
Skip·Beat!

Act 284: Sign of Spring—Awakening to an Unexpected State of Affairs

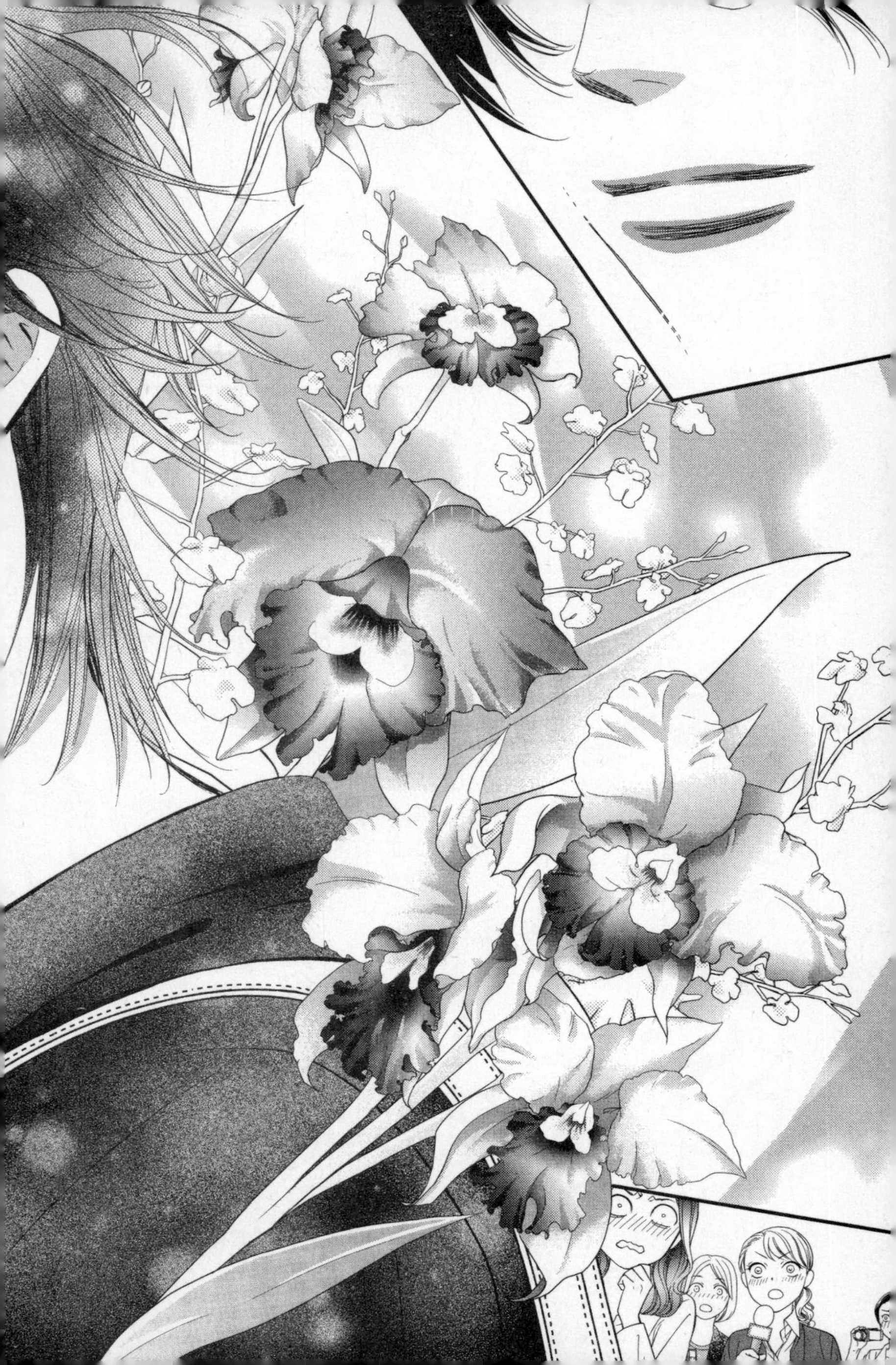

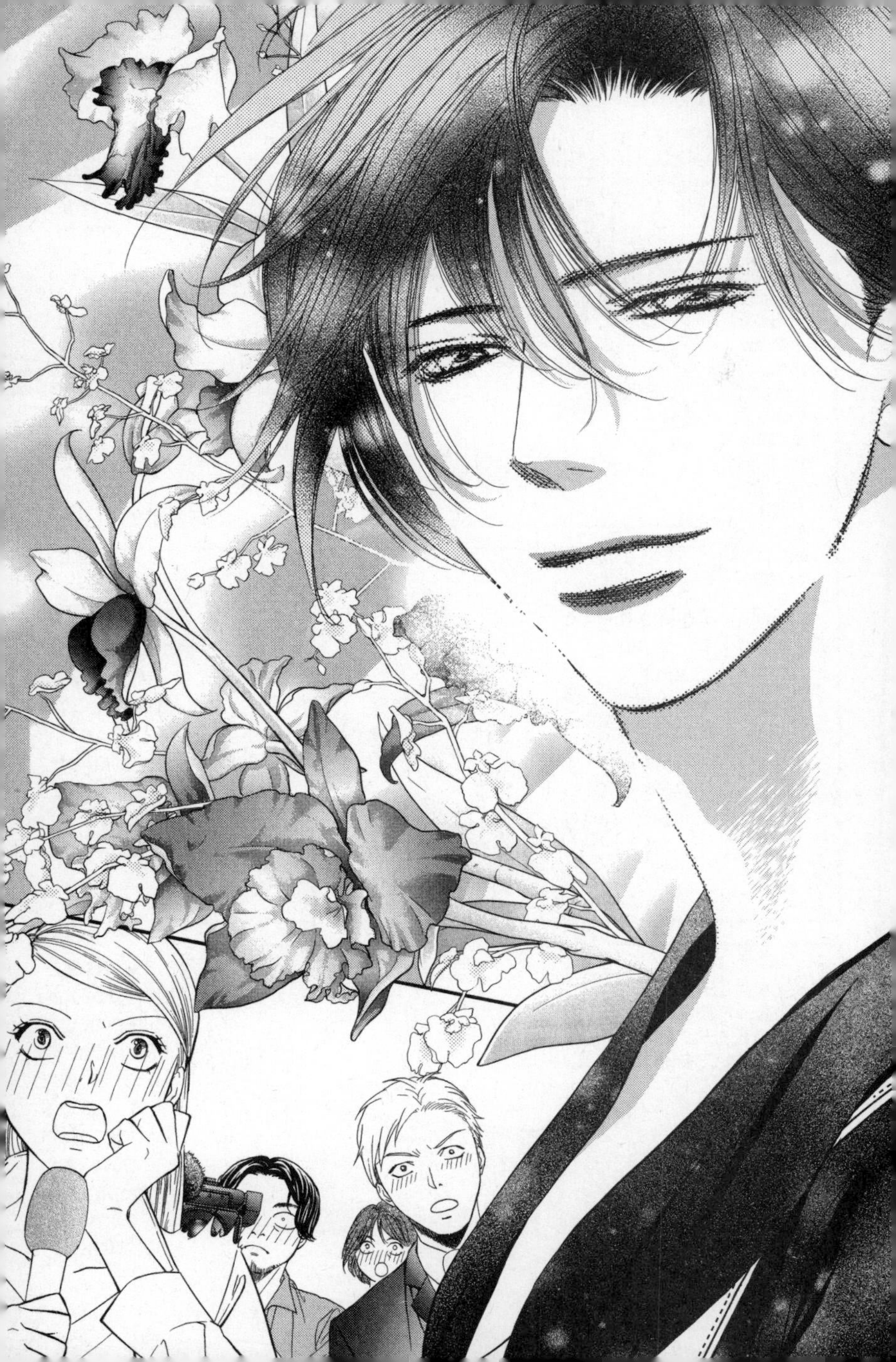

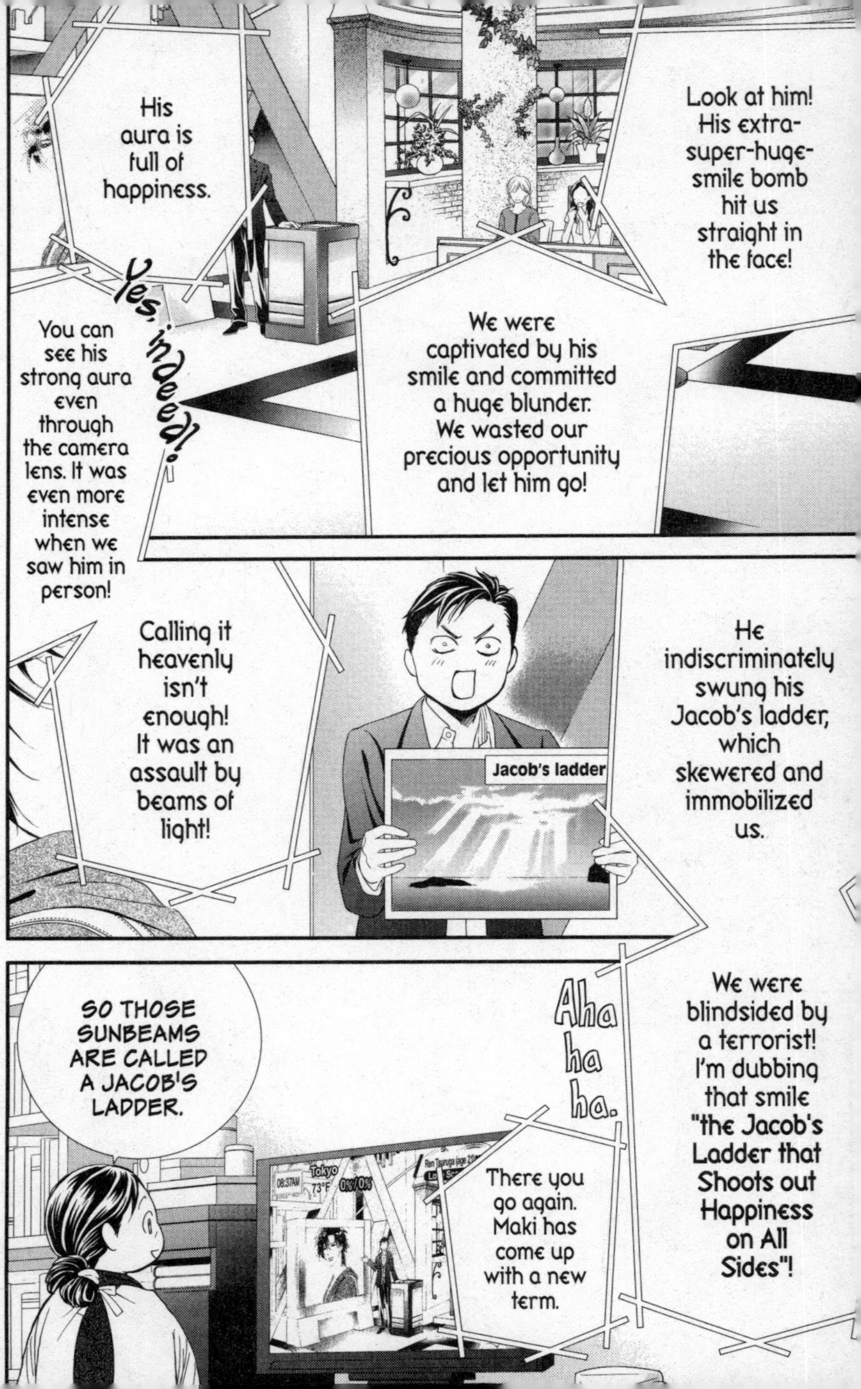
Look at him! His extra-super-huge-smile bomb hit us straight in the face!
His aura is full of happiness.
We were captivated by his smile and committed a huge blunder. We wasted our precious opportunity and let him go!
Yes, indeed!
You can see his strong aura even through the camera lens. It was even more intense when we saw him in person!
He indiscriminately swung his Jacob's ladder, which skewered and immobilized us.
Jacob's ladder
Calling it heavenly isn't enough! It was an assault by beams of light!
We were blindsided by a terrorist! I'm dubbing that smile **"the Jacob's Ladder that Shoots out Happiness on All Sides"**!
Aha ha ha.
There you go again. Maki has come up with a new term.
SO THOSE SUNBEAMS ARE CALLED A JACOB'S LADDER.

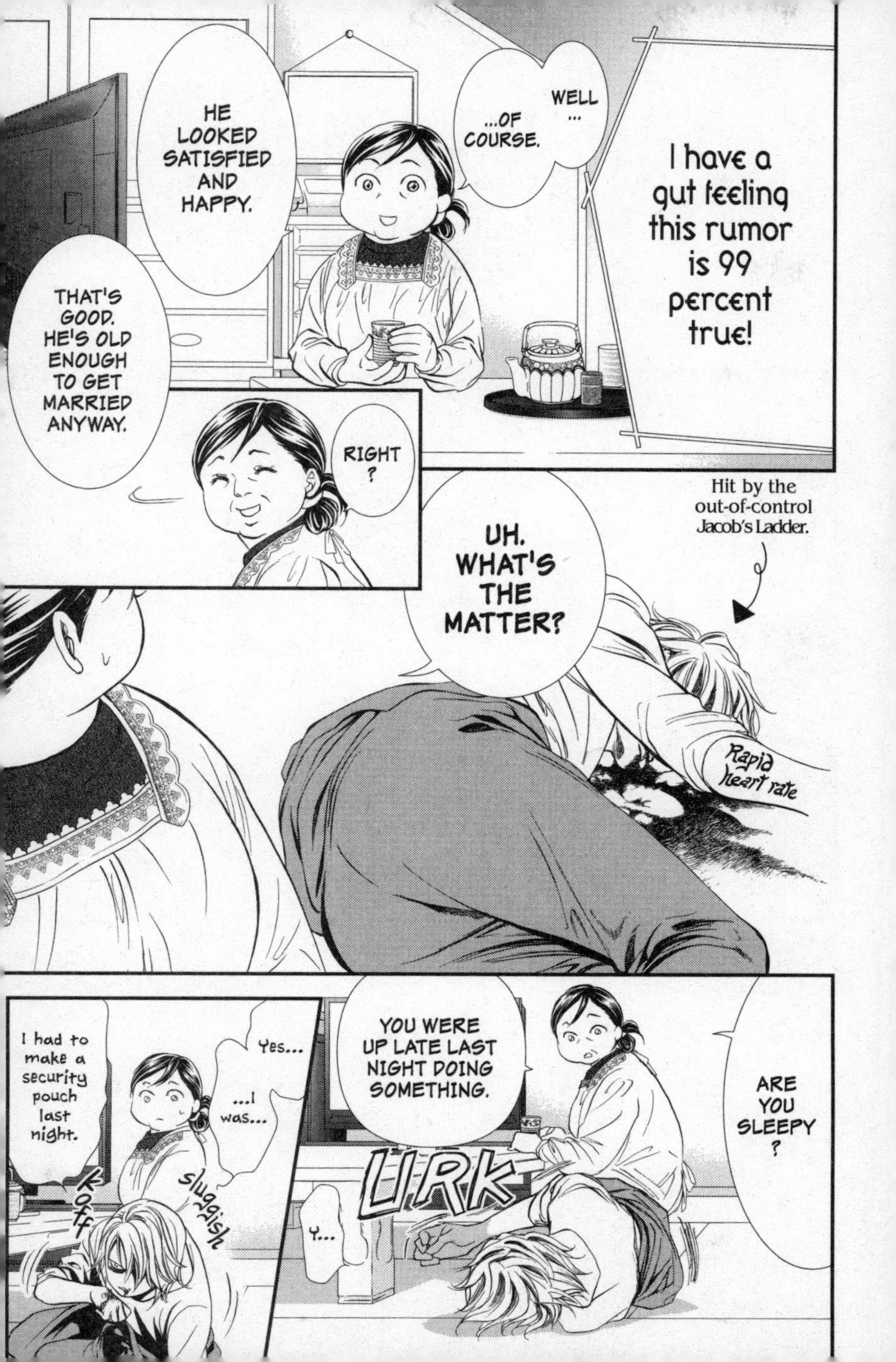
I have a gut feeling this rumor is 99 percent true!
WELL ...
...OF COURSE.
HE LOOKED SATISFIED AND HAPPY.
THAT'S GOOD. HE'S OLD ENOUGH TO GET MARRIED ANYWAY.
RIGHT ?
Hit by the out-of-control Jacob's Ladder.
Rapid heart rate
UH. WHAT'S THE MATTER?
ARE YOU SLEEPY ?
YOU WERE UP LATE LAST NIGHT DOING SOMETHING.
URK
Y...
Yes...
...I was...
I had to make a security pouch last night.
sluggish
koff

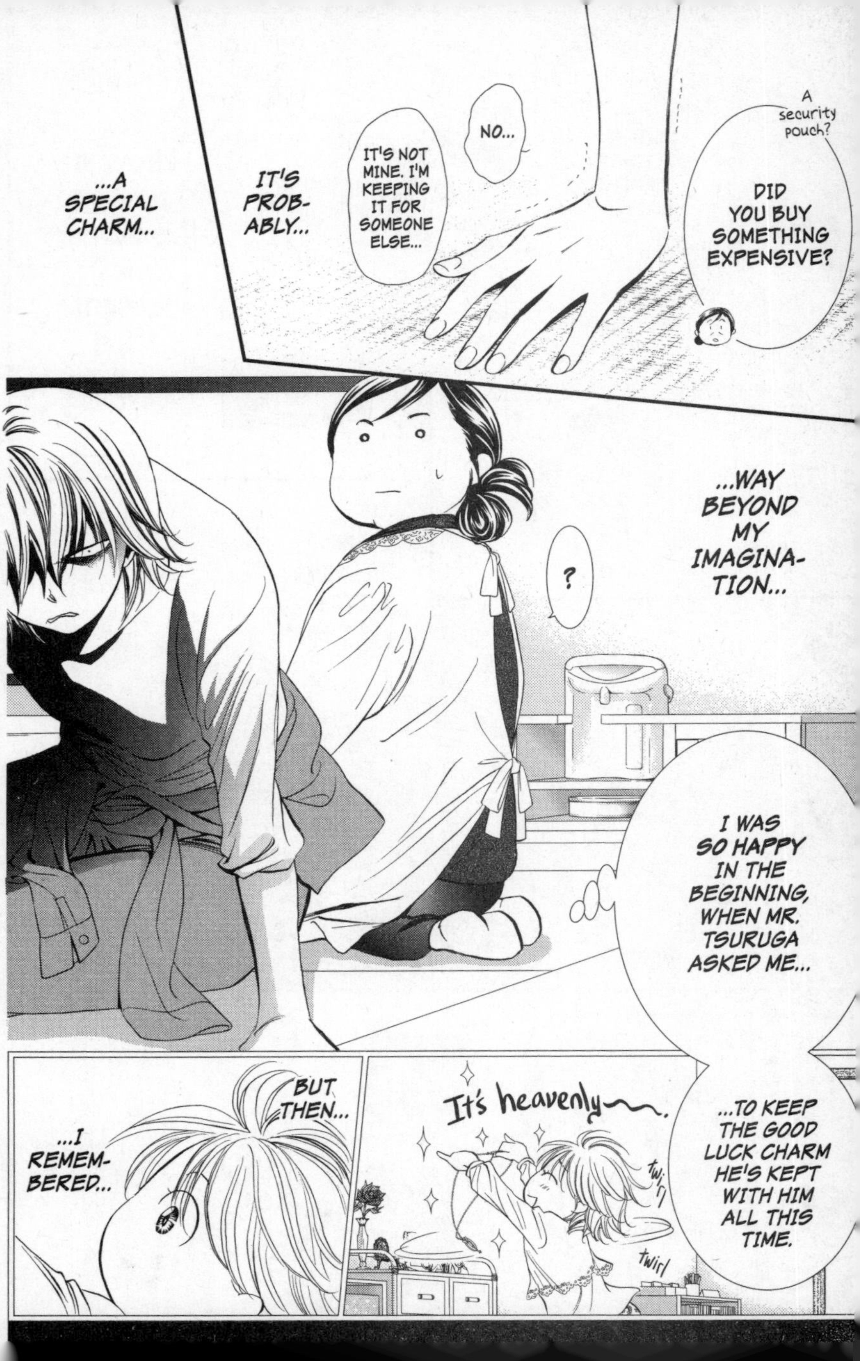
A security pouch?
DID YOU BUY SOMETHING EXPENSIVE?
NO...
IT'S NOT MINE. I'M KEEPING IT FOR SOMEONE ELSE...
IT'S PROBABLY...
...A SPECIAL CHARM...
...WAY BEYOND MY IMAGINATION...
?
I WAS SO HAPPY IN THE BEGINNING, WHEN MR. TSURUGA ASKED ME...
...TO KEEP THE GOOD LUCK CHARM HE'S KEPT WITH HIM ALL THIS TIME.
It's heavenly~.
twirl
twirl
BUT THEN...
...I REMEMBERED...

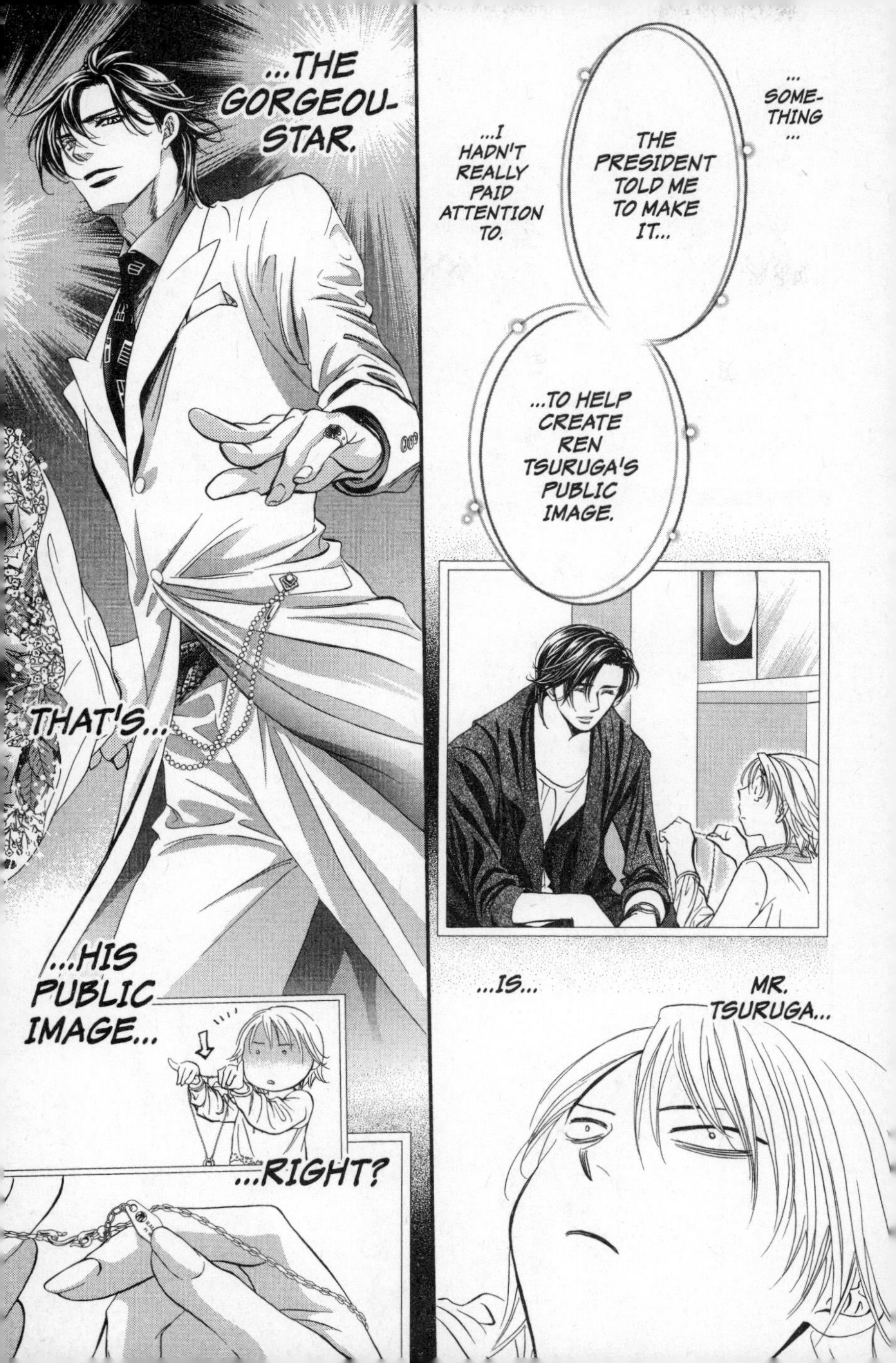
...SOMETHING...
THE PRESIDENT TOLD ME TO MAKE IT...
...I HADN'T REALLY PAID ATTENTION TO.
...TO HELP CREATE REN TSURUGA'S PUBLIC IMAGE.
MR. TSURUGA...
...IS...
...THE GORGEOU-STAR.
THAT'S...
...HIS PUBLIC IMAGE...
...RIGHT?

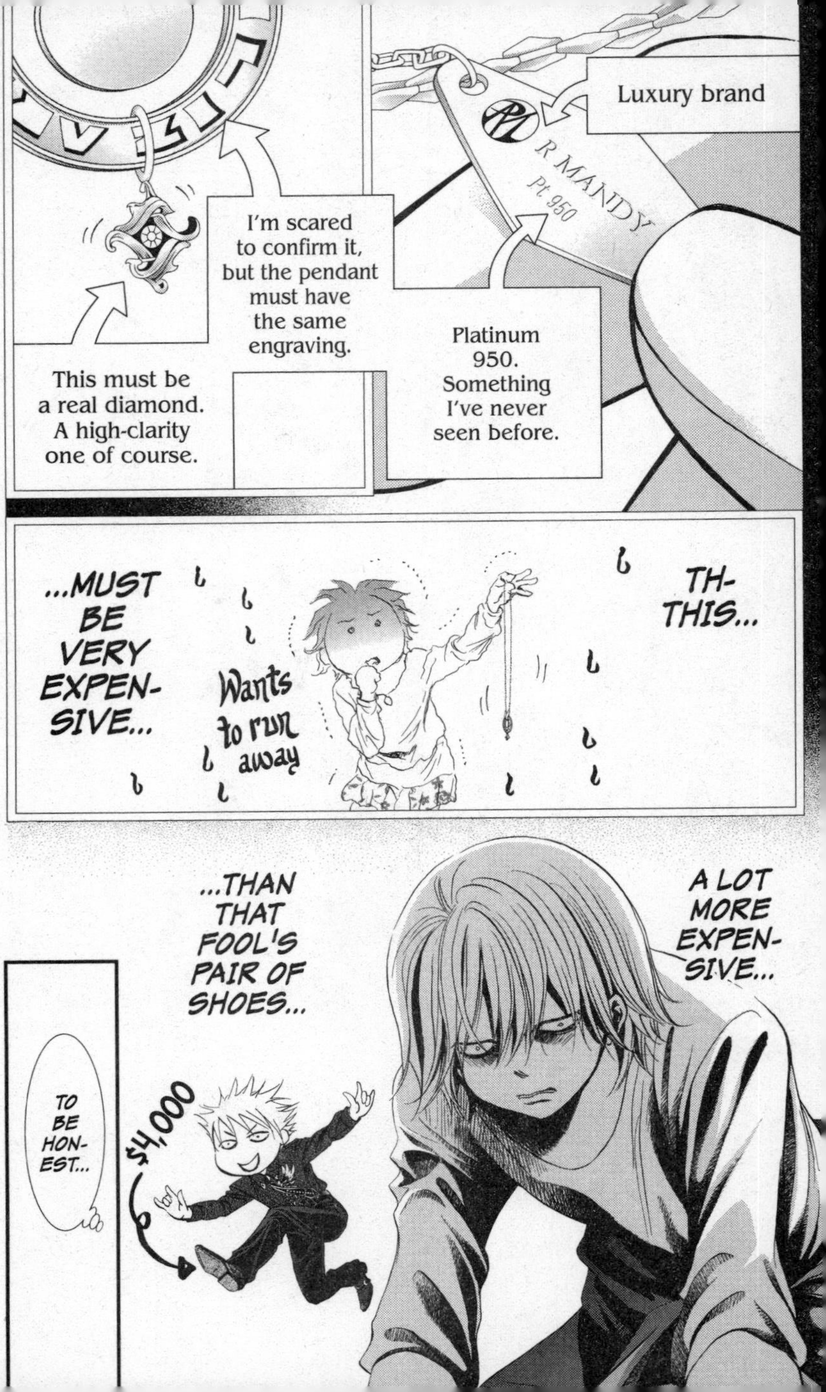
Luxury brand
R MANDY
Pt 950
Platinum 950. Something I've never seen before.
I'm scared to confirm it, but the pendant must have the same engraving.
This must be a real diamond. A high-clarity one of course.
TH-THIS...
Wants to run away
...MUST BE VERY EXPEN-SIVE...
A LOT MORE EXPEN-SIVE...
...THAN THAT FOOL'S PAIR OF SHOES...
$4,000
TO BE HON-EST...

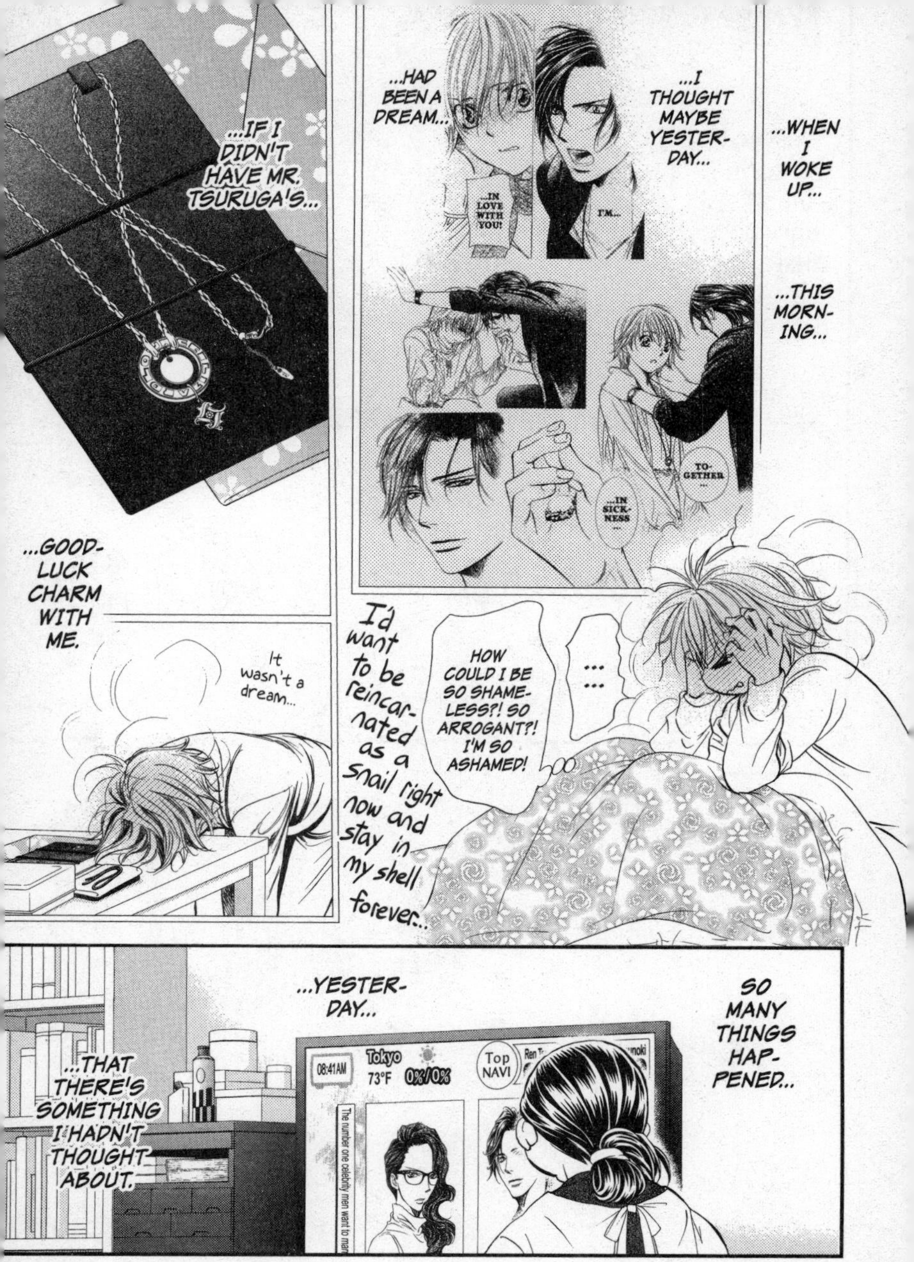
...WHEN I WOKE UP...
...THIS MORNING...
...I THOUGHT MAYBE YESTER-DAY...
I'M...
...HAD BEEN A DREAM...
...IN LOVE WITH YOU!
TO-GETHER...
...IN SICKNESS...
...IF I DIDN'T HAVE MR. TSURUGA'S...
...GOOD-LUCK CHARM WITH ME.
......
HOW COULD I BE SO SHAME-LESS?! SO ARROGANT?! I'M SO ASHAMED!
I'd want to be reincar-nated as a snail right now and stay in my shell forever...
It wasn't a dream...
SO MANY THINGS HAP-PENED...
...YESTER-DAY...
08:41AM
Tokyo
73°F 0%/0%
Top NAVI
The number one celebrity men want to mar
...THAT THERE'S SOMETHING I HADN'T THOUGHT ABOUT.

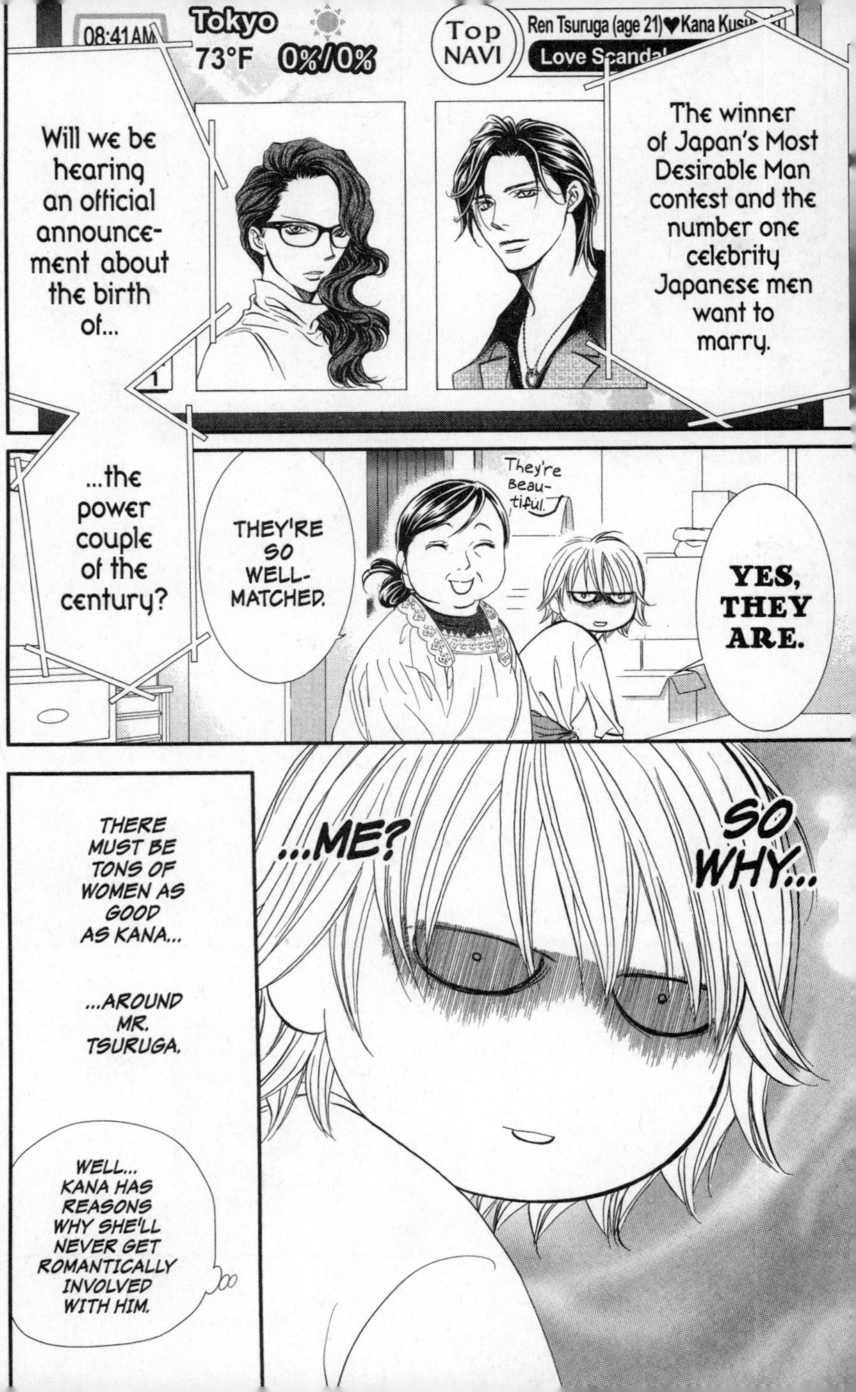
08:41AM
Tokyo
73°F
0%/0%
Top NAVI
Ren Tsuruga (age 21)♥Kana Kusu
Love Scanda
The winner of Japan's Most Desirable Man contest and the number one celebrity Japanese men want to marry.
Will we be hearing an official announcement about the birth of...
...the power couple of the century?
THEY'RE SO WELL-MATCHED.
They're beau-tiful.
YES, THEY ARE.
SO WHY...
...ME?
THERE MUST BE TONS OF WOMEN AS GOOD AS KANA...
...AROUND MR. TSURUGA.
WELL... KANA HAS REASONS WHY SHE'LL NEVER GET ROMANTICALLY INVOLVED WITH HIM.

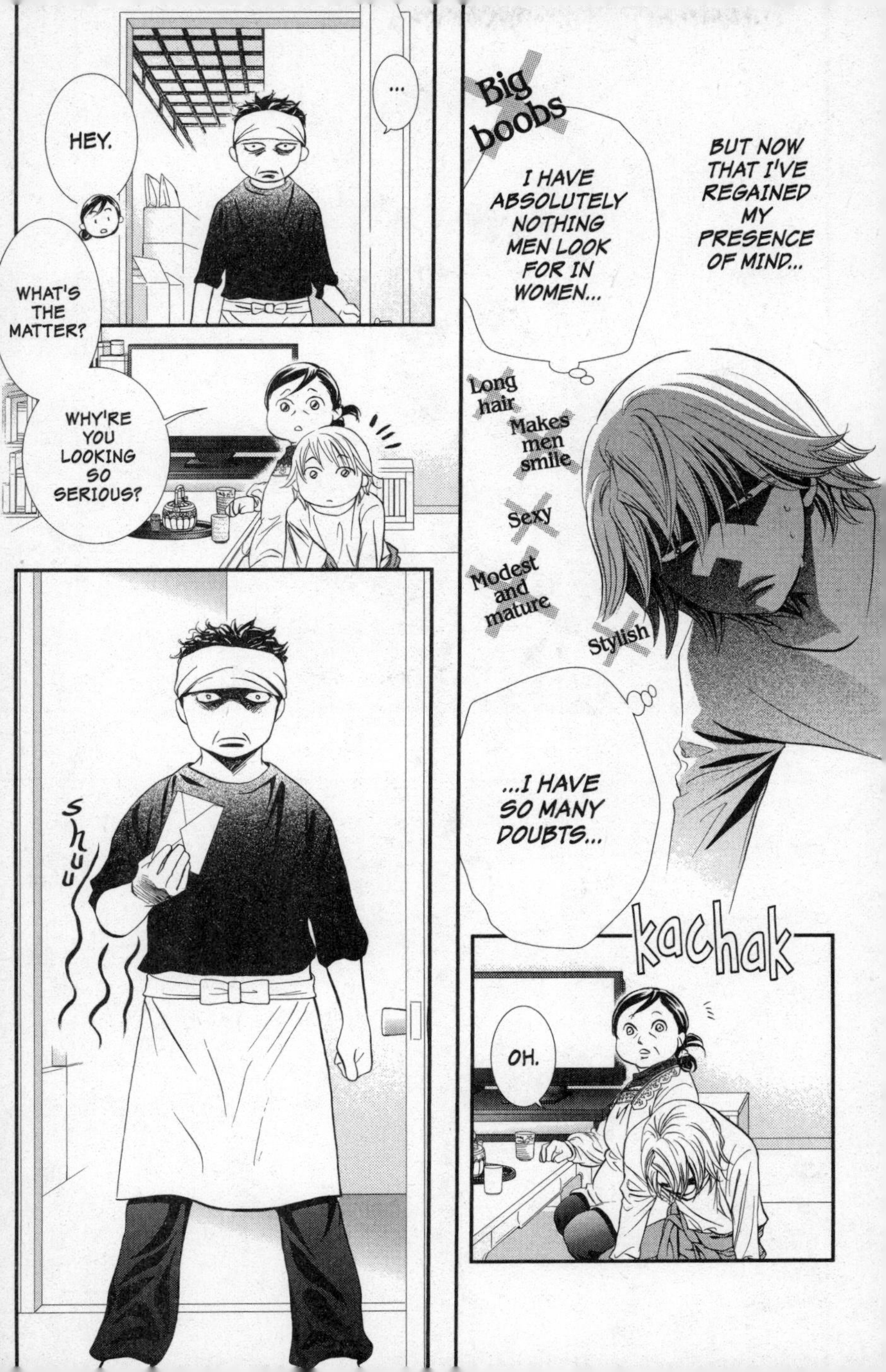
BUT NOW THAT I'VE REGAINED MY PRESENCE OF MIND...
Big boobs
I HAVE ABSOLUTELY NOTHING MEN LOOK FOR IN WOMEN...
Long hair
Makes men smile
Sexy
Modest and mature
Stylish
...I HAVE SO MANY DOUBTS...
kachak
OH.
...
HEY.
WHAT'S THE MATTER?
WHY'RE YOU LOOKING SO SERIOUS?
shuu

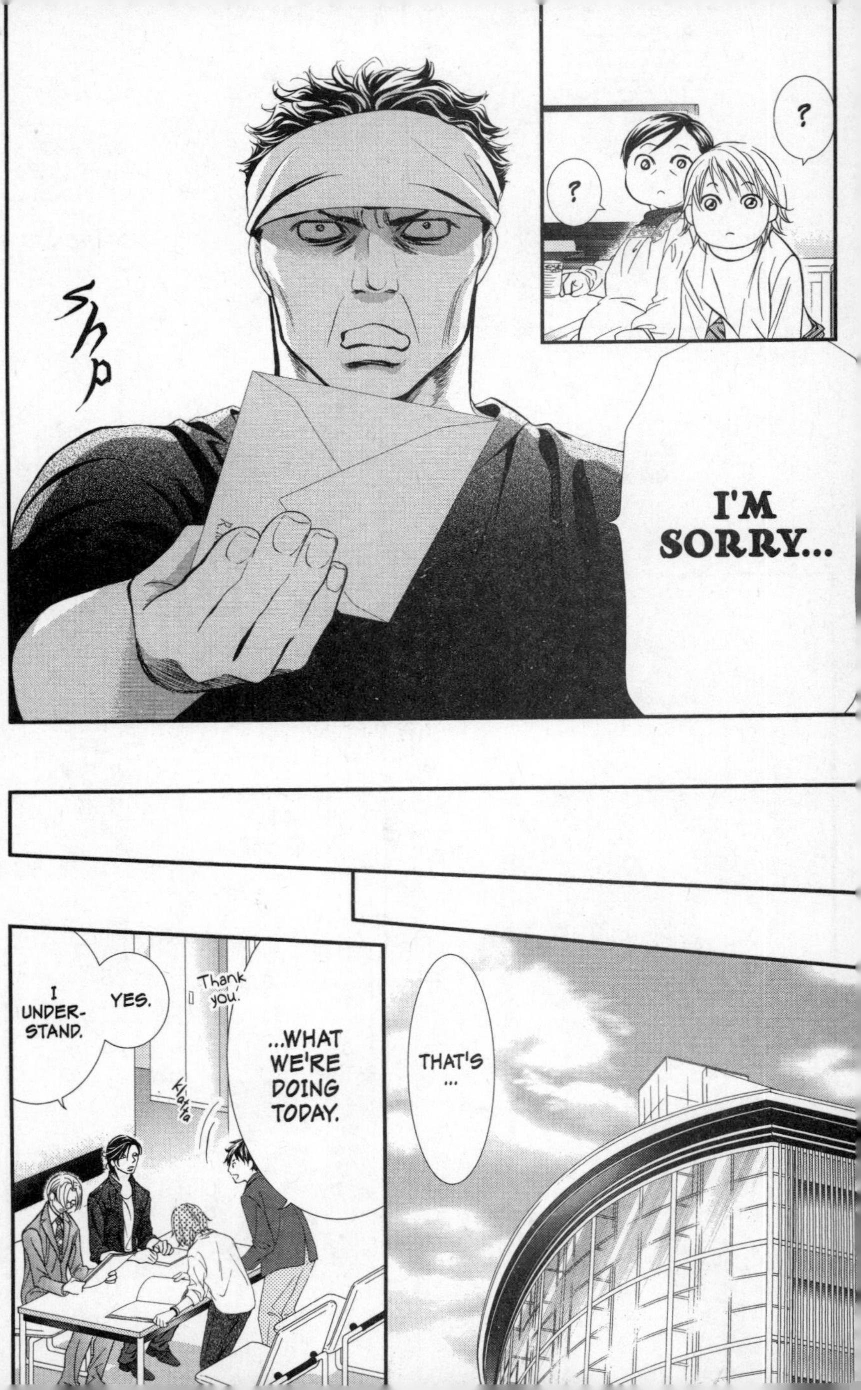
?
?
I'M SORRY...
SNP
THAT'S ...
...WHAT WE'RE DOING TODAY.
Thank you!
YES.
I UNDERSTAND.
klatta

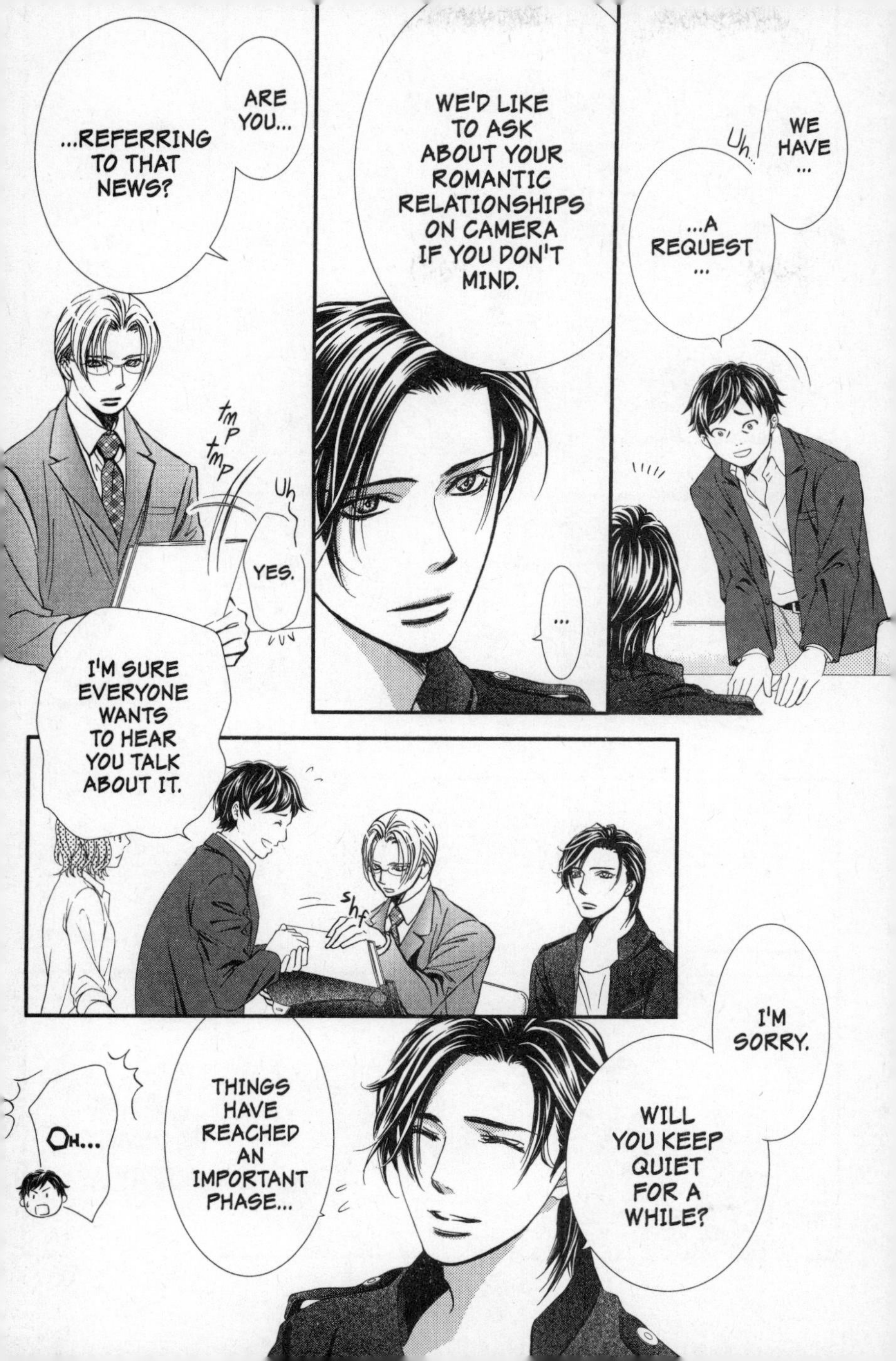
WE HAVE ...
Uh...
...A REQUEST ...
WE'D LIKE TO ASK ABOUT YOUR ROMANTIC RELATIONSHIPS ON CAMERA IF YOU DON'T MIND.
...
ARE YOU...
...REFERRING TO THAT NEWS?
tmp tmp
Uh
YES.
I'M SURE EVERYONE WANTS TO HEAR YOU TALK ABOUT IT.
shf
I'M SORRY.
WILL YOU KEEP QUIET FOR A WHILE?
THINGS HAVE REACHED AN IMPORTANT PHASE...
OH...

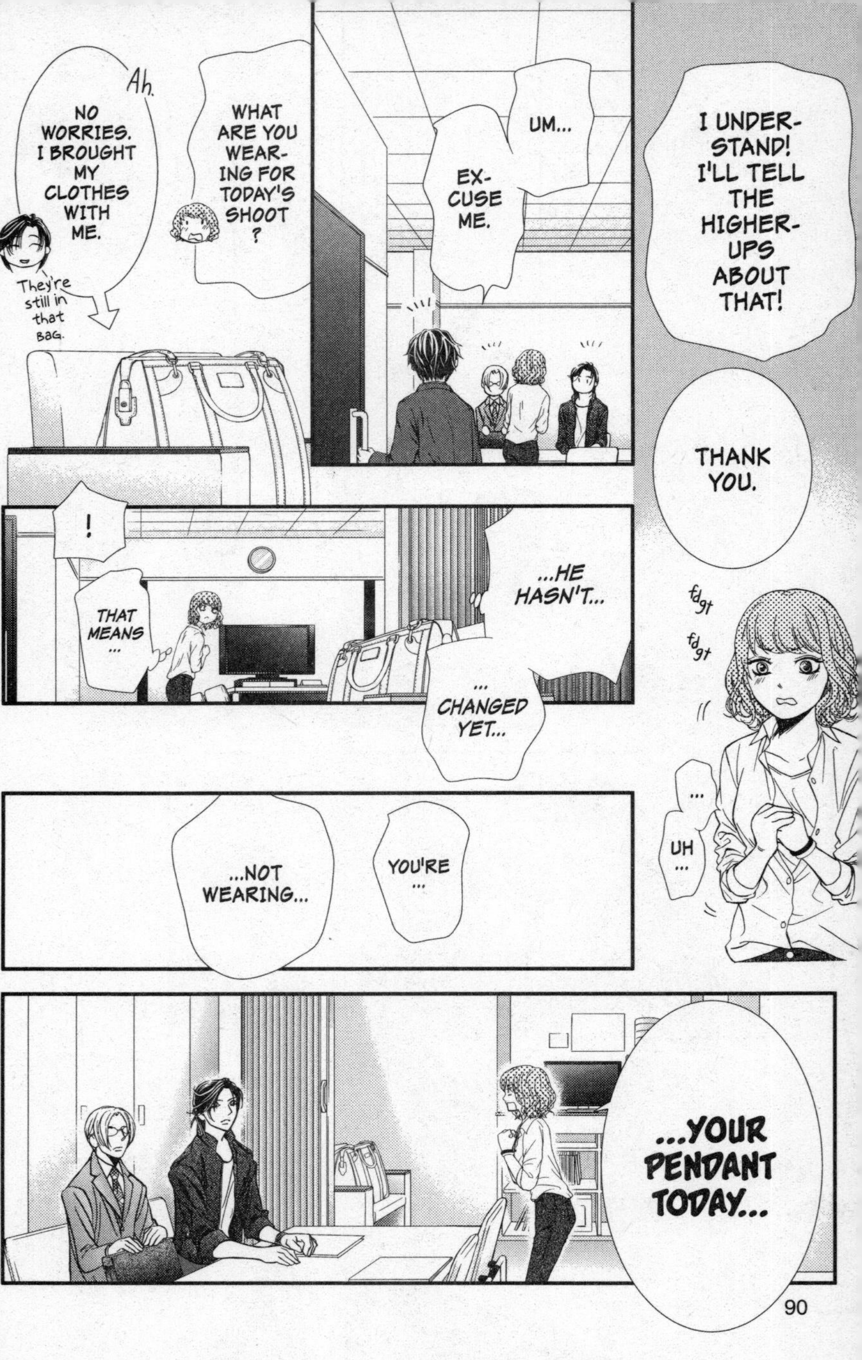
I UNDER-STAND! I'LL TELL THE HIGHER-UPS ABOUT THAT!
THANK YOU.
fdgt fdgt
...
UH...
UM...
EX-CUSE ME.
WHAT ARE YOU WEAR-ING FOR TODAY'S SHOOT?
Ah.
NO WORRIES. I BROUGHT MY CLOTHES WITH ME.
They're still in that BAG.
!
THAT MEANS...
...HE HASN'T...
...CHANGED YET...
YOU'RE...
...NOT WEARING...
...YOUR PENDANT TODAY...

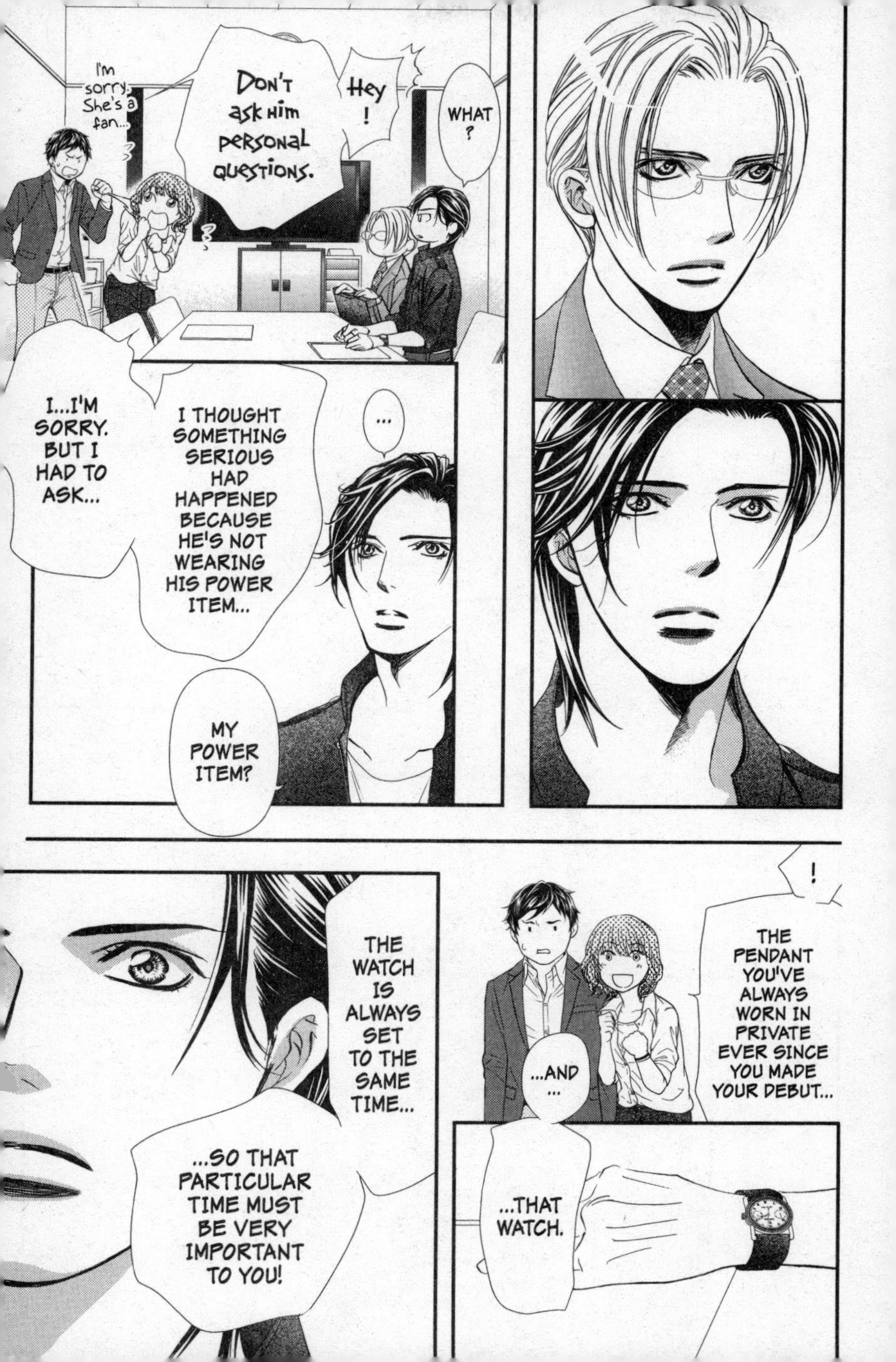
WHAT?
Hey!
Don't ask him personal questions.
I'm sorry. She's a fan...
I...I'M SORRY. BUT I HAD TO ASK...
I THOUGHT SOMETHING SERIOUS HAD HAPPENED BECAUSE HE'S NOT WEARING HIS POWER ITEM...
...
MY POWER ITEM?
!
THE PENDANT YOU'VE ALWAYS WORN IN PRIVATE EVER SINCE YOU MADE YOUR DEBUT...
...AND ...
...THAT WATCH.
THE WATCH IS ALWAYS SET TO THE SAME TIME...
...SO THAT PARTICULAR TIME MUST BE VERY IMPORTANT TO YOU!

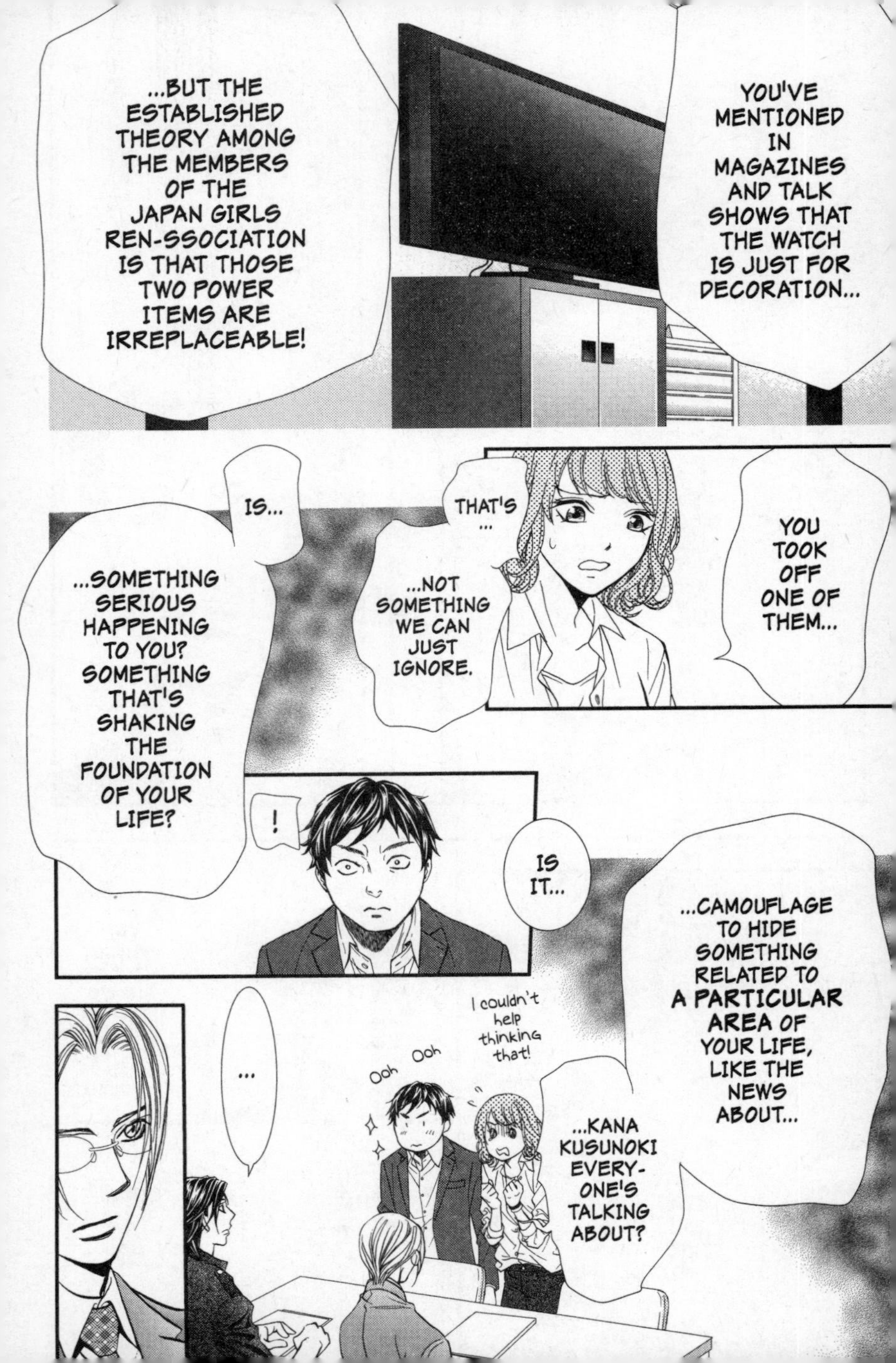
YOU'VE MENTIONED IN MAGAZINES AND TALK SHOWS THAT THE WATCH IS JUST FOR DECORATION...
...BUT THE ESTABLISHED THEORY AMONG THE MEMBERS OF THE JAPAN GIRLS REN-SSOCIATION IS THAT THOSE TWO POWER ITEMS ARE IRREPLACEABLE!
YOU TOOK OFF ONE OF THEM...
THAT'S ...
...NOT SOMETHING WE CAN JUST IGNORE.
IS...
...SOMETHING SERIOUS HAPPENING TO YOU? SOMETHING THAT'S SHAKING THE FOUNDATION OF YOUR LIFE?
!
IS IT...
...CAMOUFLAGE TO HIDE SOMETHING RELATED TO A PARTICULAR AREA OF YOUR LIFE, LIKE THE NEWS ABOUT...
...KANA KUSUNOKI EVERY-ONE'S TALKING ABOUT?
I couldn't help thinking that!
Ooh Ooh
...

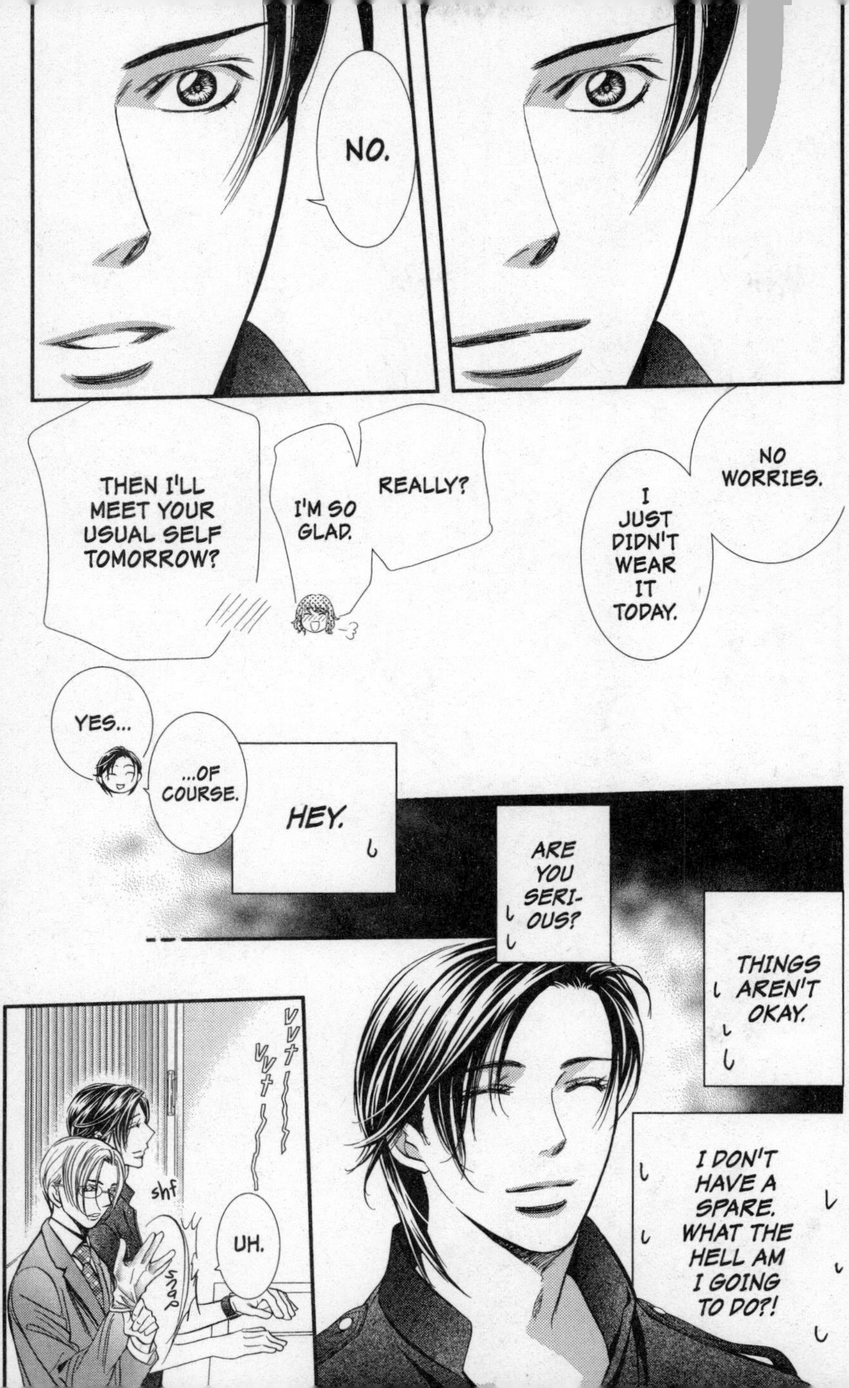
NO.
NO WORRIES.
I JUST DIDN'T WEAR IT TODAY.
REALLY?
I'M SO GLAD.
THEN I'LL MEET YOUR USUAL SELF TOMORROW?
YES...
...OF COURSE.
HEY.
ARE YOU SERIOUS?
THINGS AREN'T OKAY.
I DON'T HAVE A SPARE. WHAT THE HELL AM I GOING TO DO?!
UH.
snap
shf

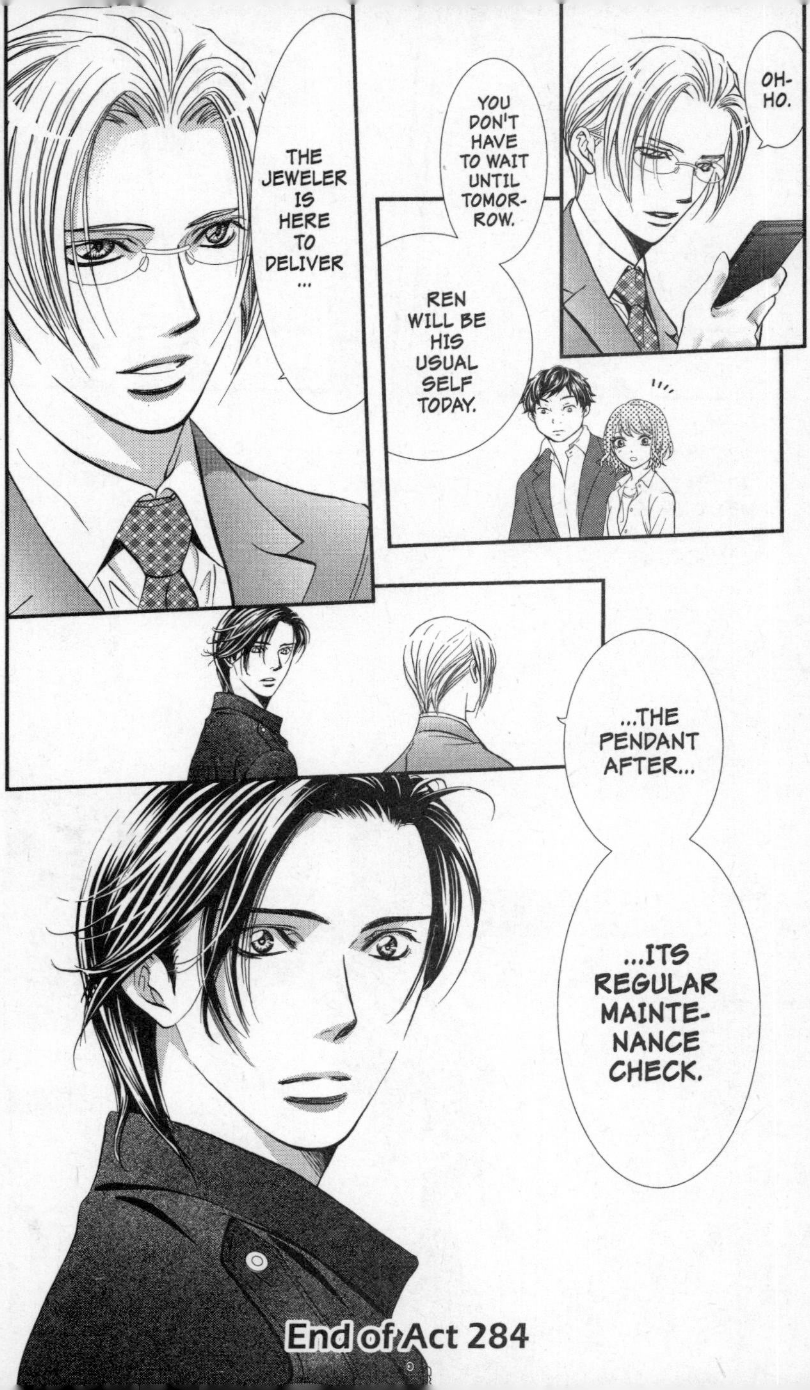
OH-HO.
YOU DON'T HAVE TO WAIT UNTIL TOMORROW.
REN WILL BE HIS USUAL SELF TODAY.
THE JEWELER IS HERE TO DELIVER...
...THE PENDANT AFTER...
...ITS REGULAR MAINTENANCE CHECK.
End of Act 284

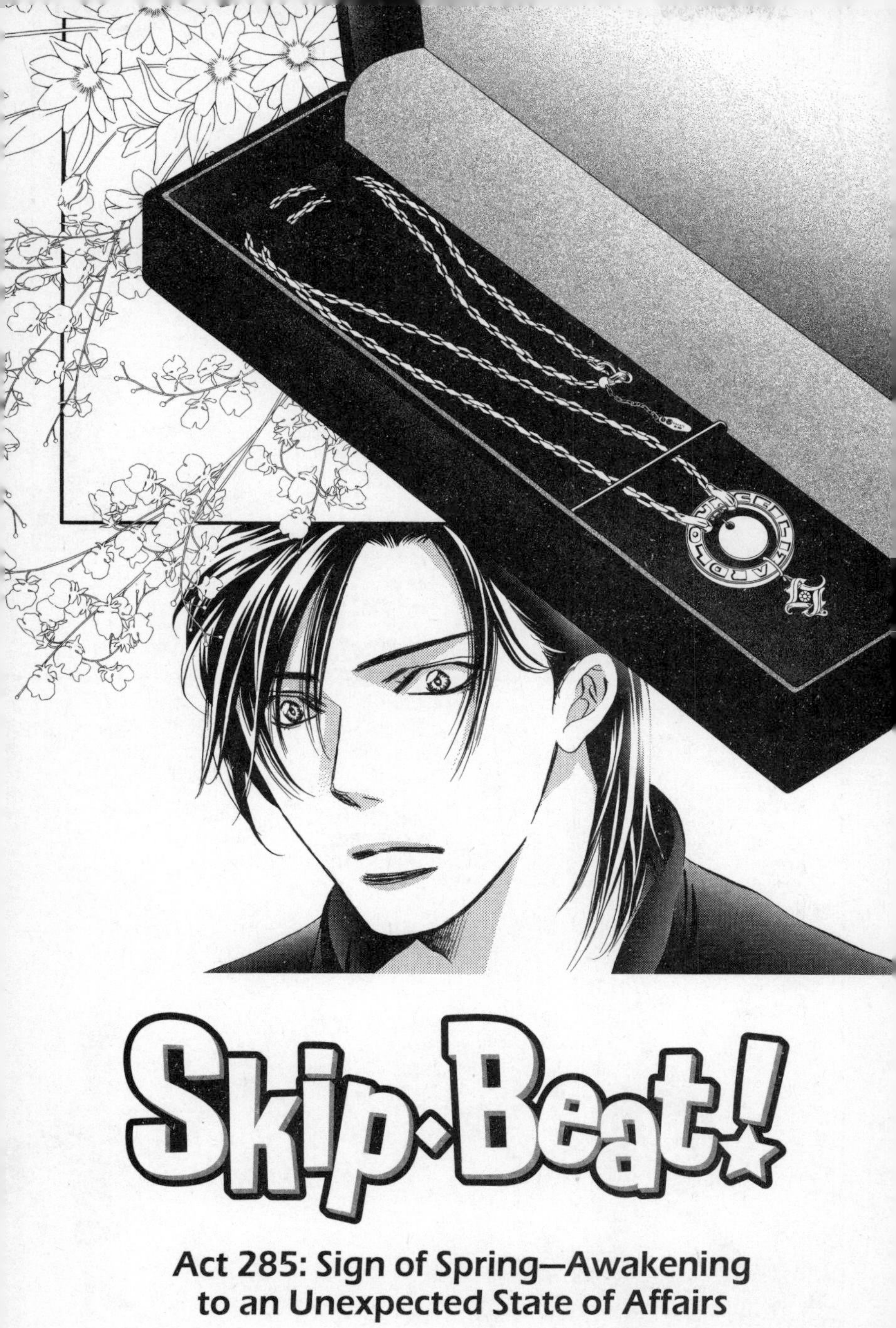

Skip·Beat!

Act 285: Sign of Spring—Awakening to an Unexpected State of Affairs

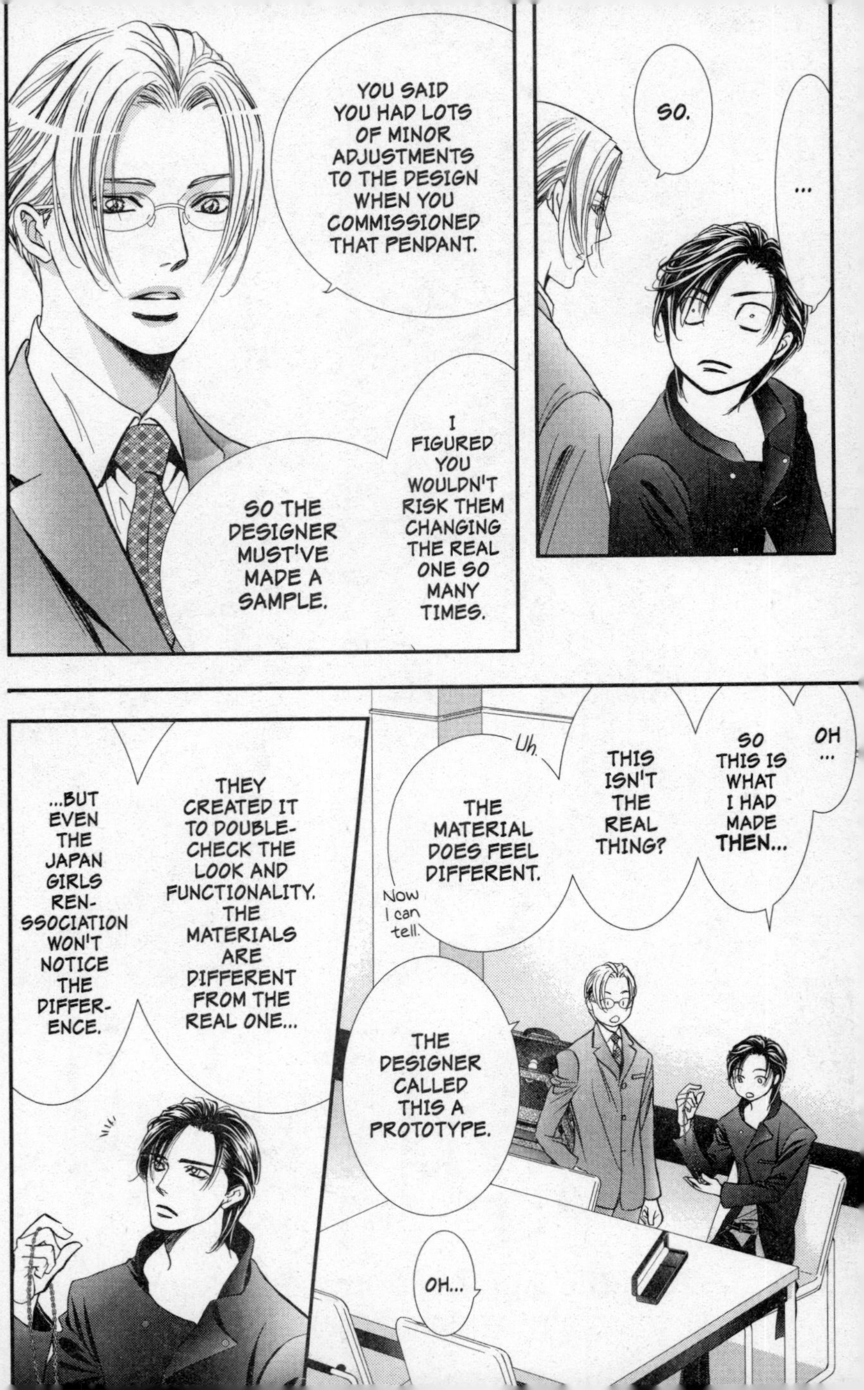
SO.
...
YOU SAID YOU HAD LOTS OF MINOR ADJUSTMENTS TO THE DESIGN WHEN YOU COMMISSIONED THAT PENDANT.
I FIGURED YOU WOULDN'T RISK THEM CHANGING THE REAL ONE SO MANY TIMES.
SO THE DESIGNER MUST'VE MADE A SAMPLE.
OH ...
SO THIS IS WHAT I HAD MADE THEN...
THIS ISN'T THE REAL THING?
Uh.
THE MATERIAL DOES FEEL DIFFERENT.
Now I can tell.
THE DESIGNER CALLED THIS A PROTOTYPE.
OH...
THEY CREATED IT TO DOUBLE-CHECK THE LOOK AND FUNCTIONALITY. THE MATERIALS ARE DIFFERENT FROM THE REAL ONE...
...BUT EVEN THE JAPAN GIRLS REN-SSOCIATION WON'T NOTICE THE DIFFER-ENCE.

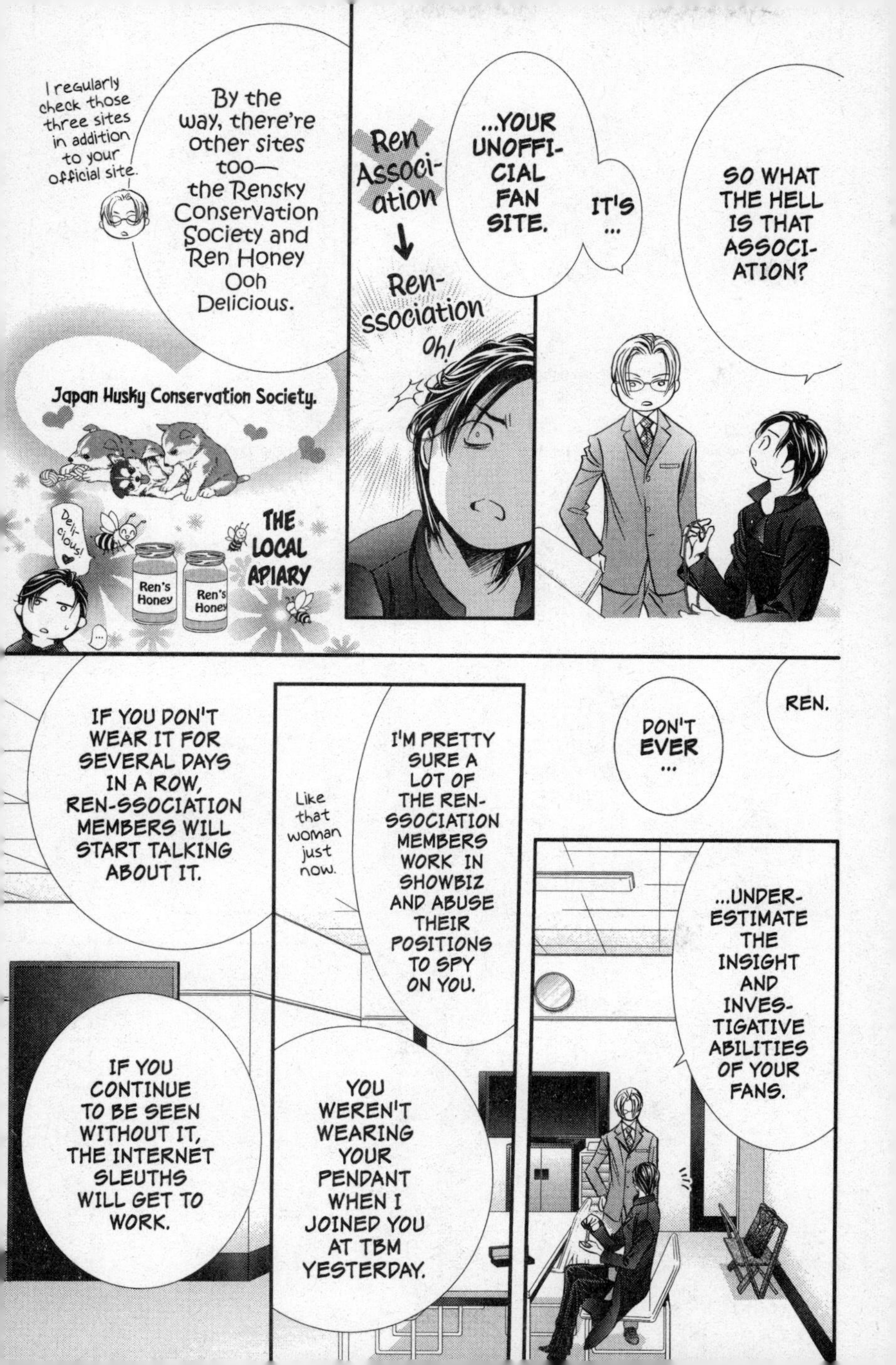

SO WHAT THE HELL IS THAT ASSOCIATION?
IT'S ...
...YOUR UNOFFICIAL FAN SITE.
Ren Association
Ren-ssociation
Oh!
By the way, there're other sites too— the Rensky Conservation Society and Ren Honey Ooh Delicious.
I regularly check those three sites in addition to your official site.
Japan Husky Conservation Society.
THE LOCAL APIARY
Deli-cious!
Ren's Honey
Ren's Honey
...
REN.
DON'T EVER ...
...UNDER-ESTIMATE THE INSIGHT AND INVES-TIGATIVE ABILITIES OF YOUR FANS.
I'M PRETTY SURE A LOT OF THE REN-SSOCIATION MEMBERS WORK IN SHOWBIZ AND ABUSE THEIR POSITIONS TO SPY ON YOU.
Like that woman just now.
YOU WEREN'T WEARING YOUR PENDANT WHEN I JOINED YOU AT TBM YESTERDAY.
IF YOU DON'T WEAR IT FOR SEVERAL DAYS IN A ROW, REN-SSOCIATION MEMBERS WILL START TALKING ABOUT IT.
IF YOU CONTINUE TO BE SEEN WITHOUT IT, THE INTERNET SLEUTHS WILL GET TO WORK.

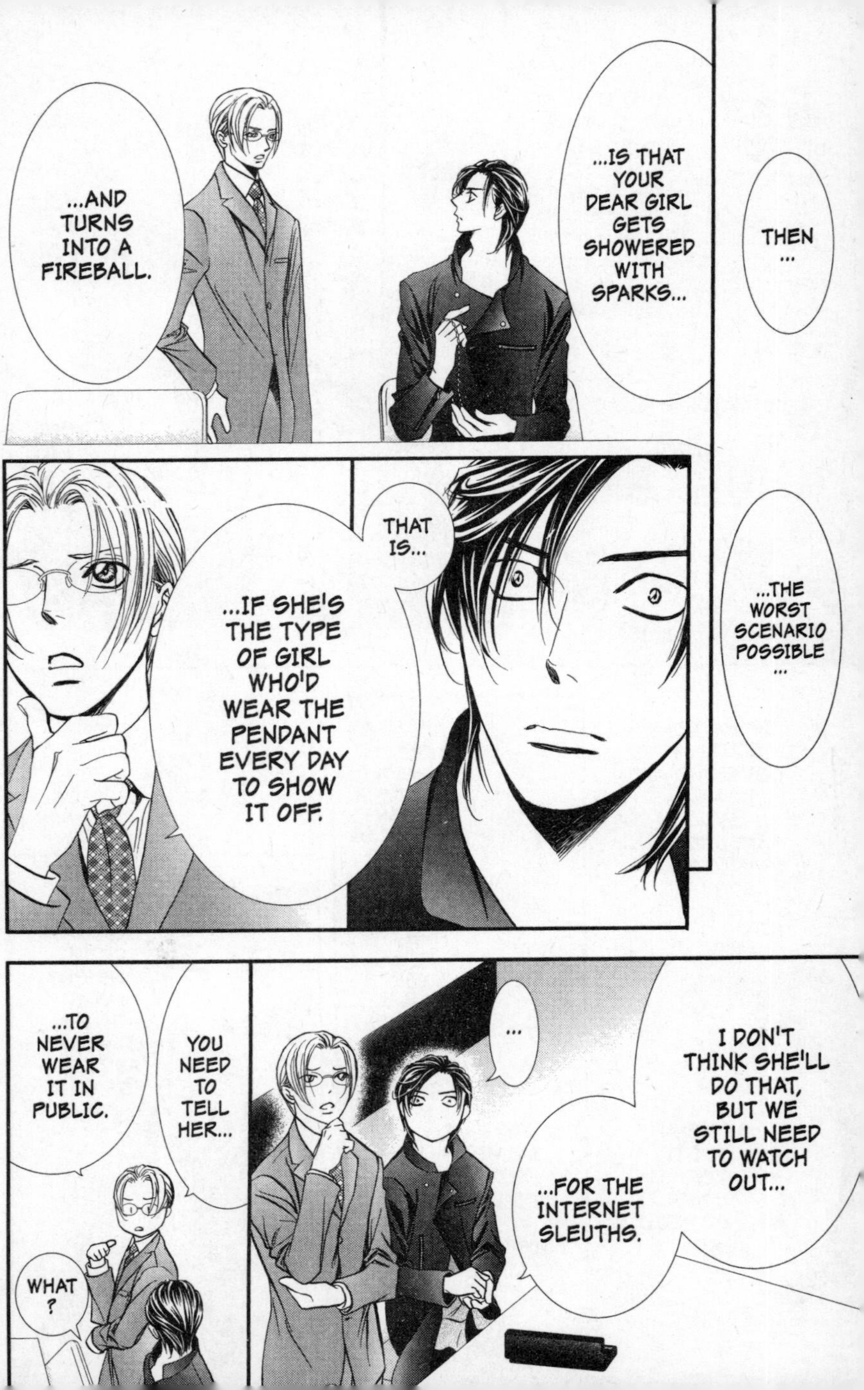
THEN ...
...THE WORST SCENARIO POSSIBLE ...
...IS THAT YOUR DEAR GIRL GETS SHOWERED WITH SPARKS...
...AND TURNS INTO A FIREBALL.
THAT IS...
...IF SHE'S THE TYPE OF GIRL WHO'D WEAR THE PENDANT EVERY DAY TO SHOW IT OFF.
I DON'T THINK SHE'LL DO THAT, BUT WE STILL NEED TO WATCH OUT...
...FOR THE INTERNET SLEUTHS.
...
YOU NEED TO TELL HER...
...TO NEVER WEAR IT IN PUBLIC.
WHAT ?

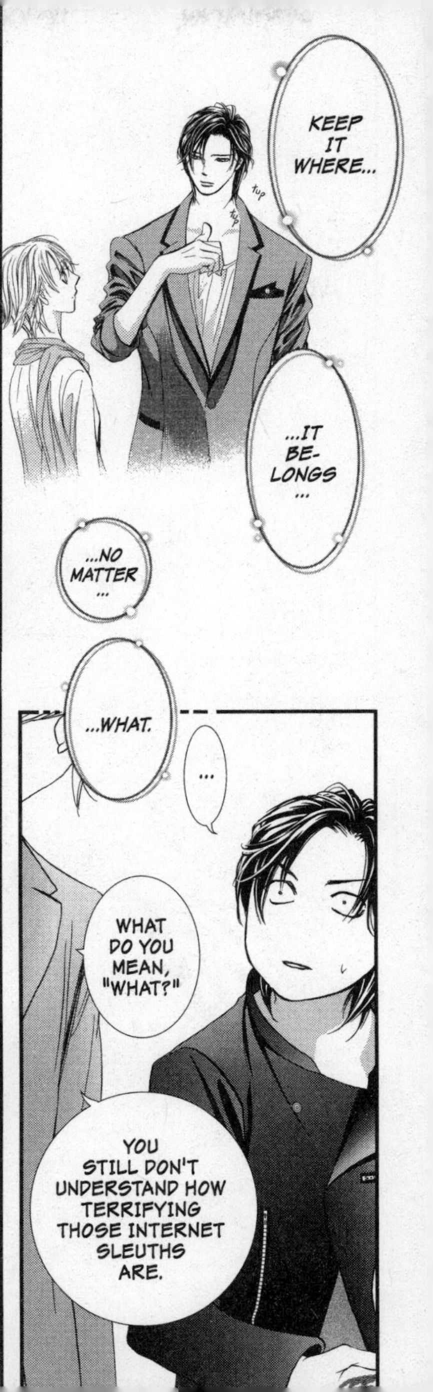
KEEP IT WHERE...
tup
tup
...IT BE-LONGS ...
...NO MATTER ...
...WHAT.
...
WHAT DO YOU MEAN, "WHAT?"
YOU STILL DON'T UNDERSTAND HOW TERRIFYING THOSE INTERNET SLEUTHS ARE.
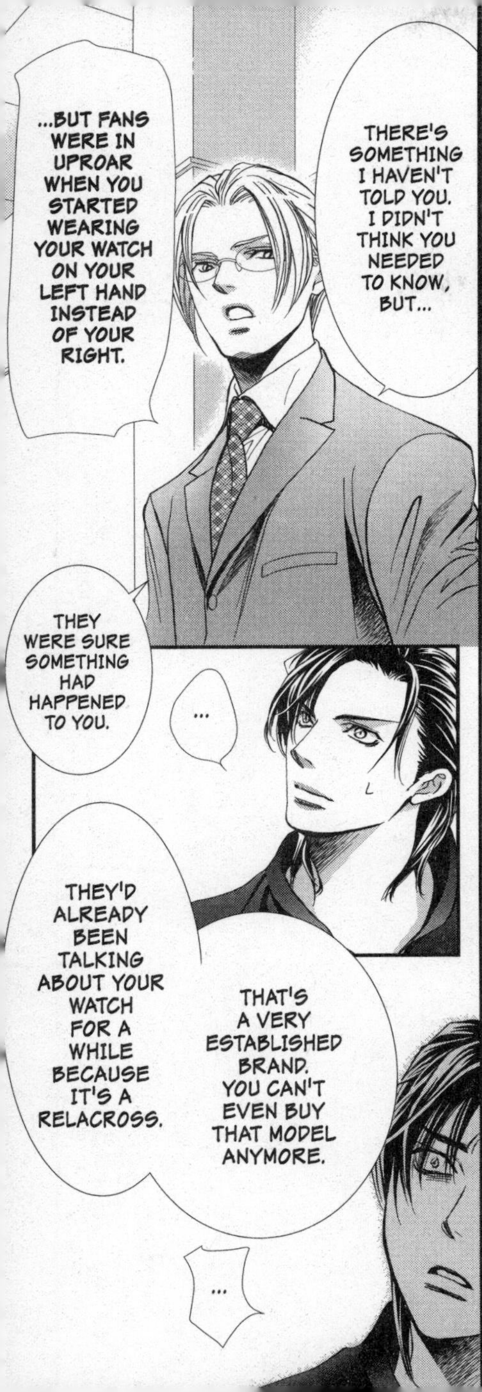
THERE'S SOMETHING I HAVEN'T TOLD YOU. I DIDN'T THINK YOU NEEDED TO KNOW, BUT...
...BUT FANS WERE IN UPROAR WHEN YOU STARTED WEARING YOUR WATCH ON YOUR LEFT HAND INSTEAD OF YOUR RIGHT.
THEY WERE SURE SOMETHING HAD HAPPENED TO YOU.
...
THEY'D ALREADY BEEN TALKING ABOUT YOUR WATCH FOR A WHILE BECAUSE IT'S A RELACROSS.
THAT'S A VERY ESTABLISHED BRAND. YOU CAN'T EVEN BUY THAT MODEL ANYMORE.
...

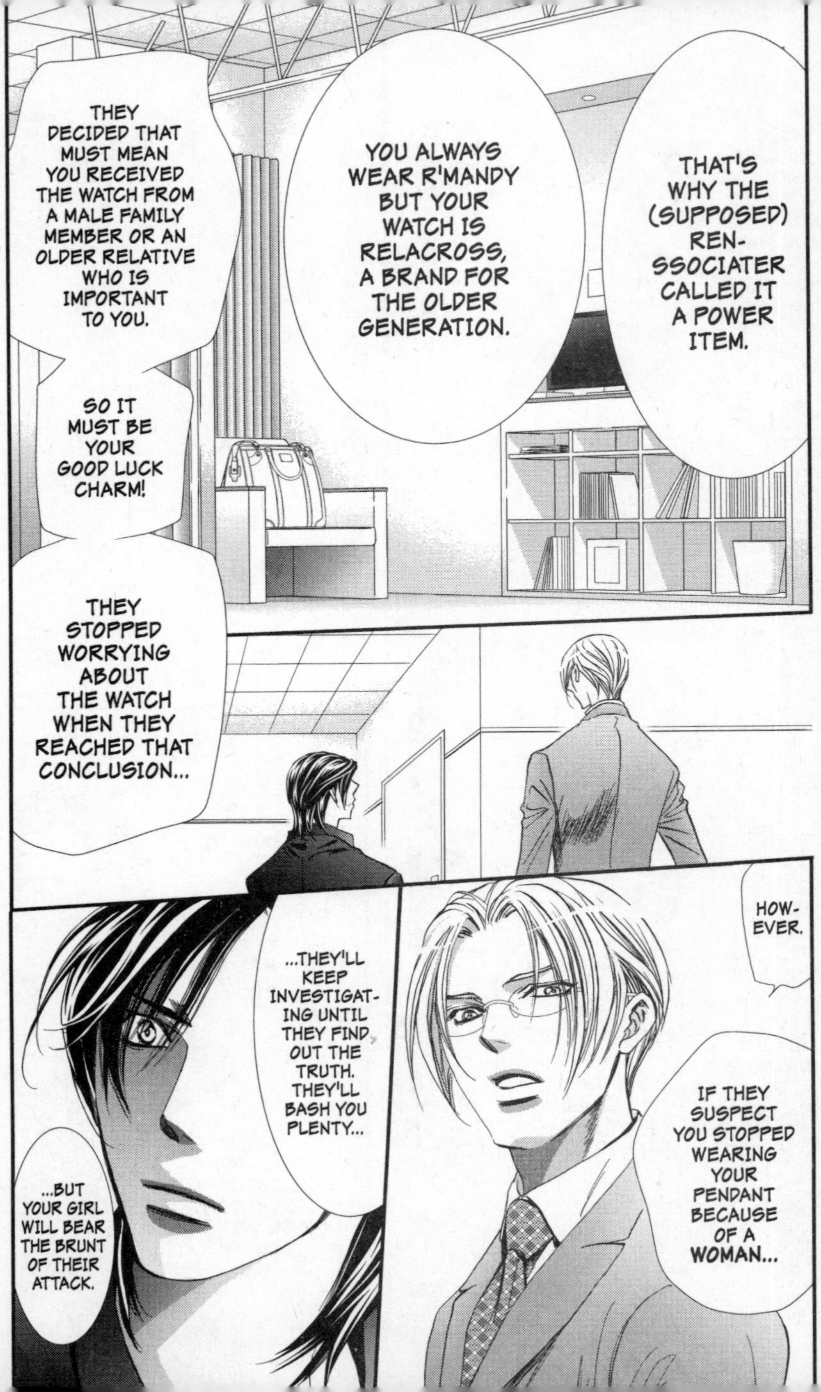
THAT'S WHY THE (SUPPOSED) REN-SSOCIATER CALLED IT A POWER ITEM.
YOU ALWAYS WEAR R'MANDY BUT YOUR WATCH IS RELACROSS, A BRAND FOR THE OLDER GENERATION.
THEY DECIDED THAT MUST MEAN YOU RECEIVED THE WATCH FROM A MALE FAMILY MEMBER OR AN OLDER RELATIVE WHO IS IMPORTANT TO YOU.
SO IT MUST BE YOUR GOOD LUCK CHARM!
THEY STOPPED WORRYING ABOUT THE WATCH WHEN THEY REACHED THAT CONCLUSION...
HOW-EVER.
IF THEY SUSPECT YOU STOPPED WEARING YOUR PENDANT BECAUSE OF A WOMAN...
...THEY'LL KEEP INVESTIGAT-ING UNTIL THEY FIND OUT THE TRUTH. THEY'LL BASH YOU PLENTY...
...BUT YOUR GIRL WILL BEAR THE BRUNT OF THEIR ATTACK.

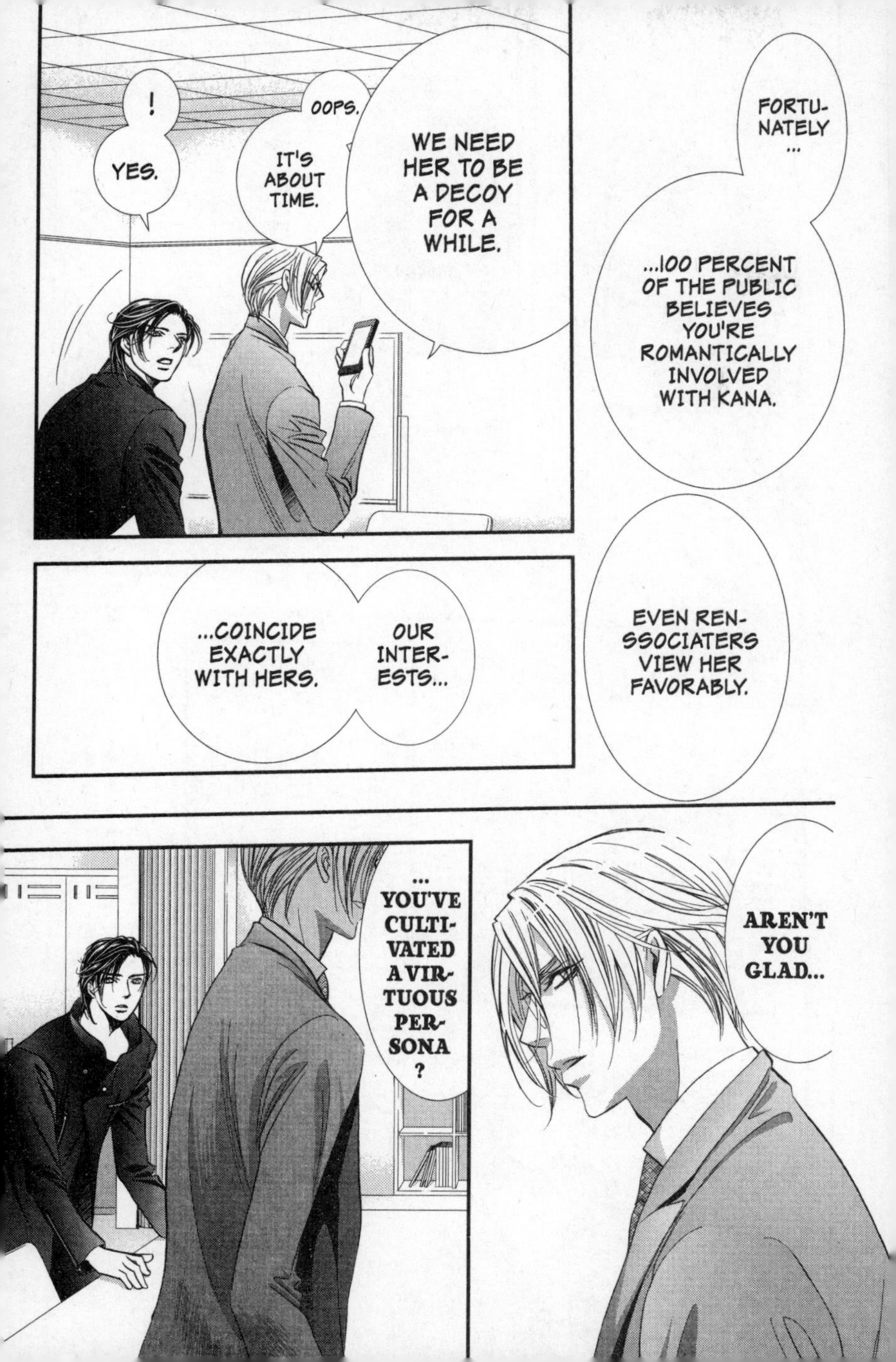
FORTU-NATELY...
...100 PERCENT OF THE PUBLIC BELIEVES YOU'RE ROMANTICALLY INVOLVED WITH KANA.
EVEN REN-SSOCIATERS VIEW HER FAVORABLY.
WE NEED HER TO BE A DECOY FOR A WHILE.
OOPS.
IT'S ABOUT TIME.
!
YES.
OUR INTER-ESTS...
...COINCIDE EXACTLY WITH HERS.
AREN'T YOU GLAD...
...YOU'VE CULTI-VATED A VIR-TUOUS PER-SONA?

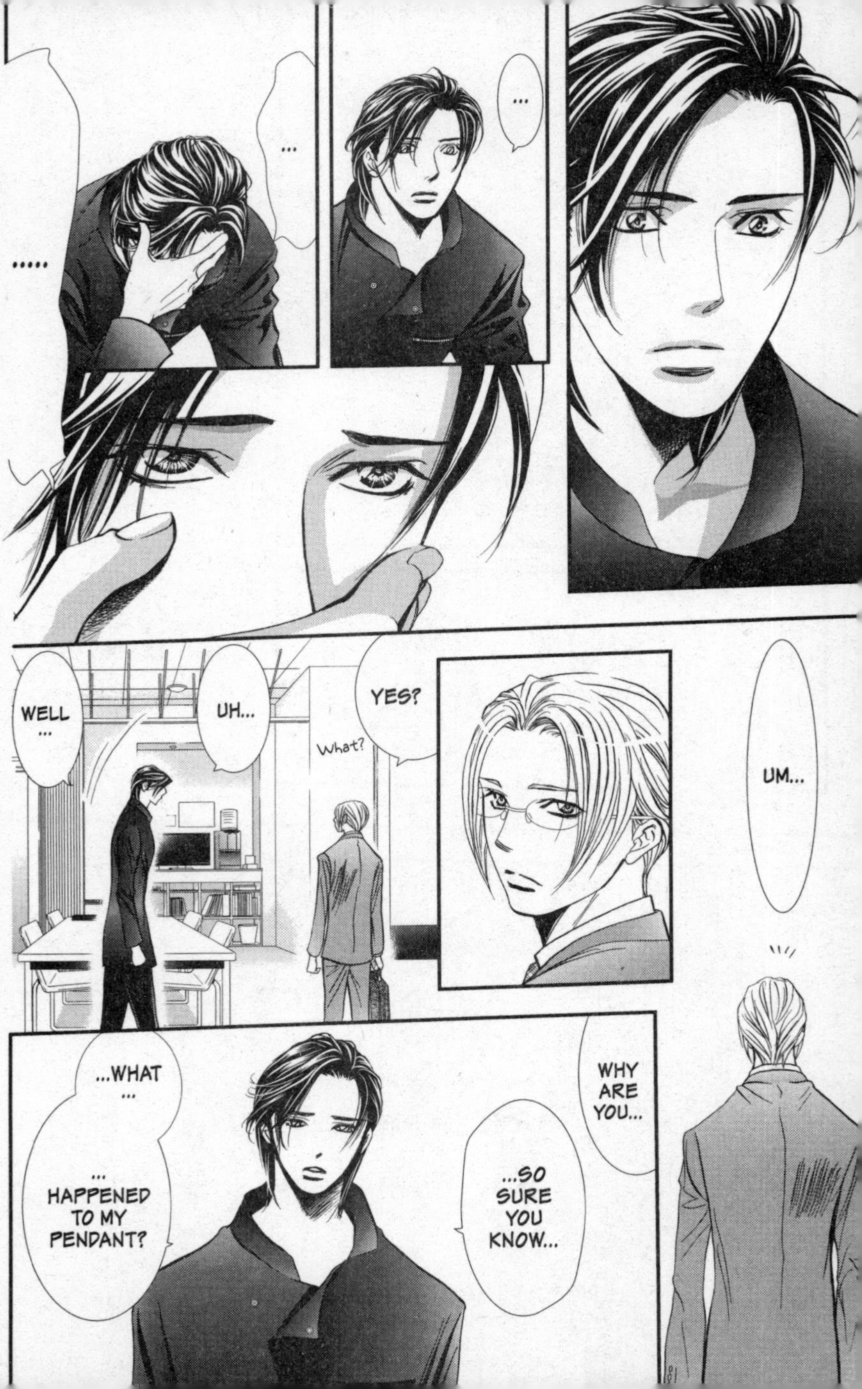
...
...
......
UM...
YES?
What?
UH...
WELL ...
WHY ARE YOU...
...SO SURE YOU KNOW...
...WHAT ...
... HAPPENED TO MY PENDANT?

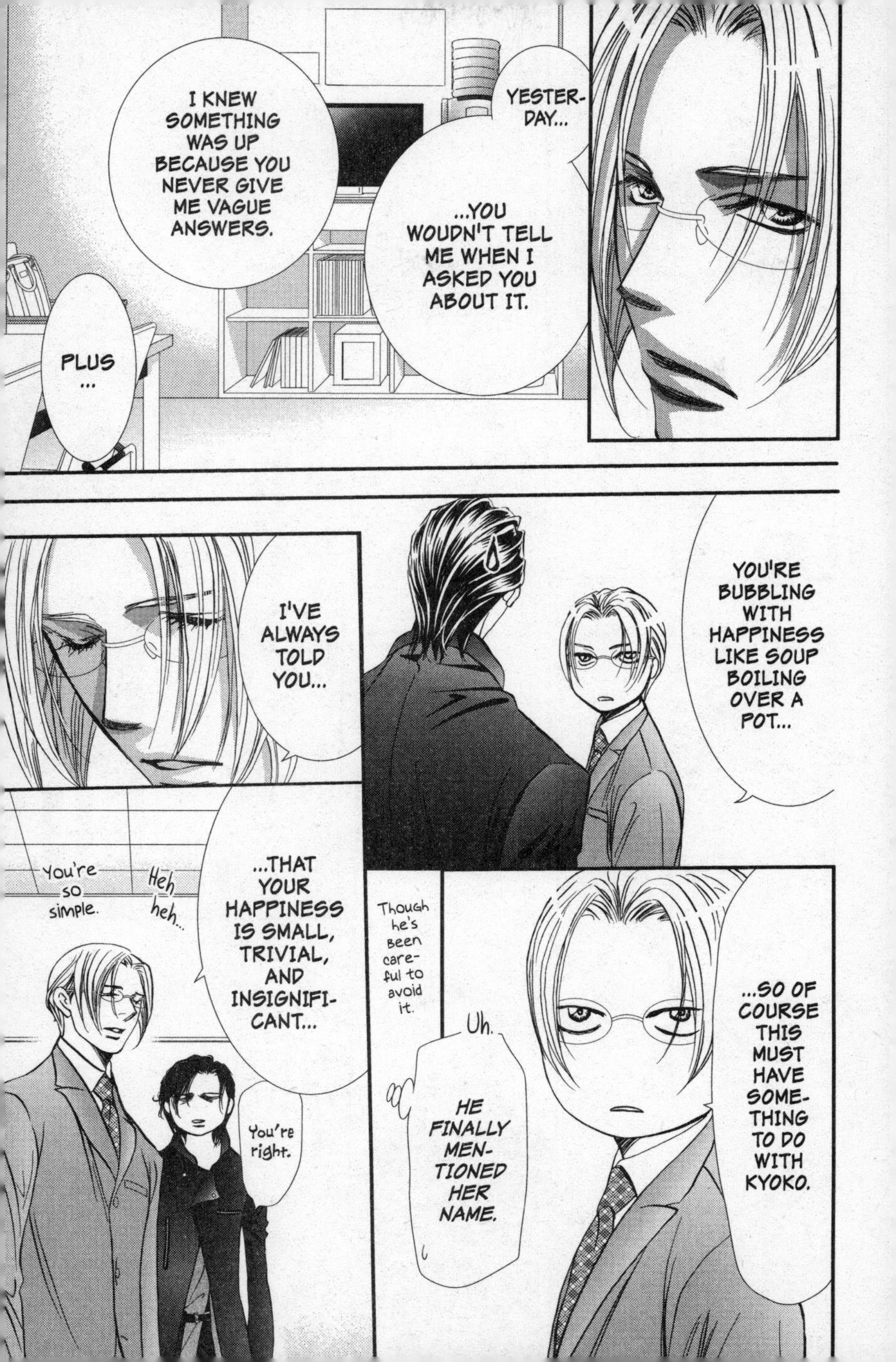
YESTER-DAY...
...YOU WOUDN'T TELL ME WHEN I ASKED YOU ABOUT IT.
I KNEW SOMETHING WAS UP BECAUSE YOU NEVER GIVE ME VAGUE ANSWERS.
PLUS...
YOU'RE BUBBLING WITH HAPPINESS LIKE SOUP BOILING OVER A POT...
I'VE ALWAYS TOLD YOU...
...THAT YOUR HAPPINESS IS SMALL, TRIVIAL, AND INSIGNIFI-CANT...
Heh heh...
You're so simple.
You're right.
...SO OF COURSE THIS MUST HAVE SOME-THING TO DO WITH KYOKO.
Uh.
HE FINALLY MEN-TIONED HER NAME.
Though he's been care-ful to avoid it.

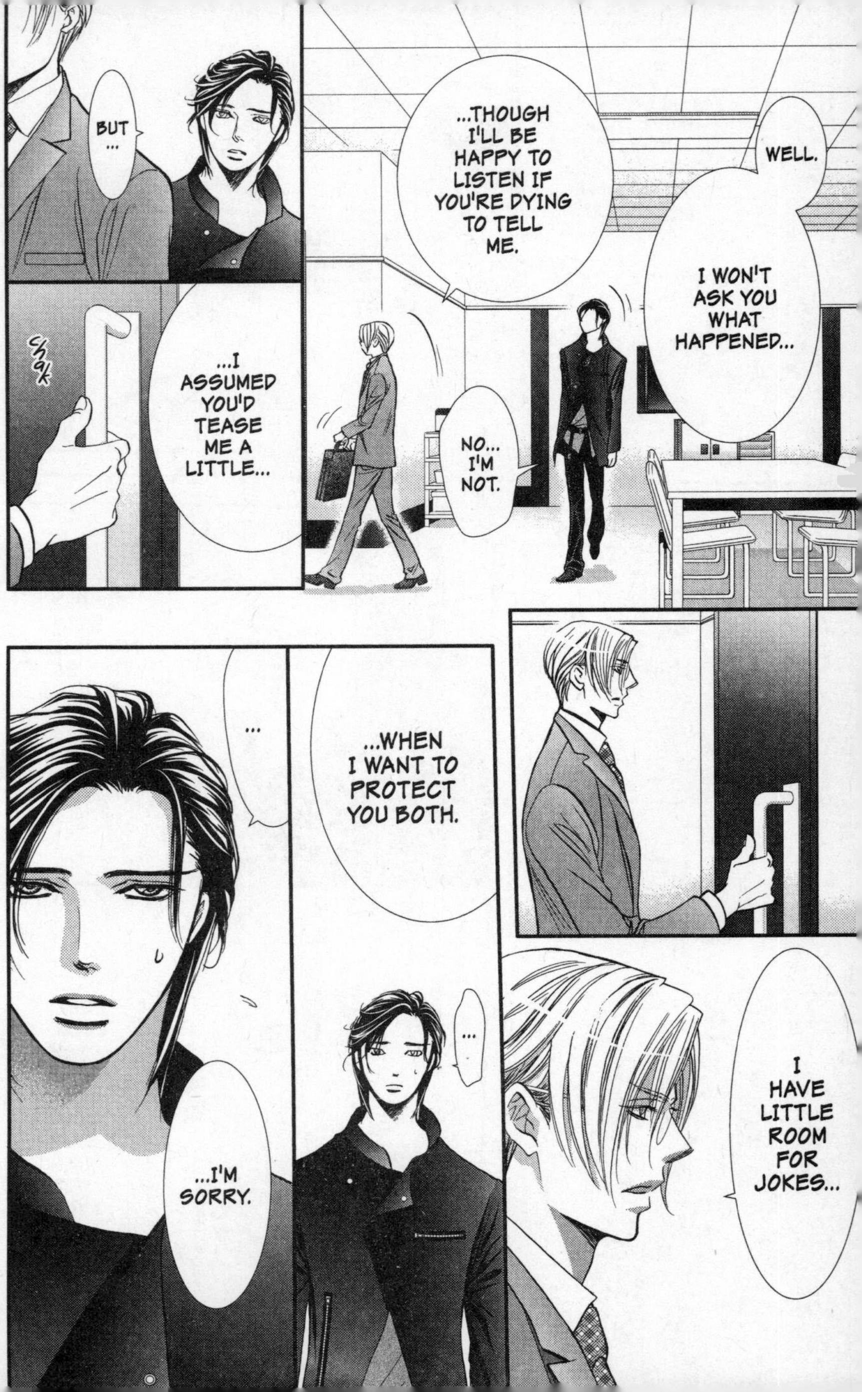
WELL.
I WON'T ASK YOU WHAT HAPPENED...
...THOUGH I'LL BE HAPPY TO LISTEN IF YOU'RE DYING TO TELL ME.
NO... I'M NOT.
BUT ...
chak
...I ASSUMED YOU'D TEASE ME A LITTLE...
I HAVE LITTLE ROOM FOR JOKES...
...WHEN I WANT TO PROTECT YOU BOTH.
...
...
...I'M SORRY.

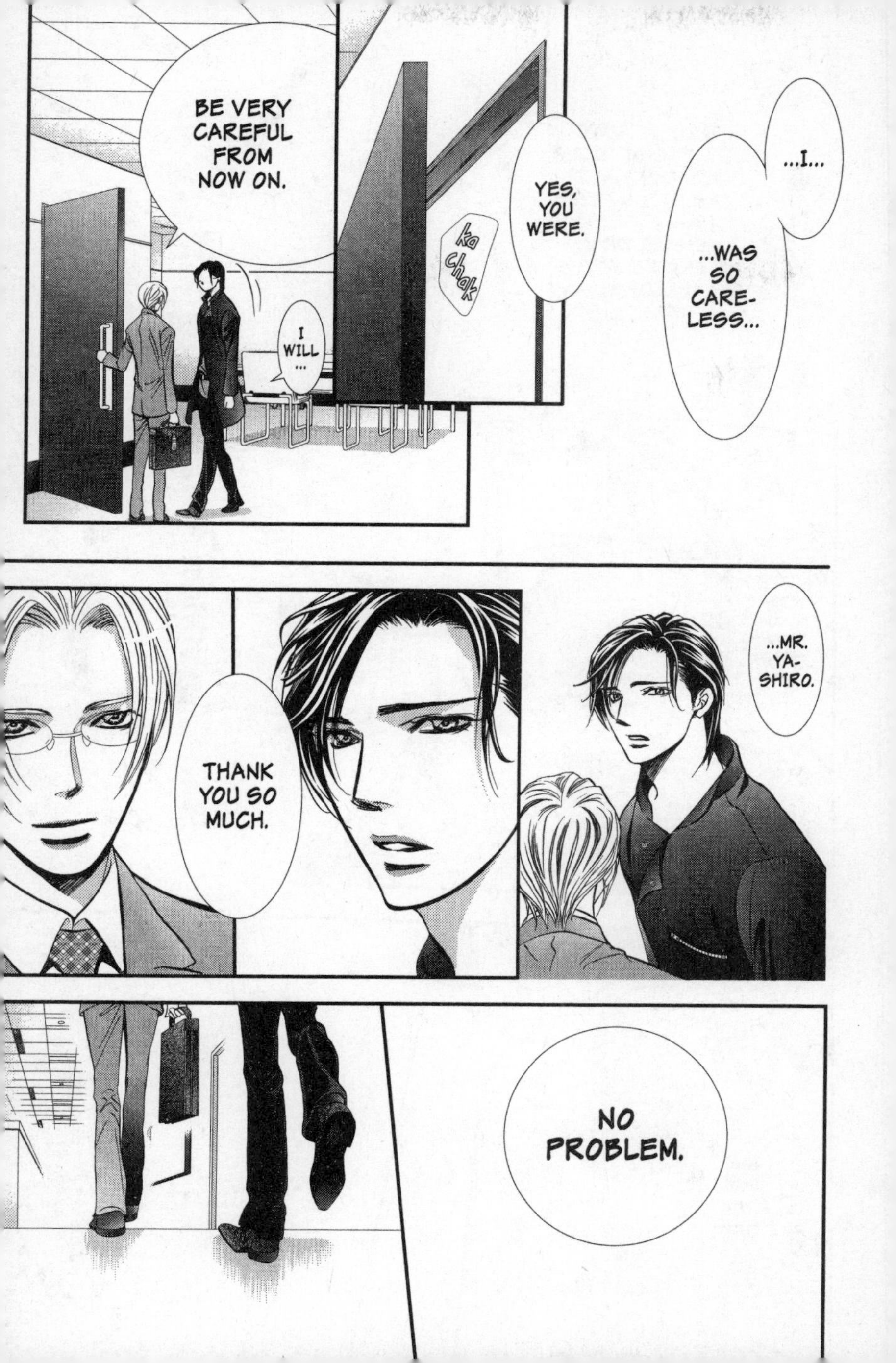
...I...
...WAS SO CARELESS...
YES, YOU WERE.
ka chak
BE VERY CAREFUL FROM NOW ON.
I WILL...
...MR. YASHIRO.
THANK YOU SO MUCH.
NO PROBLEM.

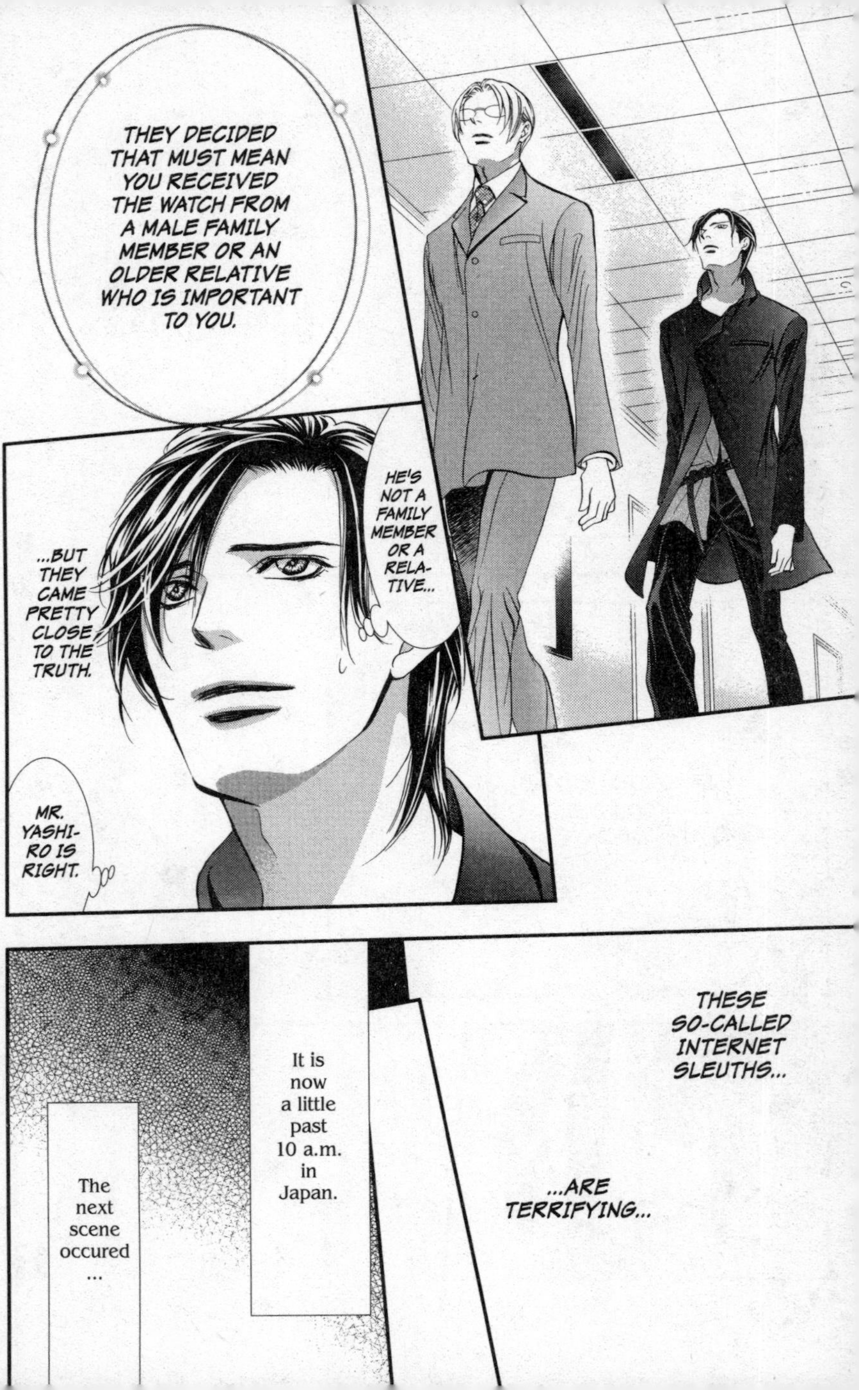
THEY DECIDED THAT MUST MEAN YOU RECEIVED THE WATCH FROM A MALE FAMILY MEMBER OR AN OLDER RELATIVE WHO IS IMPORTANT TO YOU.
HE'S NOT A FAMILY MEMBER OR A RELATIVE...
...BUT THEY CAME PRETTY CLOSE TO THE TRUTH.
MR. YASHIRO IS RIGHT.
THESE SO-CALLED INTERNET SLEUTHS...
...ARE TERRIFYING...
It is now a little past 10 a.m. in Japan.
The next scene occured ...

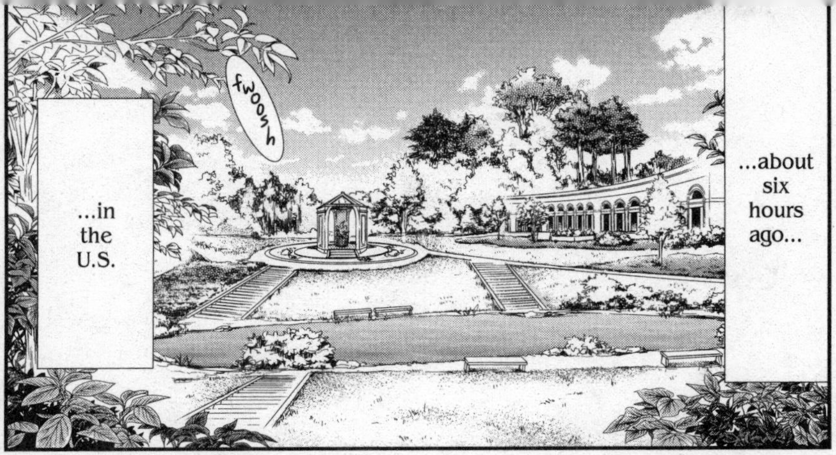
...about six hours ago...
fwoosh
...in the U.S.

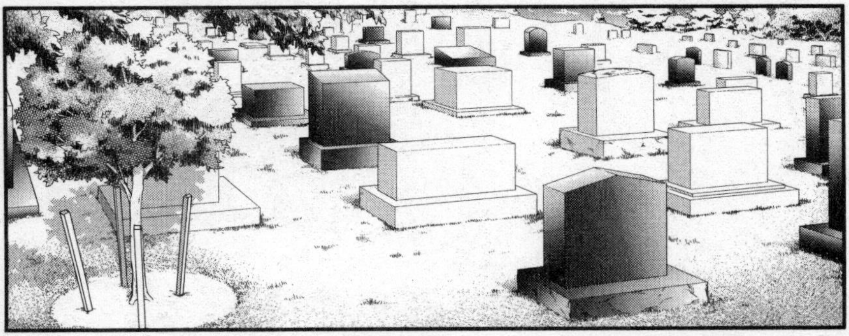

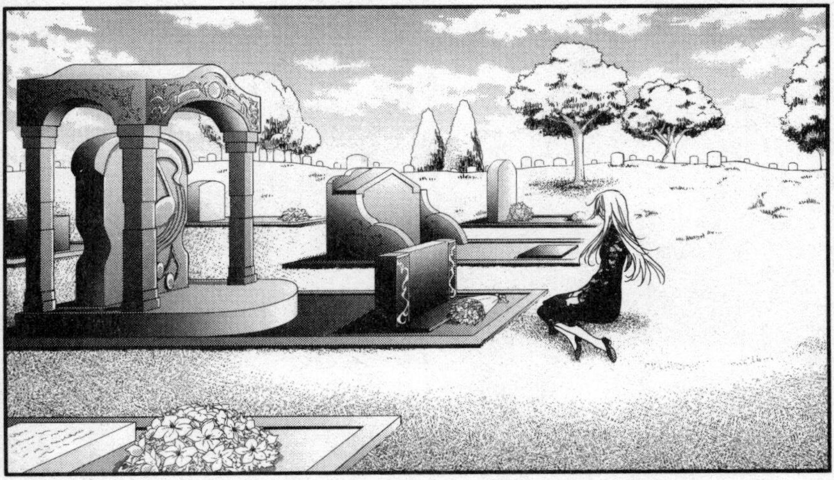

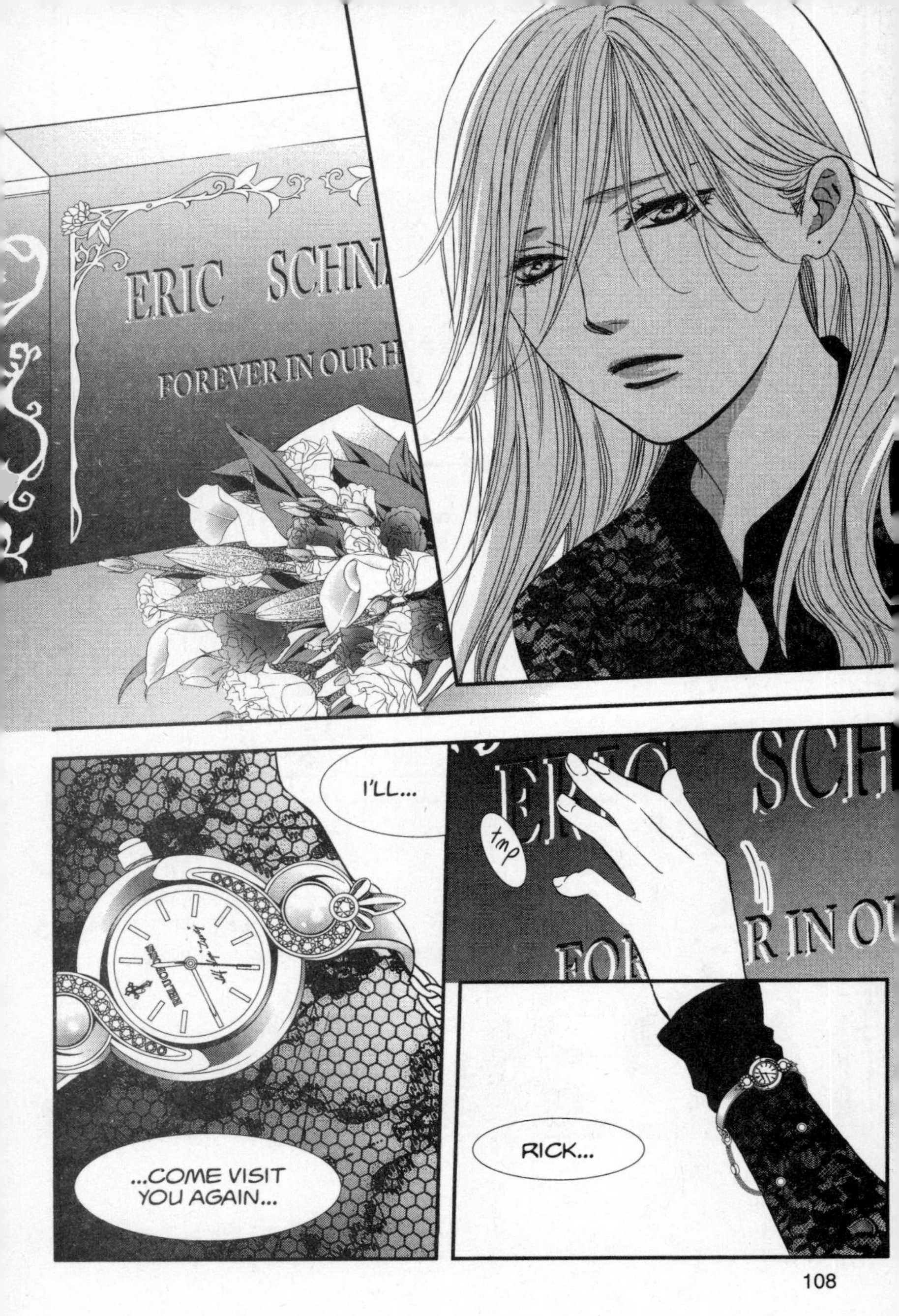
ERIC SCHN
FOREVER IN OUR H
ERIC SCH
R IN OU
RICK...
I'LL...
...COME VISIT YOU AGAIN...

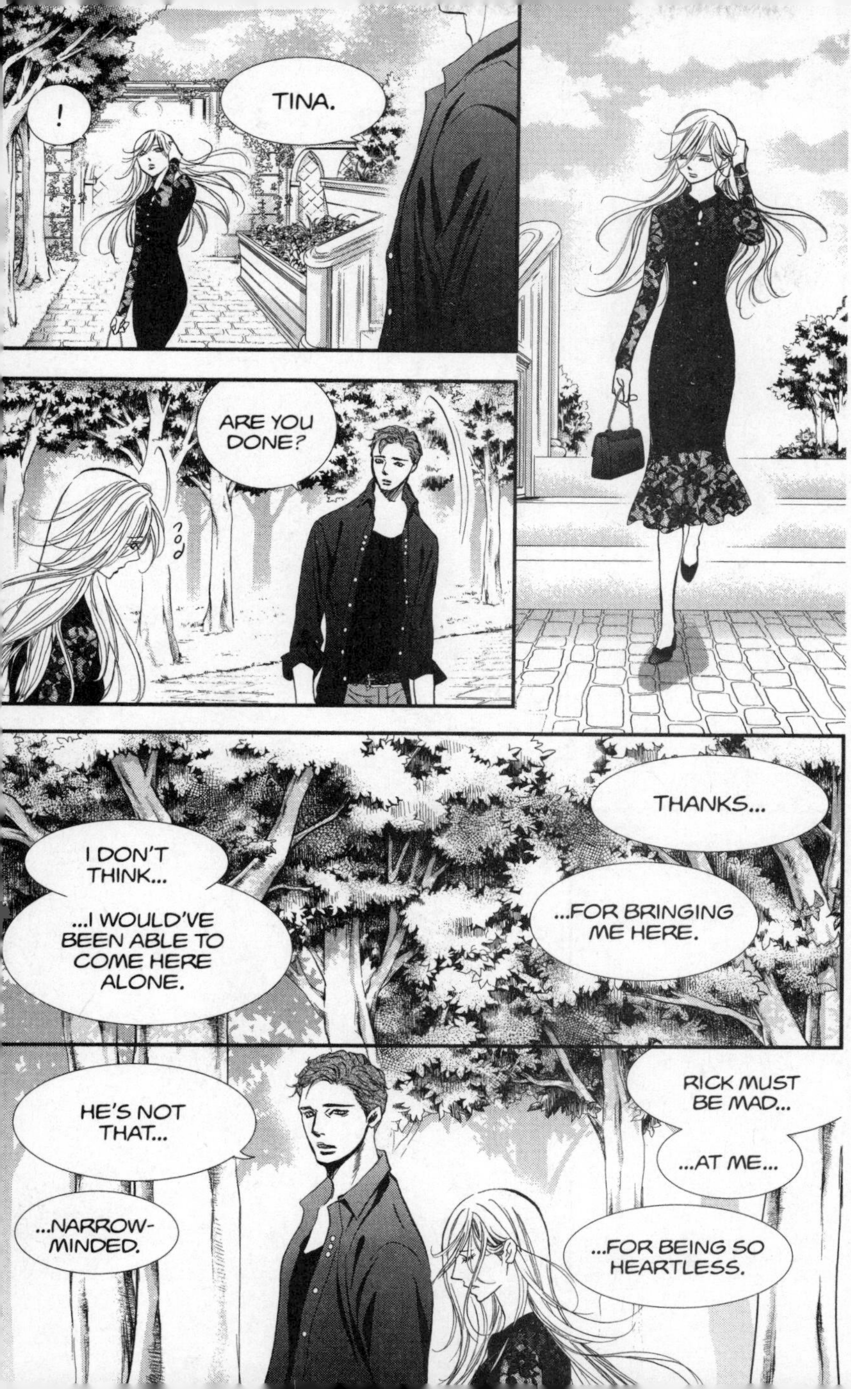
TINA.
!
ARE YOU DONE?
THANKS...
...FOR BRINGING ME HERE.
I DON'T THINK...
...I WOULD'VE BEEN ABLE TO COME HERE ALONE.
RICK MUST BE MAD...
...AT ME...
...FOR BEING SO HEARTLESS.
HE'S NOT THAT...
...NARROW-MINDED.

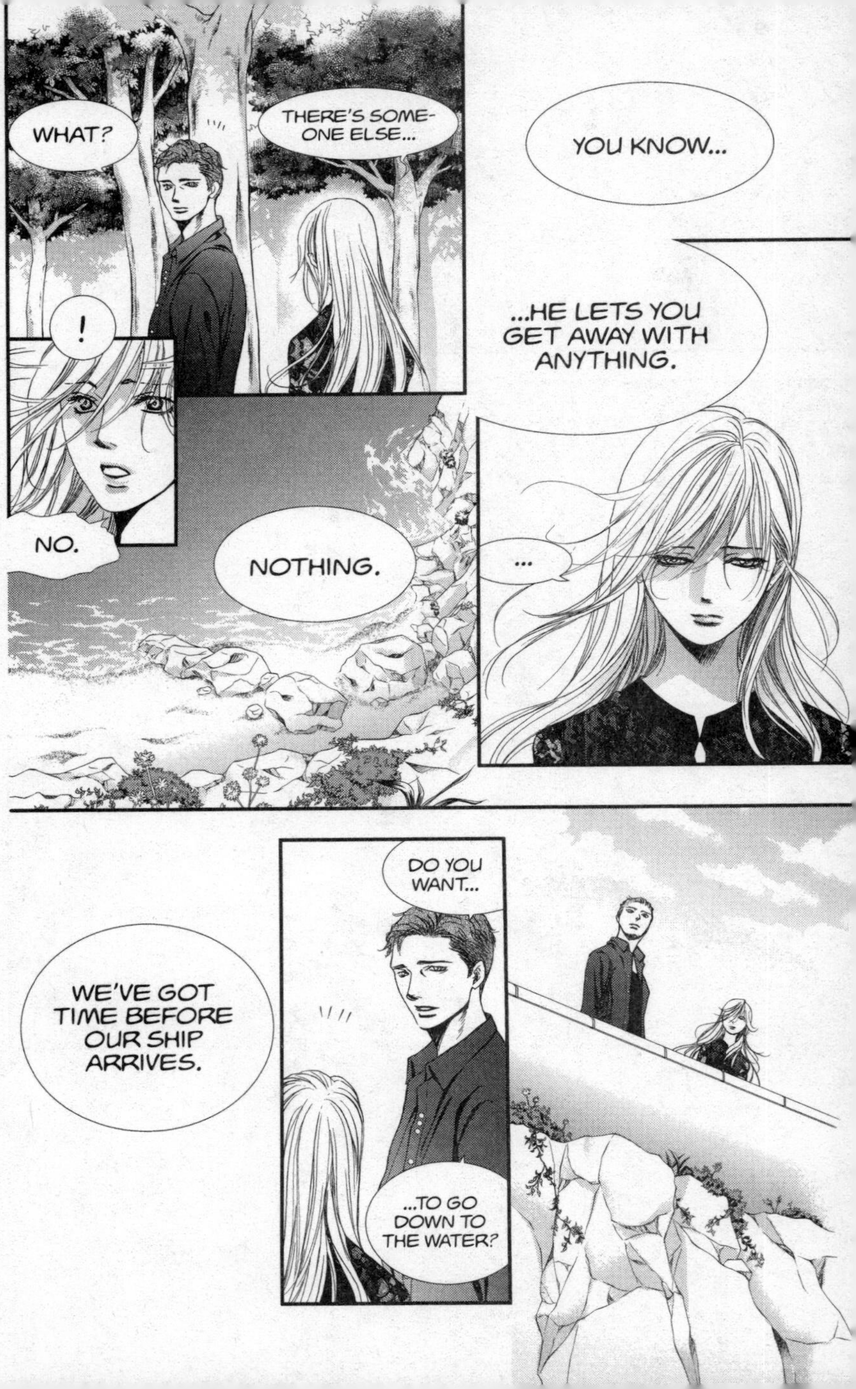
YOU KNOW...
...HE LETS YOU GET AWAY WITH ANYTHING.
...
THERE'S SOME-ONE ELSE...
WHAT?
!
NO.
NOTHING.
DO YOU WANT...
...TO GO DOWN TO THE WATER?
WE'VE GOT TIME BEFORE OUR SHIP ARRIVES.

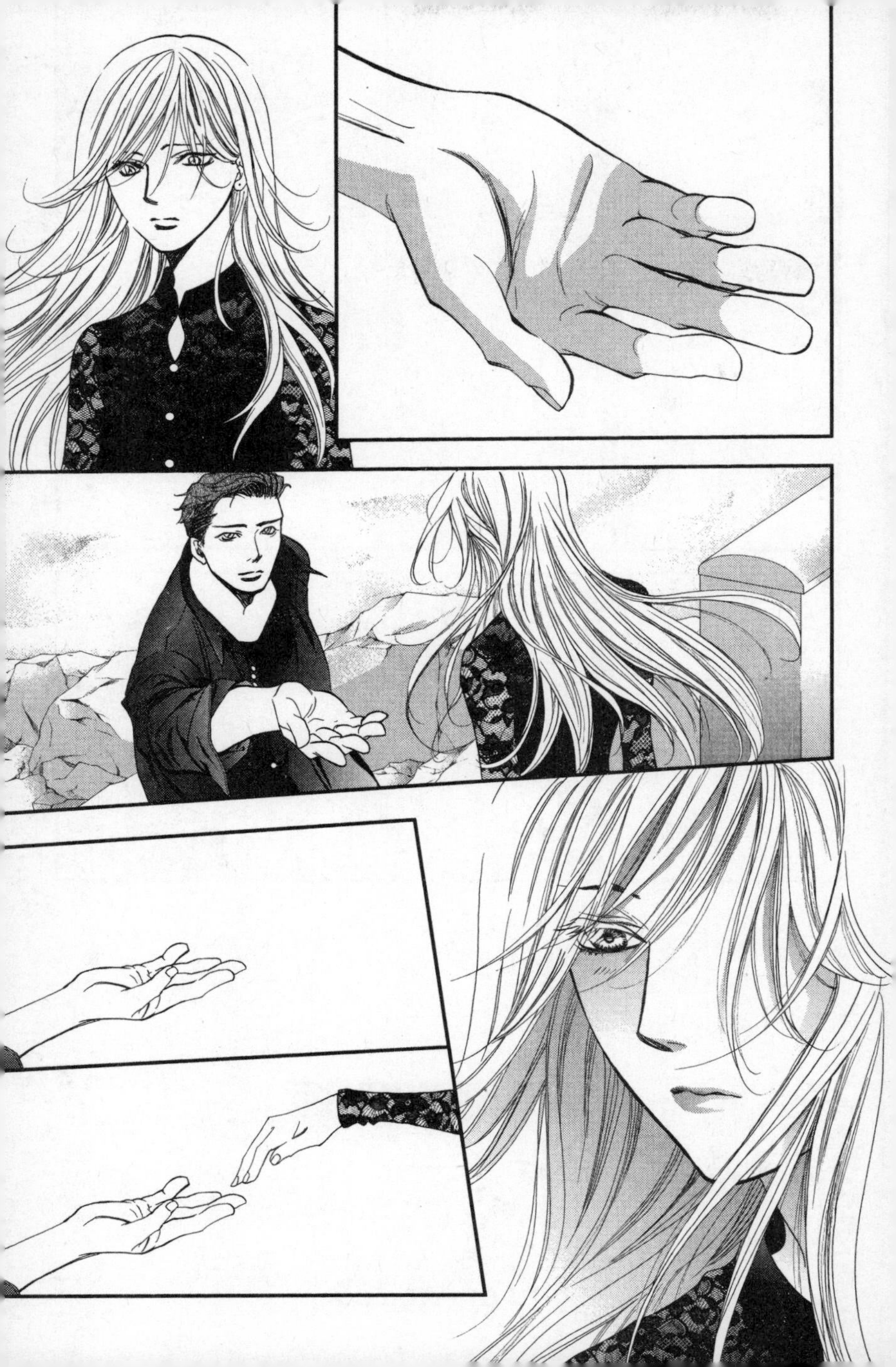

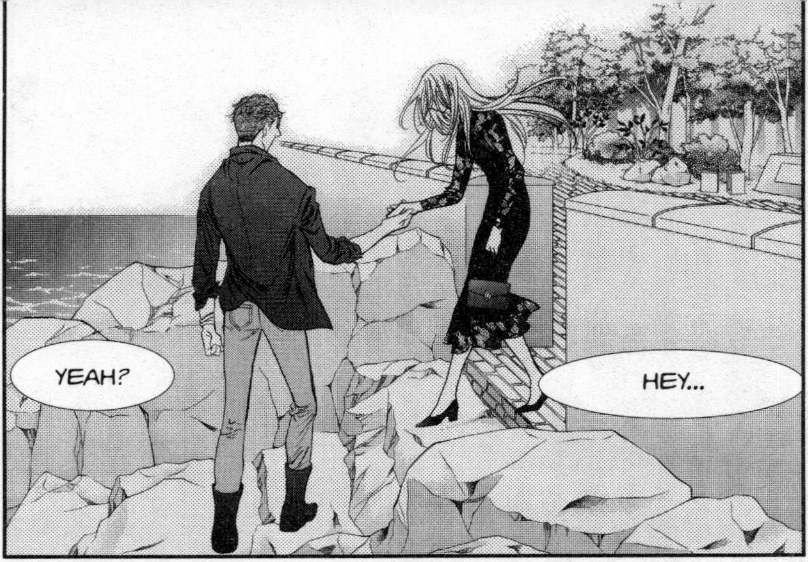
HEY...
YEAH?

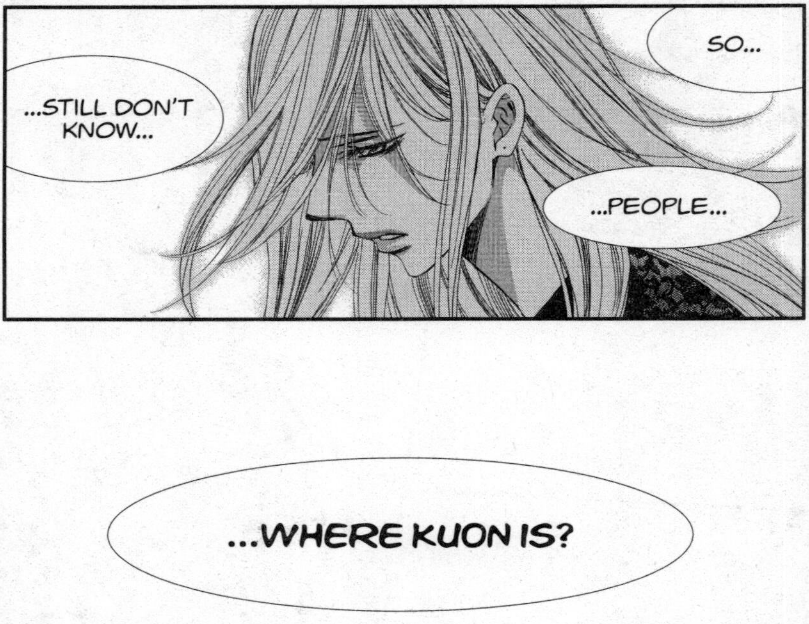
SO...
...PEOPLE...
...STILL DON'T KNOW...

...WHERE KUON IS?

End of Act 285

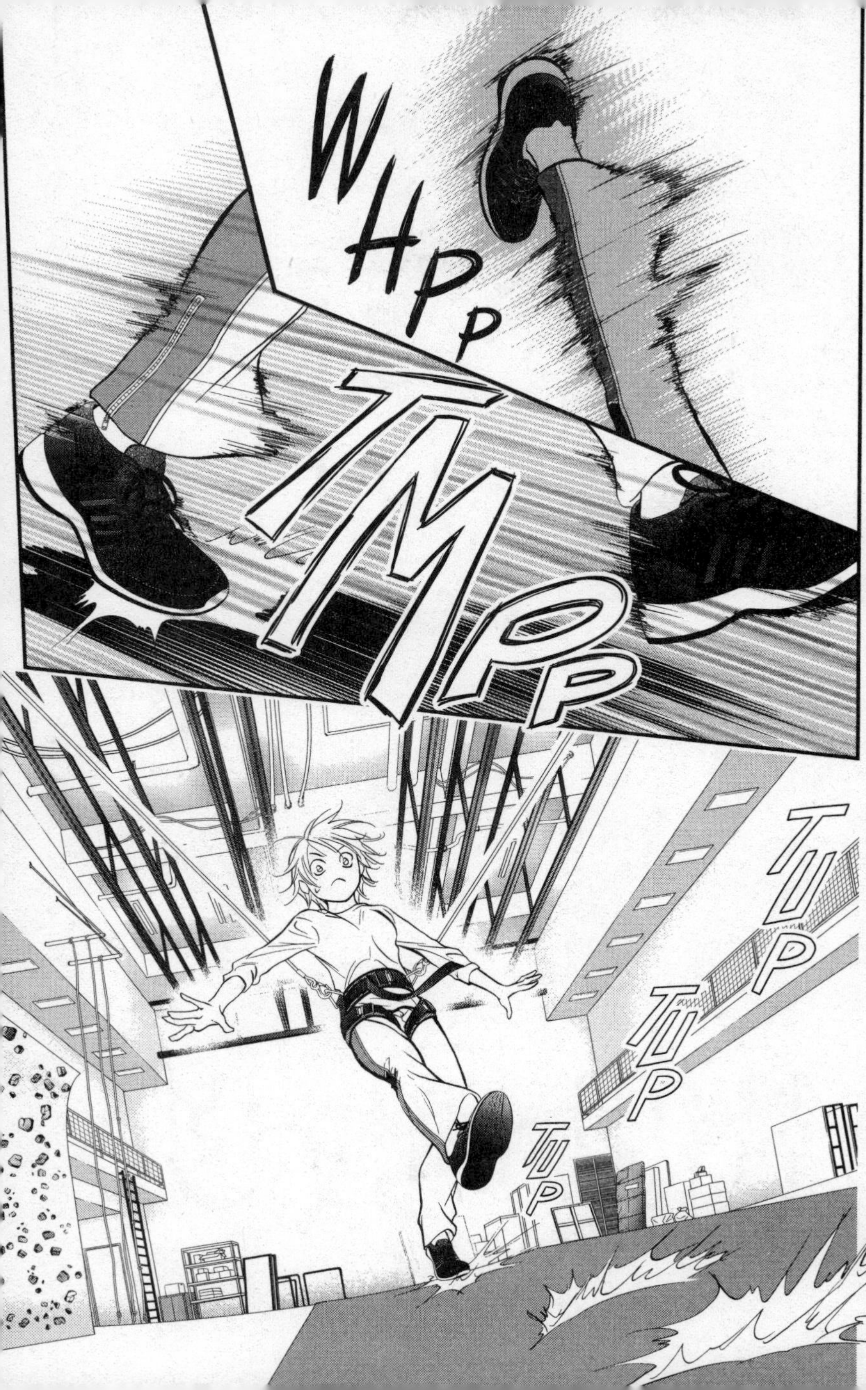
WHPP
TMPP
TUP
TUP
TUP

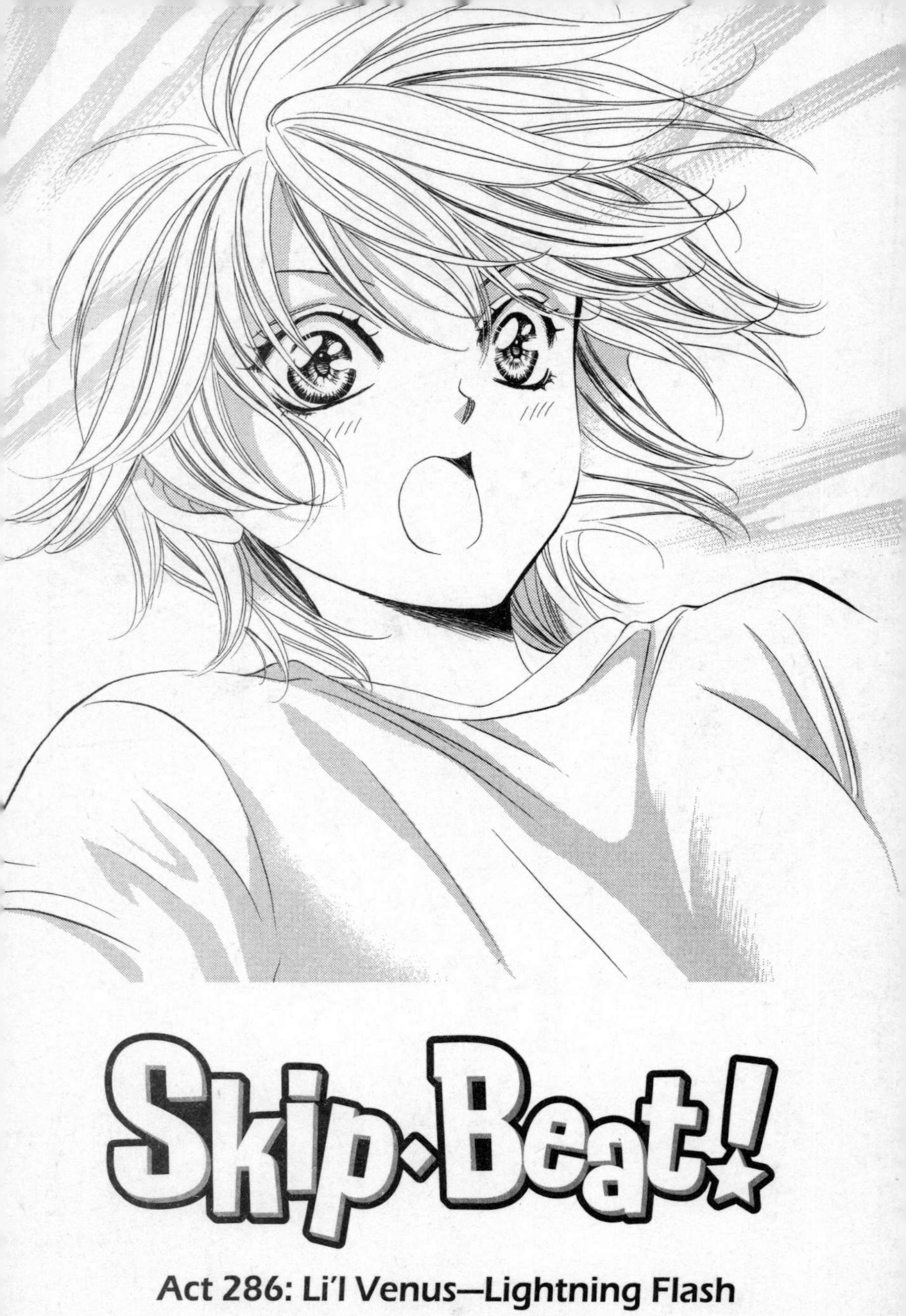

Skip·Beat!

Act 286: Li'l Venus—Lightning Flash

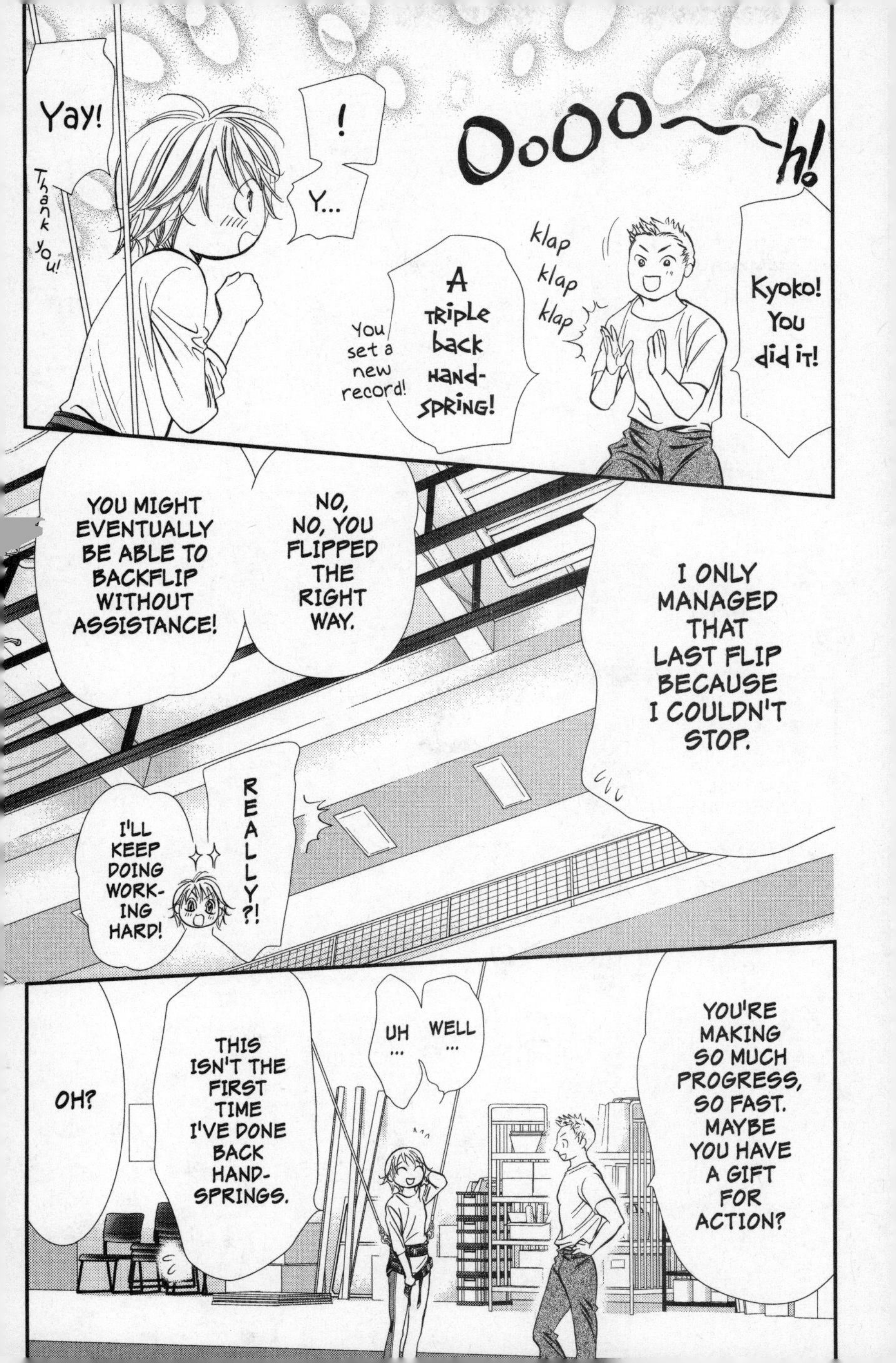
OoOO~~h!
Kyoko! You did it!
klap klap klap
A triple back hand-spring!
You set a new record!
!
Y...
Yay!
Thank you!
I ONLY MANAGED THAT LAST FLIP BECAUSE I COULDN'T STOP.
NO, NO, YOU FLIPPED THE RIGHT WAY.
YOU MIGHT EVENTUALLY BE ABLE TO BACKFLIP WITHOUT ASSISTANCE!
REALLY?!
I'LL KEEP DOING WORK-ING HARD!
YOU'RE MAKING SO MUCH PROGRESS, SO FAST. MAYBE YOU HAVE A GIFT FOR ACTION?
WELL...
UH...
THIS ISN'T THE FIRST TIME I'VE DONE BACK HAND-SPRINGS.
OH?

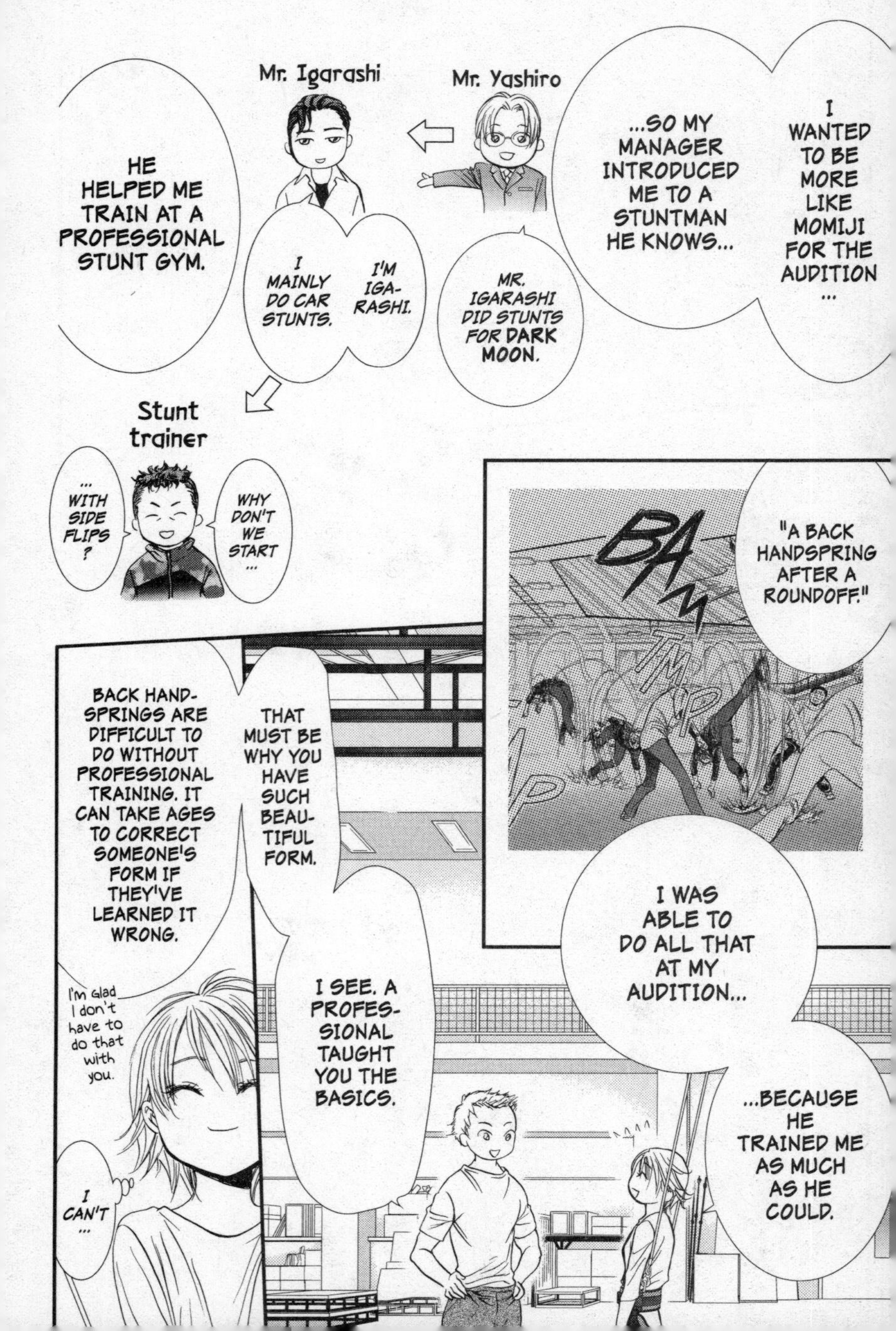

I WANTED TO BE MORE LIKE MOMIJI FOR THE AUDITION...
...SO MY MANAGER INTRODUCED ME TO A STUNTMAN HE KNOWS...
Mr. Yashiro
Mr. Igarashi
MR. IGARASHI DID STUNTS FOR DARK MOON.
I'M IGA-RASHI.
I MAINLY DO CAR STUNTS.
HE HELPED ME TRAIN AT A PROFESSIONAL STUNT GYM.
Stunt trainer
WHY DON'T WE START...
...WITH SIDE FLIPS?
"A BACK HANDSPRING AFTER A ROUNDOFF."
BAM
TMP
I WAS ABLE TO DO ALL THAT AT MY AUDITION...
...BECAUSE HE TRAINED ME AS MUCH AS HE COULD.
I SEE. A PROFES-SIONAL TAUGHT YOU THE BASICS.
THAT MUST BE WHY YOU HAVE SUCH BEAU-TIFUL FORM.
BACK HAND-SPRINGS ARE DIFFICULT TO DO WITHOUT PROFESSIONAL TRAINING. IT CAN TAKE AGES TO CORRECT SOMEONE'S FORM IF THEY'VE LEARNED IT WRONG.
I'm Glad I don't have to do that with you.
I CAN'T...

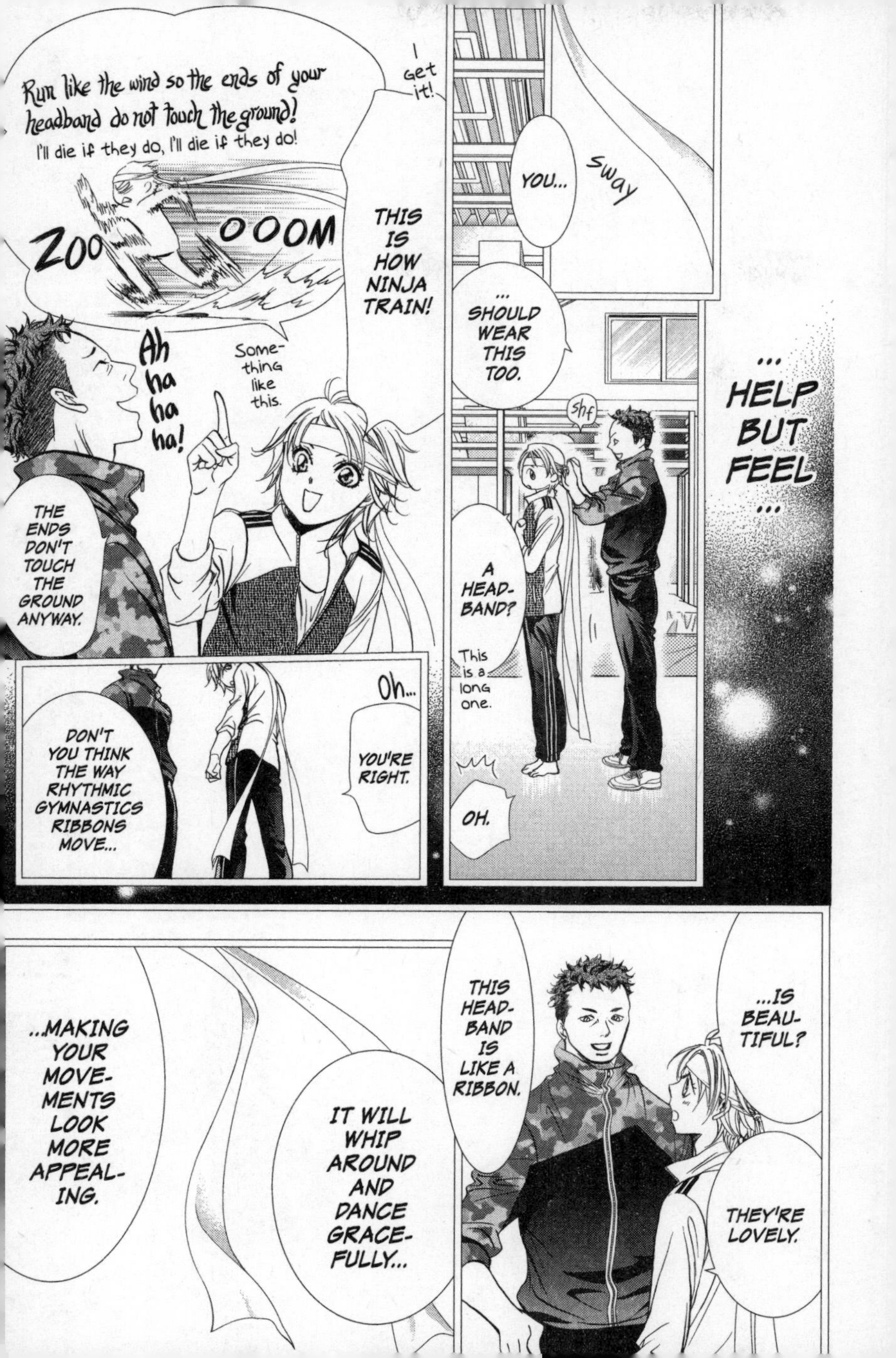
...HELP BUT FEEL...
YOU...
SWAY
...SHOULD WEAR THIS TOO.
SHF
A HEAD-BAND?
This is a long one.
OH.
I get it!
THIS IS HOW NINJA TRAIN!
Run like the wind so the ends of your headband do not touch the ground!
I'll die if they do, I'll die if they do!
ZOOOOOM
Some-thing like this.
Ah ha ha ha!
THE ENDS DON'T TOUCH THE GROUND ANYWAY.
Oh...
YOU'RE RIGHT.
DON'T YOU THINK THE WAY RHYTHMIC GYMNASTICS RIBBONS MOVE...
...IS BEAU-TIFUL?
THEY'RE LOVELY.
THIS HEAD-BAND IS LIKE A RIBBON.
IT WILL WHIP AROUND AND DANCE GRACE-FULLY...
...MAKING YOUR MOVE-MENTS LOOK MORE APPEAL-ING.

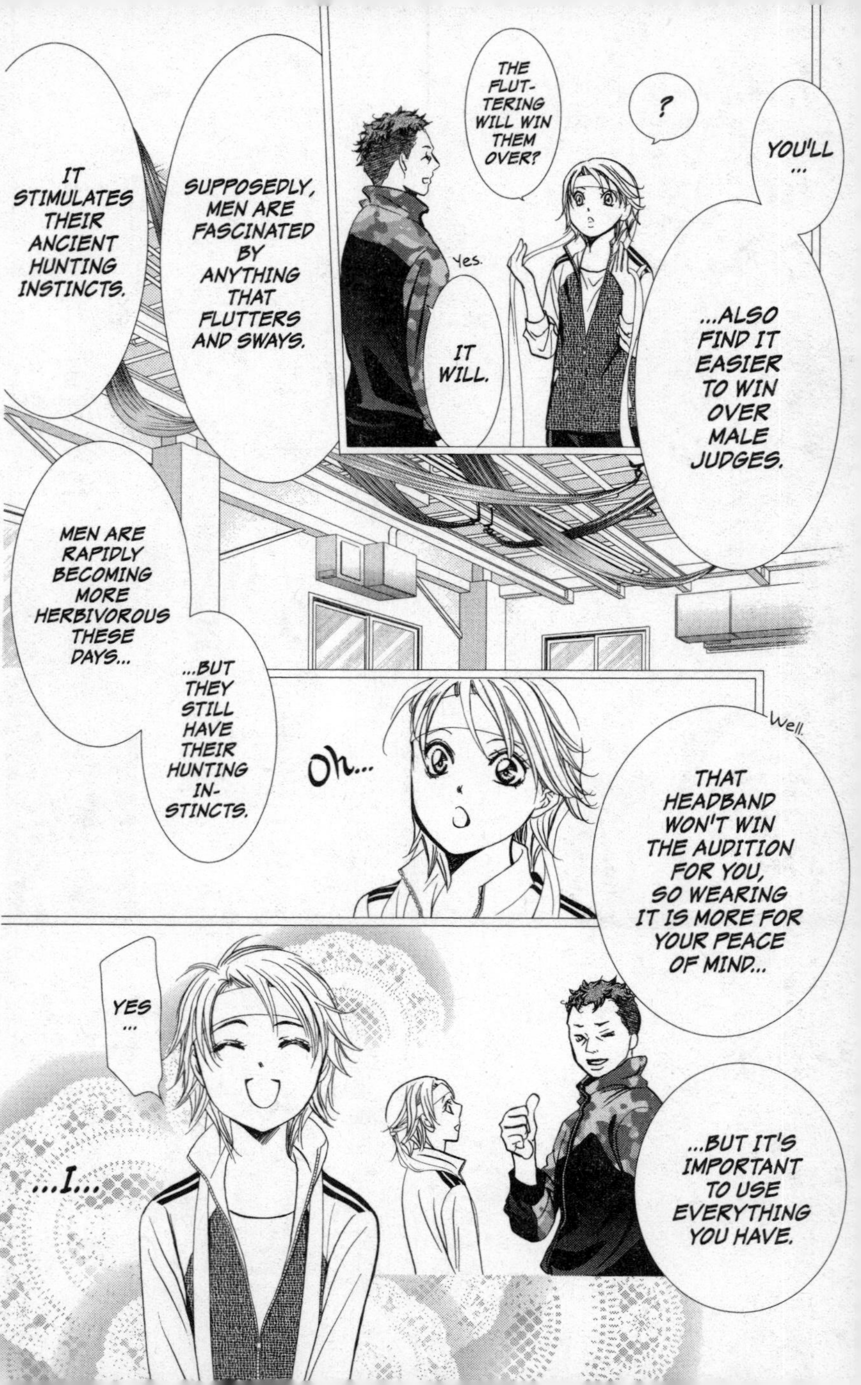

THE FLUT-TERING WILL WIN THEM OVER?
Yes.
IT WILL.
?
YOU'LL ...
...ALSO FIND IT EASIER TO WIN OVER MALE JUDGES.
SUPPOSEDLY, MEN ARE FASCINATED BY ANYTHING THAT FLUTTERS AND SWAYS.
IT STIMULATES THEIR ANCIENT HUNTING INSTINCTS.
MEN ARE RAPIDLY BECOMING MORE HERBIVOROUS THESE DAYS...
...BUT THEY STILL HAVE THEIR HUNTING IN-STINCTS.
Oh...
Well.
THAT HEADBAND WON'T WIN THE AUDITION FOR YOU, SO WEARING IT IS MORE FOR YOUR PEACE OF MIND...
...BUT IT'S IMPORTANT TO USE EVERYTHING YOU HAVE.
YES ...
...I...

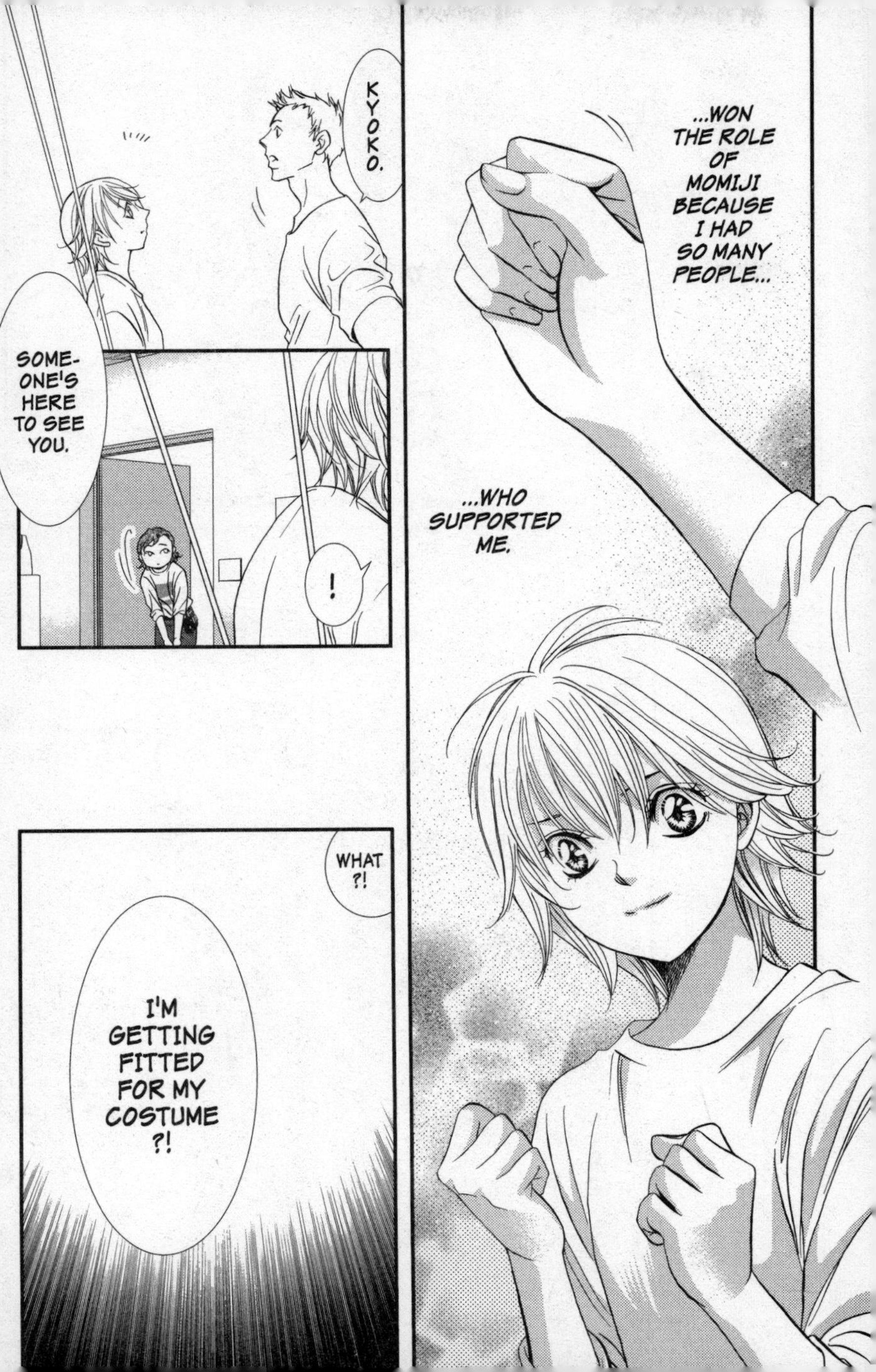
...WON THE ROLE OF MOMIJI BECAUSE I HAD SO MANY PEOPLE...
...WHO SUPPORTED ME.
KYOKO.
SOME-ONE'S HERE TO SEE YOU.
!
WHAT?!
I'M GETTING FITTED FOR MY COSTUME?!

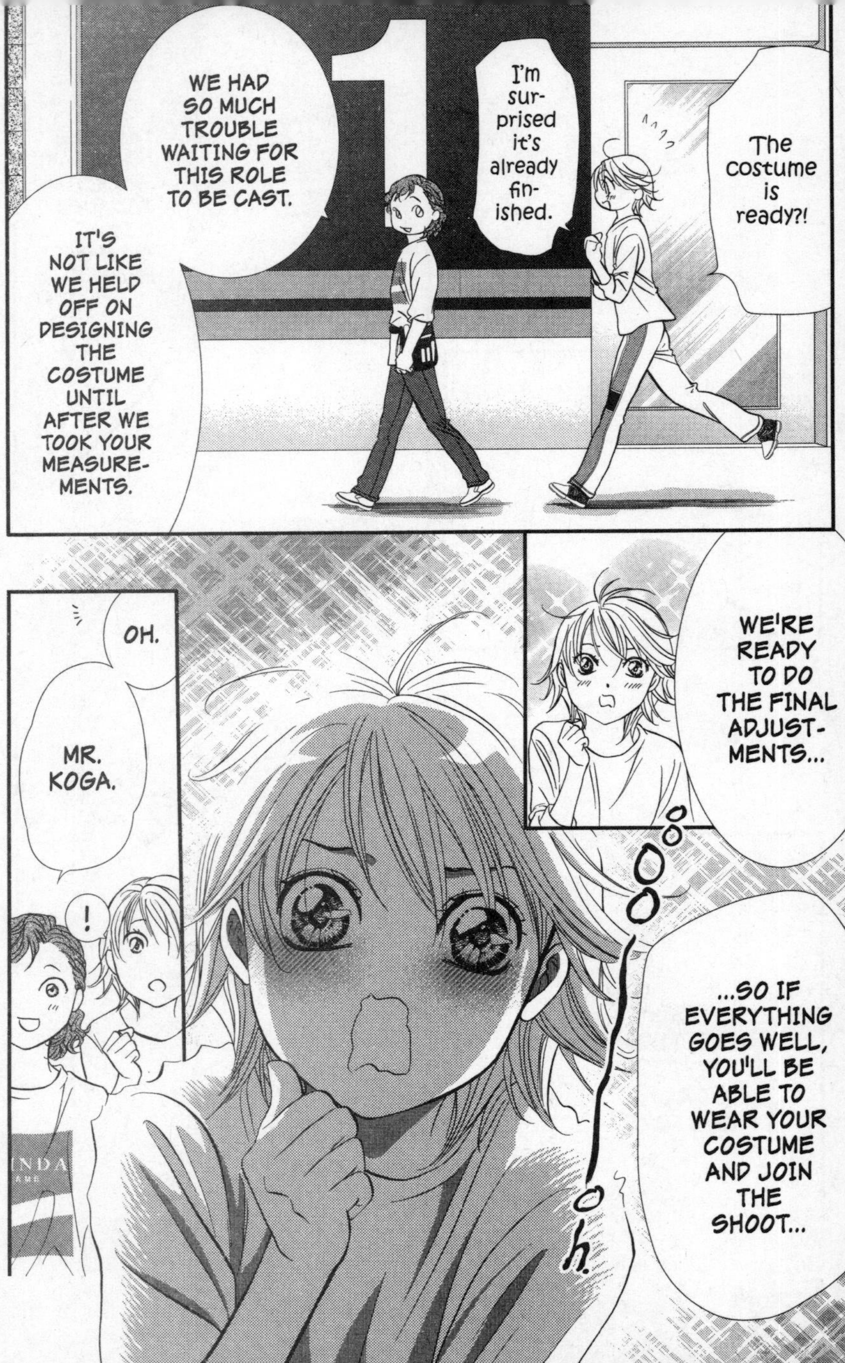
The costume is ready?!
I'm surprised it's already finished.
WE HAD SO MUCH TROUBLE WAITING FOR THIS ROLE TO BE CAST.
IT'S NOT LIKE WE HELD OFF ON DESIGNING THE COSTUME UNTIL AFTER WE TOOK YOUR MEASUREMENTS.
WE'RE READY TO DO THE FINAL ADJUSTMENTS...
...SO IF EVERYTHING GOES WELL, YOU'LL BE ABLE TO WEAR YOUR COSTUME AND JOIN THE SHOOT...
Oooo—oh.
OH.
MR. KOGA.
!

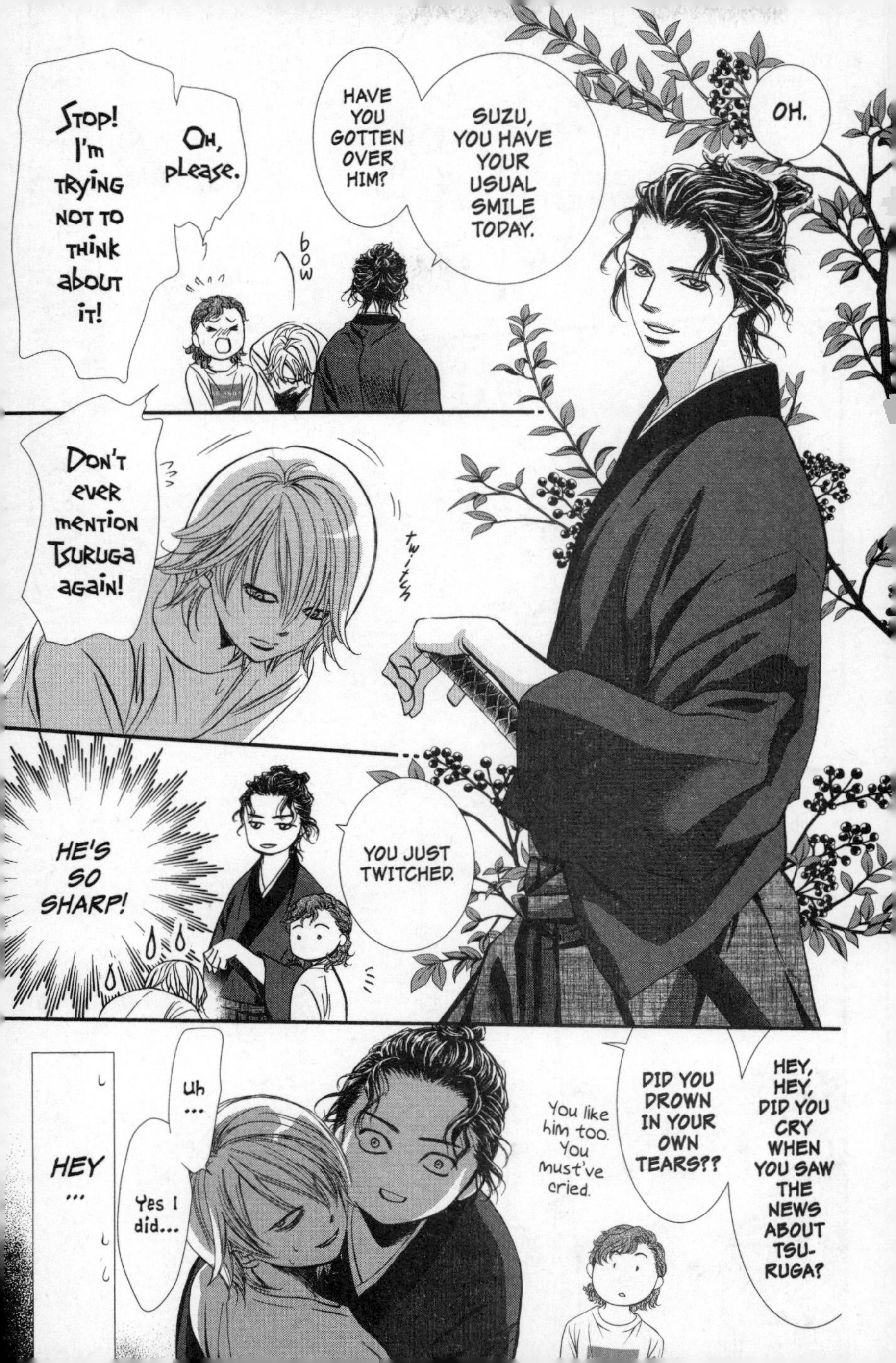
OH.
SUZU, YOU HAVE YOUR USUAL SMILE TODAY.
HAVE YOU GOTTEN OVER HIM?
Oh, please.
Stop! I'm trying not to think about it!
bow
Don't ever mention Tsuruga again!
twitch
YOU JUST TWITCHED.
HE'S SO SHARP!
HEY, HEY, DID YOU CRY WHEN YOU SAW THE NEWS ABOUT TSU-RUGA?
DID YOU DROWN IN YOUR OWN TEARS??
You like him too. You must've cried.
Uh...
Yes I did...
HEY...

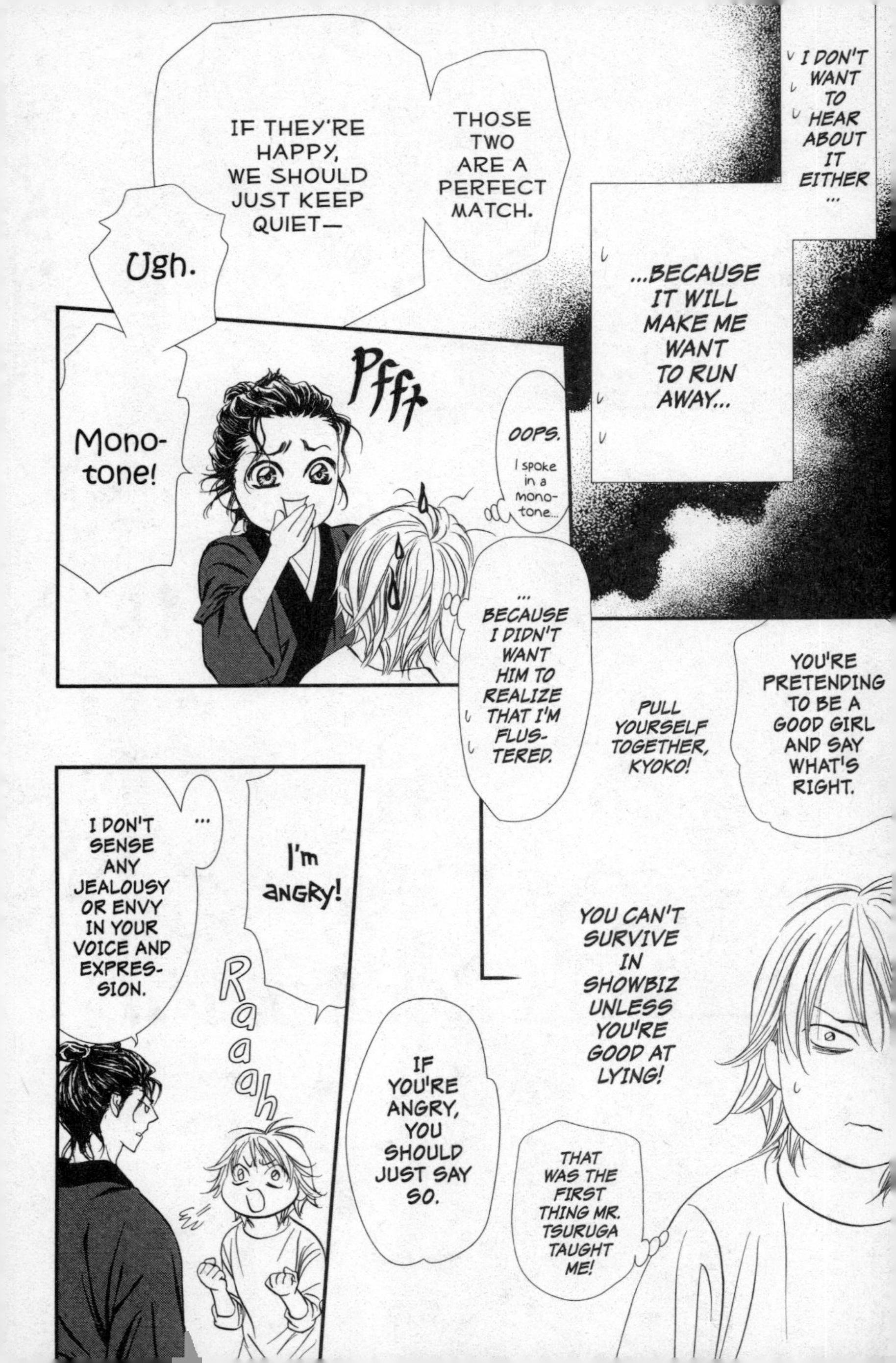

I DON'T WANT TO HEAR ABOUT IT EITHER...
...BECAUSE IT WILL MAKE ME WANT TO RUN AWAY...
THOSE TWO ARE A PERFECT MATCH.
IF THEY'RE HAPPY, WE SHOULD JUST KEEP QUIET—
Ugh.
Pfft
OOPS.
I spoke in a mono-tone...
Mono-tone!
...BECAUSE I DIDN'T WANT HIM TO REALIZE THAT I'M FLUS-TERED.
YOU'RE PRETENDING TO BE A GOOD GIRL AND SAY WHAT'S RIGHT.
PULL YOURSELF TOGETHER, KYOKO!
YOU CAN'T SURVIVE IN SHOWBIZ UNLESS YOU'RE GOOD AT LYING!
THAT WAS THE FIRST THING MR. TSURUGA TAUGHT ME!
IF YOU'RE ANGRY, YOU SHOULD JUST SAY SO.
I'm angry!
Raaah
...
I DON'T SENSE ANY JEALOUSY OR ENVY IN YOUR VOICE AND EXPRES-SION.

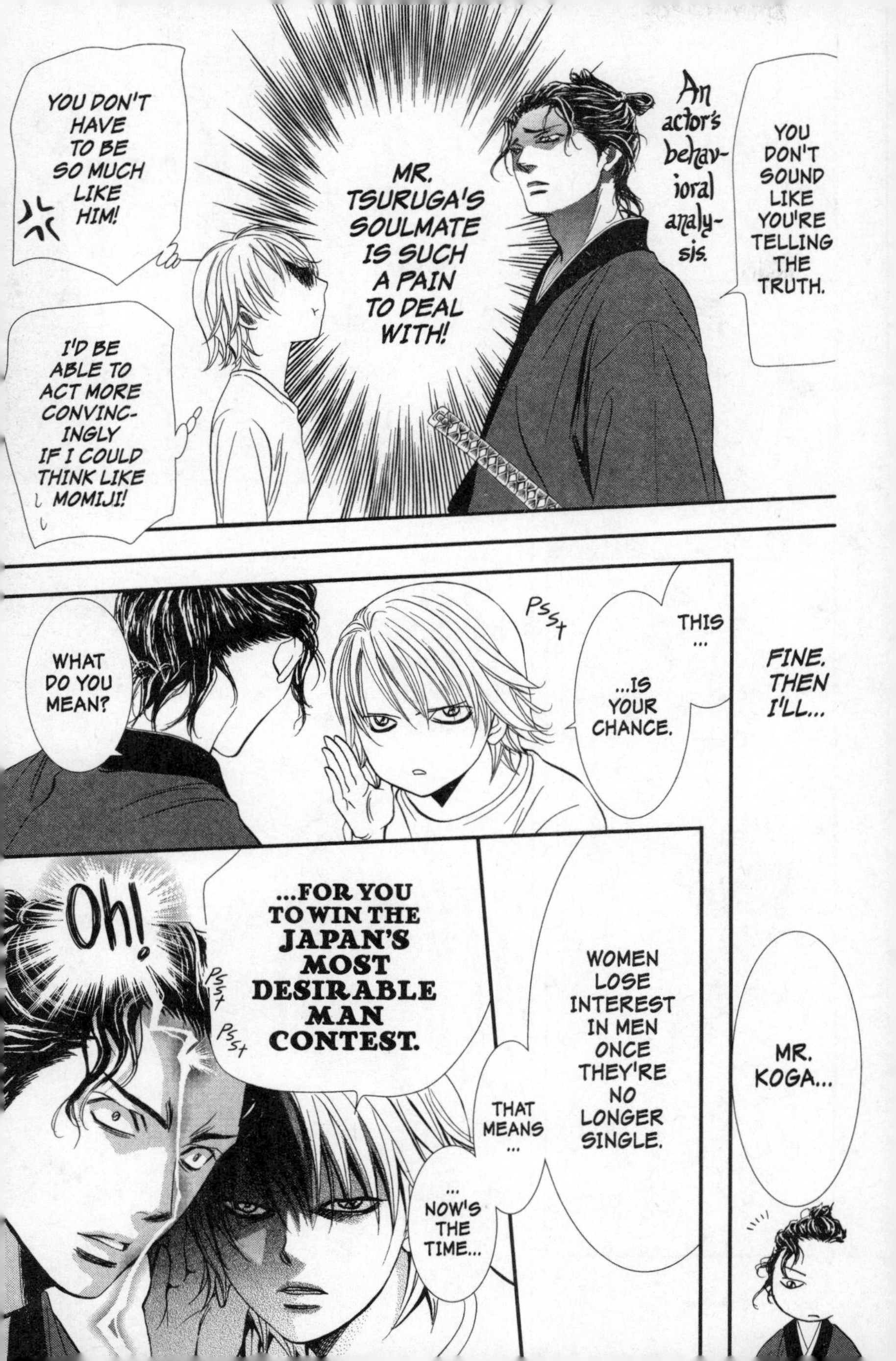
YOU DON'T SOUND LIKE YOU'RE TELLING THE TRUTH.
An actor's behavioral analysis.
MR. TSURUGA'S SOULMATE IS SUCH A PAIN TO DEAL WITH!
YOU DON'T HAVE TO BE SO MUCH LIKE HIM!
I'D BE ABLE TO ACT MORE CONVINCINGLY IF I COULD THINK LIKE MOMIJI!
FINE. THEN I'LL...
THIS...
...IS YOUR CHANCE.
Psst
WHAT DO YOU MEAN?
MR. KOGA...
WOMEN LOSE INTEREST IN MEN ONCE THEY'RE NO LONGER SINGLE.
THAT MEANS...
...NOW'S THE TIME...
...FOR YOU TO WIN THE JAPAN'S MOST DESIRABLE MAN CONTEST.
Psst
Psst
Oh!

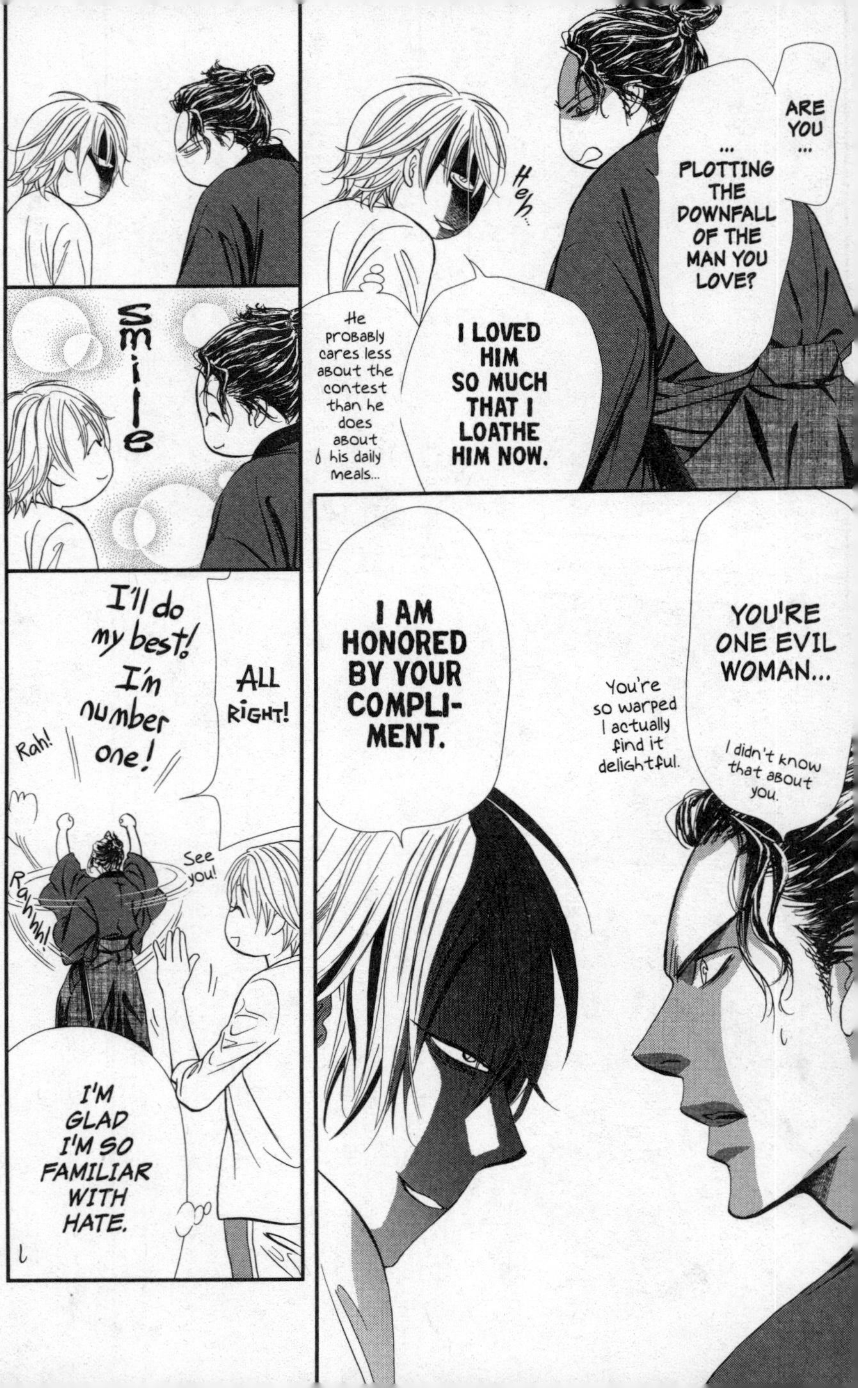
ARE YOU ... PLOTTING THE DOWNFALL OF THE MAN YOU LOVE?
Heh...
I LOVED HIM SO MUCH THAT I LOATHE HIM NOW.
He probably cares less about the contest than he does about his daily meals...
YOU'RE ONE EVIL WOMAN...
I didn't know that about you.
You're so warped I actually find it delightful.
I AM HONORED BY YOUR COMPLIMENT.
Smile
ALL RIGHT!
I'll do my best! I'm number one!
Rah!
See you!
Rahhh!
I'M GLAD I'M SO FAMILIAR WITH HATE.

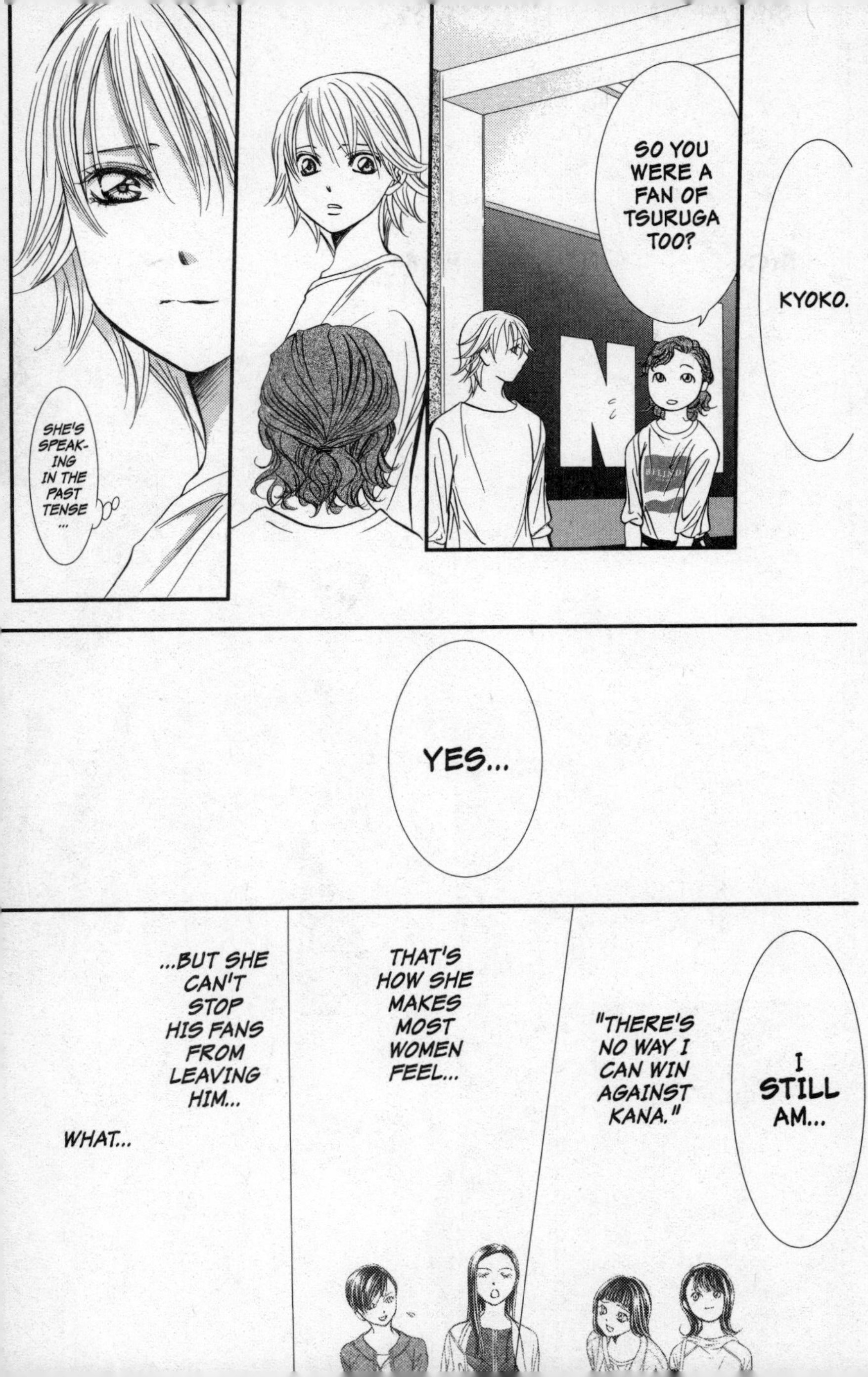
KYOKO.
SO YOU WERE A FAN OF TSURUGA TOO?
SHE'S SPEAK-ING IN THE PAST TENSE...
YES...
I STILL AM...
"THERE'S NO WAY I CAN WIN AGAINST KANA."
THAT'S HOW SHE MAKES MOST WOMEN FEEL...
...BUT SHE CAN'T STOP HIS FANS FROM LEAVING HIM...
WHAT...

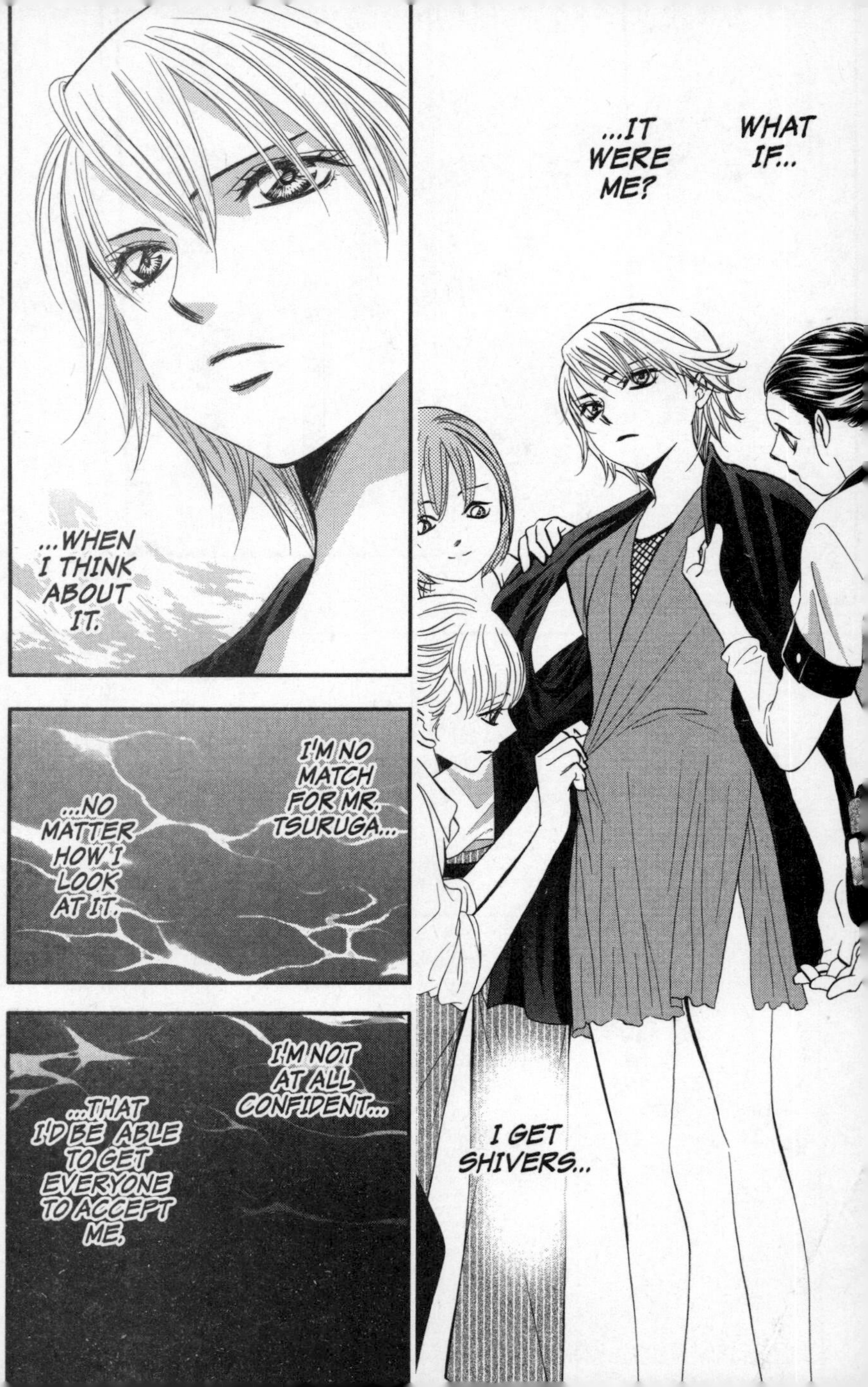
WHAT IF...
...IT WERE ME?
I GET SHIVERS...
...WHEN I THINK ABOUT IT.
I'M NO MATCH FOR MR. TSURUGA...
...NO MATTER HOW I LOOK AT IT.
I'M NOT AT ALL CONFIDENT...
...THAT I'D BE ABLE TO GET EVERYONE TO ACCEPT ME.

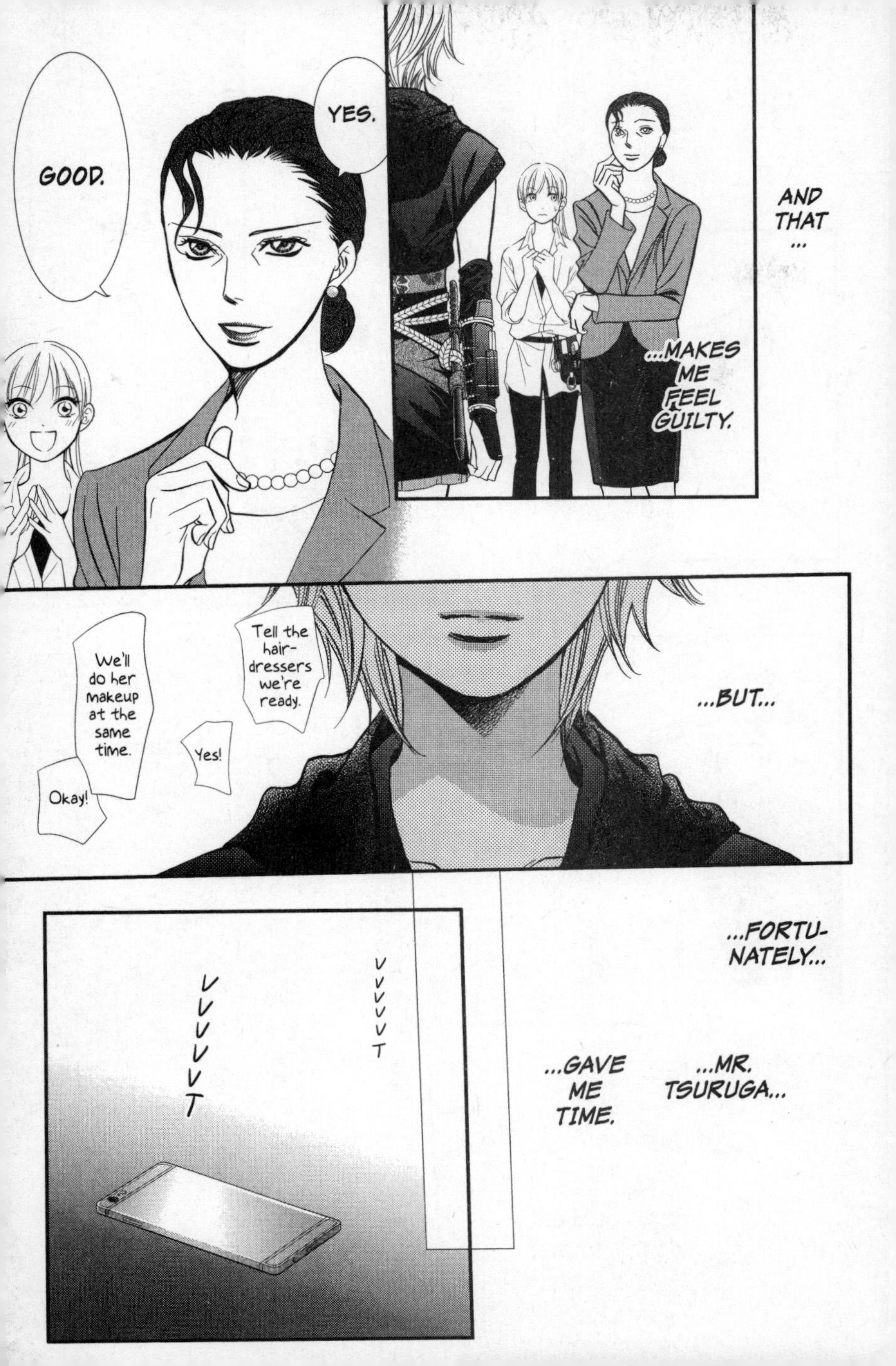
AND THAT ...
...MAKES ME FEEL GUILTY.
YES.
GOOD.
...BUT...
Tell the hair-dressers we're ready.
Yes!
We'll do her makeup at the same time.
Okay!
...FORTU-NATELY...
...MR. TSURUGA...
...GAVE ME TIME.
VVVVVT
VVVVVT

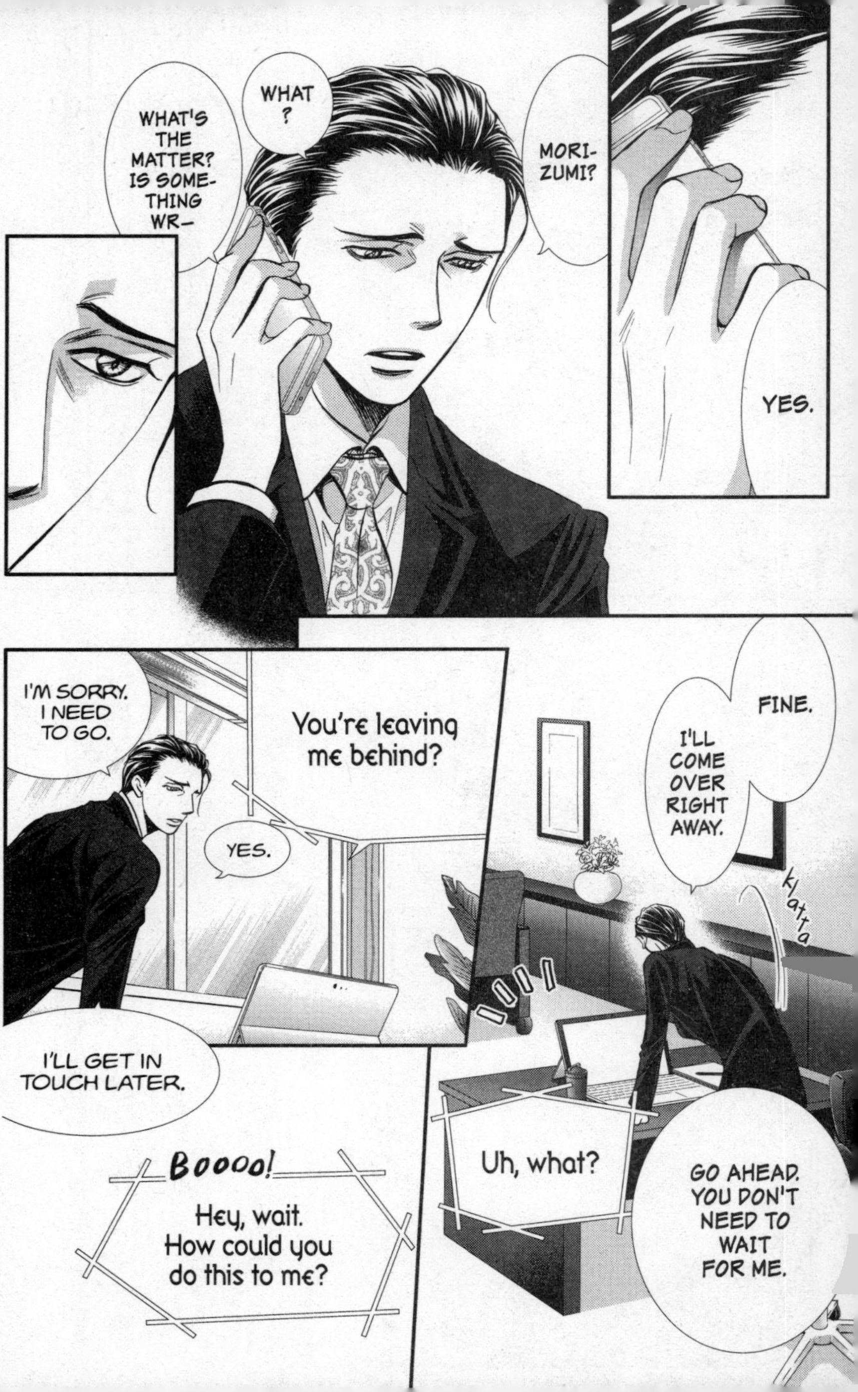
MORI-ZUMI?
YES.
WHAT?
WHAT'S THE MATTER? IS SOMETHING WR—
FINE.
I'LL COME OVER RIGHT AWAY.
klatta
GO AHEAD. YOU DON'T NEED TO WAIT FOR ME.
Uh, what?
I'M SORRY. I NEED TO GO.
You're leaving me behind?
YES.
I'LL GET IN TOUCH LATER.
Boooo!
Hey, wait. How could you do this to me?

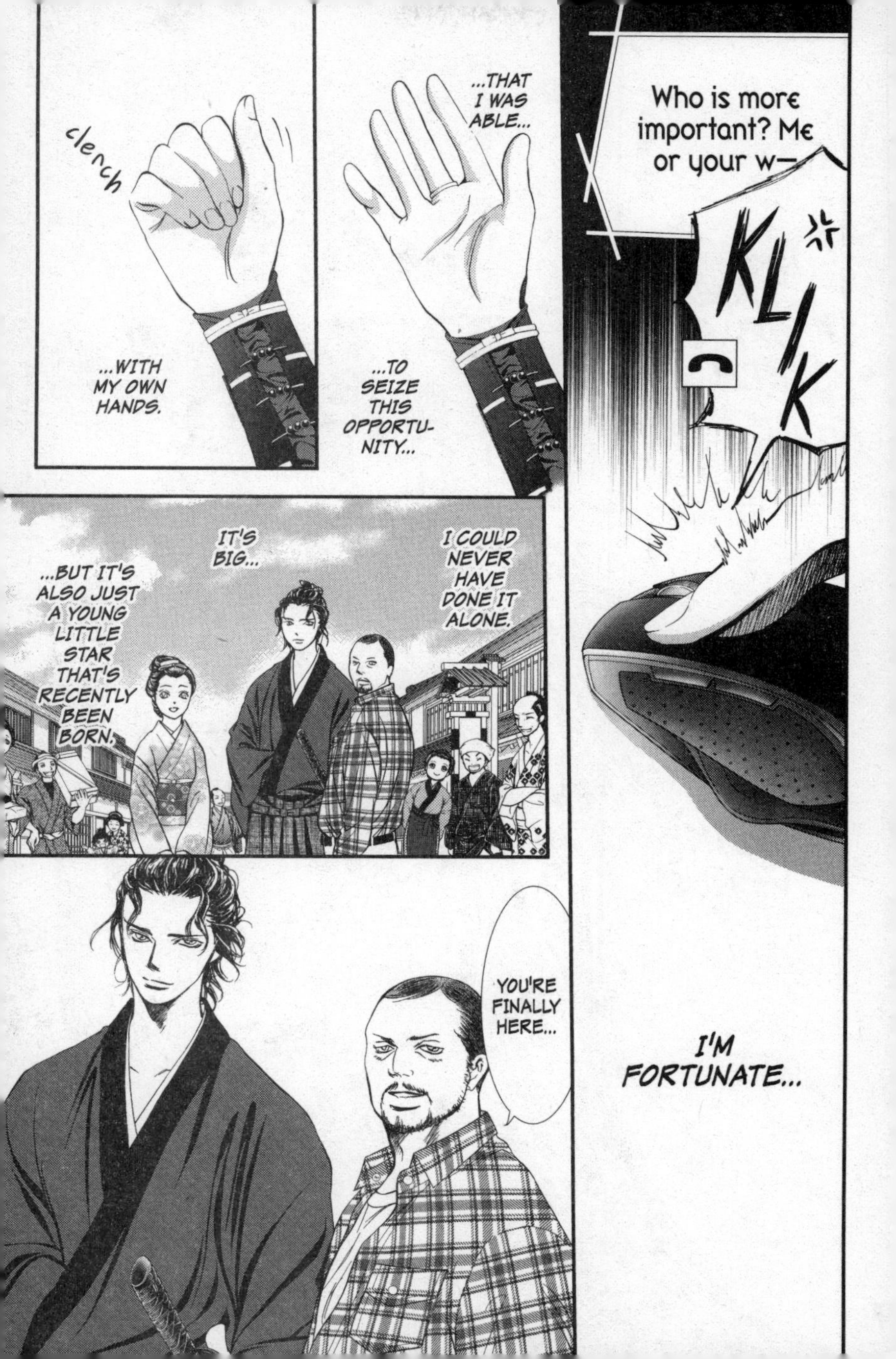

Who is more important? Me or your w—
KLIK
I'M FORTUNATE...
...THAT I WAS ABLE...
...TO SEIZE THIS OPPORTU-NITY...
clench
...WITH MY OWN HANDS.
I COULD NEVER HAVE DONE IT ALONE.
IT'S BIG...
...BUT IT'S ALSO JUST A YOUNG LITTLE STAR THAT'S RECENTLY BEEN BORN.
YOU'RE FINALLY HERE...

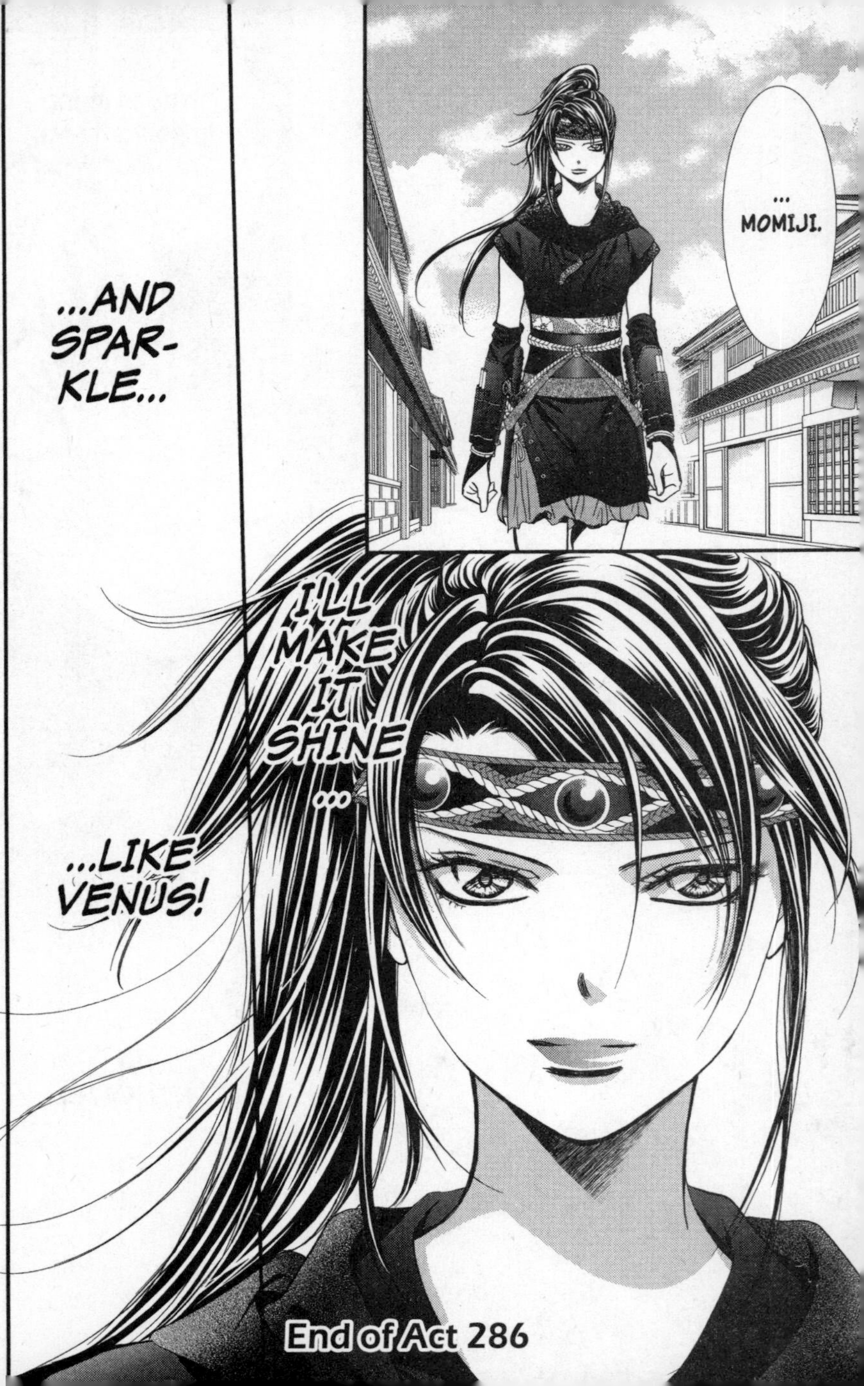
... MOMIJI.
I'LL MAKE IT SHINE...
...AND SPAR-KLE...
...LIKE VENUS!

End of Act 286

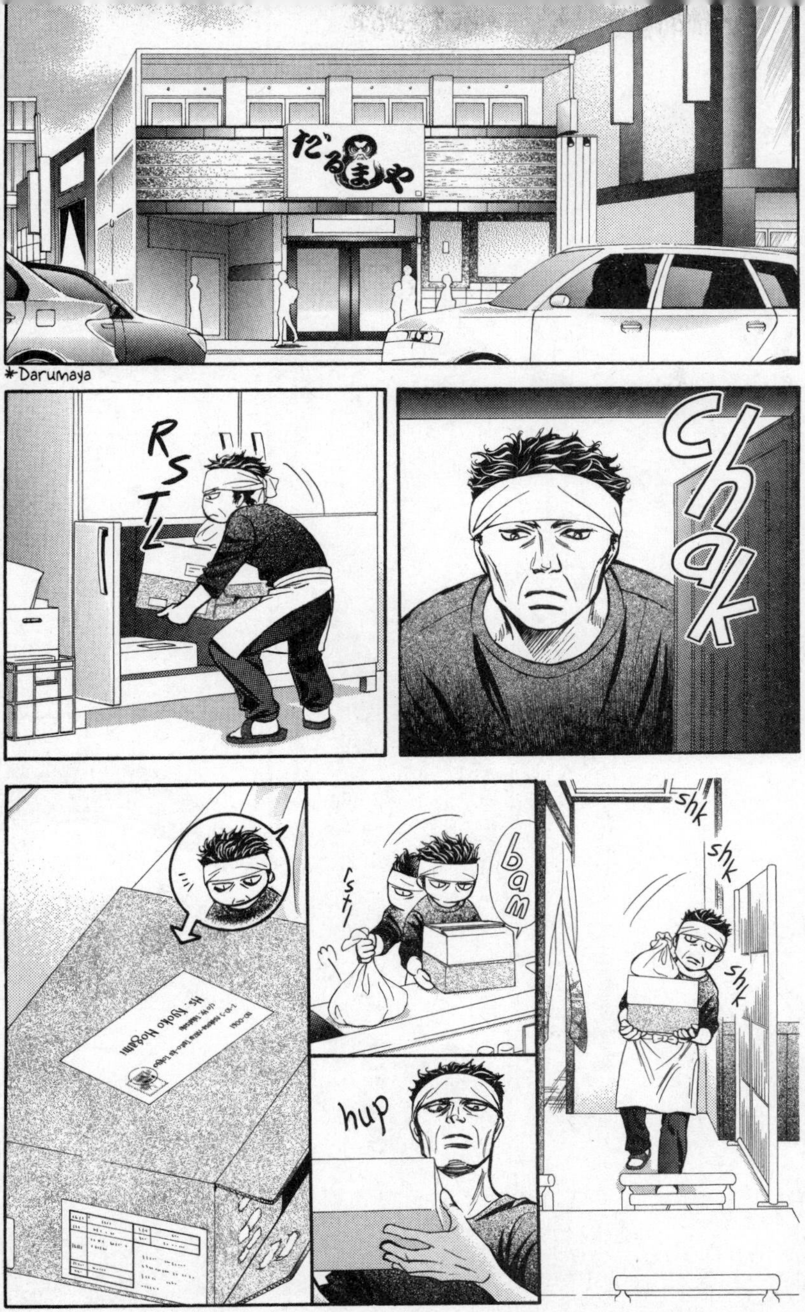
だるまや
*Darumaya
Chak
RSTL
shk
shk
shk
bam
rstl
hup

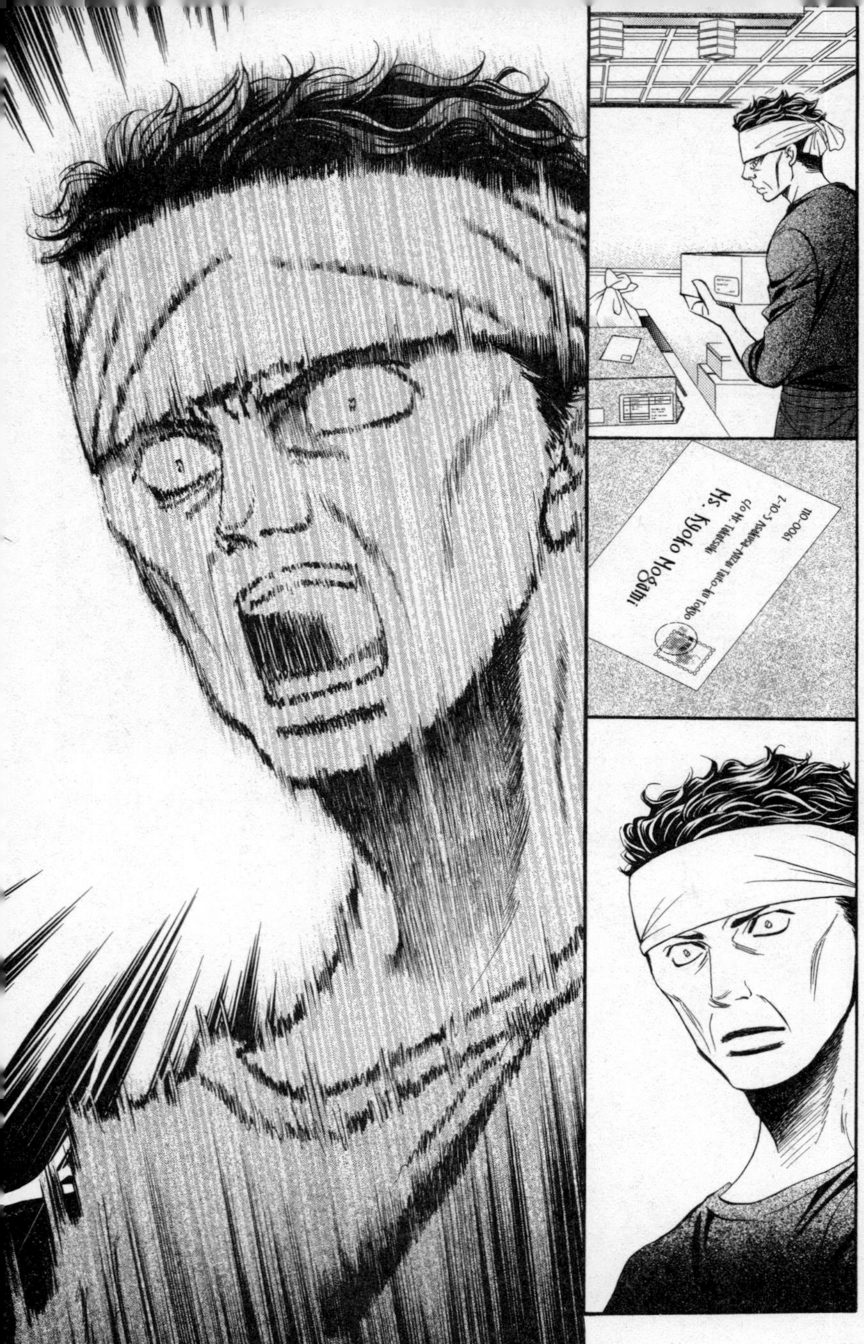
110-0061
2-10-5 Asakusa-Nizai Taito-ku Tokyo
c/o Mr. Takatsuki
Ms. Kyoko Mogami

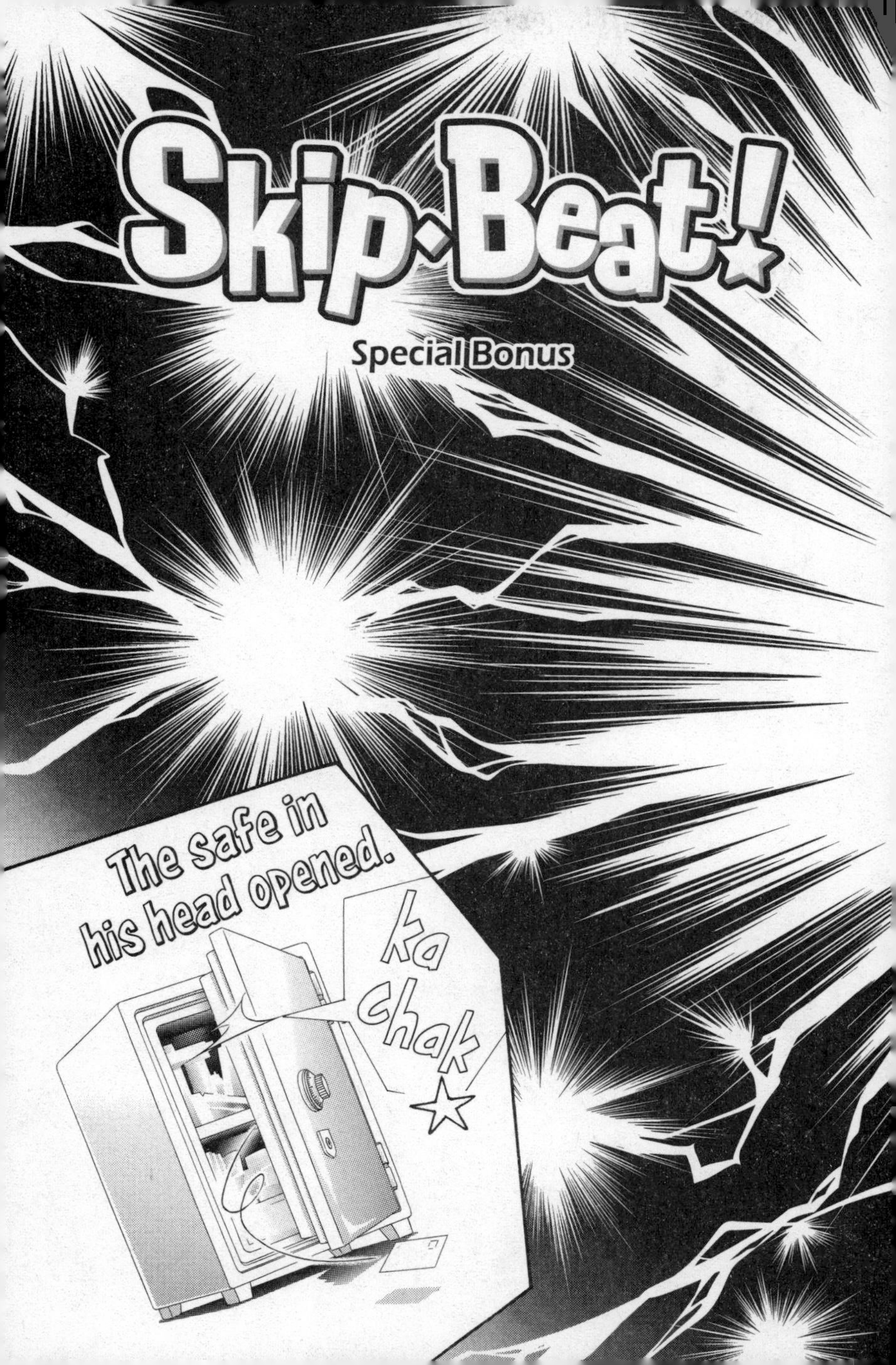
Skip·Beat!
Special Bonus
The safe in his head opened.
ka chak

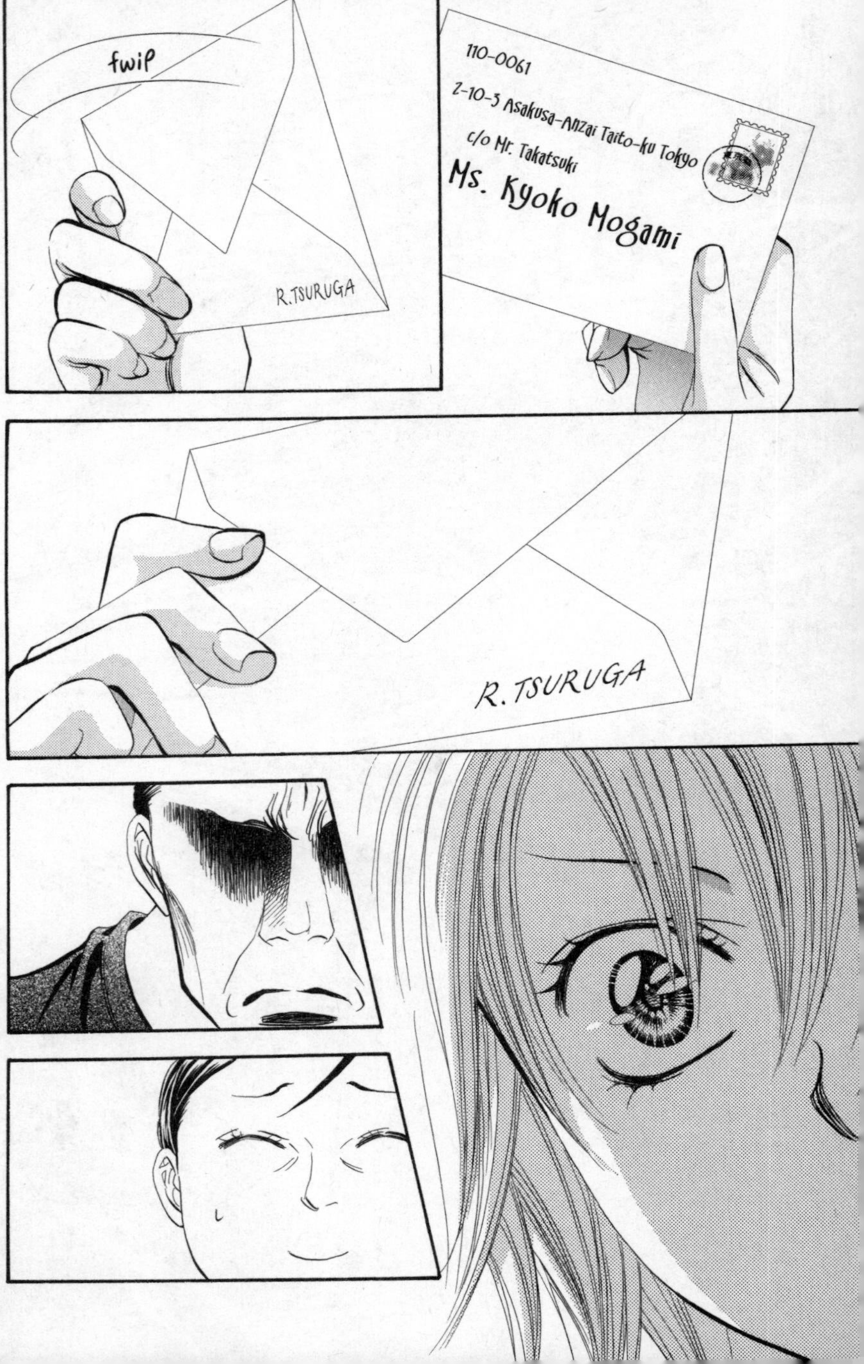
110-0061
2-10-3 Asakusa-Anzai Taito-ku Tokyo
c/o Mr. Takatsuki
Ms. Kyoko Mogami
fwip
R.TSURUGA
R. TSURUGA

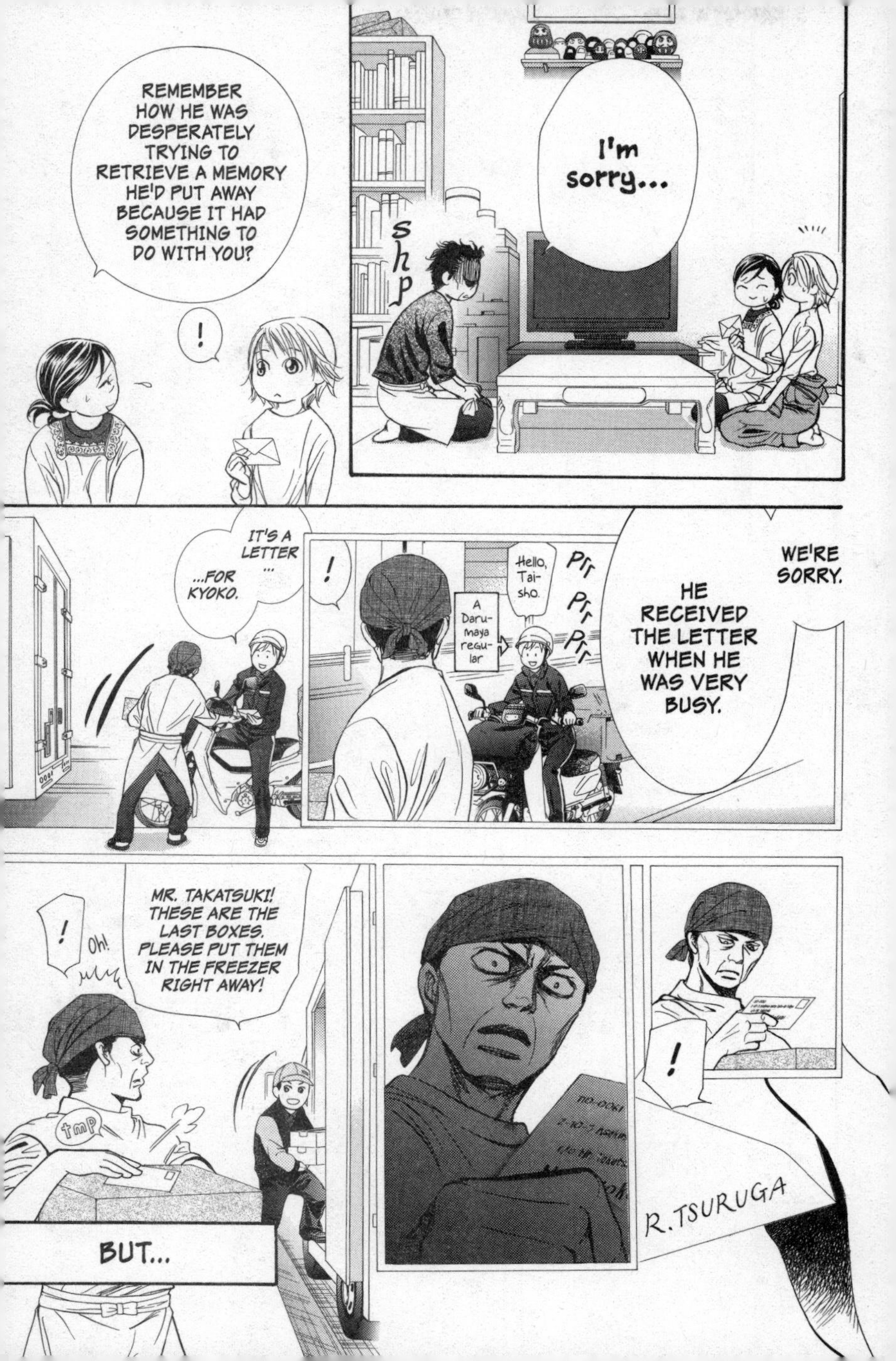

I'm sorry...
shp
REMEMBER HOW HE WAS DESPERATELY TRYING TO RETRIEVE A MEMORY HE'D PUT AWAY BECAUSE IT HAD SOMETHING TO DO WITH YOU?
!
WE'RE SORRY.
HE RECEIVED THE LETTER WHEN HE WAS VERY BUSY.
Prr Prr Prr
Hello, Tai-sho.
A Daru-maya regu-lar
!
IT'S A LETTER ...
...FOR KYOKO.
R.TSURUGA
!
MR. TAKATSUKI! THESE ARE THE LAST BOXES. PLEASE PUT THEM IN THE FREEZER RIGHT AWAY!
Oh!
!
tmp
BUT...

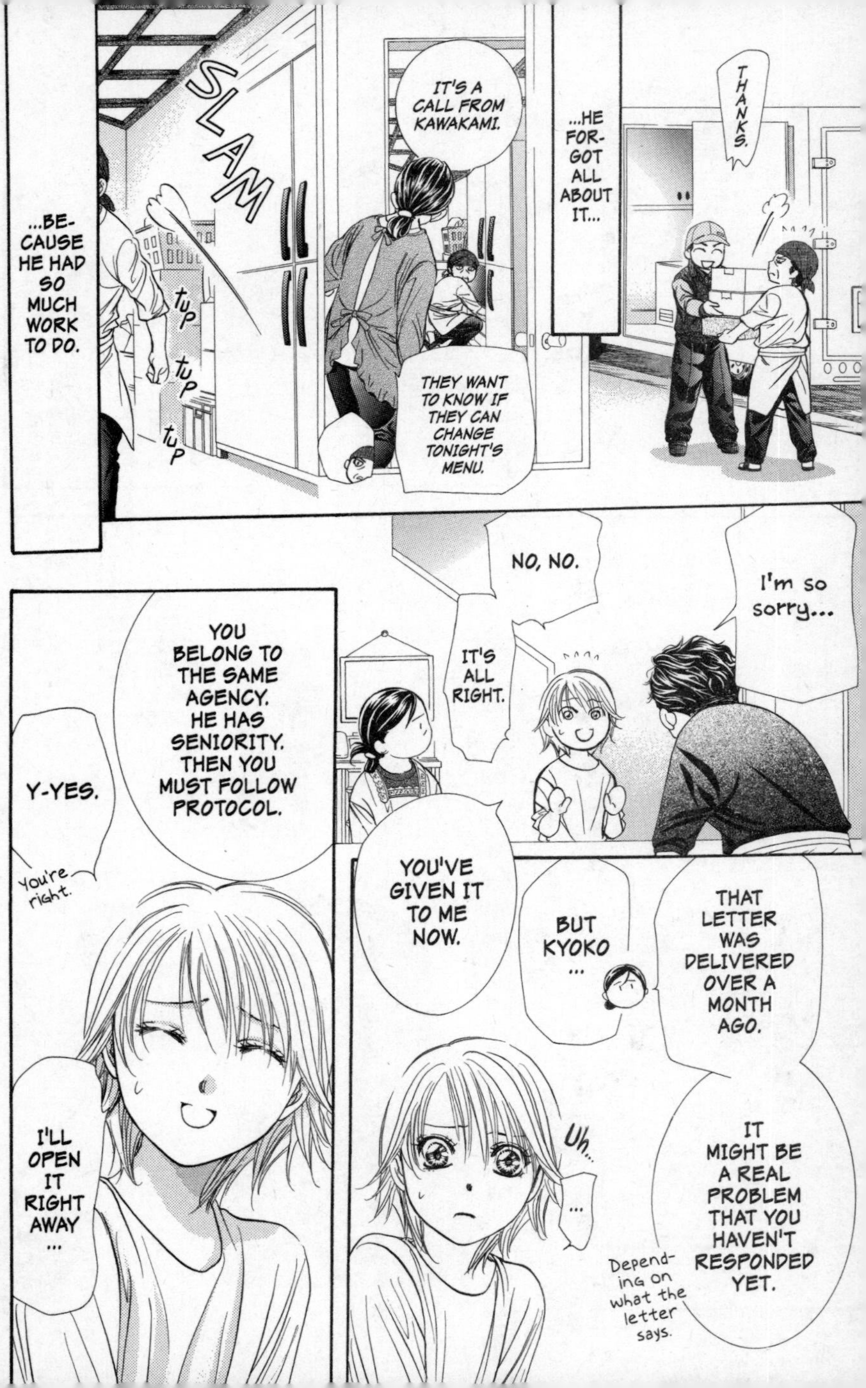
THANKS.
...HE FORGOT ALL ABOUT IT...
IT'S A CALL FROM KAWAKAMI.
THEY WANT TO KNOW IF THEY CAN CHANGE TONIGHT'S MENU.
SLAM
tup tup tup
...BECAUSE HE HAD SO MUCH WORK TO DO.
I'm so sorry...
NO, NO.
IT'S ALL RIGHT.
YOU'VE GIVEN IT TO ME NOW.
BUT KYOKO...
THAT LETTER WAS DELIVERED OVER A MONTH AGO.
IT MIGHT BE A REAL PROBLEM THAT YOU HAVEN'T RESPONDED YET.
Depending on what the letter says.
Uh...
...
YOU BELONG TO THE SAME AGENCY. HE HAS SENIORITY. THEN YOU MUST FOLLOW PROTOCOL.
Y-YES.
You're right.
I'LL OPEN IT RIGHT AWAY...

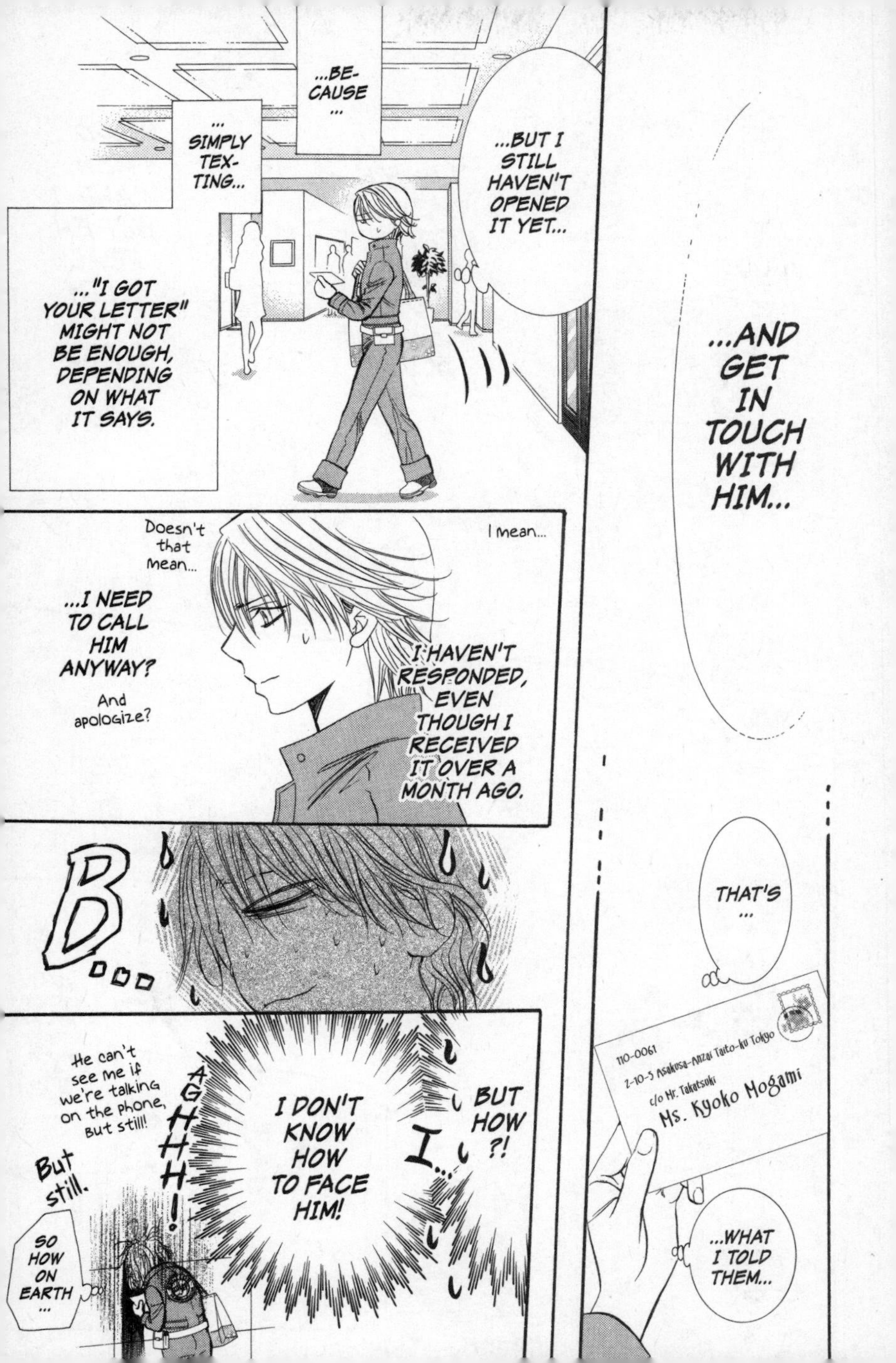
...AND GET IN TOUCH WITH HIM...
THAT'S ...
...WHAT I TOLD THEM...
110-0061
2-10-3 Asakusa-Anzai Taito-ku Tokyo
c/o Mr. Takatsuki
Ms. Kyoko Mogami
...BUT I STILL HAVEN'T OPENED IT YET...
...BE-CAUSE ...
... SIMPLY TEX-TING...
..."I GOT YOUR LETTER" MIGHT NOT BE ENOUGH, DEPENDING ON WHAT IT SAYS.
I mean...
I HAVEN'T RESPONDED, EVEN THOUGH I RECEIVED IT OVER A MONTH AGO.
Doesn't that mean...
...I NEED TO CALL HIM ANYWAY?
And apologize?
Booo
BUT HOW ?!
I...
I DON'T KNOW HOW TO FACE HIM!
AGHHH!
He can't see me if we're talking on the phone, but still!
But still.
SO HOW ON EARTH ...

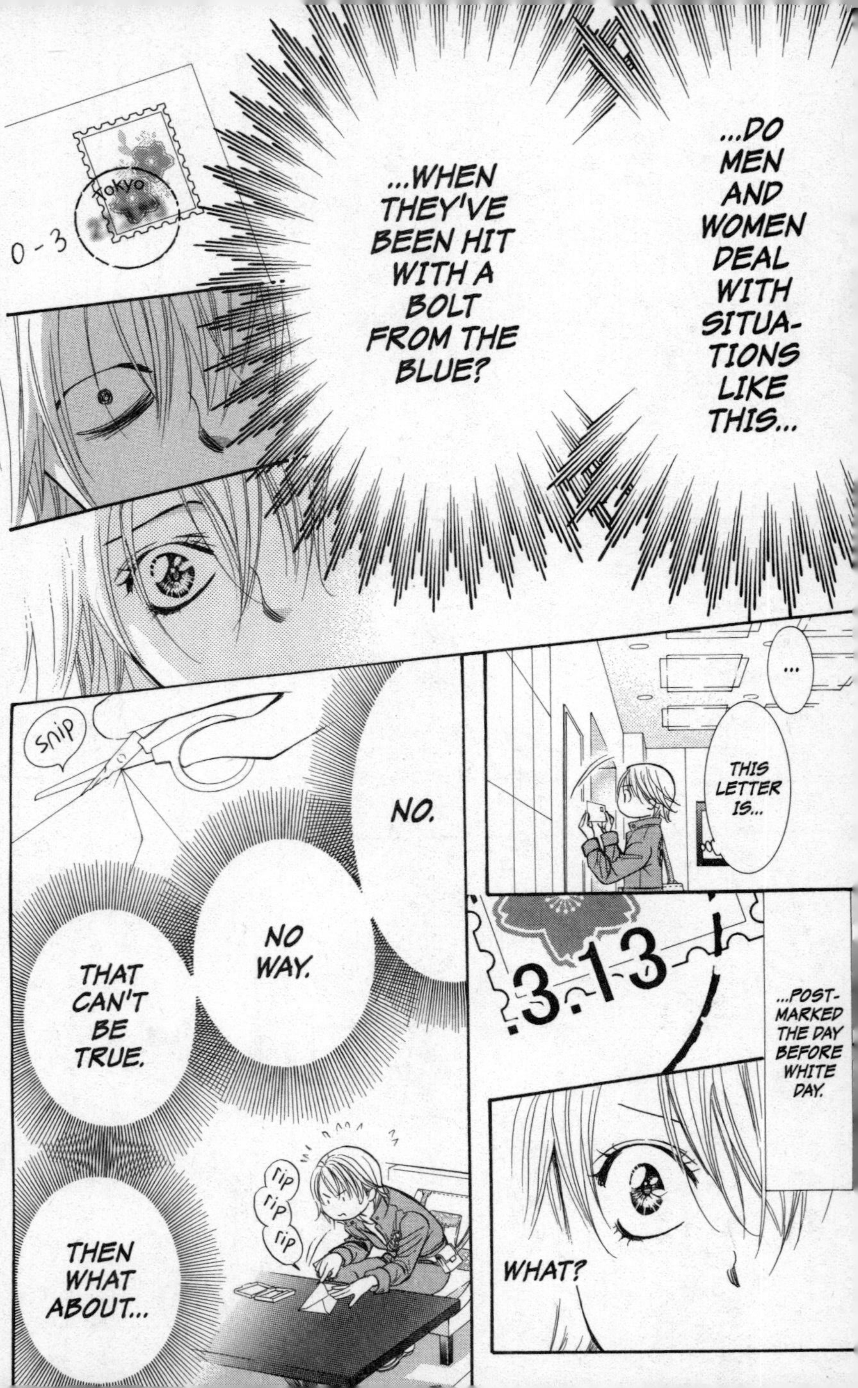
...DO MEN AND WOMEN DEAL WITH SITUATIONS LIKE THIS...
...WHEN THEY'VE BEEN HIT WITH A BOLT FROM THE BLUE?
Tokyo
0-3
...
THIS LETTER IS...
3.13
...POST-MARKED THE DAY BEFORE WHITE DAY.
WHAT?
snip
NO.
NO WAY.
THAT CAN'T BE TRUE.
rip
rip
rip
THEN WHAT ABOUT...

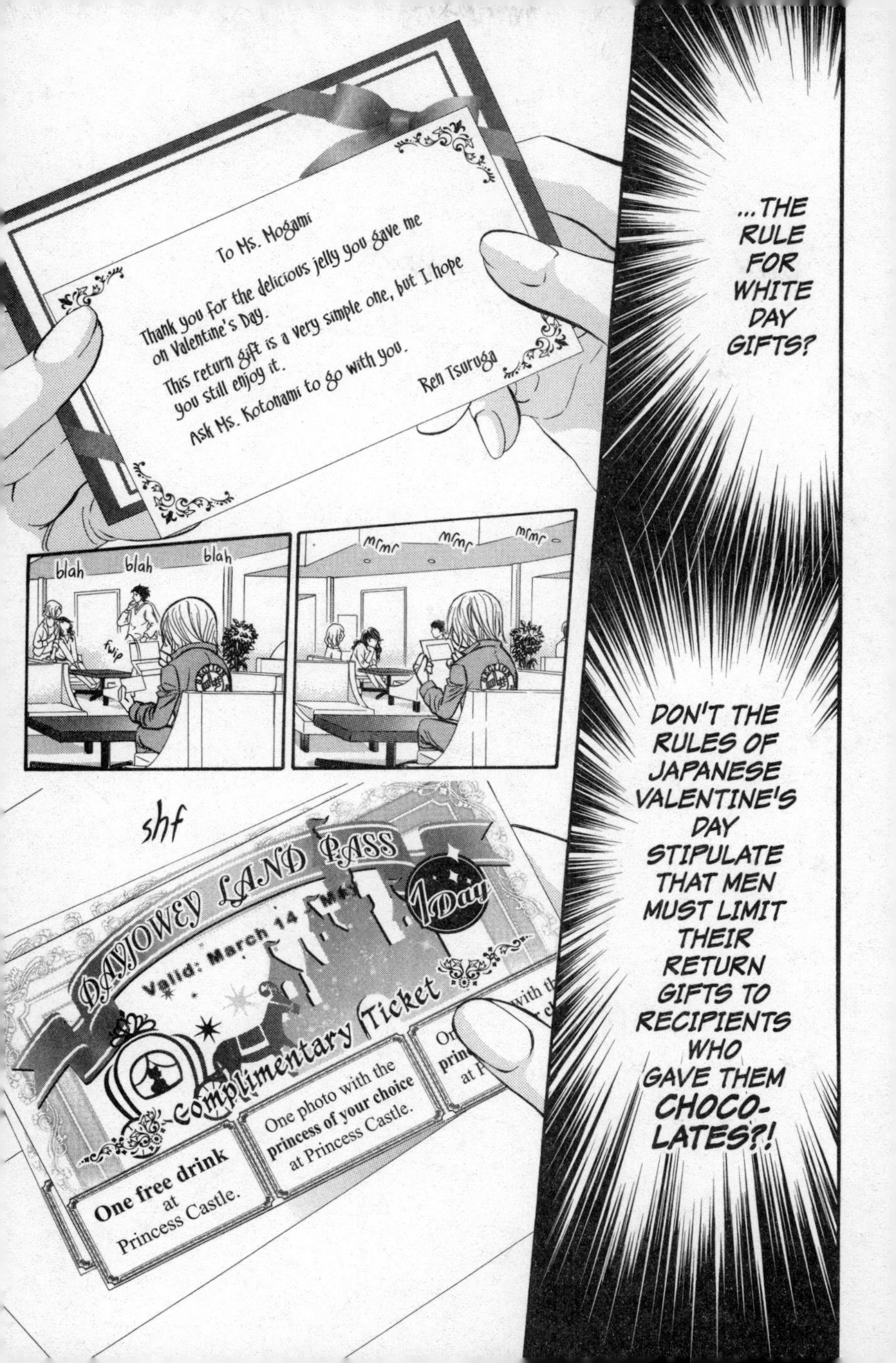
...THE RULE FOR WHITE DAY GIFTS?
DON'T THE RULES OF JAPANESE VALENTINE'S DAY STIPULATE THAT MEN MUST LIMIT THEIR RETURN GIFTS TO RECIPIENTS WHO GAVE THEM CHOCO-LATES?!
To Ms. Mogami
Thank you for the delicious jelly you gave me on Valentine's Day.
This return gift is a very simple one, but I hope you still enjoy it.
Ask Ms. Kotonami to go with you.
Ren Tsuruga
mrmr
mrmr
mrmr
blah
blah
blah
fwip
shf
DAJOWEY LAND PASS
Valid: March 14
1 Day
Complimentary Ticket
One free drink at Princess Castle.
One photo with the princess of your choice at Princess Castle.

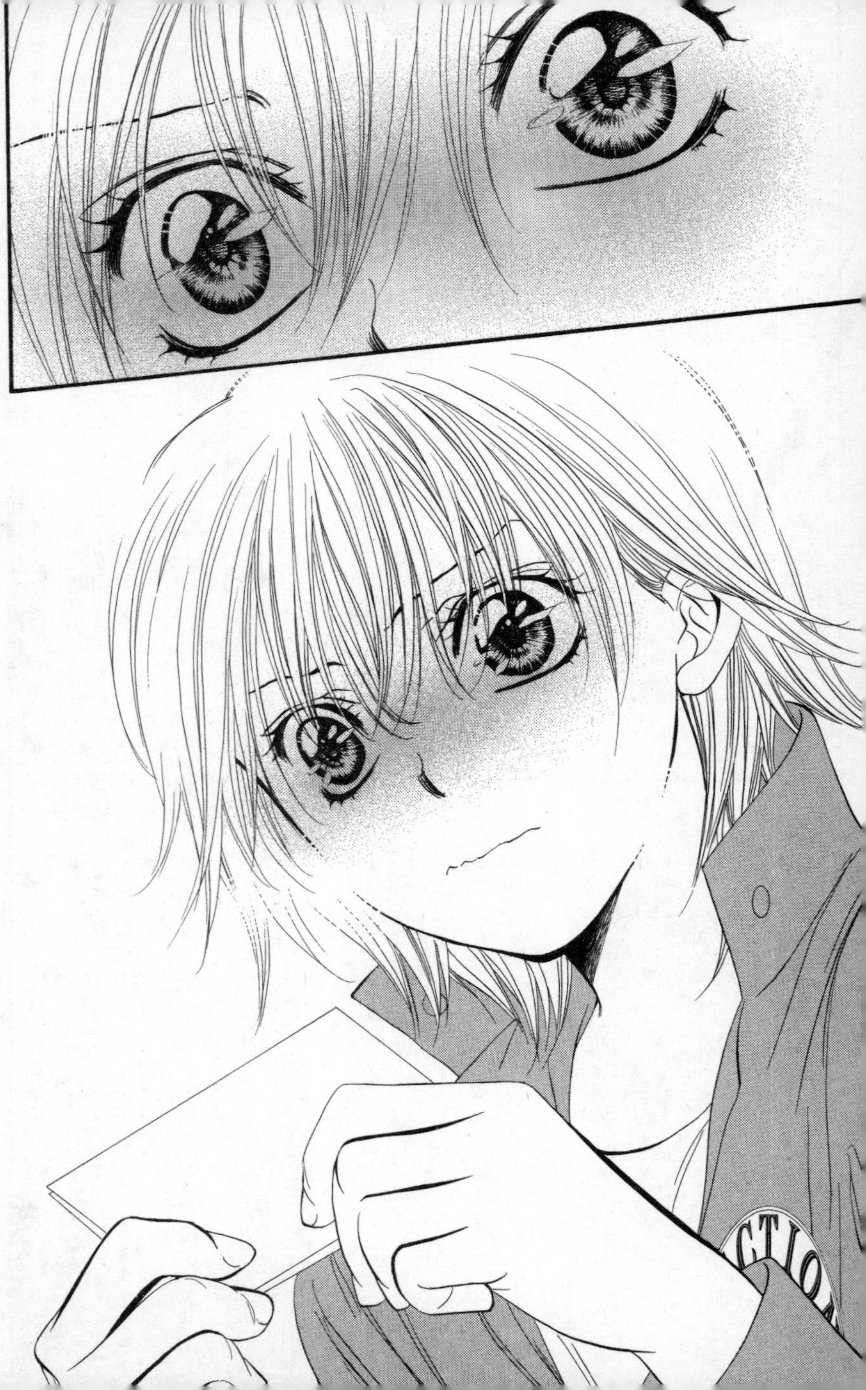

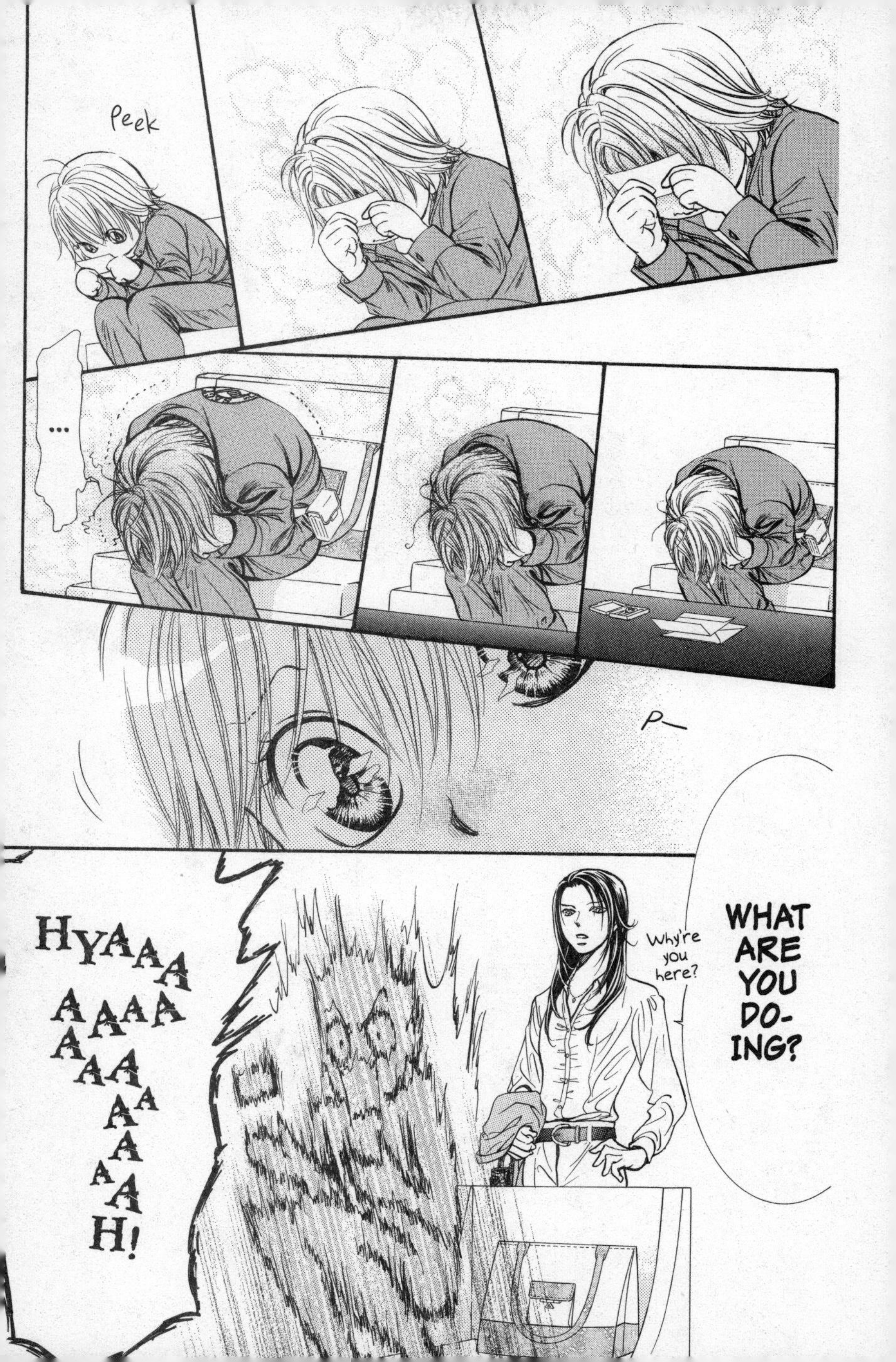
Peek
...
P—
WHAT ARE YOU DO-ING?
Why're you here?
HYAAAAAAAAAAAAAAAAAAAH!

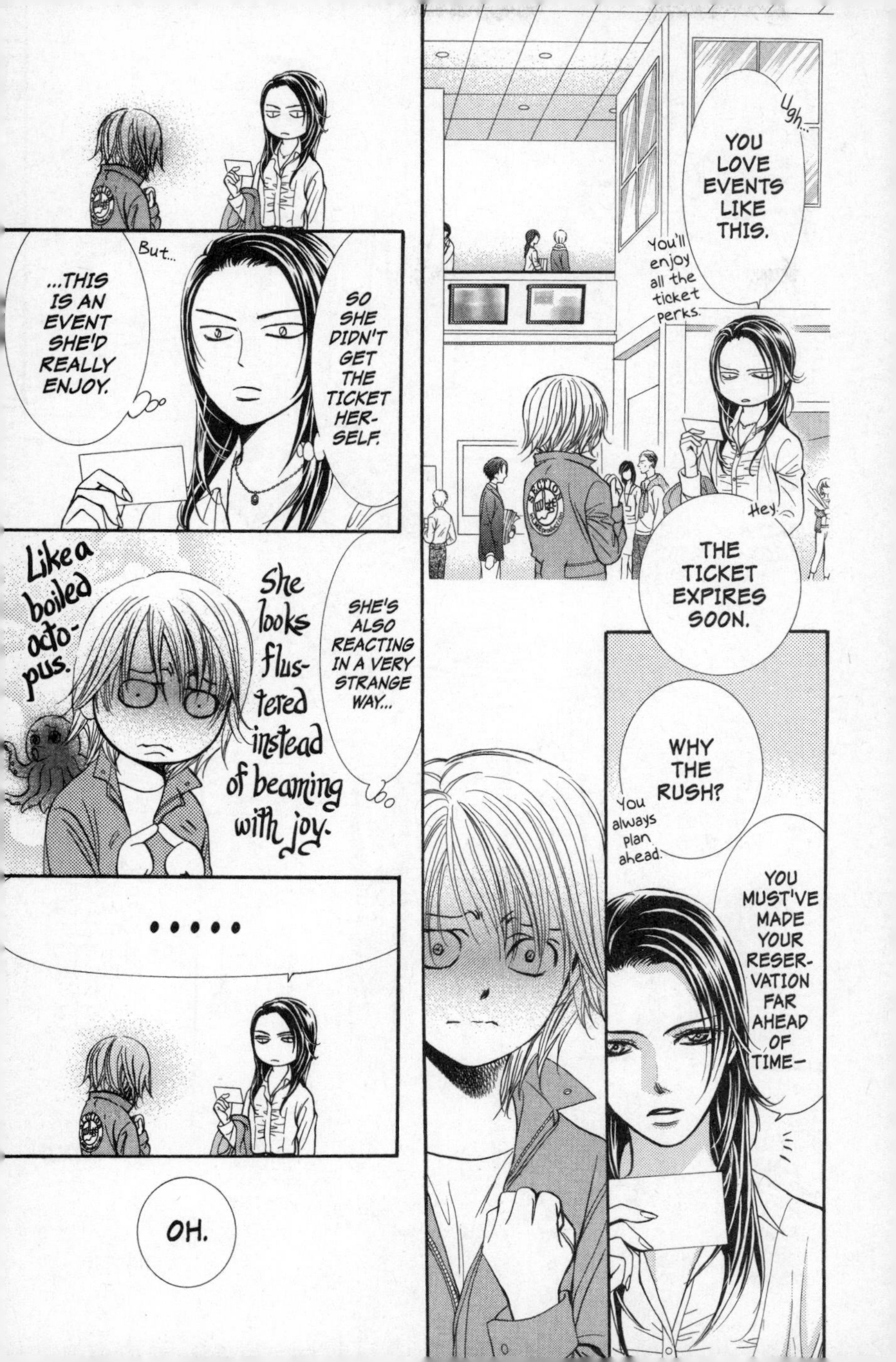
Ugh...
YOU LOVE EVENTS LIKE THIS.
You'll enjoy all the ticket perks.
Hey.
THE TICKET EXPIRES SOON.
WHY THE RUSH?
You always plan ahead.
YOU MUST'VE MADE YOUR RESERVATION FAR AHEAD OF TIME—
SO SHE DIDN'T GET THE TICKET HERSELF.
But...
...THIS IS AN EVENT SHE'D REALLY ENJOY.
SHE'S ALSO REACTING IN A VERY STRANGE WAY...
She looks flustered instead of beaming with joy.
Like a boiled octopus.
.....
OH.

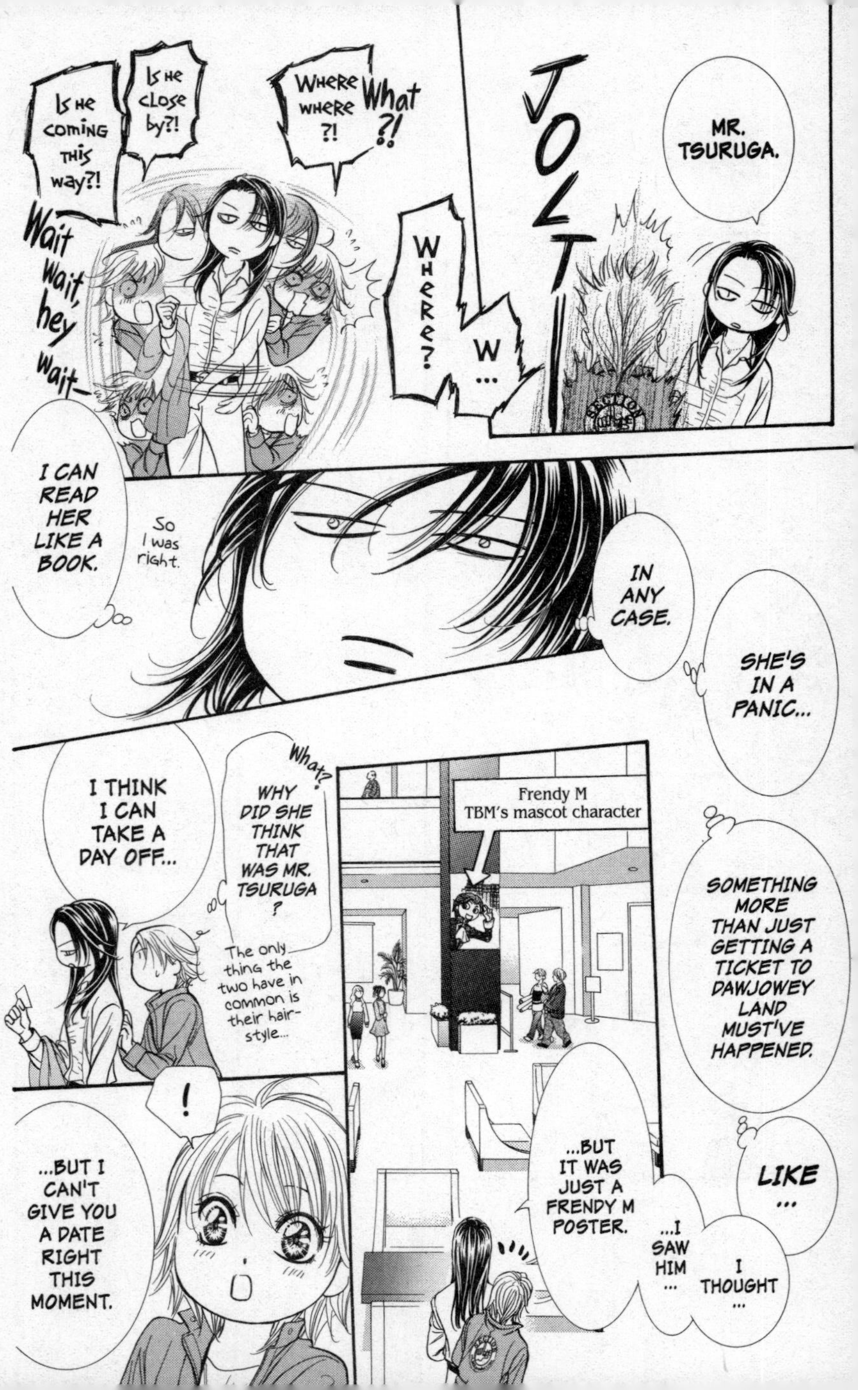
MR. TSURUGA.
JOLT
W...
WHERE?
What?!
Where where?!
Is he close by?!
Is he coming this way?!
Wait wait, hey wait—
IN ANY CASE.
SHE'S IN A PANIC...
I CAN READ HER LIKE A BOOK.
So I was right.
SOMETHING MORE THAN JUST GETTING A TICKET TO DAWJOWEY LAND MUST'VE HAPPENED.
LIKE...
I THOUGHT...
...I SAW HIM...
...BUT IT WAS JUST A FRENDY M POSTER.
Frendy M
TBM's mascot character
What?
WHY DID SHE THINK THAT WAS MR. TSURUGA?
The only thing the two have in common is their hair-style...
I THINK I CAN TAKE A DAY OFF...
!
...BUT I CAN'T GIVE YOU A DATE RIGHT THIS MOMENT.

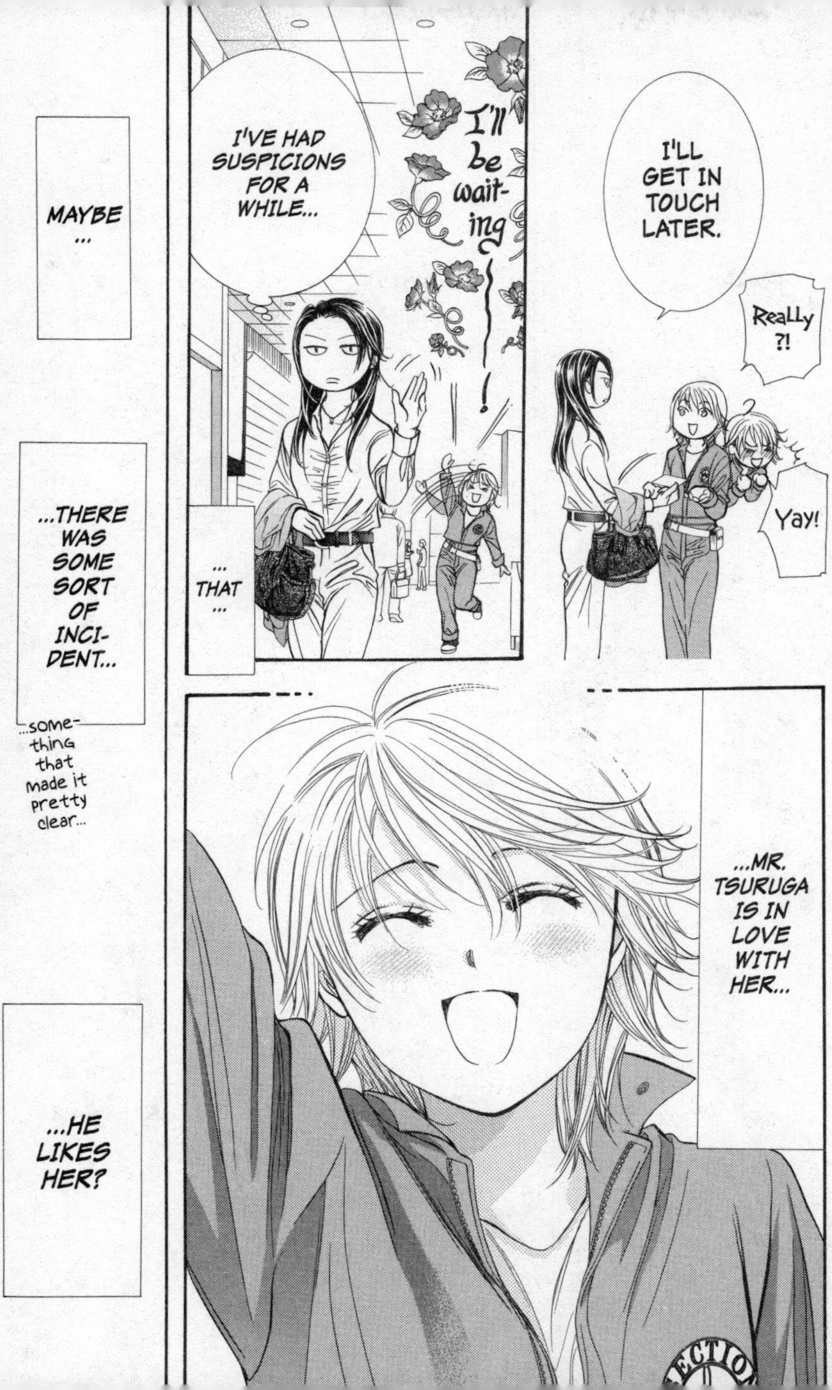
I'LL GET IN TOUCH LATER.
Really ?!
Yay!
I'VE HAD SUSPICIONS FOR A WHILE...
I'll be wait-ing—!
...THAT...
...MR. TSURUGA IS IN LOVE WITH HER...
MAYBE...
...THERE WAS SOME SORT OF INCI-DENT...
...some-thing that made it pretty clear...
...HE LIKES HER?

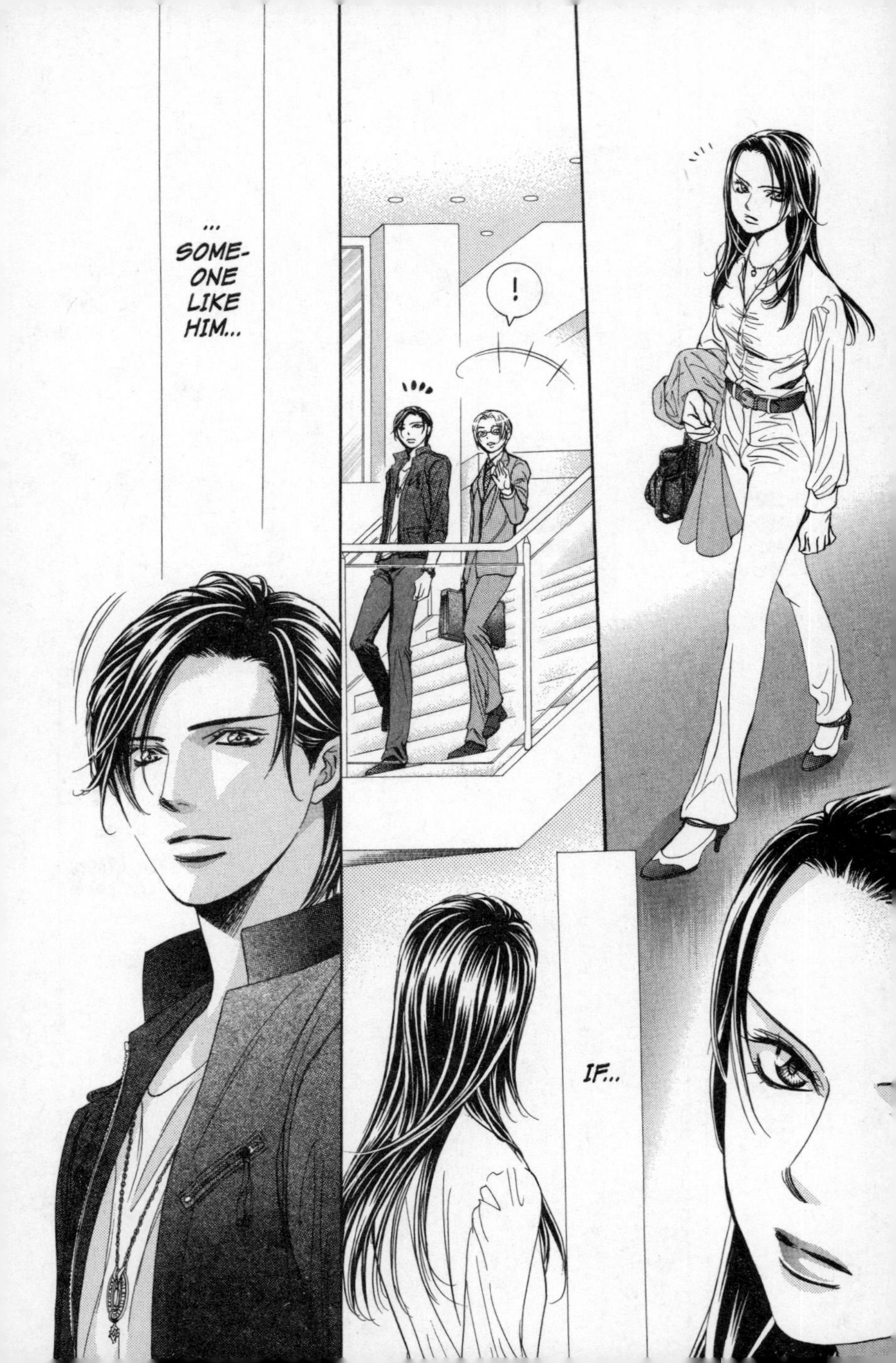
!
...SOME-ONE LIKE HIM...
IF...

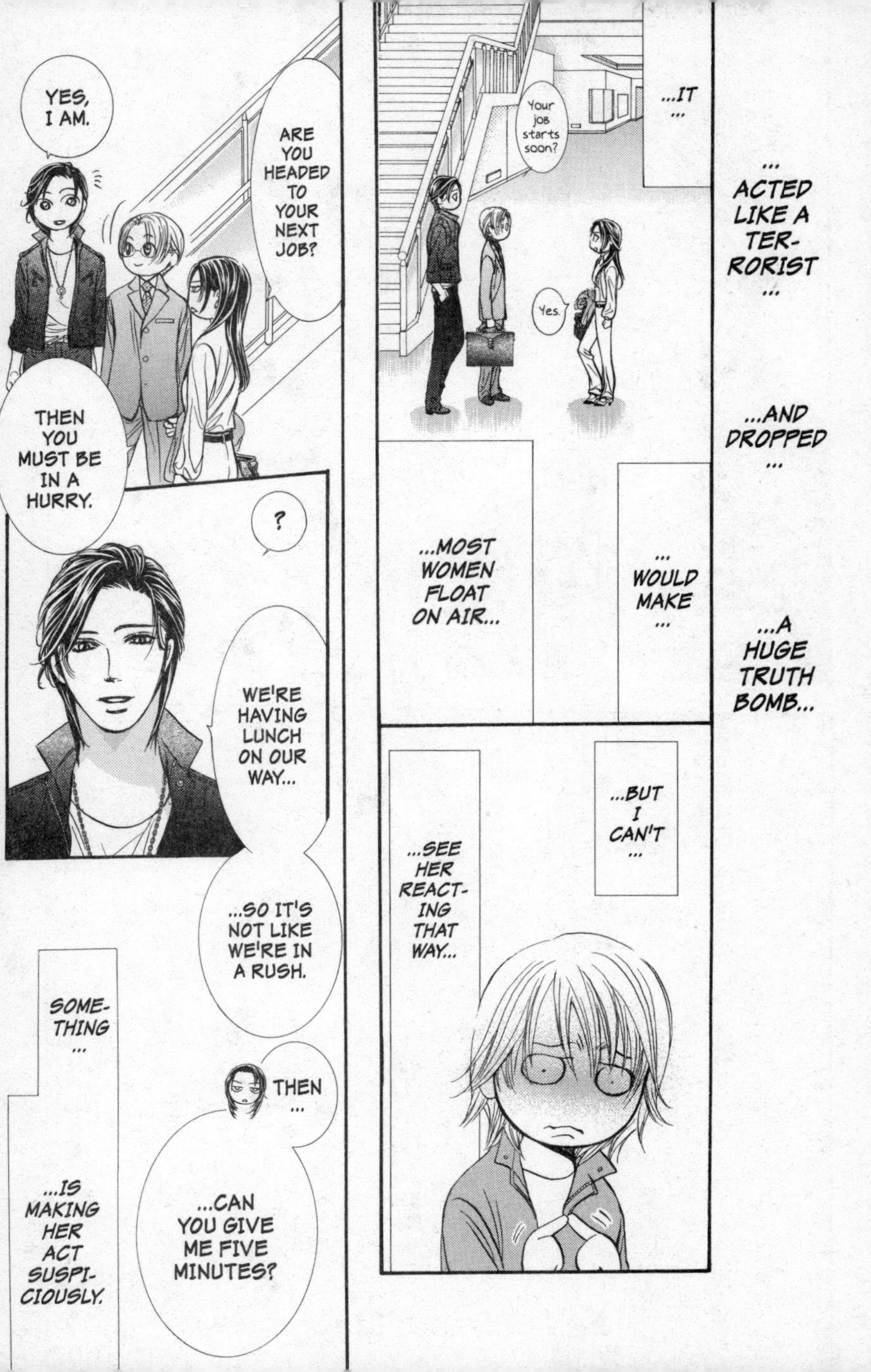
...IT...
Your job starts soon?
Yes.
...ACTED LIKE A TERRORIST...
...AND DROPPED...
...A HUGE TRUTH BOMB...
...WOULD MAKE...
...MOST WOMEN FLOAT ON AIR...
...BUT I CAN'T...
...SEE HER REACTING THAT WAY...
ARE YOU HEADED TO YOUR NEXT JOB?
YES, I AM.
THEN YOU MUST BE IN A HURRY.
?
WE'RE HAVING LUNCH ON OUR WAY...
...SO IT'S NOT LIKE WE'RE IN A RUSH.
THEN...
...CAN YOU GIVE ME FIVE MINUTES?
SOMETHING...
...IS MAKING HER ACT SUSPICIOUSLY.

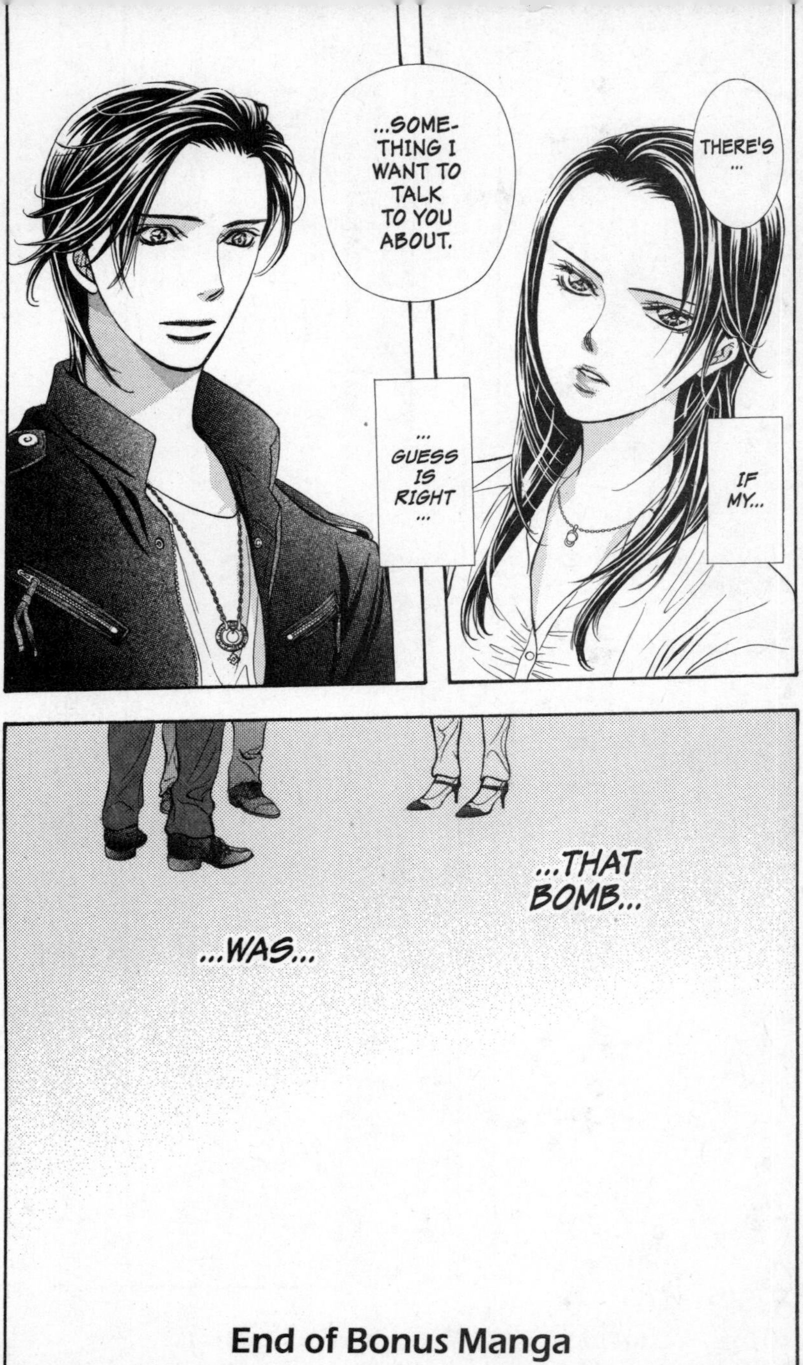
IF MY...
...
GUESS IS RIGHT
...
THERE'S
...
...SOME-
THING I WANT TO TALK TO YOU ABOUT.
...THAT BOMB...
...WAS...

End of Bonus Manga

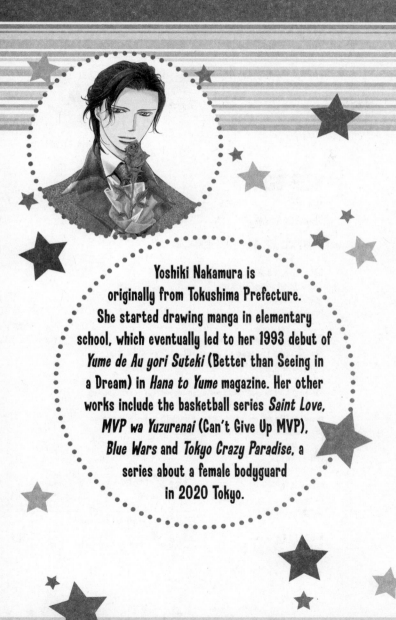

Yoshiki Nakamura is
originally from Tokushima Prefecture.
She started drawing manga in elementary
school, which eventually led to her 1993 debut of
Yume de Au yori Suteki (Better than Seeing in
a Dream) in *Hana to Yume* magazine. Her other
works include the basketball series *Saint Love*,
MVP wa Yuzurenai (Can't Give Up MVP),
Blue Wars and *Tokyo Crazy Paradise*, a
series about a female bodyguard
in 2020 Tokyo.

SKIP·BEAT!
Vol. 46
Shojo Beat Edition

STORY AND ART BY YOSHIKI NAKAMURA

English Translation & Adaptation/Tomo Kimura
Touch-up Art & Lettering/Sabrina Heep
Design/J. Shikuma
Editor/Pancha Diaz

Skip-Beat! by Yoshiki Nakamura © Yoshiki Nakamura 2021
All rights reserved. First published in Japan in 2021 by HAKUSENSHA, Inc., Tokyo.
English language translation rights arranged with HAKUSENSHA, Inc., Tokyo.

Printed in the U.S.A.

Published by VIZ Media, LLC
P.O. Box 77010
San Francisco, CA 94107

10 9 8 7 6 5 4 3 2 1
First printing, April 2022

viz.com

shojobeat.com

SLEEPY PRINCESS IN THE DEMON CASTLE

16

Story & Art by
KAGIJI KUMANOMATA

NIGHTS

196th Night: I Made It Gold and Shiny

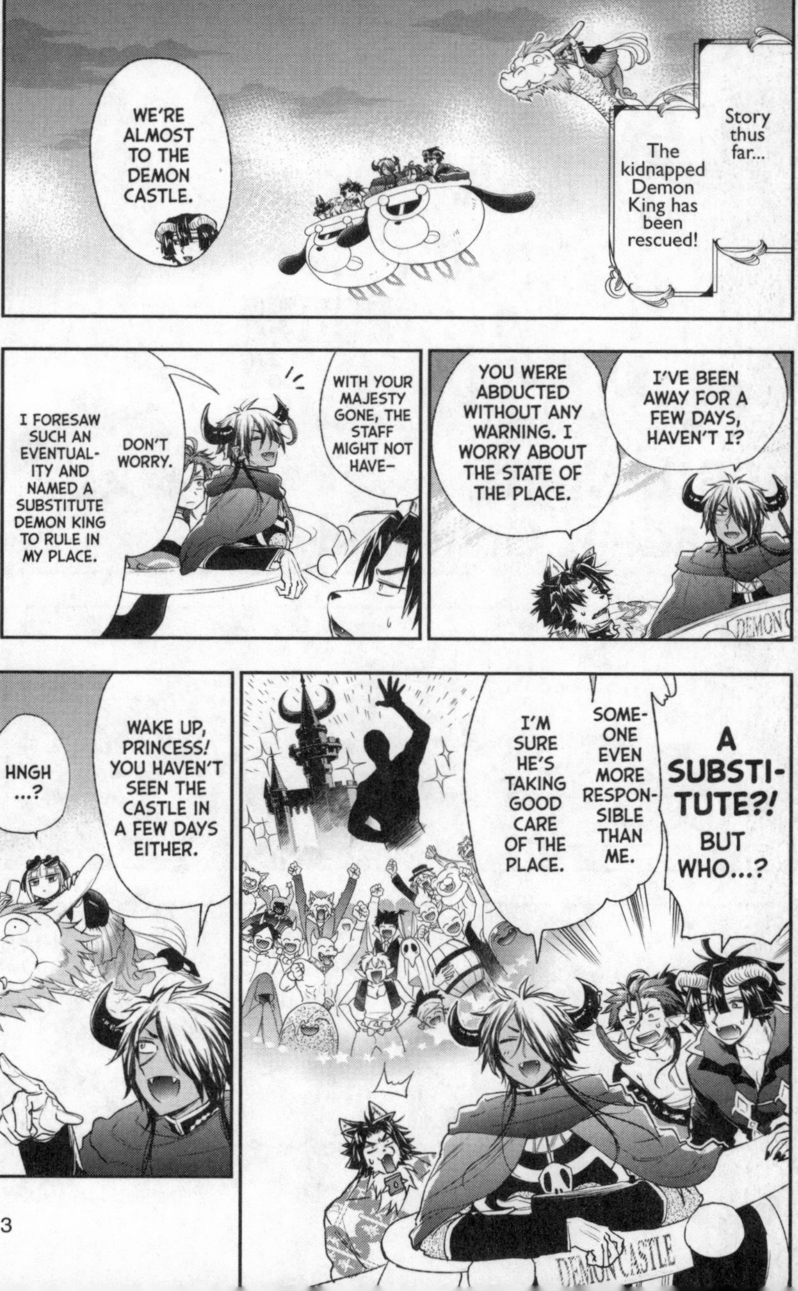

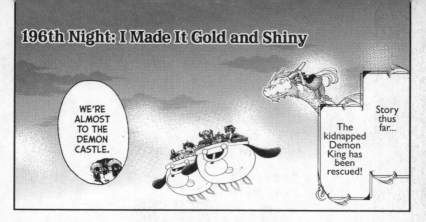

Story thus far...
The kidnapped Demon King has been rescued!
WE'RE ALMOST TO THE DEMON CASTLE.
I'VE BEEN AWAY FOR A FEW DAYS, HAVEN'T I?
YOU WERE ABDUCTED WITHOUT ANY WARNING. I WORRY ABOUT THE STATE OF THE PLACE.
WITH YOUR MAJESTY GONE, THE STAFF MIGHT NOT HAVE–
DON'T WORRY.
I FORESAW SUCH AN EVENTUALITY AND NAMED A SUBSTITUTE DEMON KING TO RULE IN MY PLACE.
A SUBSTITUTE?! BUT WHO...?
SOMEONE EVEN MORE RESPONSIBLE THAN ME.
I'M SURE HE'S TAKING GOOD CARE OF THE PLACE.
DEMON CASTLE
WAKE UP, PRINCESS! YOU HAVEN'T SEEN THE CASTLE IN A FEW DAYS EITHER.
HNGH ...?

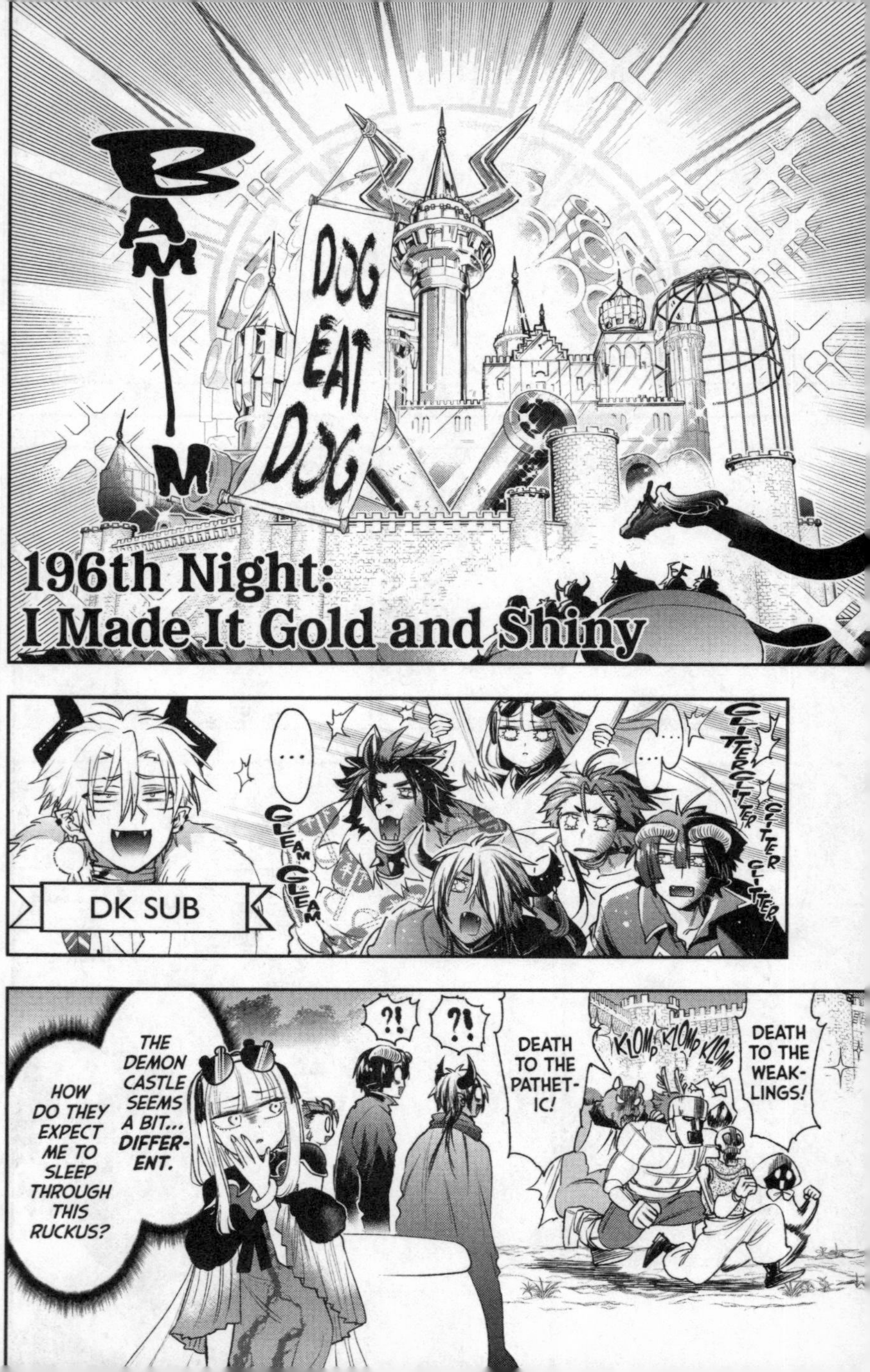
BAM
DOG EAT DOG
196th Night:
I Made It Gold and Shiny
GLITTER GLITTER GLITTER GLITTER
...
...
...
GLEAM GLEAM
DK SUB
DEATH TO THE WEAK-LINGS!
KLOMP KLOMP KLOMP
DEATH TO THE PATHET-IC!
?!
?!
THE DEMON CASTLE SEEMS A BIT... DIFFER-ENT.
HOW DO THEY EXPECT ME TO SLEEP THROUGH THIS RUCKUS?

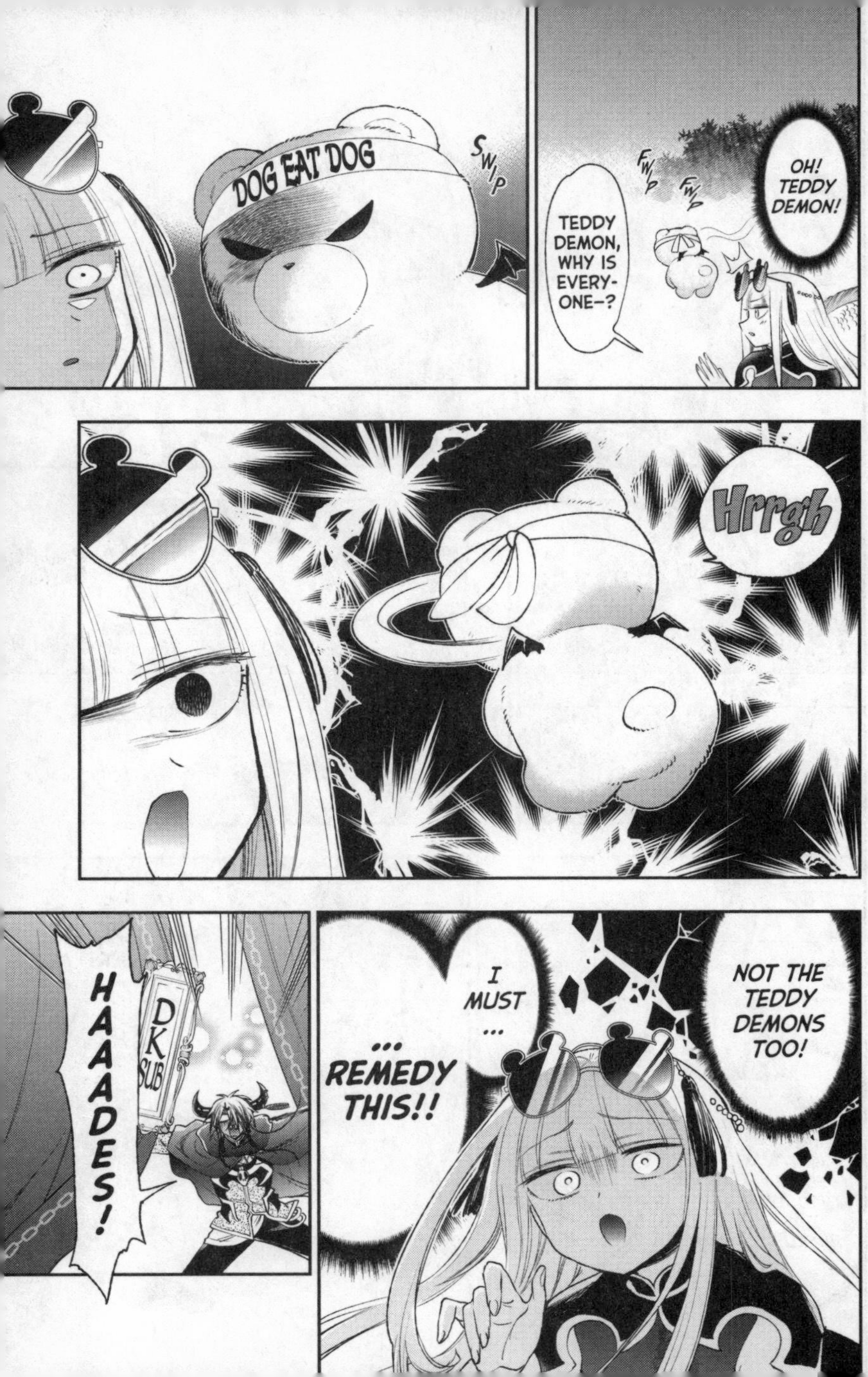
OH! TEDDY DEMON!
FWIP
FWIP
TEDDY DEMON, WHY IS EVERY-ONE--?
SWIP
DOG EAT DOG
Hrrgh
NOT THE TEDDY DEMONS TOO!
I MUST...
...REMEDY THIS!!
DK SUB
HAAADES!

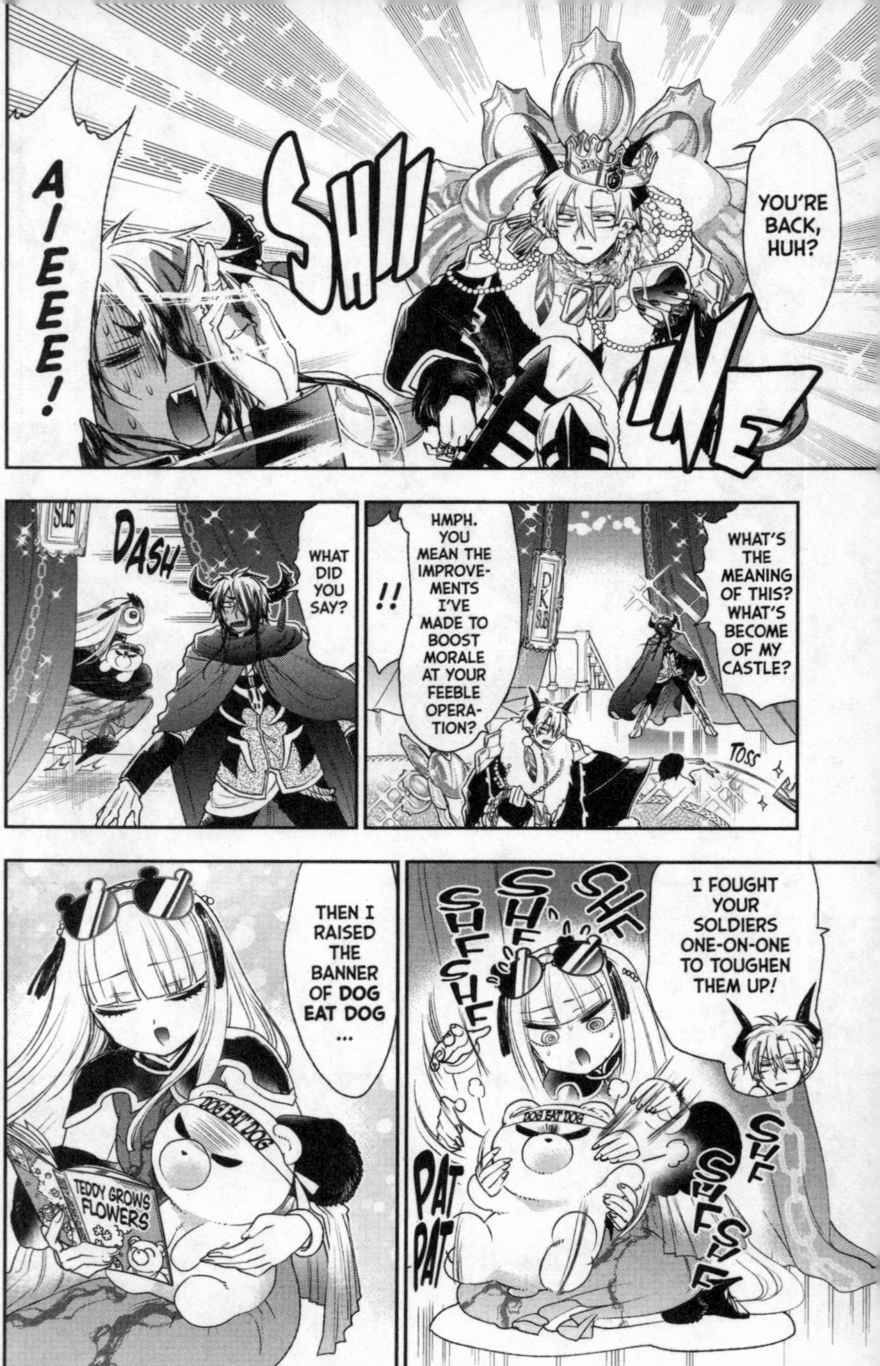
YOU'RE BACK, HUH?
SHIIINE
AIEEEE!
WHAT'S THE MEANING OF THIS? WHAT'S BECOME OF MY CASTLE?
TOSS
HMPH. YOU MEAN THE IMPROVEMENTS I'VE MADE TO BOOST MORALE AT YOUR FEEBLE OPERATION?
!!
WHAT DID YOU SAY?
DASH
I FOUGHT YOUR SOLDIERS ONE-ON-ONE TO TOUGHEN THEM UP!
SHF SHF SHF SHF SHF
DOG EAT DOG
SHF SHF SHF SHF
PAT PAT
THEN I RAISED THE BANNER OF DOG EAT DOG ...
DOG EAT DOG
TEDDY GROWS FLOWERS

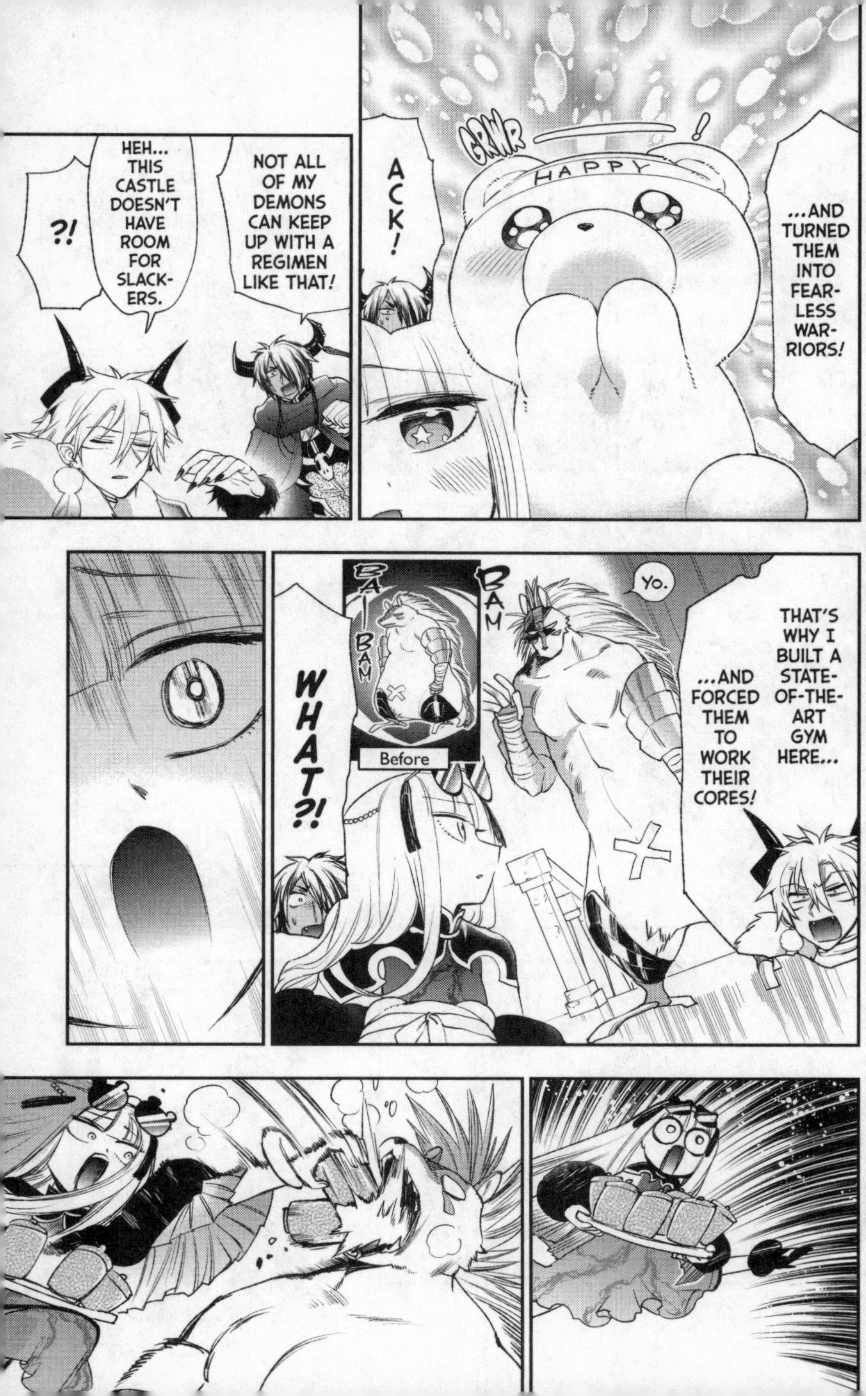
GRWR
!
HAPPY
...AND TURNED THEM INTO FEARLESS WARRIORS!
ACK!
NOT ALL OF MY DEMONS CAN KEEP UP WITH A REGIMEN LIKE THAT!
HEH... THIS CASTLE DOESN'T HAVE ROOM FOR SLACKERS.
?!
THAT'S WHY I BUILT A STATE-OF-THE-ART GYM HERE...
...AND FORCED THEM TO WORK THEIR CORES!
Yo.
BAM
BA-BAM
Before
WHAT?!

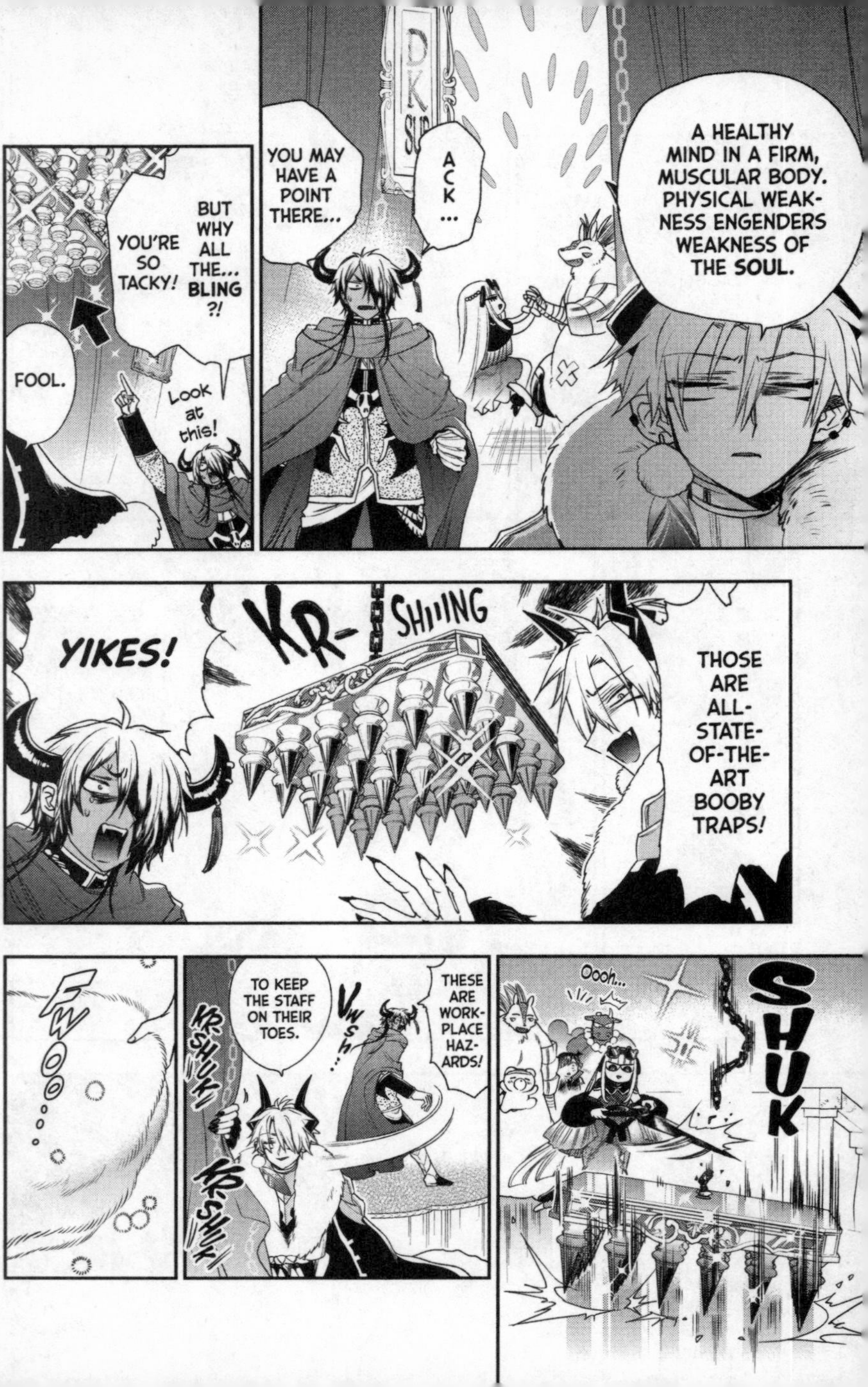
A HEALTHY MIND IN A FIRM, MUSCULAR BODY. PHYSICAL WEAK-NESS ENGENDERS WEAKNESS OF THE SOUL.
ACK ...
YOU MAY HAVE A POINT THERE...
BUT WHY ALL THE... BLING ?!
YOU'RE SO TACKY!
Look at this!
FOOL.
KR-SHIIING
THOSE ARE ALL-STATE-OF-THE-ART BOOBY TRAPS!
YIKES!
SHUK
Oooh...
THESE ARE WORK-PLACE HAZ-ARDS!
Vwsh...
TO KEEP THE STAFF ON THEIR TOES.
KR-SHUK!
KR-SHUK
FWOOO...

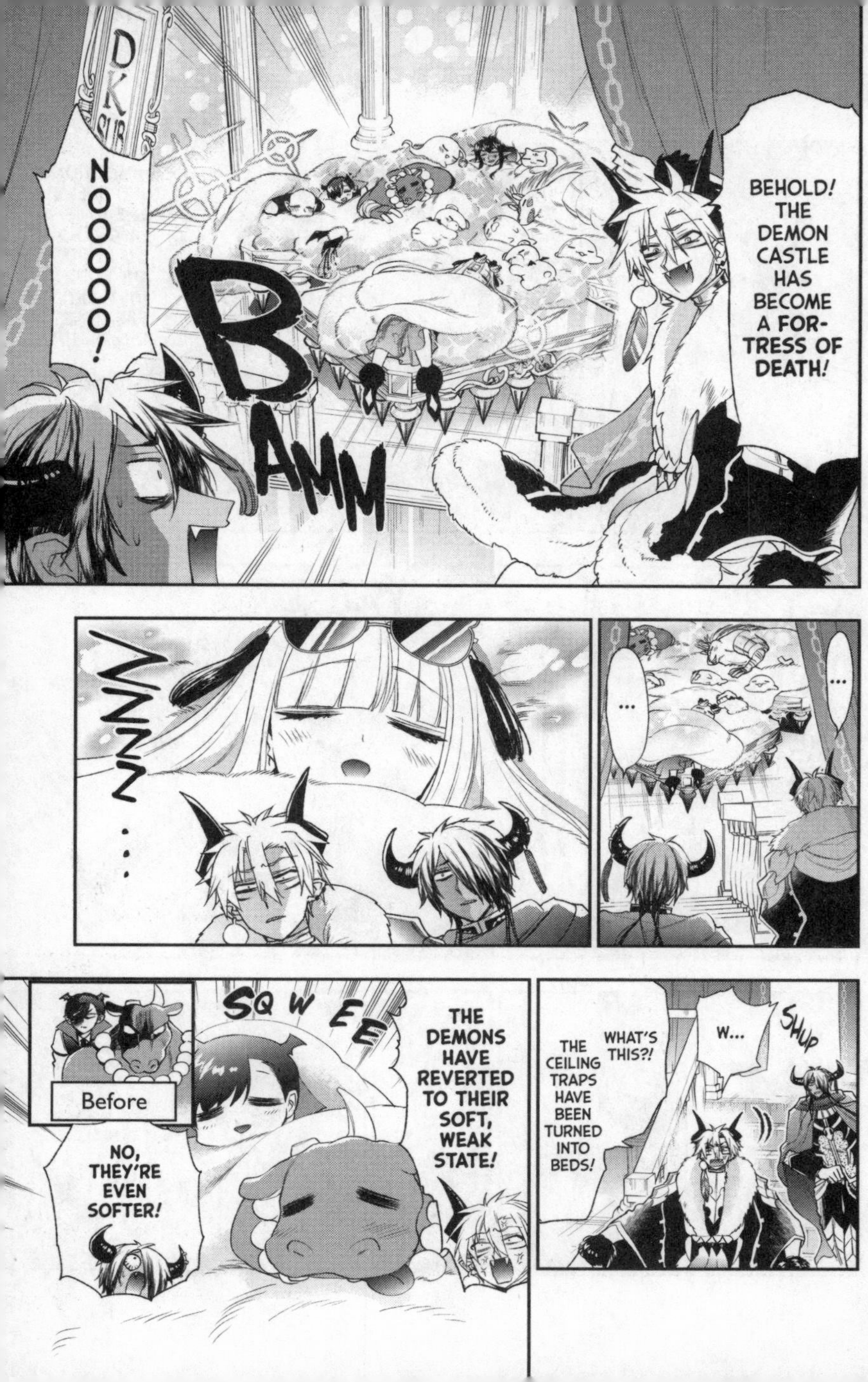
BEHOLD! THE DEMON CASTLE HAS BECOME A FORTRESS OF DEATH!
BAMM
NOOOOOO!
...
...
ZZZZ ...
SHUP
W...
WHAT'S THIS?!
THE CEILING TRAPS HAVE BEEN TURNED INTO BEDS!
THE DEMONS HAVE REVERTED TO THEIR SOFT, WEAK STATE!
SQWEE
Before
NO, THEY'RE EVEN SOFTER!

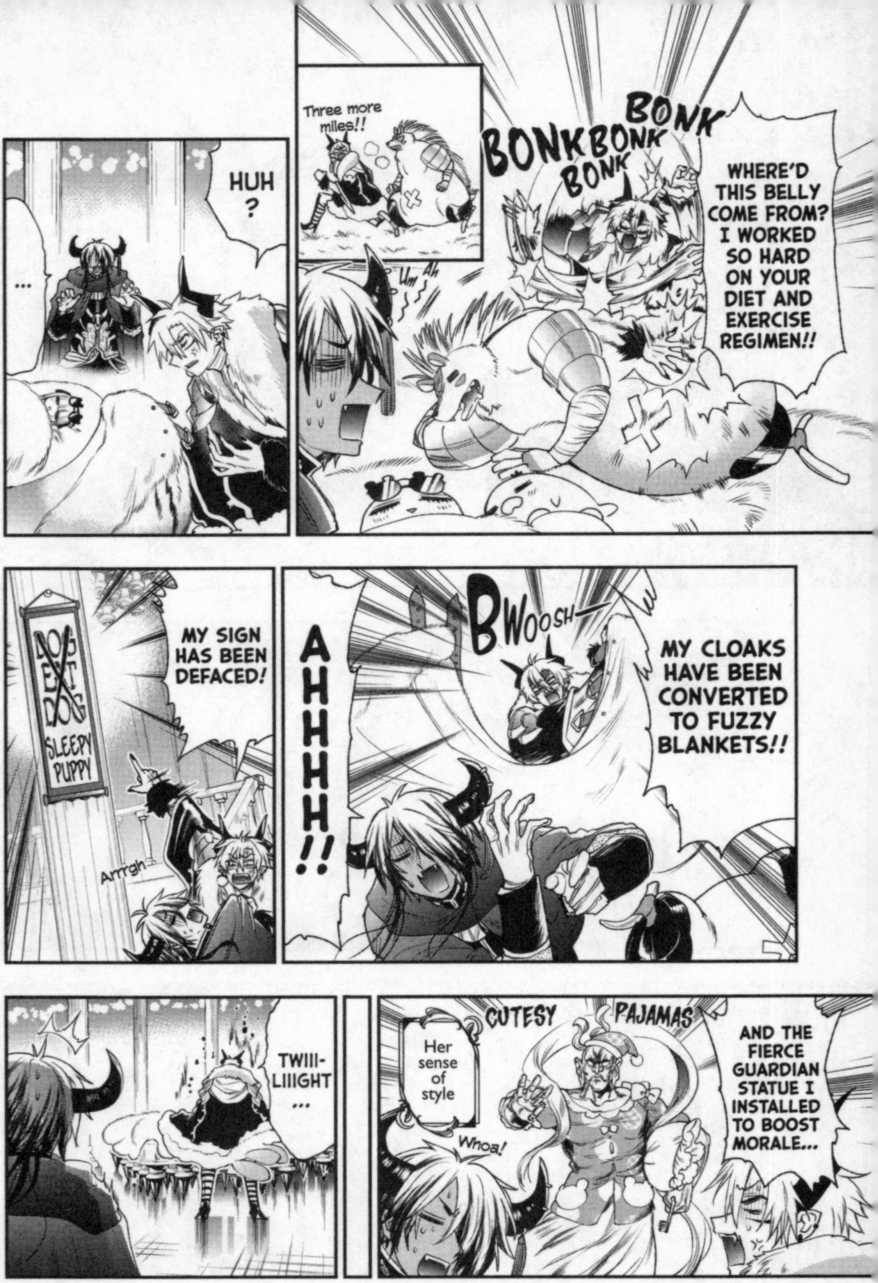
BONKBONK BONK BONK
WHERE'D THIS BELLY COME FROM? I WORKED SO HARD ON YOUR DIET AND EXERCISE REGIMEN!!
Three more miles!!
Um Ah
HUH?
...
BWOOSH
MY CLOAKS HAVE BEEN CONVERTED TO FUZZY BLANKETS!!
AHHHHH!!
MY SIGN HAS BEEN DEFACED!
SLEEPY PUPPY
Arrrgh
CUTESY PAJAMAS
AND THE FIERCE GUARDIAN STATUE I INSTALLED TO BOOST MORALE...
Her sense of style
Whoa!
TWIII-LIIIGHT...

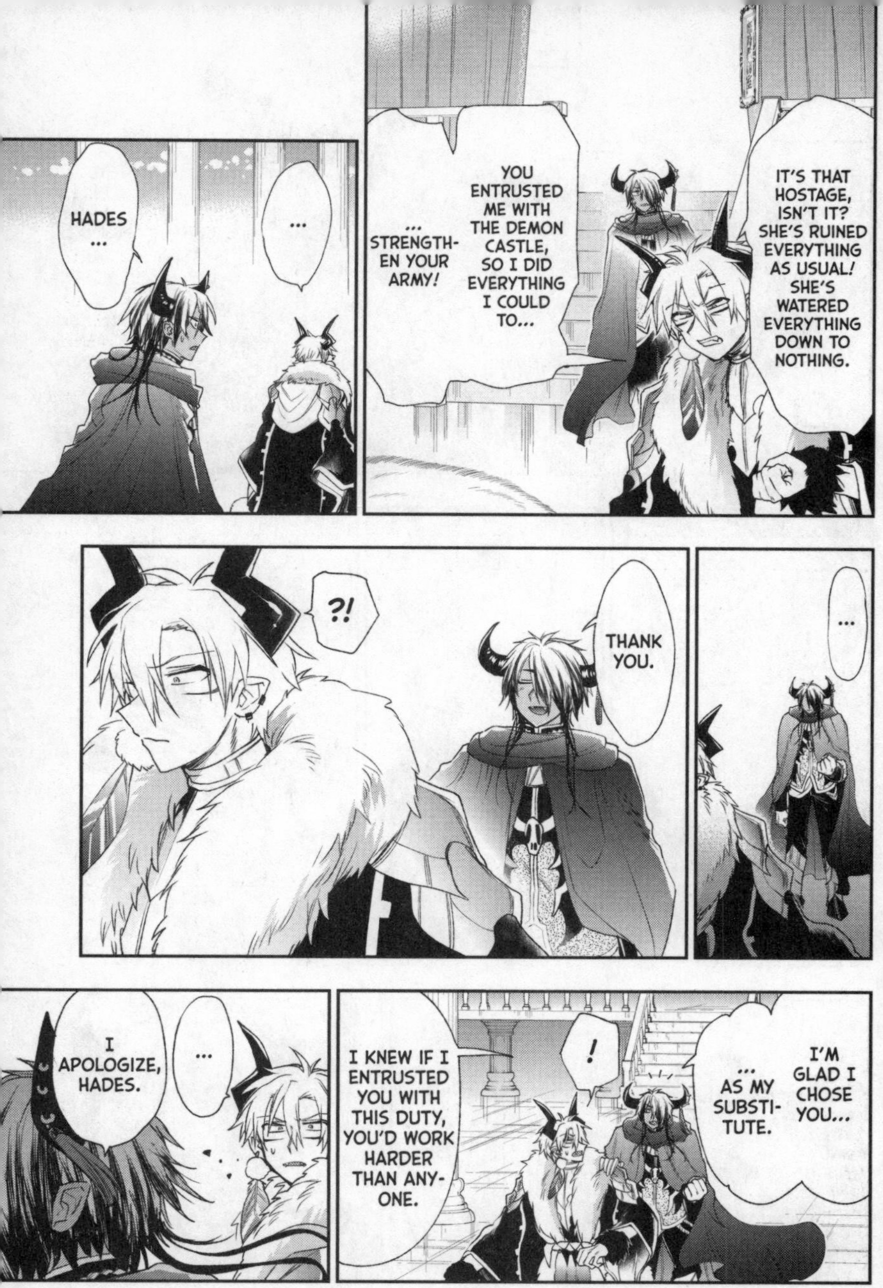
IT'S THAT HOSTAGE, ISN'T IT? SHE'S RUINED EVERYTHING AS USUAL! SHE'S WATERED EVERYTHING DOWN TO NOTHING.
YOU ENTRUSTED ME WITH THE DEMON CASTLE, SO I DID EVERYTHING I COULD TO...
... STRENGTH-EN YOUR ARMY!
...
HADES ...
...
THANK YOU.
?!
I'M GLAD I CHOSE YOU...
... AS MY SUBSTI-TUTE.
!
I KNEW IF I ENTRUSTED YOU WITH THIS DUTY, YOU'D WORK HARDER THAN ANY-ONE.
...
I APOLOGIZE, HADES.

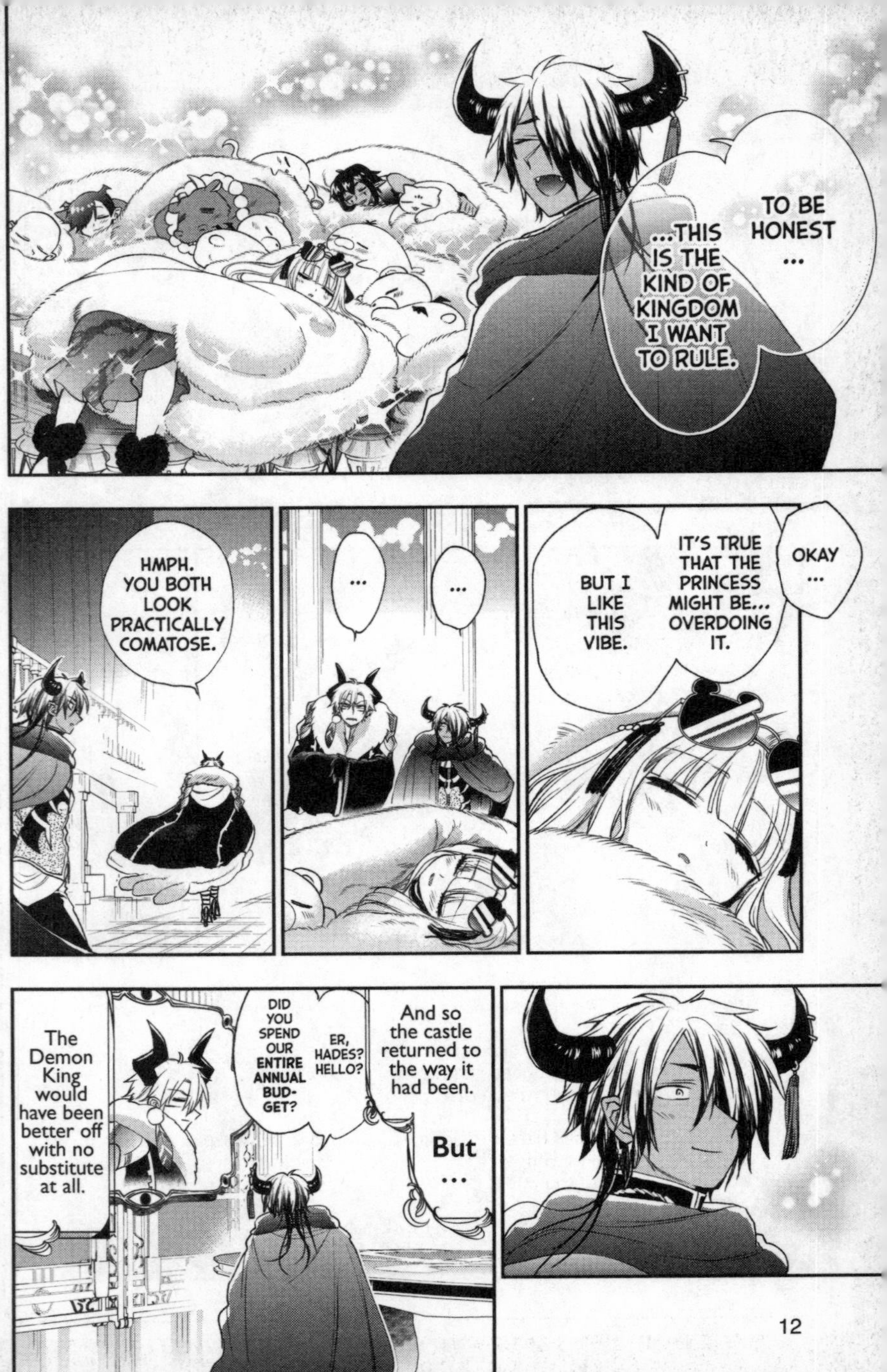
TO BE HONEST ...
...THIS IS THE KIND OF KINGDOM I WANT TO RULE.
OKAY ...
IT'S TRUE THAT THE PRINCESS MIGHT BE... OVERDOING IT.
BUT I LIKE THIS VIBE.
...
...
HMPH. YOU BOTH LOOK PRACTICALLY COMATOSE.
And so the castle returned to the way it had been.
ER, HADES? HELLO?
DID YOU SPEND OUR ENTIRE ANNUAL BUD-GET?
But ...
The Demon King would have been better off with no substitute at all.

NOT MANY QUESTIONS THIS VOLUME

Why not?

Q Who would win a castlewide staring contest?

A Teddy Demon. Those who stared at him would wind up with big smiles on their faces.

Q In volume 1, the princess asked Alazif for the complete works of Osamu Tezuka. What kind of manga does everyone like to read?

A

Princess: Adventure manga	Bussy: Comedy manga
Demon King: Historical fiction with lots of battles	Harpy: Romantic comedy manga
Demon Cleric: Doesn't read manga	Cursed Musician: Doesn't read manga
Furry Dog: Doesn't read manga	Quilladillo: Fighting manga (shared with his circle of friends)
Poseidon: Battle manga	Gobbly Gobbly Goblin: Same as above
Hades: Doesn't read manga	Minotaur: Same as above
Alraune: Bishonen romance manga	Frankenzombie: Same as above
Fire Venom Dragon: Gambling manga	Vampire: Splatter manga
Sand Dragon: Relaxing four-panel funnies	Agave: Doesn't read manga
M.O.T.H.E.R.: Doesn't read manga	Scissors Sorcerer: Autobiographical manga
Zeus: Mystery manga	Hypnos: All kinds of manga
	Narmie: Everything in *Shonen Someday* magazine

Q What do Quilladillo, Minotaur, Castle Grunt Goblin, and Frankenzombie call each other?

A Usually "Quill," "Minotaur," "Goblin," and "Franken."
But sometimes, for fun, they use the nicknames the princess gave them.

Q Nemlis is called the queen and not the queen consort. Does that mean she rules alongside the king?

A She does have a lot of royal duties, but they're a little different from her husband's. Some of her most important work is done out of the public eye.

Q Are there more subspecies of Teddy Demon?

A There are probably as many types as there are breeds of dogs.

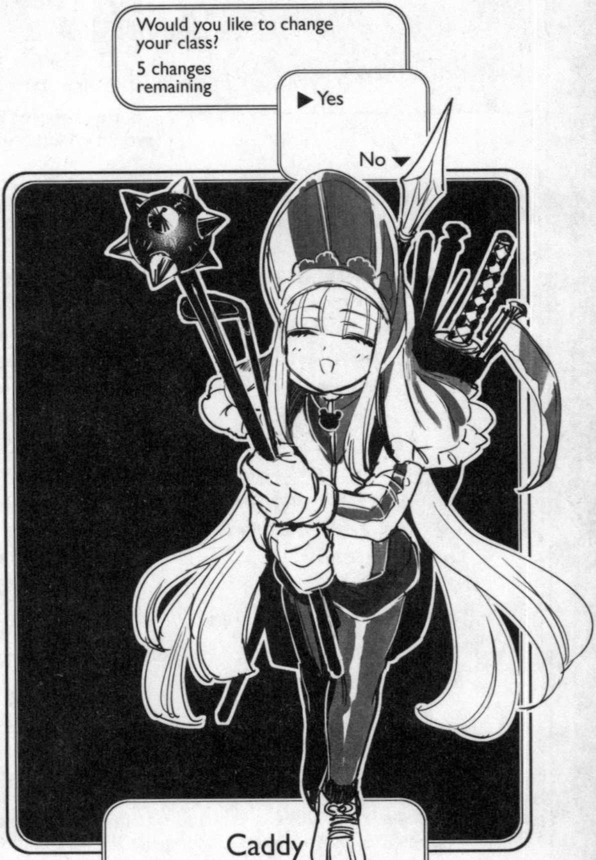

Would you like to change your class?
5 changes remaining
▶Yes
No
Caddy
"Looovely club you've got there!"

197th Night: Hostage Princess vs. Trespassing Dragon

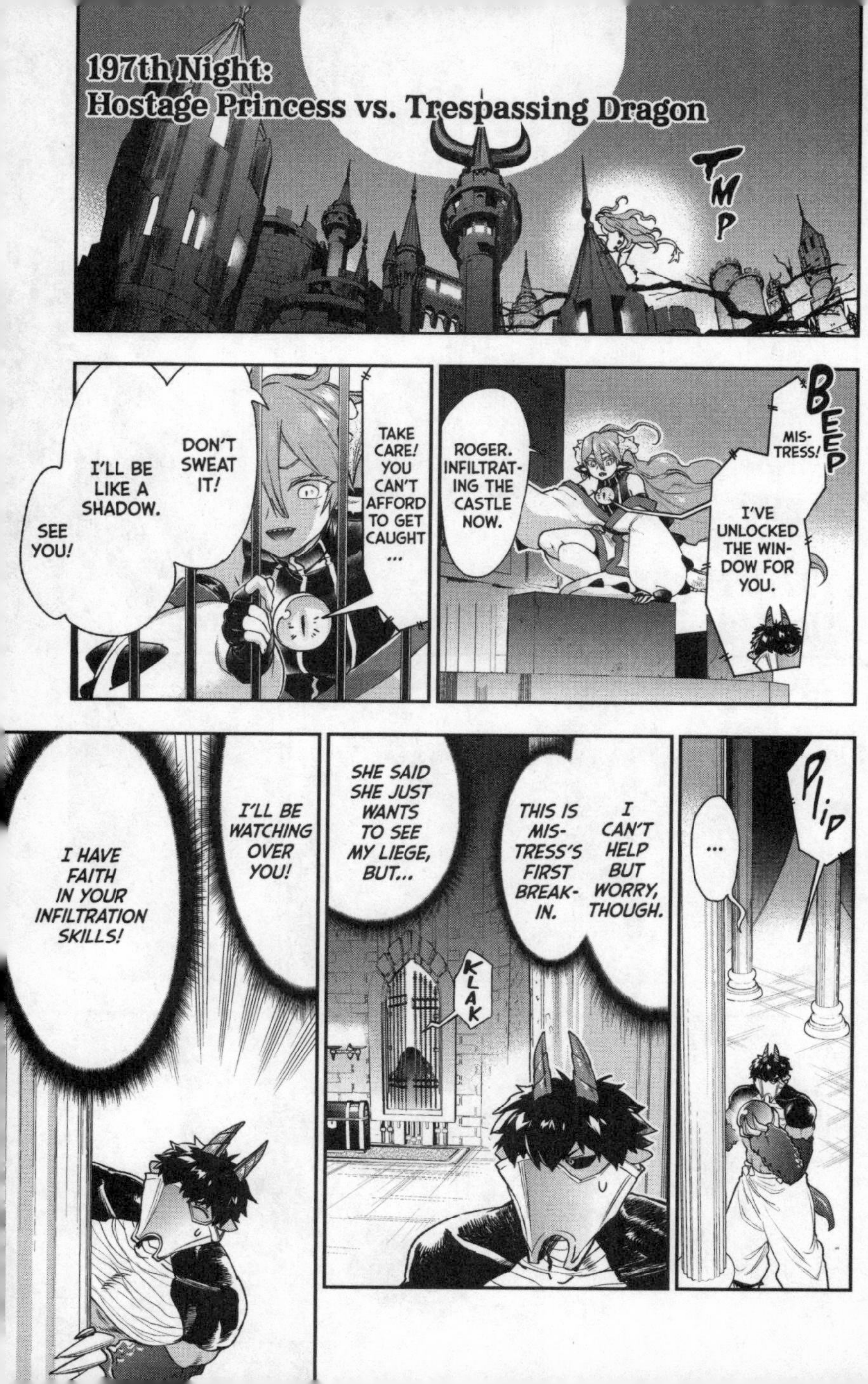
TMP
BEEP
MIS-TRESS!
I'VE UNLOCKED THE WIN-DOW FOR YOU.
ROGER. INFILTRAT-ING THE CASTLE NOW.
TAKE CARE! YOU CAN'T AFFORD TO GET CAUGHT...
DON'T SWEAT IT!
I'LL BE LIKE A SHADOW.
SEE YOU!
Plip
...
I CAN'T HELP BUT WORRY, THOUGH.
THIS IS MIS-TRESS'S FIRST BREAK-IN.
SHE SAID SHE JUST WANTS TO SEE MY LIEGE, BUT...
KLAK
I'LL BE WATCHING OVER YOU!
I HAVE FAITH IN YOUR INFILTRATION SKILLS!

197th Night: Hostage Princess vs. Trespassing Dragon

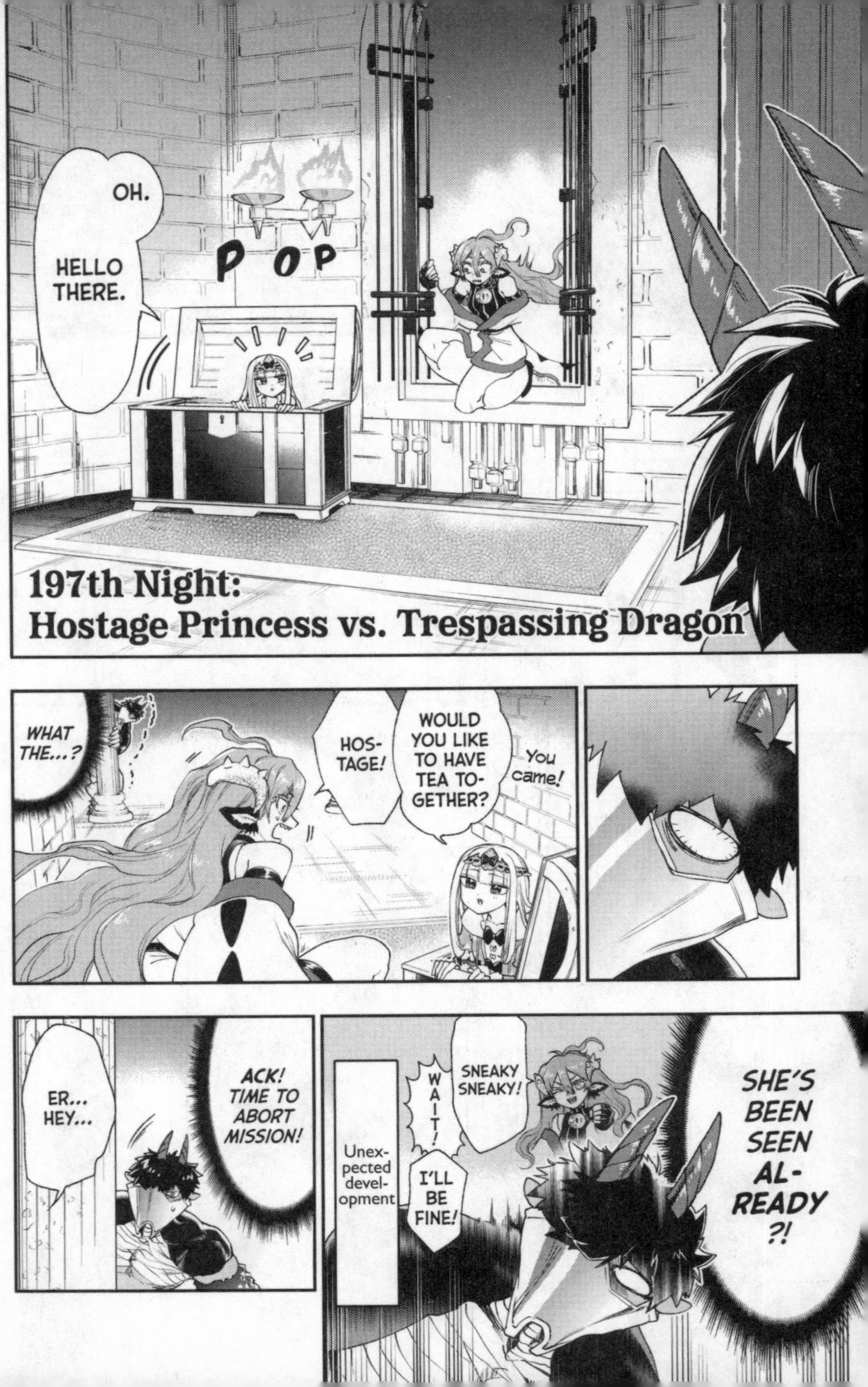
OH.
HELLO THERE.
POP
You came!
WOULD YOU LIKE TO HAVE TEA TO-GETHER?
HOS-TAGE!
WHAT THE...?
SHE'S BEEN SEEN AL-READY?!
SNEAKY SNEAKY!
WAIT!
I'LL BE FINE!
Unex-pected devel-opment
ACK! TIME TO ABORT MISSION!
ER... HEY...

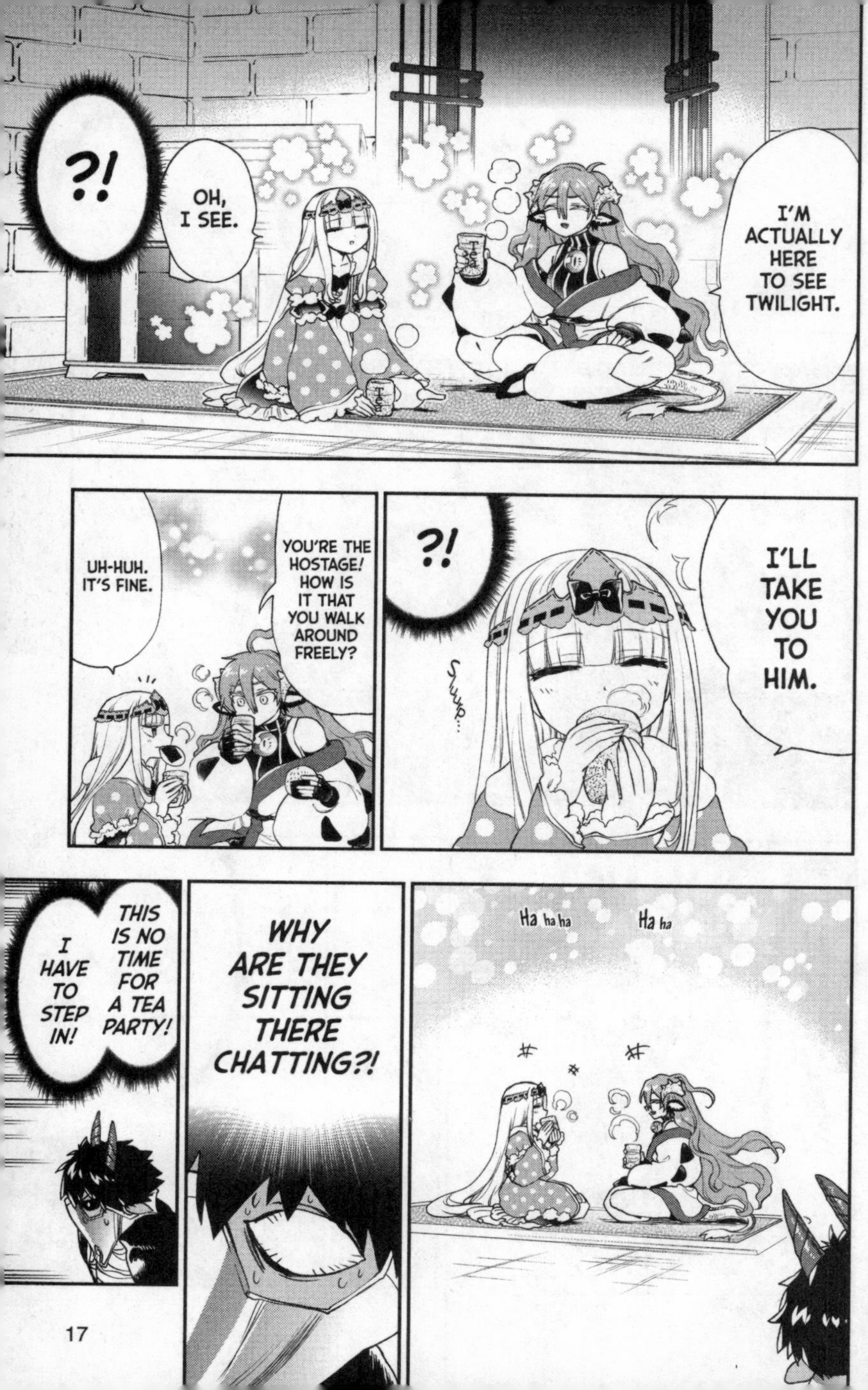
I'M ACTUALLY HERE TO SEE TWILIGHT.
OH, I SEE.
?!
I'LL TAKE YOU TO HIM.
Sluuup...
?!
YOU'RE THE HOSTAGE! HOW IS IT THAT YOU WALK AROUND FREELY?
UH-HUH. IT'S FINE.
Ha ha
Ha ha ha
WHY ARE THEY SITTING THERE CHATTING?!
THIS IS NO TIME FOR A TEA PARTY!
I HAVE TO STEP IN!

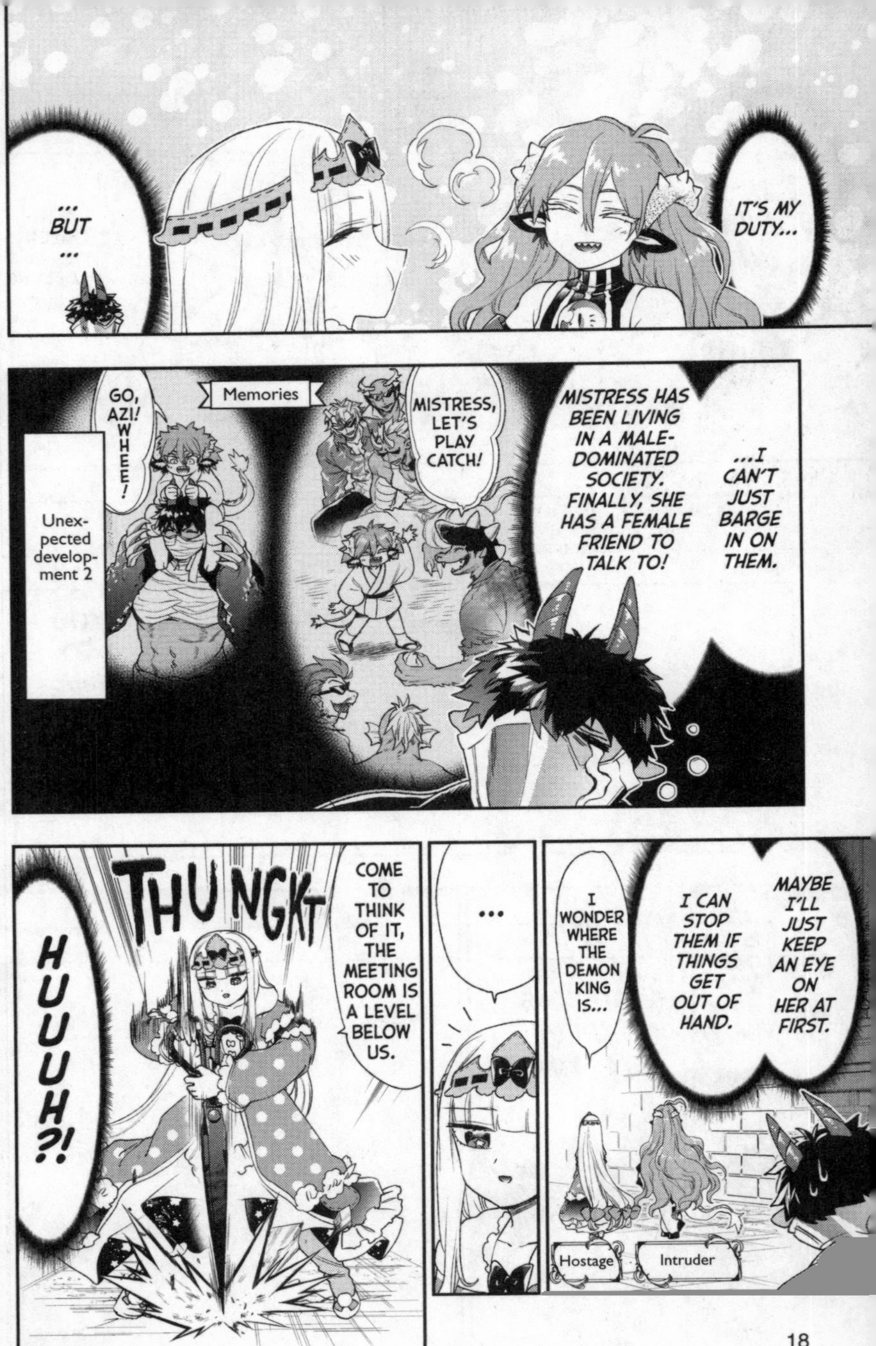
IT'S MY DUTY...
... BUT ...
...I CAN'T JUST BARGE IN ON THEM.
MISTRESS HAS BEEN LIVING IN A MALE-DOMINATED SOCIETY. FINALLY, SHE HAS A FEMALE FRIEND TO TALK TO!
MISTRESS, LET'S PLAY CATCH!
Memories
GO, AZI!
WHEEE!
Unexpected development 2
MAYBE I'LL JUST KEEP AN EYE ON HER AT FIRST.
I CAN STOP THEM IF THINGS GET OUT OF HAND.
I WONDER WHERE THE DEMON KING IS...
Intruder
Hostage
...
COME TO THINK OF IT, THE MEETING ROOM IS A LEVEL BELOW US.
THUNGKT
HUUUUH?!

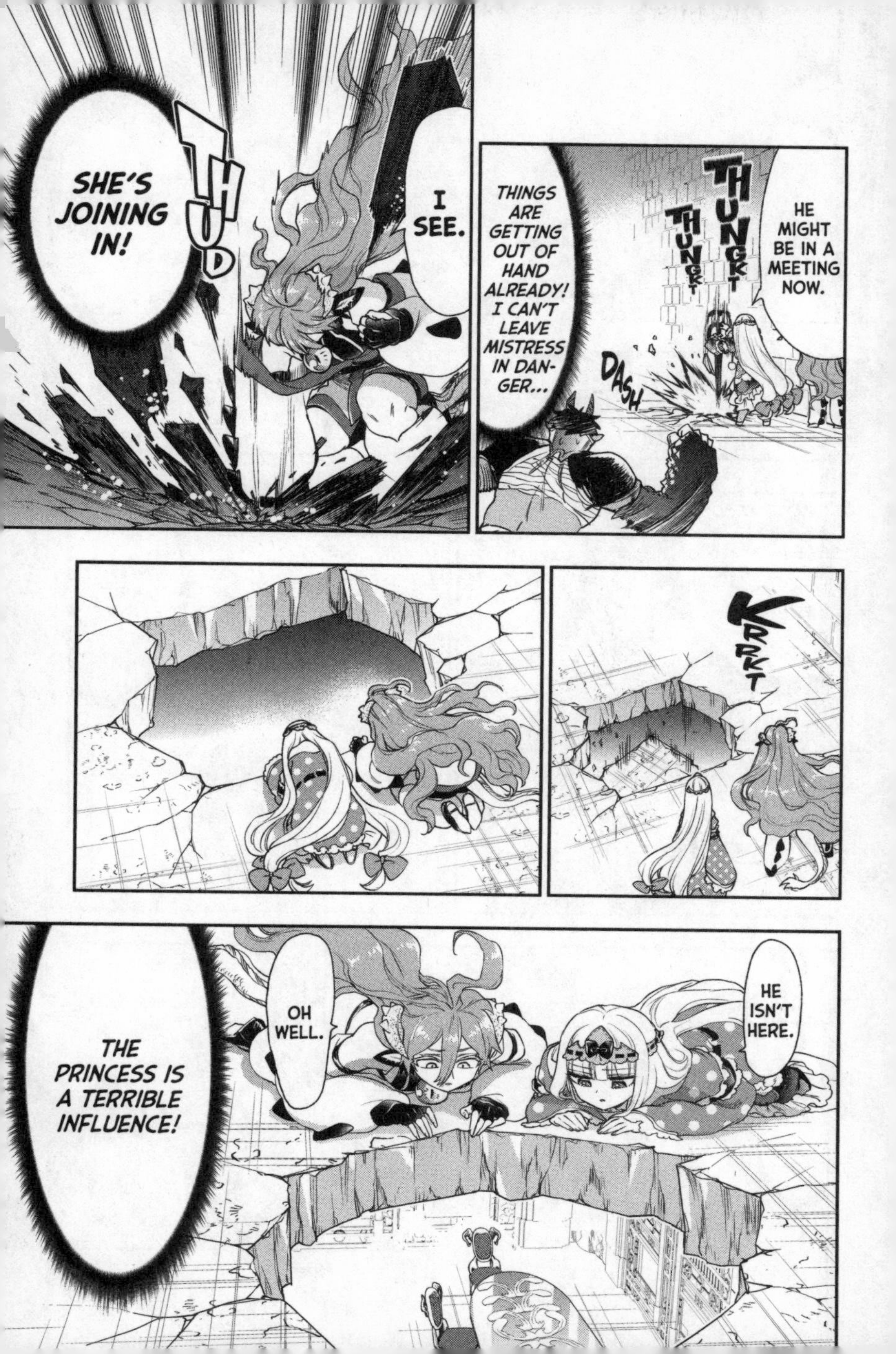

HE MIGHT BE IN A MEETING NOW.
THUNGKT
THUNGKT
THINGS ARE GETTING OUT OF HAND ALREADY! I CAN'T LEAVE MISTRESS IN DAN-GER...
DASH
I SEE.
THUD
SHE'S JOINING IN!
KRRKT
HE ISN'T HERE.
OH WELL.
THE PRINCESS IS A TERRIBLE INFLUENCE!

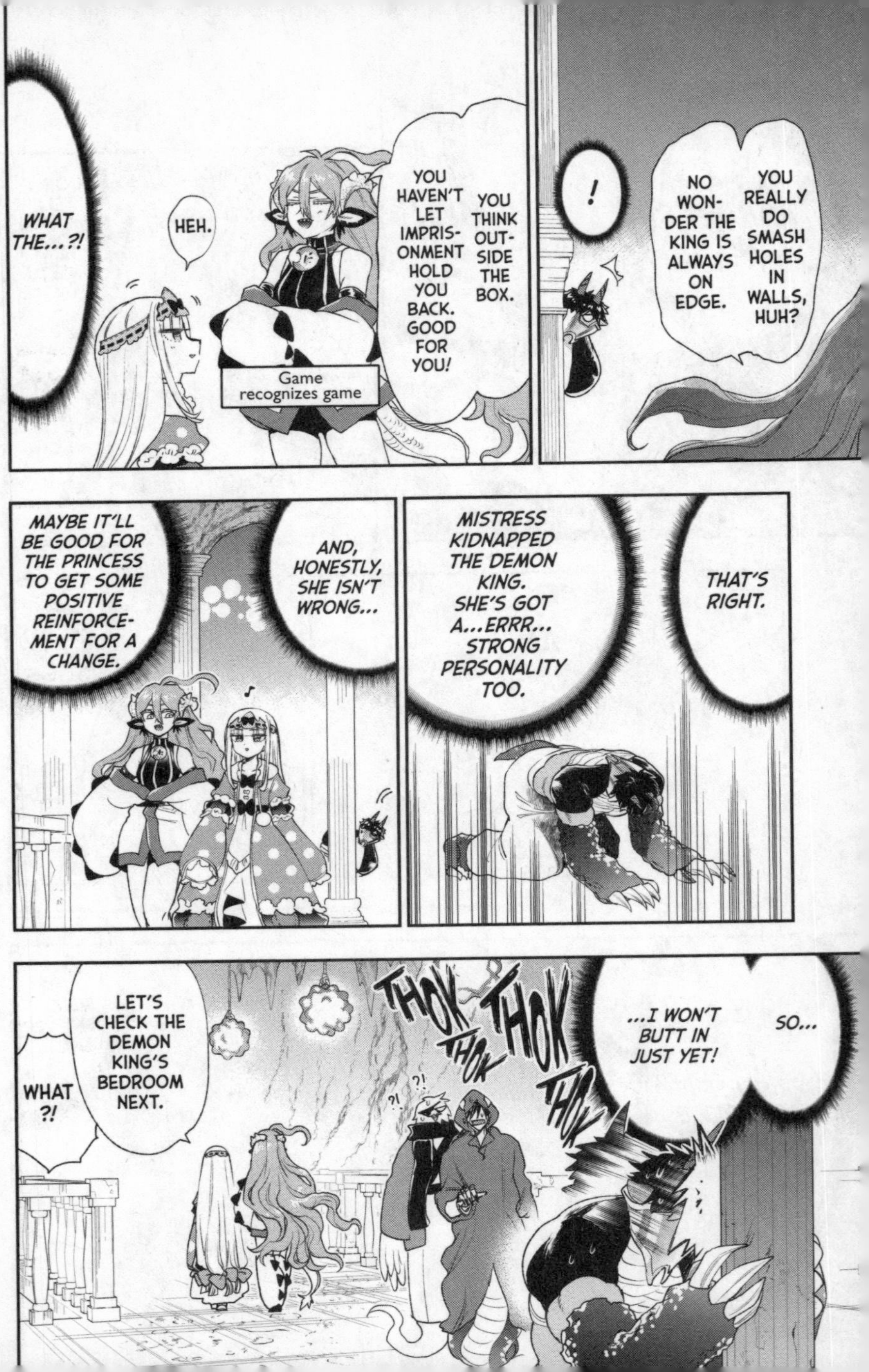
YOU REALLY DO SMASH HOLES IN WALLS, HUH?
NO WON-DER THE KING IS ALWAYS ON EDGE.
!
YOU THINK OUT-SIDE THE BOX.
YOU HAVEN'T LET IMPRIS-ONMENT HOLD YOU BACK. GOOD FOR YOU!
HEH.
Game recognizes game
WHAT THE...?!
THAT'S RIGHT.
MISTRESS KIDNAPPED THE DEMON KING. SHE'S GOT A...ERRR... STRONG PERSONALITY TOO.
AND, HONESTLY, SHE ISN'T WRONG...
MAYBE IT'LL BE GOOD FOR THE PRINCESS TO GET SOME POSITIVE REINFORCE-MENT FOR A CHANGE.
SO...
...I WON'T BUTT IN JUST YET!
THOK THOK THOK THOK
LET'S CHECK THE DEMON KING'S BEDROOM NEXT.
WHAT ?!

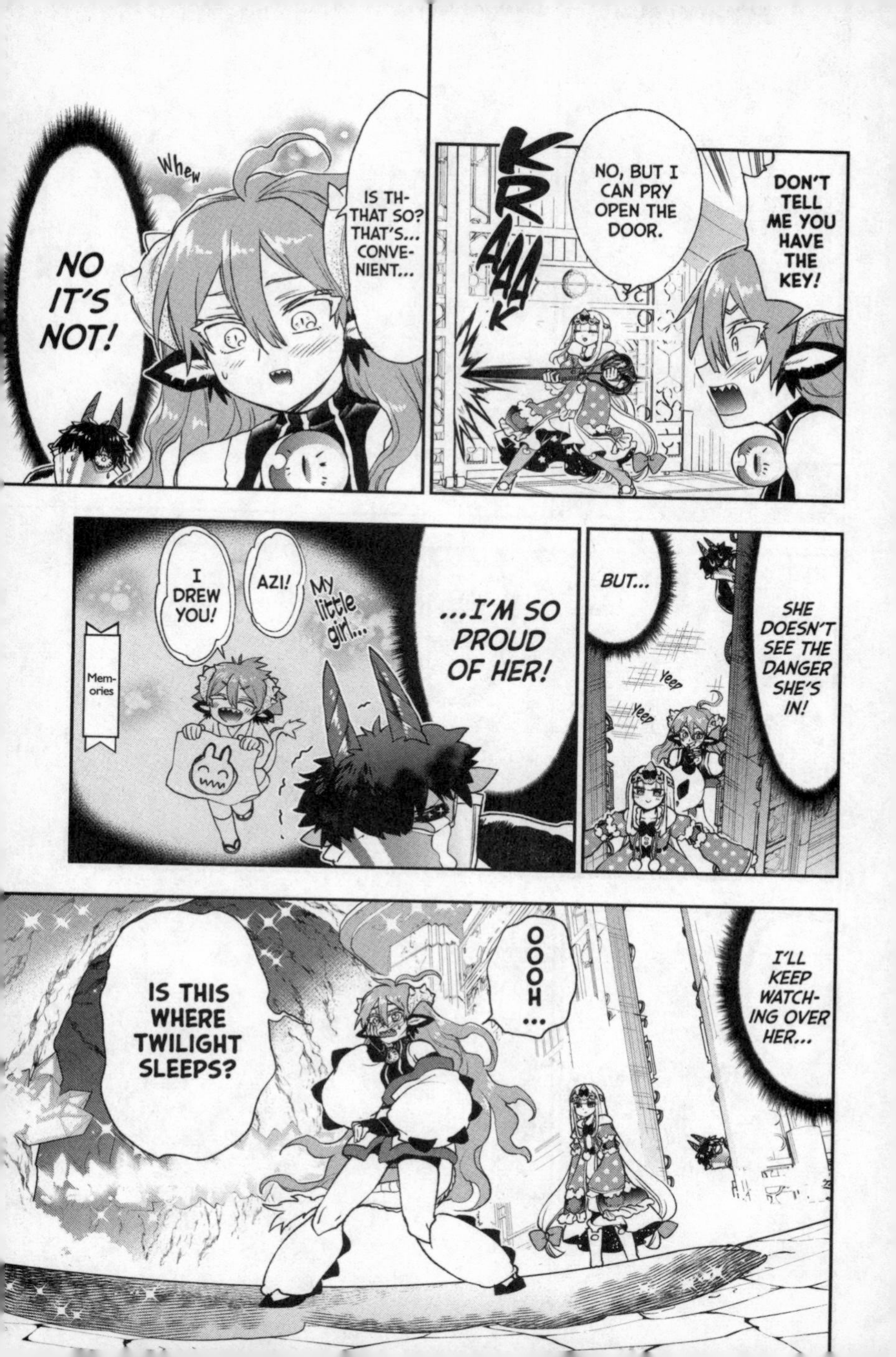
DON'T TELL ME YOU HAVE THE KEY!
NO, BUT I CAN PRY OPEN THE DOOR.
KRAAAK
IS TH-THAT SO? THAT'S... CONVE-NIENT...
Whew
NO IT'S NOT!
SHE DOESN'T SEE THE DANGER SHE'S IN!
BUT...
Yeep
Yeep
...I'M SO PROUD OF HER!
My little girl...
AZI!
I DREW YOU!
Mem-ories
I'LL KEEP WATCH-ING OVER HER...
OOOH...
IS THIS WHERE TWILIGHT SLEEPS?

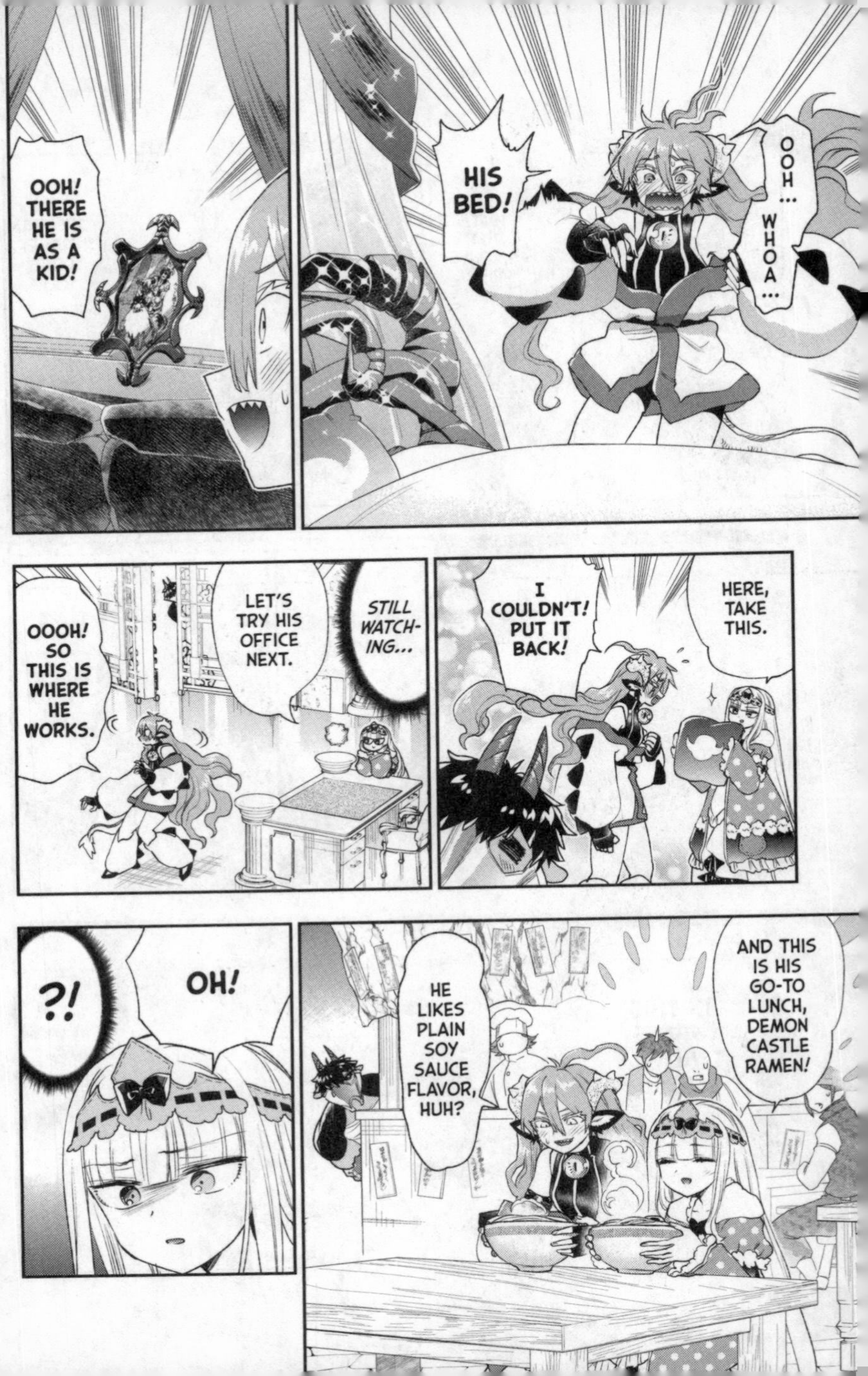
OOH... WHOA...
HIS BED!
OOH! THERE HE IS AS A KID!
HERE, TAKE THIS.
I COULDN'T! PUT IT BACK!
STILL WATCHING...
LET'S TRY HIS OFFICE NEXT.
OOOH! SO THIS IS WHERE HE WORKS.
AND THIS IS HIS GO-TO LUNCH, DEMON CASTLE RAMEN!
HE LIKES PLAIN SOY SAUCE FLAVOR, HUH?
OH!
?!

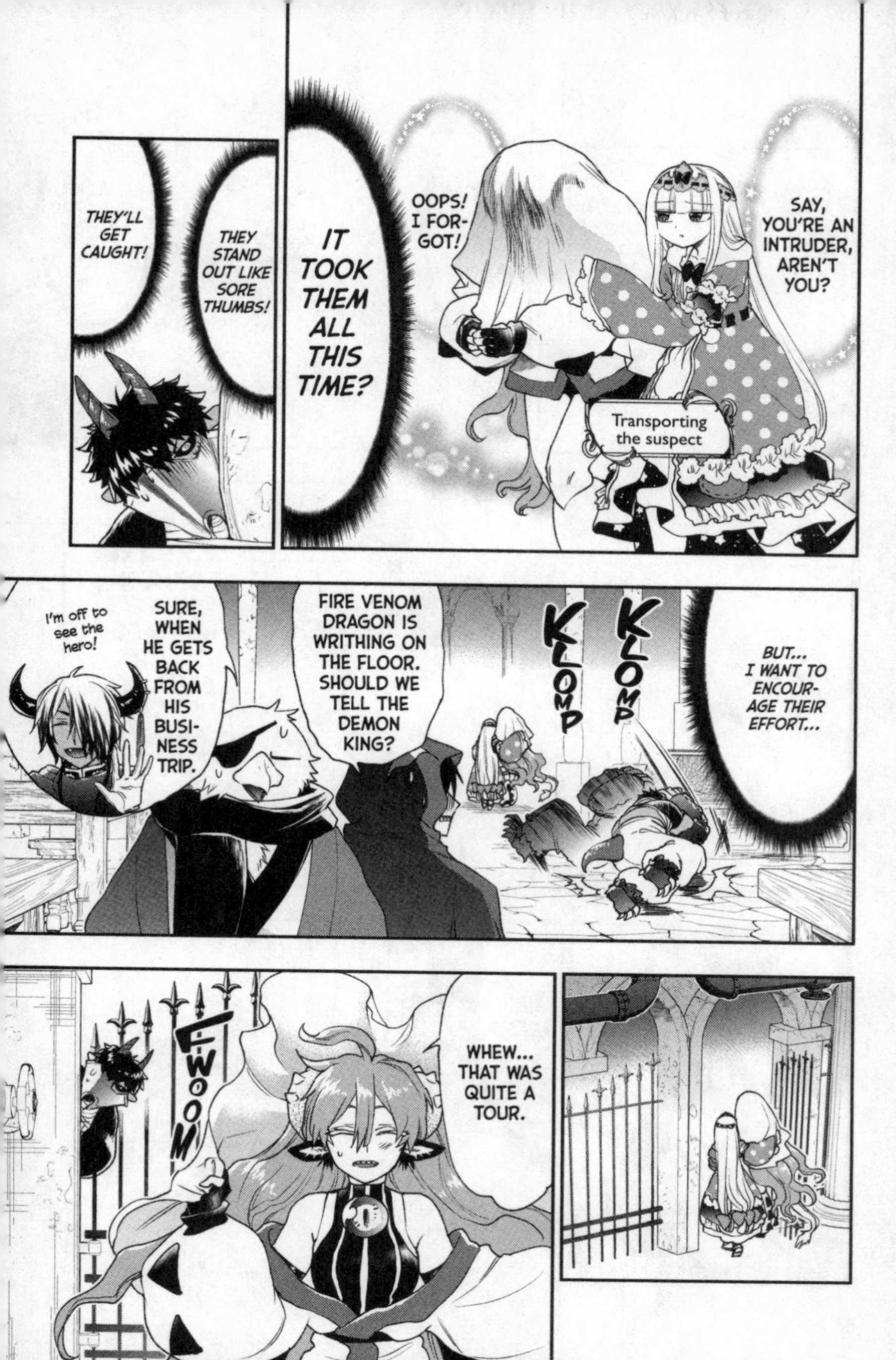
SAY, YOU'RE AN INTRUDER, AREN'T YOU?
OOPS! I FOR-GOT!
Transporting the suspect
IT TOOK THEM ALL THIS TIME?
THEY STAND OUT LIKE SORE THUMBS!
THEY'LL GET CAUGHT!
BUT... I WANT TO ENCOUR-AGE THEIR EFFORT...
KLOMP
KLOMP
FIRE VENOM DRAGON IS WRITHING ON THE FLOOR. SHOULD WE TELL THE DEMON KING?
SURE, WHEN HE GETS BACK FROM HIS BUSI-NESS TRIP.
I'm off to see the hero!
WHEW... THAT WAS QUITE A TOUR.
FWOOM

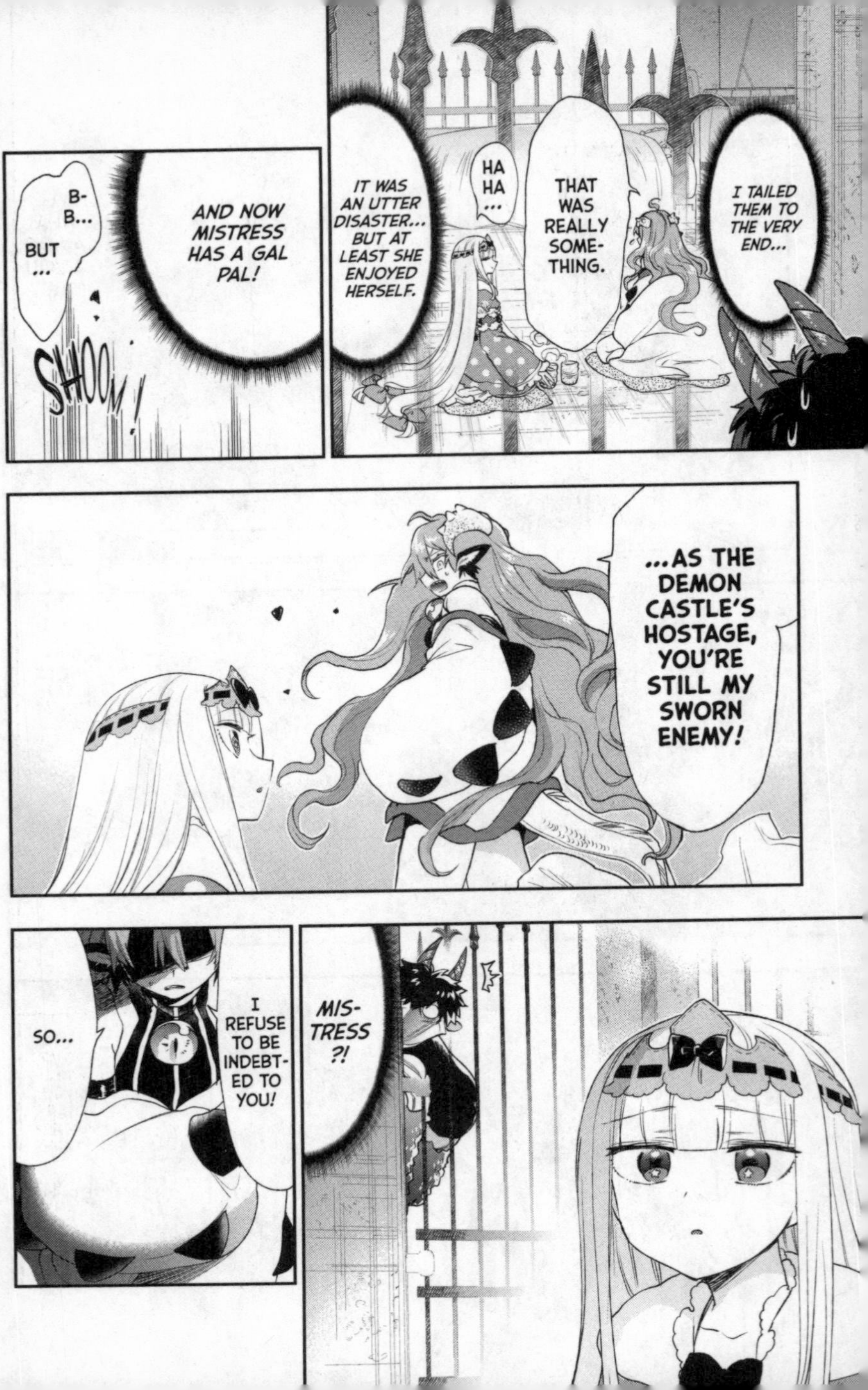
I TAILED THEM TO THE VERY END...
THAT WAS REALLY SOME-THING.
HA HA ...
IT WAS AN UTTER DISASTER... BUT AT LEAST SHE ENJOYED HERSELF.
AND NOW MISTRESS HAS A GAL PAL!
B- B... BUT ...
SHOOM!
...AS THE DEMON CASTLE'S HOSTAGE, YOU'RE STILL MY SWORN ENEMY!
MIS-TRESS ?!
I REFUSE TO BE INDEBT-ED TO YOU!
SO...

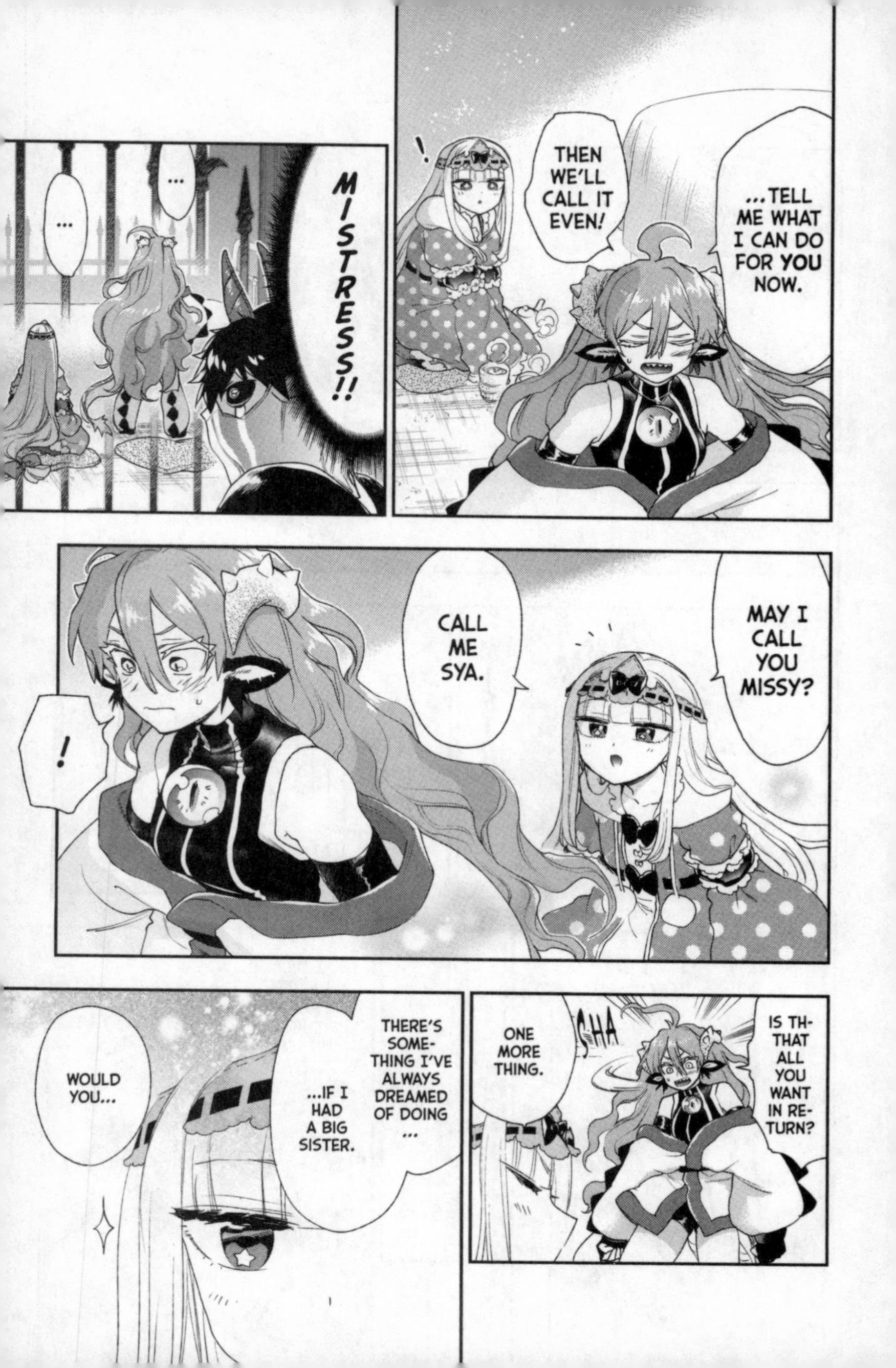

...TELL ME WHAT I CAN DO FOR YOU NOW.
THEN WE'LL CALL IT EVEN!
!
MISTRESS!!
...
...
MAY I CALL YOU MISSY?
CALL ME SYA.
!
IS TH-THAT ALL YOU WANT IN RE-TURN?
SHA
ONE MORE THING.
THERE'S SOME-THING I'VE ALWAYS DREAMED OF DOING ...
...IF I HAD A BIG SISTER.
WOULD YOU...

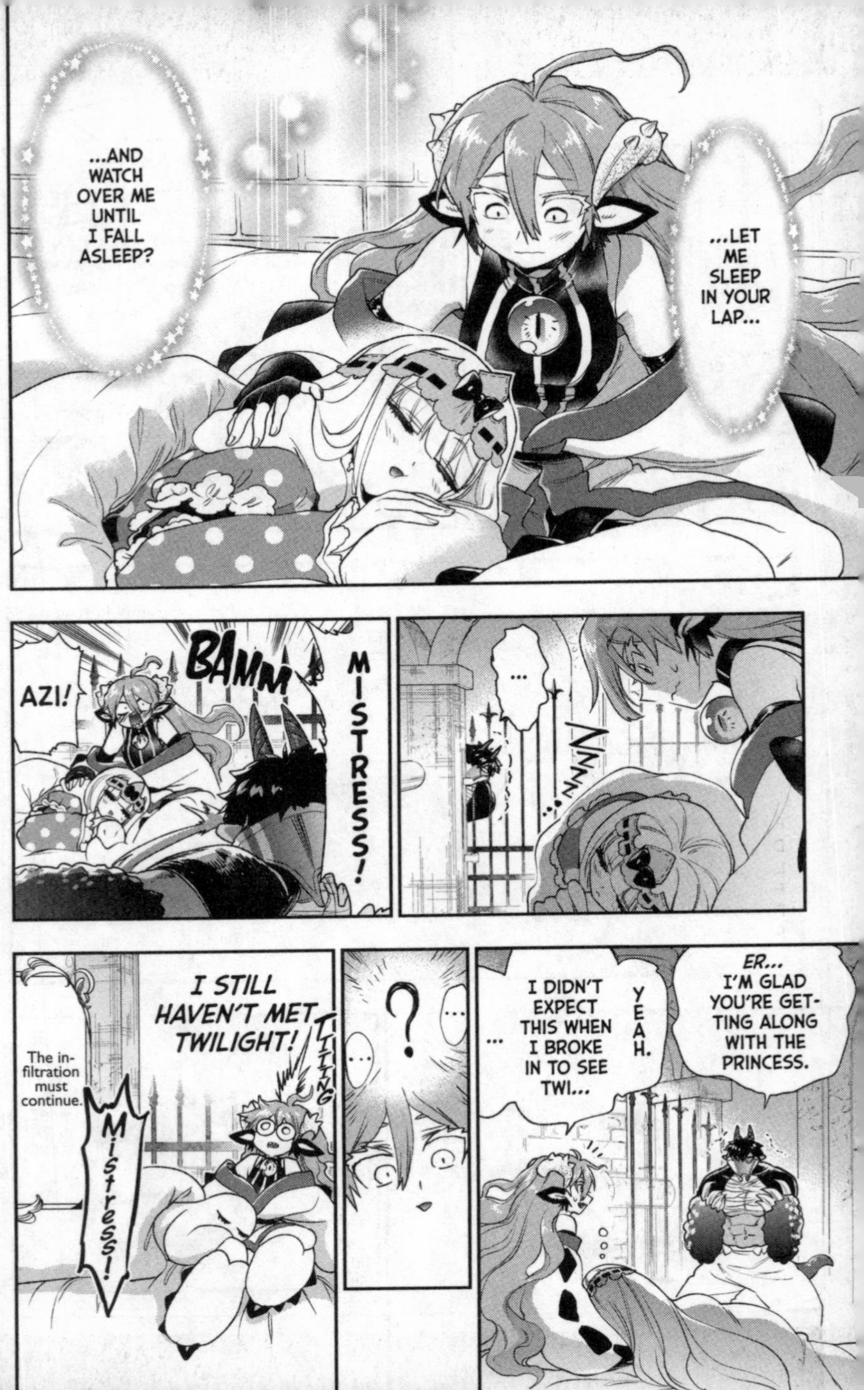
...LET ME SLEEP IN YOUR LAP...
...AND WATCH OVER ME UNTIL I FALL ASLEEP?
...
ZNNN...
MISTRESS!
BAMM
AZI!
ER... I'M GLAD YOU'RE GETTING ALONG WITH THE PRINCESS.
YEAH.
I DIDN'T EXPECT THIS WHEN I BROKE IN TO SEE TWI...
...
...
?
...
I STILL HAVEN'T MET TWILIGHT!
TIIING
Mistress!
The infiltration must continue.

2
La la la

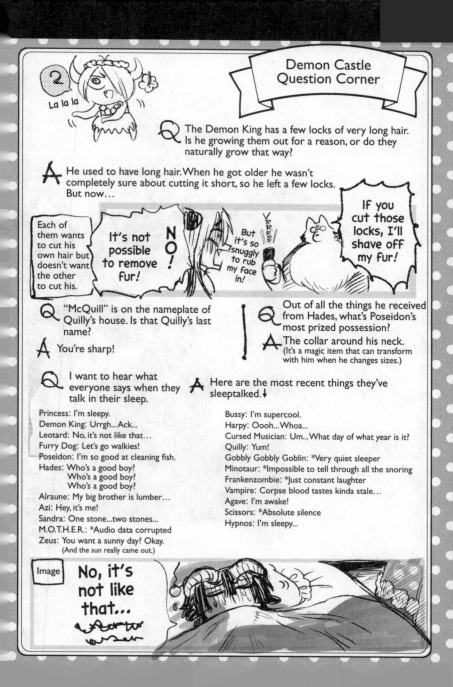

Demon Castle Question Corner

Q The Demon King has a few locks of very long hair. Is he growing them out for a reason, or do they naturally grow that way?

A He used to have long hair. When he got older he wasn't completely sure about cutting it short, so he left a few locks. But now…

If you cut those locks, I'll shave off my fur!
VRRRR
But it's so snuggly to rub my face in!
NO!
It's not possible to remove fur!
Each of them wants to cut his own hair but doesn't want the other to cut his.

Q "McQuill" is on the nameplate of Quilly's house. Is that Quilly's last name?

A You're sharp!

Q Out of all the things he received from Hades, what's Poseidon's most prized possession?

A The collar around his neck.
(It's a magic item that can transform with him when he changes sizes.)

Q I want to hear what everyone says when they talk in their sleep.

A Here are the most recent things they've sleeptalked.↓

Princess: I'm sleepy.
Demon King: Urrgh...Ack...
Leotard: No, it's not like that…
Furry Dog: Let's go walkies!
Poseidon: I'm so good at cleaning fish.
Hades: Who's a good boy?
Who's a good boy?
Who's a good boy?
Alraune: My big brother is lumber…
Azi: Hey, it's me!
Sandra: One stone...two stones...
M.O.T.H.E.R.: *Audio data corrupted
Zeus: You want a sunny day? Okay.
(And the sun really came out.)

Bussy: I'm supercool.
Harpy: Oooh...Whoa...
Cursed Musician: Um...What day of what year is it?
Quilly: Yum!
Gobbly Gobbly Goblin: *Very quiet sleeper
Minotaur: *Impossible to tell through all the snoring
Frankenzombie: *Just constant laughter
Vampire: Corpse blood tastes kinda stale…
Agave: I'm awake!
Scissors: *Absolute silence
Hypnos: I'm sleepy...

Image
No, it's not like that...

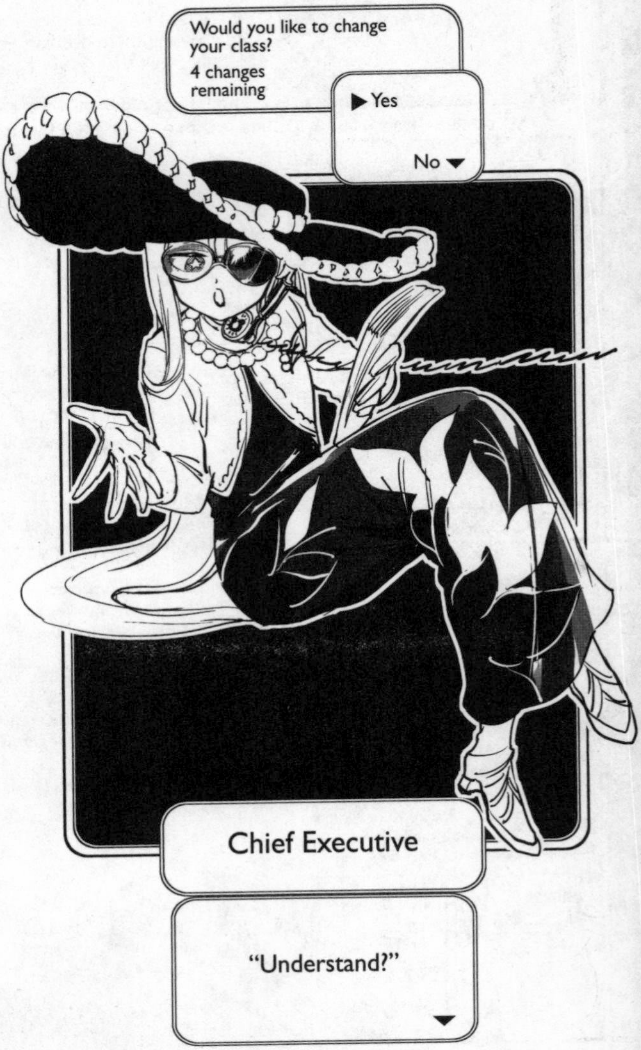
Would you like to change your class?
4 changes remaining
▶ Yes
No
Chief Executive
"Understand?"

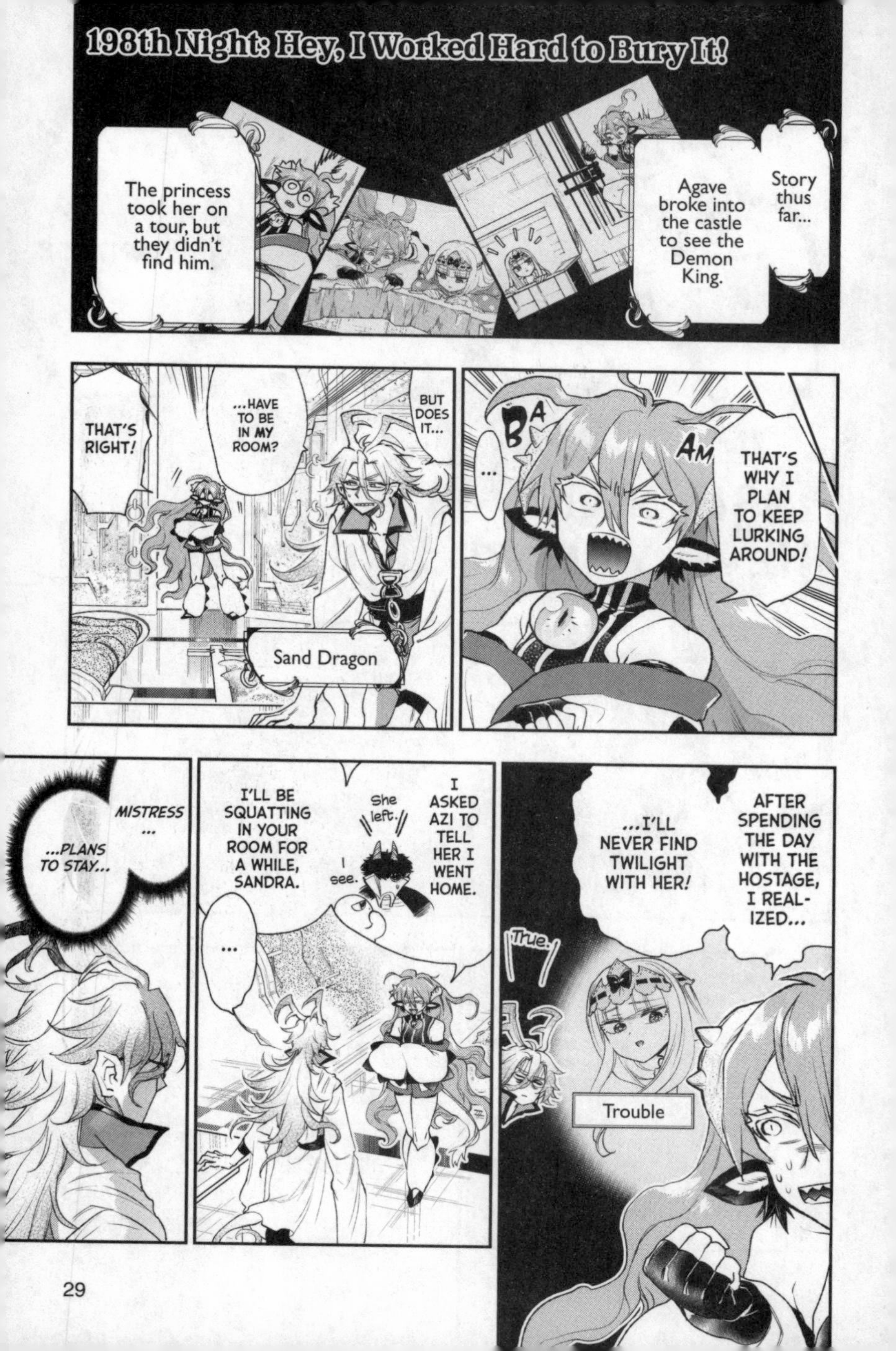
198th Night: Hey, I Worked Hard to Bury It!
Story thus far...
Agave broke into the castle to see the Demon King.
The princess took her on a tour, but they didn't find him.
BAAM
THAT'S WHY I PLAN TO KEEP LURKING AROUND!
...
BUT DOES IT...
...HAVE TO BE IN MY ROOM?
THAT'S RIGHT!
Sand Dragon
AFTER SPENDING THE DAY WITH THE HOSTAGE, I REAL-IZED...
...I'LL NEVER FIND TWILIGHT WITH HER!
True.
Trouble
I ASKED AZI TO TELL HER I WENT HOME.
She left.
I see.
I'LL BE SQUATTING IN YOUR ROOM FOR A WHILE, SANDRA.
...
MISTRESS ...
...PLANS TO STAY...

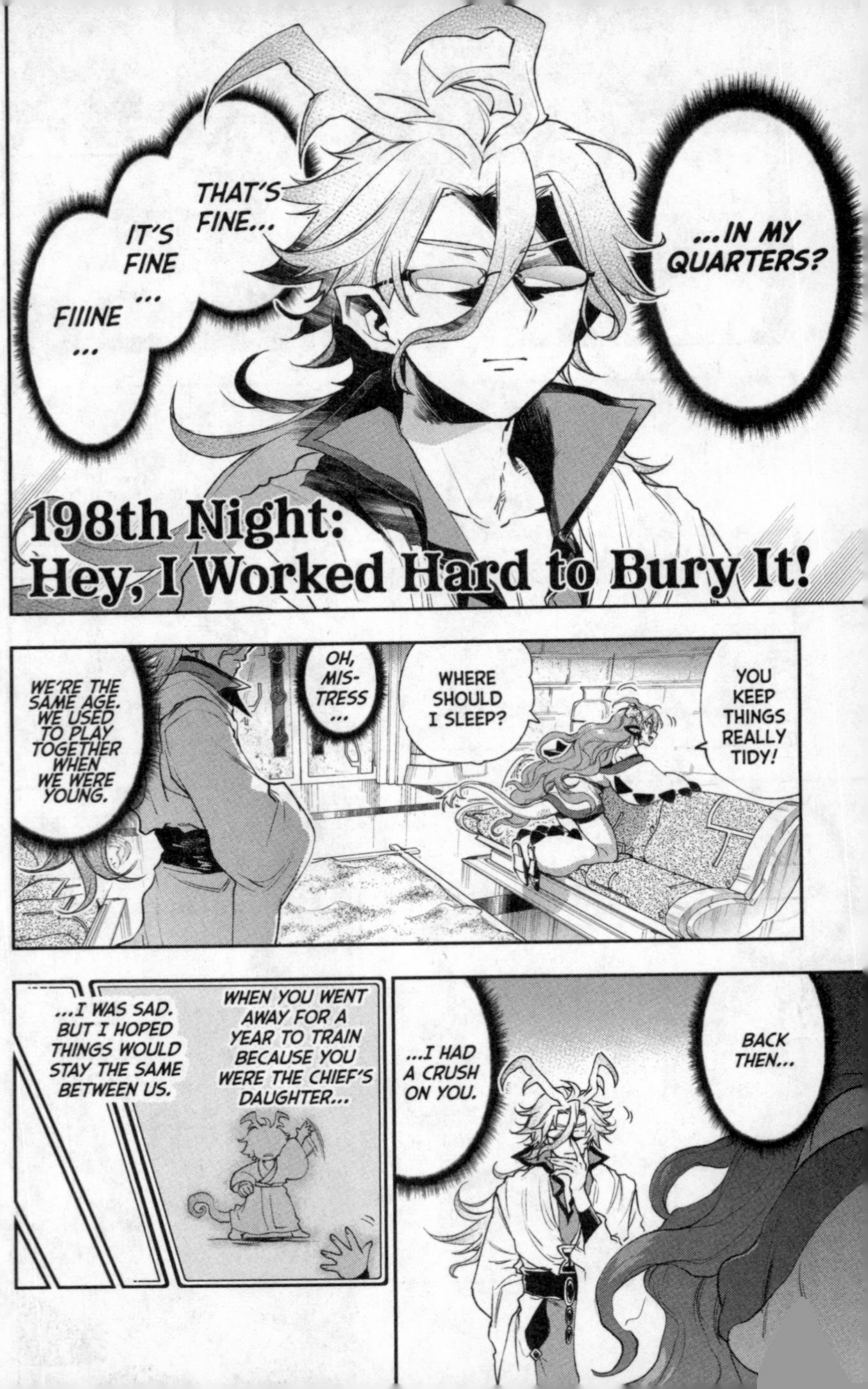
...IN MY QUARTERS?
THAT'S FINE...
IT'S FINE...
FIIINE...
198th Night: Hey, I Worked Hard to Bury It!
YOU KEEP THINGS REALLY TIDY!
WHERE SHOULD I SLEEP?
OH, MISTRESS...
WE'RE THE SAME AGE. WE USED TO PLAY TOGETHER WHEN WE WERE YOUNG.
BACK THEN...
...I HAD A CRUSH ON YOU.
WHEN YOU WENT AWAY FOR A YEAR TO TRAIN BECAUSE YOU WERE THE CHIEF'S DAUGHTER...
...I WAS SAD. BUT I HOPED THINGS WOULD STAY THE SAME BETWEEN US.

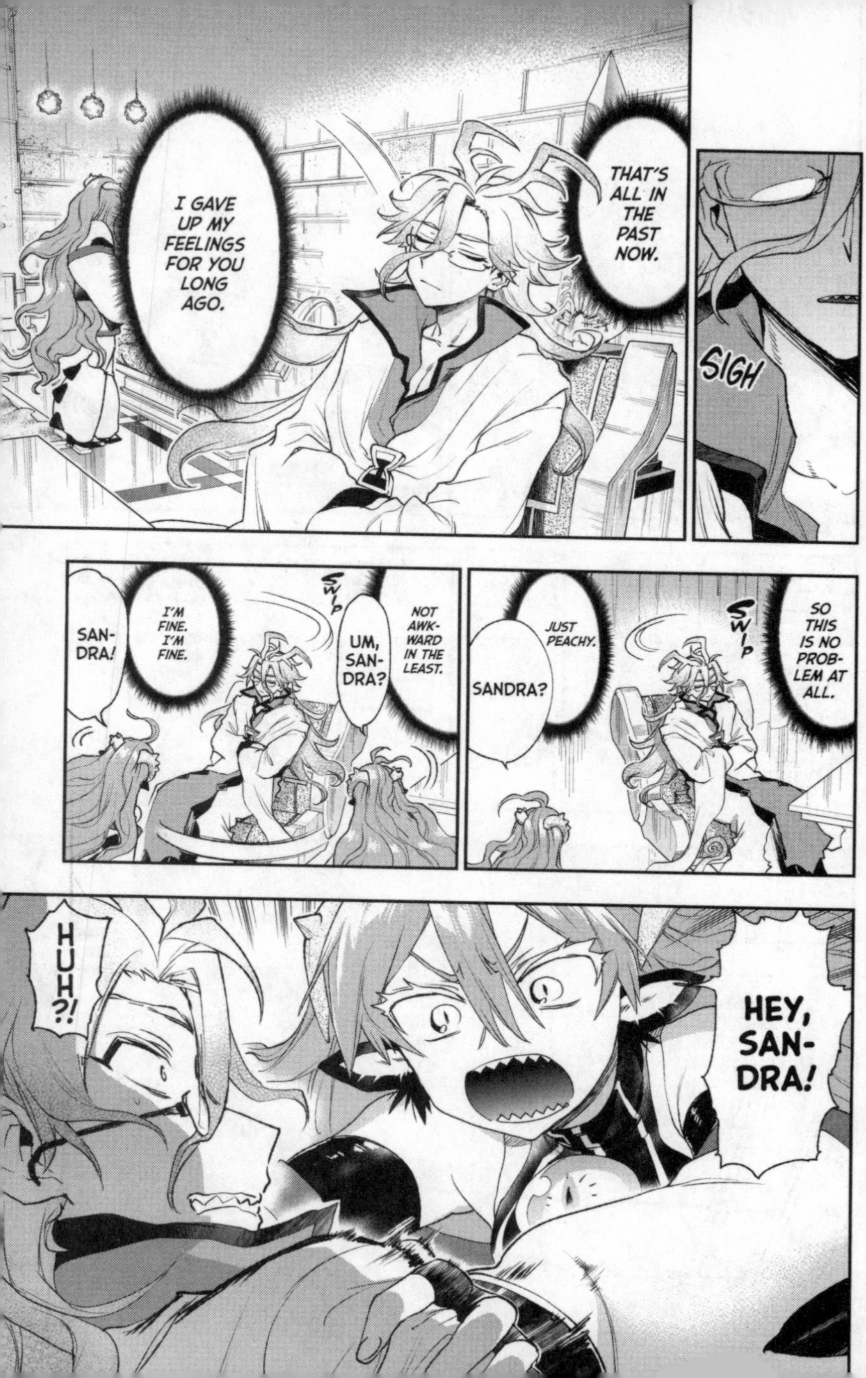
SIGH
THAT'S ALL IN THE PAST NOW.
I GAVE UP MY FEELINGS FOR YOU LONG AGO.
SWIP
SO THIS IS NO PROBLEM AT ALL.
JUST PEACHY.
SANDRA?
NOT AWKWARD IN THE LEAST.
SWIP
UM, SANDRA?
I'M FINE. I'M FINE.
SANDRA!
HEY, SANDRA!
HUH?!

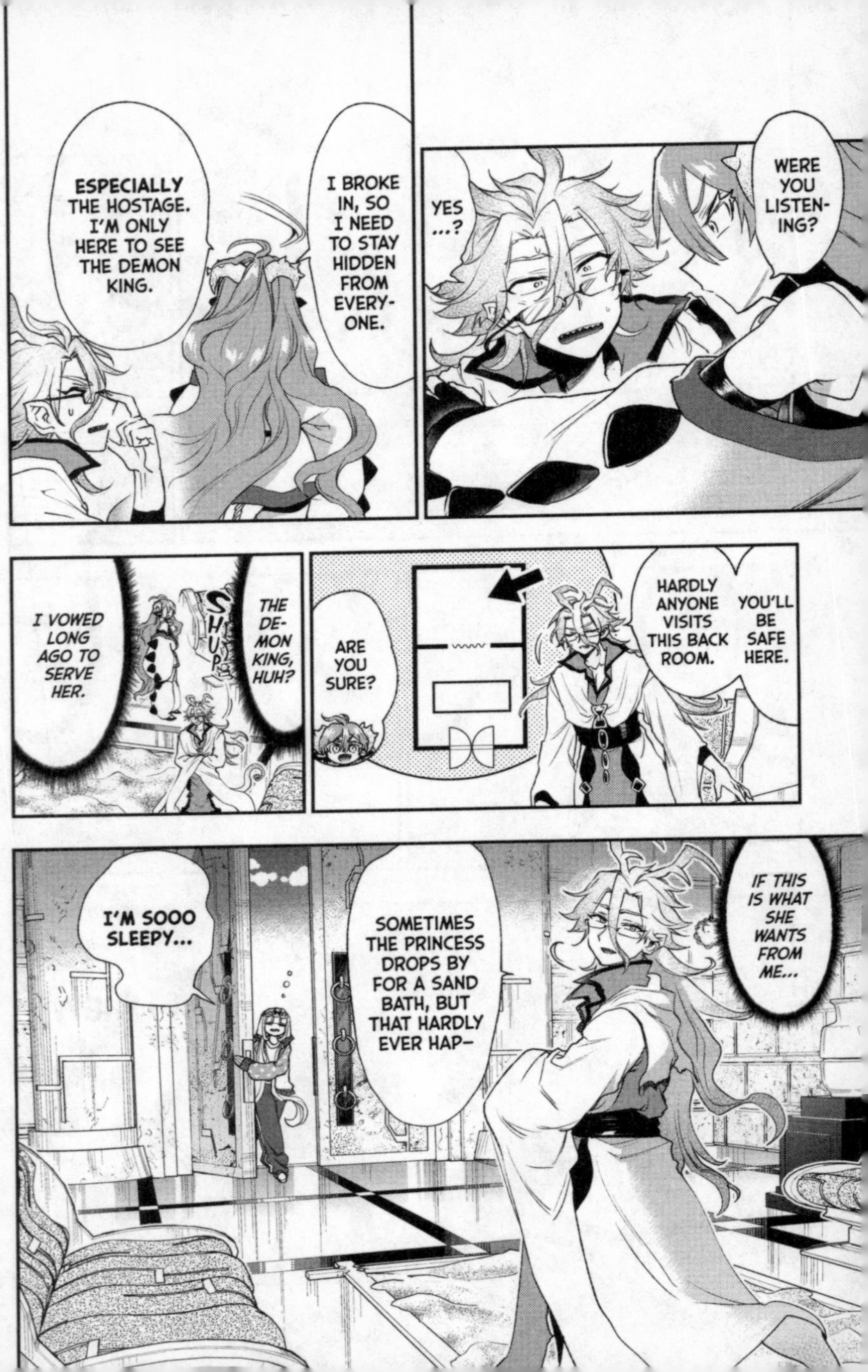
WERE YOU LISTEN-ING?
YES ...?
I BROKE IN, SO I NEED TO STAY HIDDEN FROM EVERY-ONE.
ESPECIALLY THE HOSTAGE. I'M ONLY HERE TO SEE THE DEMON KING.
YOU'LL BE SAFE HERE.
HARDLY ANYONE VISITS THIS BACK ROOM.
ARE YOU SURE?
THE DE-MON KING, HUH?
SHUP
I VOWED LONG AGO TO SERVE HER.
IF THIS IS WHAT SHE WANTS FROM ME...
SOMETIMES THE PRINCESS DROPS BY FOR A SAND BATH, BUT THAT HARDLY EVER HAP–
I'M SOOO SLEEPY...

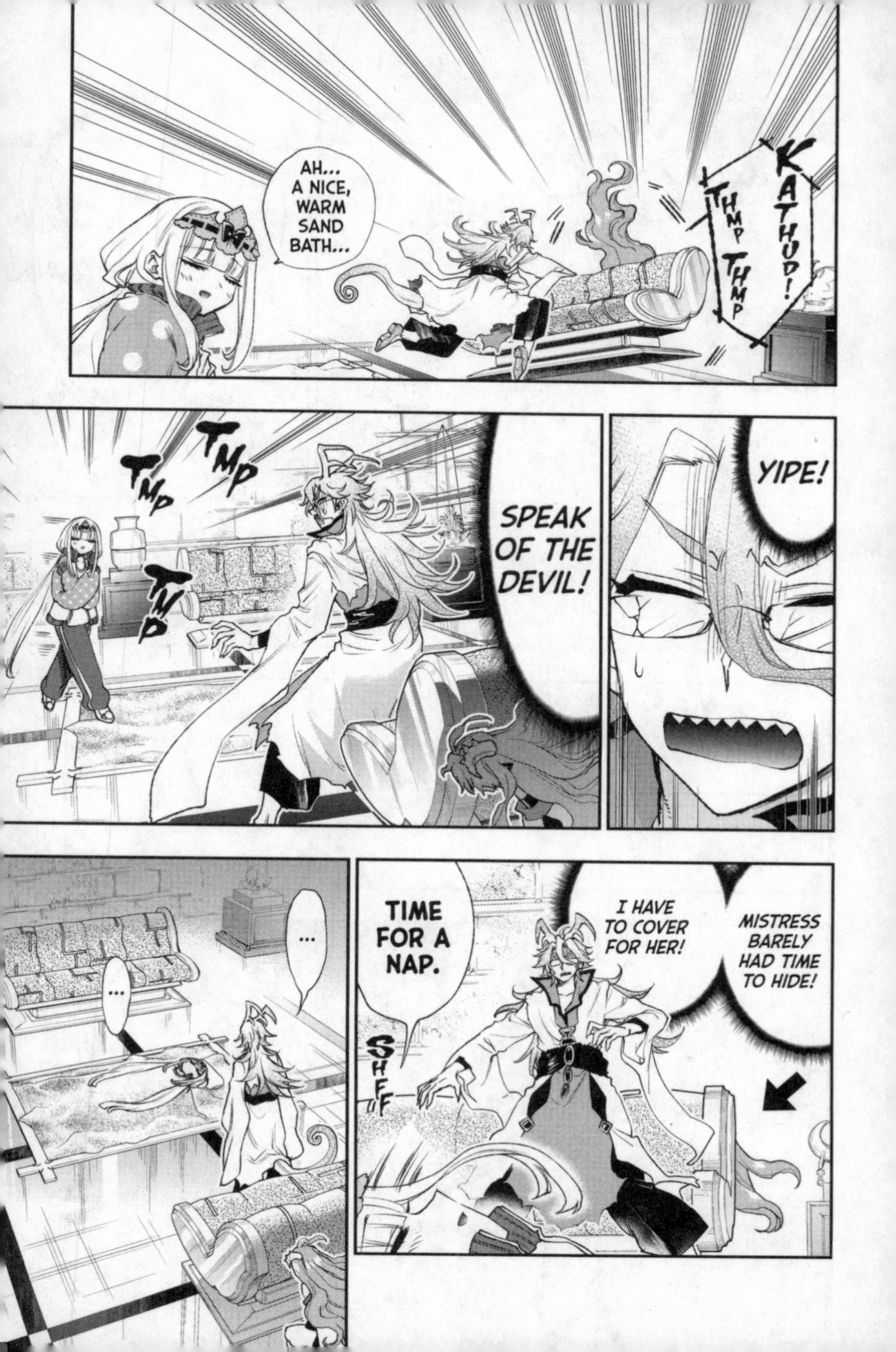
KATHUD!
THMP THMP
AH... A NICE, WARM SAND BATH...
YIPE!
SPEAK OF THE DEVIL!
TMP TMP
TMP
MISTRESS BARELY HAD TIME TO HIDE!
I HAVE TO COVER FOR HER!
TIME FOR A NAP.
SHFF
...
...

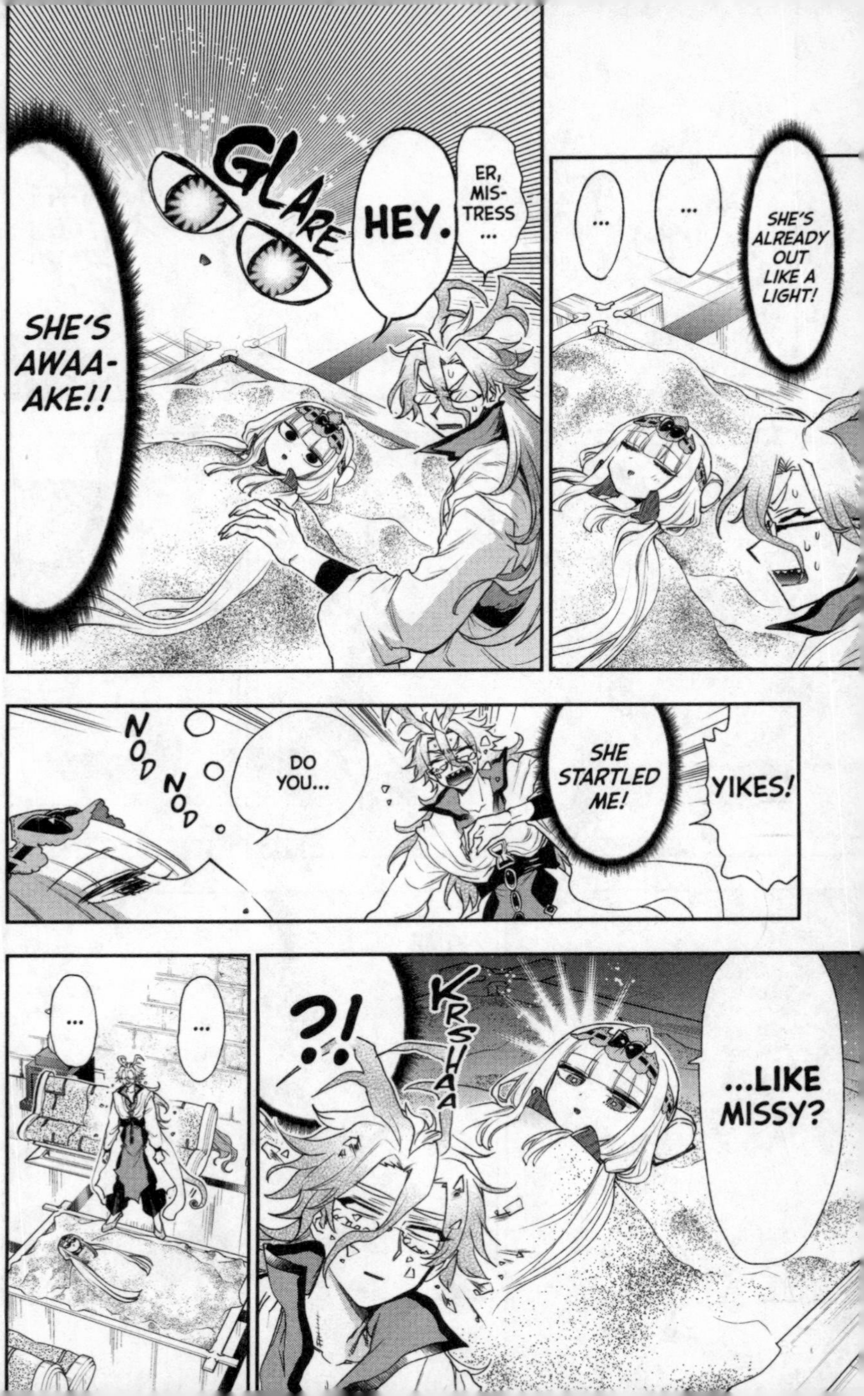
SHE'S ALREADY OUT LIKE A LIGHT!
...
...
ER, MISTRESS...
HEY.
GLARE
SHE'S AWAAA-AKE!!
YIKES!
SHE STARTLED ME!
DO YOU...
NOD NOD
...LIKE MISSY?
KRSHAA
?!
...
...

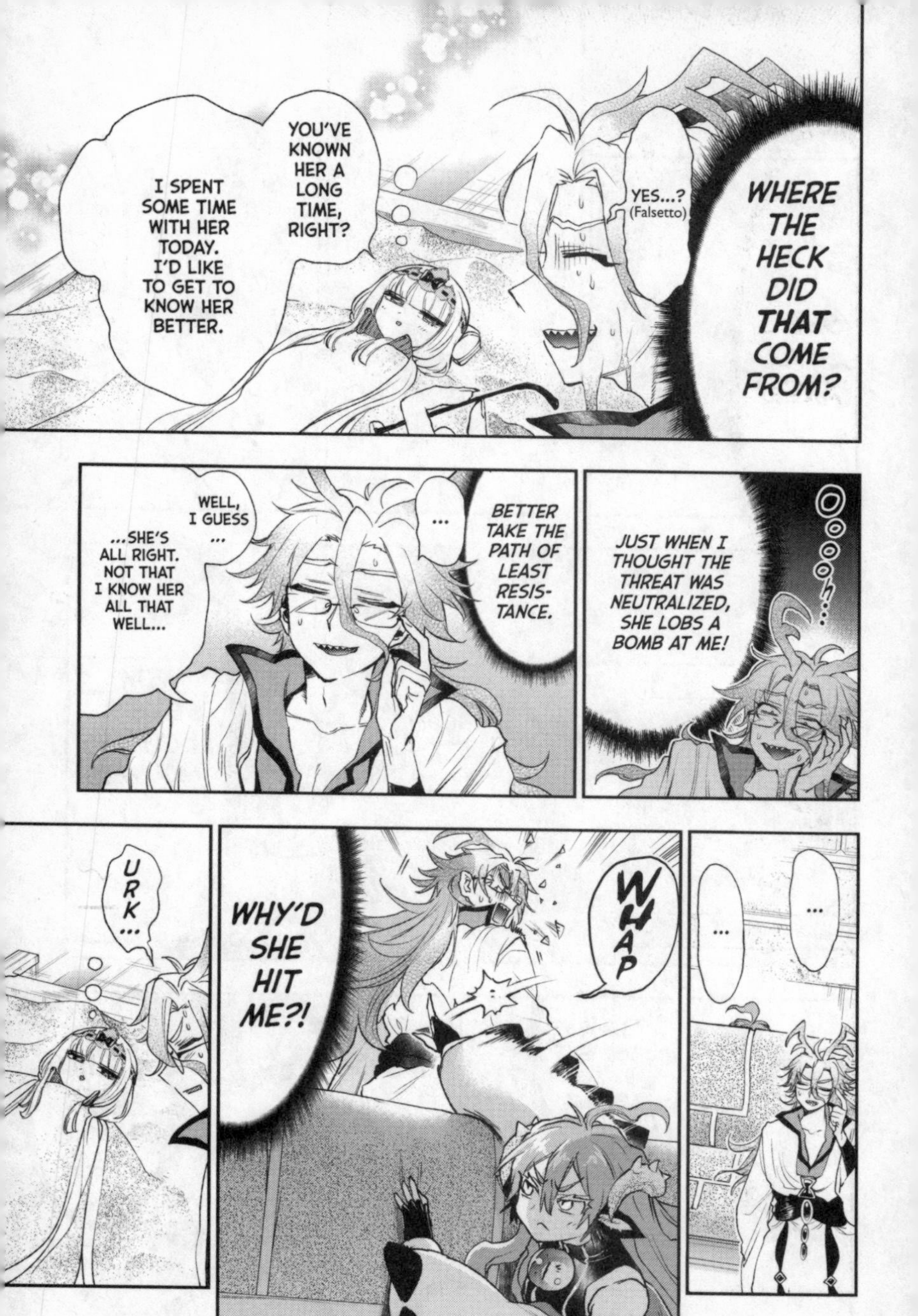
WHERE THE HECK DID THAT COME FROM?
YES...? (Falsetto)
YOU'VE KNOWN HER A LONG TIME, RIGHT?
I SPENT SOME TIME WITH HER TODAY. I'D LIKE TO GET TO KNOW HER BETTER.
Ooooh...
JUST WHEN I THOUGHT THE THREAT WAS NEUTRALIZED, SHE LOBS A BOMB AT ME!
BETTER TAKE THE PATH OF LEAST RESIS-TANCE.
...
WELL, I GUESS ...
...SHE'S ALL RIGHT. NOT THAT I KNOW HER ALL THAT WELL...
...
...
WHAP
WHY'D SHE HIT ME?!
URK...

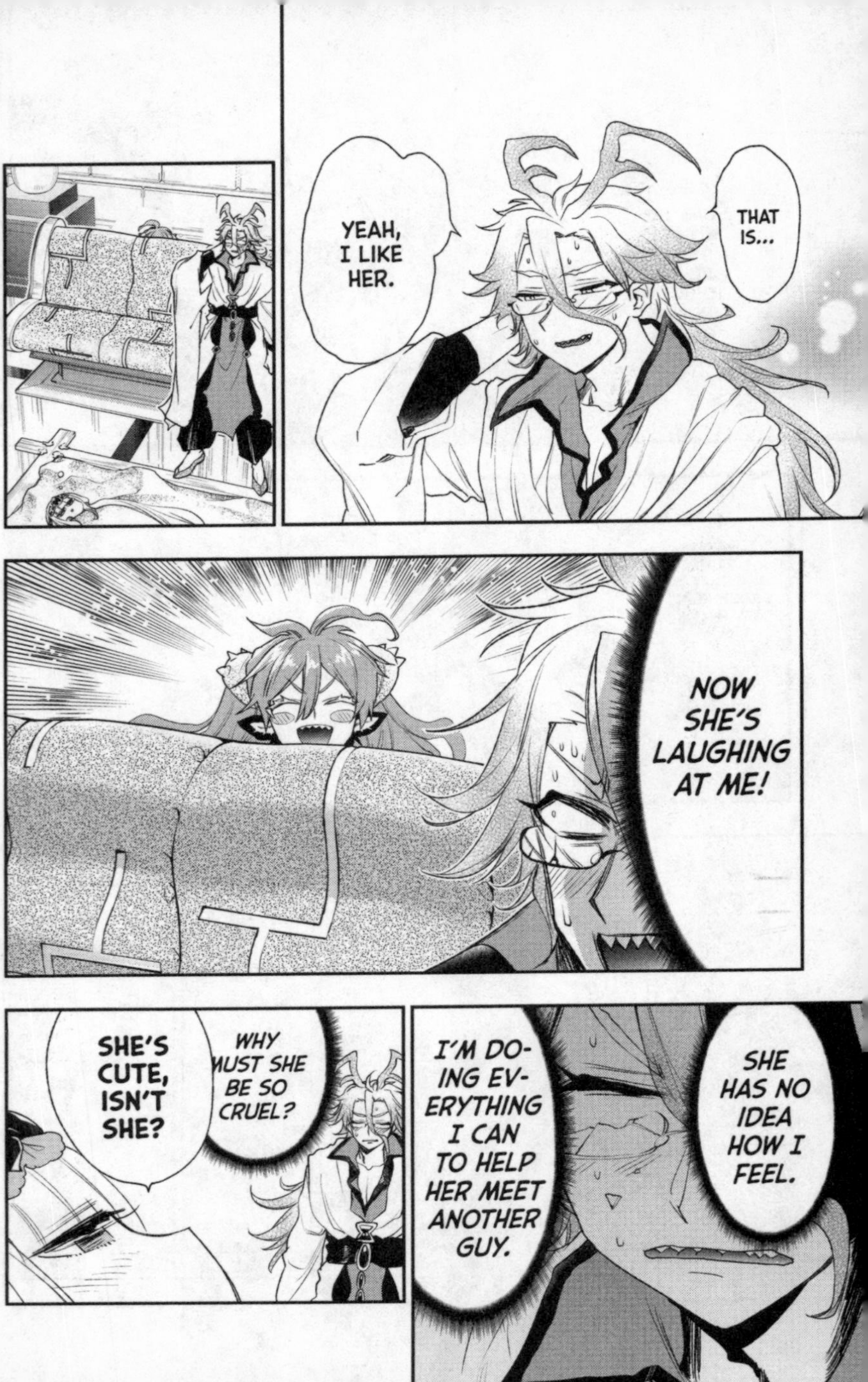
THAT IS...
YEAH, I LIKE HER.
NOW SHE'S LAUGHING AT ME!
SHE HAS NO IDEA HOW I FEEL.
I'M DOING EVERYTHING I CAN TO HELP HER MEET ANOTHER GUY.
WHY MUST SHE BE SO CRUEL?
SHE'S CUTE, ISN'T SHE?

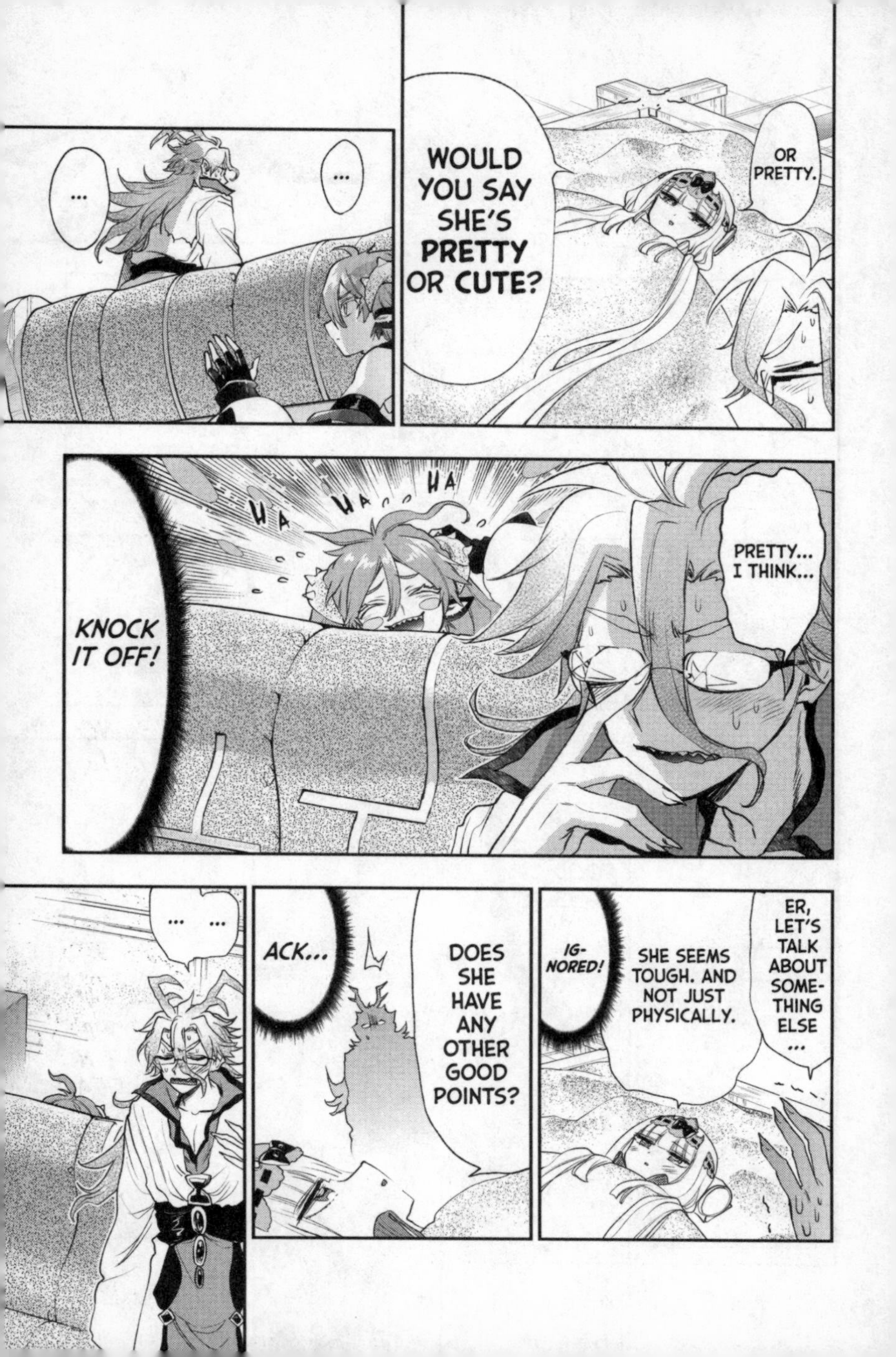
WOULD YOU SAY SHE'S PRETTY OR CUTE?
OR PRETTY.
...
...
PRETTY... I THINK...
HA HA HA HA
KNOCK IT OFF!
ER, LET'S TALK ABOUT SOME-THING ELSE...
SHE SEEMS TOUGH. AND NOT JUST PHYSICALLY.
IG-NORED!
DOES SHE HAVE ANY OTHER GOOD POINTS?
ACK...
... ...

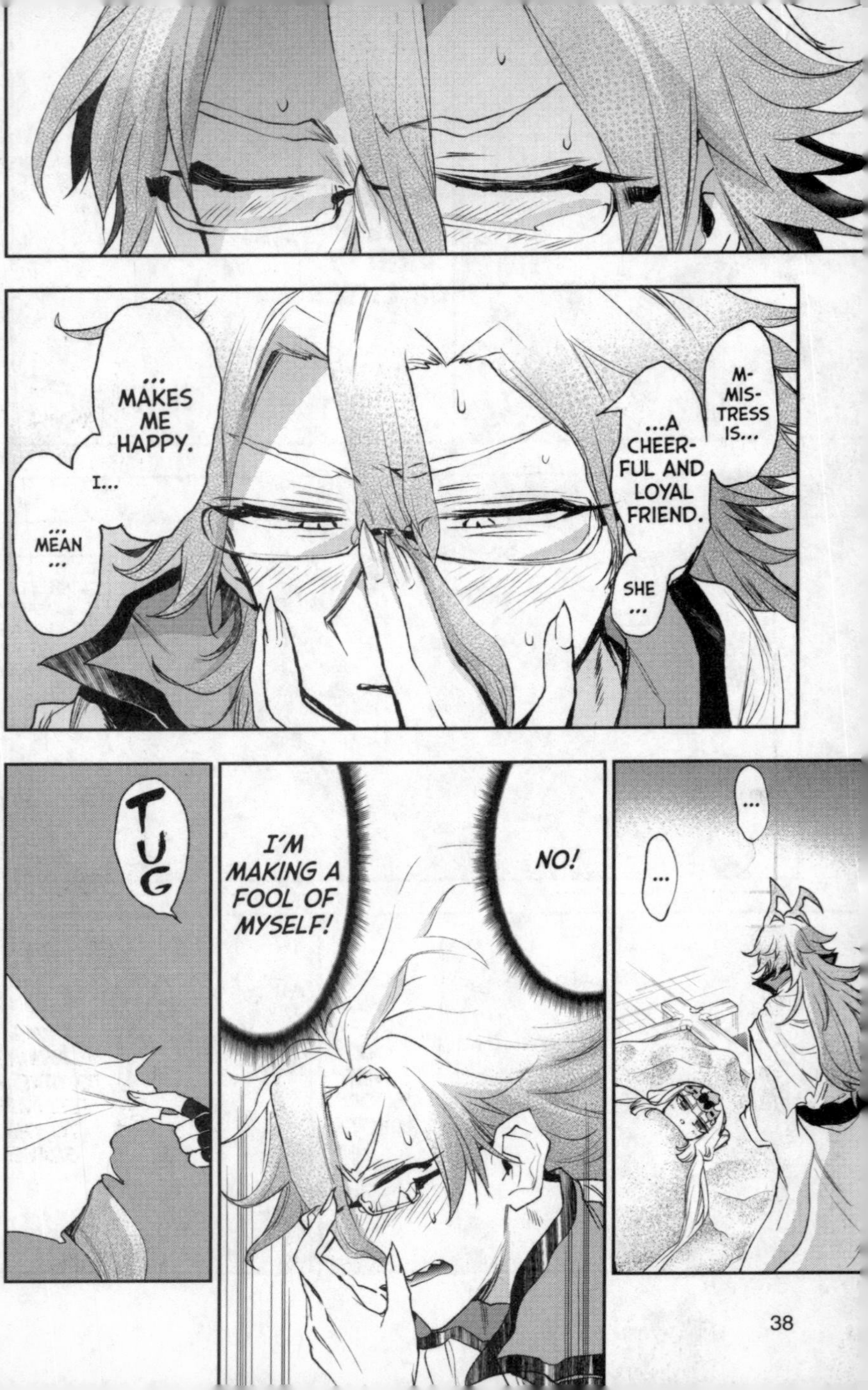
M-MISTRESS IS...
...A CHEERFUL AND LOYAL FRIEND.
SHE ...
...MAKES ME HAPPY.
I...
...MEAN ...
...
...
NO!
I'M MAKING A FOOL OF MYSELF!
TUG

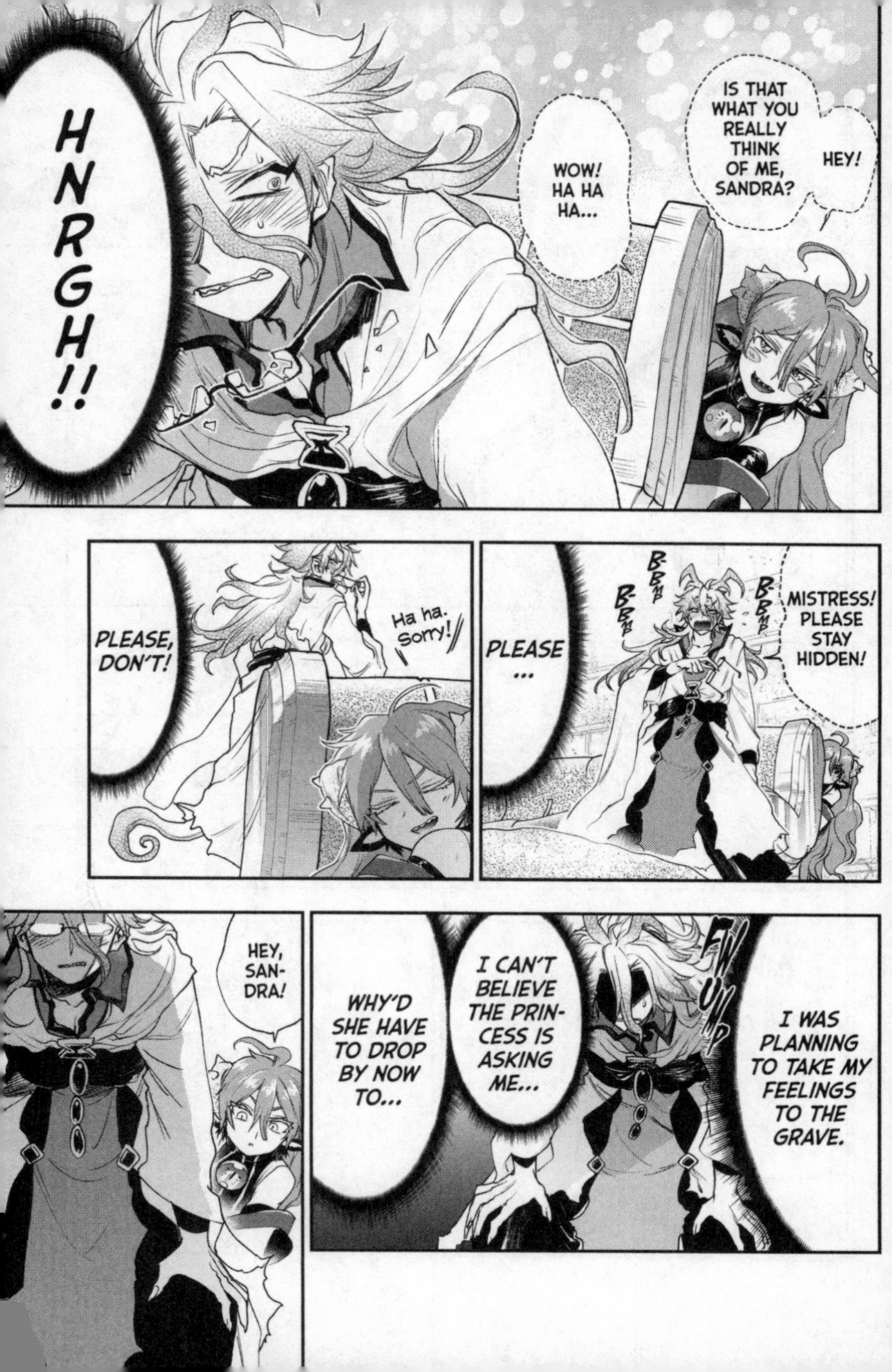
HEY!
IS THAT WHAT YOU REALLY THINK OF ME, SANDRA?
WOW! HA HA HA...
HNRGH!!
MISTRESS! PLEASE STAY HIDDEN!
B-BMP
B-BMP
PLEASE...
Ha ha. Sorry!
PLEASE, DON'T!
I WAS PLANNING TO TAKE MY FEELINGS TO THE GRAVE.
FWUMP
I CAN'T BELIEVE THE PRINCESS IS ASKING ME...
WHY'D SHE HAVE TO DROP BY NOW TO...
HEY, SANDRA!

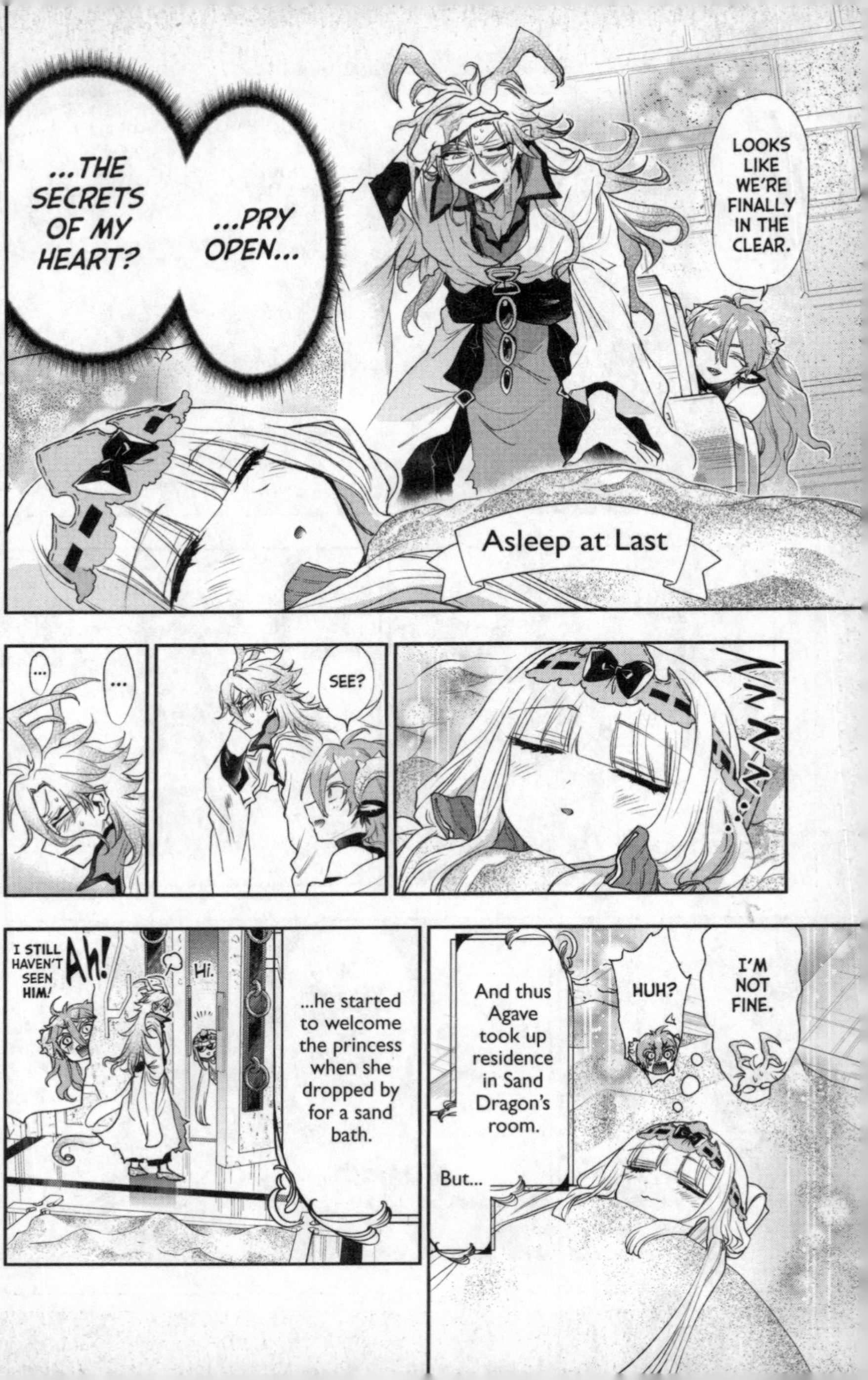
LOOKS LIKE WE'RE FINALLY IN THE CLEAR.
...PRY OPEN...
...THE SECRETS OF MY HEART?
Asleep at Last
SEE?
...
...
I'M NOT FINE.
HUH?
And thus Agave took up residence in Sand Dragon's room.
But...
...he started to welcome the princess when she dropped by for a sand bath.
Hi.
Ah!
I STILL HAVEN'T SEEN HIM!

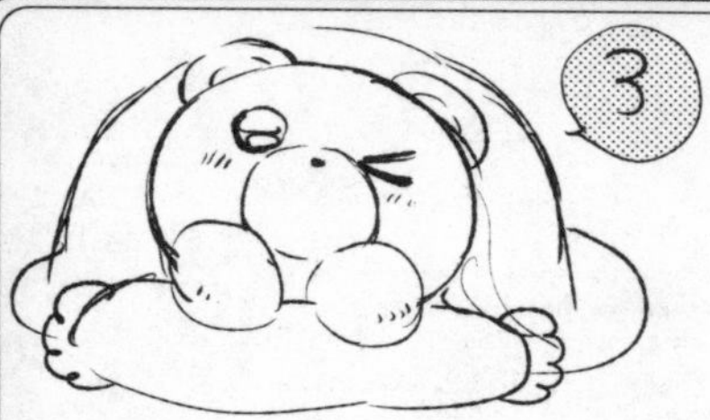
3

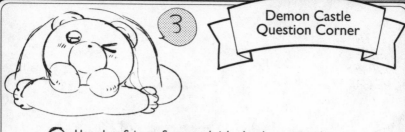

Demon Castle Question Corner

Q How does Scissors Sorcerer shrink when he meets with the Ten Guardians?

A He uses a small remote-controlled body to take part in meetings.

Q Where did the princess get the Chinese-style dress she wore in volume 13?

A She altered a training gown from the castle's armor shop.

Q I'd like to know the new characters' birthdays!

A Agave—September 6, Kowloon Island Commemoration Day
Sand Dragon—March 10
Chamos—first of the 111th month
(He doesn't remember, so he wrote down a made-up date.)

Q Does Great Red Siberian have a dark secret from his past that he doesn't want anyone to find out about?

A During his four-legged days, he used to get unruly and lick everybody's face.

Q How quickly do the Demon King's horns grow back after he sheds them?

A

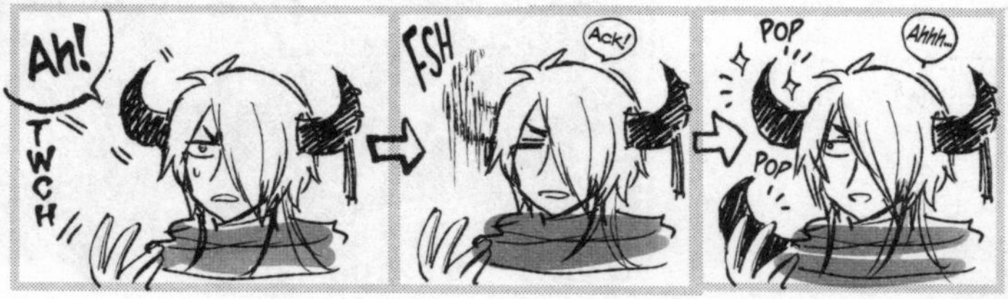
Ah!
TWCH
FSH
Ack!
POP
Ahhh...
POP

Q Who has the longest eyelashes?

A Midnight by a landslide because of his sheer size.
Agave and Sexy Girl have quite long eyelashes too.

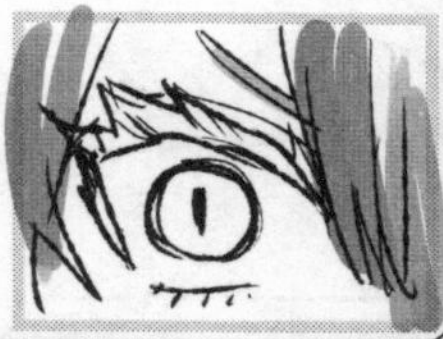

Would you like to change your class?

3 changes remaining

▶ Yes

No ▼

Silk Spinner

"Look at all these thorns."

▼

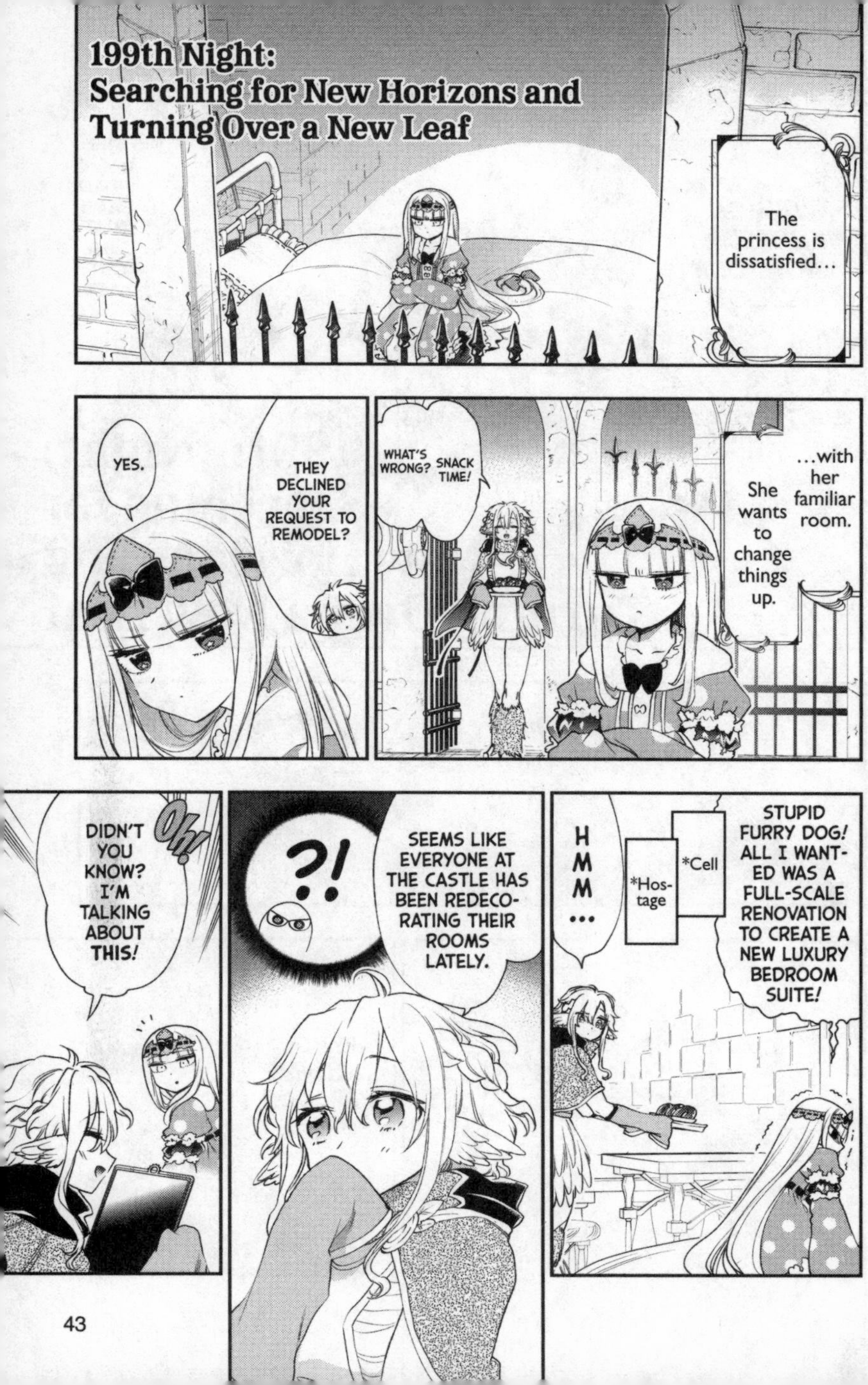
199th Night:
Searching for New Horizons and Turning Over a New Leaf
The princess is dissatisfied...
...with her familiar room.
She wants to change things up.
WHAT'S WRONG? SNACK TIME!
THEY DECLINED YOUR REQUEST TO REMODEL?
YES.
STUPID FURRY DOG! ALL I WANT-ED WAS A FULL-SCALE RENOVATION TO CREATE A NEW LUXURY BEDROOM SUITE!
*Cell
*Hos-tage
HMM...
?!
SEEMS LIKE EVERYONE AT THE CASTLE HAS BEEN REDECO-RATING THEIR ROOMS LATELY.
Oh!
DIDN'T YOU KNOW? I'M TALKING ABOUT THIS!

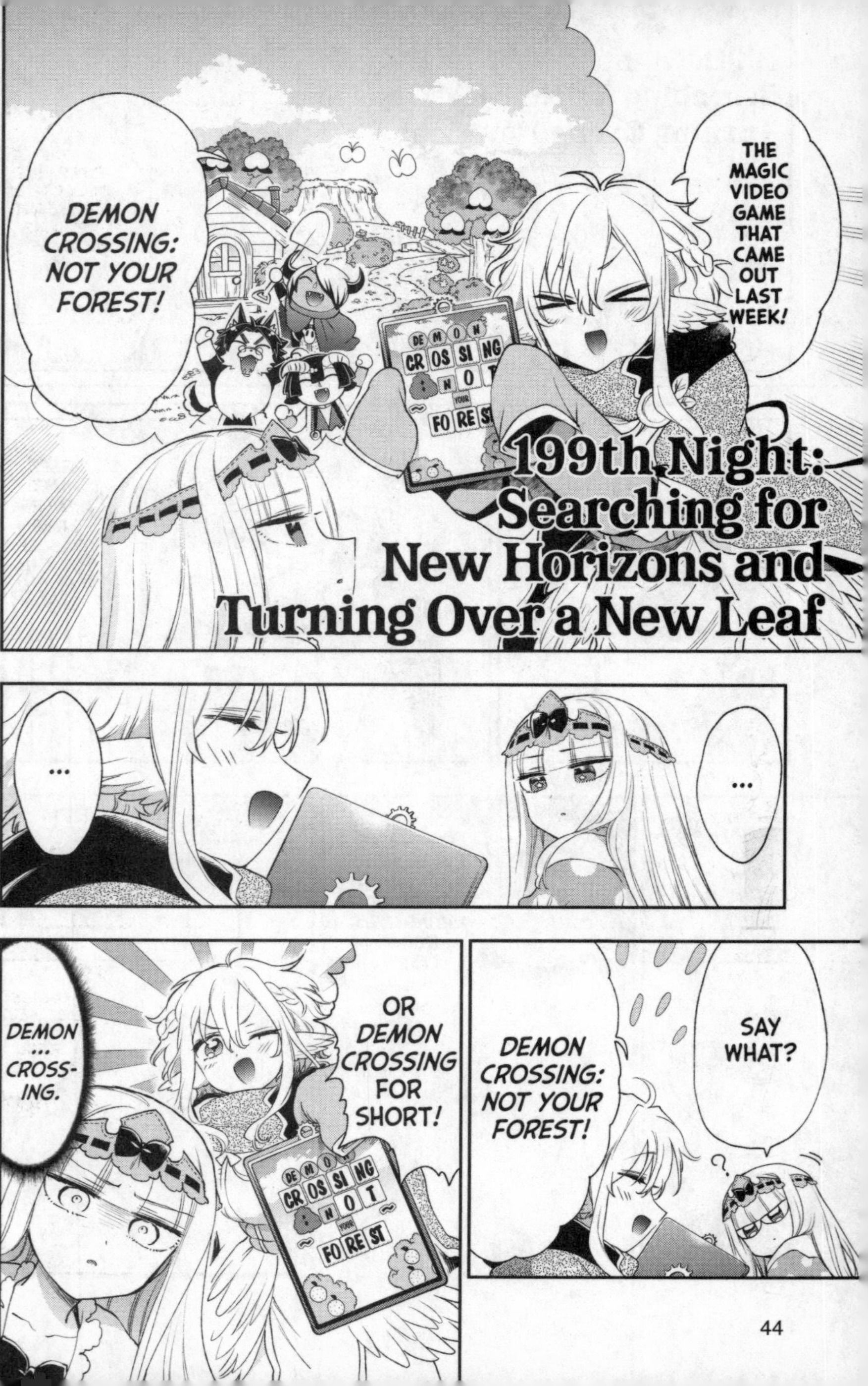
THE MAGIC VIDEO GAME THAT CAME OUT LAST WEEK!
DEMON CROSSING: NOT YOUR FOREST!
199th Night: Searching for New Horizons and Turning Over a New Leaf
...
...
SAY WHAT?
DEMON CROSSING: NOT YOUR FOREST!
OR DEMON CROSSING FOR SHORT!
DEMON... CROSS-ING.

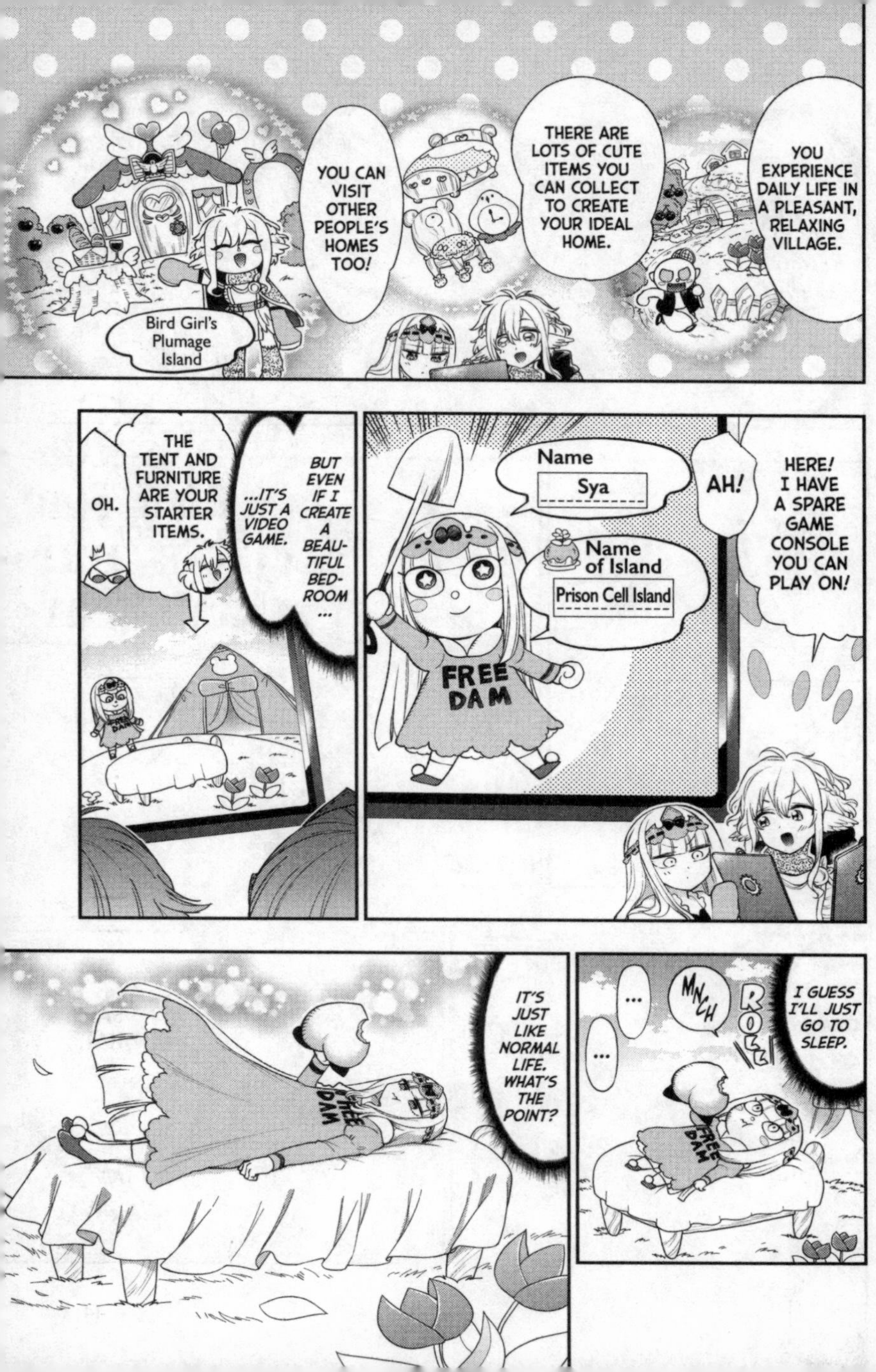
YOU EXPERIENCE DAILY LIFE IN A PLEASANT, RELAXING VILLAGE.
THERE ARE LOTS OF CUTE ITEMS YOU CAN COLLECT TO CREATE YOUR IDEAL HOME.
YOU CAN VISIT OTHER PEOPLE'S HOMES TOO!
Bird Girl's Plumage Island
HERE! I HAVE A SPARE GAME CONSOLE YOU CAN PLAY ON!
AH!
Name
Sya
Name of Island
Prison Cell Island
FREE DAM
BUT EVEN IF I CREATE A BEAUTIFUL BEDROOM...
...IT'S JUST A VIDEO GAME.
THE TENT AND FURNITURE ARE YOUR STARTER ITEMS.
OH.
I GUESS I'LL JUST GO TO SLEEP.
ROLL
MNCH
...
...
IT'S JUST LIKE NORMAL LIFE. WHAT'S THE POINT?
FREE DAM

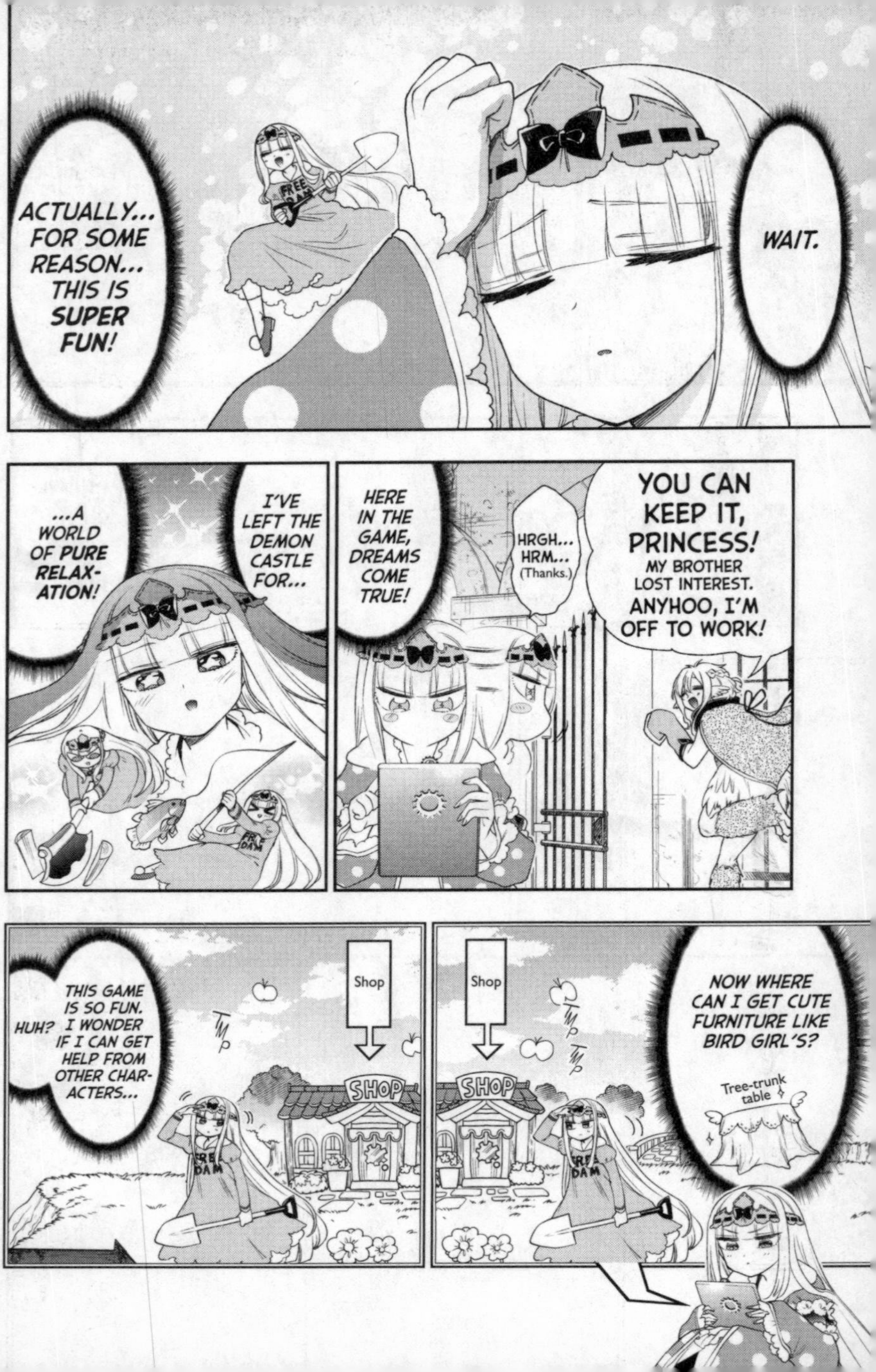
WAIT.
ACTUALLY... FOR SOME REASON... THIS IS SUPER FUN!
FREE DAM
YOU CAN KEEP IT, PRINCESS! MY BROTHER LOST INTEREST. ANYHOO, I'M OFF TO WORK!
HRGH... HRM... (Thanks.)
HERE IN THE GAME, DREAMS COME TRUE!
I'VE LEFT THE DEMON CASTLE FOR...
...A WORLD OF PURE RELAXATION!
NOW WHERE CAN I GET CUTE FURNITURE LIKE BIRD GIRL'S?
Tree-trunk table
Shop
SHOP
TMP TMP
Shop
SHOP
TMP
HUH?
THIS GAME IS SO FUN. I WONDER IF I CAN GET HELP FROM OTHER CHARACTERS...

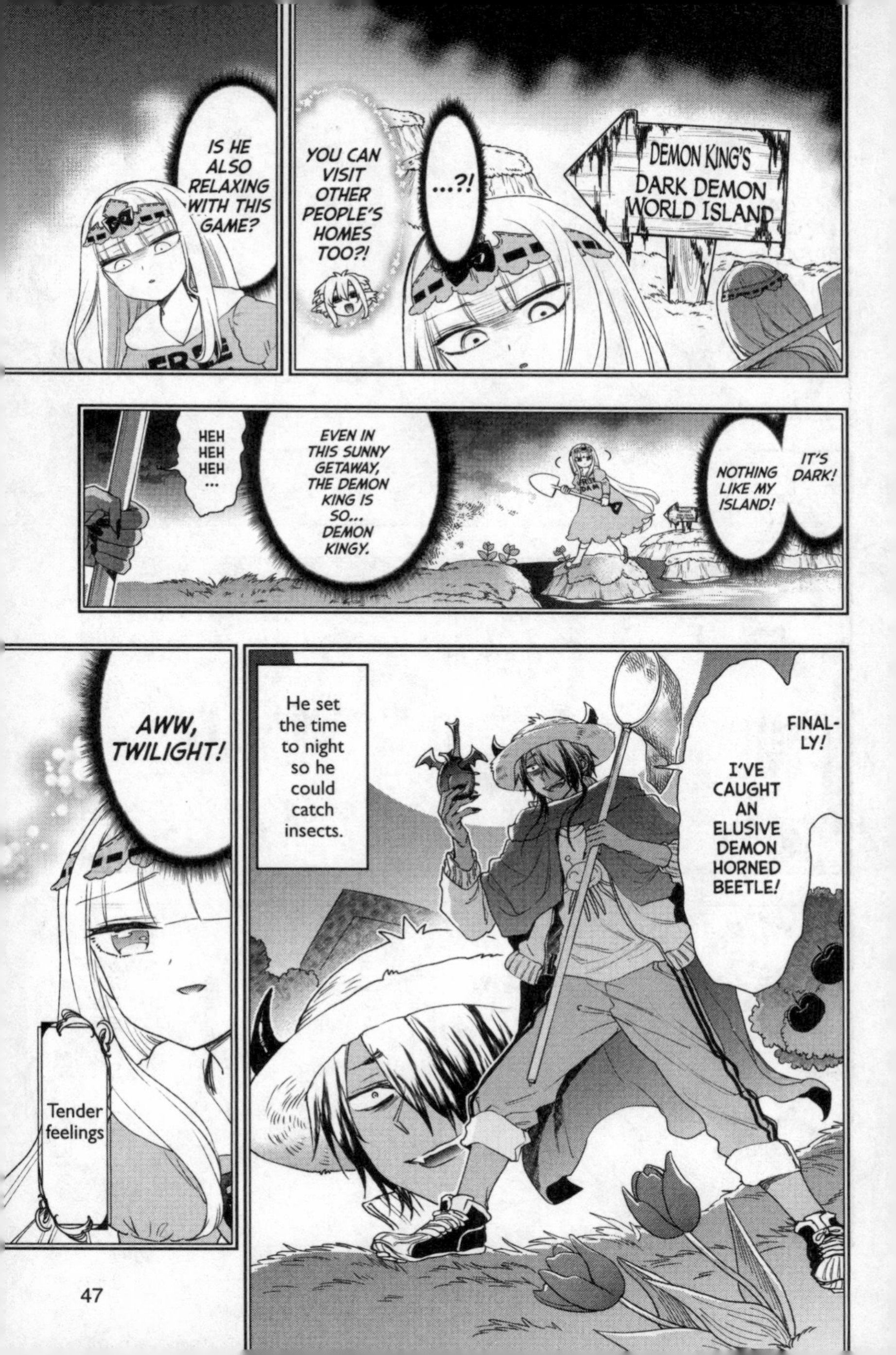
DEMON KING'S DARK DEMON WORLD ISLAND
...?!
YOU CAN VISIT OTHER PEOPLE'S HOMES TOO?!
IS HE ALSO RELAXING WITH THIS GAME?
IT'S DARK!
NOTHING LIKE MY ISLAND!
EVEN IN THIS SUNNY GETAWAY, THE DEMON KING IS SO... DEMON KINGY.
HEH HEH HEH ...
FINAL-LY!
I'VE CAUGHT AN ELUSIVE DEMON HORNED BEETLE!
He set the time to night so he could catch insects.
AWW, TWILIGHT!
Tender feelings

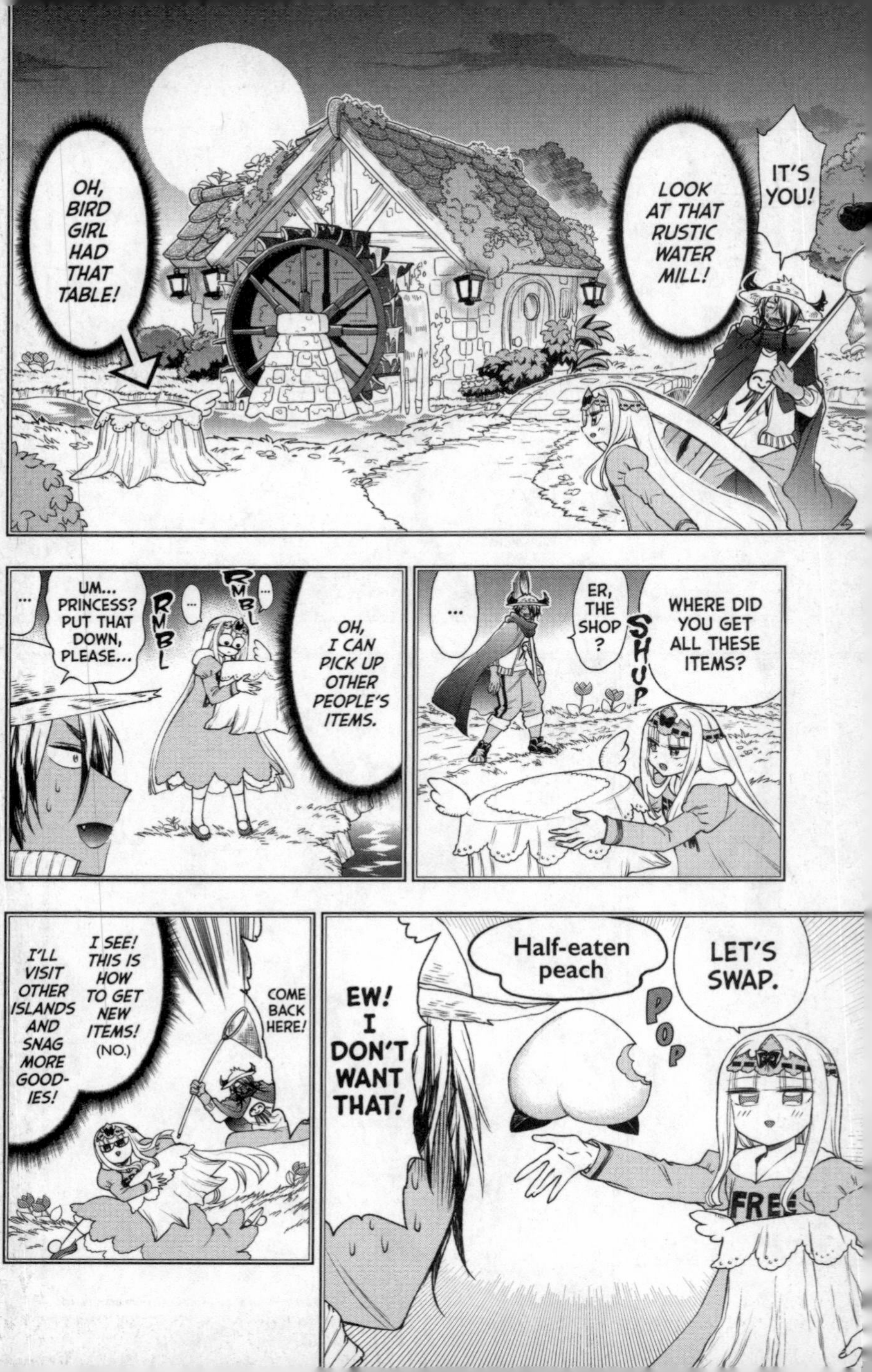
IT'S YOU!
LOOK AT THAT RUSTIC WATER MILL!
OH, BIRD GIRL HAD THAT TABLE!
WHERE DID YOU GET ALL THESE ITEMS?
SHUP
ER, THE SHOP?
...
OH, I CAN PICK UP OTHER PEOPLE'S ITEMS.
RMBL
RMBL
...
...
UM... PRINCESS? PUT THAT DOWN, PLEASE...
...
LET'S SWAP.
Half-eaten peach
POP
EW! I DON'T WANT THAT!
COME BACK HERE!
I SEE! THIS IS HOW TO GET NEW ITEMS! (NO.)
I'LL VISIT OTHER ISLANDS AND SNAG MORE GOOD-IES!

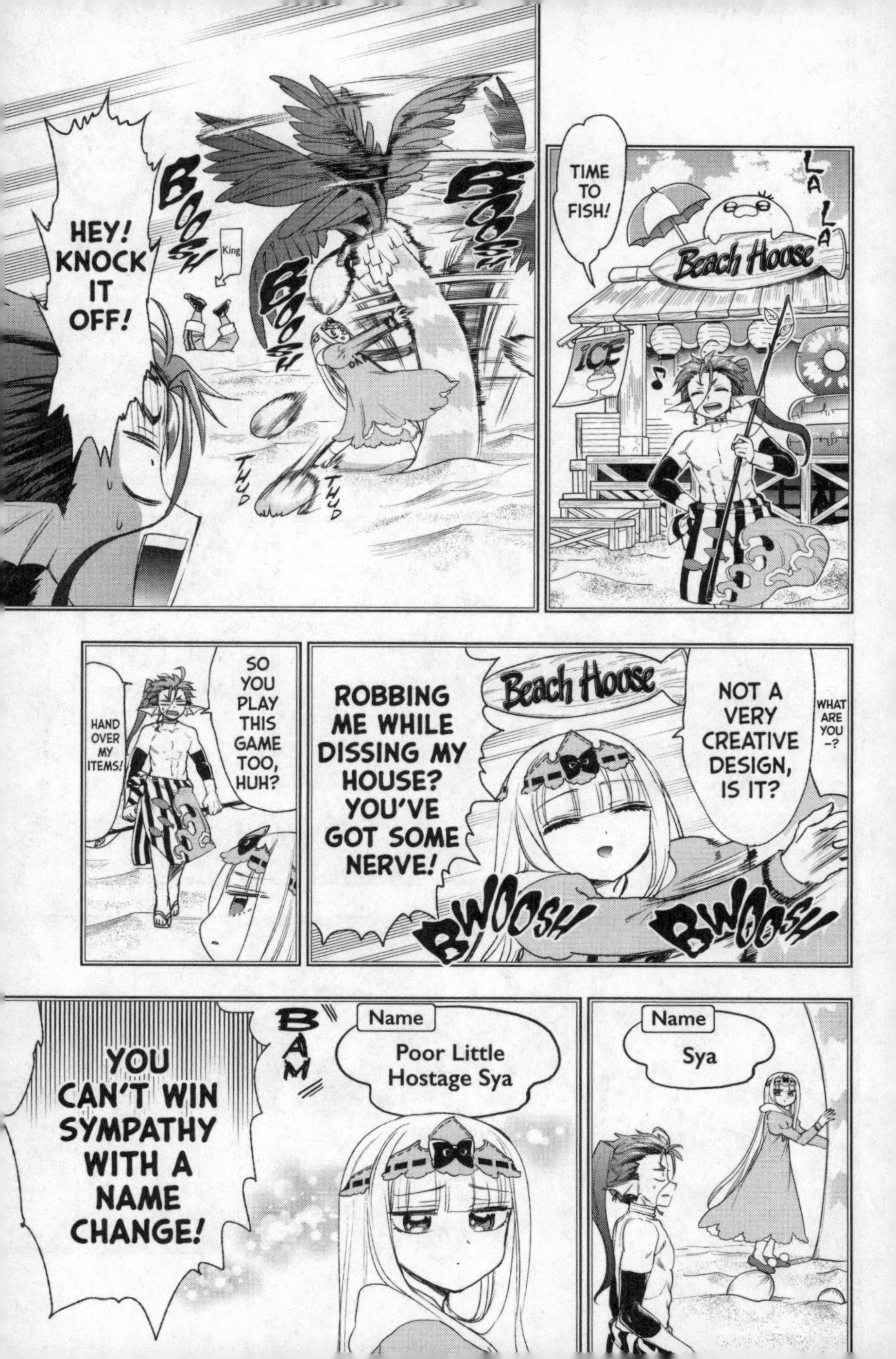
TIME TO FISH!
LA LA LA
Beach House
ICE
BOOOSH
BOOOSH
BOOOSH
King
HEY! KNOCK IT OFF!
THUD
THUD
WHAT ARE YOU –?
NOT A VERY CREATIVE DESIGN, IS IT?
Beach House
ROBBING ME WHILE DISSING MY HOUSE? YOU'VE GOT SOME NERVE!
BWOOSH
BWOOSH
SO YOU PLAY THIS GAME TOO, HUH?
HAND OVER MY ITEMS!
Name
Sya
BAM
Name
Poor Little Hostage Sya
YOU CAN'T WIN SYMPATHY WITH A NAME CHANGE!

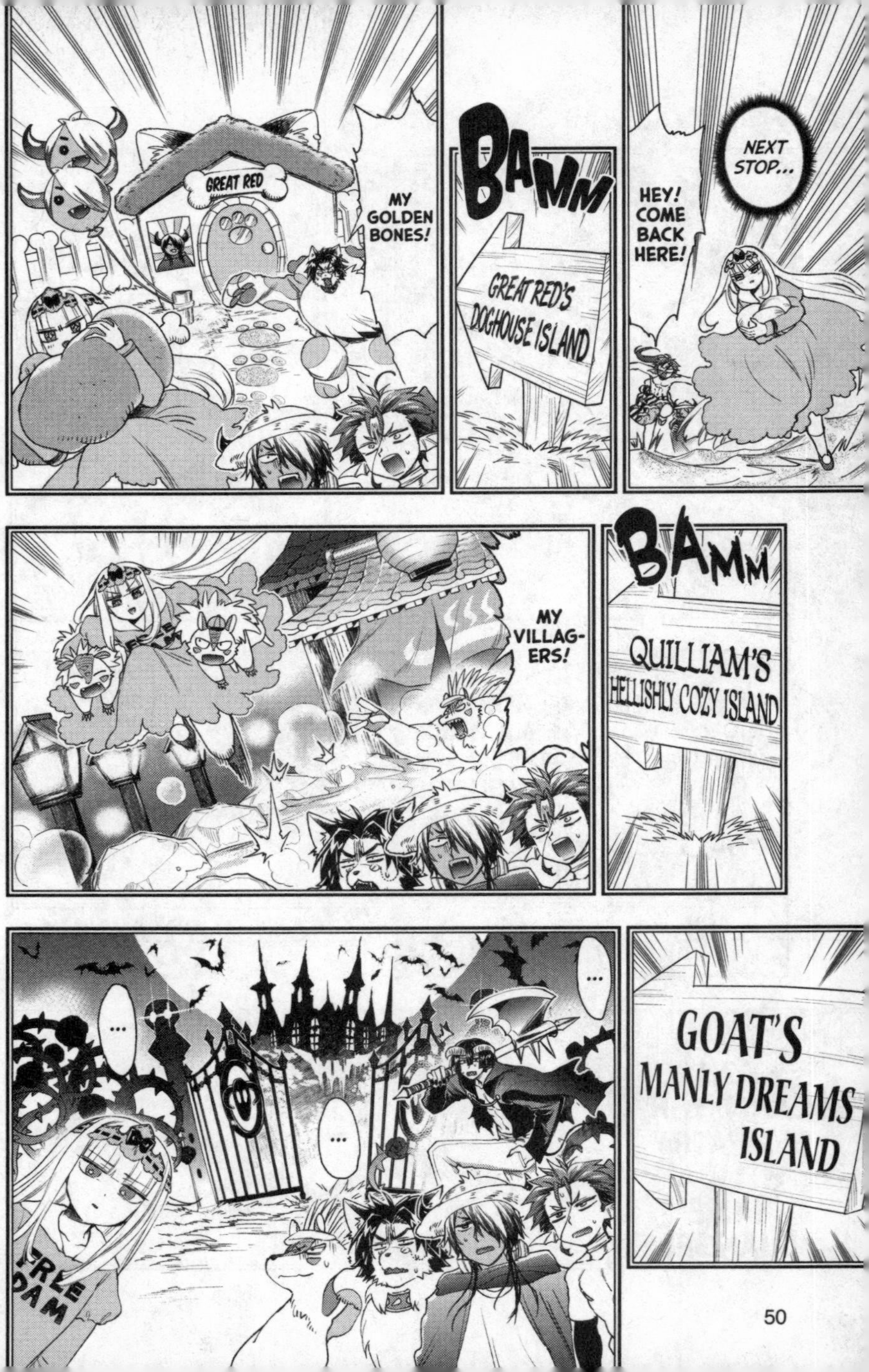
NEXT STOP...
HEY! COME BACK HERE!
BAMM
GREAT RED'S DOGHOUSE ISLAND
MY GOLDEN BONES!
GREAT RED
BAMM
QUILLIAM'S HELLISHLY COZY ISLAND
MY VILLAG-ERS!
GOAT'S MANLY DREAMS ISLAND
...
...
...
FREE DAM

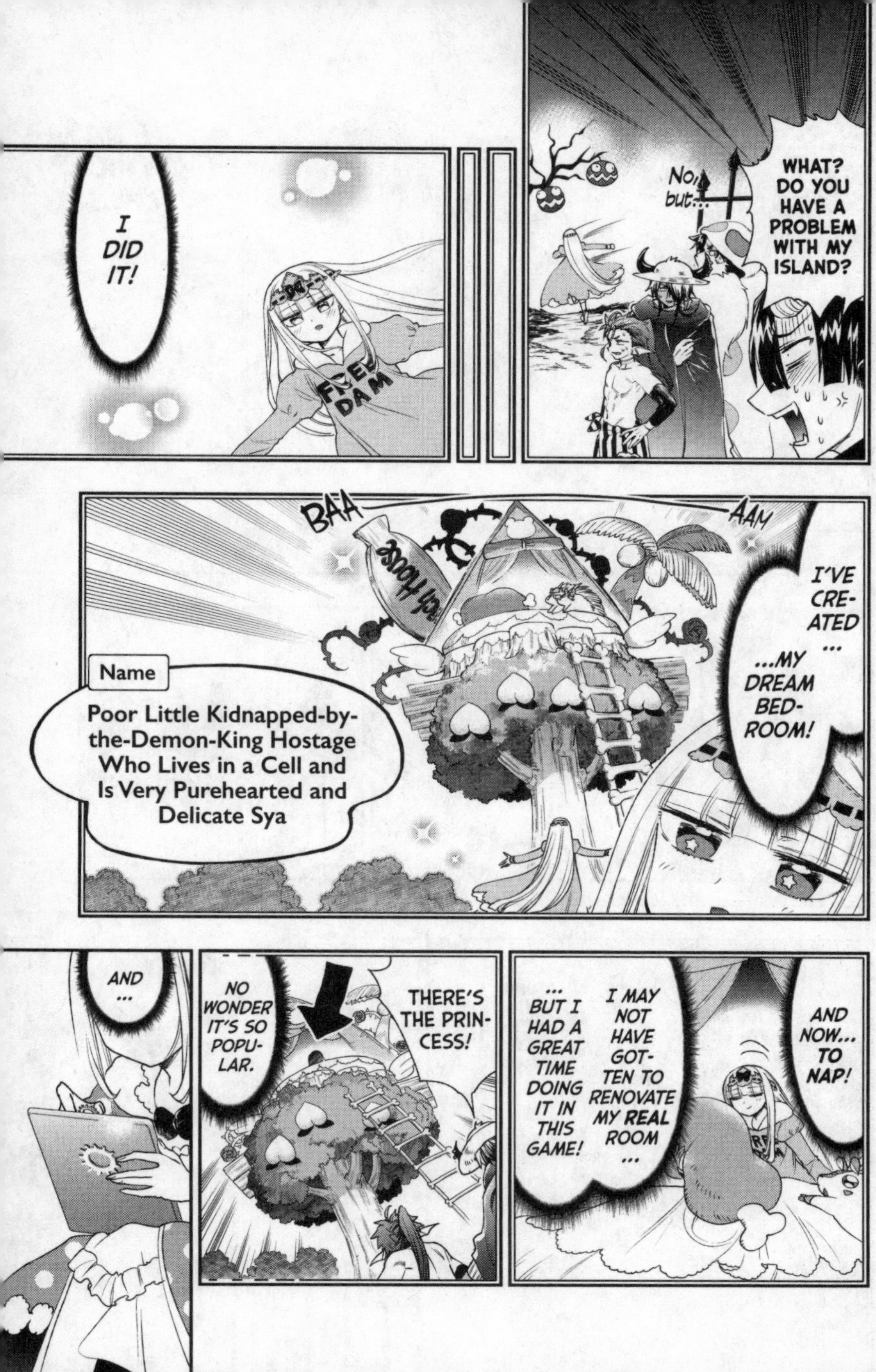
WHAT? DO YOU HAVE A PROBLEM WITH MY ISLAND?
No, but...
I DID IT!
BAA
AAM
I'VE CREATED...
...MY DREAM BEDROOM!
Name
Poor Little Kidnapped-by-the-Demon-King Hostage Who Lives in a Cell and Is Very Purehearted and Delicate Sya
I MAY NOT HAVE GOTTEN TO RENOVATE MY REAL ROOM...
...BUT I HAD A GREAT TIME DOING IT IN THIS GAME!
AND NOW... TO NAP!
THERE'S THE PRINCESS!
NO WONDER IT'S SO POPULAR.
AND...

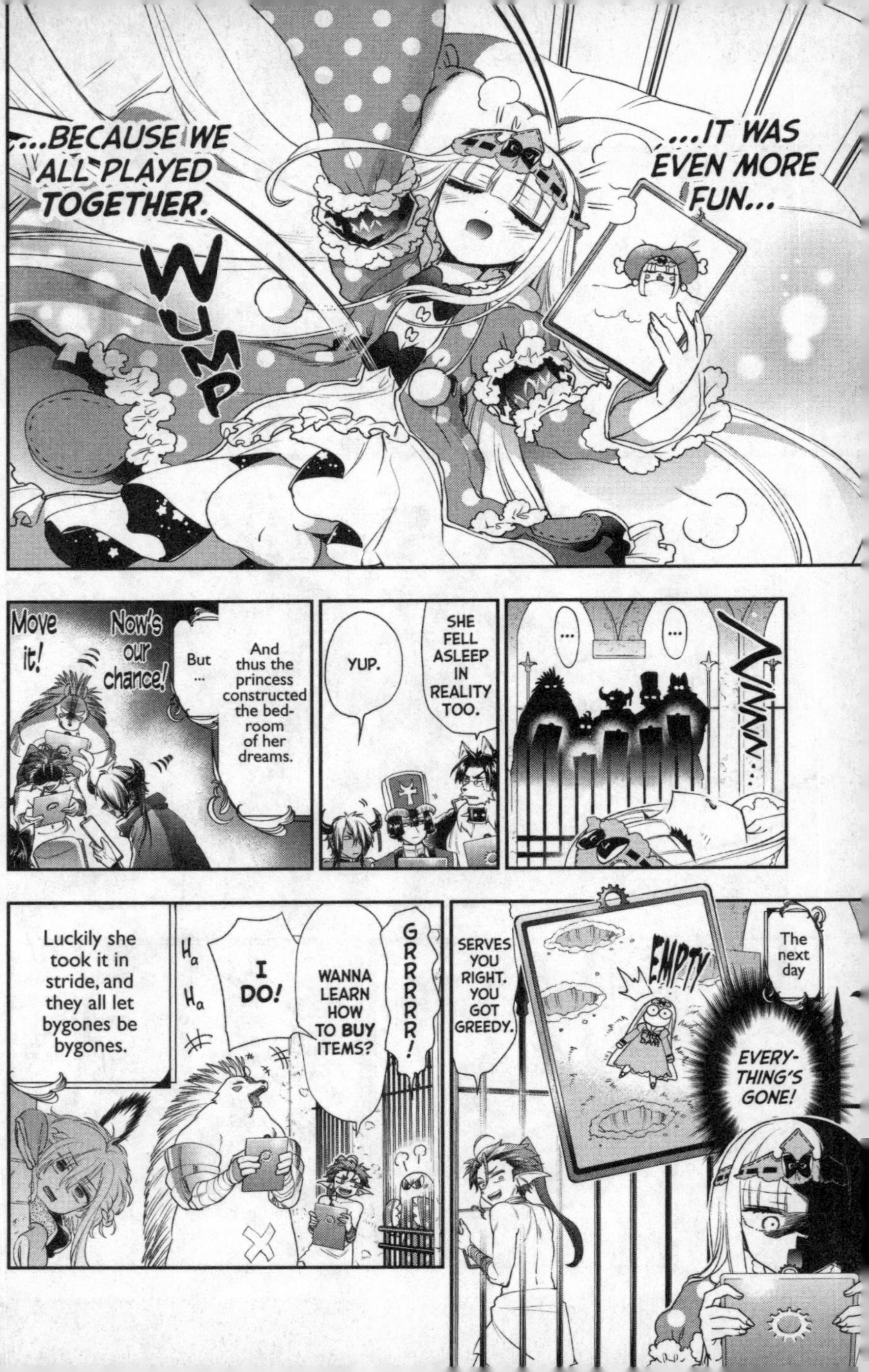
...IT WAS EVEN MORE FUN...
...BECAUSE WE ALL PLAYED TOGETHER.
WUMP
...
...
SHE FELL ASLEEP IN REALITY TOO.
YUP.
And thus the princess constructed the bedroom of her dreams.
But ...
Now's our chance!
Move it!
The next day
EMPTY
EVERYTHING'S GONE!
SERVES YOU RIGHT. YOU GOT GREEDY.
GRRRRR!
WANNA LEARN HOW TO BUY ITEMS?
I DO!
Ha Ha
Luckily she took it in stride, and they all let bygones be bygones.

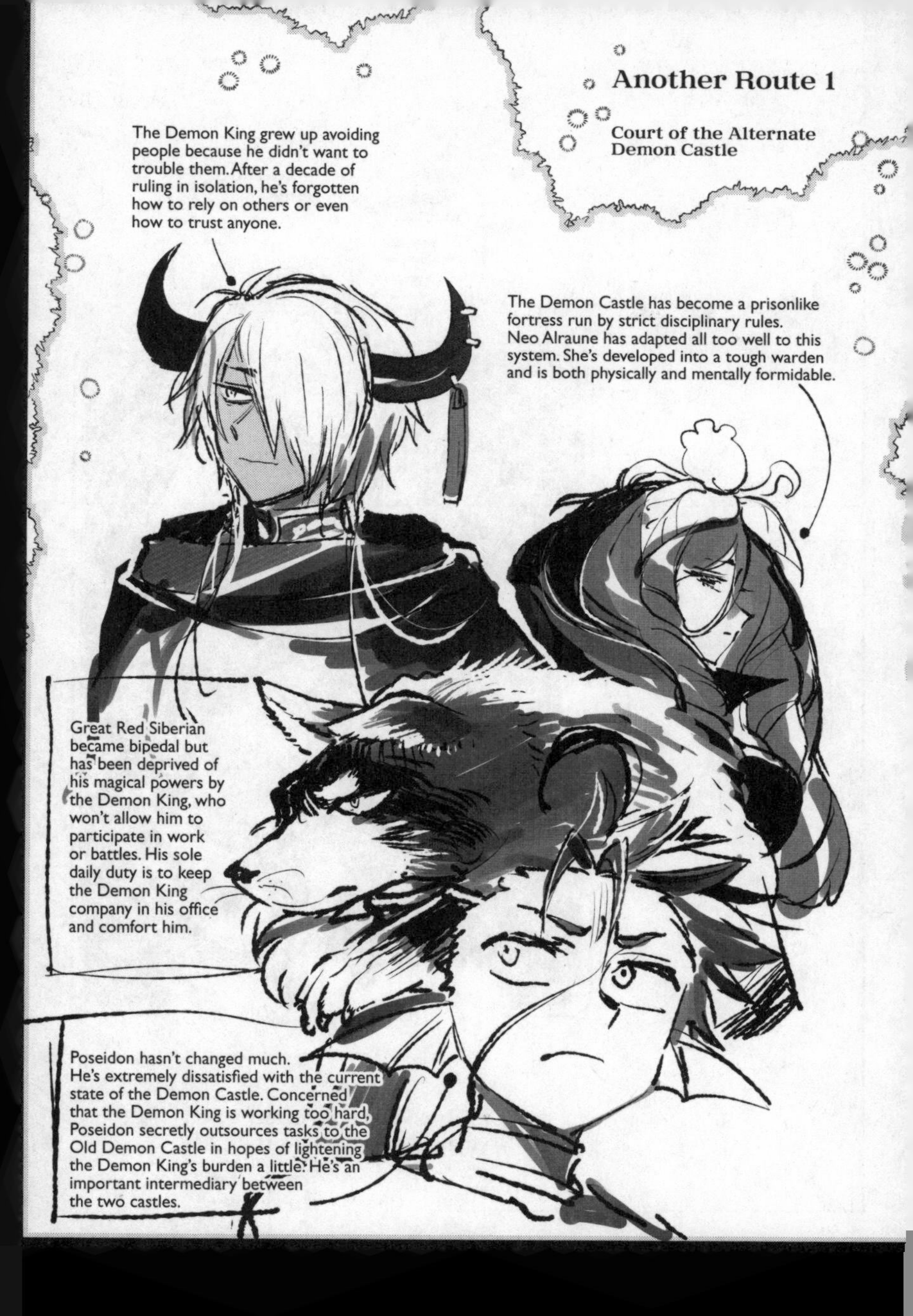
Another Route 1
Court of the Alternate Demon Castle
The Demon King grew up avoiding people because he didn't want to trouble them. After a decade of ruling in isolation, he's forgotten how to rely on others or even how to trust anyone.
The Demon Castle has become a prisonlike fortress run by strict disciplinary rules. Neo Alraune has adapted all too well to this system. She's developed into a tough warden and is both physically and mentally formidable.
Great Red Siberian became bipedal but has been deprived of his magical powers by the Demon King, who won't allow him to participate in work or battles. His sole daily duty is to keep the Demon King company in his office and comfort him.
Poseidon hasn't changed much. He's extremely dissatisfied with the current state of the Demon Castle. Concerned that the Demon King is working too hard, Poseidon secretly outsources tasks to the Old Demon Castle in hopes of lightening the Demon King's burden a little. He's an important intermediary between the two castles.

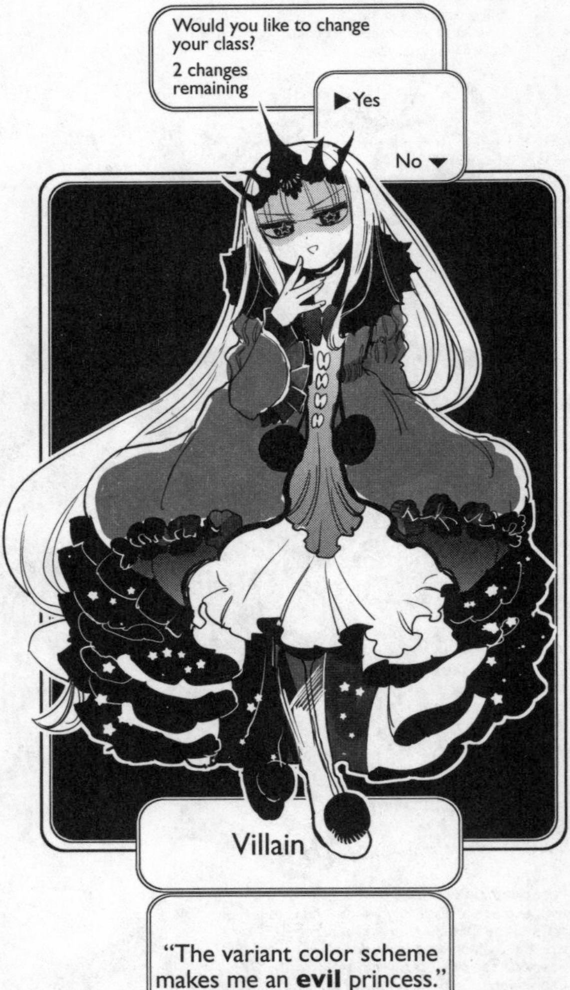
Would you like to change your class?
2 changes remaining
▶Yes
No ▼
Villain
"The variant color scheme makes me an **evil** princess."

200th Night: Accidental Leap

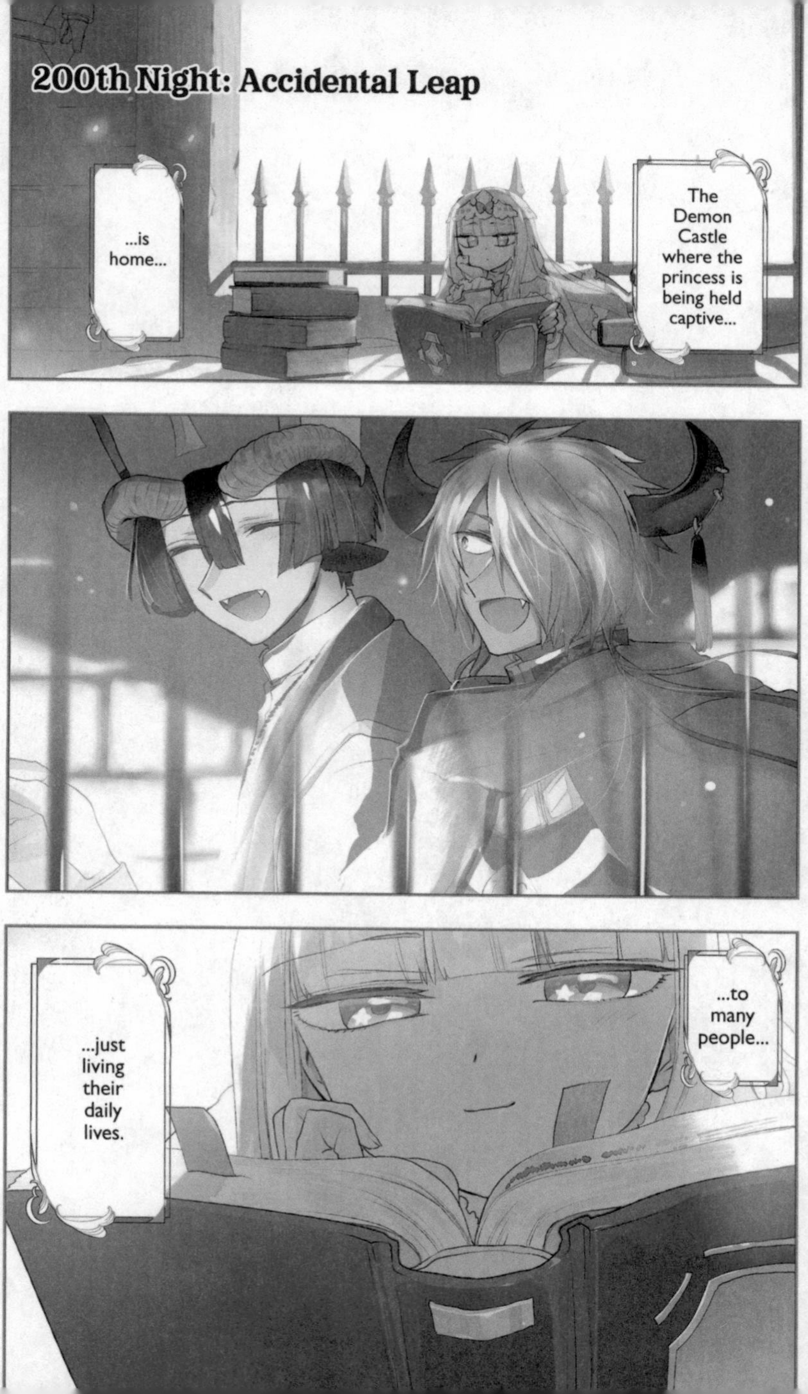
The Demon Castle where the princess is being held captive...
...is home...
...to many people...
...just living their daily lives.

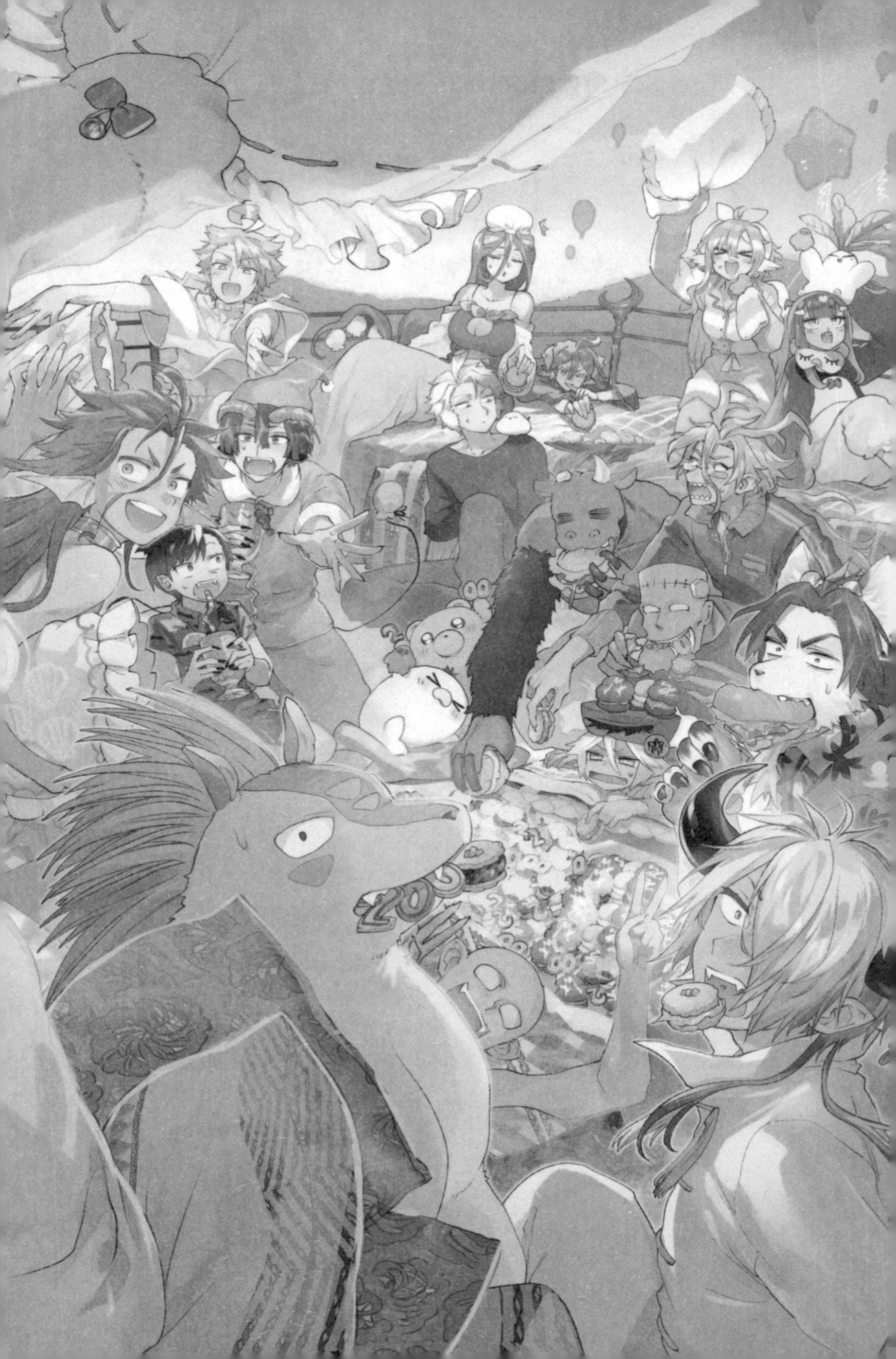

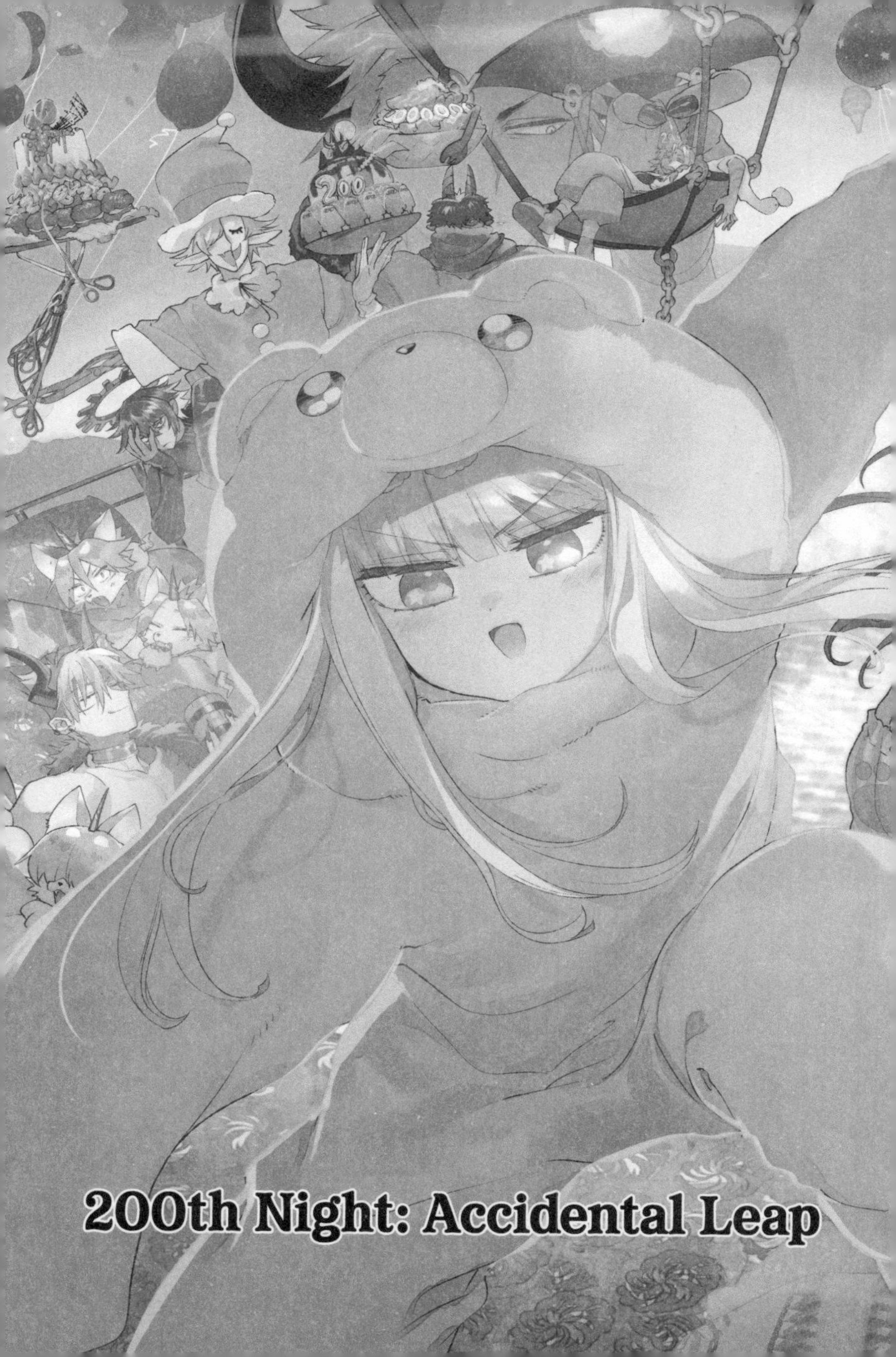

200th Night: Accidental Leap

SLEEPY PRINCESS
IN THE
DEMON CASTLE

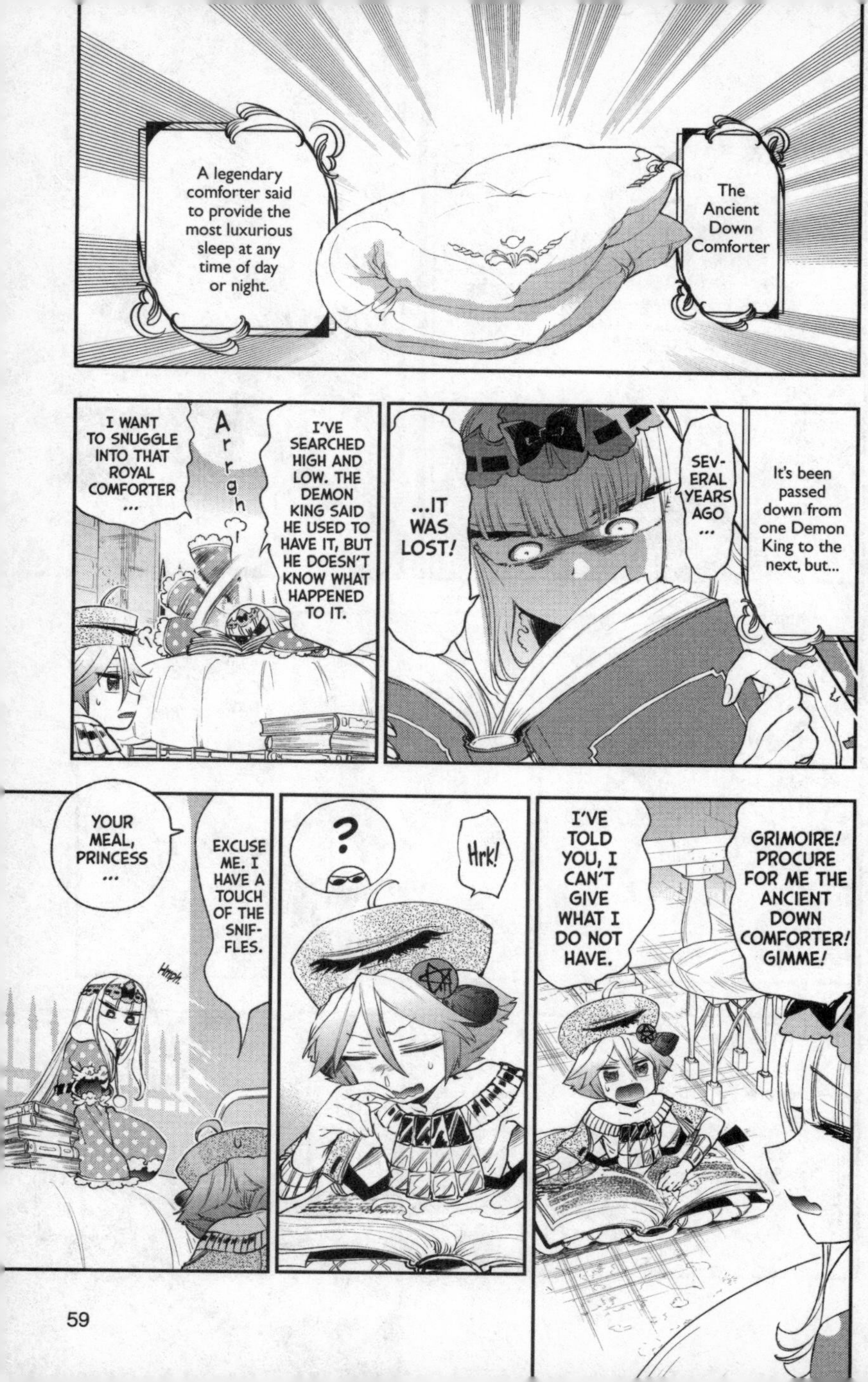

The Ancient Down Comforter
A legendary comforter said to provide the most luxurious sleep at any time of day or night.
It's been passed down from one Demon King to the next, but...
SEV-ERAL YEARS AGO...
...IT WAS LOST!
I'VE SEARCHED HIGH AND LOW. THE DEMON KING SAID HE USED TO HAVE IT, BUT HE DOESN'T KNOW WHAT HAPPENED TO IT.
Arrgh!
I WANT TO SNUGGLE INTO THAT ROYAL COMFORTER...
GRIMOIRE! PROCURE FOR ME THE ANCIENT DOWN COMFORTER! GIMME!
I'VE TOLD YOU, I CAN'T GIVE WHAT I DO NOT HAVE.
Hrk!
?
EXCUSE ME. I HAVE A TOUCH OF THE SNIF-FLES.
YOUR MEAL, PRINCESS...
Hmph.

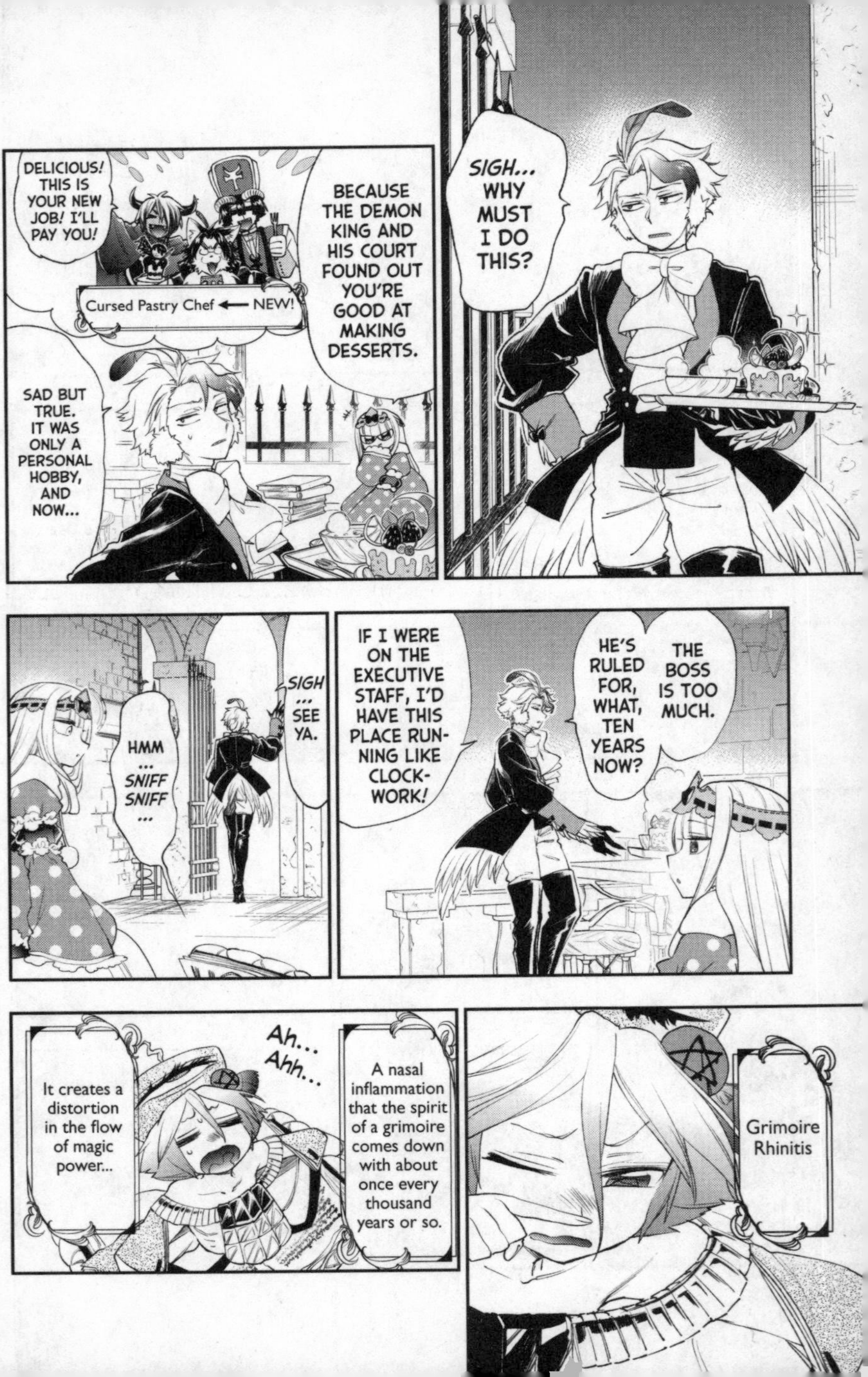
SIGH... WHY MUST I DO THIS?
BECAUSE THE DEMON KING AND HIS COURT FOUND OUT YOU'RE GOOD AT MAKING DESSERTS.
DELICIOUS! THIS IS YOUR NEW JOB! I'LL PAY YOU!
Cursed Pastry Chef ← NEW!
SAD BUT TRUE. IT WAS ONLY A PERSONAL HOBBY, AND NOW...
THE BOSS IS TOO MUCH.
HE'S RULED FOR, WHAT, TEN YEARS NOW?
IF I WERE ON THE EXECUTIVE STAFF, I'D HAVE THIS PLACE RUN-NING LIKE CLOCK-WORK!
SIGH ... SEE YA.
HMM ... SNIFF SNIFF ...
Grimoire Rhinitis
A nasal inflammation that the spirit of a grimoire comes down with about once every thousand years or so.
Ah... Ahh...
It creates a distortion in the flow of magic power...

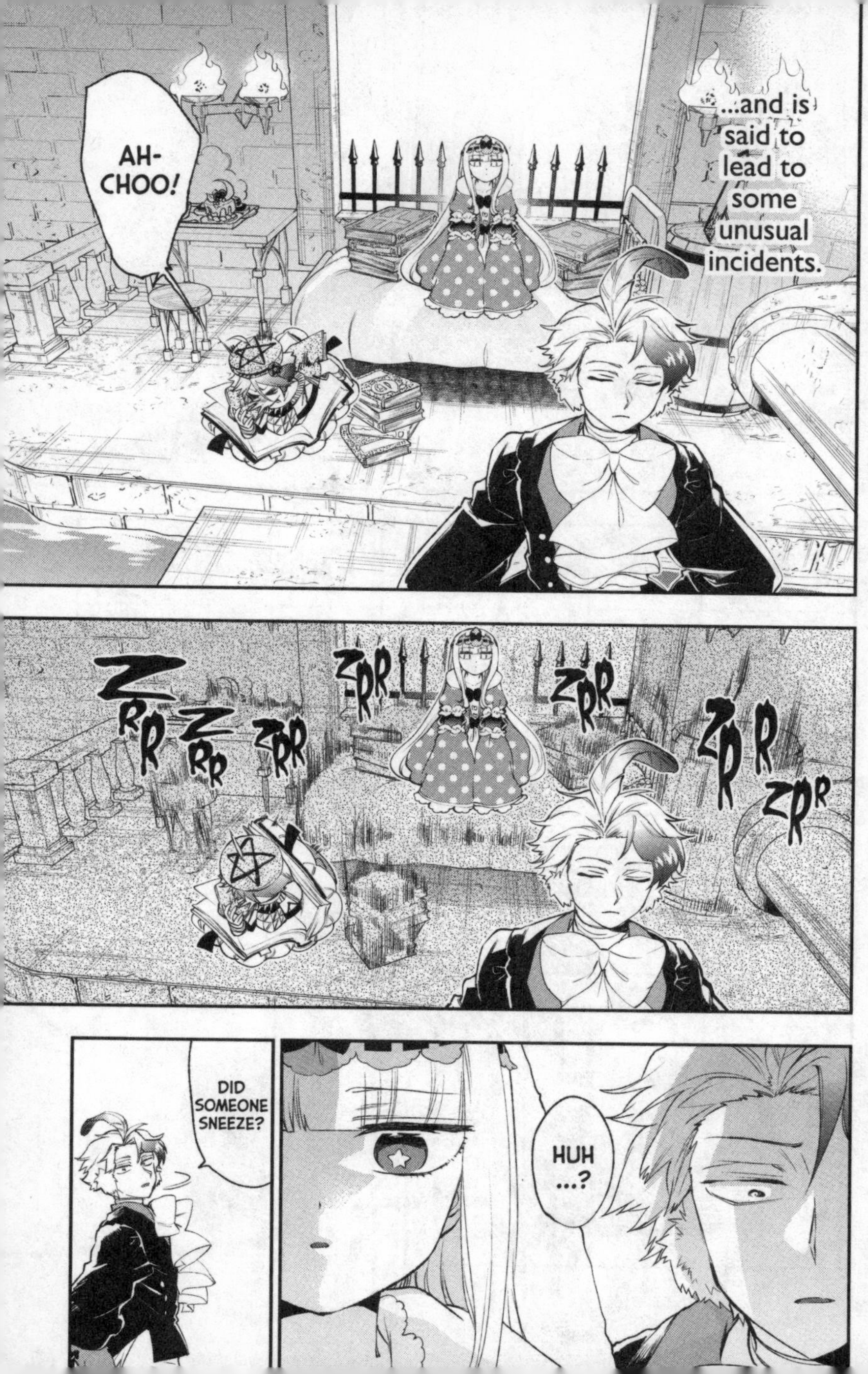
...and is said to lead to some unusual incidents.
AH-CHOO!
ZRR
ZRR
ZRR
ZRR
ZRR
ZRR
ZRR
HUH ...?
DID SOMEONE SNEEZE?

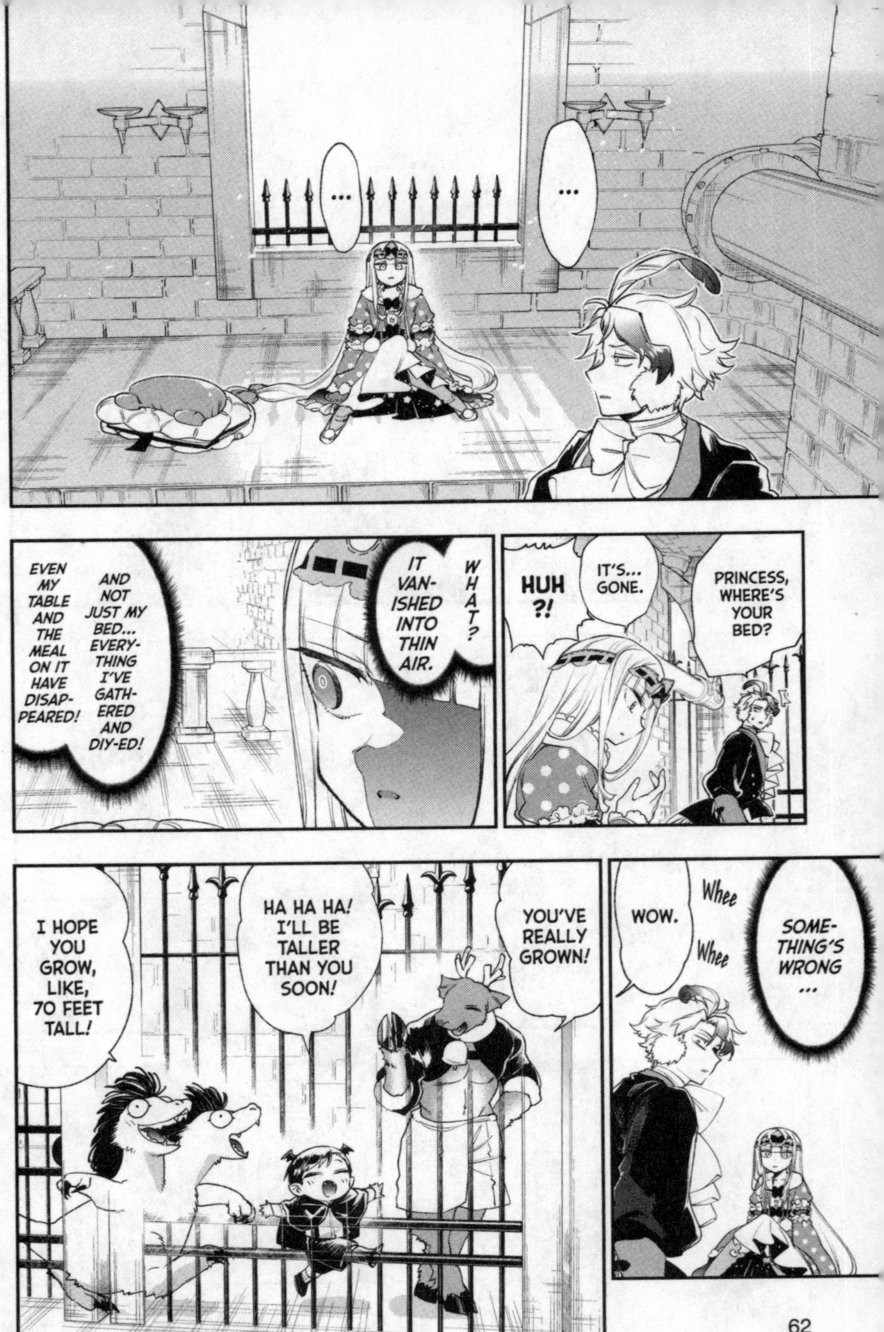
...
...
PRINCESS, WHERE'S YOUR BED?
IT'S... GONE.
HUH ?!
WHAT?
IT VAN-ISHED INTO THIN AIR.
AND NOT JUST MY BED... EVERY-THING I'VE GATH-ERED AND DIY-ED!
EVEN MY TABLE AND THE MEAL ON IT HAVE DISAP-PEARED!
SOME-THING'S WRONG ...
Whee
Whee
WOW.
YOU'VE REALLY GROWN!
HA HA HA! I'LL BE TALLER THAN YOU SOON!
I HOPE YOU GROW, LIKE, 70 FEET TALL!

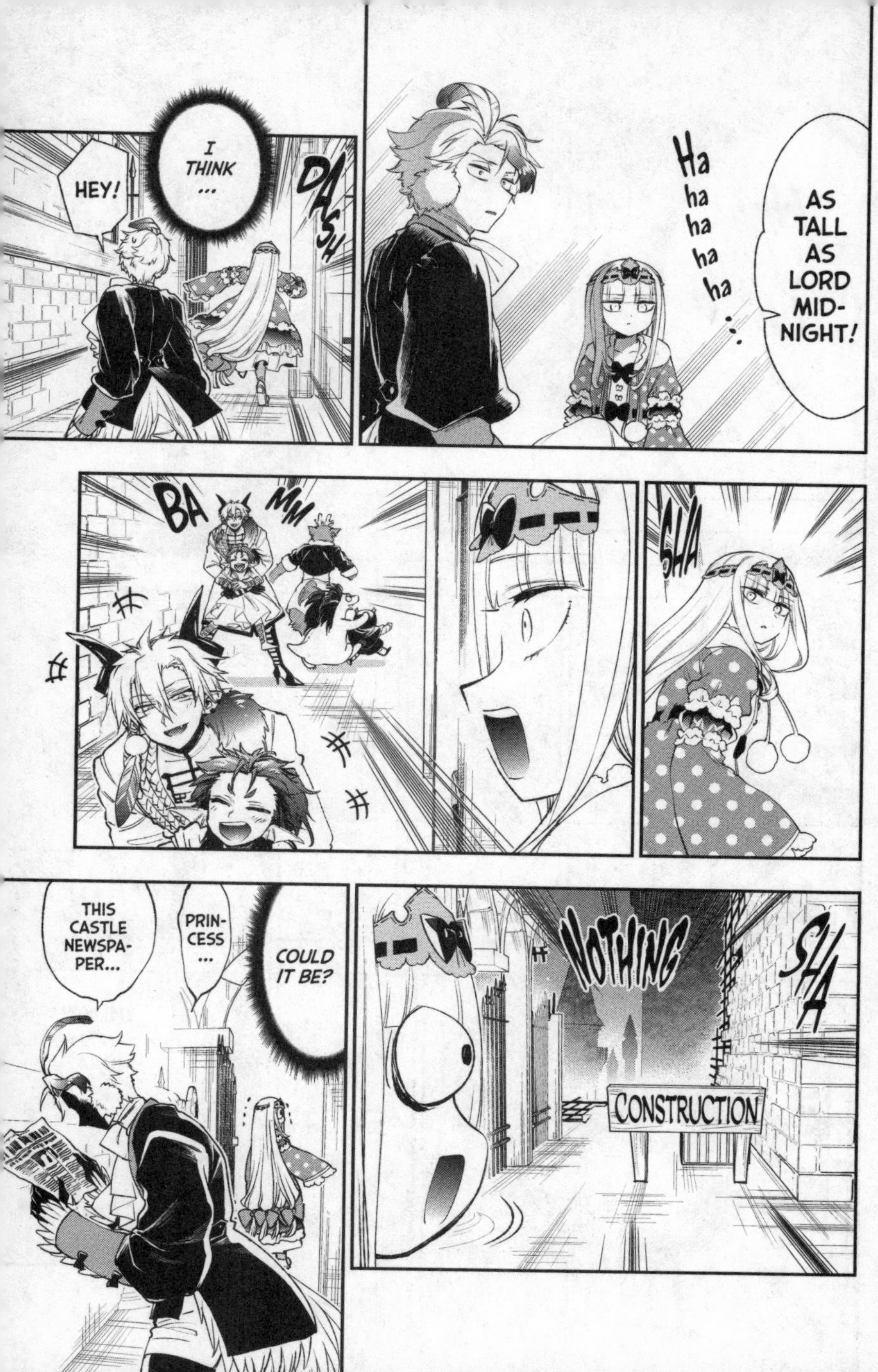
AS TALL AS LORD MID-NIGHT!
Ha ha ha ha ha ...
I THINK ...
DASH
HEY!
SHA
BAMM
SHA
NOTHING
CONSTRUCTION
COULD IT BE?
PRIN-CESS ...
THIS CASTLE NEWSPA-PER...

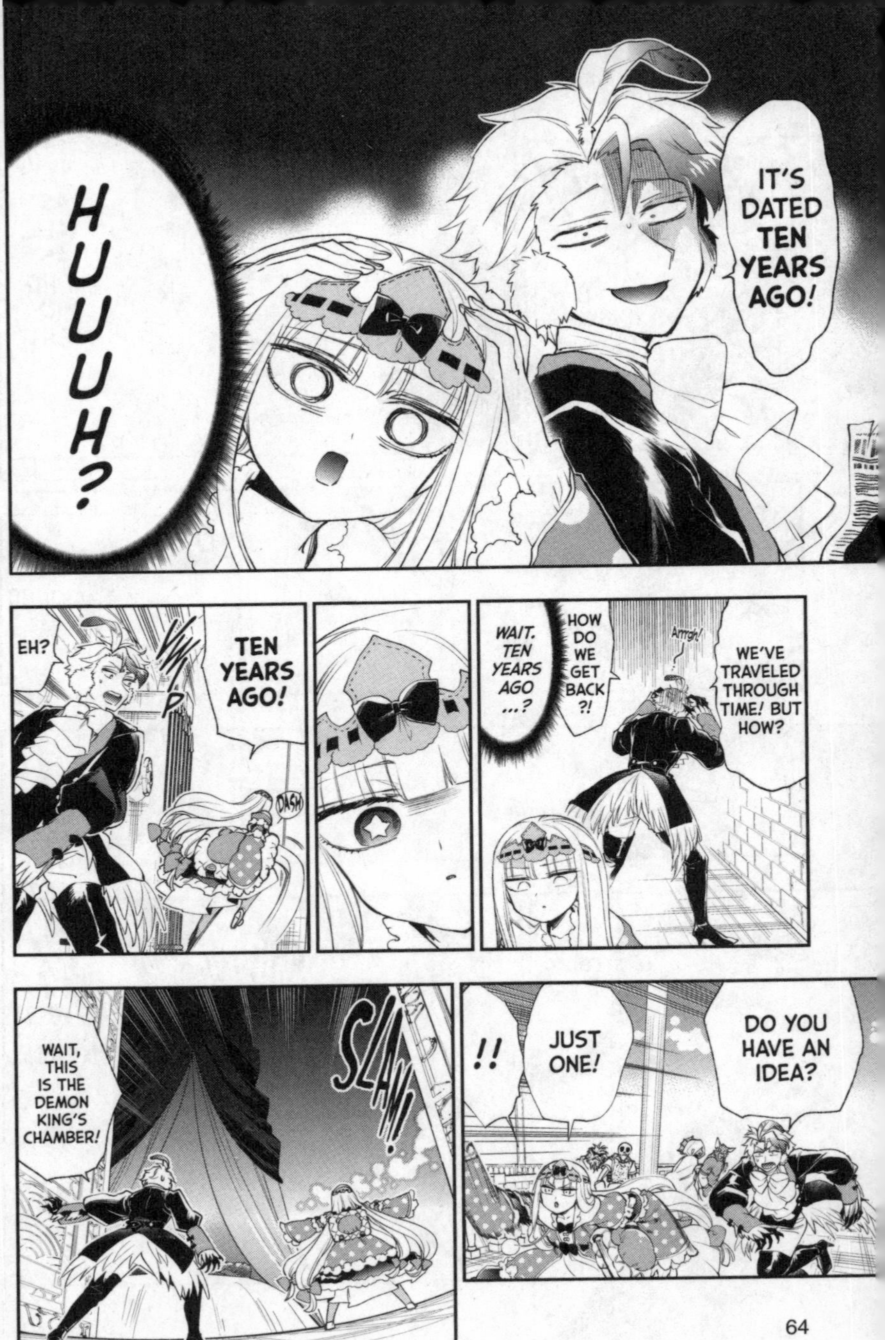
IT'S DATED TEN YEARS AGO!
HUUUUH?
WE'VE TRAVELED THROUGH TIME! BUT HOW?
Arrrgh!
HOW DO WE GET BACK?!
WAIT. TEN YEARS AGO ...?
TEN YEARS AGO!
VWIP
EH?
DASH
DO YOU HAVE AN IDEA?
JUST ONE!
!!
SLAM!
WAIT, THIS IS THE DEMON KING'S CHAMBER!

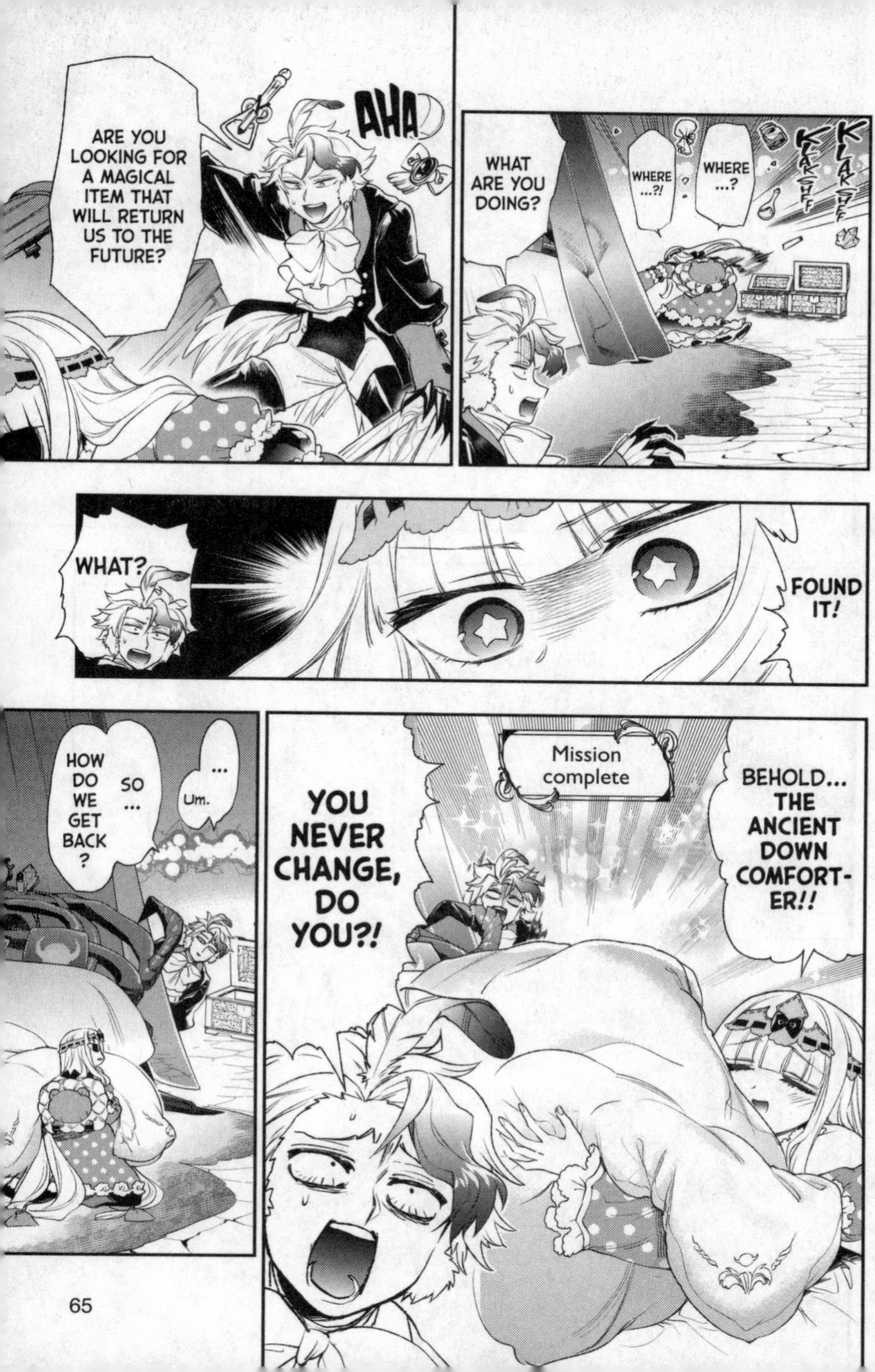
KLAK SHFF
KLAK SHFF
WHERE ...?
WHERE ...?!
WHAT ARE YOU DOING?
AHA
ARE YOU LOOKING FOR A MAGICAL ITEM THAT WILL RETURN US TO THE FUTURE?
FOUND IT!
WHAT?
BEHOLD... THE ANCIENT DOWN COMFORT-ER!!
Mission complete
YOU NEVER CHANGE, DO YOU?!
... Um.
SO ...
HOW DO WE GET BACK?

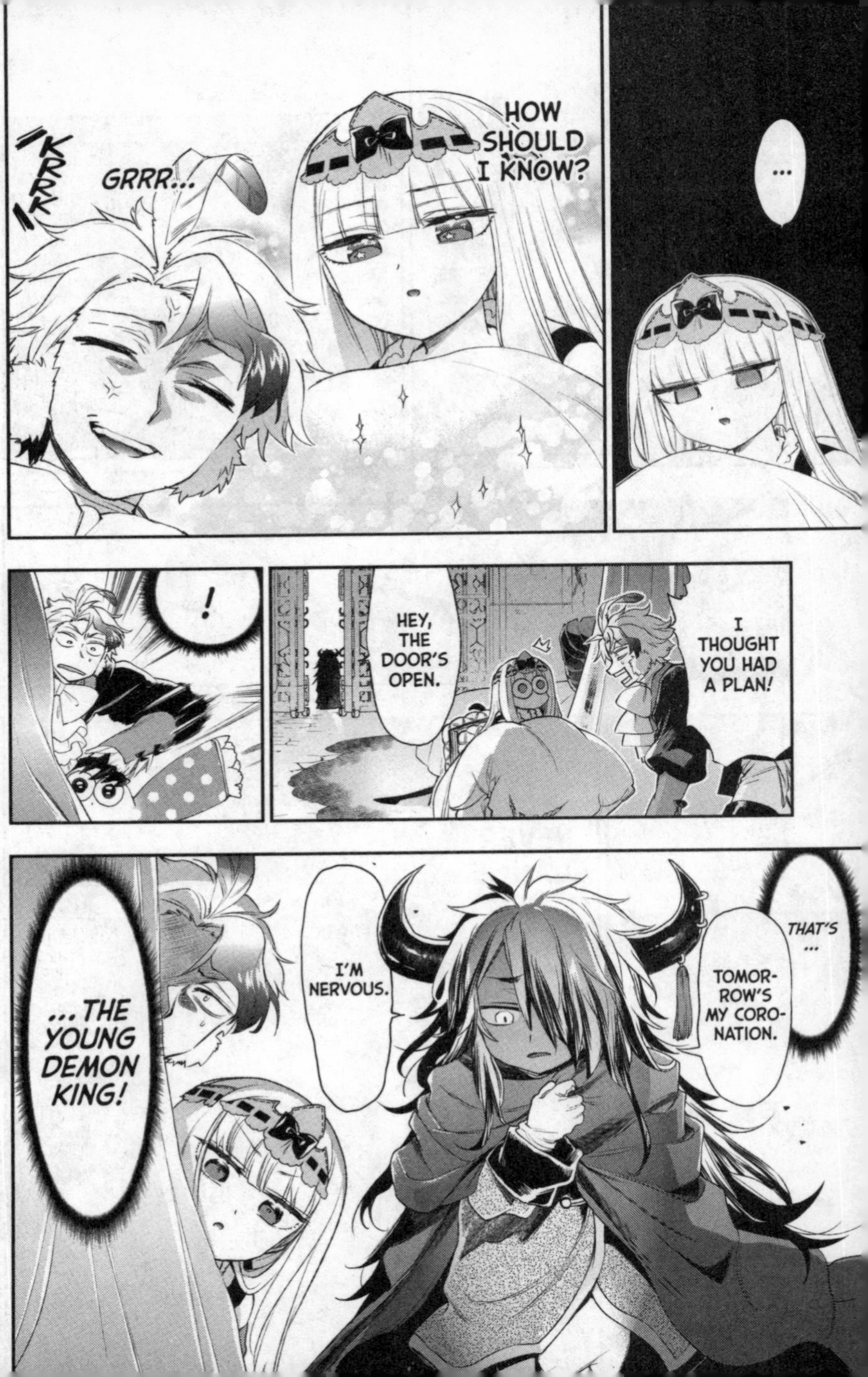
...
HOW SHOULD I KNOW?
GRRR...
KRRK
I THOUGHT YOU HAD A PLAN!
HEY, THE DOOR'S OPEN.
!
THAT'S ...
TOMORROW'S MY CORONATION.
I'M NERVOUS.
...THE YOUNG DEMON KING!

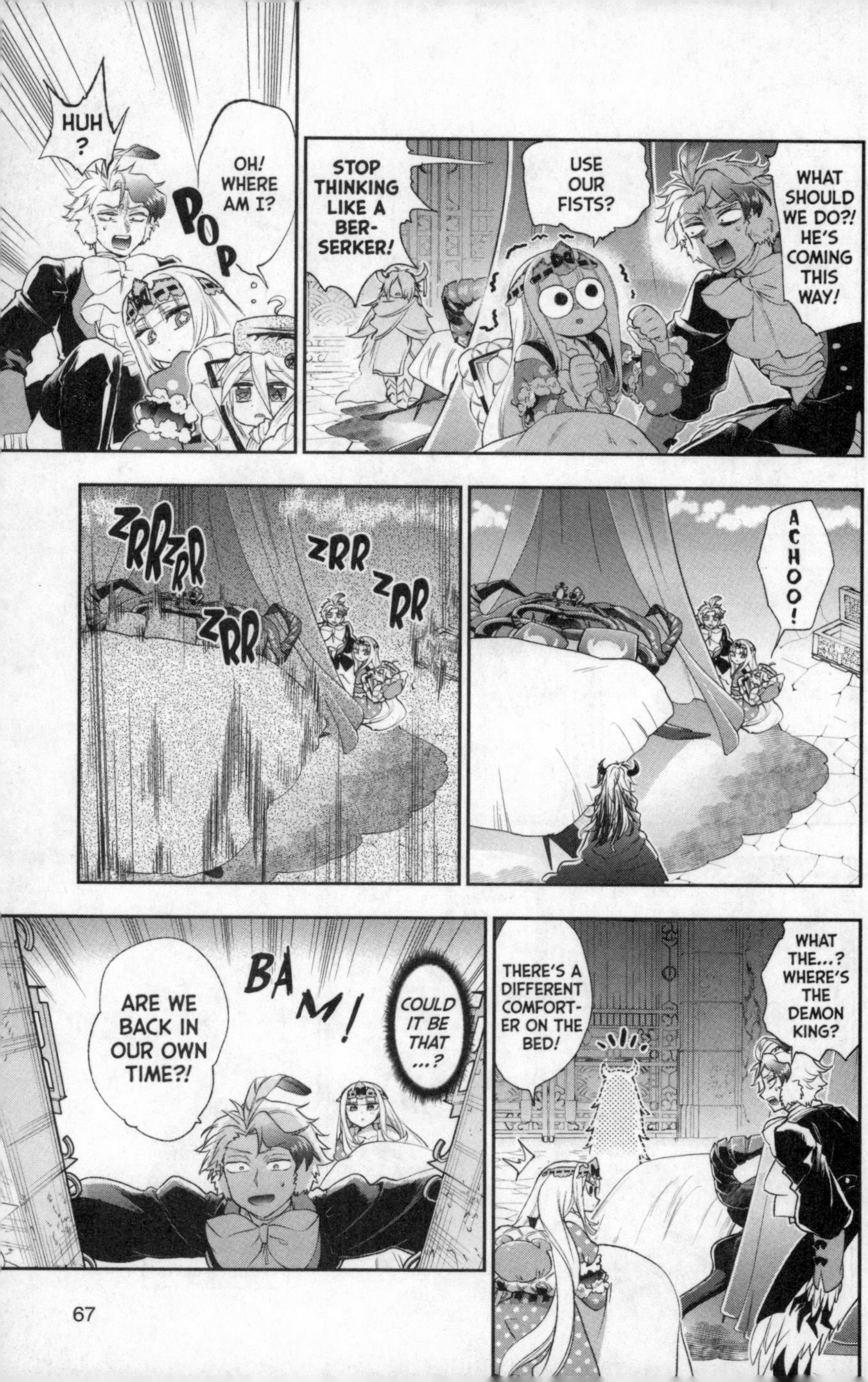
WHAT SHOULD WE DO?! HE'S COMING THIS WAY!
USE OUR FISTS?
STOP THINKING LIKE A BER-SERKER!
OH! WHERE AM I?
POP
HUH?
ACHOO!
ZRRZRR
ZRR ZRR
ZRR
WHAT THE...? WHERE'S THE DEMON KING?
THERE'S A DIFFERENT COMFORT-ER ON THE BED!
COULD IT BE THAT ...?
BAM!
ARE WE BACK IN OUR OWN TIME?!

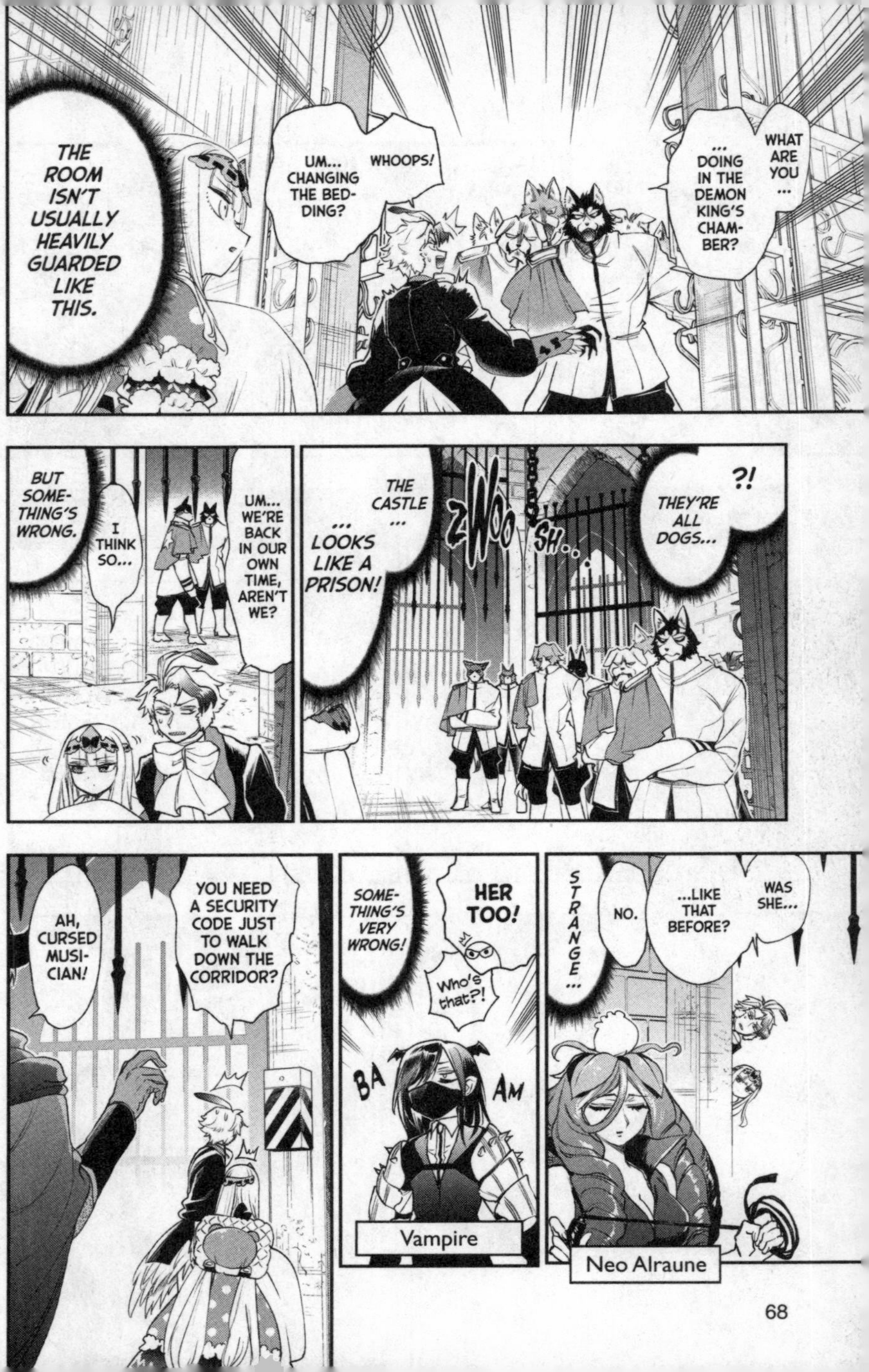
WHAT ARE YOU ...
... DOING IN THE DEMON KING'S CHAMBER?
WHOOPS!
UM... CHANGING THE BEDDING?
THE ROOM ISN'T USUALLY HEAVILY GUARDED LIKE THIS.
?!
THEY'RE ALL DOGS...
ZWOOSH...
THE CASTLE ...
... LOOKS LIKE A PRISON!
UM... WE'RE BACK IN OUR OWN TIME, AREN'T WE?
I THINK SO...
BUT SOMETHING'S WRONG.
WAS SHE...
...LIKE THAT BEFORE?
NO.
STRANGE...
Neo Alraune
HER TOO!
Who's that?!
SOMETHING'S VERY WRONG!
BAAM
Vampire
YOU NEED A SECURITY CODE JUST TO WALK DOWN THE CORRIDOR?
AH, CURSED MUSICIAN!

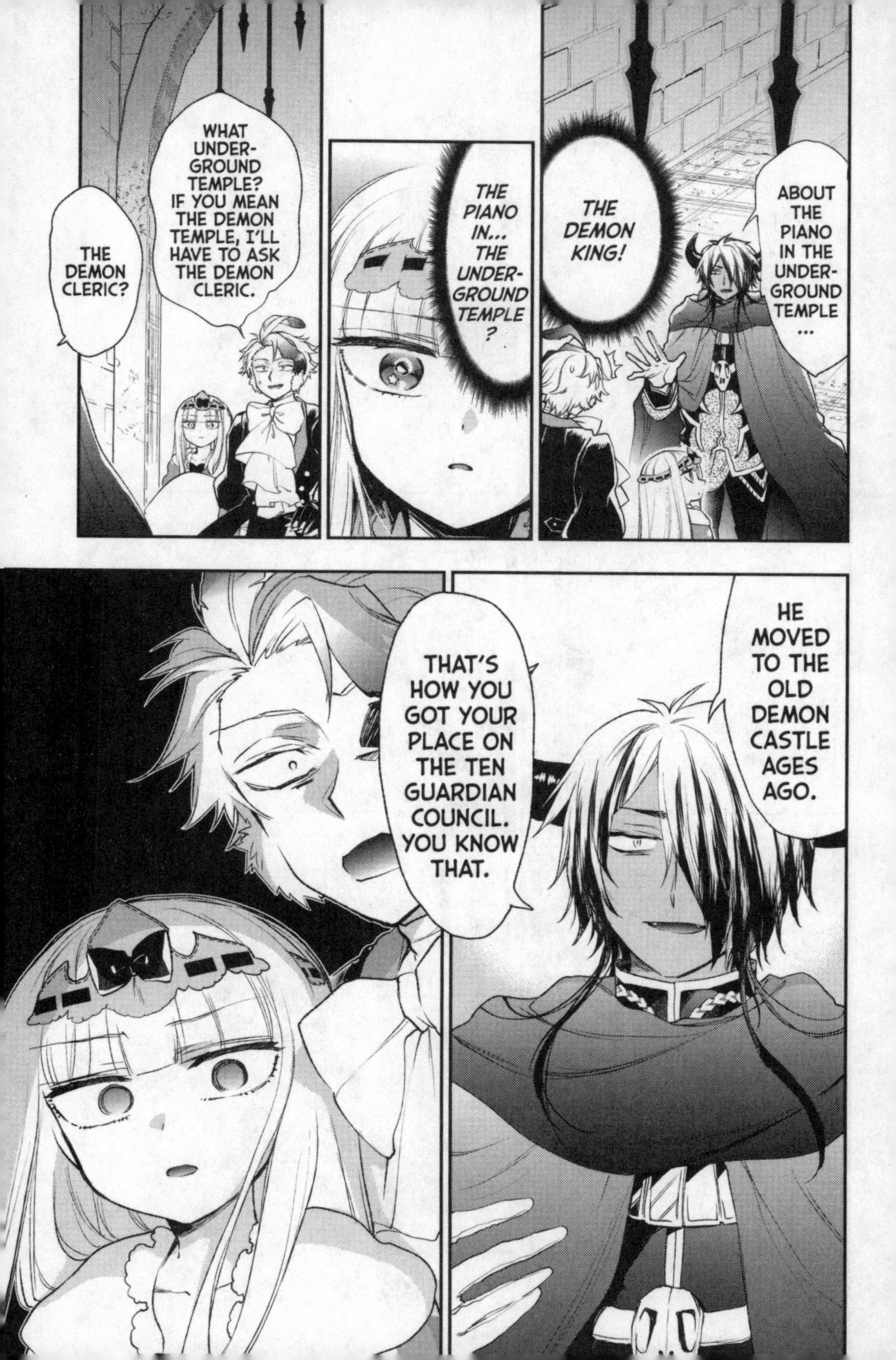
ABOUT THE PIANO IN THE UNDER-GROUND TEMPLE...
THE DEMON KING!
THE PIANO IN... THE UNDER-GROUND TEMPLE?
WHAT UNDER-GROUND TEMPLE? IF YOU MEAN THE DEMON TEMPLE, I'LL HAVE TO ASK THE DEMON CLERIC.
THE DEMON CLERIC?
HE MOVED TO THE OLD DEMON CASTLE AGES AGO.
THAT'S HOW YOU GOT YOUR PLACE ON THE TEN GUARDIAN COUNCIL. YOU KNOW THAT.

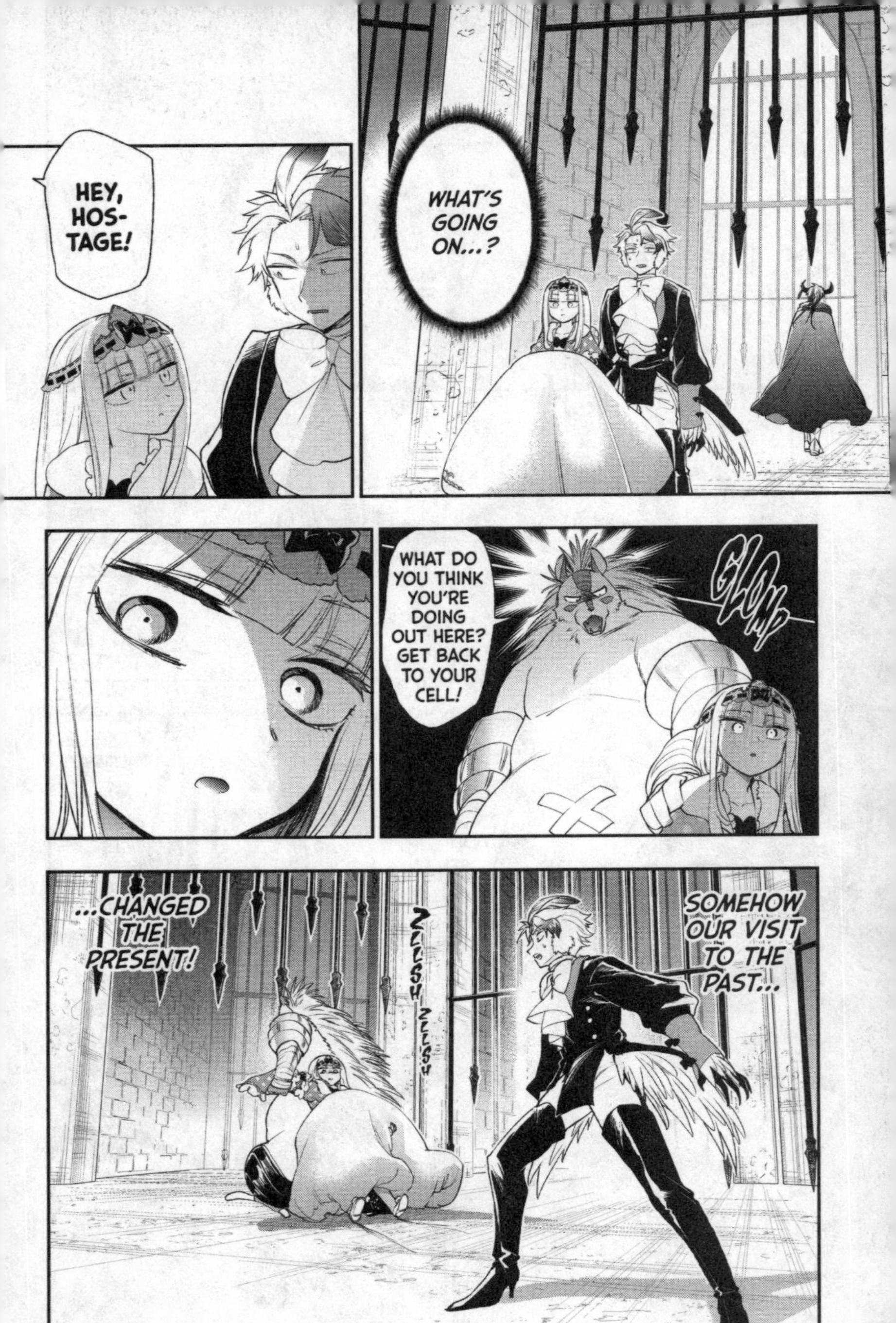
WHAT'S GOING ON...?
HEY, HOS-TAGE!
GLOMP
WHAT DO YOU THINK YOU'RE DOING OUT HERE? GET BACK TO YOUR CELL!
SOMEHOW OUR VISIT TO THE PAST...
ZEESH ZEESH
...CHANGED THE PRESENT!

201st Night: Another Route

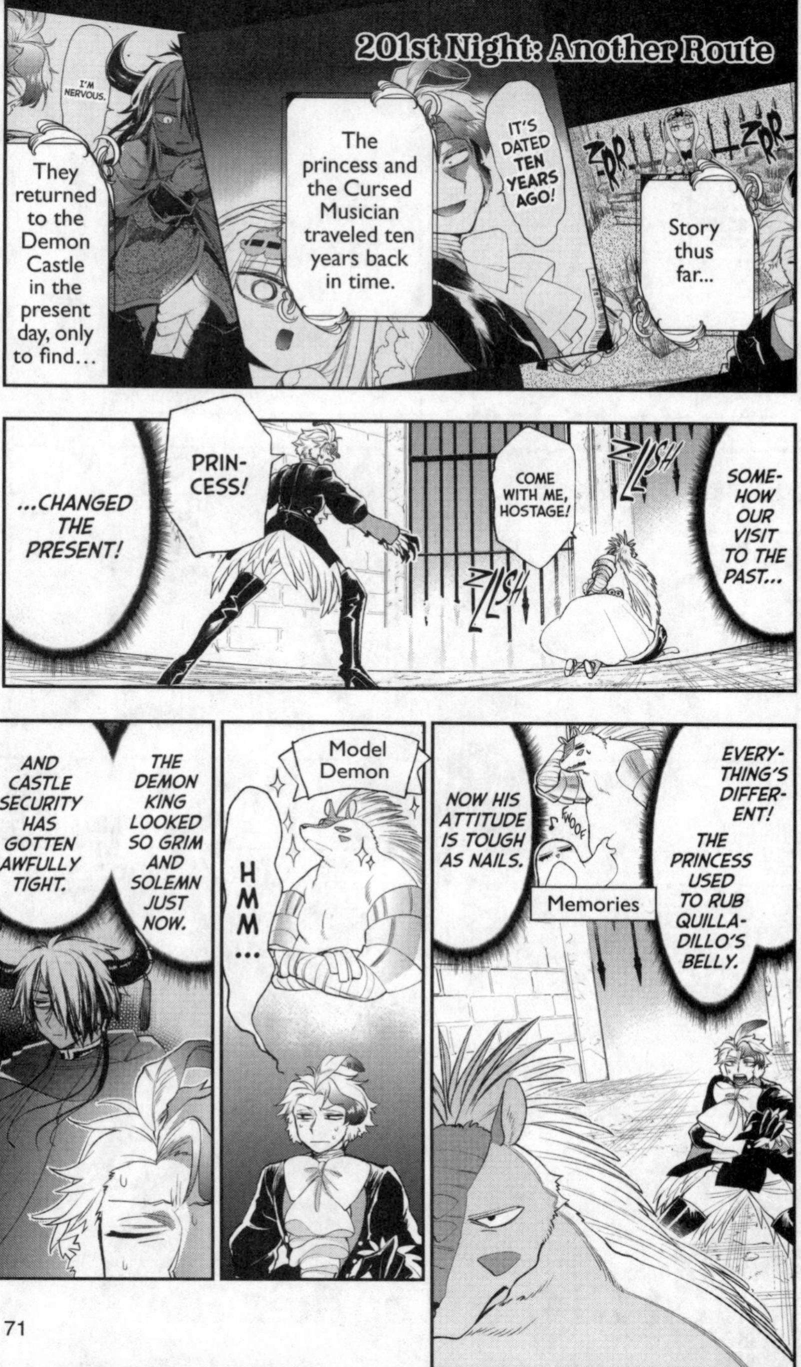
Story thus far...
ZRR
ZRR
IT'S DATED TEN YEARS AGO!
The princess and the Cursed Musician traveled ten years back in time.
I'M NERVOUS.
They returned to the Demon Castle in the present day, only to find…
SOME-HOW OUR VISIT TO THE PAST...
ZLLSH
COME WITH ME, HOSTAGE!
ZLLSH
PRIN-CESS!
...CHANGED THE PRESENT!
EVERY-THING'S DIFFER-ENT!
THE PRINCESS USED TO RUB QUILLA-DILLO'S BELLY.
FWOOF
Memories
NOW HIS ATTITUDE IS TOUGH AS NAILS.
Model Demon
HMM...
THE DEMON KING LOOKED SO GRIM AND SOLEMN JUST NOW.
AND CASTLE SECURITY HAS GOTTEN AWFULLY TIGHT.

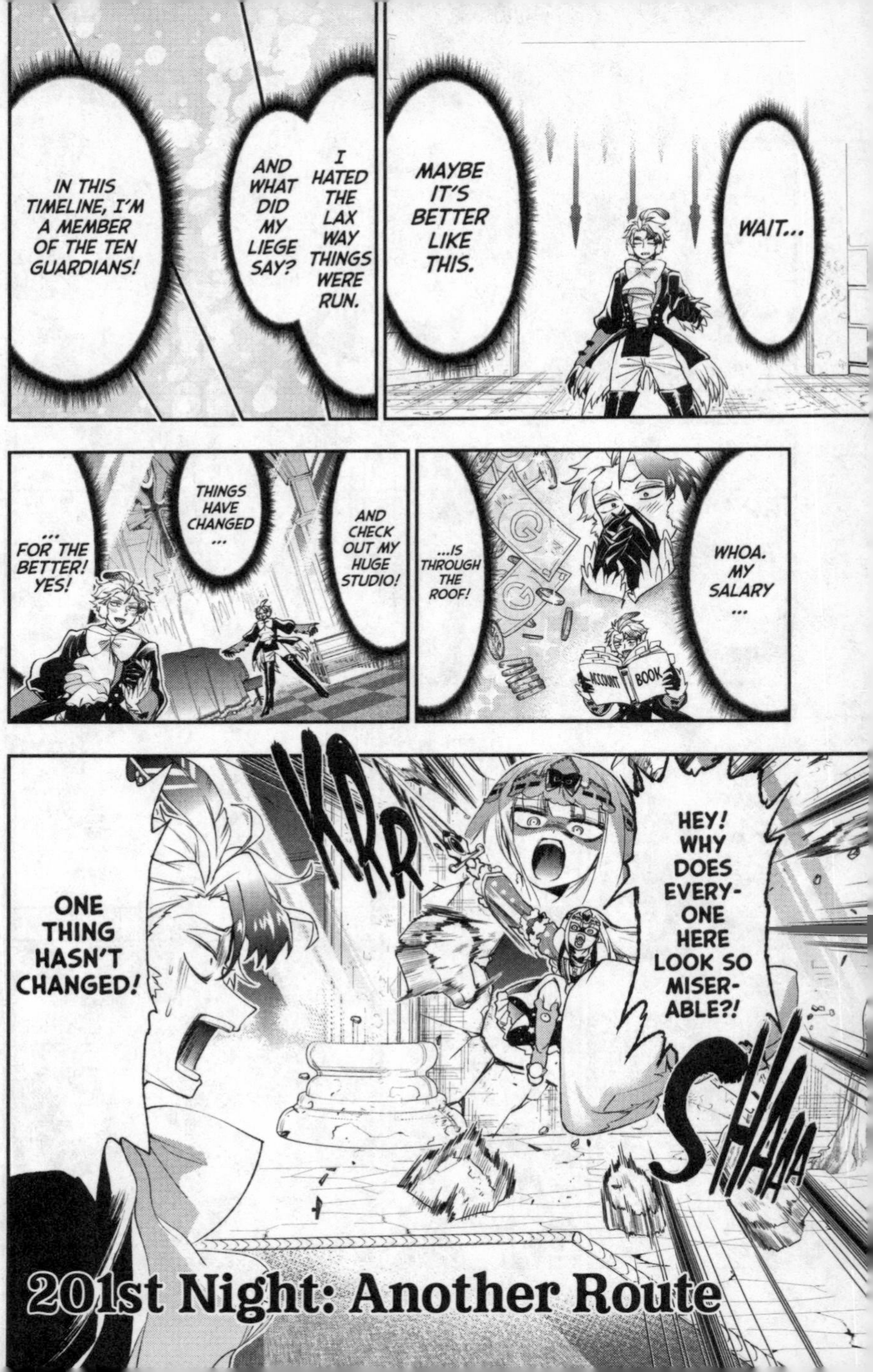
WAIT...
MAYBE IT'S BETTER LIKE THIS.
I HATED THE LAX WAY THINGS WERE RUN.
AND WHAT DID MY LIEGE SAY?
IN THIS TIMELINE, I'M A MEMBER OF THE TEN GUARDIANS!
WHOA. MY SALARY...
...IS THROUGH THE ROOF!
ACCOUNT BOOK
AND CHECK OUT MY HUGE STUDIO!
THINGS HAVE CHANGED...
...FOR THE BETTER! YES!
HEY! WHY DOES EVERY-ONE HERE LOOK SO MISER-ABLE?!
KRRR
SHAAA
ONE THING HASN'T CHANGED!

201st Night: Another Route

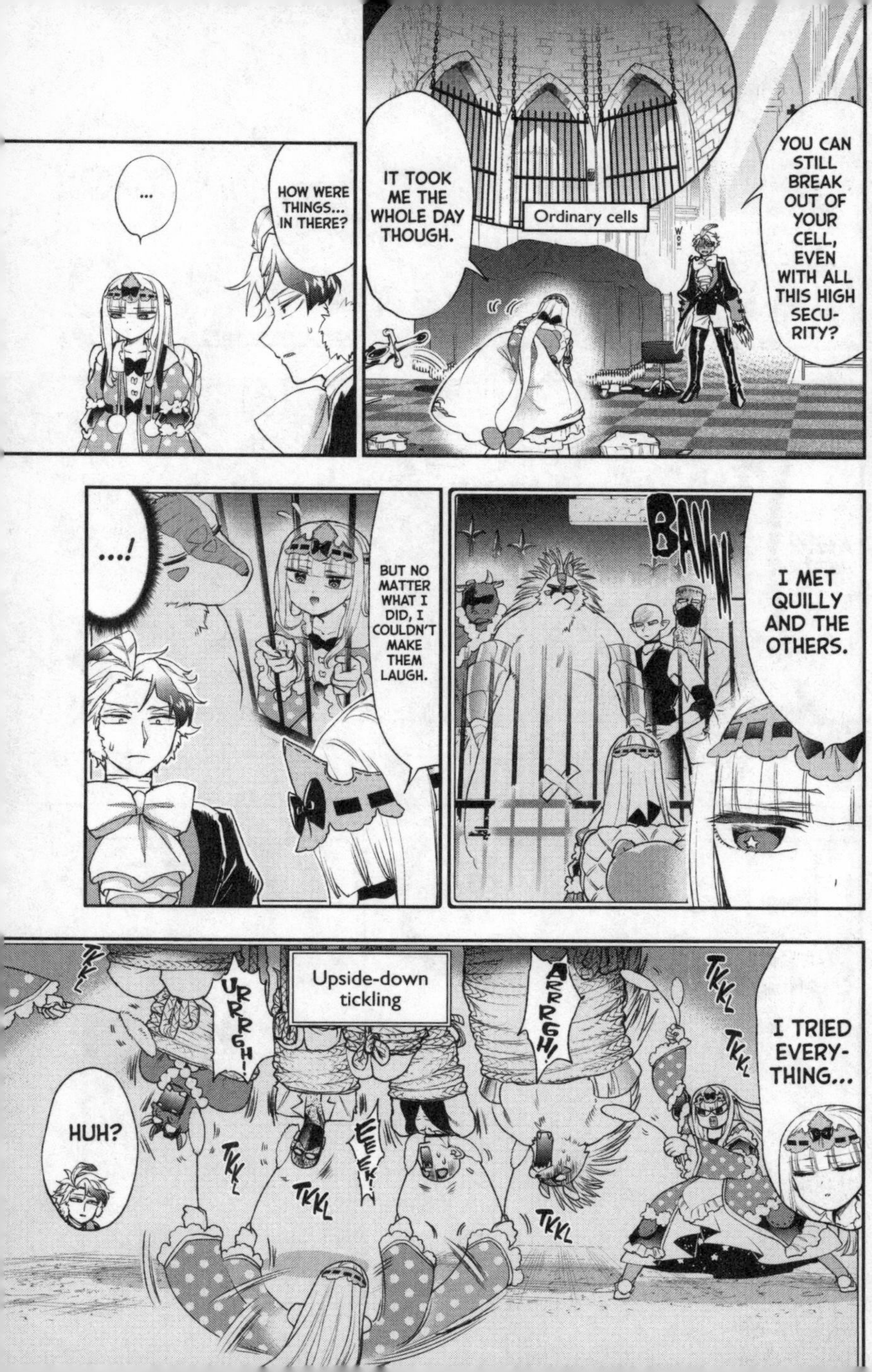
YOU CAN STILL BREAK OUT OF YOUR CELL, EVEN WITH ALL THIS HIGH SECURITY?
IT TOOK ME THE WHOLE DAY THOUGH.
Ordinary cells
HOW WERE THINGS... IN THERE?
...
BAMM
I MET QUILLY AND THE OTHERS.
BUT NO MATTER WHAT I DID, I COULDN'T MAKE THEM LAUGH.
...!
I TRIED EVERYTHING...
TKKL
TKKL
Upside-down tickling
ARRRGH!
URRRGH!
TKKL
EEEEK!
TKKL
TKKL
TKKL
HUH?

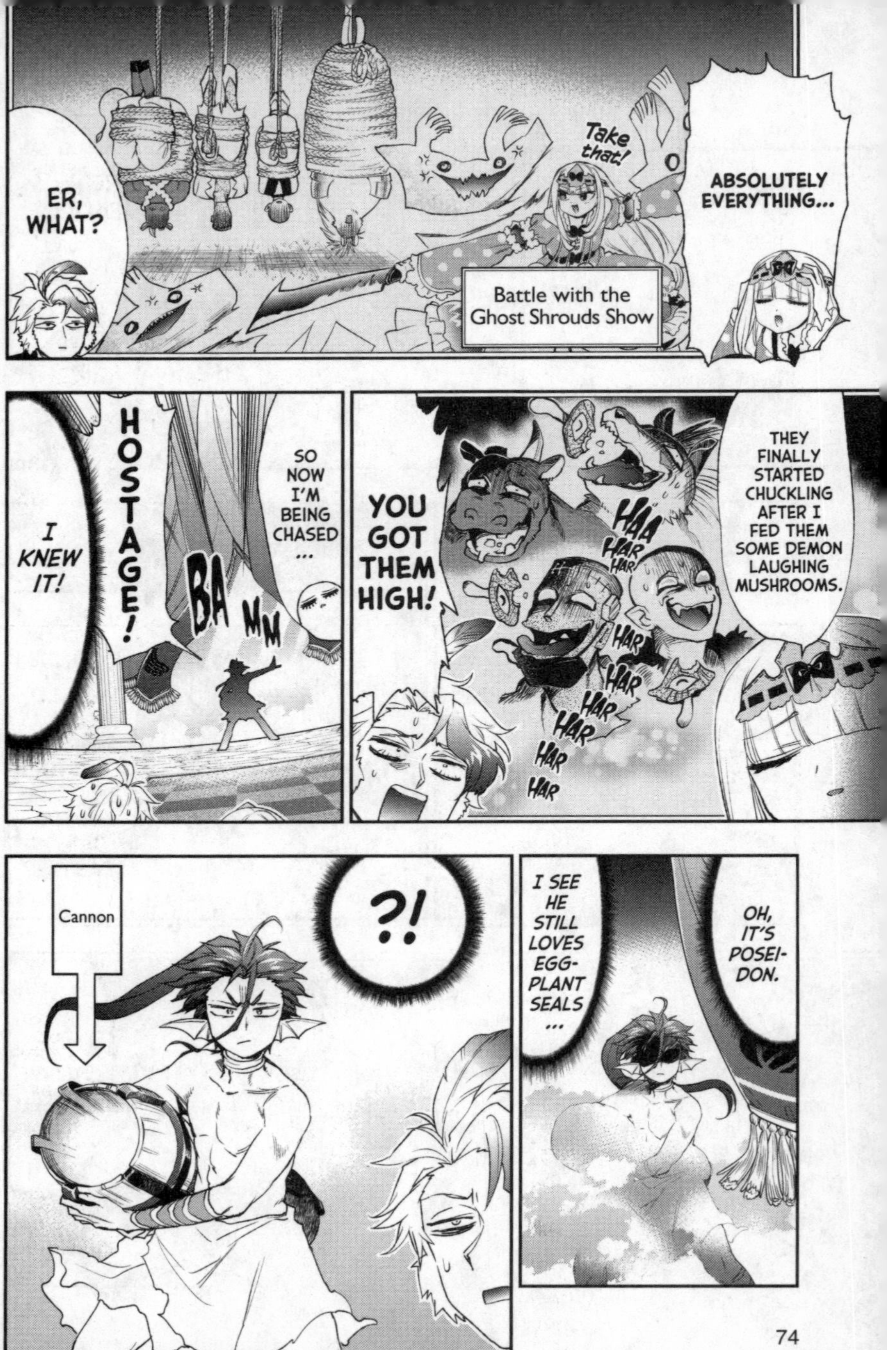
ABSOLUTELY EVERYTHING...
Take that!
Battle with the Ghost Shrouds Show
ER, WHAT?
THEY FINALLY STARTED CHUCKLING AFTER I FED THEM SOME DEMON LAUGHING MUSHROOMS.
HAA HAR HAR HAR HAR HAR HAR HAR HAR HAR
YOU GOT THEM HIGH!
SO NOW I'M BEING CHASED...
HOSTAGE!
BAMM
I KNEW IT!
OH, IT'S POSEI-DON.
I SEE HE STILL LOVES EGG-PLANT SEALS...
?!
Cannon

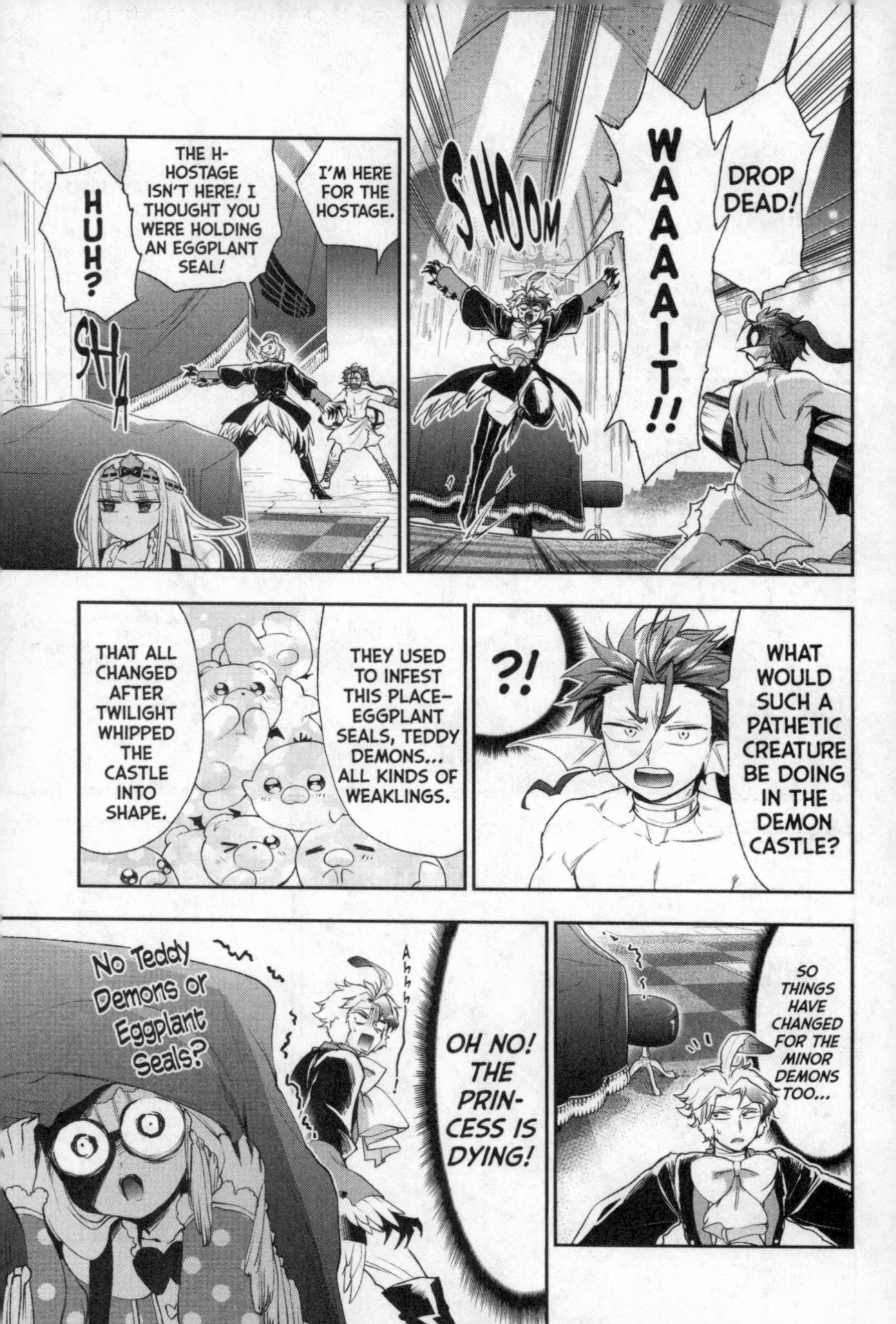
DROP DEAD!
WAAAAIT!!
SHOOM
I'M HERE FOR THE HOSTAGE.
THE H-HOSTAGE ISN'T HERE! I THOUGHT YOU WERE HOLDING AN EGGPLANT SEAL!
HUH?
SHA
WHAT WOULD SUCH A PATHETIC CREATURE BE DOING IN THE DEMON CASTLE?
?!
THEY USED TO INFEST THIS PLACE—EGGPLANT SEALS, TEDDY DEMONS... ALL KINDS OF WEAKLINGS.
THAT ALL CHANGED AFTER TWILIGHT WHIPPED THE CASTLE INTO SHAPE.
SO THINGS HAVE CHANGED FOR THE MINOR DEMONS TOO...
OH NO! THE PRINCESS IS DYING!
Ahh
No Teddy Demons or Eggplant Seals?

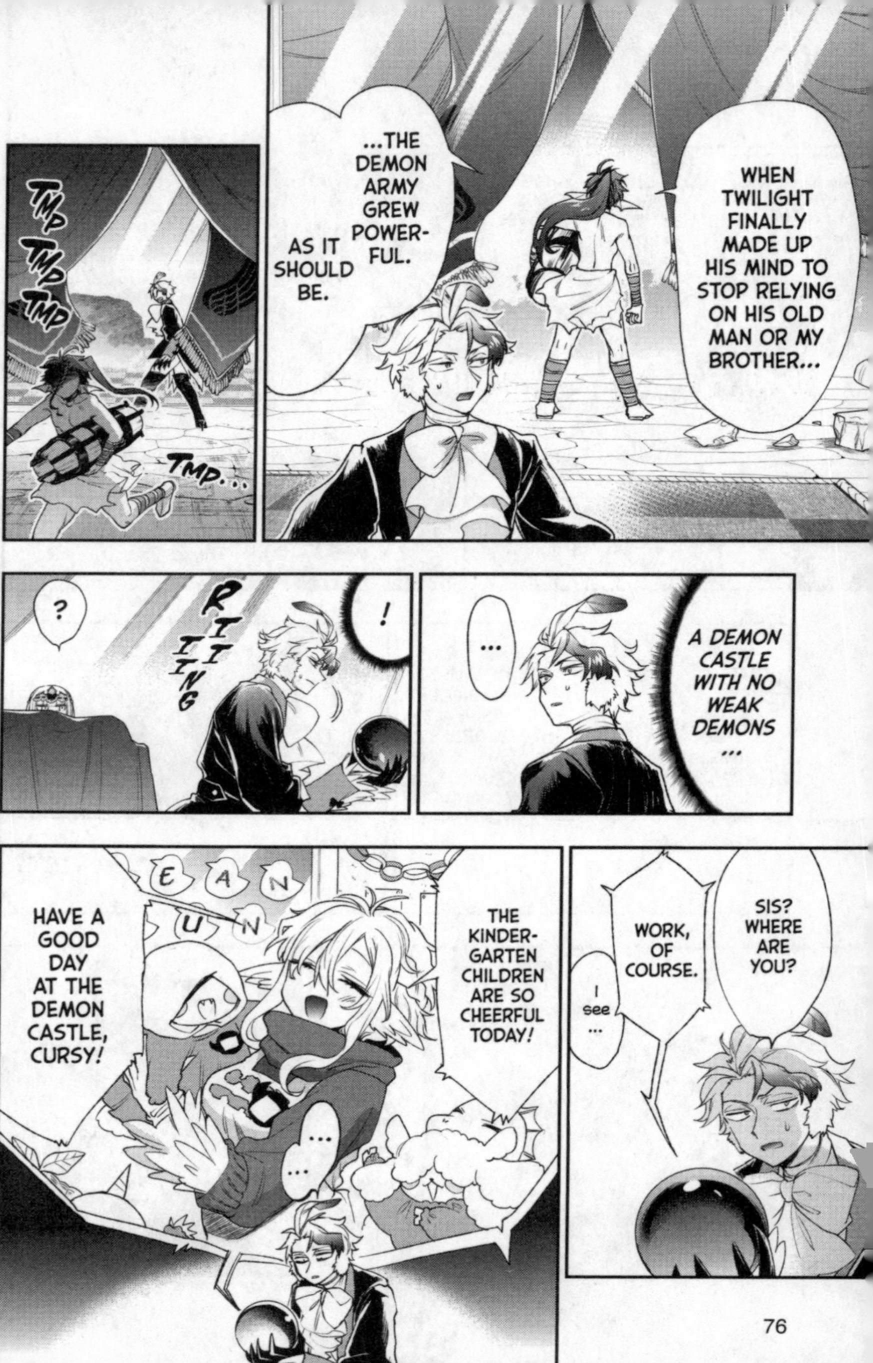
WHEN TWILIGHT FINALLY MADE UP HIS MIND TO STOP RELYING ON HIS OLD MAN OR MY BROTHER...
...THE DEMON ARMY GREW POWERFUL.
AS IT SHOULD BE.
TMP TMP TMP TMP
TMP...
...
A DEMON CASTLE WITH NO WEAK DEMONS...
!
RIIIIING
?
SIS? WHERE ARE YOU?
WORK, OF COURSE.
I see...
THE KINDERGARTEN CHILDREN ARE SO CHEERFUL TODAY!
E A N U N
HAVE A GOOD DAY AT THE DEMON CASTLE, CURSY!
...
...

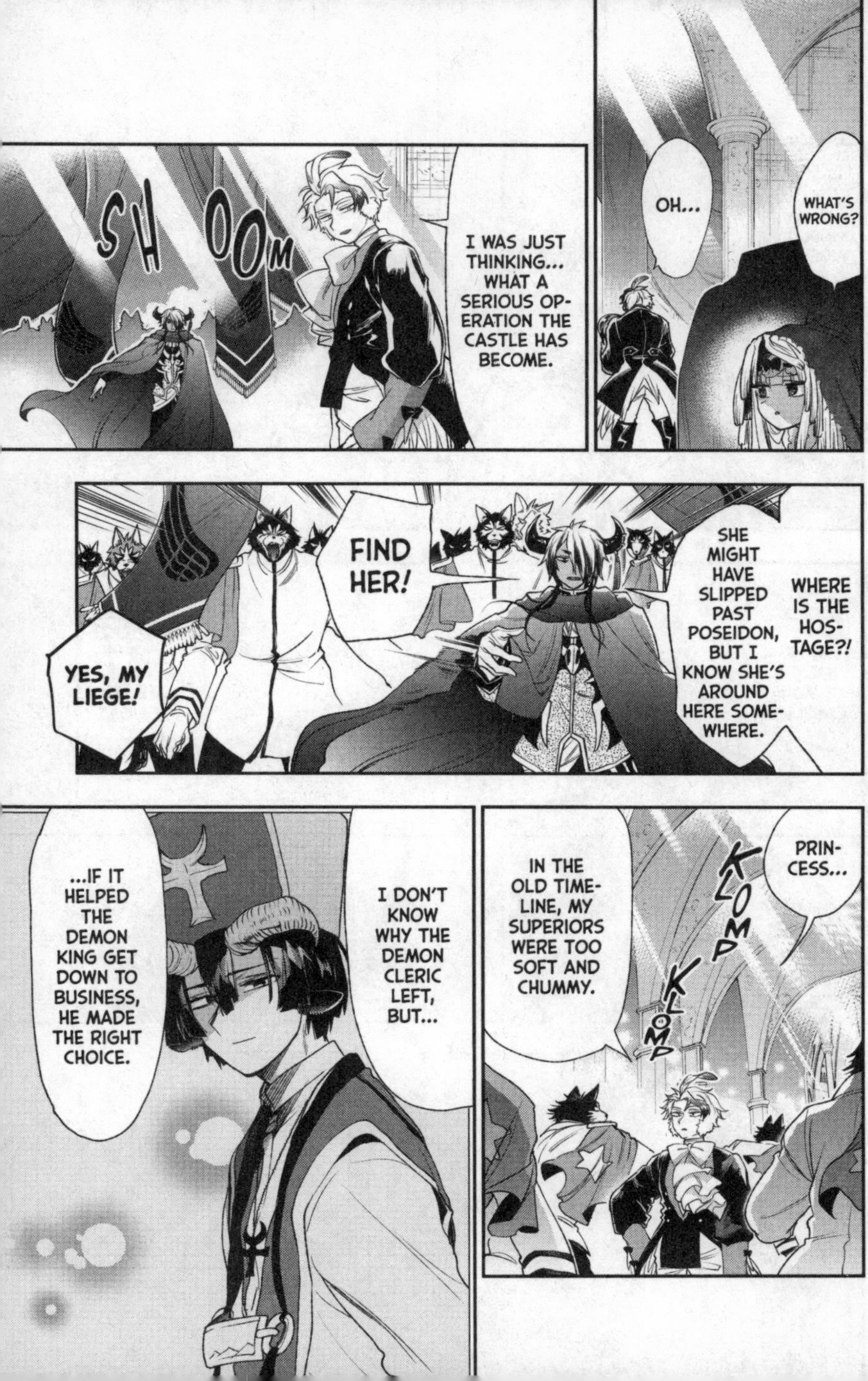
WHAT'S WRONG?
OH...
SHOOM
I WAS JUST THINKING... WHAT A SERIOUS OP-ERATION THE CASTLE HAS BECOME.
WHERE IS THE HOS-TAGE?!
SHE MIGHT HAVE SLIPPED PAST POSEIDON, BUT I KNOW SHE'S AROUND HERE SOME-WHERE.
FIND HER!
YES, MY LIEGE!
PRIN-CESS...
KLOMP
KLOMP
IN THE OLD TIME-LINE, MY SUPERIORS WERE TOO SOFT AND CHUMMY.
I DON'T KNOW WHY THE DEMON CLERIC LEFT, BUT...
...IF IT HELPED THE DEMON KING GET DOWN TO BUSINESS, HE MADE THE RIGHT CHOICE.

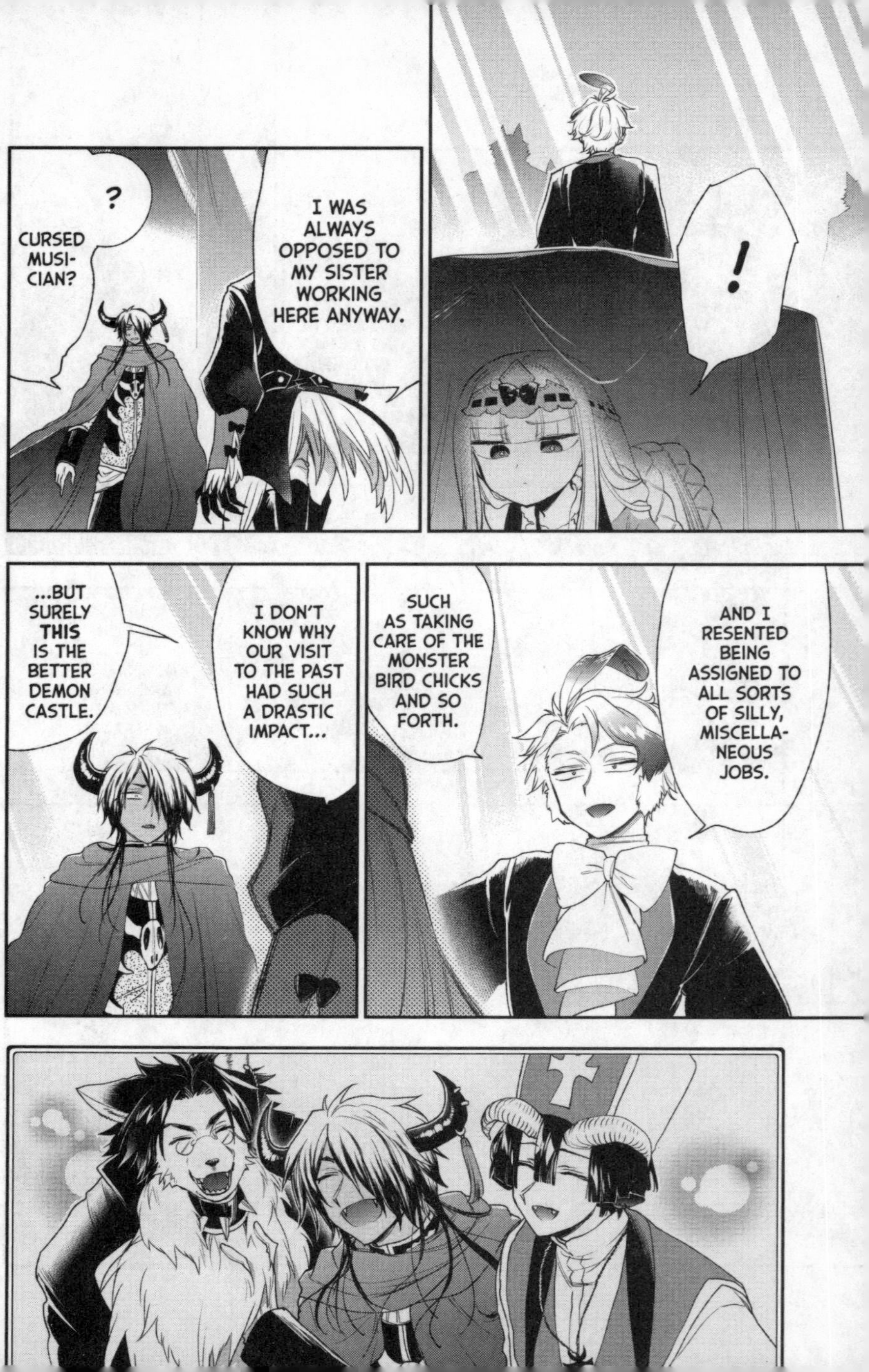
!
I WAS ALWAYS OPPOSED TO MY SISTER WORKING HERE ANYWAY.
?
CURSED MUSI-CIAN?
AND I RESENTED BEING ASSIGNED TO ALL SORTS OF SILLY, MISCELLA-NEOUS JOBS.
SUCH AS TAKING CARE OF THE MONSTER BIRD CHICKS AND SO FORTH.
I DON'T KNOW WHY OUR VISIT TO THE PAST HAD SUCH A DRASTIC IMPACT...
...BUT SURELY **THIS** IS THE BETTER DEMON CASTLE.

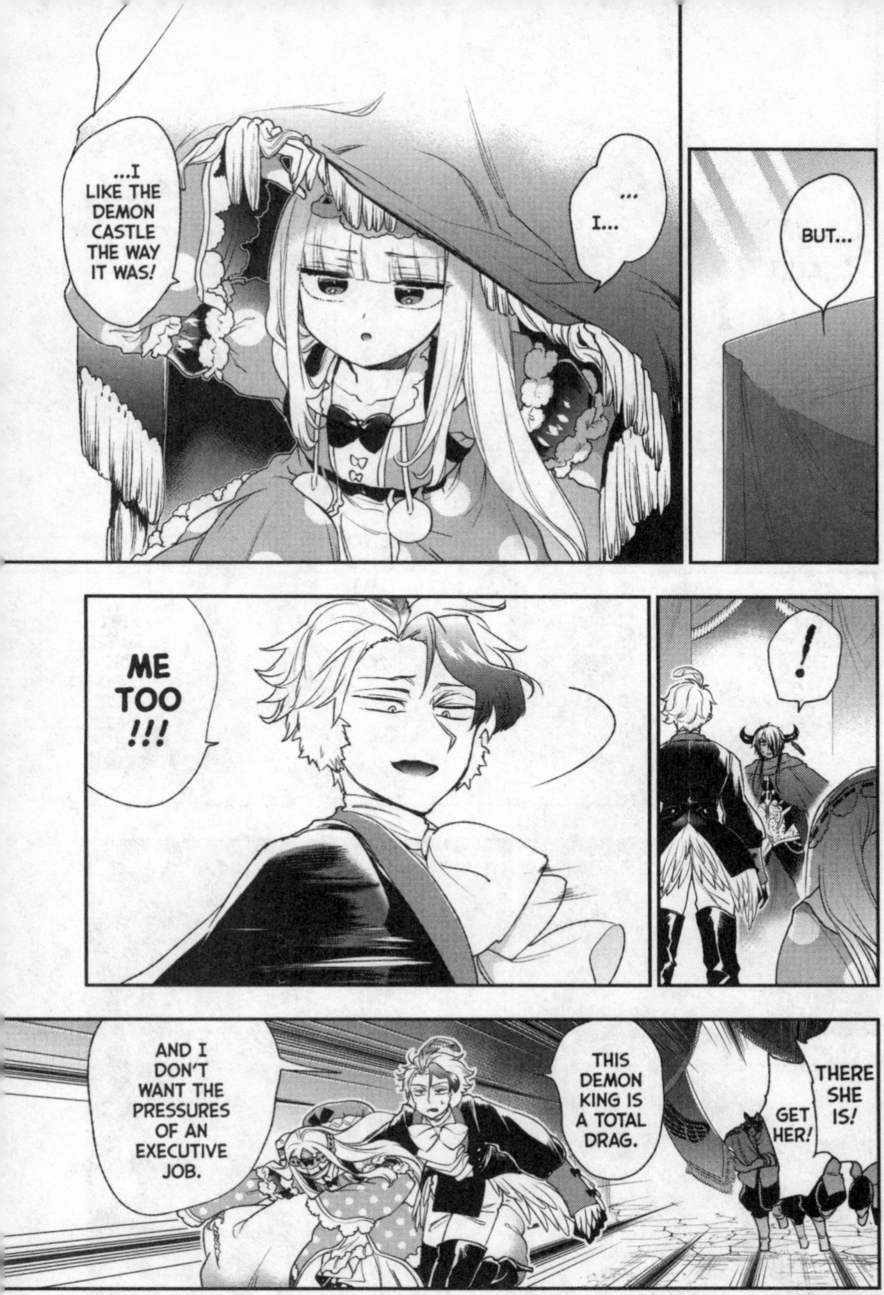
BUT...
... I...
...I LIKE THE DEMON CASTLE THE WAY IT WAS!
!
ME TOO!!!
THERE SHE IS!
GET HER!
THIS DEMON KING IS A TOTAL DRAG.
AND I DON'T WANT THE PRESSURES OF AN EXECUTIVE JOB.

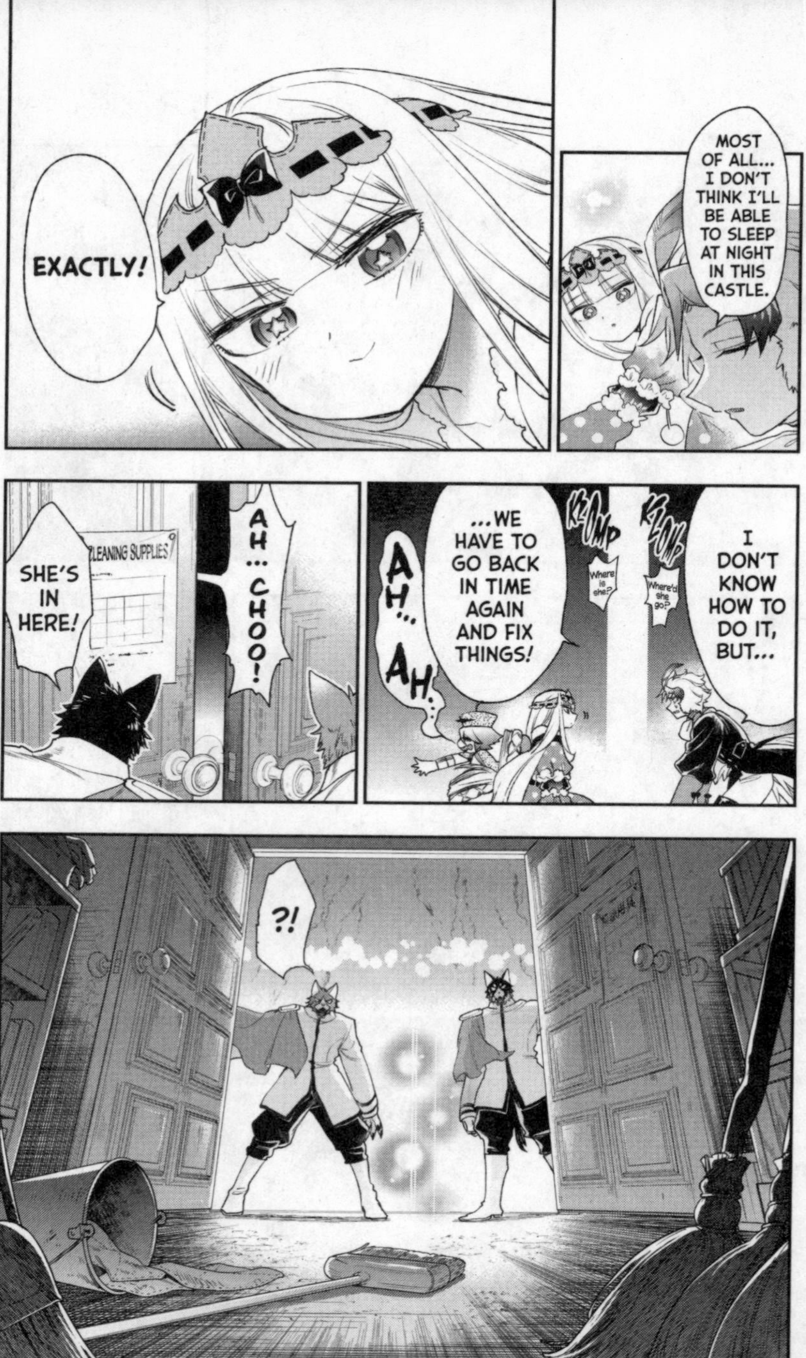
MOST OF ALL... I DON'T THINK I'LL BE ABLE TO SLEEP AT NIGHT IN THIS CASTLE.
EXACTLY!
I DON'T KNOW HOW TO DO IT, BUT...
KLOMP
Where'd she go?
KLOMP
Where is she?
...WE HAVE TO GO BACK IN TIME AGAIN AND FIX THINGS!
AH... AH...
AH... CHOO!
CLEANING SUPPLIES
SHE'S IN HERE!
?!

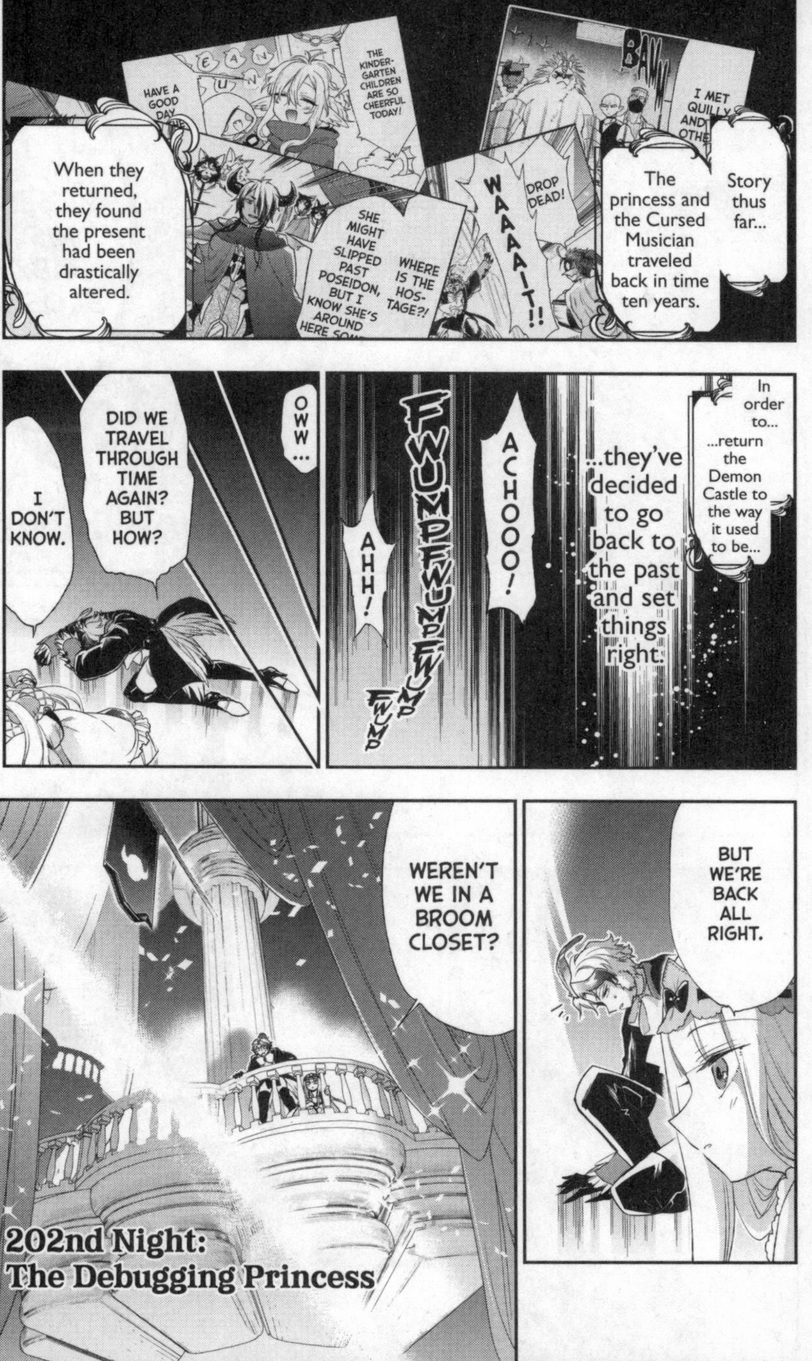
Story thus far...
The princess and the Cursed Musician traveled back in time ten years.
BAM
I MET QUILLY AND OTHE
DROP DEAD!
WAAAAIT!!
WHERE IS THE HOS-TAGE?!
SHE MIGHT HAVE SLIPPED PAST POSEIDON, BUT I KNOW SHE'S AROUND HERE SOM
THE KINDER-GARTEN CHILDREN ARE SO CHEERFUL TODAY!
HAVE A GOOD DAY
When they returned, they found the present had been drastically altered.
In order to...
...return the Demon Castle to the way it used to be...
...they've decided to go back to the past and set things right.
ACHOOOO!
FWUMPFWUMPFWUMP
AHH!
FWUMP
OWW...
DID WE TRAVEL THROUGH TIME AGAIN? BUT HOW?
I DON'T KNOW.
BUT WE'RE BACK ALL RIGHT.
WEREN'T WE IN A BROOM CLOSET?

202nd Night: The Debugging Princess

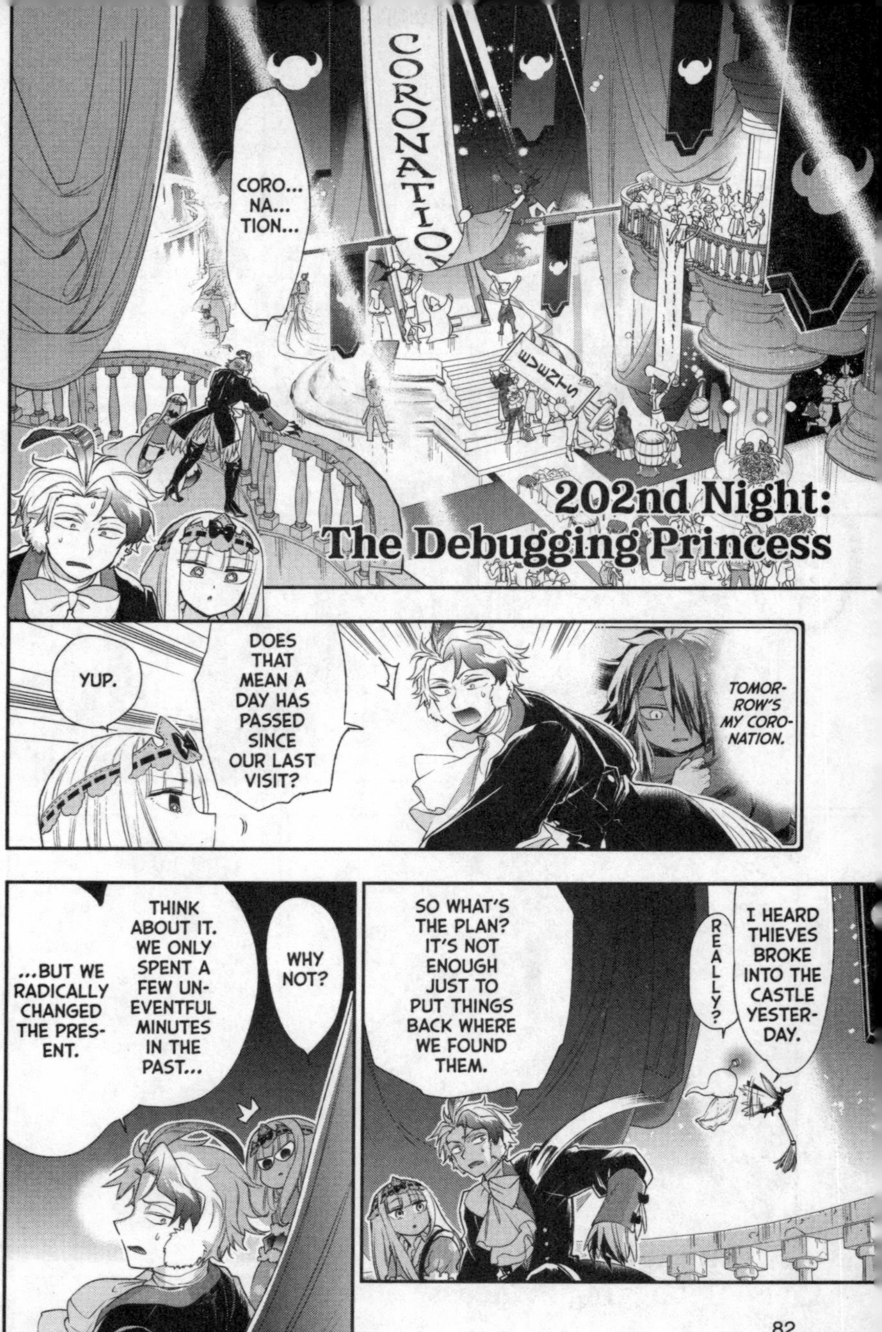
CORONATION
CORO... NA... TION...
202nd Night: The Debugging Princess
TOMORROW'S MY CORONATION.
DOES THAT MEAN A DAY HAS PASSED SINCE OUR LAST VISIT?
YUP.
I HEARD THIEVES BROKE INTO THE CASTLE YESTERDAY.
REALLY?
SO WHAT'S THE PLAN? IT'S NOT ENOUGH JUST TO PUT THINGS BACK WHERE WE FOUND THEM.
WHY NOT?
THINK ABOUT IT. WE ONLY SPENT A FEW UNEVENTFUL MINUTES IN THE PAST...
...BUT WE RADICALLY CHANGED THE PRESENT.

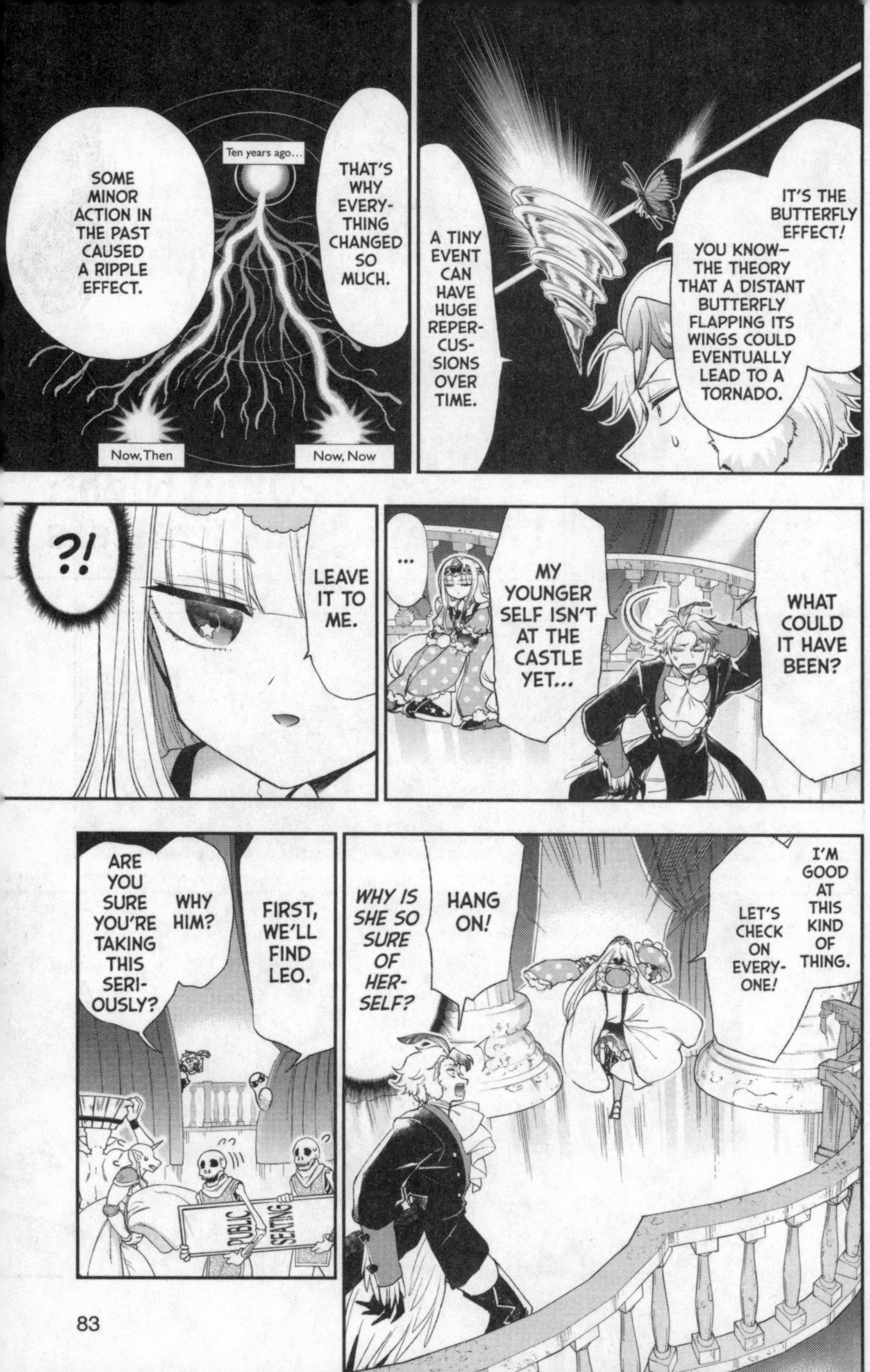
IT'S THE BUTTERFLY EFFECT!
YOU KNOW— THE THEORY THAT A DISTANT BUTTERFLY FLAPPING ITS WINGS COULD EVENTUALLY LEAD TO A TORNADO.
A TINY EVENT CAN HAVE HUGE REPERCUSSIONS OVER TIME.
THAT'S WHY EVERYTHING CHANGED SO MUCH.
Ten years ago…
SOME MINOR ACTION IN THE PAST CAUSED A RIPPLE EFFECT.
Now, Now
Now, Then
WHAT COULD IT HAVE BEEN?
MY YOUNGER SELF ISN'T AT THE CASTLE YET…
…
LEAVE IT TO ME.
?!
I'M GOOD AT THIS KIND OF THING.
LET'S CHECK ON EVERYONE!
HANG ON!
WHY IS SHE SO SURE OF HERSELF?
FIRST, WE'LL FIND LEO.
WHY HIM?
ARE YOU SURE YOU'RE TAKING THIS SERIOUSLY?
PUBLIC SEATING

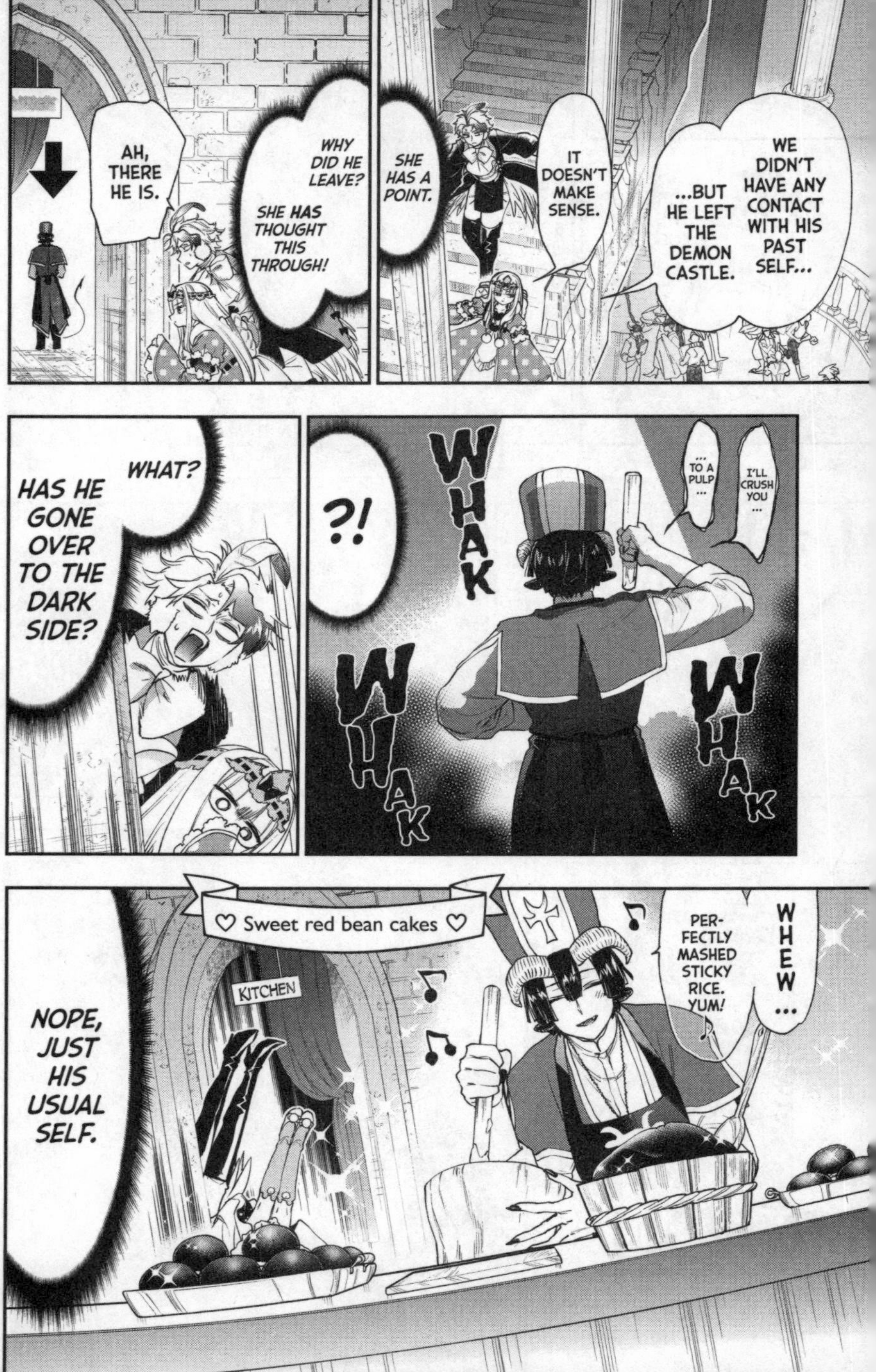
WE DIDN'T HAVE ANY CONTACT WITH HIS PAST SELF...
...BUT HE LEFT THE DEMON CASTLE.
IT DOESN'T MAKE SENSE.
SHE HAS A POINT.
WHY DID HE LEAVE?
SHE HAS THOUGHT THIS THROUGH!
AH, THERE HE IS.
I'LL CRUSH YOU...
...TO A PULP...
WHAK
WHAK
WHAK
?!
WHAT?
HAS HE GONE OVER TO THE DARK SIDE?
♡ Sweet red bean cakes ♡
WHEW...
PERFECTLY MASHED STICKY RICE. YUM!
KITCHEN
NOPE, JUST HIS USUAL SELF.

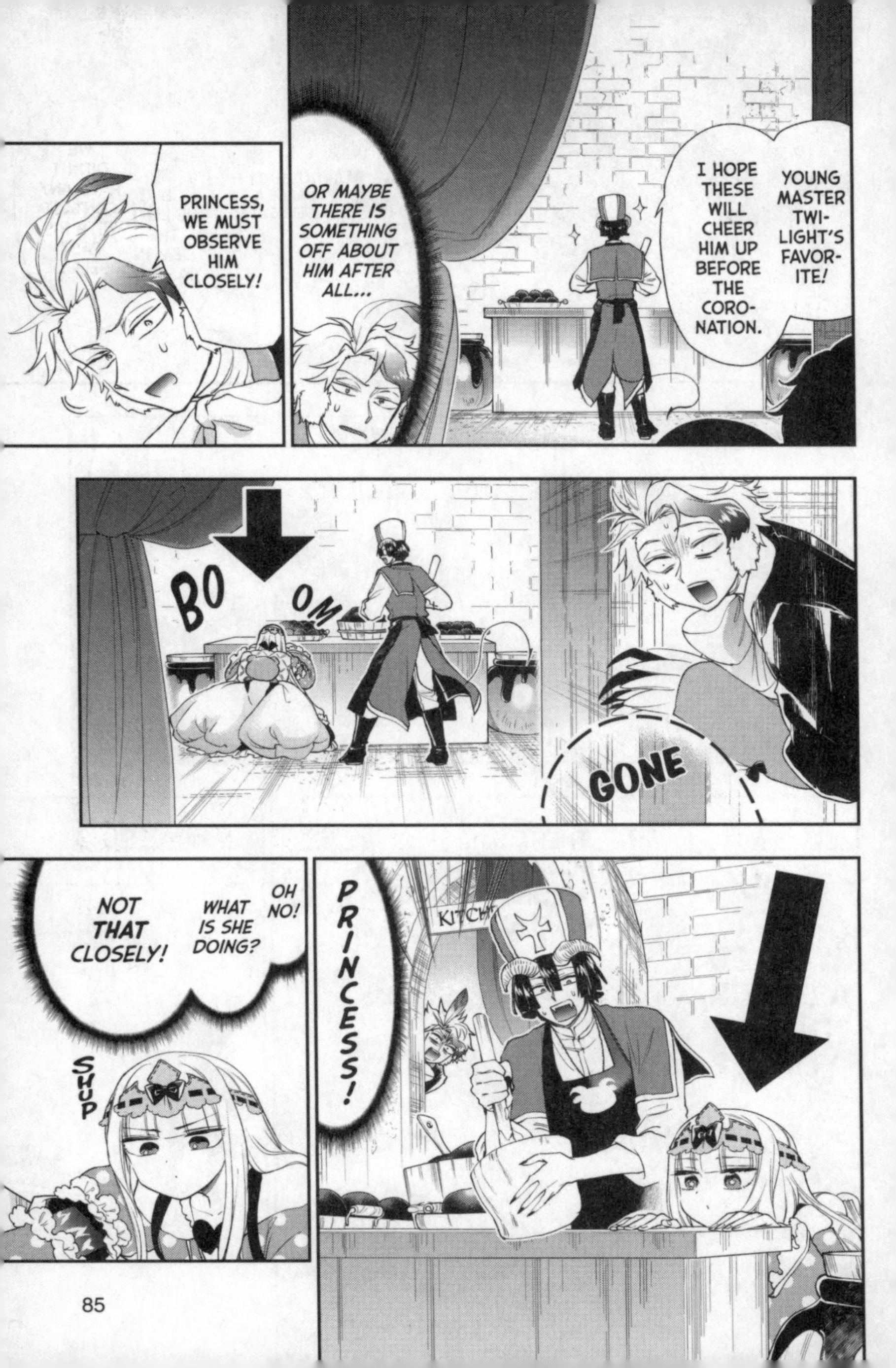
YOUNG MASTER TWILIGHT'S FAVORITE!
I HOPE THESE WILL CHEER HIM UP BEFORE THE CORONATION.
OR MAYBE THERE IS SOMETHING OFF ABOUT HIM AFTER ALL...
PRINCESS, WE MUST OBSERVE HIM CLOSELY!
GONE
BOOM
PRINCESS!
OH NO!
WHAT IS SHE DOING?
NOT THAT CLOSELY!
SHUP

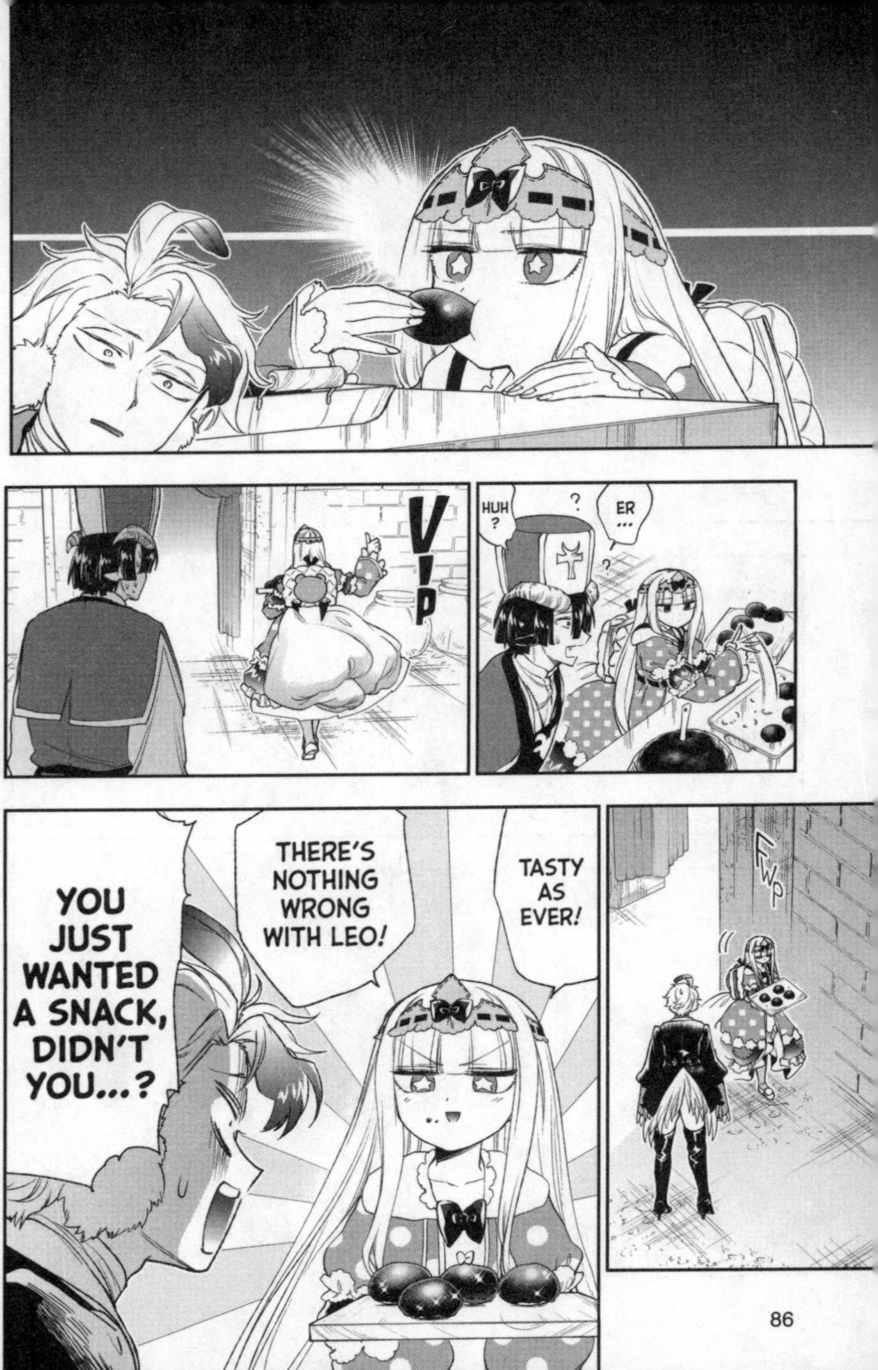
HUH?
?
ER...
?
VIP
FWP
TASTY AS EVER!
THERE'S NOTHING WRONG WITH LEO!
YOU JUST WANTED A SNACK, DIDN'T YOU...?

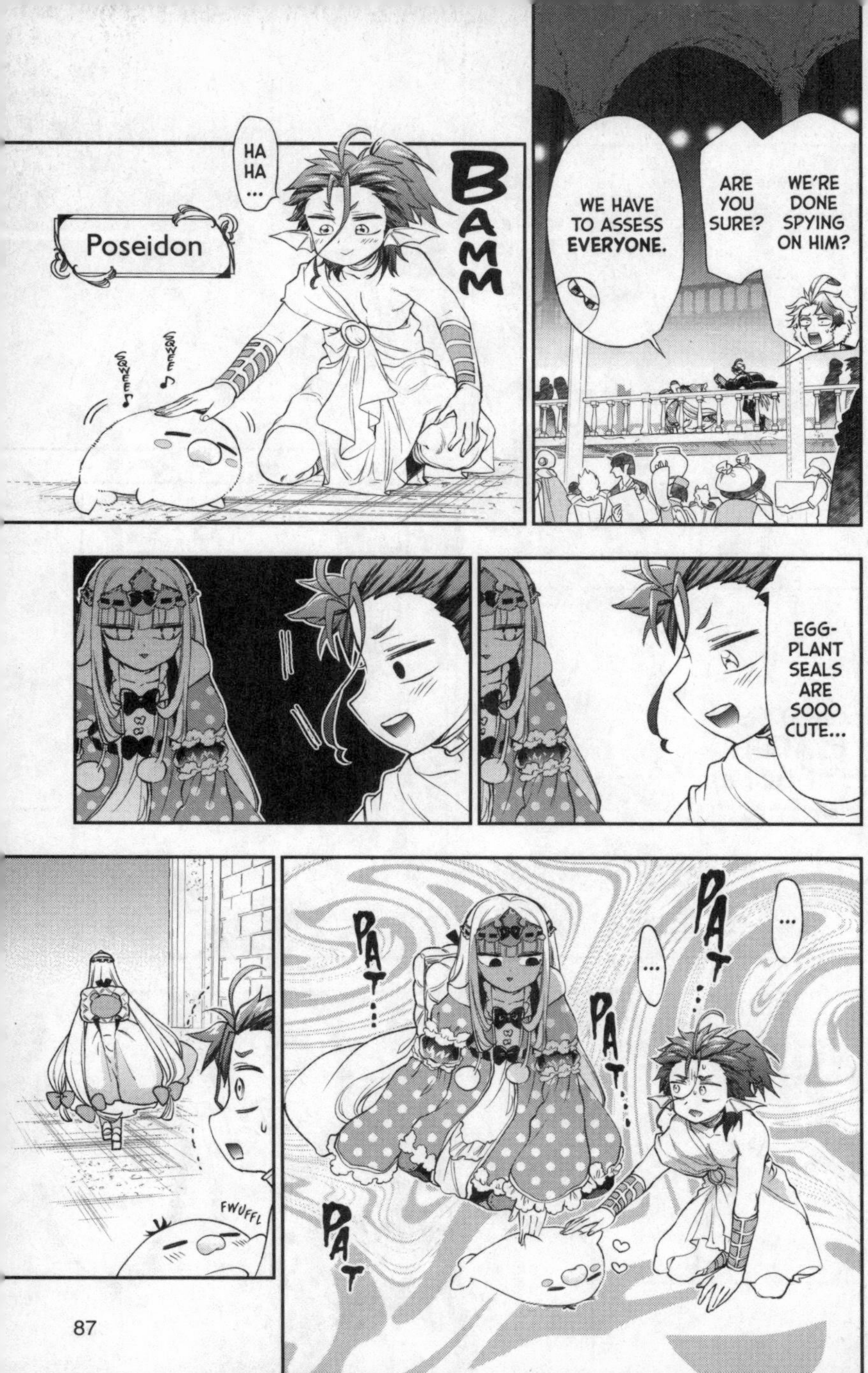
WE'RE DONE SPYING ON HIM?
ARE YOU SURE?
WE HAVE TO ASSESS EVERYONE.
BAMM
HA HA ...
Poseidon
SQWEE♪
SQWEE♪
EGG-PLANT SEALS ARE SOOO CUTE...
...
...
PAT...
PAT
PAT...
PAT...
PAT
FWUFFL

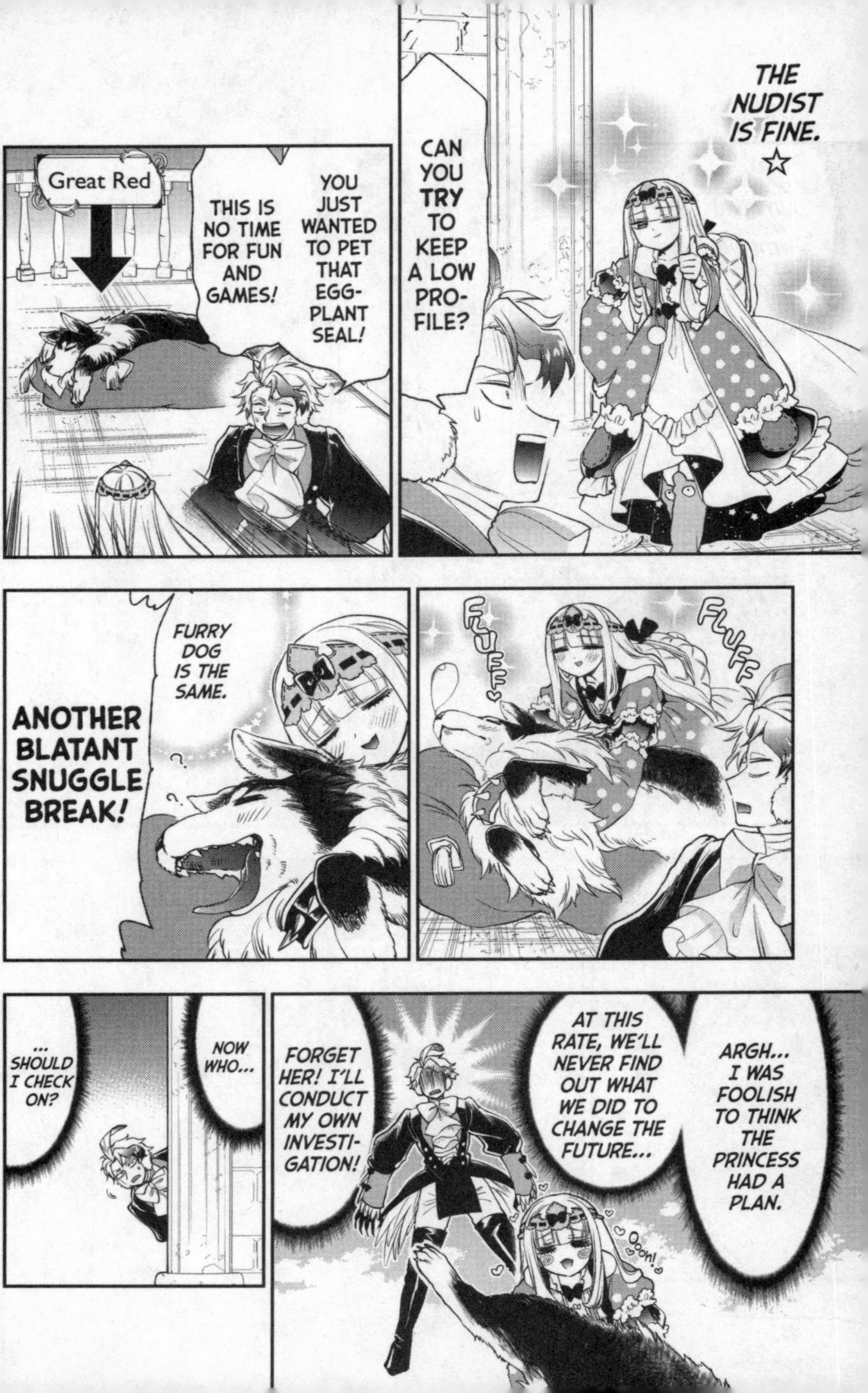
THE NUDIST IS FINE. ☆
CAN YOU TRY TO KEEP A LOW PRO-FILE?
YOU JUST WANTED TO PET THAT EGG-PLANT SEAL!
THIS IS NO TIME FOR FUN AND GAMES!
Great Red
FLUFF
FLUFF
FURRY DOG IS THE SAME.
ANOTHER BLATANT SNUGGLE BREAK!
ARGH... I WAS FOOLISH TO THINK THE PRINCESS HAD A PLAN.
AT THIS RATE, WE'LL NEVER FIND OUT WHAT WE DID TO CHANGE THE FUTURE...
FORGET HER! I'LL CONDUCT MY OWN INVESTI-GATION!
Oooh!
NOW WHO...
...SHOULD I CHECK ON?

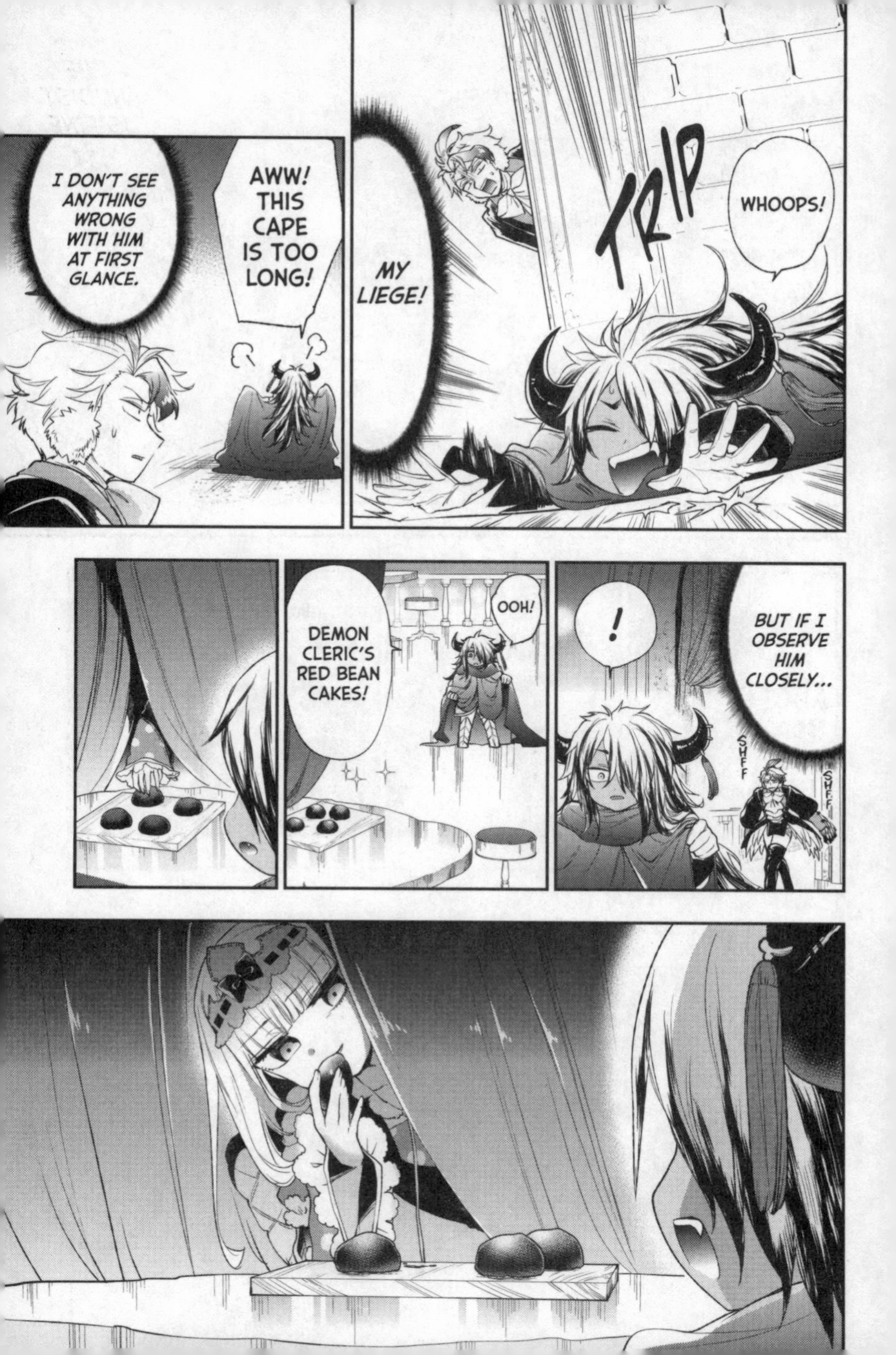
WHOOPS!
TRIP
MY LIEGE!
AWW! THIS CAPE IS TOO LONG!
I DON'T SEE ANYTHING WRONG WITH HIM AT FIRST GLANCE.
BUT IF I OBSERVE HIM CLOSELY...
SHFF
SHFF
!
OOH!
DEMON CLERIC'S RED BEAN CAKES!

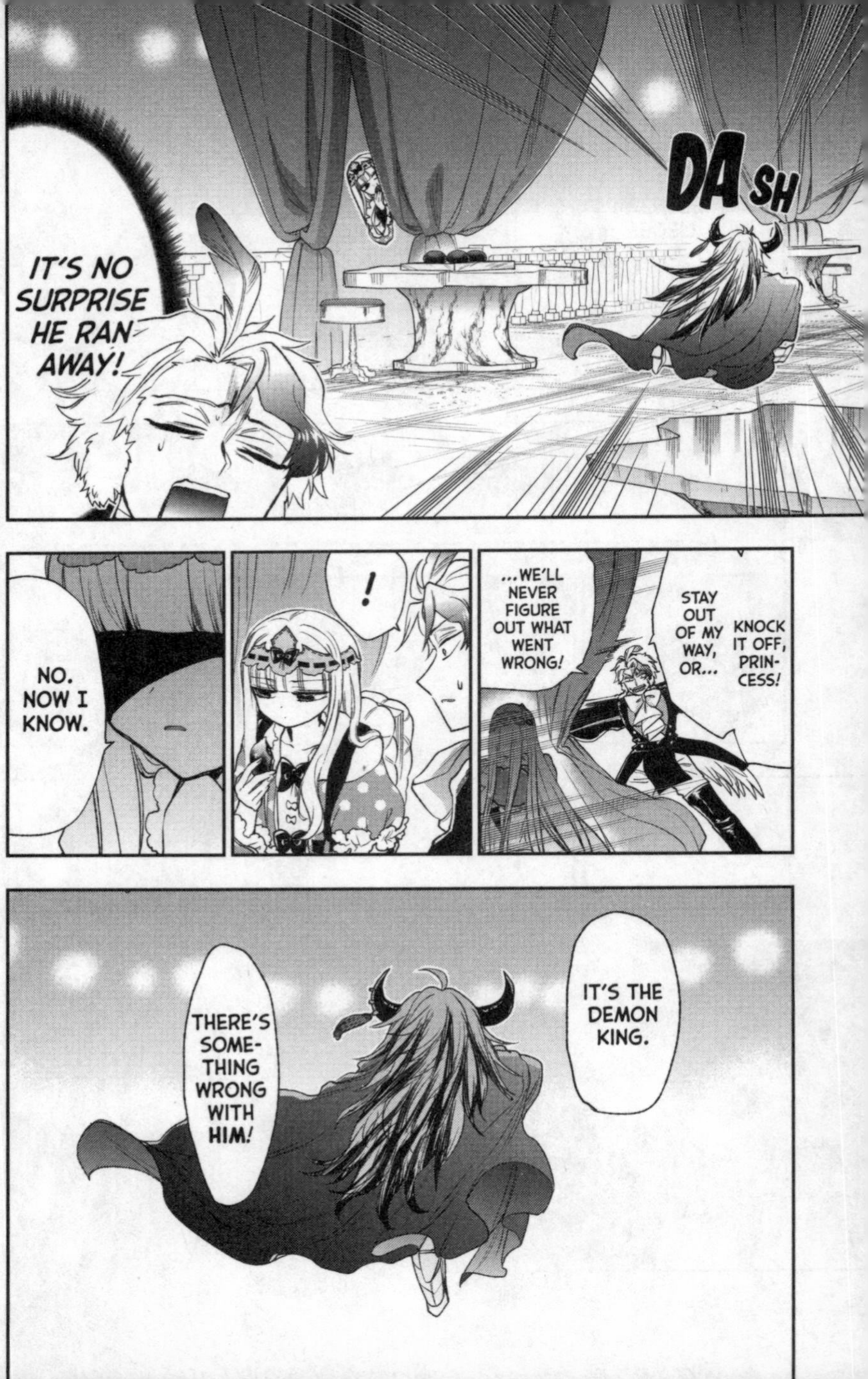
DASH
IT'S NO SURPRISE HE RAN AWAY!
KNOCK IT OFF, PRINCESS!
STAY OUT OF MY WAY, OR...
...WE'LL NEVER FIGURE OUT WHAT WENT WRONG!
!
NO. NOW I KNOW.
IT'S THE DEMON KING.
THERE'S SOMETHING WRONG WITH HIM!

203rd Night: You Shall Be King

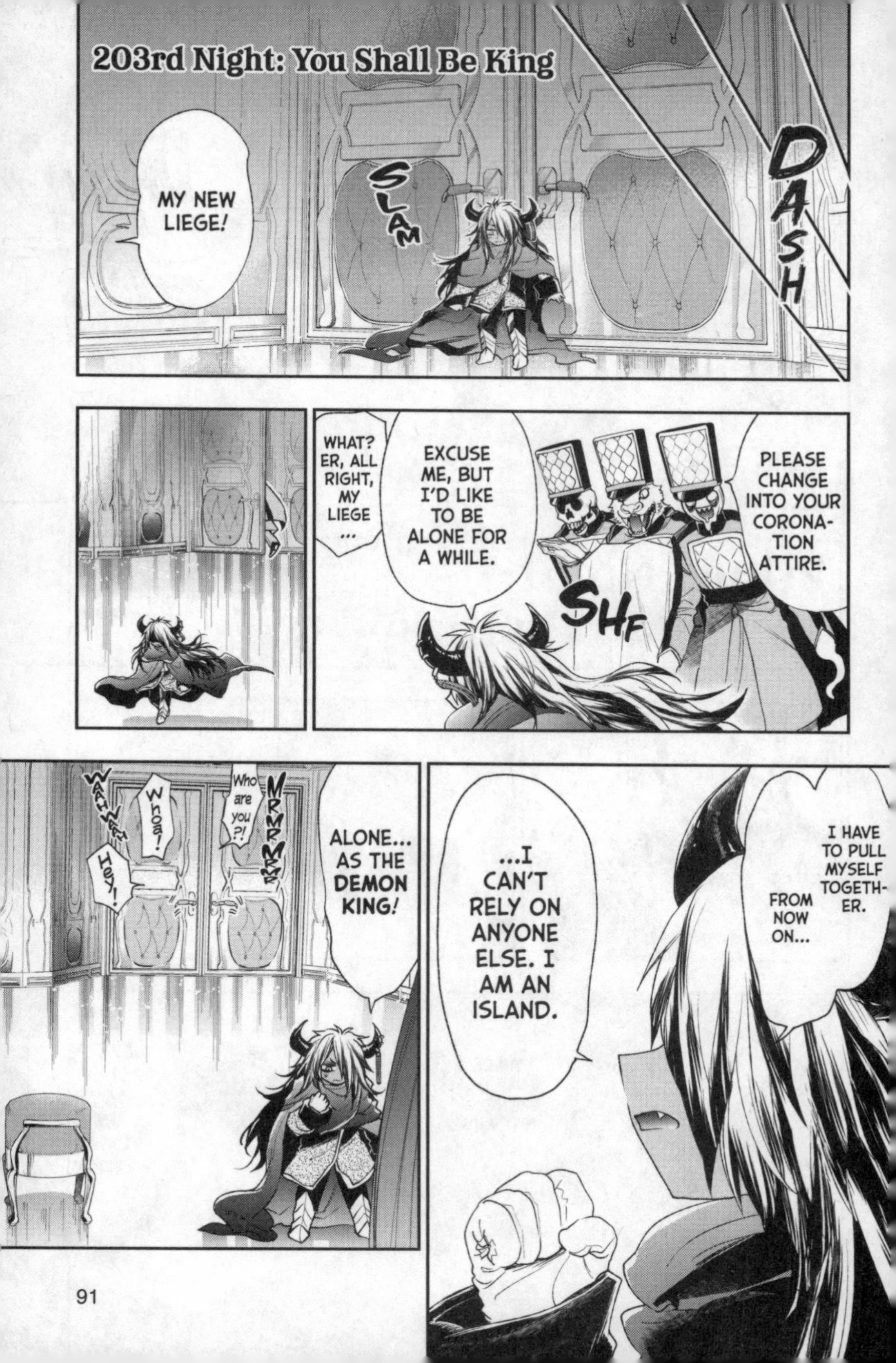
DASH
SLAM
MY NEW LIEGE!
PLEASE CHANGE INTO YOUR CORONATION ATTIRE.
SHF
EXCUSE ME, BUT I'D LIKE TO BE ALONE FOR A WHILE.
WHAT? ER, ALL RIGHT, MY LIEGE...
FROM NOW ON... I HAVE TO PULL MYSELF TOGETHER.
...I CAN'T RELY ON ANYONE ELSE. I AM AN ISLAND.
ALONE... AS THE DEMON KING!
MRMRMRMR
Who are you?!
Whoa!
Hey!
WAAHWAH

203rd Night: You Shall Be King

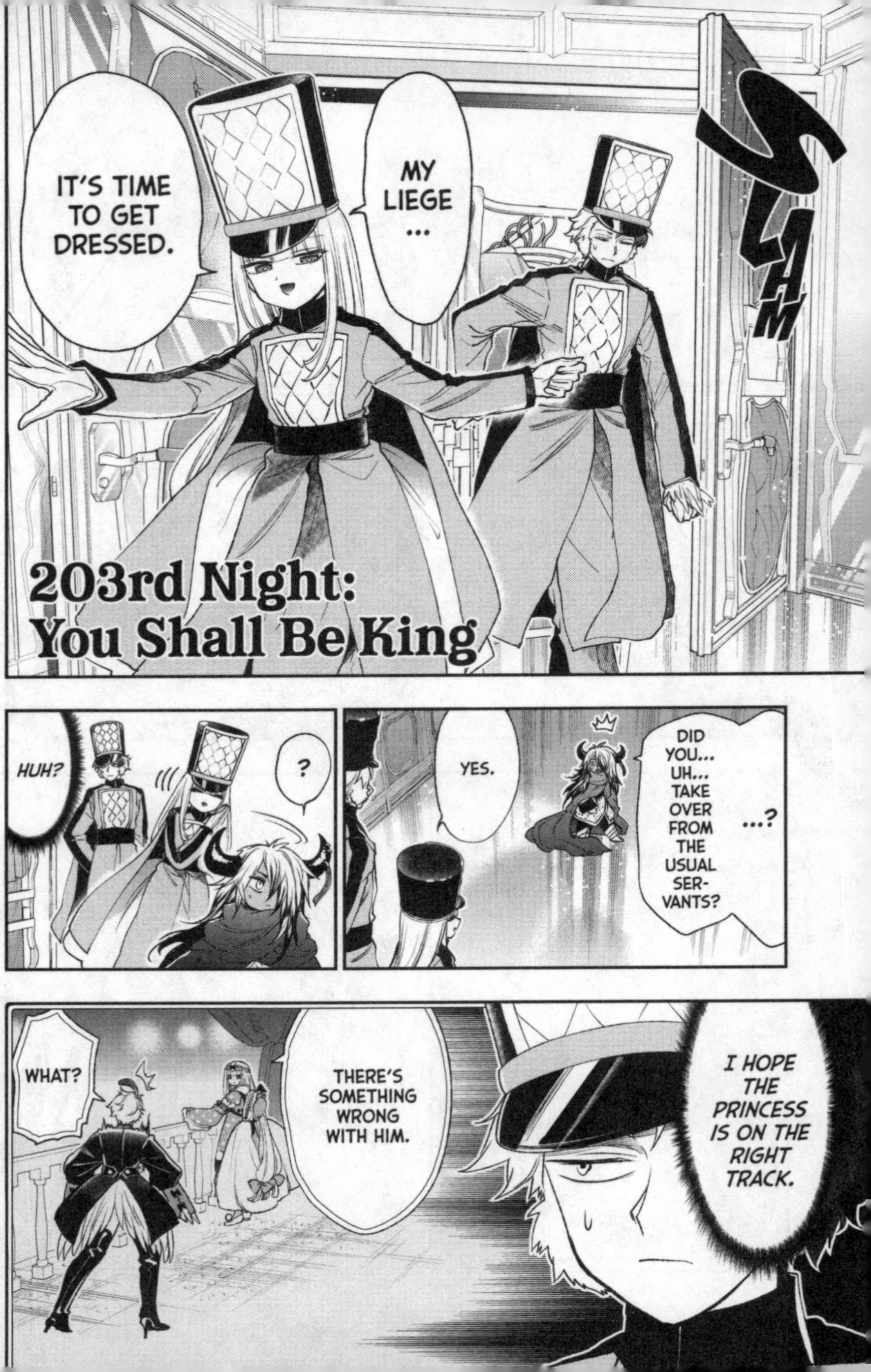
SLAM
MY LIEGE ...
IT'S TIME TO GET DRESSED.
DID YOU... UH... TAKE OVER FROM THE USUAL SER-VANTS?
...?
YES.
?
HUH?
I HOPE THE PRINCESS IS ON THE RIGHT TRACK.
THERE'S SOMETHING WRONG WITH HIM.
WHAT?

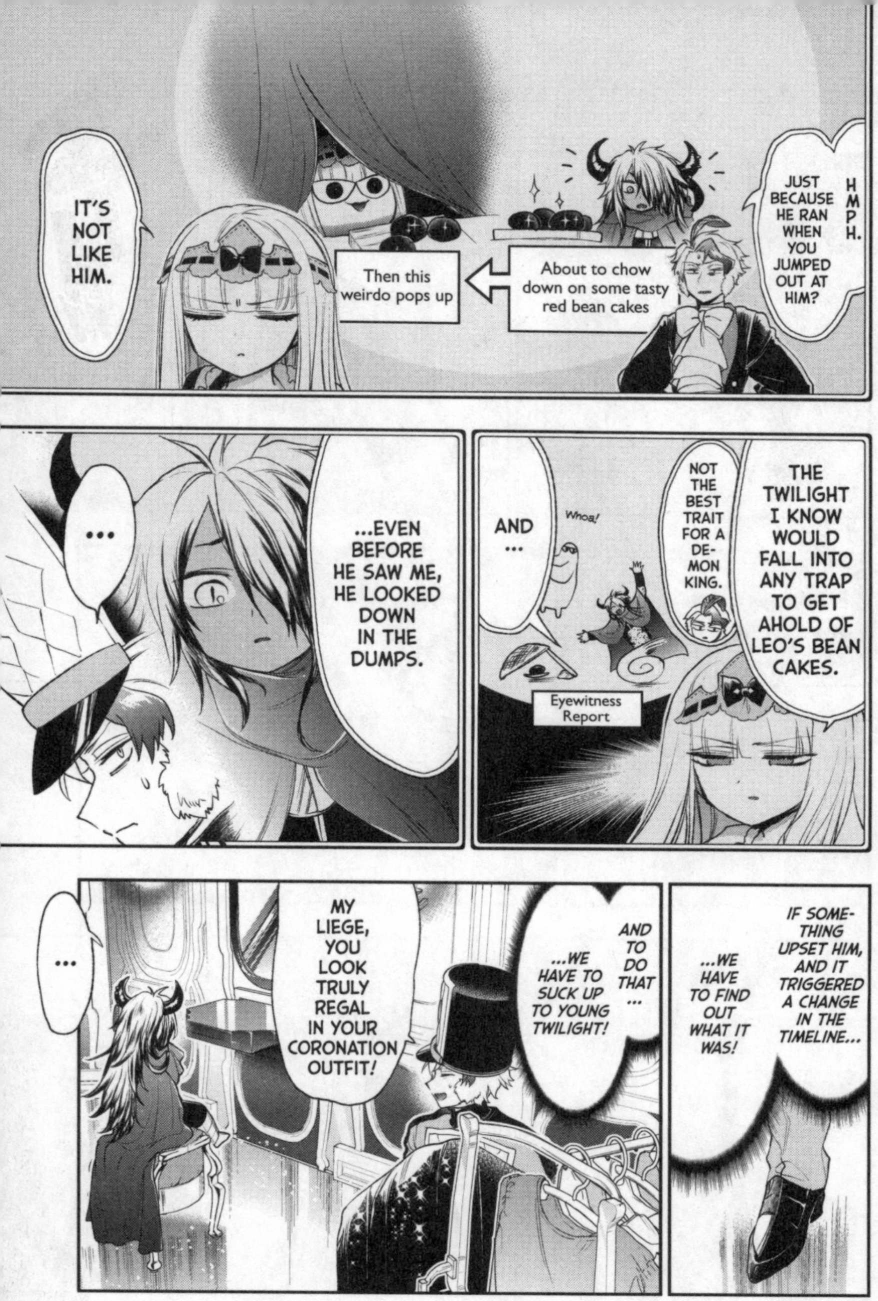
HMPH.
JUST BECAUSE HE RAN WHEN YOU JUMPED OUT AT HIM?
About to chow down on some tasty red bean cakes
Then this weirdo pops up
IT'S NOT LIKE HIM.
THE TWILIGHT I KNOW WOULD FALL INTO ANY TRAP TO GET AHOLD OF LEO'S BEAN CAKES.
NOT THE BEST TRAIT FOR A DEMON KING.
Whoa!
Eyewitness Report
AND ...
...EVEN BEFORE HE SAW ME, HE LOOKED DOWN IN THE DUMPS.
...
IF SOMETHING UPSET HIM, AND IT TRIGGERED A CHANGE IN THE TIMELINE...
...WE HAVE TO FIND OUT WHAT IT WAS!
AND TO DO THAT ...
...WE HAVE TO SUCK UP TO YOUNG TWILIGHT!
MY LIEGE, YOU LOOK TRULY REGAL IN YOUR CORONATION OUTFIT!
...

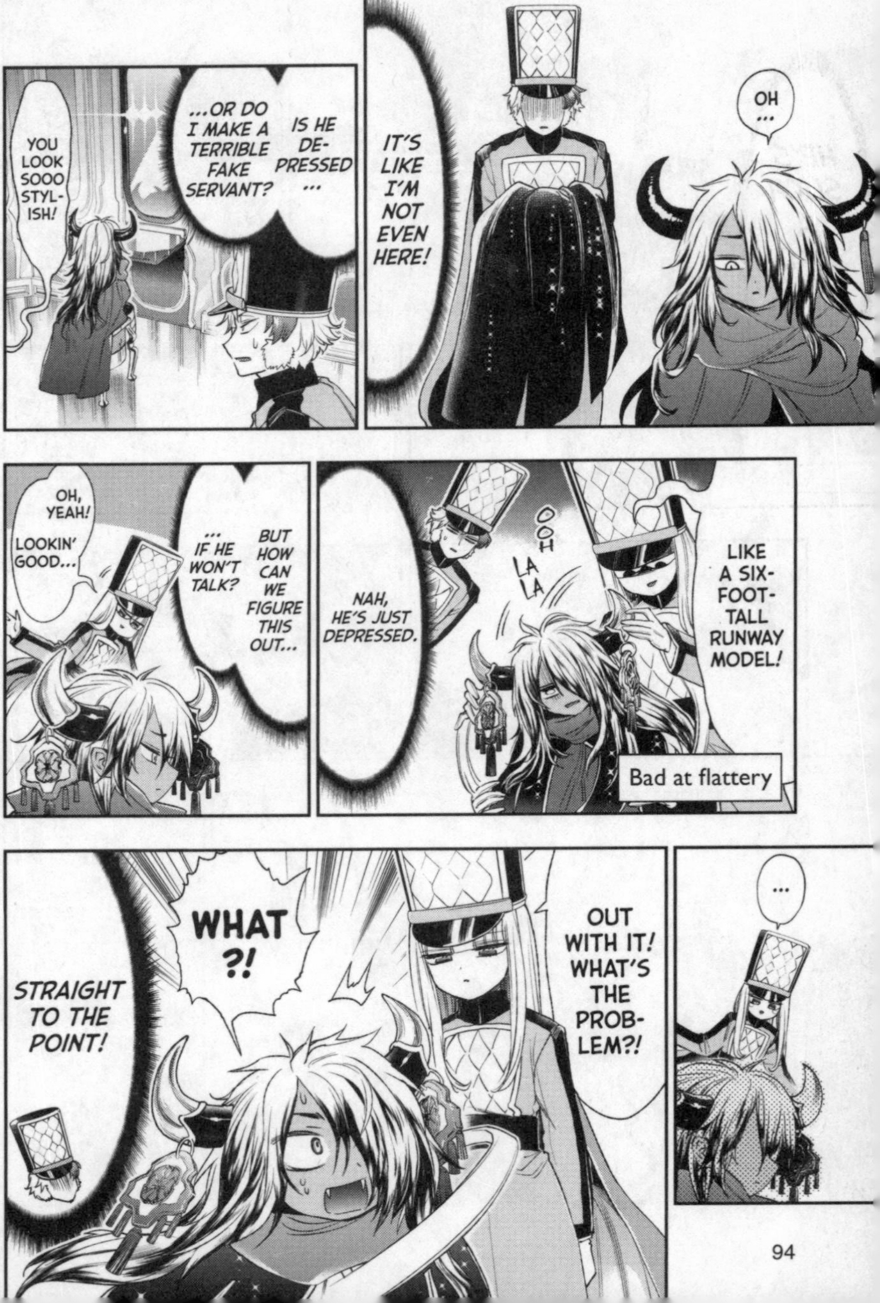
OH ...
IT'S LIKE I'M NOT EVEN HERE!
IS HE DE-PRESSED ...
...OR DO I MAKE A TERRIBLE FAKE SERVANT?
YOU LOOK SOOO STYL-ISH!
LIKE A SIX-FOOT-TALL RUNWAY MODEL!
OOH LA LA
NAH, HE'S JUST DEPRESSED.
Bad at flattery
BUT HOW CAN WE FIGURE THIS OUT...
...IF HE WON'T TALK?
OH, YEAH!
LOOKIN' GOOD...
...
OUT WITH IT! WHAT'S THE PROB-LEM?!
WHAT ?!
STRAIGHT TO THE POINT!

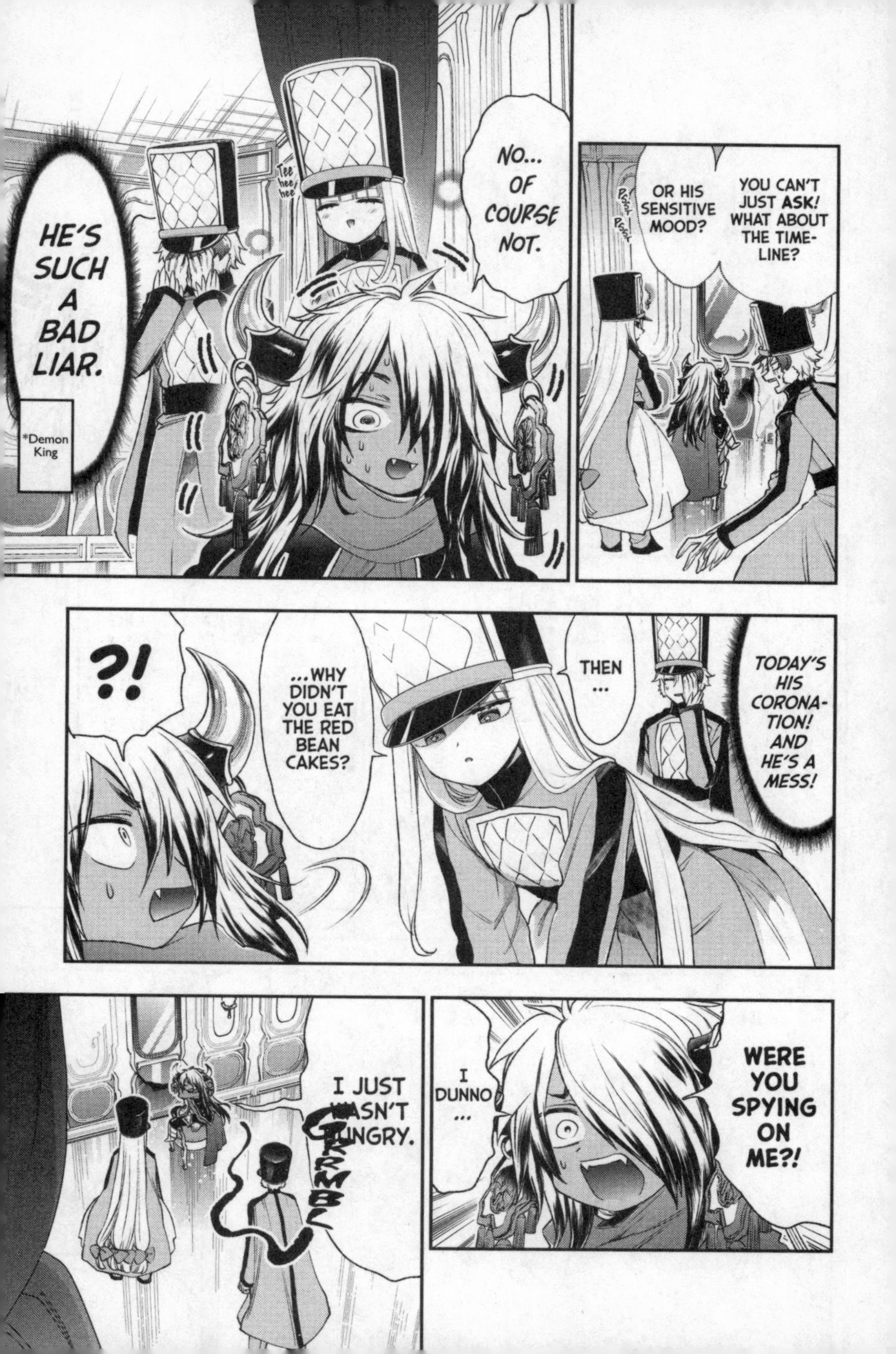
YOU CAN'T JUST ASK! WHAT ABOUT THE TIME-LINE?
Pssst Pssst
OR HIS SENSITIVE MOOD?
NO... OF COURSE NOT.
Tee hee hee
HE'S SUCH A BAD LIAR.
*Demon King
TODAY'S HIS CORONATION! AND HE'S A MESS!
THEN ...
...WHY DIDN'T YOU EAT THE RED BEAN CAKES?
?!
WERE YOU SPYING ON ME?!
I DUNNO ...
I JUST WASN'T HUNGRY.
GRRMBL

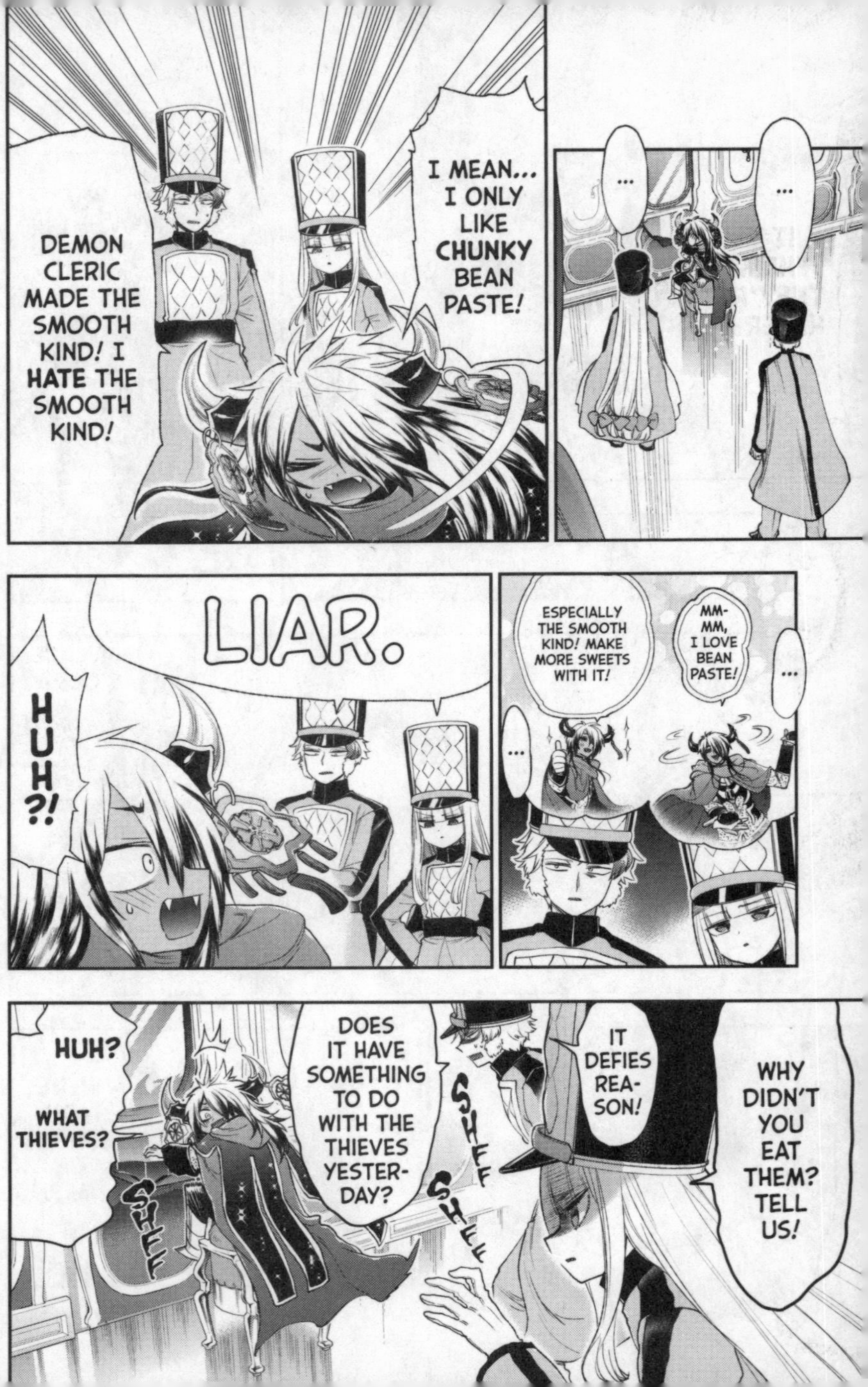
...
...
I MEAN... I ONLY LIKE CHUNKY BEAN PASTE!
DEMON CLERIC MADE THE SMOOTH KIND! I HATE THE SMOOTH KIND!
...
MM-MM, I LOVE BEAN PASTE!
ESPECIALLY THE SMOOTH KIND! MAKE MORE SWEETS WITH IT!
...
LIAR.
HUH?!
WHY DIDN'T YOU EAT THEM? TELL US!
IT DEFIES REA-SON!
SHFF
SHFF
DOES IT HAVE SOMETHING TO DO WITH THE THIEVES YESTER-DAY?
HUH?
WHAT THIEVES?
SHFF

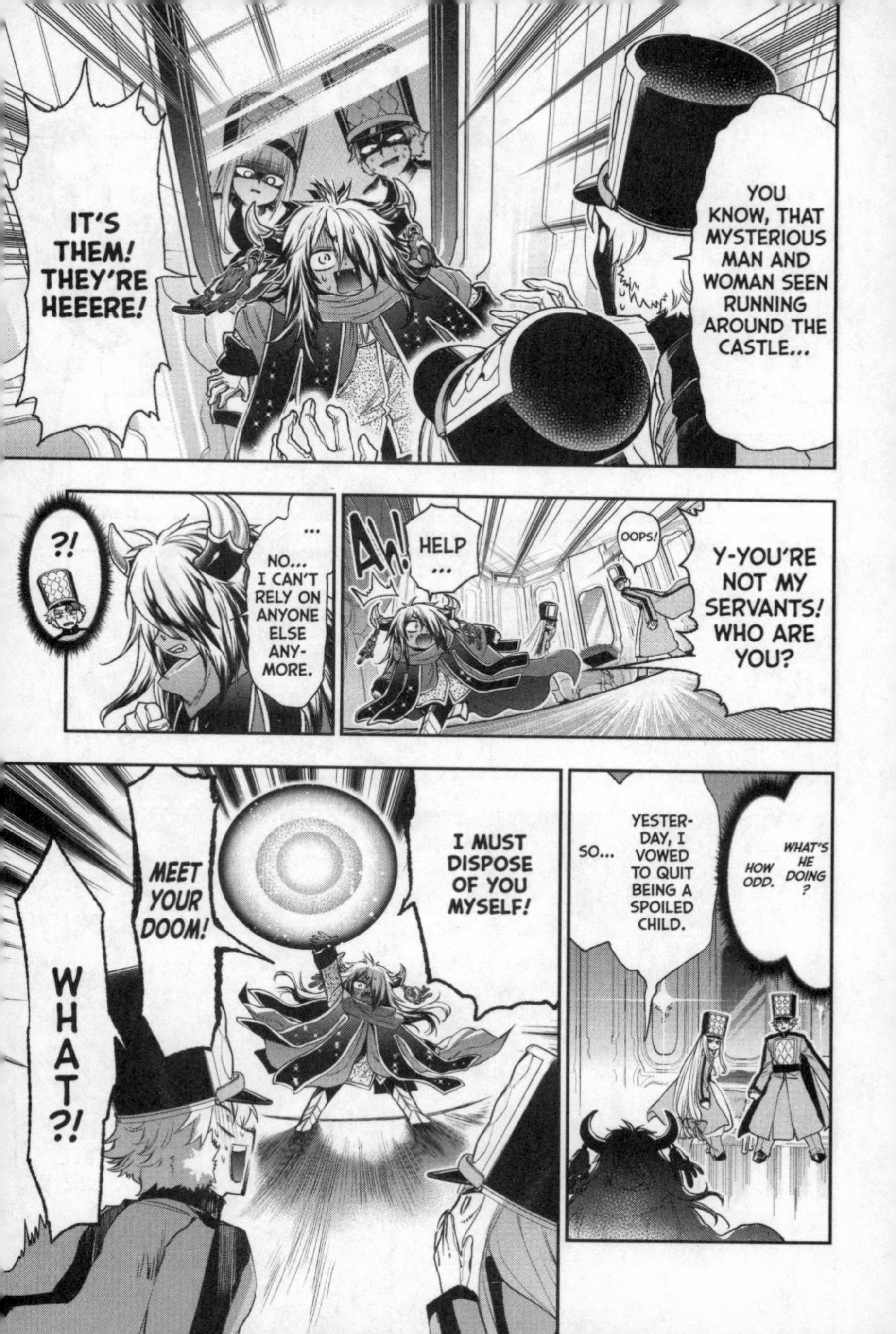
YOU KNOW, THAT MYSTERIOUS MAN AND WOMAN SEEN RUNNING AROUND THE CASTLE...
IT'S THEM! THEY'RE HEEERE!
Y-YOU'RE NOT MY SERVANTS! WHO ARE YOU?
OOPS!
Ah!
HELP ...
... NO... I CAN'T RELY ON ANYONE ELSE ANY-MORE.
?!
WHAT'S HE DOING?
HOW ODD.
YESTER-DAY, I VOWED TO QUIT BEING A SPOILED CHILD.
SO...
I MUST DISPOSE OF YOU MYSELF!
MEET YOUR DOOM!
WHAT?!

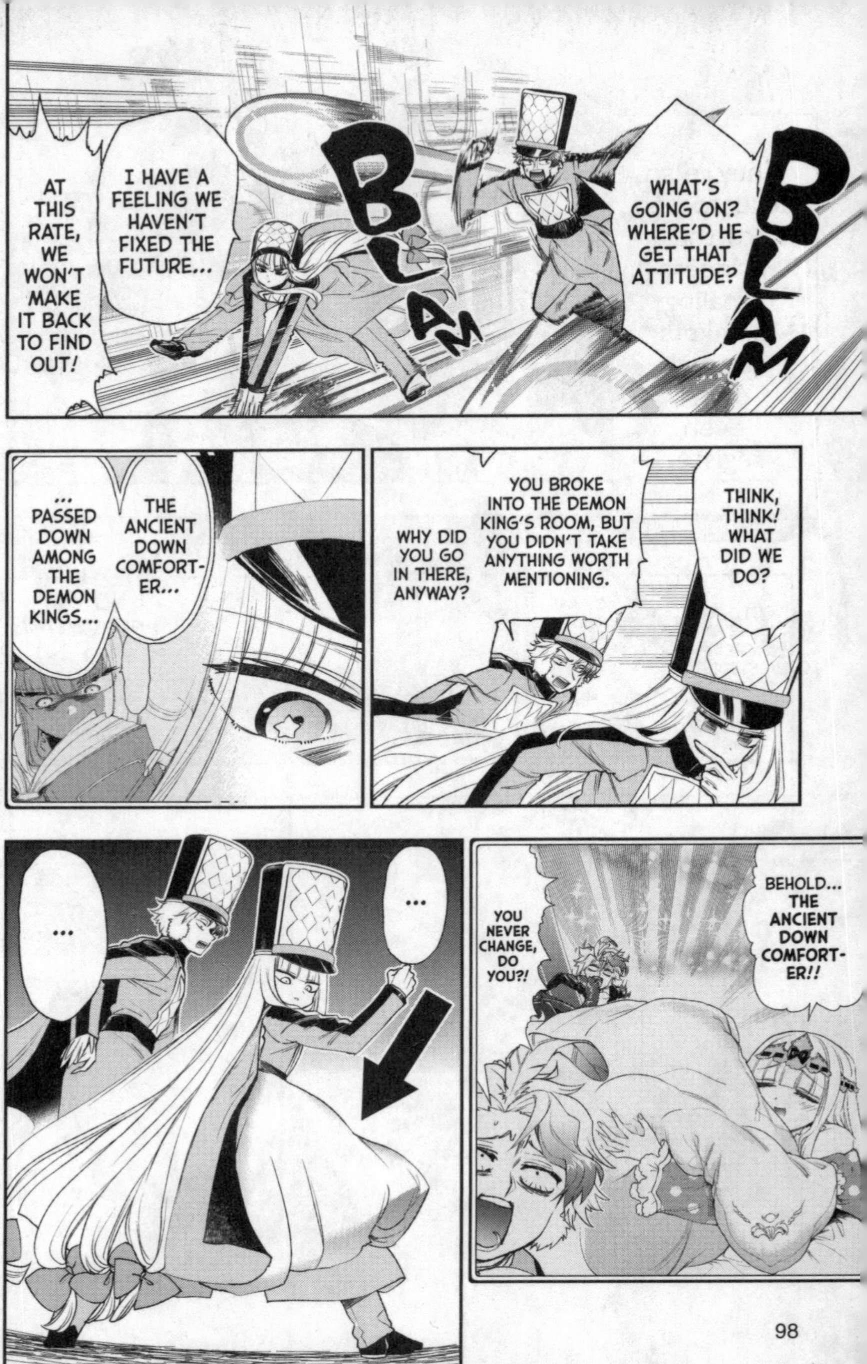
WHAT'S GOING ON? WHERE'D HE GET THAT ATTITUDE?
BLAM
BLAM
I HAVE A FEELING WE HAVEN'T FIXED THE FUTURE...
AT THIS RATE, WE WON'T MAKE IT BACK TO FIND OUT!
THINK, THINK! WHAT DID WE DO?
YOU BROKE INTO THE DEMON KING'S ROOM, BUT YOU DIDN'T TAKE ANYTHING WORTH MENTIONING.
WHY DID YOU GO IN THERE, ANYWAY?
THE ANCIENT DOWN COMFORT-ER...
...PASSED DOWN AMONG THE DEMON KINGS...
BEHOLD... THE ANCIENT DOWN COMFORT-ER!!
YOU NEVER CHANGE, DO YOU?!
...
...

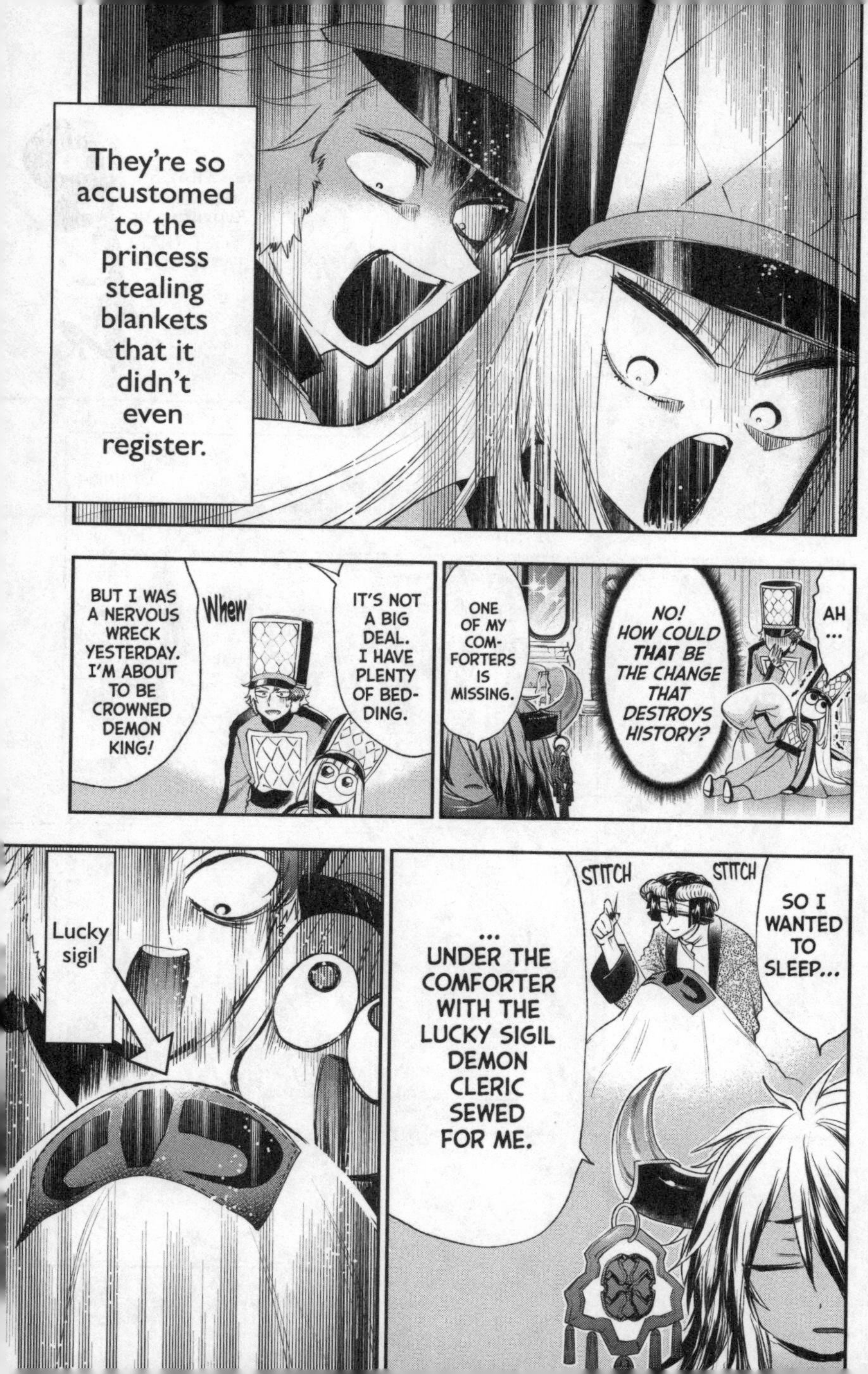
They're so accustomed to the princess stealing blankets that it didn't even register.
AH ...
NO! HOW COULD THAT BE THE CHANGE THAT DESTROYS HISTORY?
ONE OF MY COM-FORTERS IS MISSING.
IT'S NOT A BIG DEAL. I HAVE PLENTY OF BED-DING.
Whew
BUT I WAS A NERVOUS WRECK YESTERDAY. I'M ABOUT TO BE CROWNED DEMON KING!
SO I WANTED TO SLEEP...
STITCH
STITCH
... UNDER THE COMFORTER WITH THE LUCKY SIGIL DEMON CLERIC SEWED FOR ME.
Lucky sigil

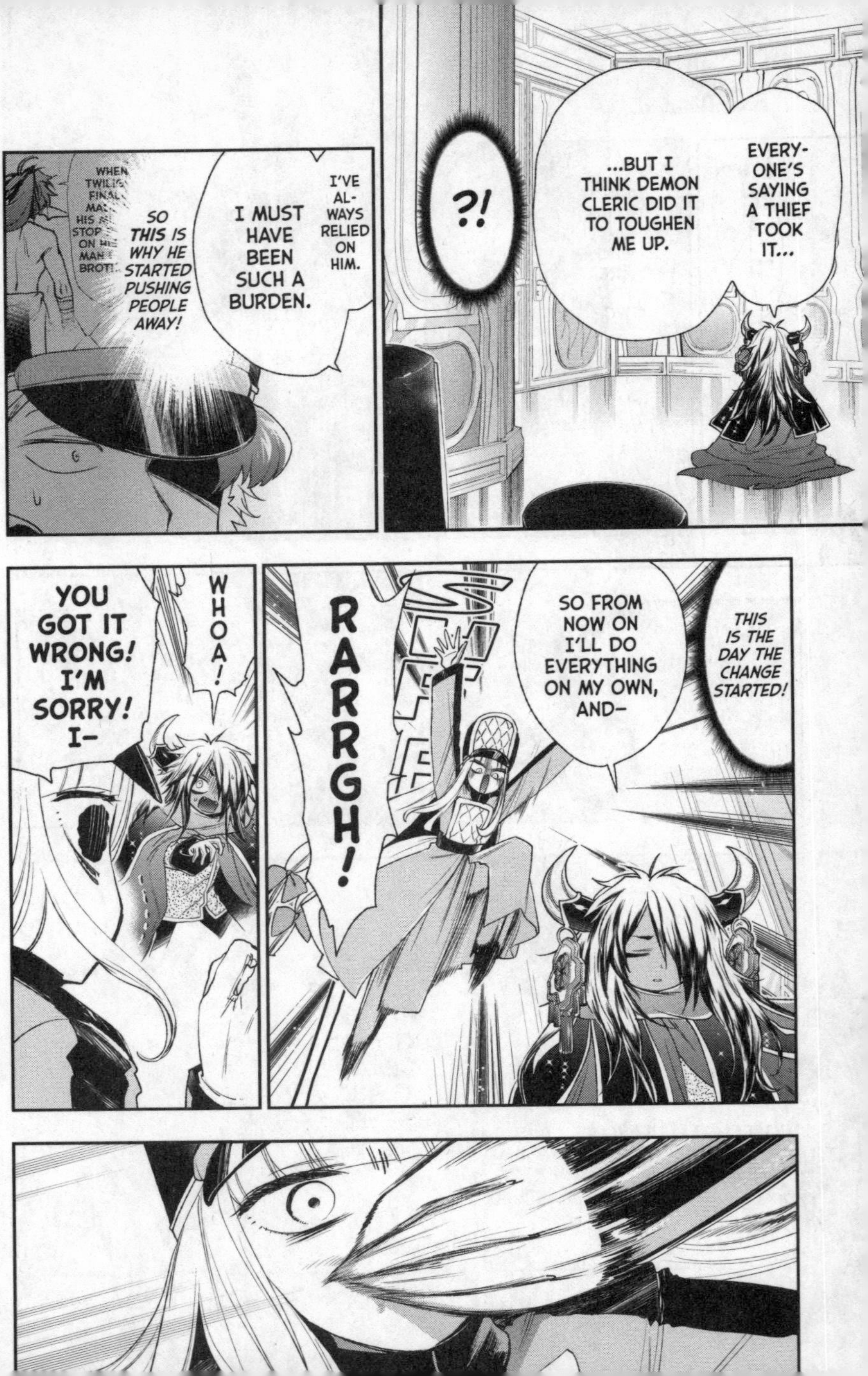
EVERY-ONE'S SAYING A THIEF TOOK IT...
...BUT I THINK DEMON CLERIC DID IT TO TOUGHEN ME UP.
?!
I'VE AL-WAYS RELIED ON HIM.
I MUST HAVE BEEN SUCH A BURDEN.
SO THIS IS WHY HE STARTED PUSHING PEOPLE AWAY!
THIS IS THE DAY THE CHANGE STARTED!
SO FROM NOW ON I'LL DO EVERYTHING ON MY OWN, AND–
RARRGH!
WHOA!
YOU GOT IT WRONG! I'M SORRY! I–

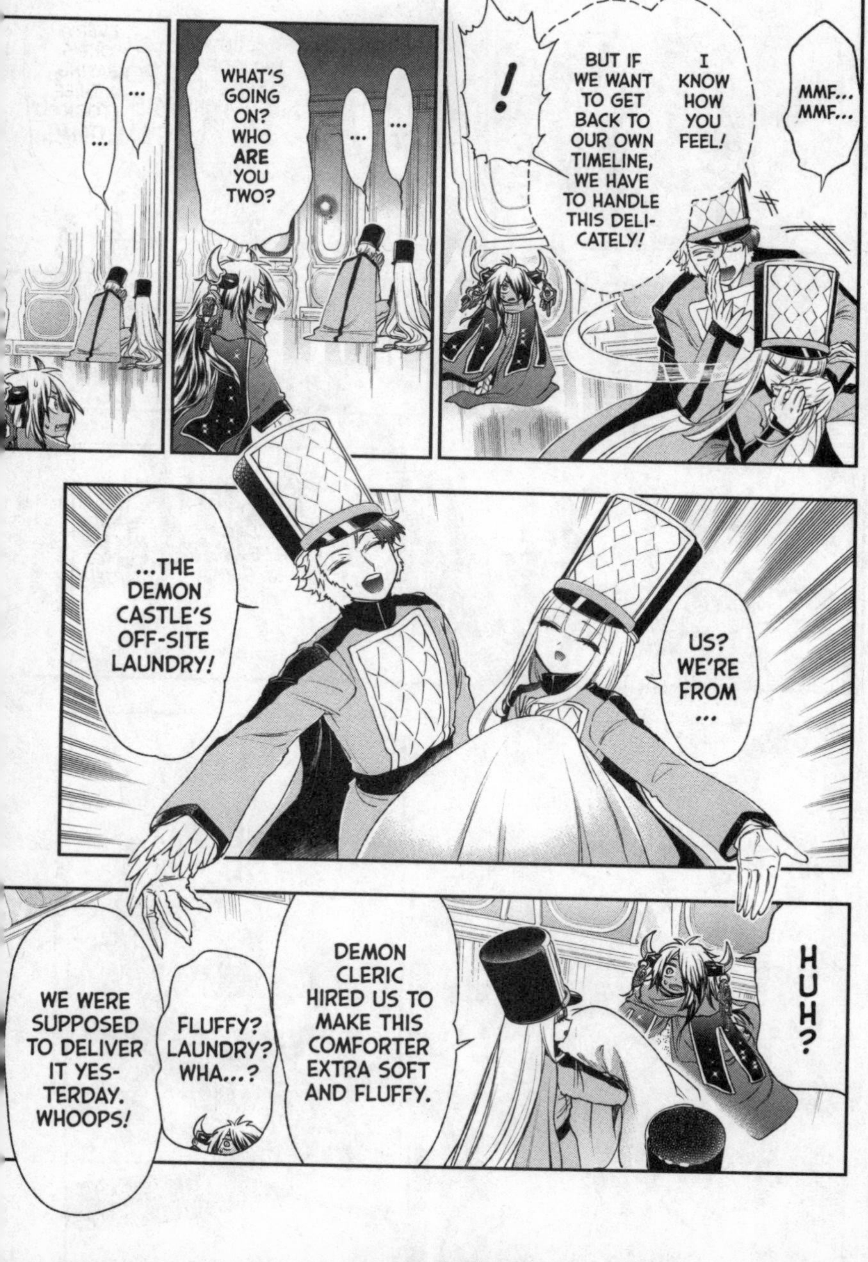
MMF... MMF...
I KNOW HOW YOU FEEL!
BUT IF WE WANT TO GET BACK TO OUR OWN TIMELINE, WE HAVE TO HANDLE THIS DELI-CATELY!
!
...
...
WHAT'S GOING ON? WHO ARE YOU TWO?
...
...
US? WE'RE FROM ...
...THE DEMON CASTLE'S OFF-SITE LAUNDRY!
HUH?
DEMON CLERIC HIRED US TO MAKE THIS COMFORTER EXTRA SOFT AND FLUFFY.
FLUFFY? LAUNDRY? WHA...?
WE WERE SUPPOSED TO DELIVER IT YES-TERDAY. WHOOPS!

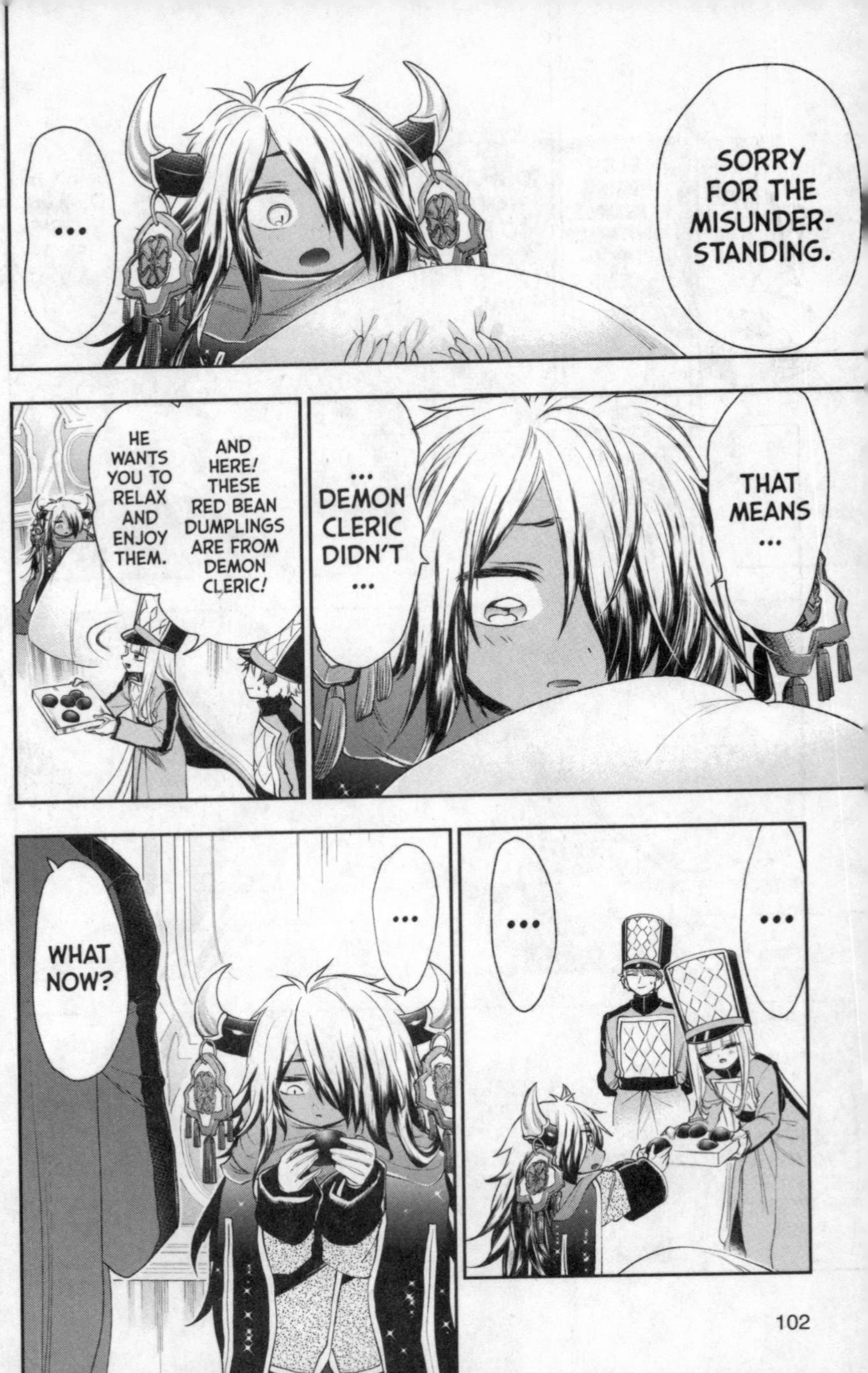
SORRY FOR THE MISUNDER-STANDING.
...
THAT MEANS ...
... DEMON CLERIC DIDN'T ...
AND HERE! THESE RED BEAN DUMPLINGS ARE FROM DEMON CLERIC!
HE WANTS YOU TO RELAX AND ENJOY THEM.
...
...
...
WHAT NOW?

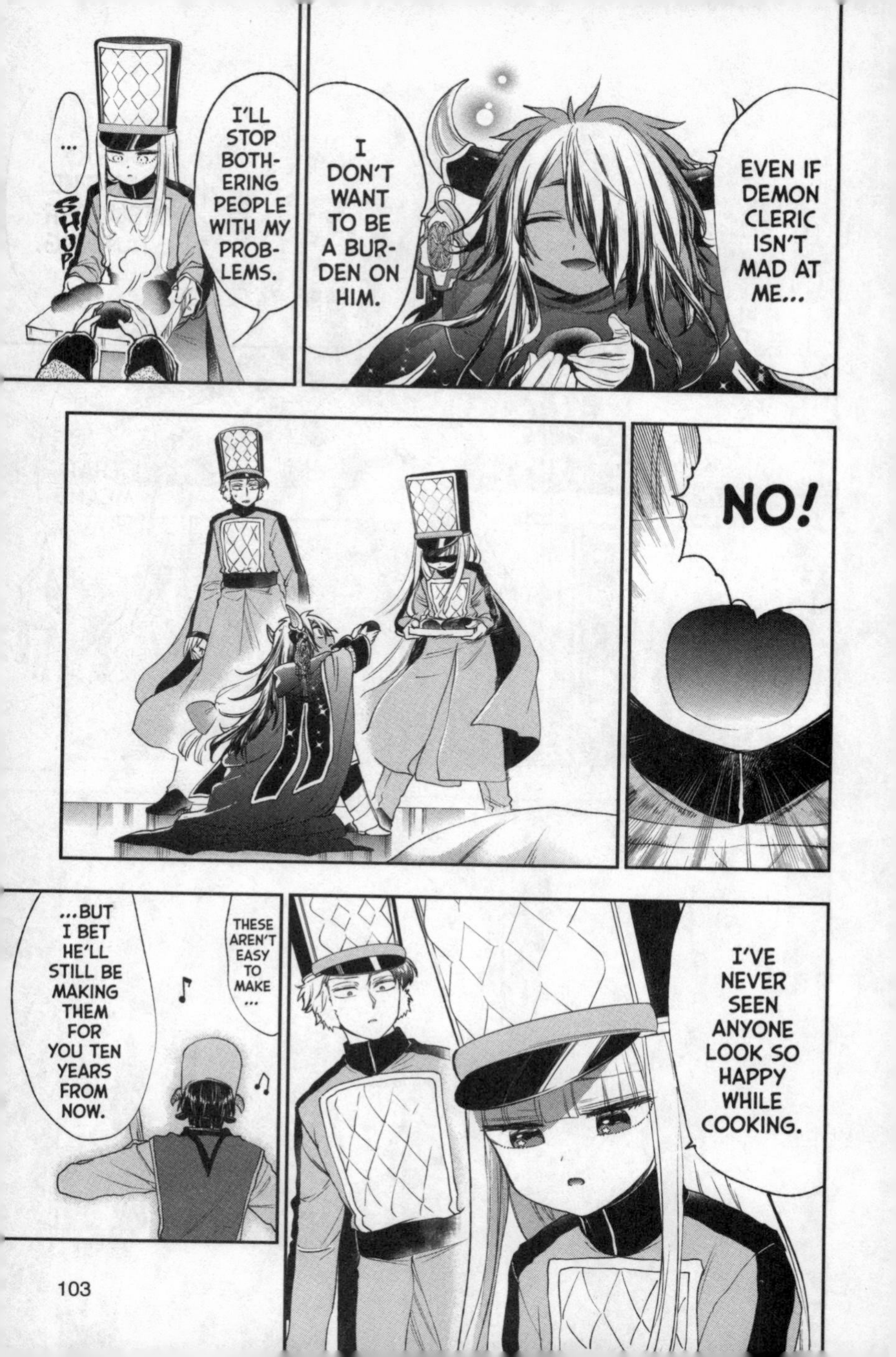
EVEN IF DEMON CLERIC ISN'T MAD AT ME...
I DON'T WANT TO BE A BURDEN ON HIM.
I'LL STOP BOTHERING PEOPLE WITH MY PROBLEMS.
...
SHUP
NO!
I'VE NEVER SEEN ANYONE LOOK SO HAPPY WHILE COOKING.
THESE AREN'T EASY TO MAKE...
...BUT I BET HE'LL STILL BE MAKING THEM FOR YOU TEN YEARS FROM NOW.

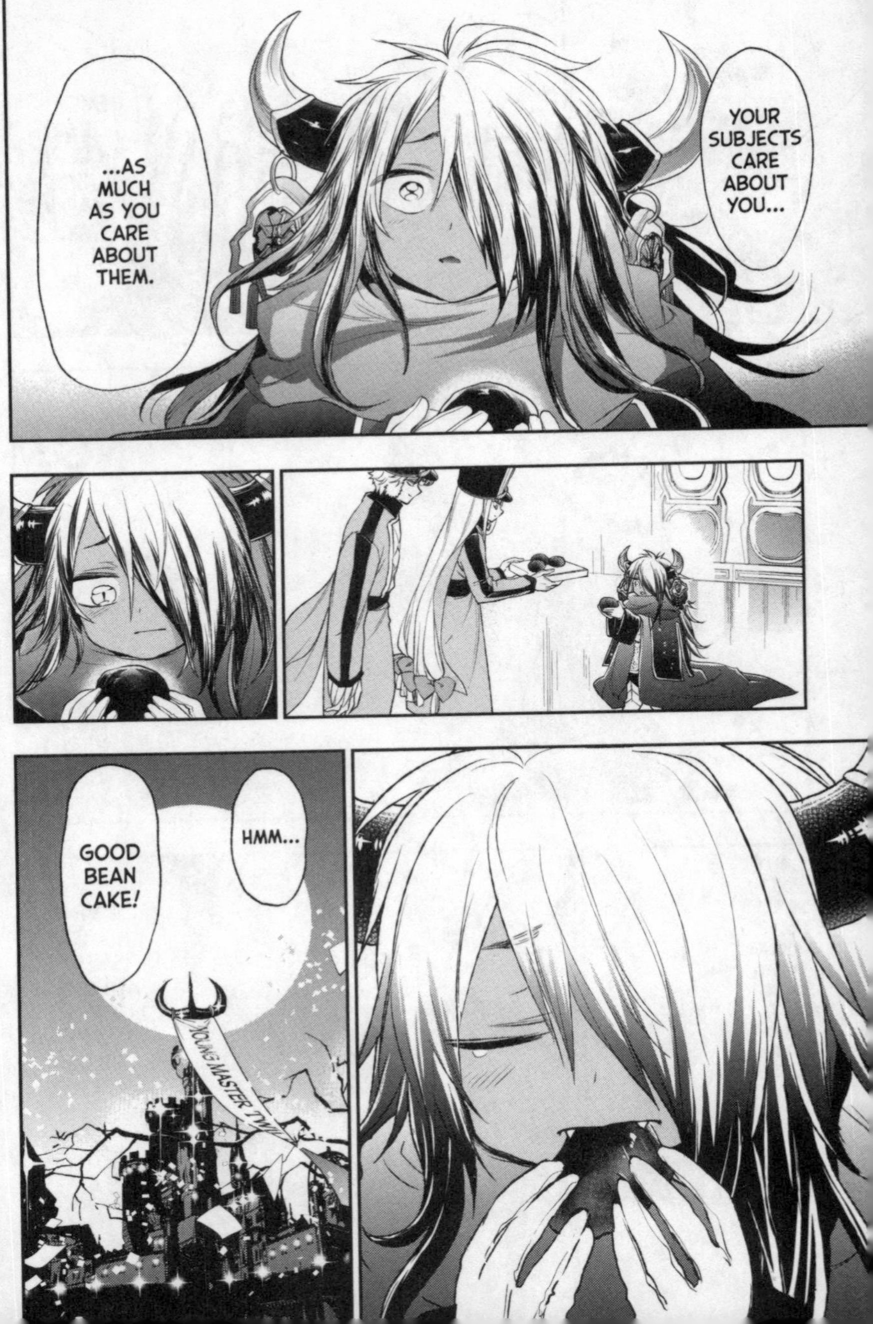
YOUR SUBJECTS CARE ABOUT YOU...
...AS MUCH AS YOU CARE ABOUT THEM.
HMM...
GOOD BEAN CAKE!
YOUNG MASTER

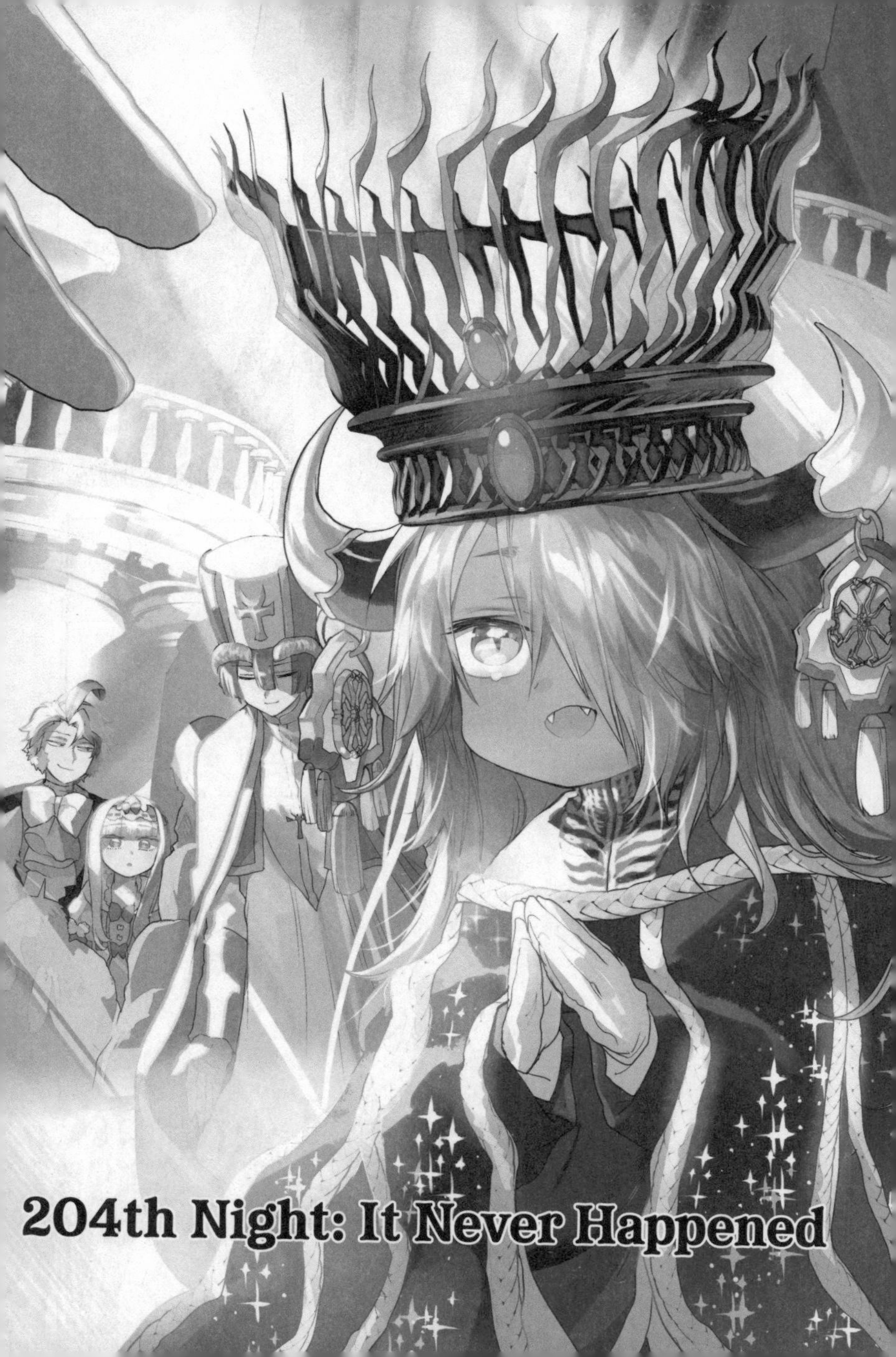
204th Night: It Never Happened

SLEEPY PRINCESS
IN THE DEMON CASTLE

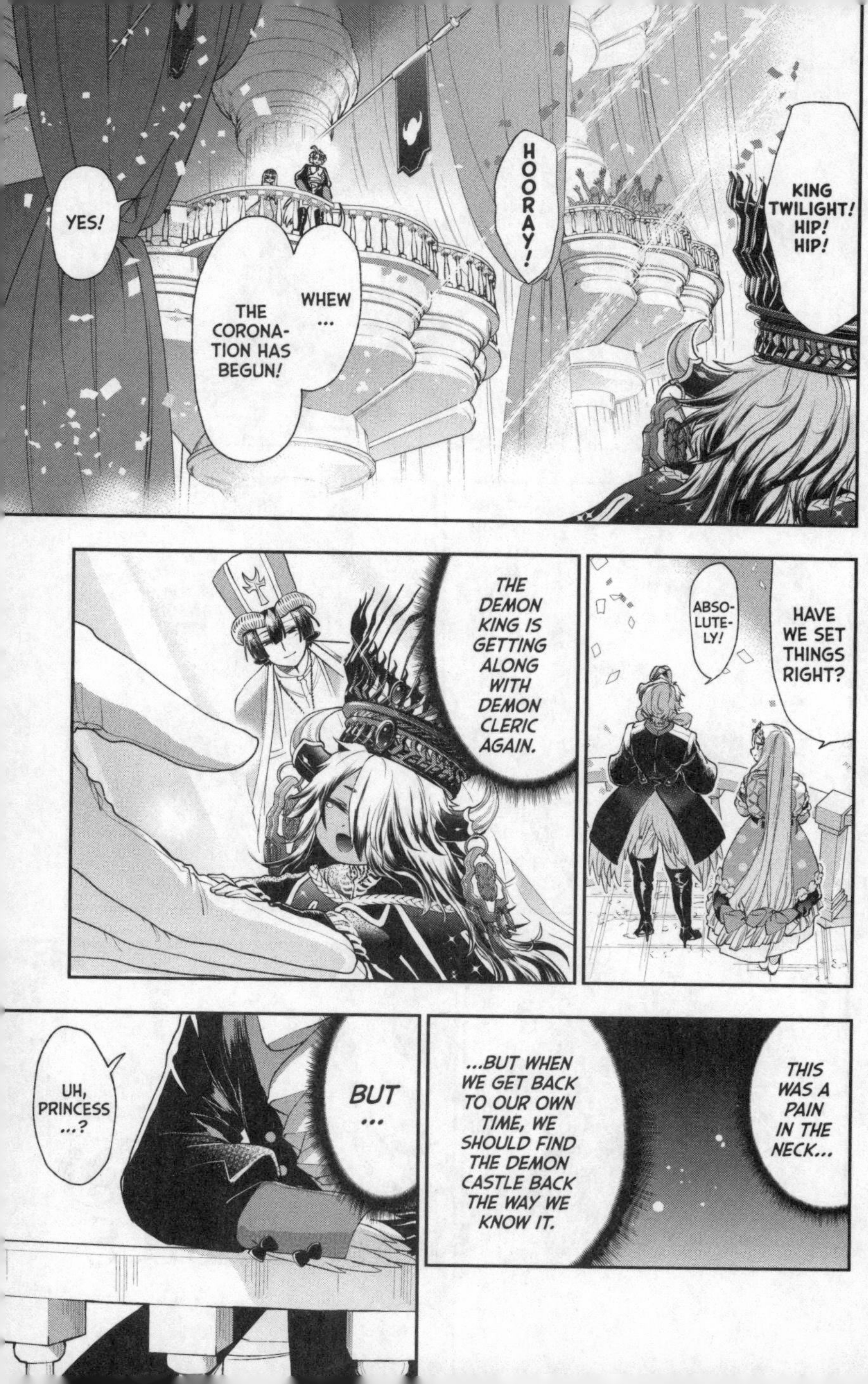
KING TWILIGHT! HIP! HIP!
HOORAY!
WHEW ... THE CORONATION HAS BEGUN!
YES!
HAVE WE SET THINGS RIGHT?
ABSOLUTELY!
THE DEMON KING IS GETTING ALONG WITH DEMON CLERIC AGAIN.
THIS WAS A PAIN IN THE NECK...
...BUT WHEN WE GET BACK TO OUR OWN TIME, WE SHOULD FIND THE DEMON CASTLE BACK THE WAY WE KNOW IT.
BUT ...
UH, PRINCESS ...?

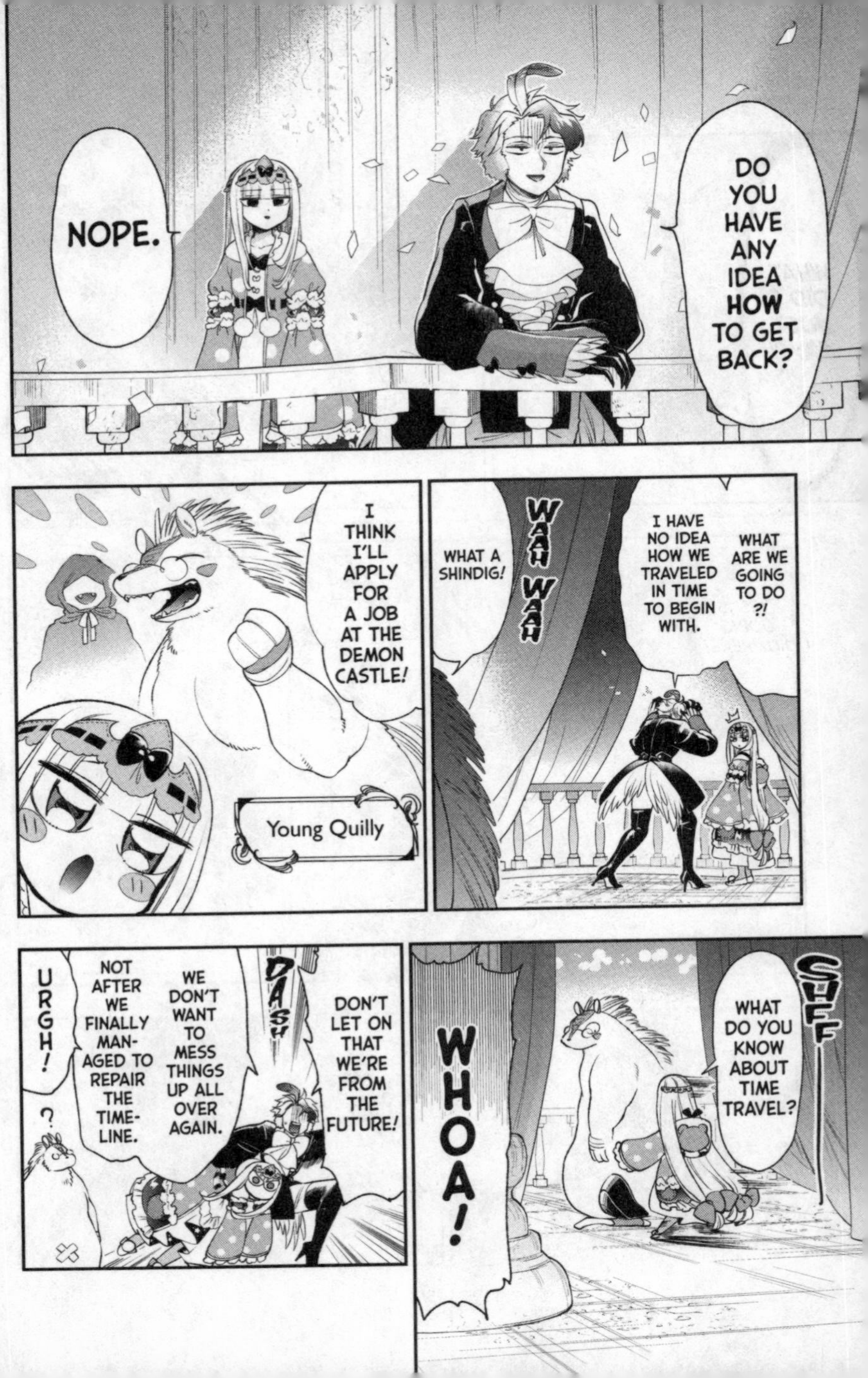
DO YOU HAVE ANY IDEA HOW TO GET BACK?
NOPE.
WHAT ARE WE GOING TO DO ?!
I HAVE NO IDEA HOW WE TRAVELED IN TIME TO BEGIN WITH.
WAAH WAAH
WHAT A SHINDIG!
I THINK I'LL APPLY FOR A JOB AT THE DEMON CASTLE!
Young Quilly
SHFF
WHAT DO YOU KNOW ABOUT TIME TRAVEL?
WHOA!
DON'T LET ON THAT WE'RE FROM THE FUTURE!
DASH
WE DON'T WANT TO MESS THINGS UP ALL OVER AGAIN.
NOT AFTER WE FINALLY MAN-AGED TO REPAIR THE TIME-LINE.
URGH!
?

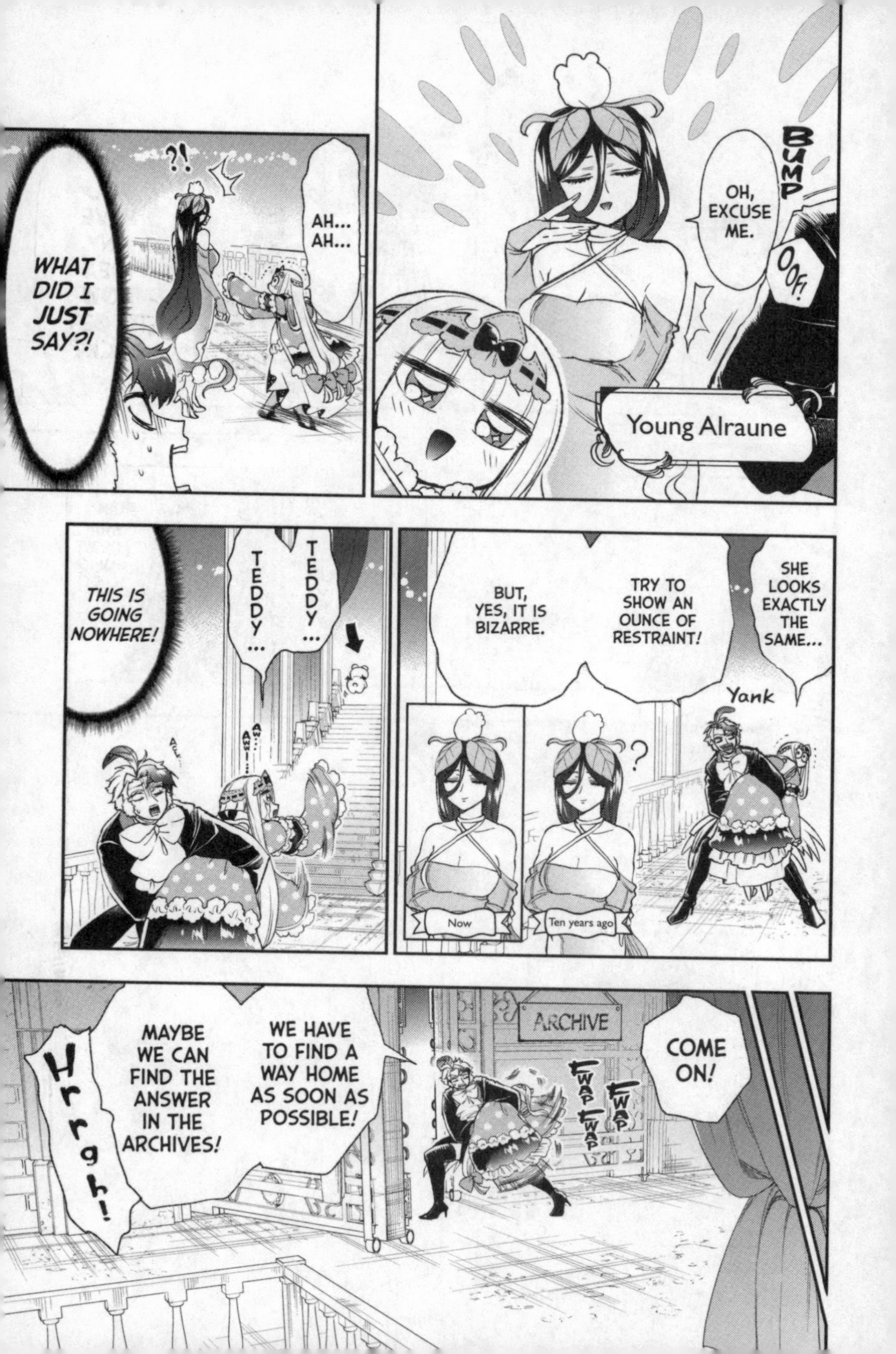
BUMP
OOF!
OH, EXCUSE ME.
Young Alraune
?!
AH... AH...
WHAT DID I JUST SAY?!
SHE LOOKS EXACTLY THE SAME...
TRY TO SHOW AN OUNCE OF RESTRAINT!
BUT, YES, IT IS BIZARRE.
Yank
?
Now
Ten years ago
TEDDY...
TEDDY...
THIS IS GOING NOWHERE!
COME ON!
ARCHIVE
FWAP
FWAP
FWAP
FWAP
WE HAVE TO FIND A WAY HOME AS SOON AS POSSIBLE!
MAYBE WE CAN FIND THE ANSWER IN THE ARCHIVES!
Hrrgh!

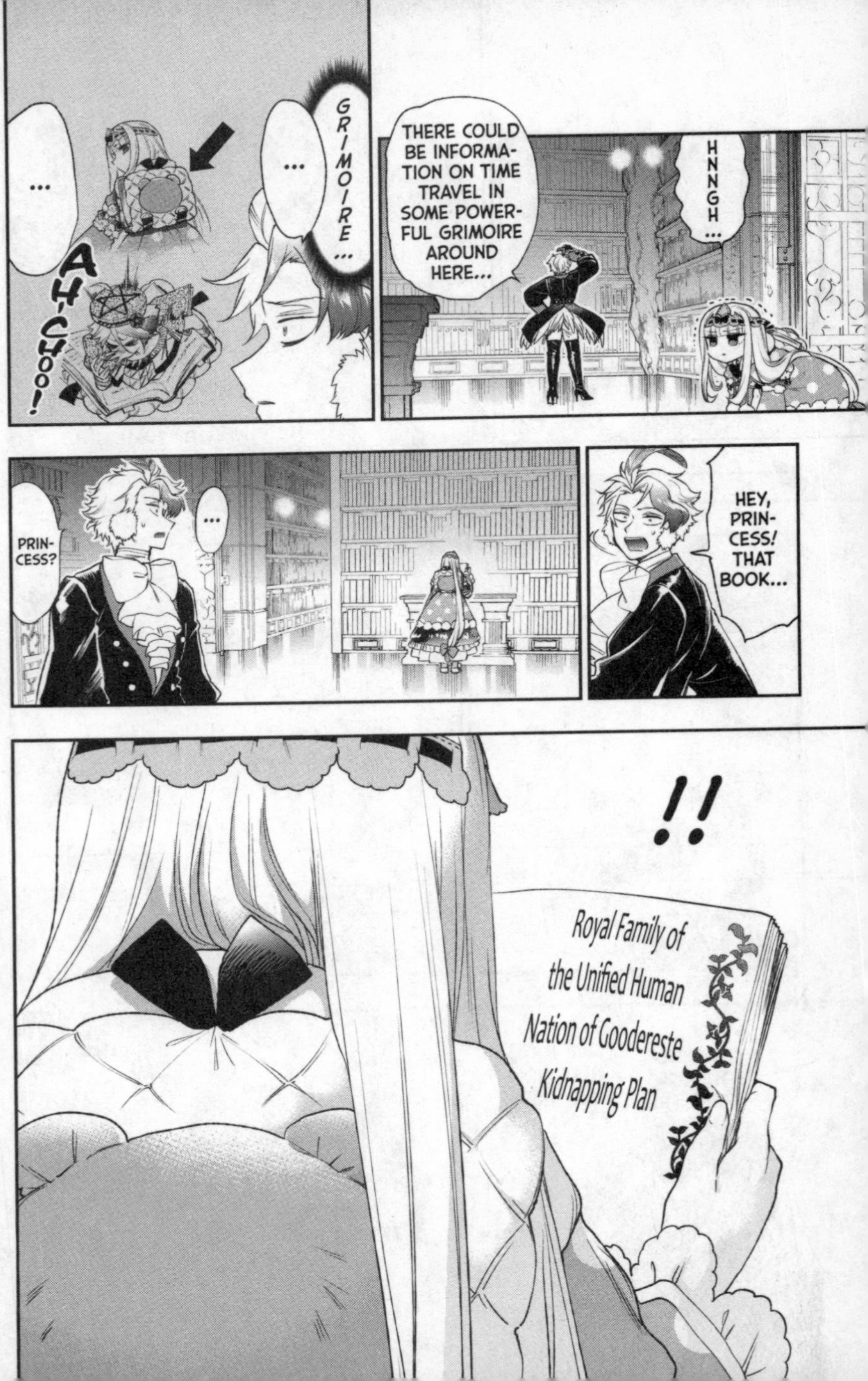
HNNGH...
THERE COULD BE INFORMATION ON TIME TRAVEL IN SOME POWERFUL GRIMOIRE AROUND HERE...
GRIMOIRE...
...
...
AH-CHOO!
HEY, PRINCESS! THAT BOOK...
...
PRINCESS?
!!
Royal Family of the Unified Human Nation of Goodereste Kidnapping Plan

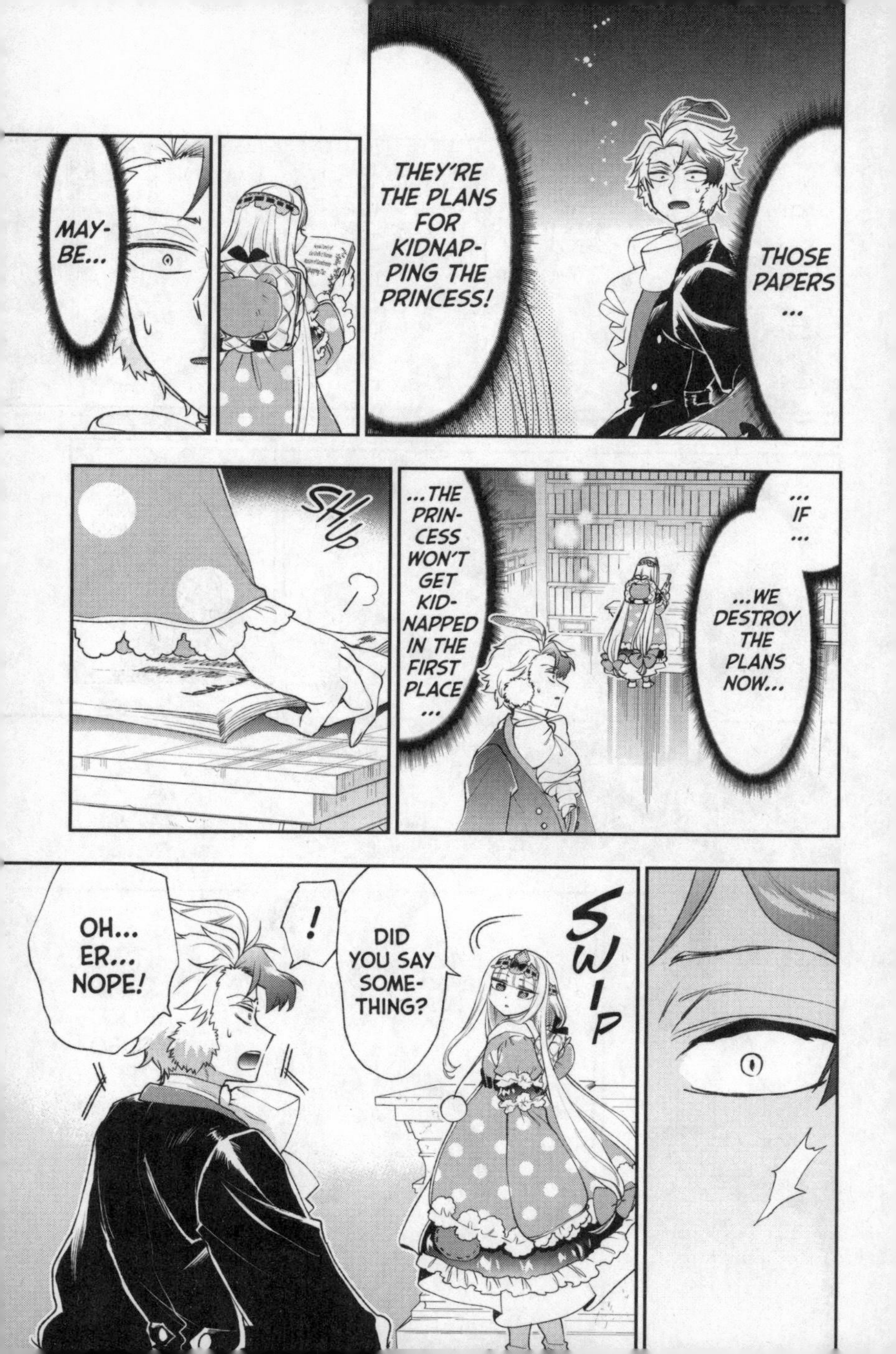
THOSE PAPERS ...
THEY'RE THE PLANS FOR KIDNAP-PING THE PRINCESS!
MAY-BE...
... IF ...
...WE DESTROY THE PLANS NOW...
...THE PRIN-CESS WON'T GET KID-NAPPED IN THE FIRST PLACE ...
SHUP
SWIP
DID YOU SAY SOME-THING?
!
OH... ER... NOPE!

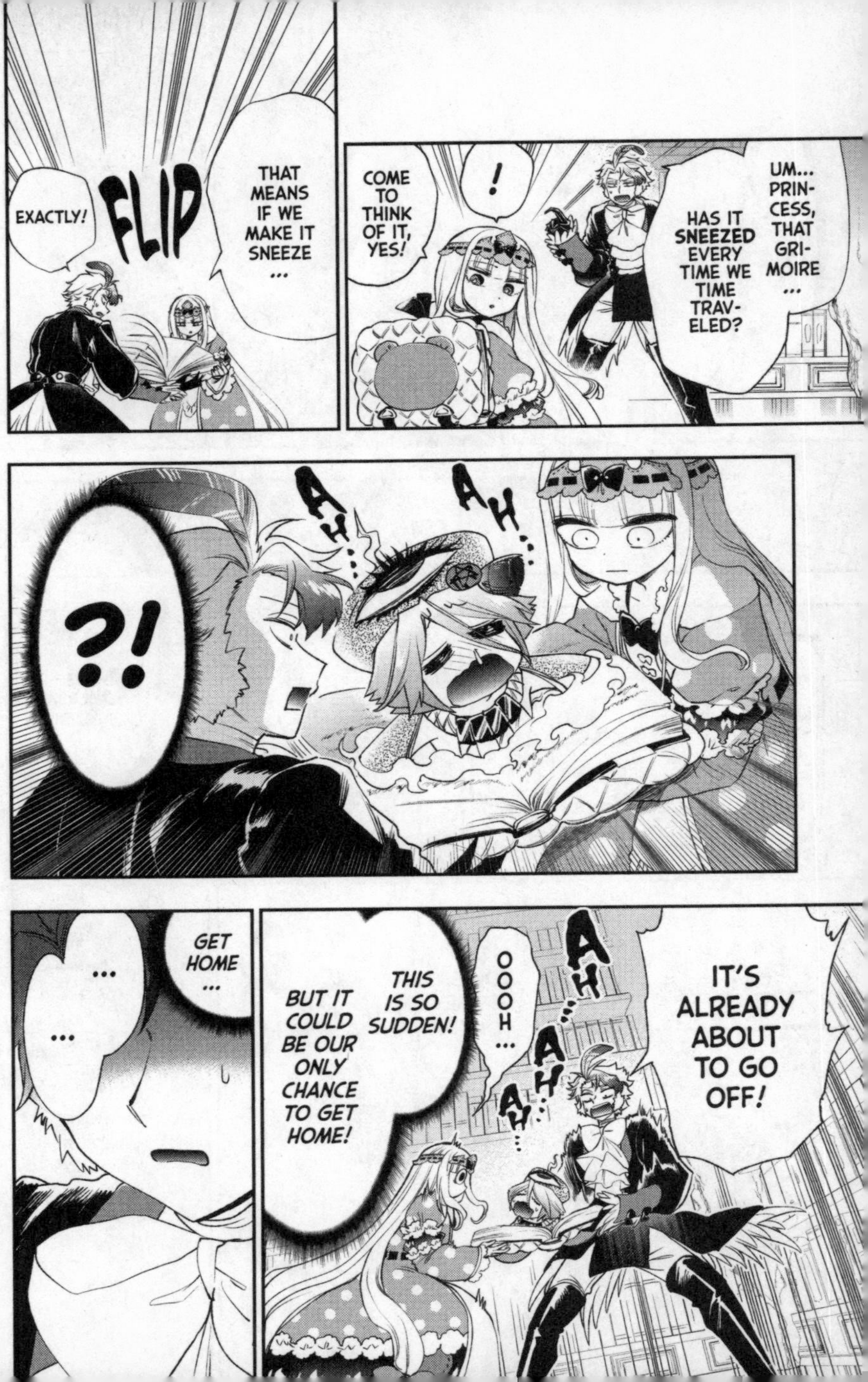
UM... PRIN-CESS, THAT GRI-MOIRE ...
HAS IT SNEEZED EVERY TIME WE TIME TRAV-ELED?
!
COME TO THINK OF IT, YES!
THAT MEANS IF WE MAKE IT SNEEZE ...
FLIP
EXACTLY!
AH...
AH...
?!
IT'S ALREADY ABOUT TO GO OFF!
AH... AH... AH...
OOOH...
THIS IS SO SUDDEN!
BUT IT COULD BE OUR ONLY CHANCE TO GET HOME!
GET HOME ...
...
...

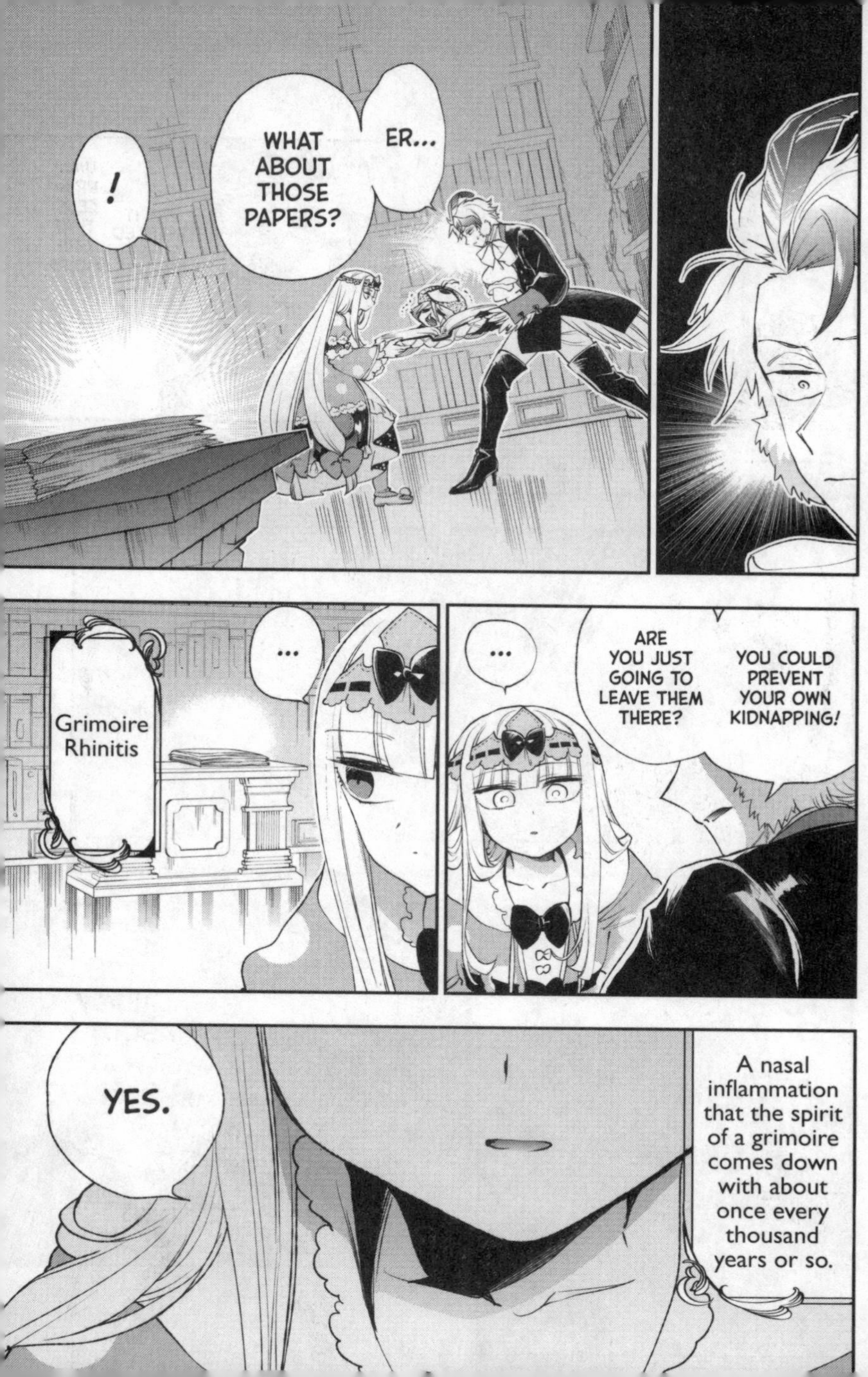
ER...
WHAT ABOUT THOSE PAPERS?
!
YOU COULD PREVENT YOUR OWN KIDNAPPING!
ARE YOU JUST GOING TO LEAVE THEM THERE?
...
...
Grimoire Rhinitis
A nasal inflammation that the spirit of a grimoire comes down with about once every thousand years or so.
YES.

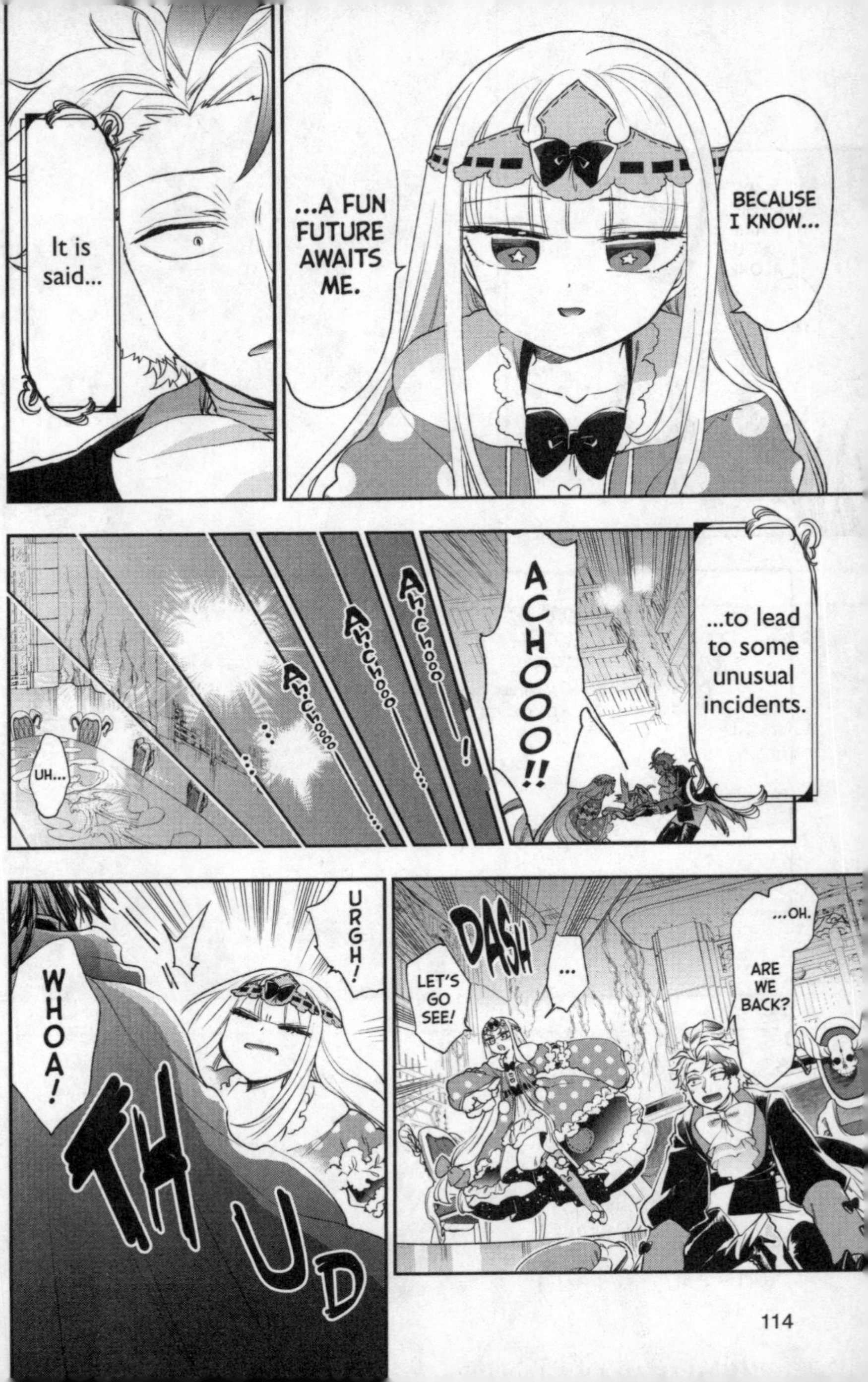
BECAUSE I KNOW...
...A FUN FUTURE AWAITS ME.
It is said...
...to lead to some unusual incidents.
ACHOOOO!!
Ah-chooo—!
Ah-chooo—...
Ah-chooooo...
UH...
...OH.
ARE WE BACK?
...
DASH
LET'S GO SEE!
URGH!
WHOA!
THUD

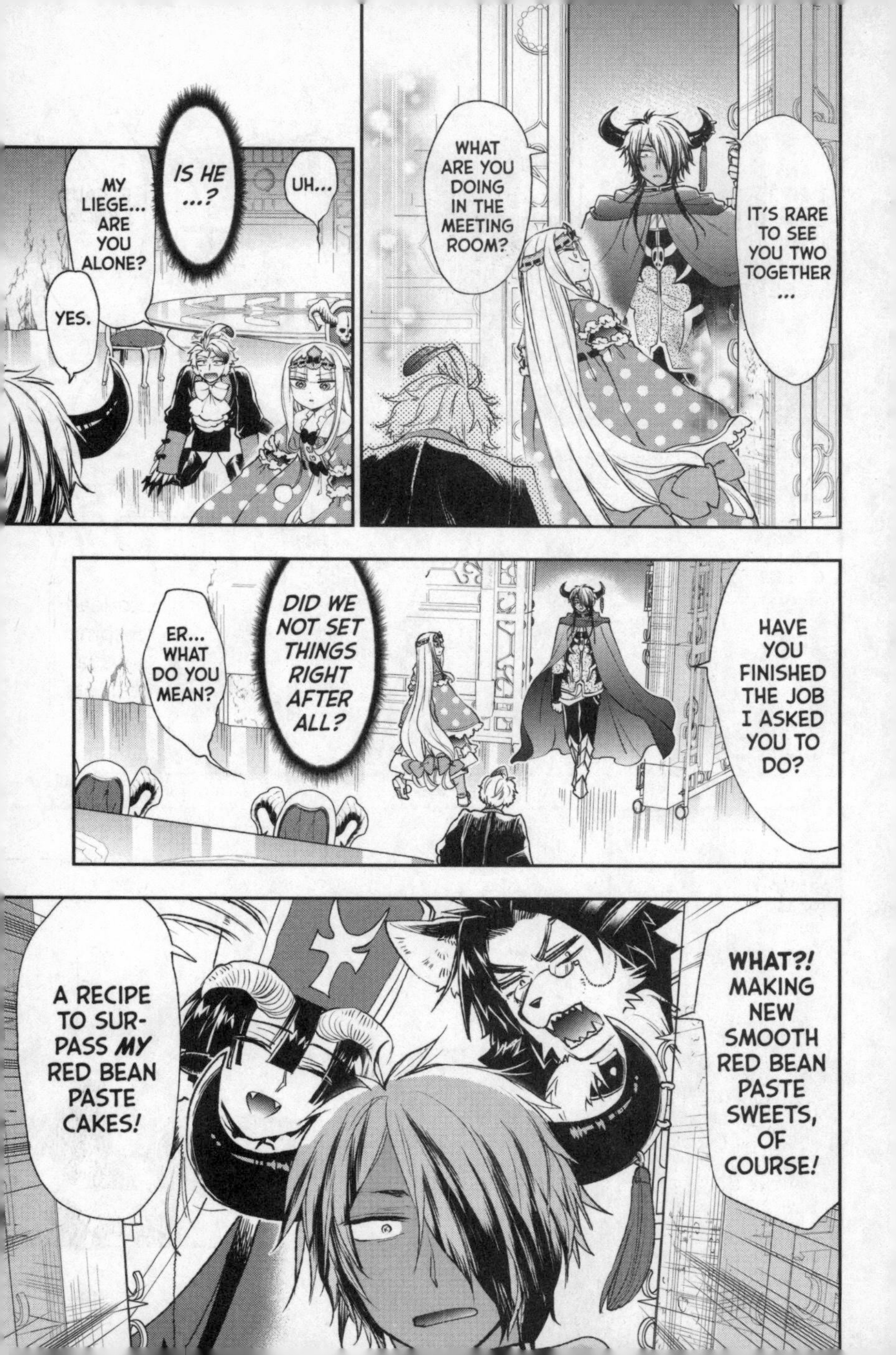
IT'S RARE TO SEE YOU TWO TOGETHER...
WHAT ARE YOU DOING IN THE MEETING ROOM?
UH...
IS HE ...?
MY LIEGE... ARE YOU ALONE?
YES.
HAVE YOU FINISHED THE JOB I ASKED YOU TO DO?
DID WE NOT SET THINGS RIGHT AFTER ALL?
ER... WHAT DO YOU MEAN?
WHAT?! MAKING NEW SMOOTH RED BEAN PASTE SWEETS, OF COURSE!
A RECIPE TO SURPASS MY RED BEAN PASTE CAKES!

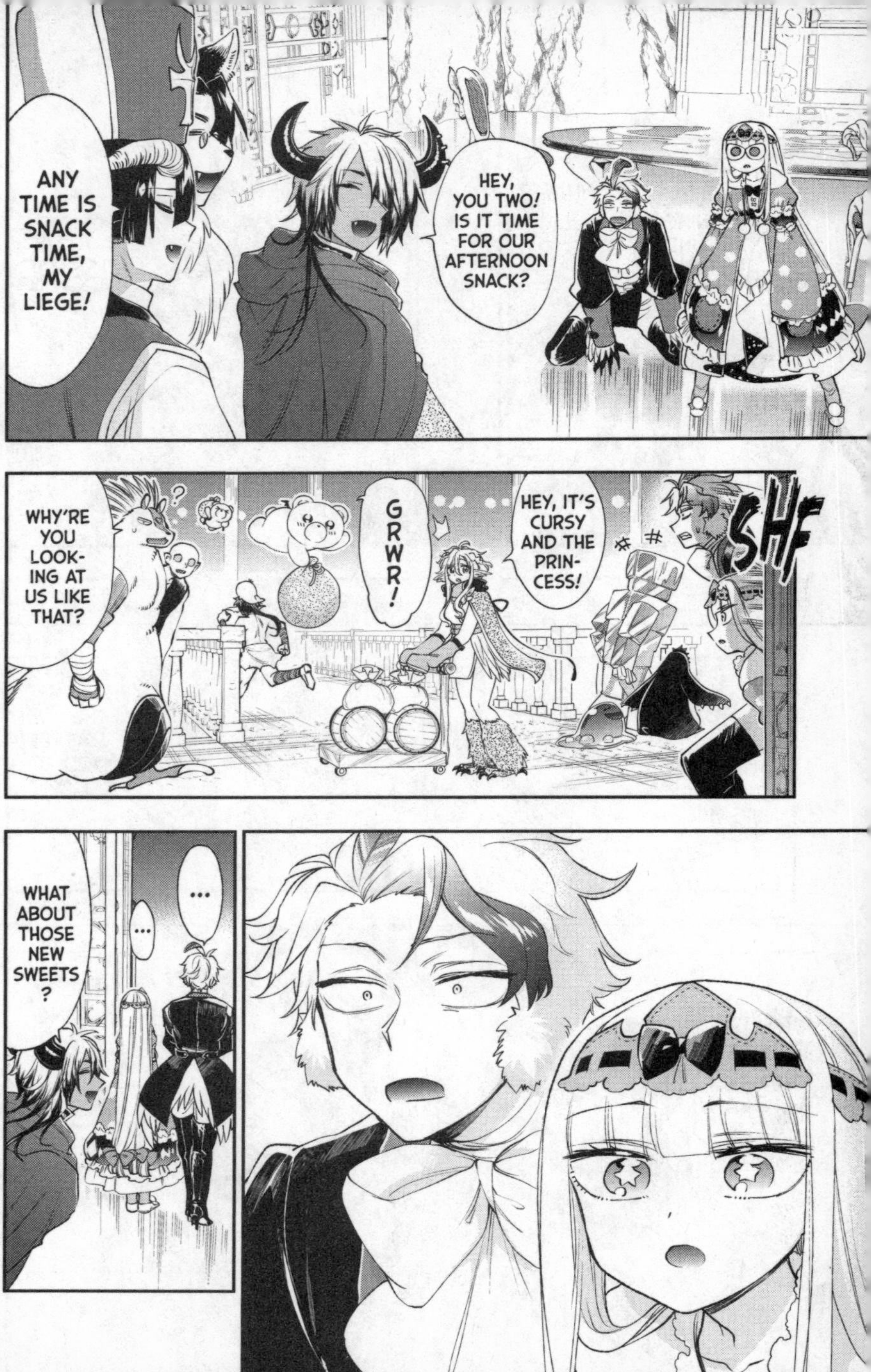
HEY, YOU TWO! IS IT TIME FOR OUR AFTERNOON SNACK?
ANY TIME IS SNACK TIME, MY LIEGE!
SHF
HEY, IT'S CURSY AND THE PRIN-CESS!
GRWR!
WHY'RE YOU LOOKING AT US LIKE THAT?
...
...
WHAT ABOUT THOSE NEW SWEETS?

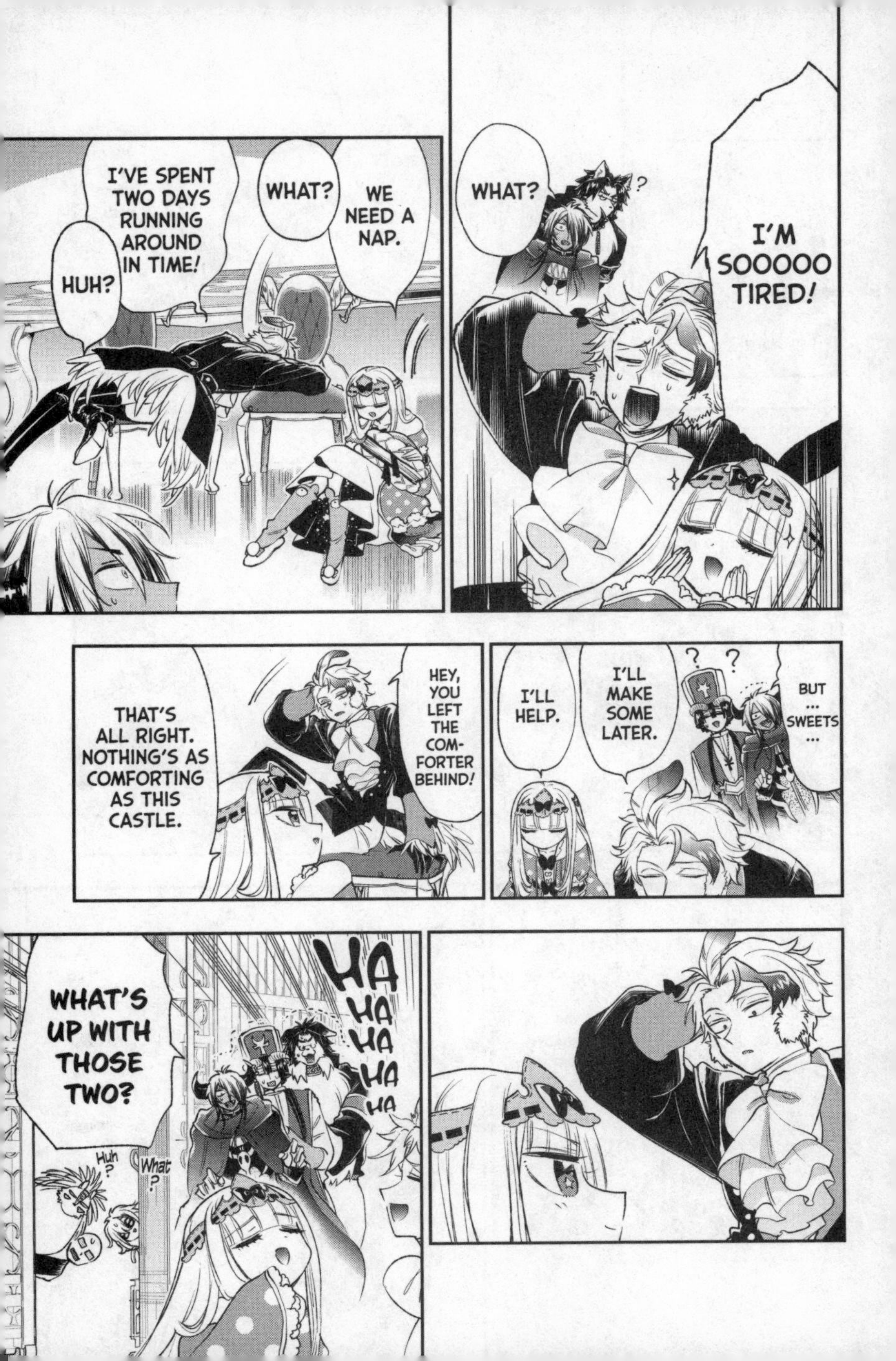
I'M SOOOOO TIRED!
WHAT?
WE NEED A NAP.
WHAT?
I'VE SPENT TWO DAYS RUNNING AROUND IN TIME!
HUH?
BUT ... SWEETS ...
I'LL MAKE SOME LATER.
I'LL HELP.
HEY, YOU LEFT THE COM-FORTER BEHIND!
THAT'S ALL RIGHT. NOTHING'S AS COMFORTING AS THIS CASTLE.
HA HA HA HA HA HA
WHAT'S UP WITH THOSE TWO?
What?
Huh?

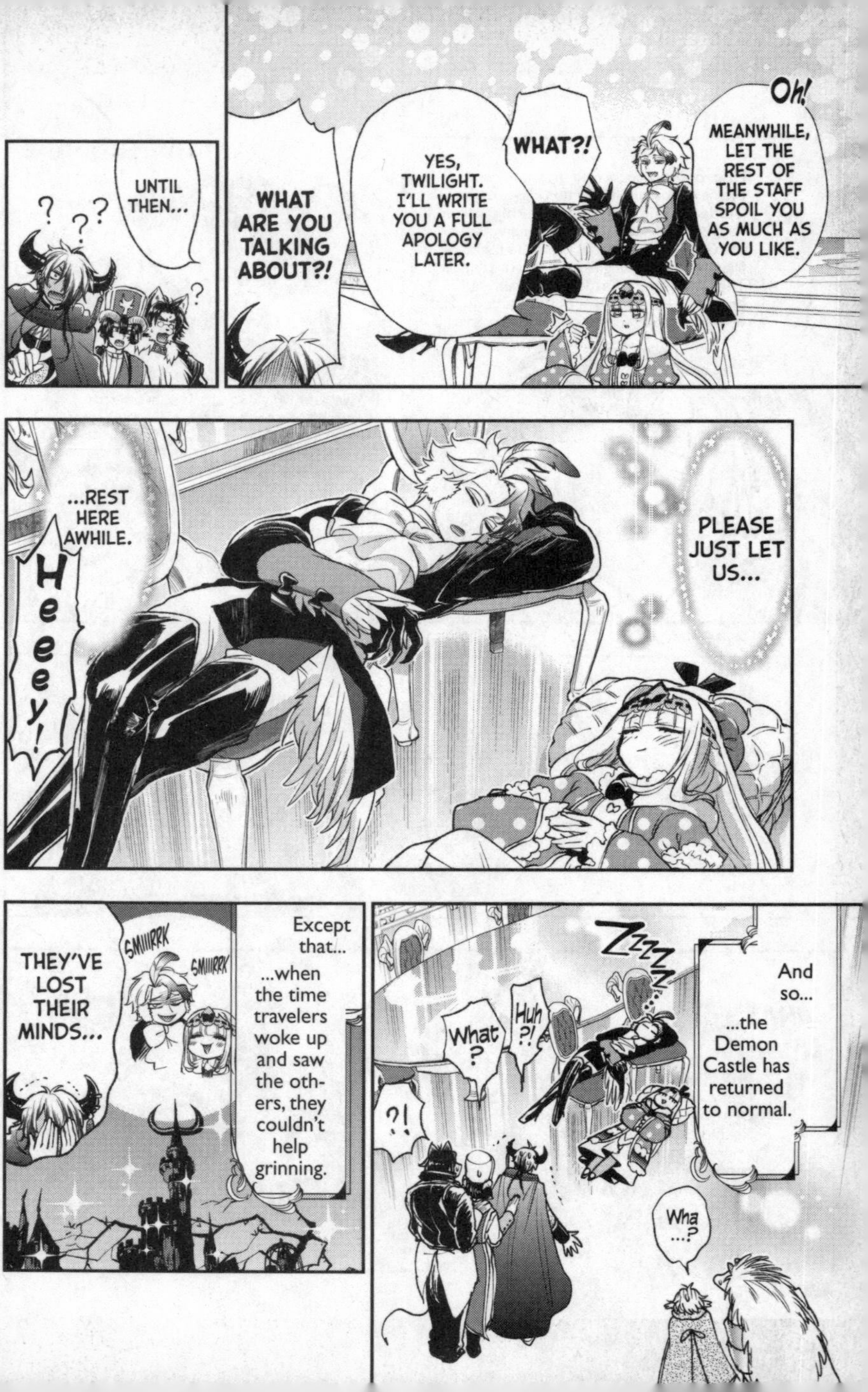
Oh!
MEANWHILE, LET THE REST OF THE STAFF SPOIL YOU AS MUCH AS YOU LIKE.
WHAT?!
YES, TWILIGHT. I'LL WRITE YOU A FULL APOLOGY LATER.
WHAT ARE YOU TALKING ABOUT?!
UNTIL THEN...
PLEASE JUST LET US...
...REST HERE AWHILE.
Heeey!
And so...
...the Demon Castle has returned to normal.
ZZZZZ
Huh?!
What?
?!
Wha...?
Except that...
...when the time travelers woke up and saw the others, they couldn't help grinning.
SMIIIRRK
SMIIIRRK
THEY'VE LOST THEIR MINDS...

Another Route 2

Court of the Alternate Demon Castle

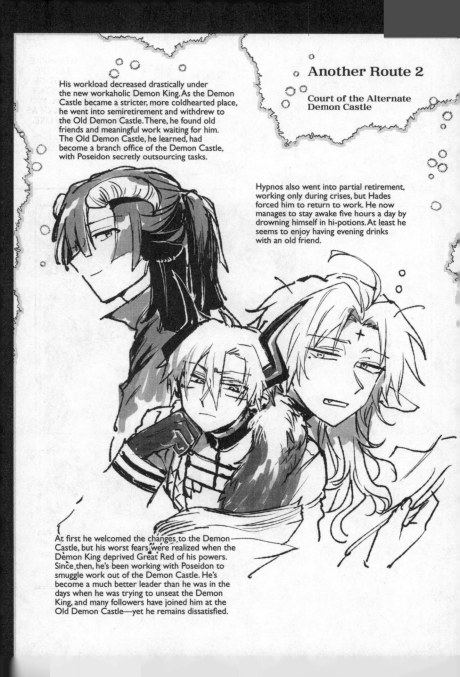

His workload decreased drastically under the new workaholic Demon King. As the Demon Castle became a stricter, more coldhearted place, he went into semiretirement and withdrew to the Old Demon Castle. There, he found old friends and meaningful work waiting for him. The Old Demon Castle, he learned, had become a branch office of the Demon Castle, with Poseidon secretly outsourcing tasks.

Hypnos also went into partial retirement, working only during crises, but Hades forced him to return to work. He now manages to stay awake five hours a day by drowning himself in hi-potions. At least he seems to enjoy having evening drinks with an old friend.

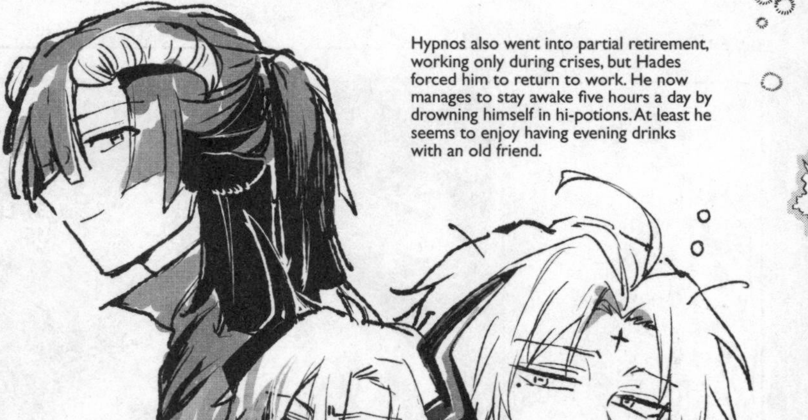

At first he welcomed the changes to the Demon Castle, but his worst fears were realized when the Demon King deprived Great Red of his powers. Since then, he's been working with Poseidon to smuggle work out of the Demon Castle. He's become a much better leader than he was in the days when he was trying to unseat the Demon King, and many followers have joined him at the Old Demon Castle—yet he remains dissatisfied.

Would you like to change your class?

1 change remaining

▶ Yes

No ▼

Time Traveler

"So close and yet so far."

▼

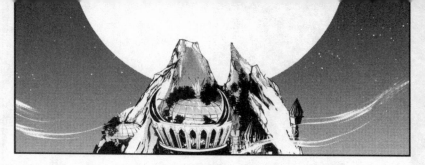

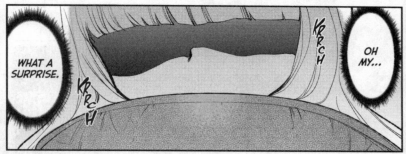

OH MY...

WHAT A SURPRISE.

THIS...

...WAS NOT AT ALL WHAT I EXPECTED.

205th Night: Massage Bro

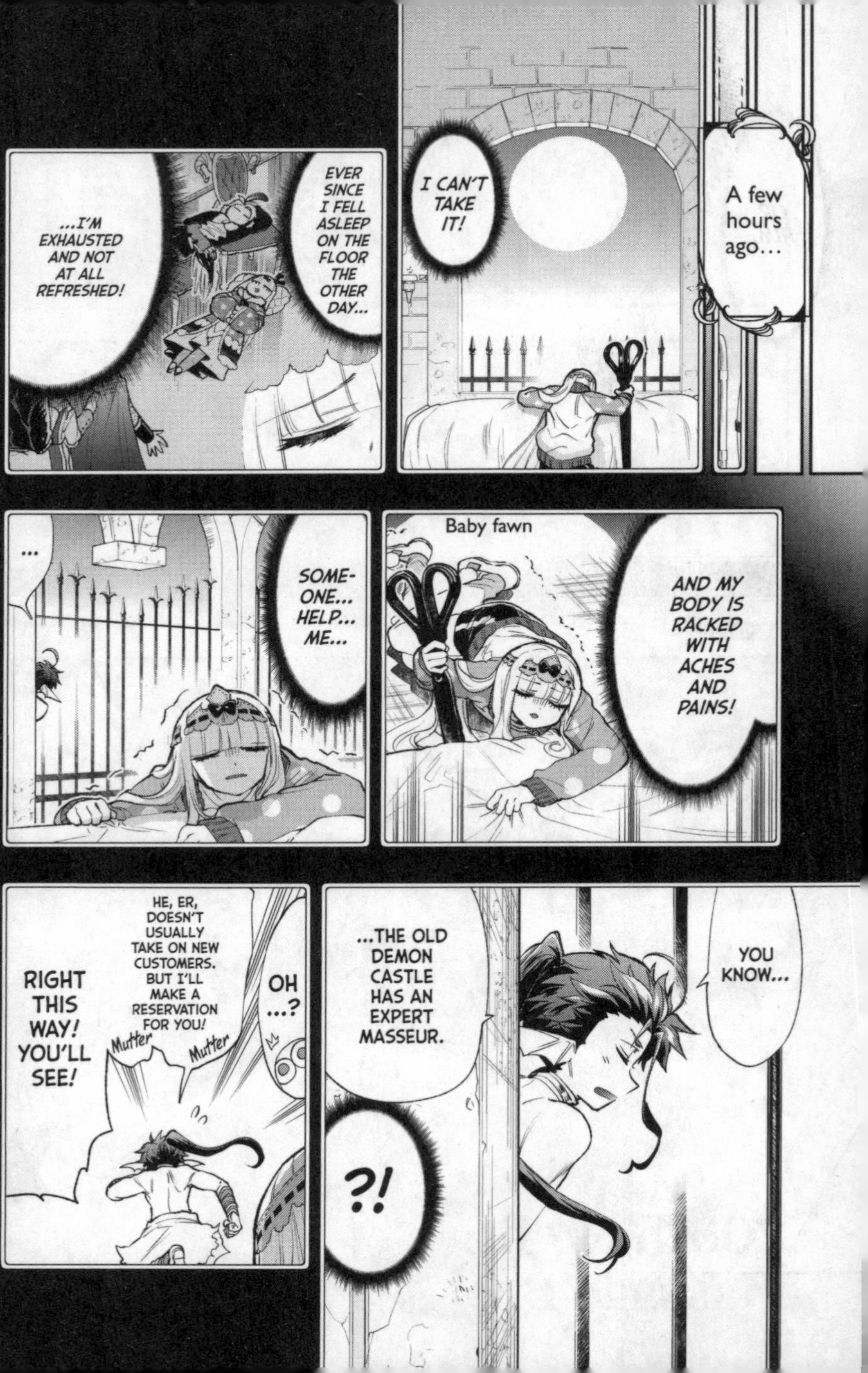
A few hours ago...
I CAN'T TAKE IT!
EVER SINCE I FELL ASLEEP ON THE FLOOR THE OTHER DAY...
...I'M EXHAUSTED AND NOT AT ALL REFRESHED!
Baby fawn
AND MY BODY IS RACKED WITH ACHES AND PAINS!
SOME-ONE... HELP... ME...
...
YOU KNOW...
...THE OLD DEMON CASTLE HAS AN EXPERT MASSEUR.
?!
OH ...?
HE, ER, DOESN'T USUALLY TAKE ON NEW CUSTOMERS. BUT I'LL MAKE A RESERVATION FOR YOU!
Mutter
Mutter
RIGHT THIS WAY! YOU'LL SEE!

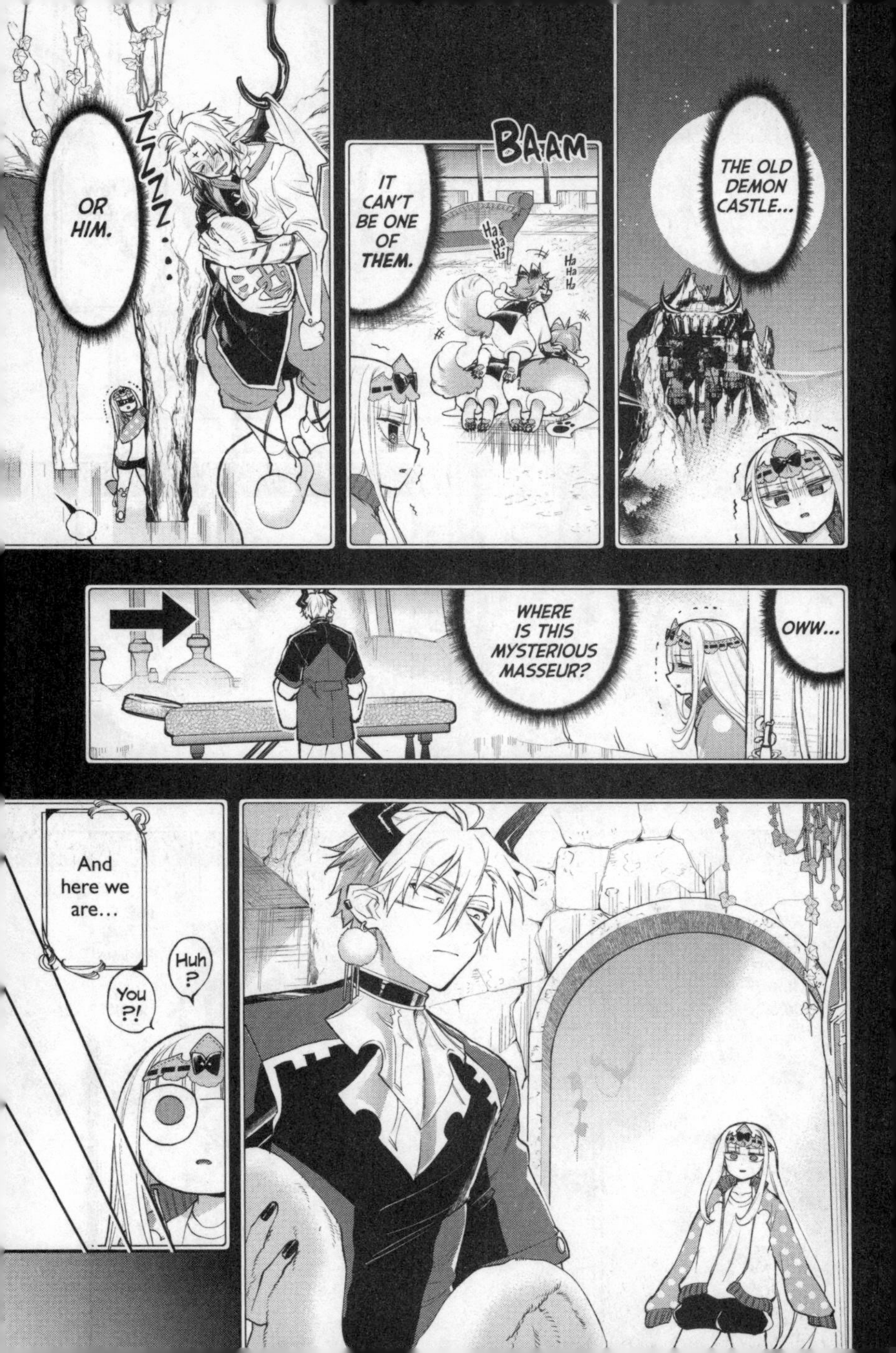
THE OLD DEMON CASTLE...
BAAM
IT CAN'T BE ONE OF THEM.
Ha Ha Ha
Ha Ha Ha
OR HIM.
ZZZZ...
OWW...
WHERE IS THIS MYSTERIOUS MASSEUR?
And here we are...
Huh?
You?!

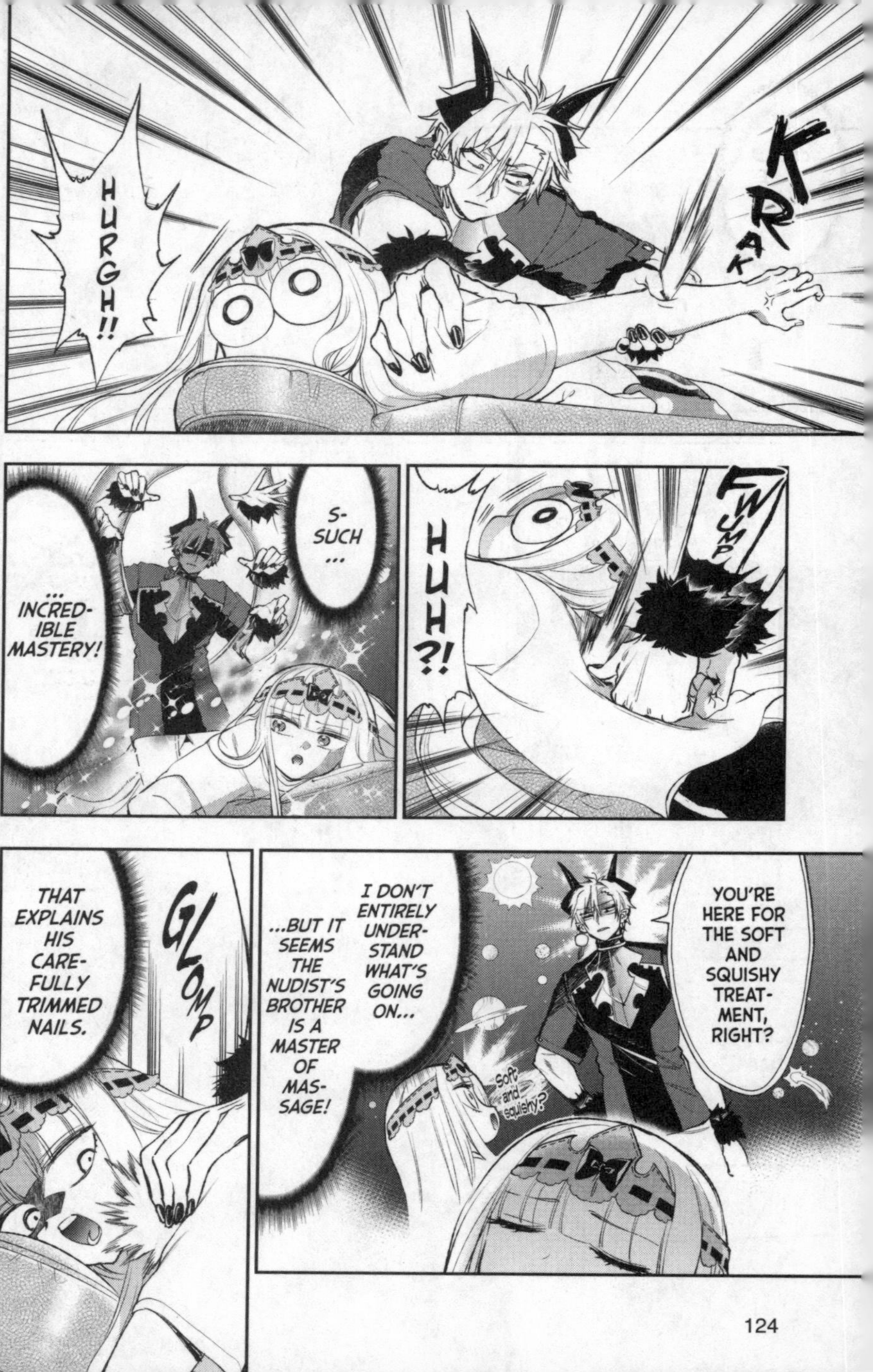
KRAK
HURGH!!
FWUMP
HUH?!
S-SUCH...
...INCREDIBLE MASTERY!
YOU'RE HERE FOR THE SOFT AND SQUISHY TREATMENT, RIGHT?
Soft and squishy?
I DON'T ENTIRELY UNDERSTAND WHAT'S GOING ON...
...BUT IT SEEMS THE NUDIST'S BROTHER IS A MASTER OF MASSAGE!
GLOMP
THAT EXPLAINS HIS CAREFULLY TRIMMED NAILS.

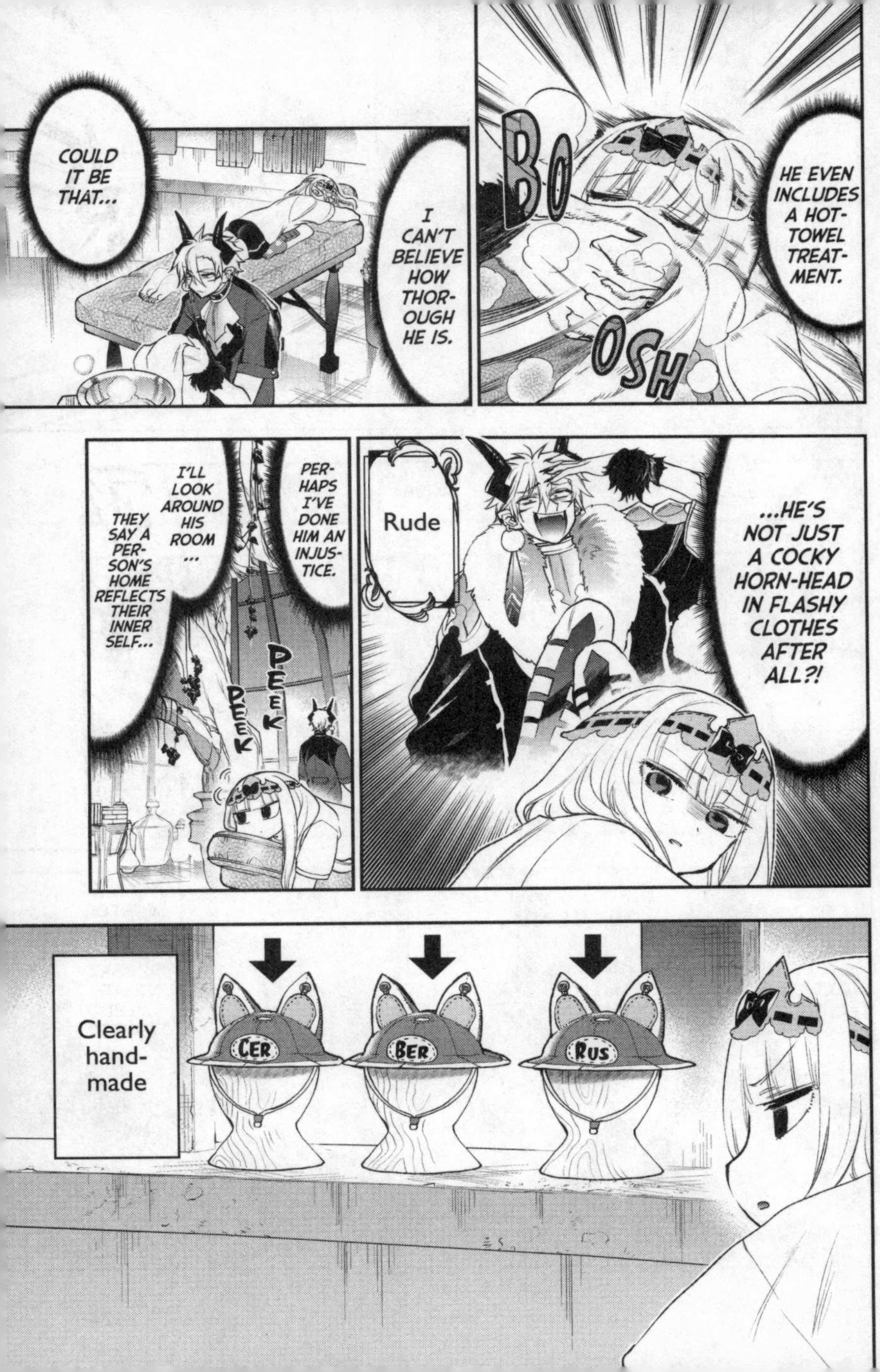
HE EVEN INCLUDES A HOT-TOWEL TREAT-MENT.
BOOSH
I CAN'T BELIEVE HOW THOR-OUGH HE IS.
COULD IT BE THAT...
...HE'S NOT JUST A COCKY HORN-HEAD IN FLASHY CLOTHES AFTER ALL?!
Rude
PER-HAPS I'VE DONE HIM AN INJUS-TICE.
I'LL LOOK AROUND HIS ROOM ...
THEY SAY A PER-SON'S HOME REFLECTS THEIR INNER SELF...
PEEK
PEEK
CER
BER
RUS
Clearly hand-made

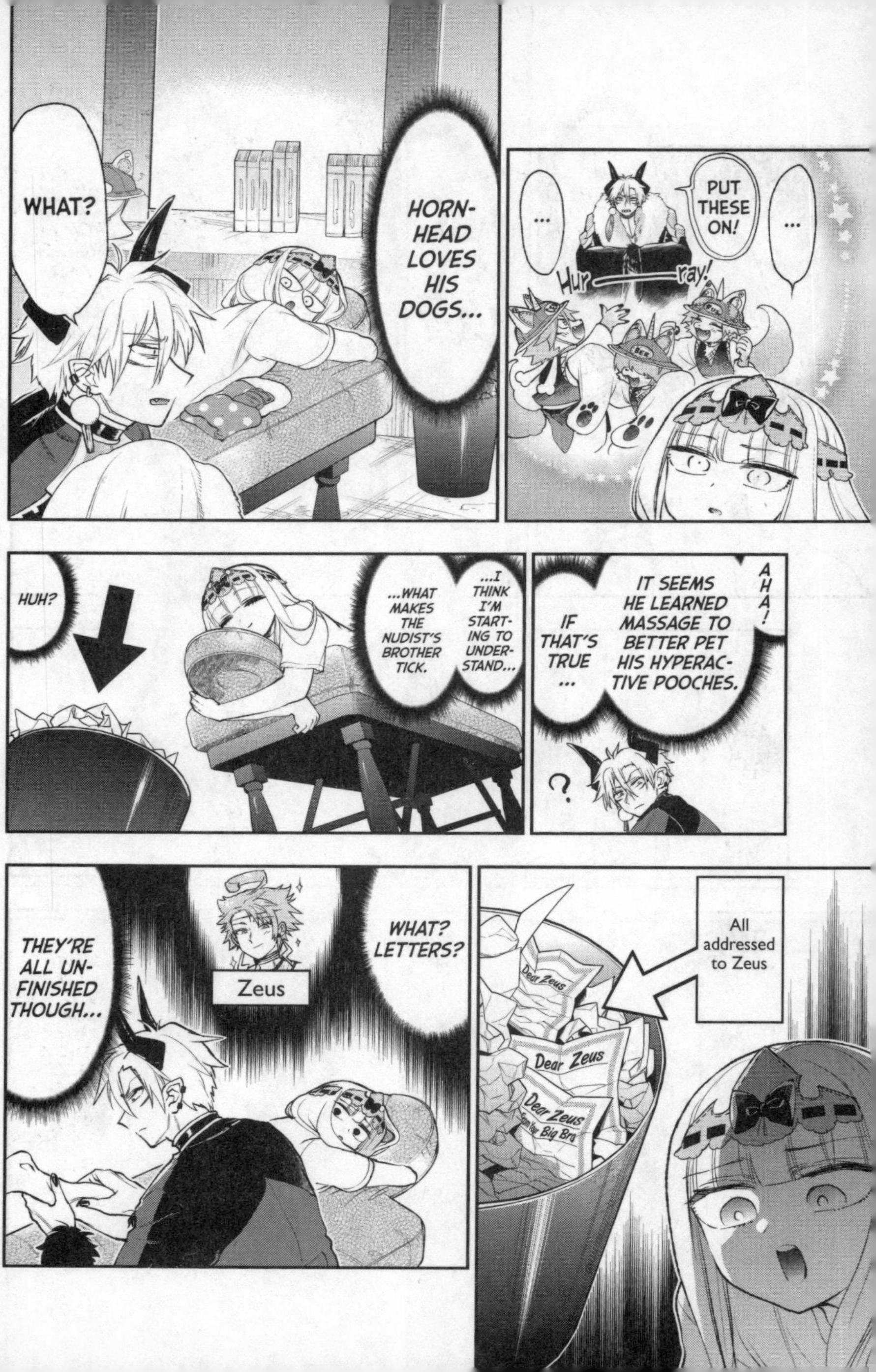
...
PUT THESE ON!
...
Hur——ray!
HORN-HEAD LOVES HIS DOGS...
WHAT?
AHA!
IT SEEMS HE LEARNED MASSAGE TO BETTER PET HIS HYPERACTIVE POOCHES.
IF THAT'S TRUE ...
...I THINK I'M STARTING TO UNDERSTAND...
...WHAT MAKES THE NUDIST'S BROTHER TICK.
HUH?
All addressed to Zeus
Dear Zeus
Dear Zeus
Dear Zeus From Your Big Bro
WHAT? LETTERS?
Zeus
THEY'RE ALL UNFINISHED THOUGH...

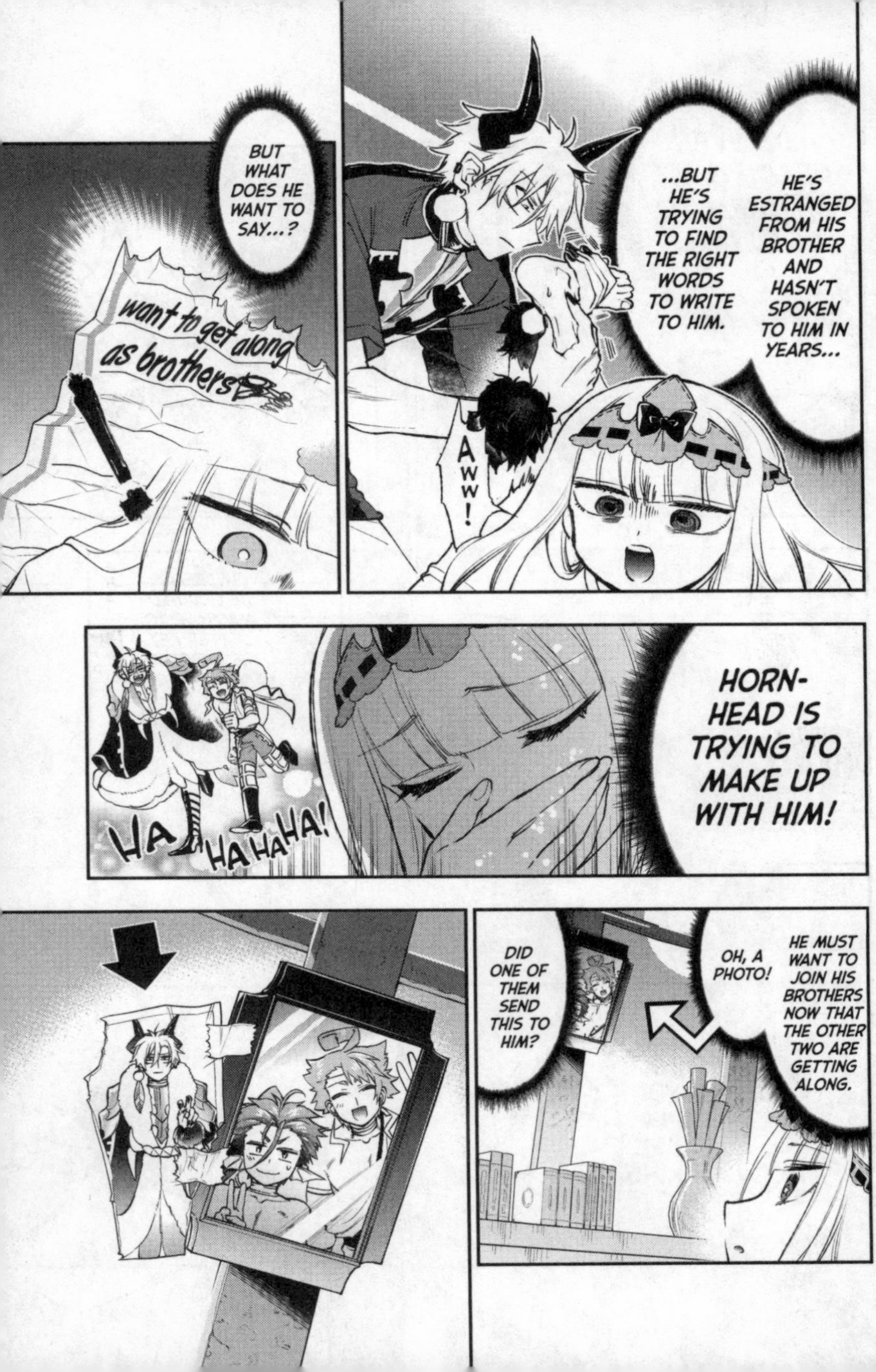
HE'S ESTRANGED FROM HIS BROTHER AND HASN'T SPOKEN TO HIM IN YEARS...
...BUT HE'S TRYING TO FIND THE RIGHT WORDS TO WRITE TO HIM.
AWW!
BUT WHAT DOES HE WANT TO SAY...?
want to get along as brothers
HORN-HEAD IS TRYING TO MAKE UP WITH HIM!
HA HA HAHAHA!
HE MUST WANT TO JOIN HIS BROTHERS NOW THAT THE OTHER TWO ARE GETTING ALONG.
OH, A PHOTO!
DID ONE OF THEM SEND THIS TO HIM?

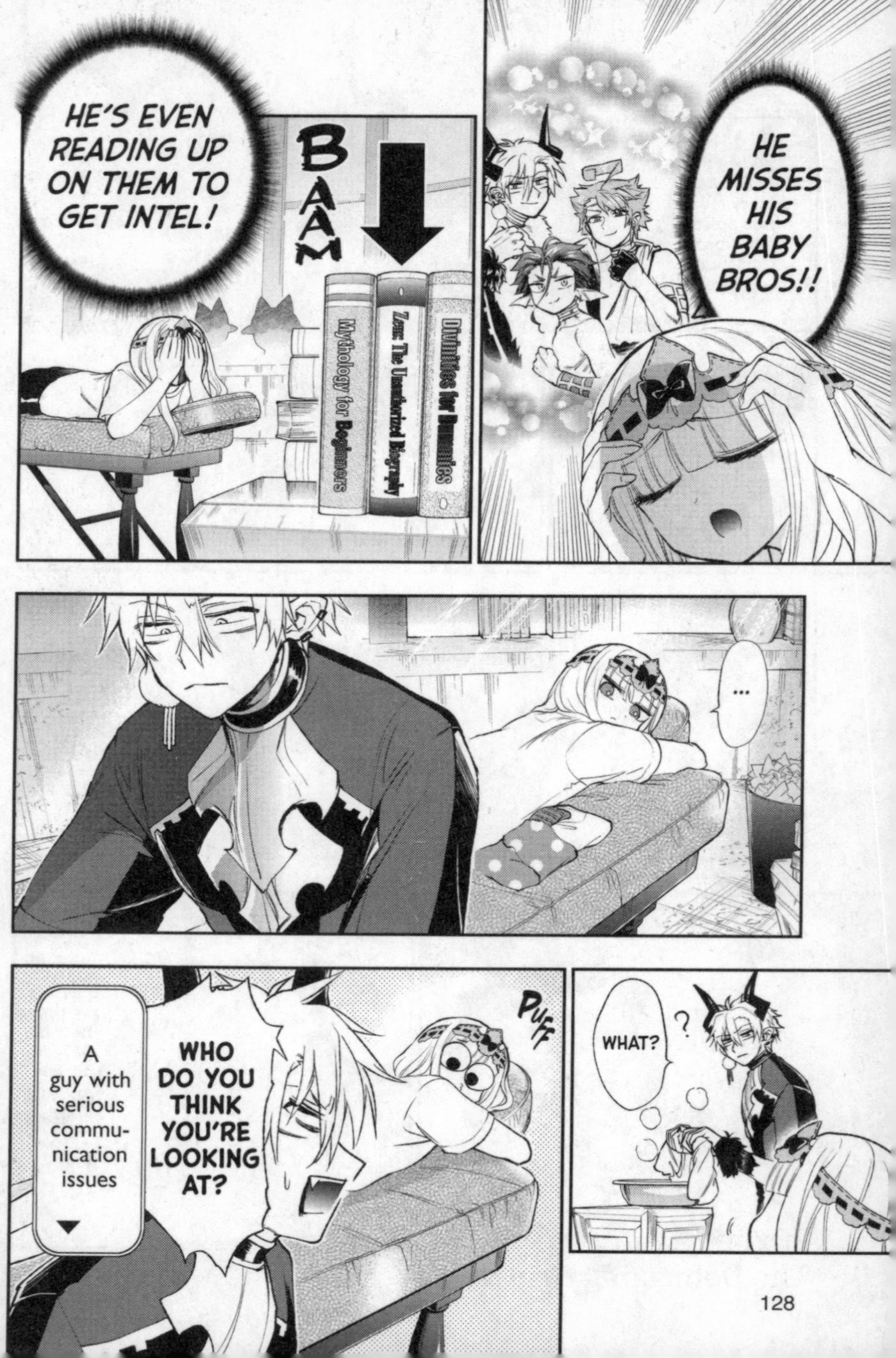
HE MISSES HIS BABY BROS!!
HE'S EVEN READING UP ON THEM TO GET INTEL!
BAAM
Divinities for Dummies
Zeus: The Unauthorized Biography
Mythology for Beginners
...
WHAT?
?
PUFF
WHO DO YOU THINK YOU'RE LOOKING AT?
A guy with serious communication issues

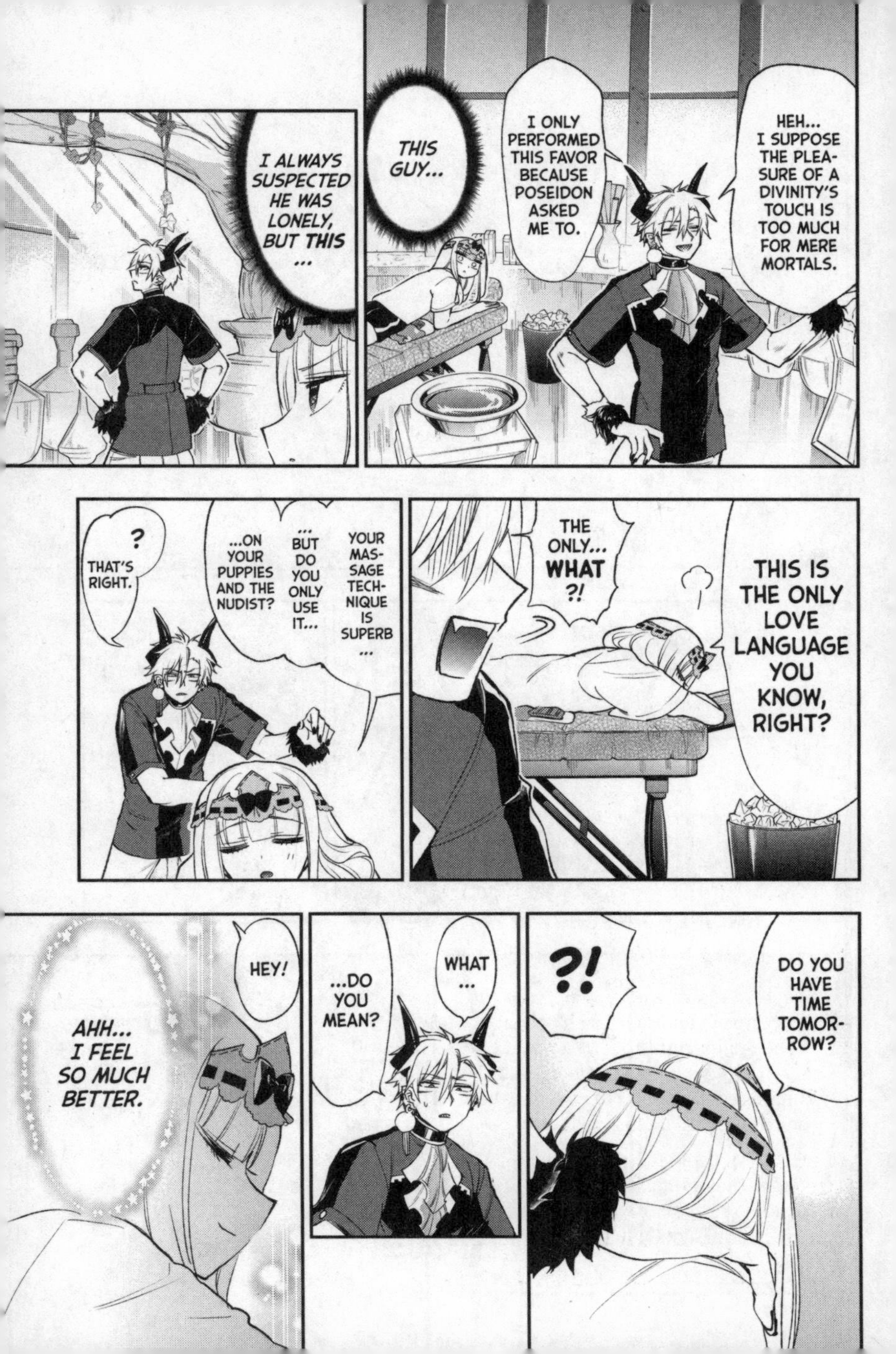
HEH... I SUPPOSE THE PLEA-SURE OF A DIVINITY'S TOUCH IS TOO MUCH FOR MERE MORTALS.
I ONLY PERFORMED THIS FAVOR BECAUSE POSEIDON ASKED ME TO.
THIS GUY...
I ALWAYS SUSPECTED HE WAS LONELY, BUT THIS ...
THIS IS THE ONLY LOVE LANGUAGE YOU KNOW, RIGHT?
THE ONLY... WHAT ?!
YOUR MAS-SAGE TECH-NIQUE IS SUPERB ...
... BUT DO YOU ONLY USE IT...
...ON YOUR PUPPIES AND THE NUDIST?
?
THAT'S RIGHT.
DO YOU HAVE TIME TOMOR-ROW?
?!
WHAT ...
...DO YOU MEAN?
HEY!
AHH... I FEEL SO MUCH BETTER.

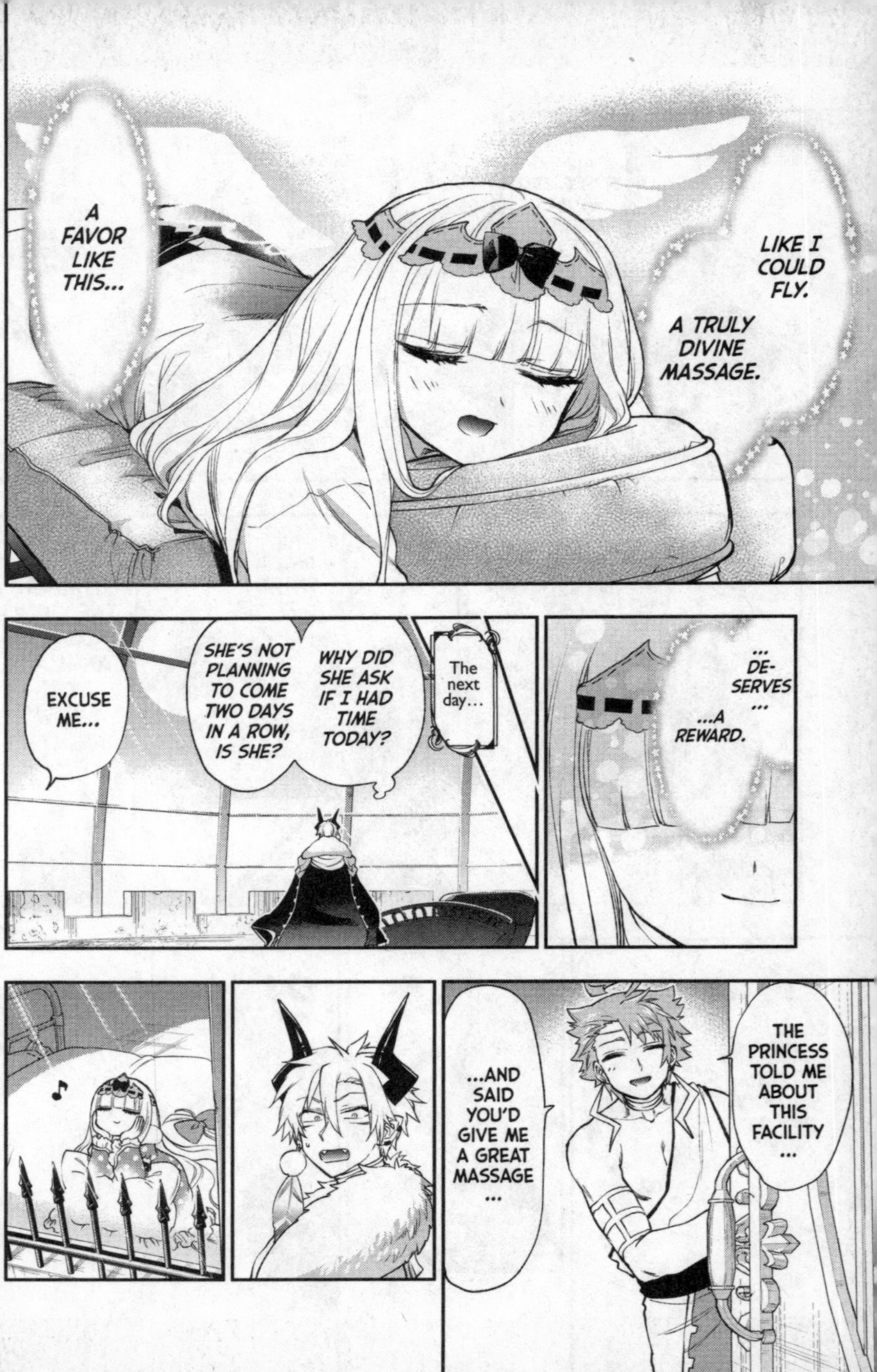

LIKE I COULD FLY.
A TRULY DIVINE MASSAGE.
A FAVOR LIKE THIS...
...DE-SERVES...
...A REWARD.
The next day…
WHY DID SHE ASK IF I HAD TIME TODAY?
SHE'S NOT PLANNING TO COME TWO DAYS IN A ROW, IS SHE?
EXCUSE ME...
THE PRINCESS TOLD ME ABOUT THIS FACILITY...
...AND SAID YOU'D GIVE ME A GREAT MASSAGE...
♪

Another Route 3

Court of the Alternate Demon Castle

An elitist who went to work for the Demon Castle and joined the Ten Guardians after Demon Cleric left. Being a jack-of-all-trades, he keeps busy, so he was away from the castle during the time-travel incident due to an urgent trip to the fortress. He believes the Demon King is about to collapse and is trying his best to keep him from falling apart.

After being kidnapped, she had nothing to do except sleep, but she found the castle uncomfortable and didn't care for its atmosphere. She executed a carefully developed escape plan shortly before the time-travel incident, so she was not in residence at the castle at that time. The demons discovered the breakout but captured the **other** princess instead, so she got away scott free. She has just encountered her first Teddy Demon in a forest outside the Demon Castle…

Would you like to change your class?
0 changes remaining

Executor

"Bow to your fate."

206th Night: Quality Service from Kowloon Construction

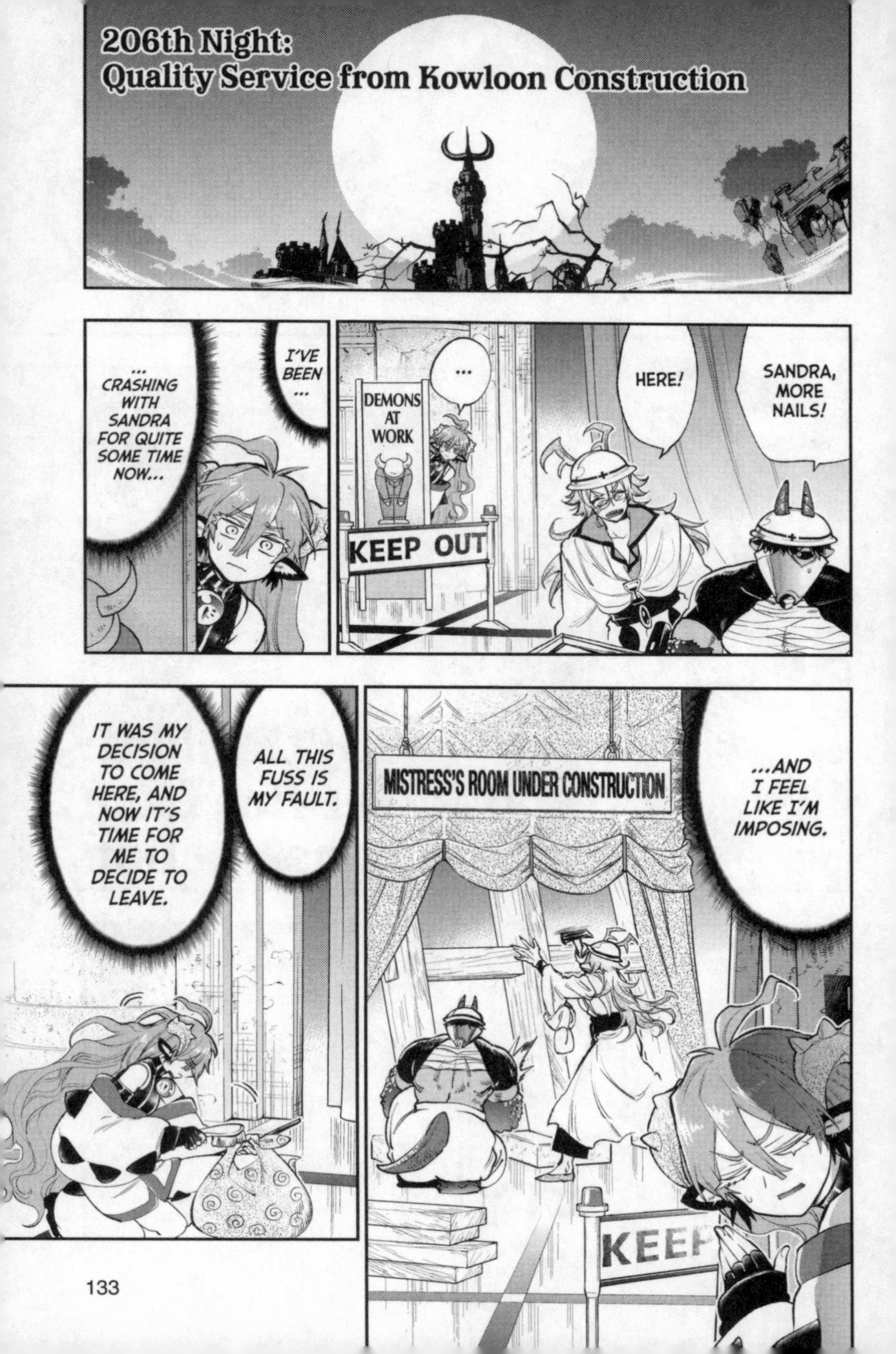
SANDRA, MORE NAILS!
HERE!
...
DEMONS AT WORK
KEEP OUT
I'VE BEEN...
...CRASHING WITH SANDRA FOR QUITE SOME TIME NOW...
MISTRESS'S ROOM UNDER CONSTRUCTION
...AND I FEEL LIKE I'M IMPOSING.
KEEP
ALL THIS FUSS IS MY FAULT.
IT WAS MY DECISION TO COME HERE, AND NOW IT'S TIME FOR ME TO DECIDE TO LEAVE.

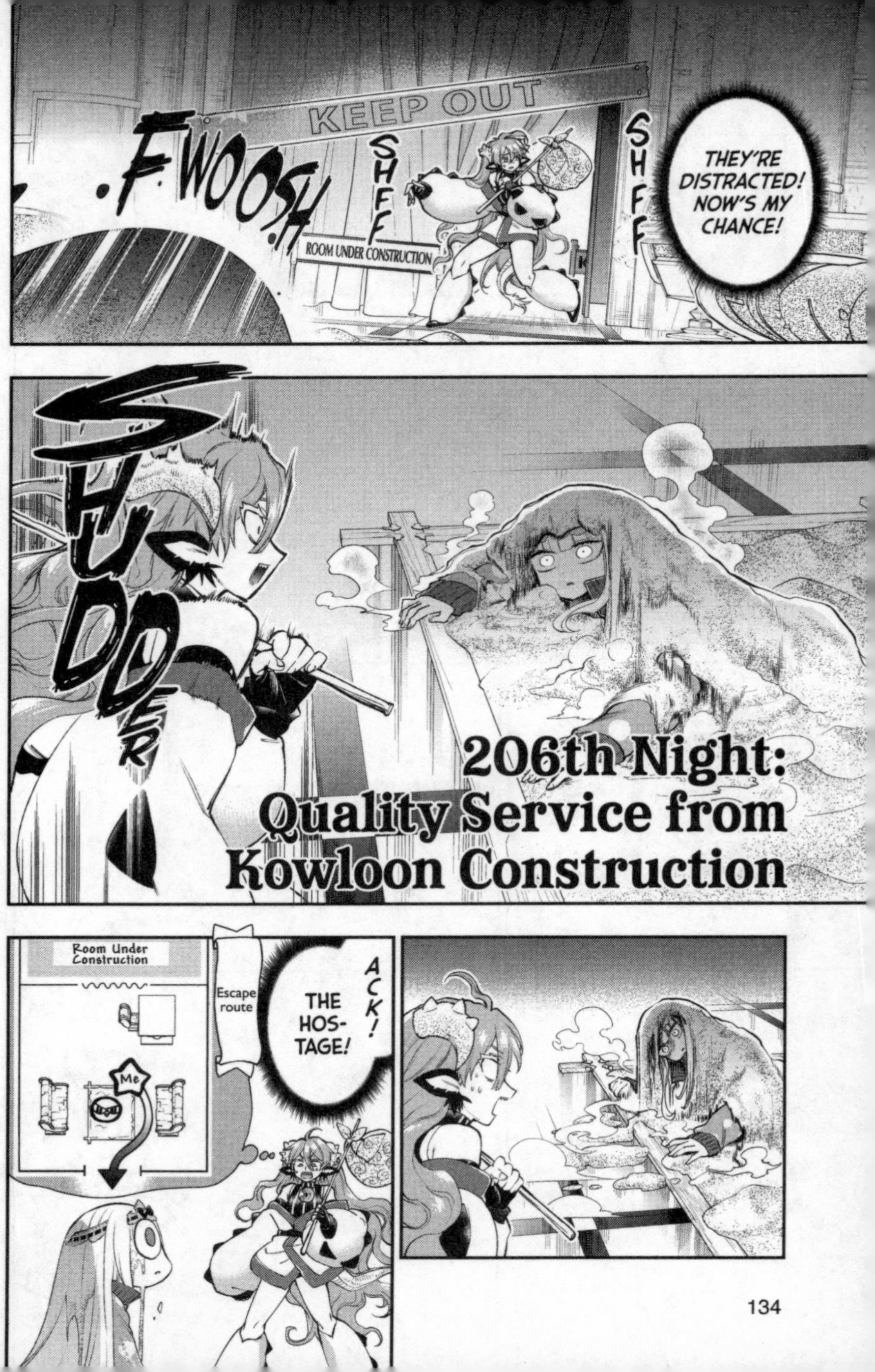
THEY'RE DISTRACTED! NOW'S MY CHANCE!
SHFF
KEEP OUT
SHFF
ROOM UNDER CONSTRUCTION
FWOOSH
SHUDDER
206th Night: Quality Service from Kowloon Construction
ACK!
THE HOS-TAGE!
Escape route
Room Under Construction
Me

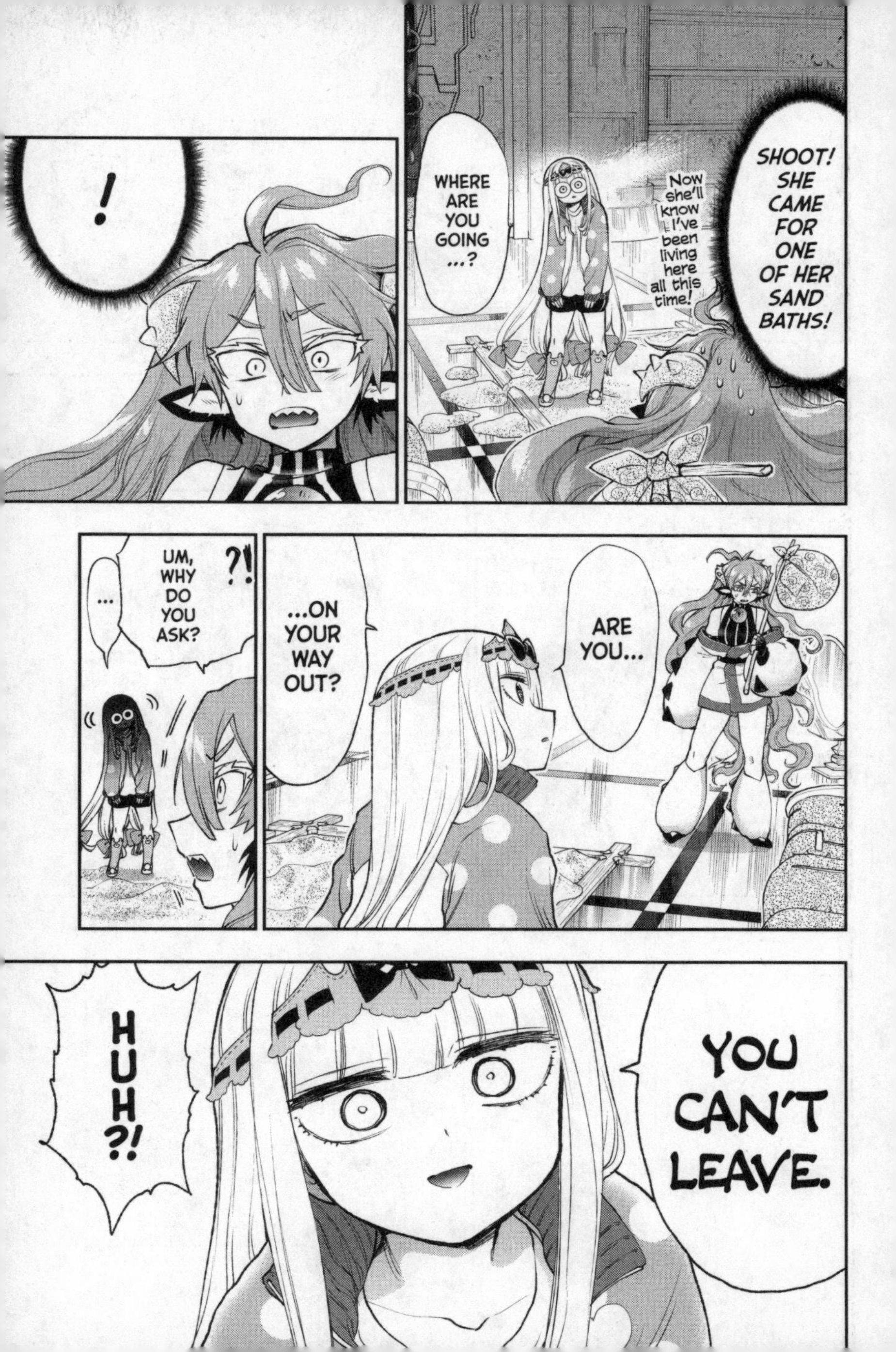
SHOOT! SHE CAME FOR ONE OF HER SAND BATHS!
Now she'll know I've been living here all this time!
WHERE ARE YOU GOING ...?
!
ARE YOU...
...ON YOUR WAY OUT?
?!
UM, WHY DO YOU ASK?
...
YOU CAN'T LEAVE.
HUH?!

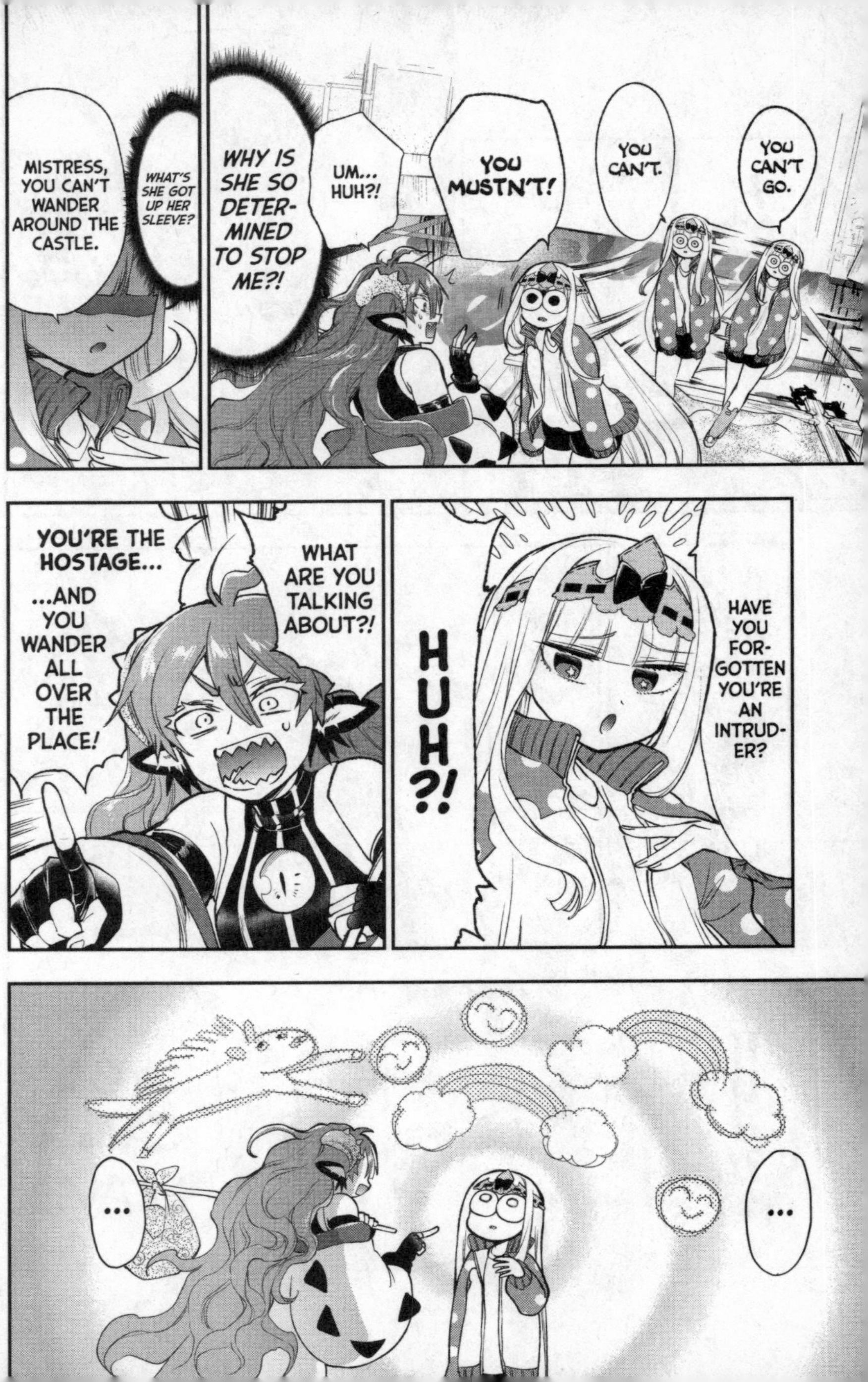
YOU CAN'T GO.
YOU CAN'T.
YOU MUSTN'T!
UM... HUH?!
WHY IS SHE SO DETER-MINED TO STOP ME?!
WHAT'S SHE GOT UP HER SLEEVE?
MISTRESS, YOU CAN'T WANDER AROUND THE CASTLE.
HAVE YOU FOR-GOTTEN YOU'RE AN INTRUD-ER?
HUH?!
WHAT ARE YOU TALKING ABOUT?!
YOU'RE THE HOSTAGE...
...AND YOU WANDER ALL OVER THE PLACE!
...
...

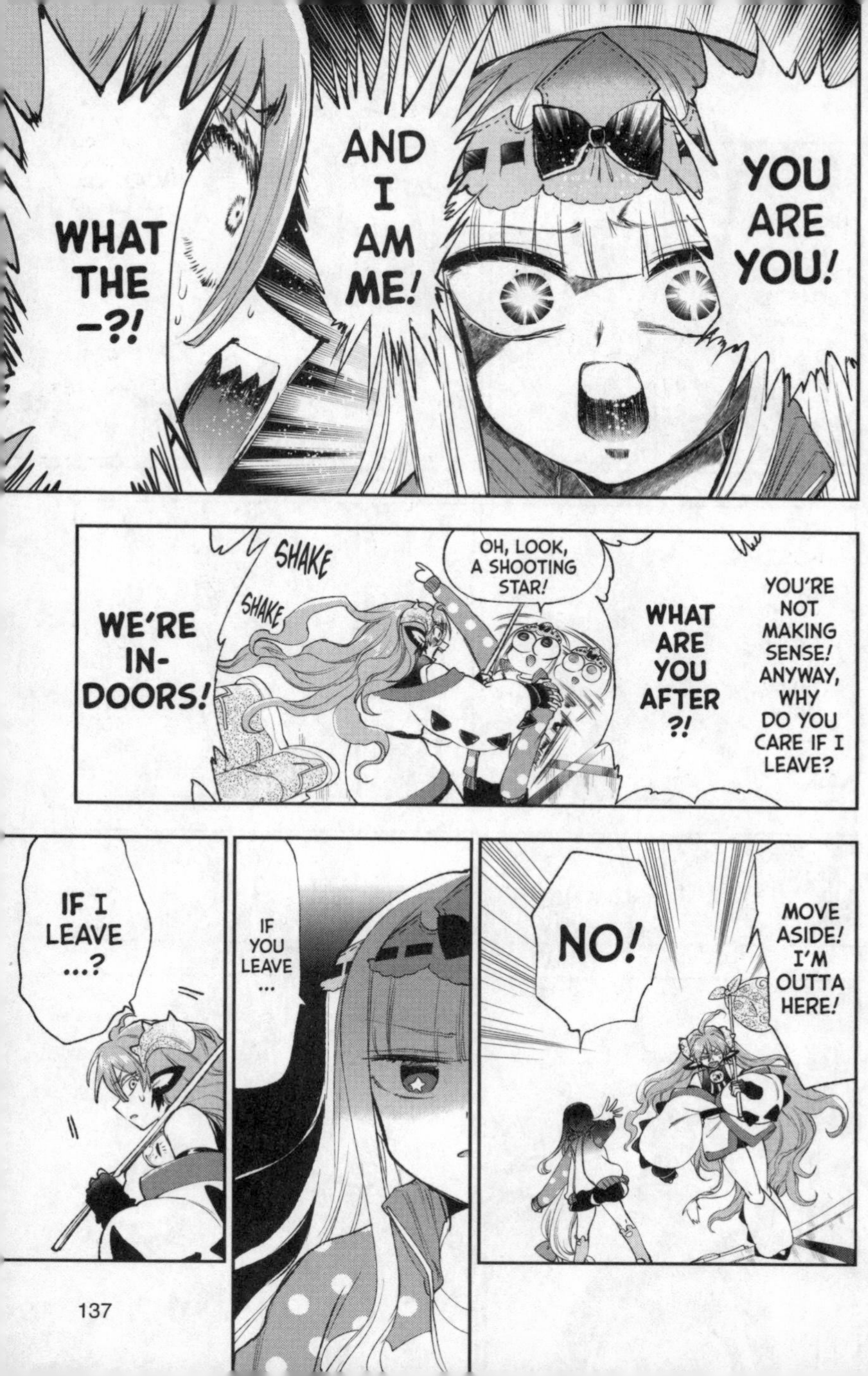
YOU ARE YOU!
AND I AM ME!
WHAT THE—?!
YOU'RE NOT MAKING SENSE! ANYWAY, WHY DO YOU CARE IF I LEAVE?
WHAT ARE YOU AFTER?!
OH, LOOK, A SHOOTING STAR!
SHAKE
SHAKE
WE'RE IN-DOORS!
MOVE ASIDE! I'M OUTTA HERE!
NO!
IF YOU LEAVE ...
IF I LEAVE ...?

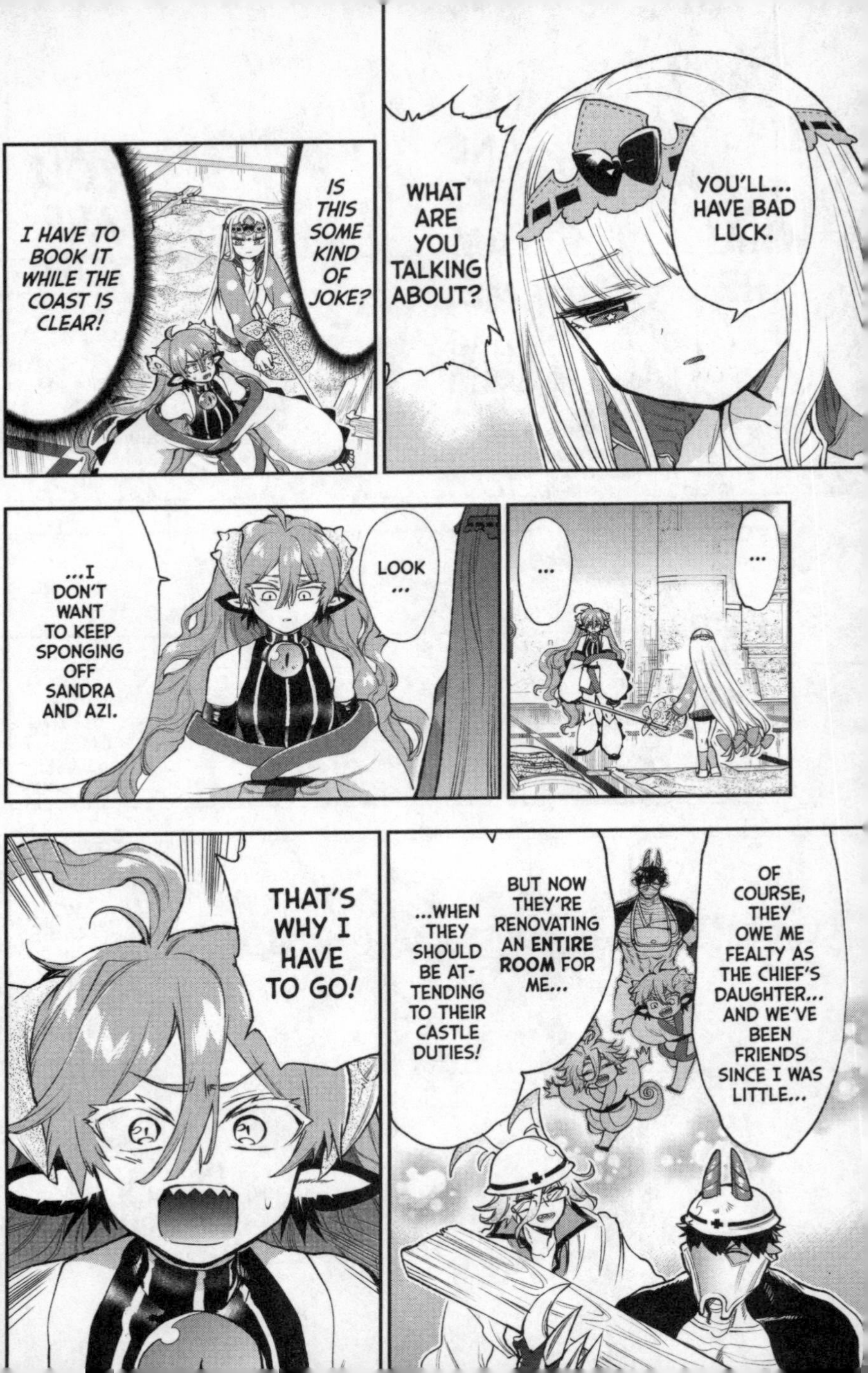

YOU'LL... HAVE BAD LUCK.
WHAT ARE YOU TALKING ABOUT?
IS THIS SOME KIND OF JOKE?
I HAVE TO BOOK IT WHILE THE COAST IS CLEAR!
...
...
LOOK ...
...I DON'T WANT TO KEEP SPONGING OFF SANDRA AND AZI.
OF COURSE, THEY OWE ME FEALTY AS THE CHIEF'S DAUGHTER... AND WE'VE BEEN FRIENDS SINCE I WAS LITTLE...
BUT NOW THEY'RE RENOVATING AN **ENTIRE ROOM** FOR ME...
...WHEN THEY SHOULD BE AT-TENDING TO THEIR CASTLE DUTIES!
THAT'S WHY I HAVE TO GO!

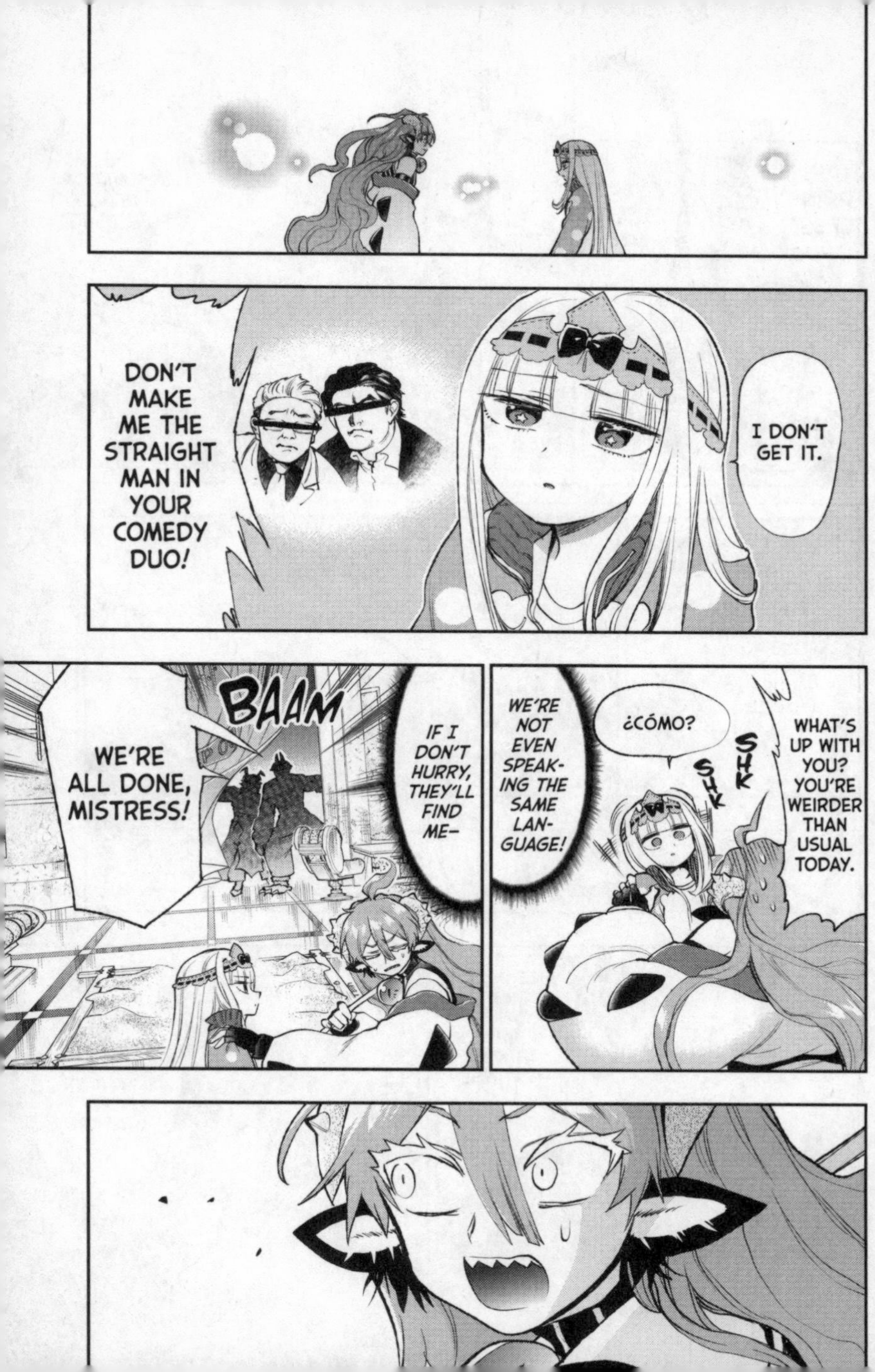
I DON'T GET IT.
DON'T MAKE ME THE STRAIGHT MAN IN YOUR COMEDY DUO!
WHAT'S UP WITH YOU? YOU'RE WEIRDER THAN USUAL TODAY.
¿CÓMO?
SHK SHK
WE'RE NOT EVEN SPEAKING THE SAME LANGUAGE!
IF I DON'T HURRY, THEY'LL FIND ME–
BAAM
WE'RE ALL DONE, MISTRESS!

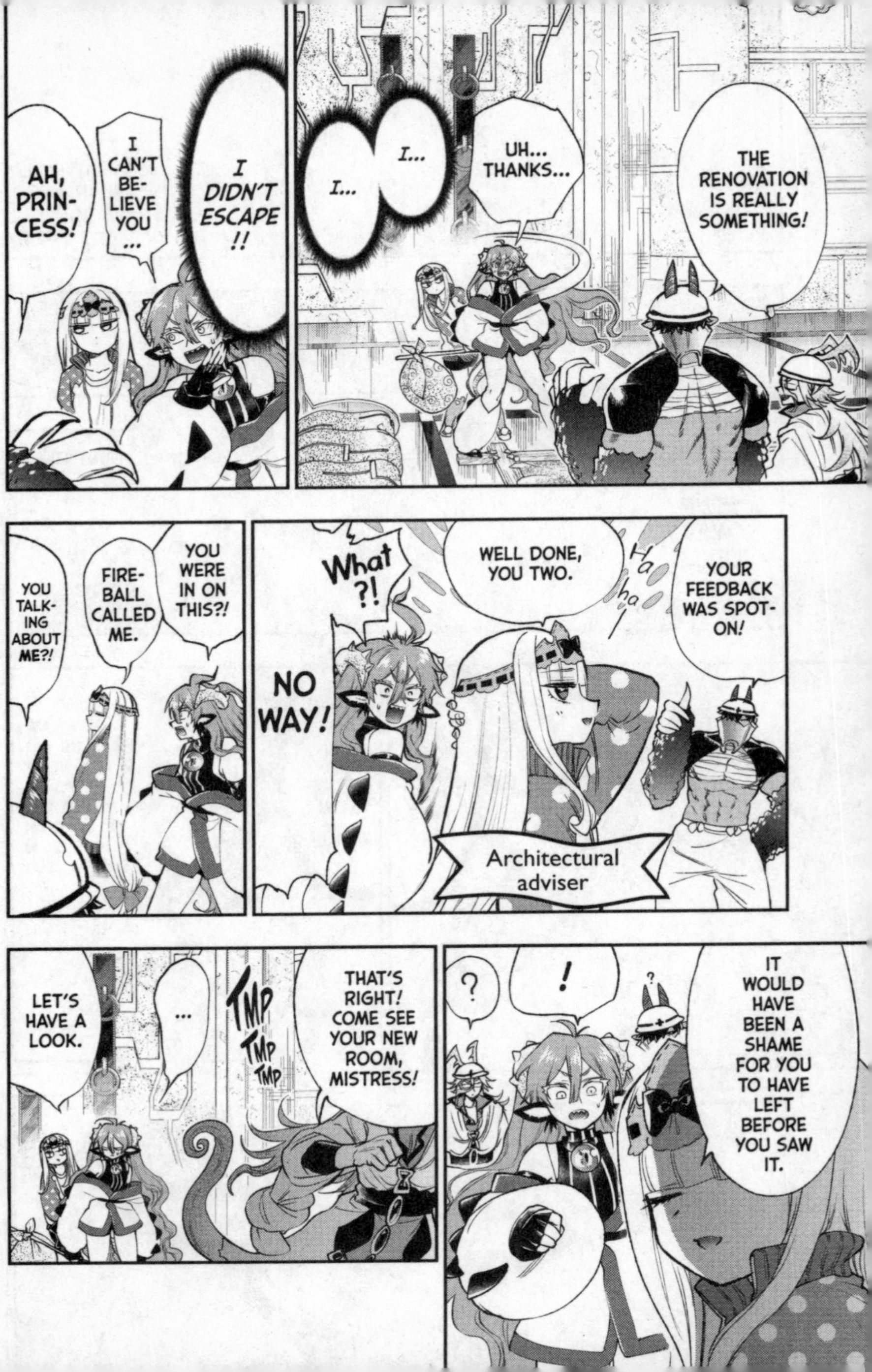
THE RENOVATION IS REALLY SOMETHING!
UH... THANKS...
I...
I...
I DIDN'T ESCAPE!!
I CAN'T BELIEVE YOU...
AH, PRINCESS!
YOUR FEEDBACK WAS SPOT-ON!
Ha ha ha
WELL DONE, YOU TWO.
What?!
NO WAY!
Architectural adviser
YOU WERE IN ON THIS?!
FIREBALL CALLED ME.
YOU TALKING ABOUT ME?!
IT WOULD HAVE BEEN A SHAME FOR YOU TO HAVE LEFT BEFORE YOU SAW IT.
?
!
?
THAT'S RIGHT! COME SEE YOUR NEW ROOM, MISTRESS!
TMP TMP TMP
...
LET'S HAVE A LOOK.

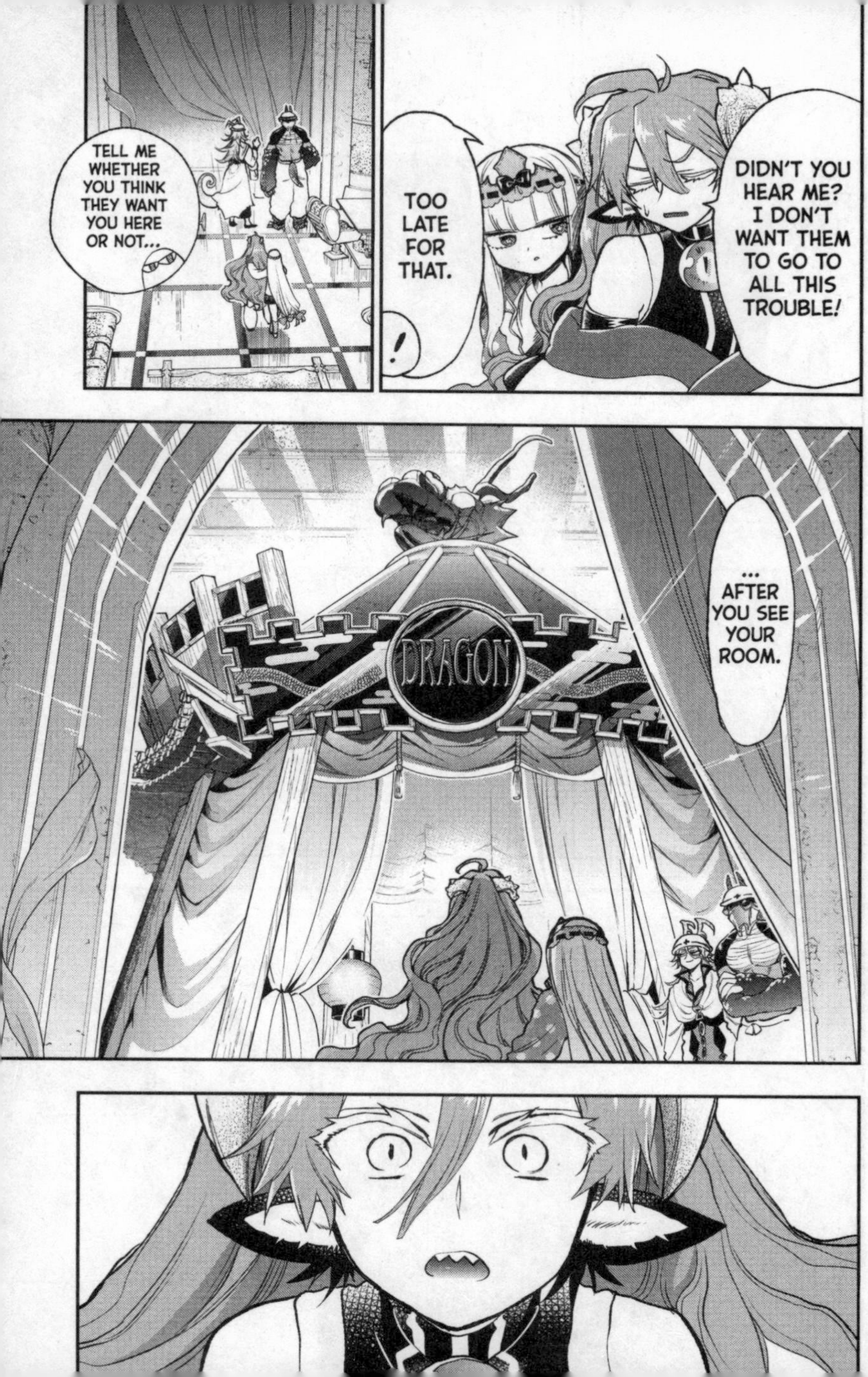
DIDN'T YOU HEAR ME? I DON'T WANT THEM TO GO TO ALL THIS TROUBLE!
TOO LATE FOR THAT.
!
TELL ME WHETHER YOU THINK THEY WANT YOU HERE OR NOT...
... AFTER YOU SEE YOUR ROOM.
DRAGON

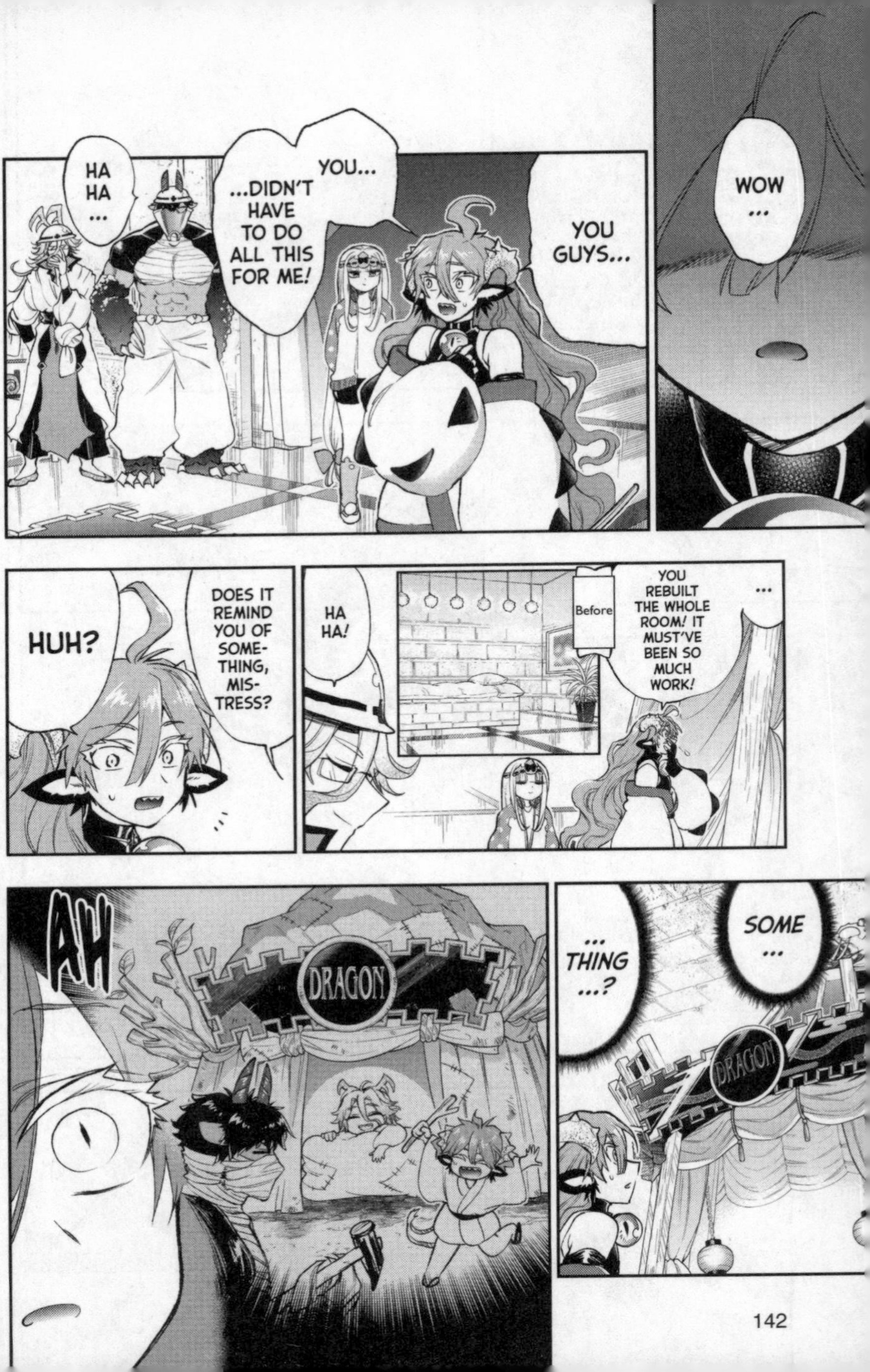
WOW ...
YOU GUYS...
YOU... ...DIDN'T HAVE TO DO ALL THIS FOR ME!
HA HA ...
...
YOU REBUILT THE WHOLE ROOM! IT MUST'VE BEEN SO MUCH WORK!
Before
HA HA!
DOES IT REMIND YOU OF SOME-THING, MIS-TRESS?
HUH?
SOME ...
... THING ...?
DRAGON
AH
DRAGON

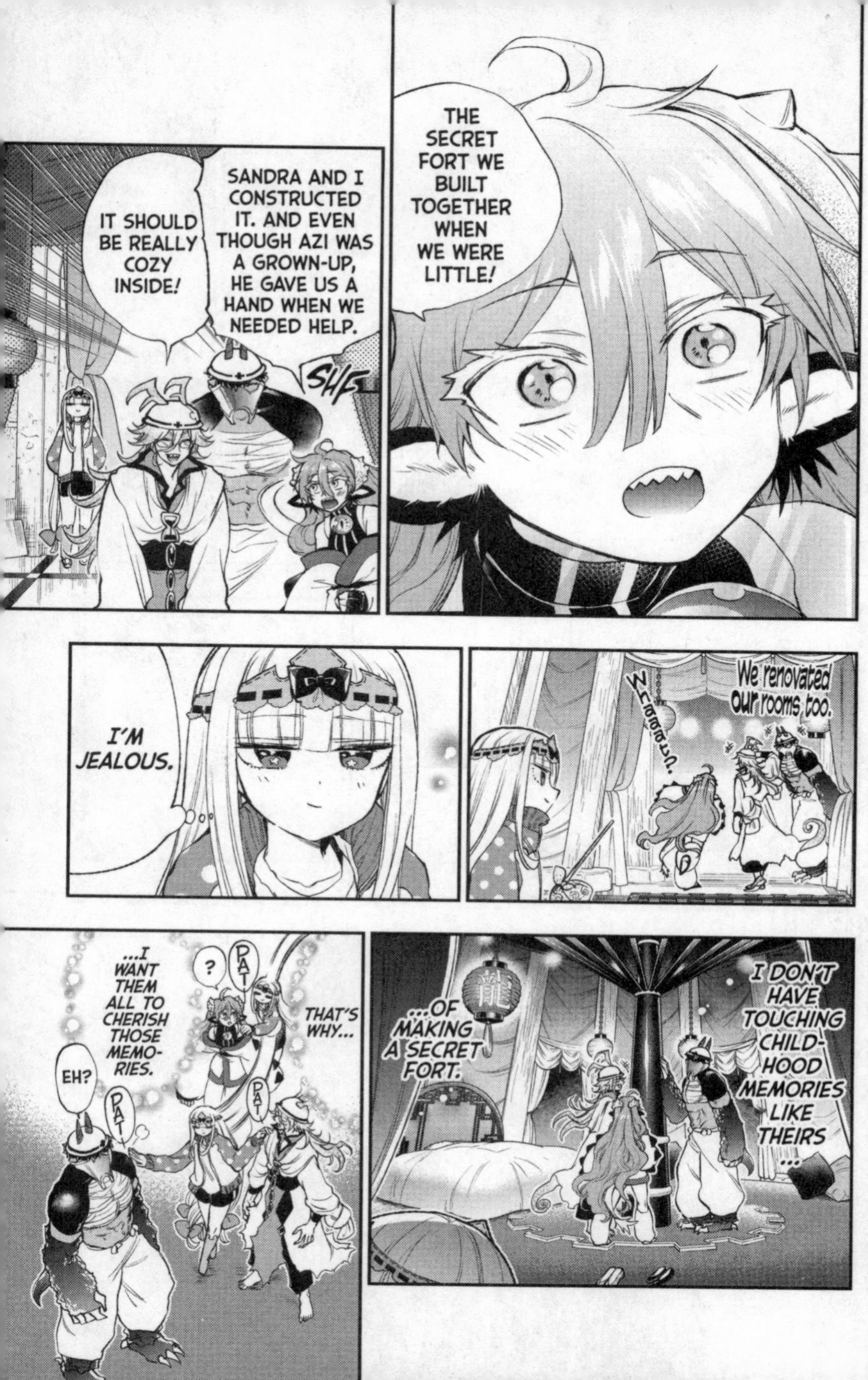
THE SECRET FORT WE BUILT TOGETHER WHEN WE WERE LITTLE!
SANDRA AND I CONSTRUCTED IT. AND EVEN THOUGH AZI WAS A GROWN-UP, HE GAVE US A HAND WHEN WE NEEDED HELP.
IT SHOULD BE REALLY COZY INSIDE!
SHF
We renovated our rooms, too.
Whoooa.
I'M JEALOUS.
I DON'T HAVE TOUCHING CHILD-HOOD MEMORIES LIKE THEIRS...
...OF MAKING A SECRET FORT.
THAT'S WHY...
...I WANT THEM ALL TO CHERISH THOSE MEMO-RIES.
PAT
?
EH?
PAT
PAT

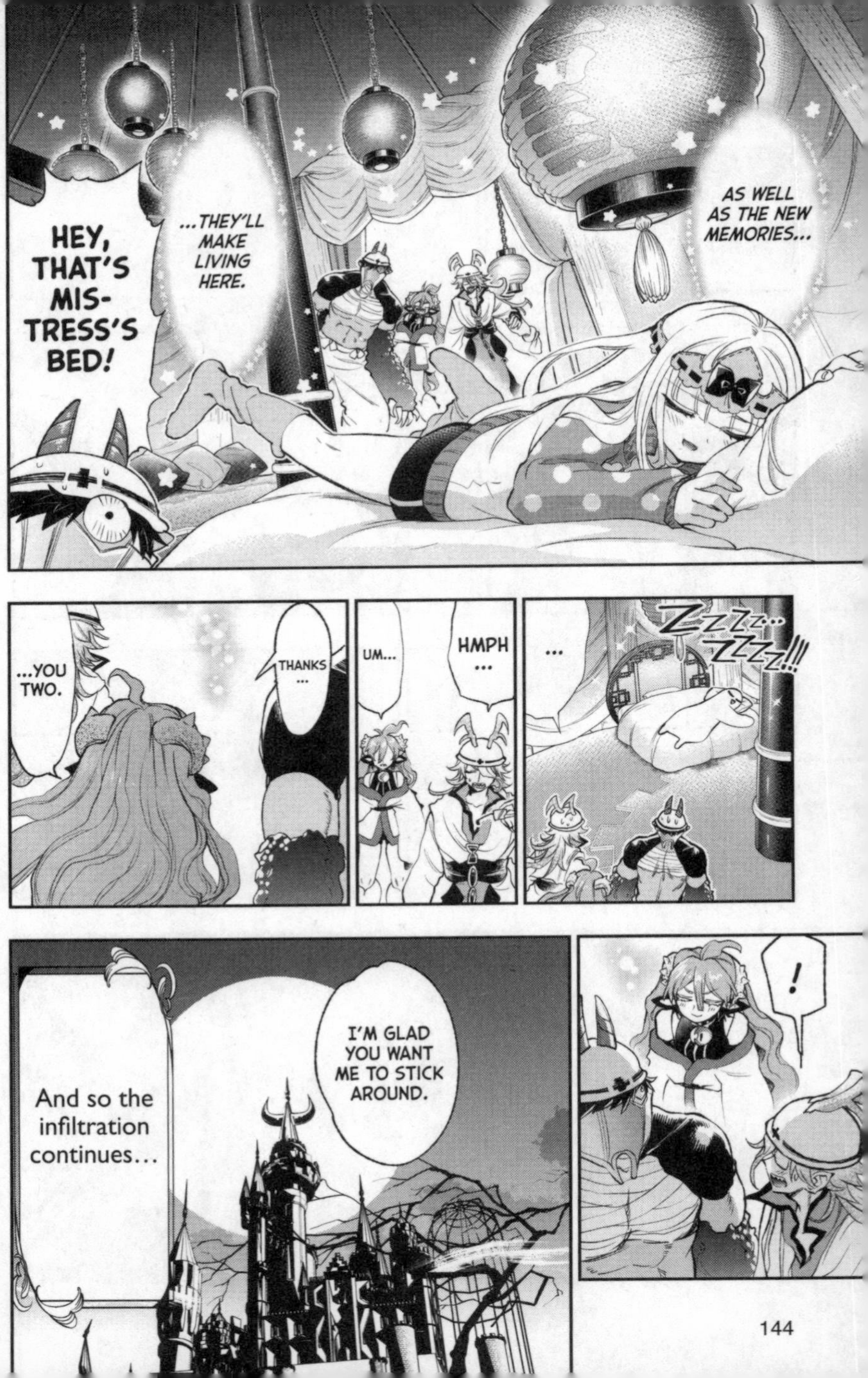
AS WELL AS THE NEW MEMORIES...
...THEY'LL MAKE LIVING HERE.
HEY, THAT'S MIS-TRESS'S BED!
...
ZZZZZ... ZZZZ!!!
HMPH ...
UM...
THANKS ...
...YOU TWO.
!
I'M GLAD YOU WANT ME TO STICK AROUND.
And so the infiltration continues…

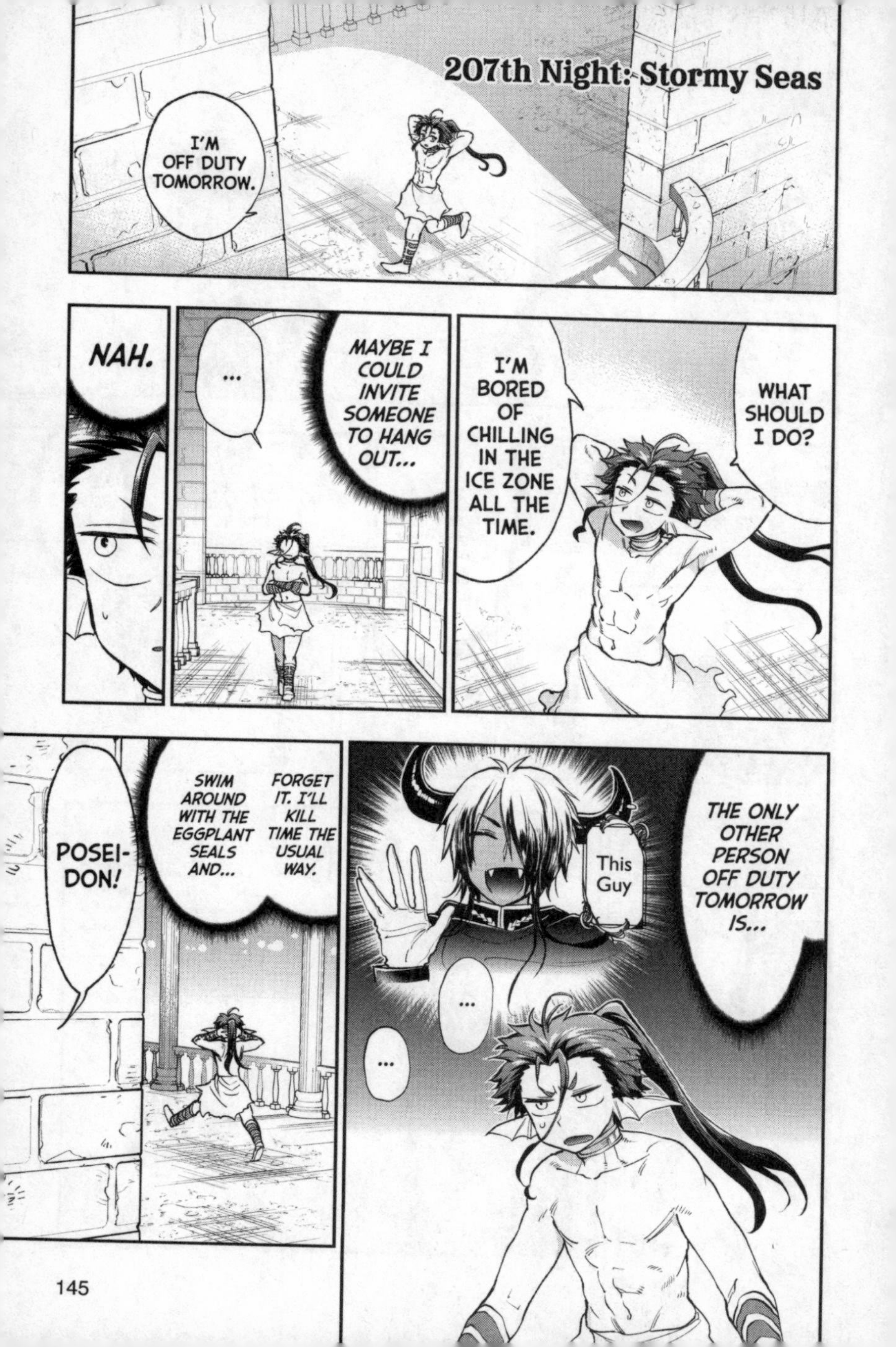
207th Night: Stormy Seas
I'M OFF DUTY TOMORROW.
WHAT SHOULD I DO?
I'M BORED OF CHILLING IN THE ICE ZONE ALL THE TIME.
MAYBE I COULD INVITE SOMEONE TO HANG OUT...
...
NAH.
THE ONLY OTHER PERSON OFF DUTY TOMORROW IS...
This Guy
...
...
FORGET IT. I'LL KILL TIME THE USUAL WAY.
SWIM AROUND WITH THE EGGPLANT SEALS AND...
POSEI-DON!

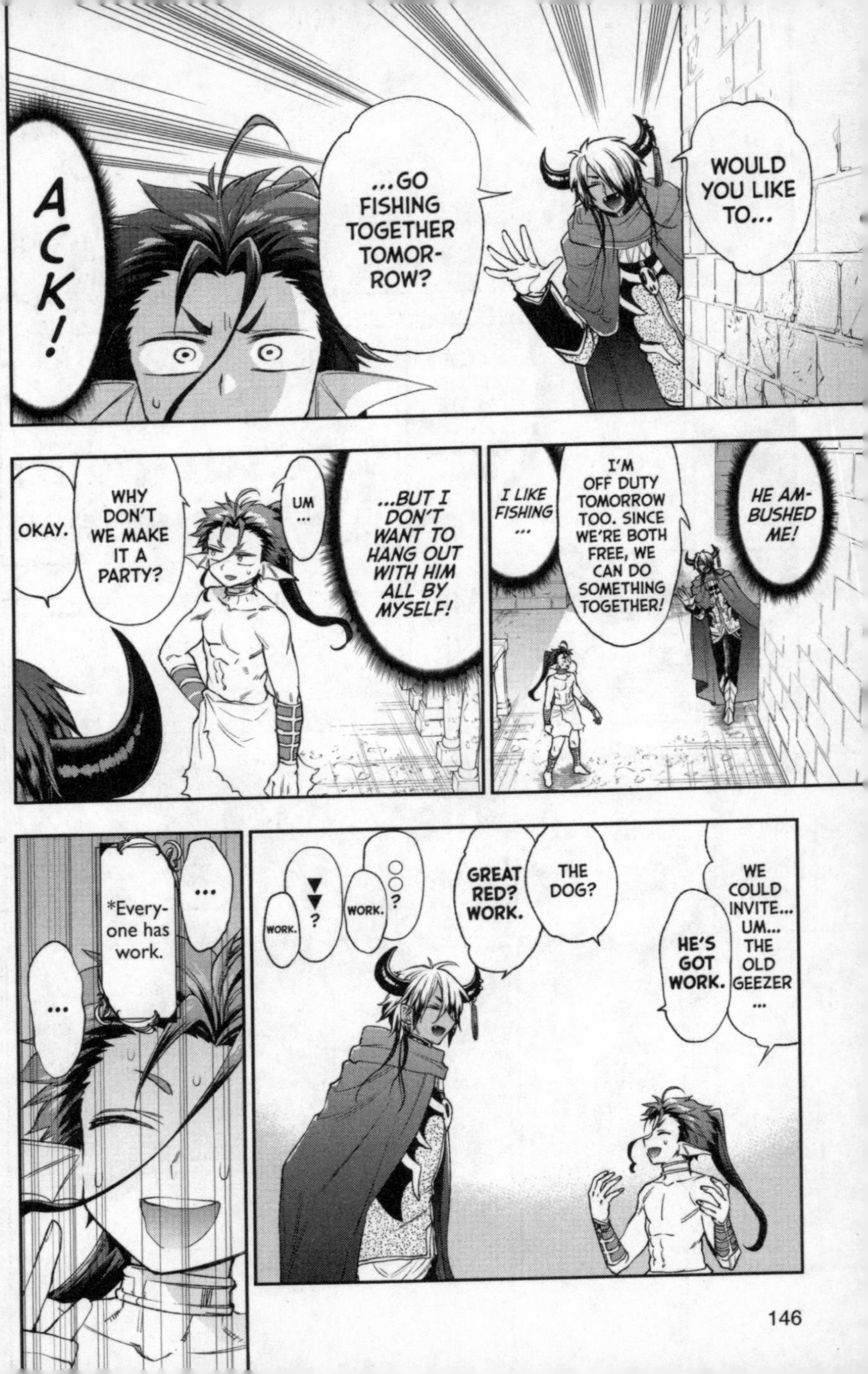
WOULD YOU LIKE TO...
...GO FISHING TOGETHER TOMOR-ROW?
ACK!
HE AM-BUSHED ME!
I'M OFF DUTY TOMORROW TOO. SINCE WE'RE BOTH FREE, WE CAN DO SOMETHING TOGETHER!
I LIKE FISHING ...
...BUT I DON'T WANT TO HANG OUT WITH HIM ALL BY MYSELF!
UM ...
WHY DON'T WE MAKE IT A PARTY?
OKAY.
WE COULD INVITE... UM... THE OLD GEEZER ...
HE'S GOT WORK.
THE DOG?
GREAT RED? WORK.
○○○?
WORK.
▼▼?
WORK.
...
*Every-one has work.
...

207th Night: Stormy Seas

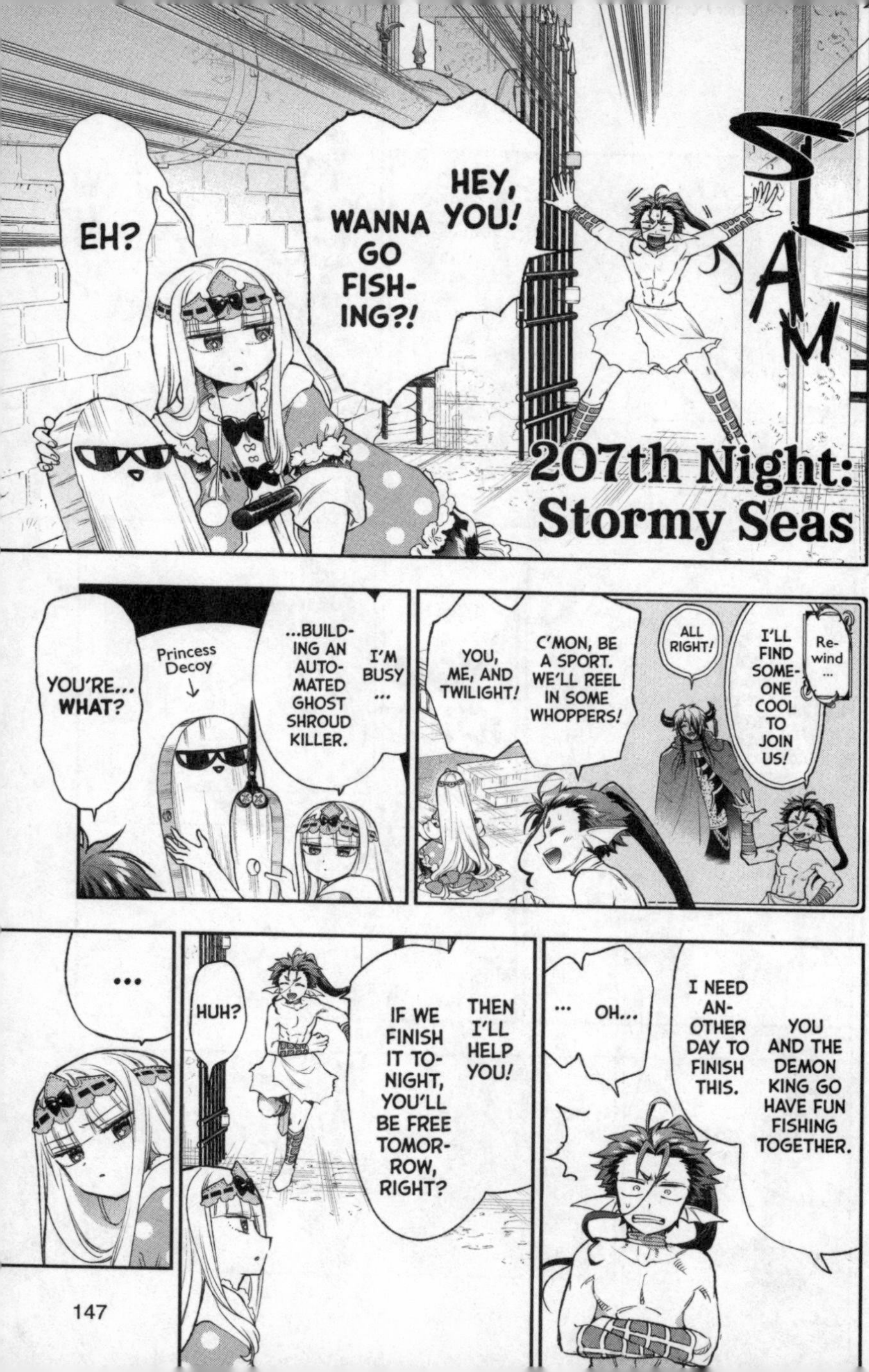
SLAM
HEY, YOU! WANNA GO FISHING?!
EH?
Re-wind...
I'LL FIND SOMEONE COOL TO JOIN US!
ALL RIGHT!
C'MON, BE A SPORT. WE'LL REEL IN SOME WHOPPERS!
YOU, ME, AND TWILIGHT!
I'M BUSY...
...BUILDING AN AUTOMATED GHOST SHROUD KILLER.
Princess Decoy
YOU'RE... WHAT?
YOU AND THE DEMON KING GO HAVE FUN FISHING TOGETHER.
I NEED ANOTHER DAY TO FINISH THIS.
... OH...
THEN I'LL HELP YOU!
IF WE FINISH IT TONIGHT, YOU'LL BE FREE TOMORROW, RIGHT?
HUH?
...

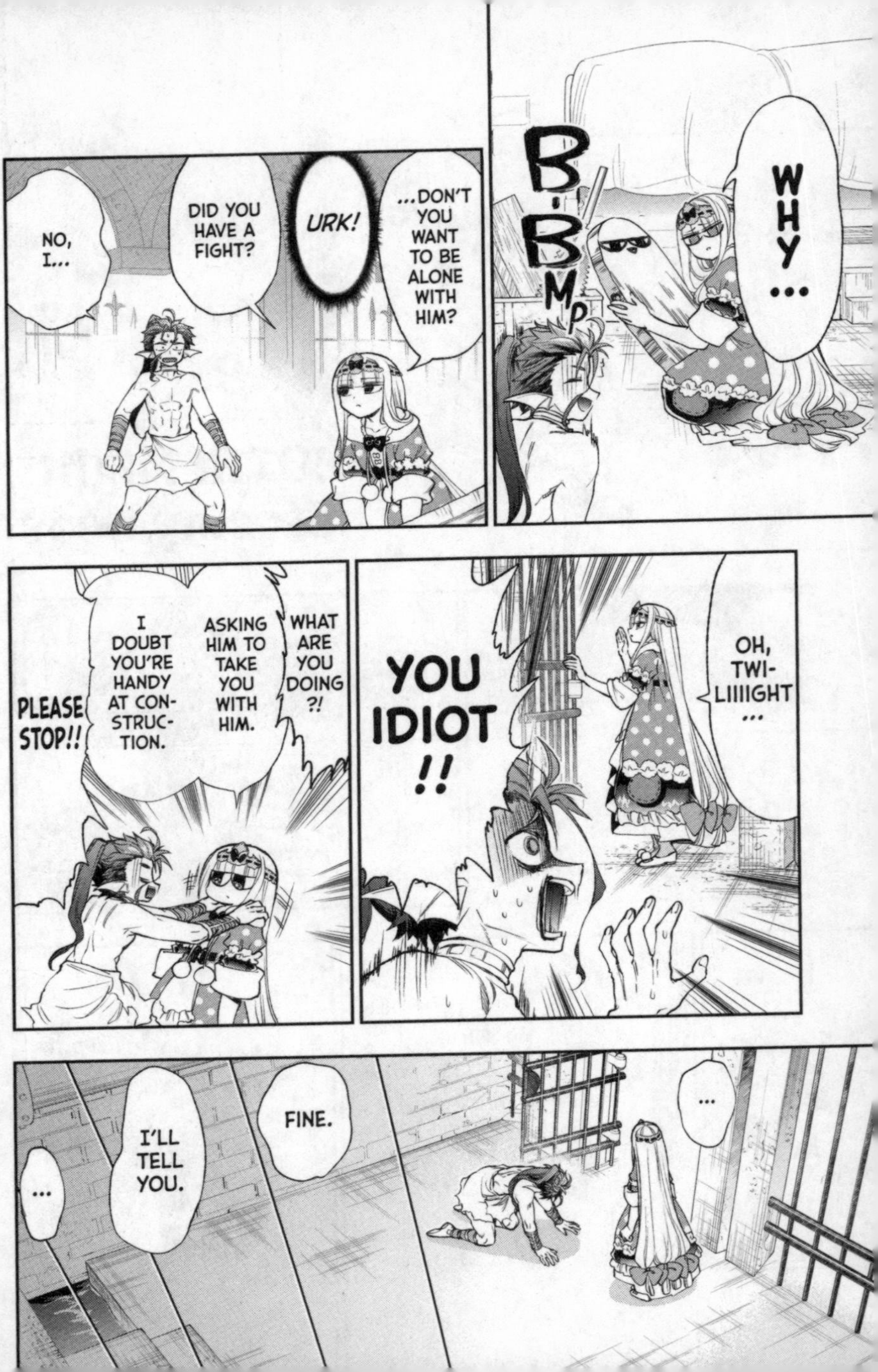
WHY...
B-BMP
...DON'T YOU WANT TO BE ALONE WITH HIM?
URK!
DID YOU HAVE A FIGHT?
NO, I...
OH, TWI-LIIIIGHT...
YOU IDIOT!!
WHAT ARE YOU DOING?!
ASKING HIM TO TAKE YOU WITH HIM.
I DOUBT YOU'RE HANDY AT CON-STRUC-TION.
PLEASE STOP!!
...
FINE.
I'LL TELL YOU.
...

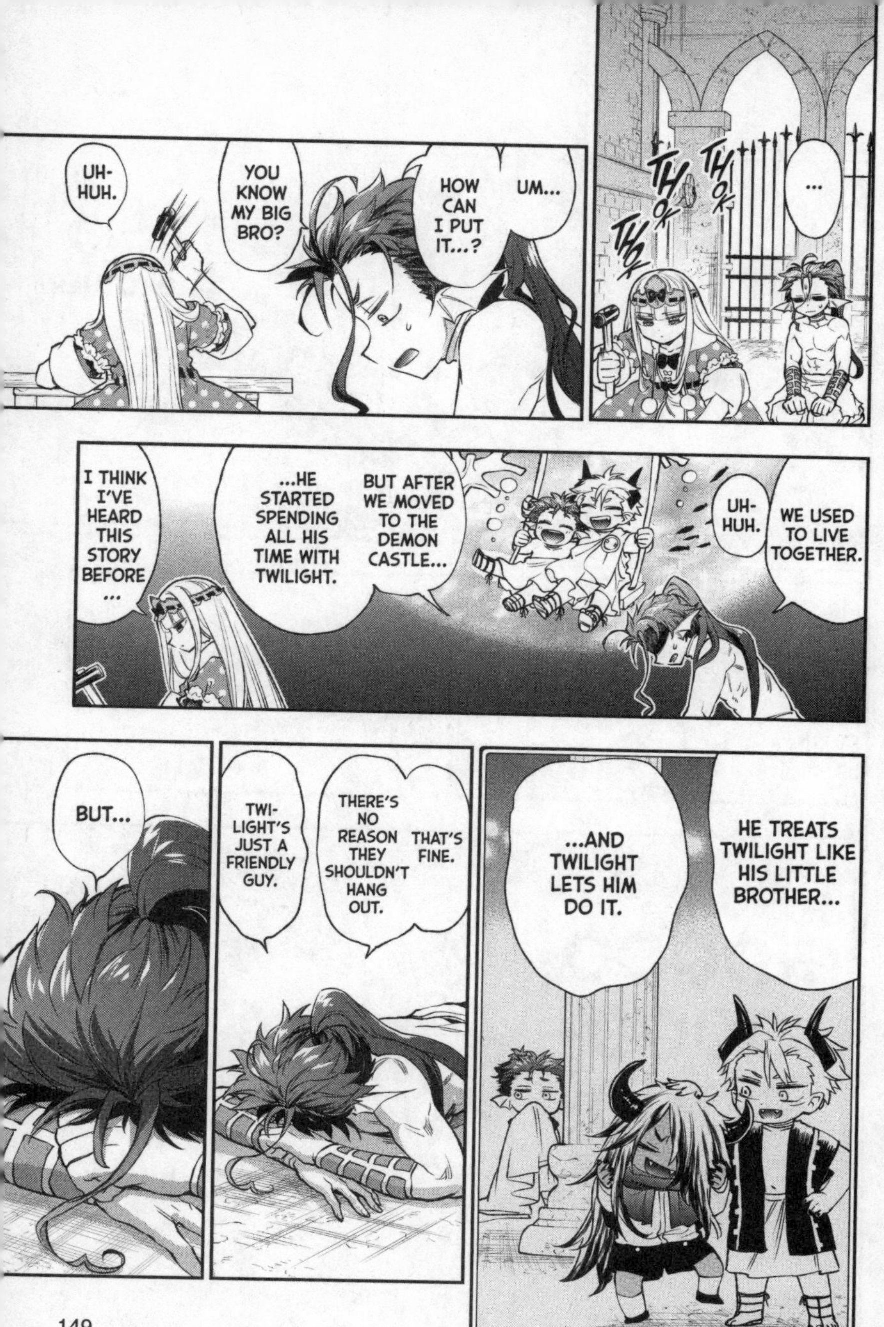
...
THOK THOK THOK
UM...
HOW CAN I PUT IT...?
YOU KNOW MY BIG BRO?
UH-HUH.
WE USED TO LIVE TOGETHER.
UH-HUH.
BUT AFTER WE MOVED TO THE DEMON CASTLE...
...HE STARTED SPENDING ALL HIS TIME WITH TWILIGHT.
I THINK I'VE HEARD THIS STORY BEFORE...
HE TREATS TWILIGHT LIKE HIS LITTLE BROTHER...
...AND TWILIGHT LETS HIM DO IT.
THAT'S FINE.
THERE'S NO REASON THEY SHOULDN'T HANG OUT.
TWILIGHT'S JUST A FRIENDLY GUY.
BUT...

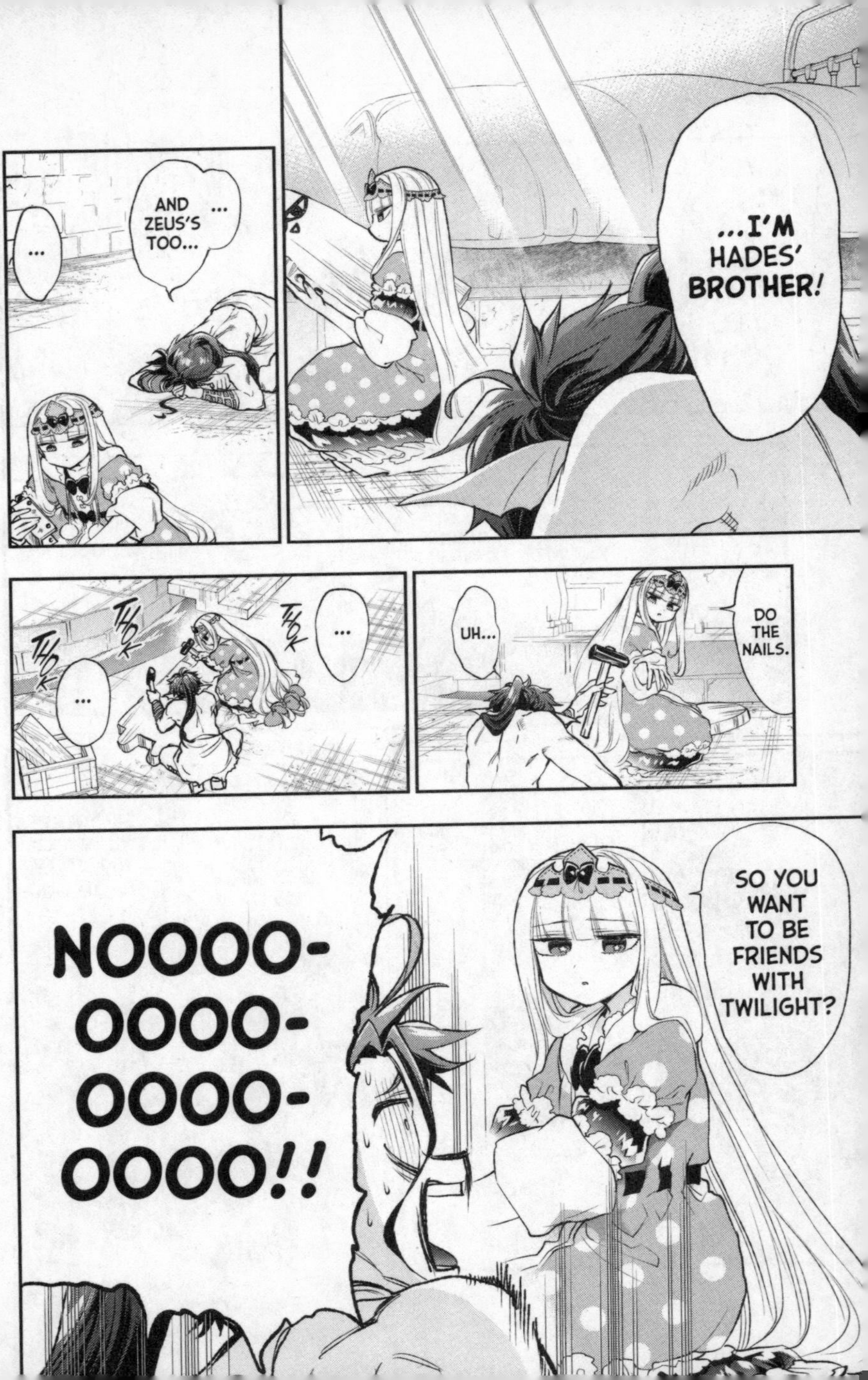
...I'M HADES' BROTHER!
AND ZEUS'S TOO... ...
...
DO THE NAILS.
UH...
...
THOK
THOK
THOK
...
SO YOU WANT TO BE FRIENDS WITH TWILIGHT?
NOOOO-OOOO-OOOO-OOOO!!

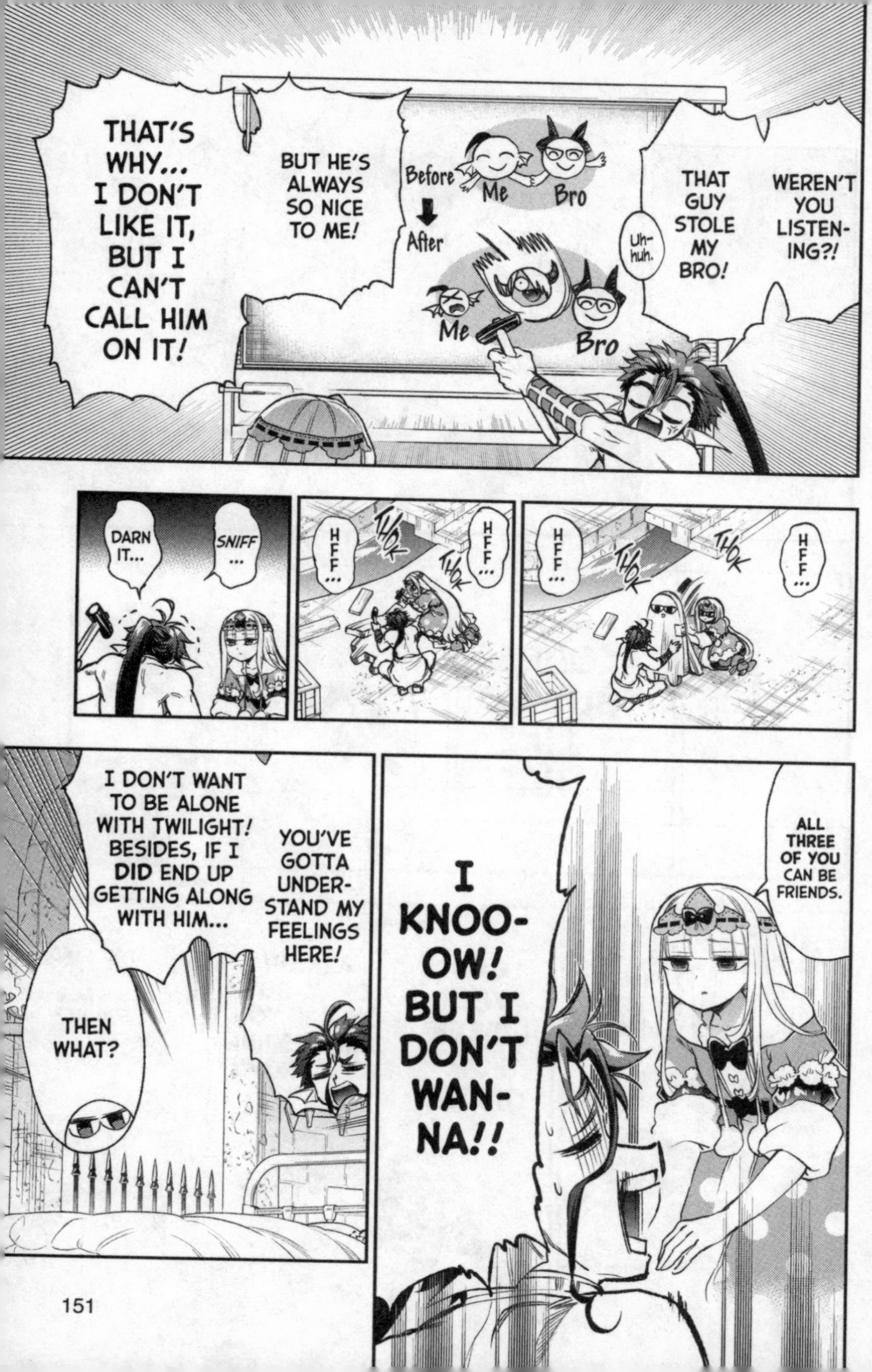
WEREN'T YOU LISTEN-ING?!
THAT GUY STOLE MY BRO!
Uh-huh.
Before
Me
Bro
After
Me
Bro
BUT HE'S ALWAYS SO NICE TO ME!
THAT'S WHY... I DON'T LIKE IT, BUT I CAN'T CALL HIM ON IT!
HFF...
THOK
THOK
HFF...
HFF...
THOK
HFF...
SNIFF...
DARN IT...
ALL THREE OF YOU CAN BE FRIENDS.
I KNOO-OW! BUT I DON'T WAN-NA!!
THEN WHAT?
I DON'T WANT TO BE ALONE WITH TWILIGHT! BESIDES, IF I DID END UP GETTING ALONG WITH HIM...
YOU'VE GOTTA UNDER-STAND MY FEELINGS HERE!

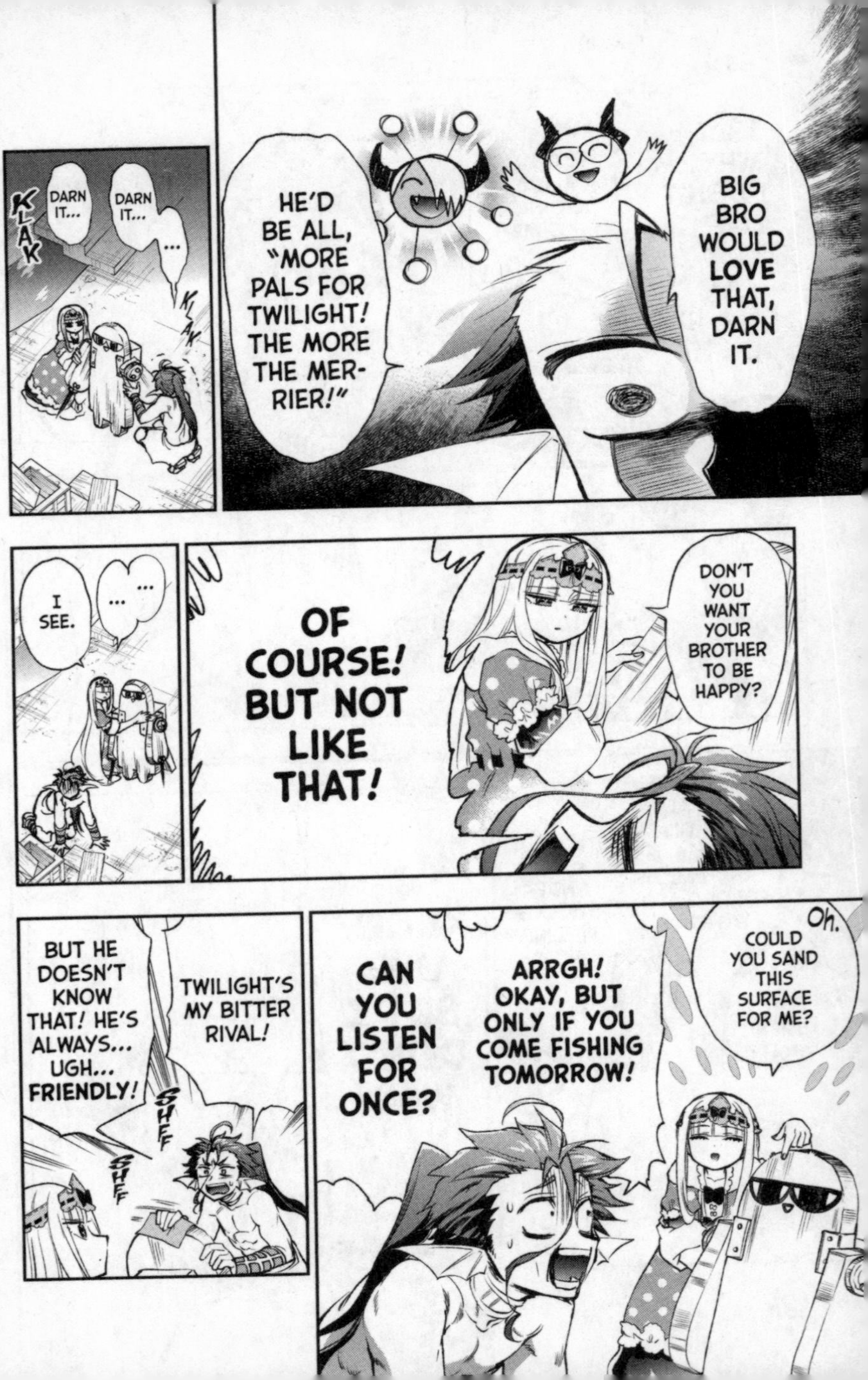
BIG BRO WOULD LOVE THAT, DARN IT.
HE'D BE ALL, "MORE PALS FOR TWILIGHT! THE MORE THE MERRIER!"
DARN IT...
DARN IT...
...
KLAK
KLAK
DON'T YOU WANT YOUR BROTHER TO BE HAPPY?
OF COURSE! BUT NOT LIKE THAT!
... ...
I SEE.
Oh.
COULD YOU SAND THIS SURFACE FOR ME?
ARRGH! OKAY, BUT ONLY IF YOU COME FISHING TOMORROW!
CAN YOU LISTEN FOR ONCE?
TWILIGHT'S MY BITTER RIVAL!
BUT HE DOESN'T KNOW THAT! HE'S ALWAYS... UGH... FRIENDLY!
SHFF
SHFF

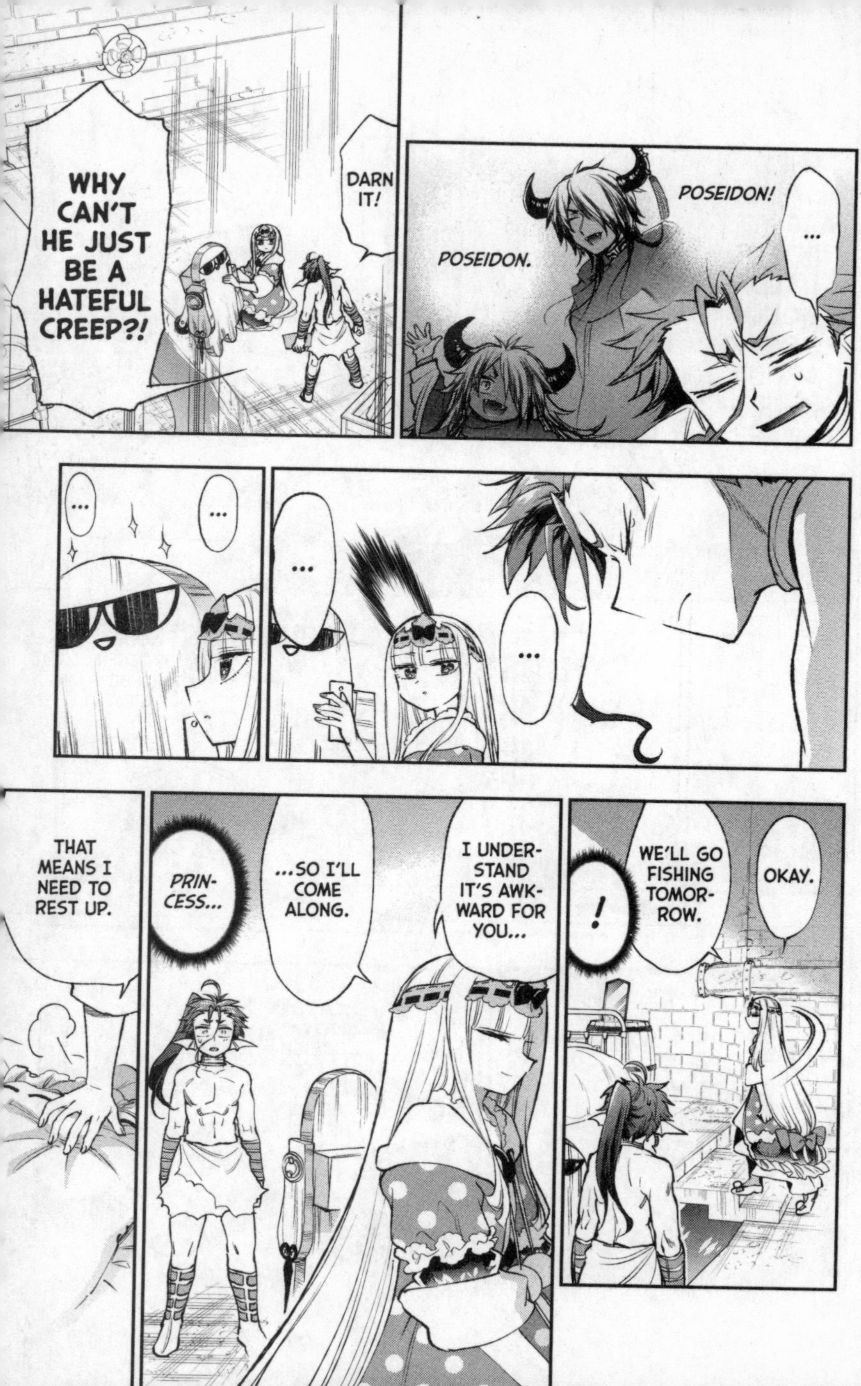
...
POSEIDON!
POSEIDON.
DARN IT!
WHY CAN'T HE JUST BE A HATEFUL CREEP?!
...
...
...
...
OKAY.
WE'LL GO FISHING TOMORROW.
!
I UNDERSTAND IT'S AWKWARD FOR YOU...
...SO I'LL COME ALONG.
PRINCESS...
THAT MEANS I NEED TO REST UP.

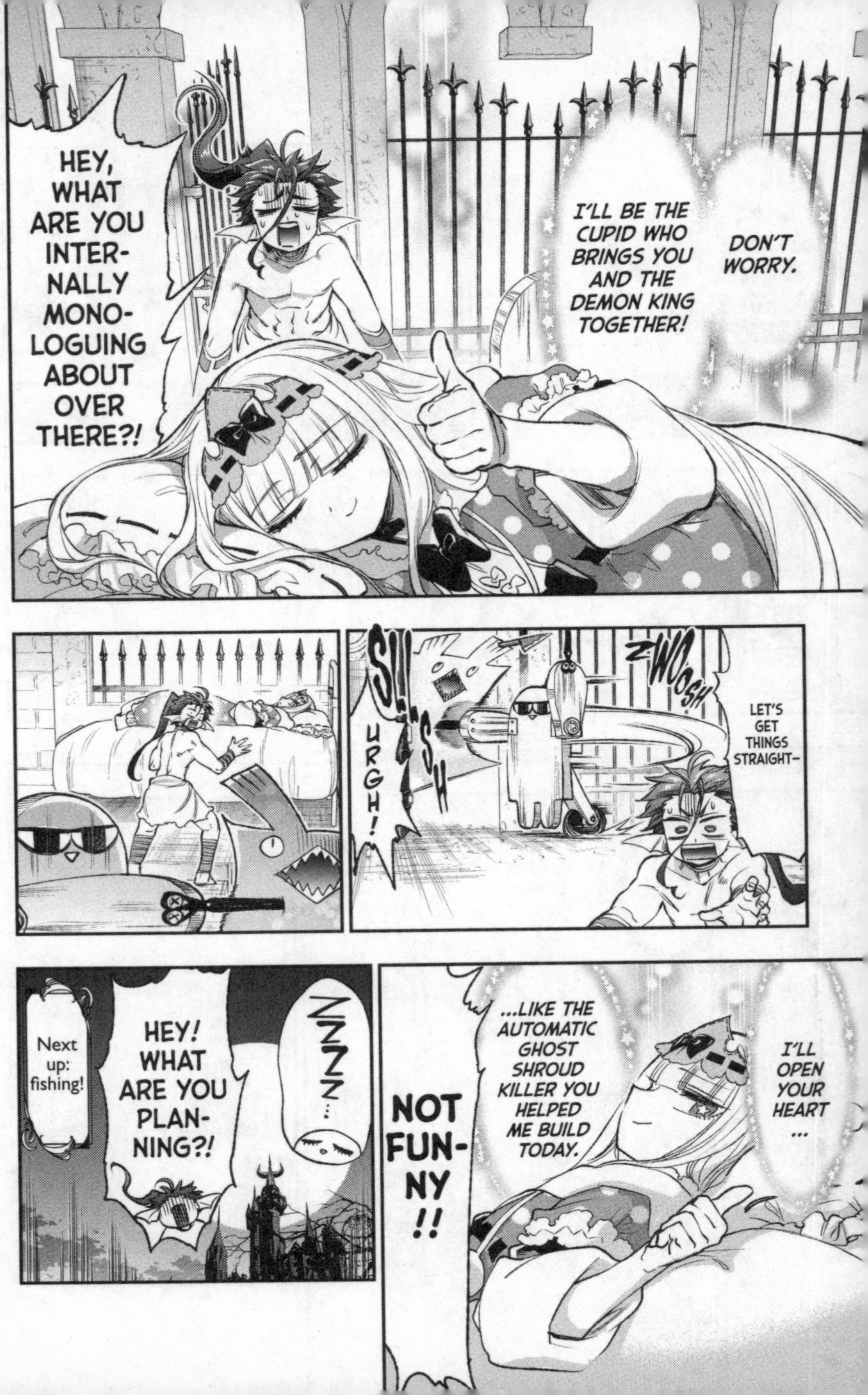
DON'T WORRY.
I'LL BE THE CUPID WHO BRINGS YOU AND THE DEMON KING TOGETHER!
HEY, WHAT ARE YOU INTER-NALLY MONO-LOGUING ABOUT OVER THERE?!
LET'S GET THINGS STRAIGHT—
ZWOOSH
URGH!
I'LL OPEN YOUR HEART...
...LIKE THE AUTOMATIC GHOST SHROUD KILLER YOU HELPED ME BUILD TODAY.
NOT FUN-NY!!
ZZZ...
HEY! WHAT ARE YOU PLAN-NING?!
Next up: fishing!

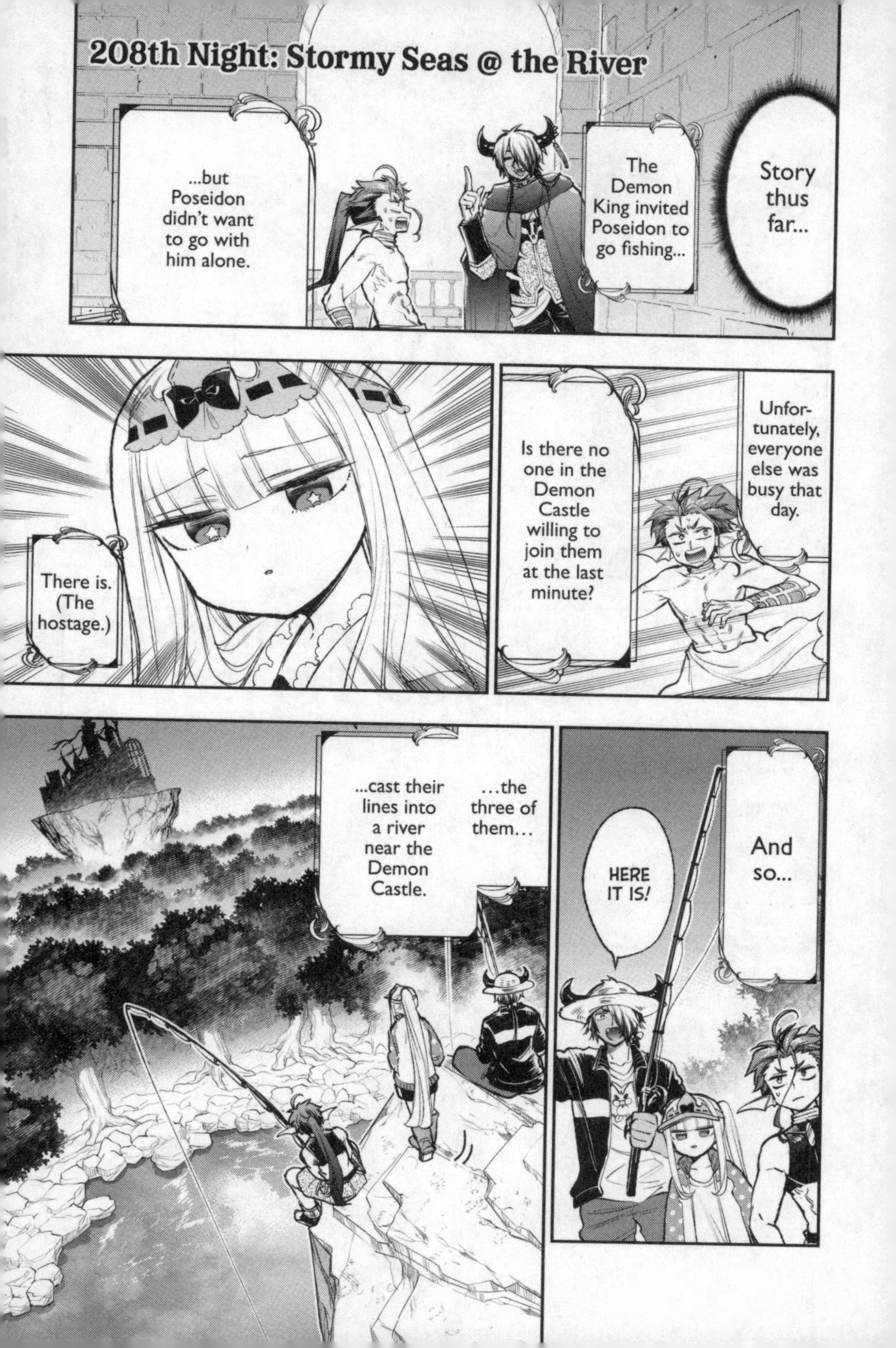
208th Night: Stormy Seas @ the River
Story thus far...
The Demon King invited Poseidon to go fishing...
...but Poseidon didn't want to go with him alone.
Unfor-tunately, everyone else was busy that day.
Is there no one in the Demon Castle willing to join them at the last minute?
There is. (The hostage.)
And so...
HERE IT IS!
…the three of them…
...cast their lines into a river near the Demon Castle.

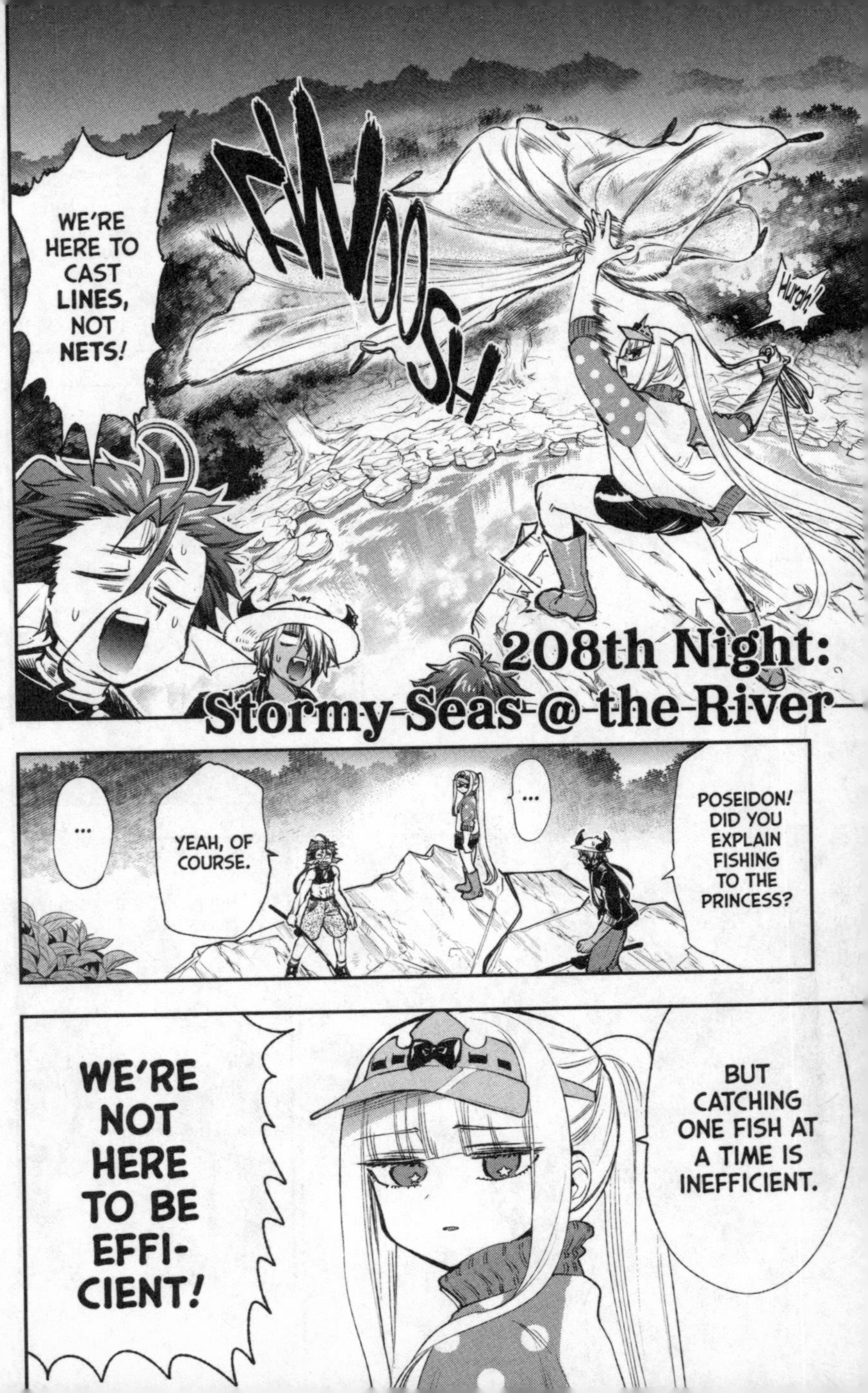
Hurgh!?
FWOOSH
WE'RE HERE TO CAST LINES, NOT NETS!
208th Night: Stormy Seas @ the River
POSEIDON! DID YOU EXPLAIN FISHING TO THE PRINCESS?
...
YEAH, OF COURSE.
...
BUT CATCHING ONE FISH AT A TIME IS INEFFICIENT.
WE'RE NOT HERE TO BE EFFI-CIENT!

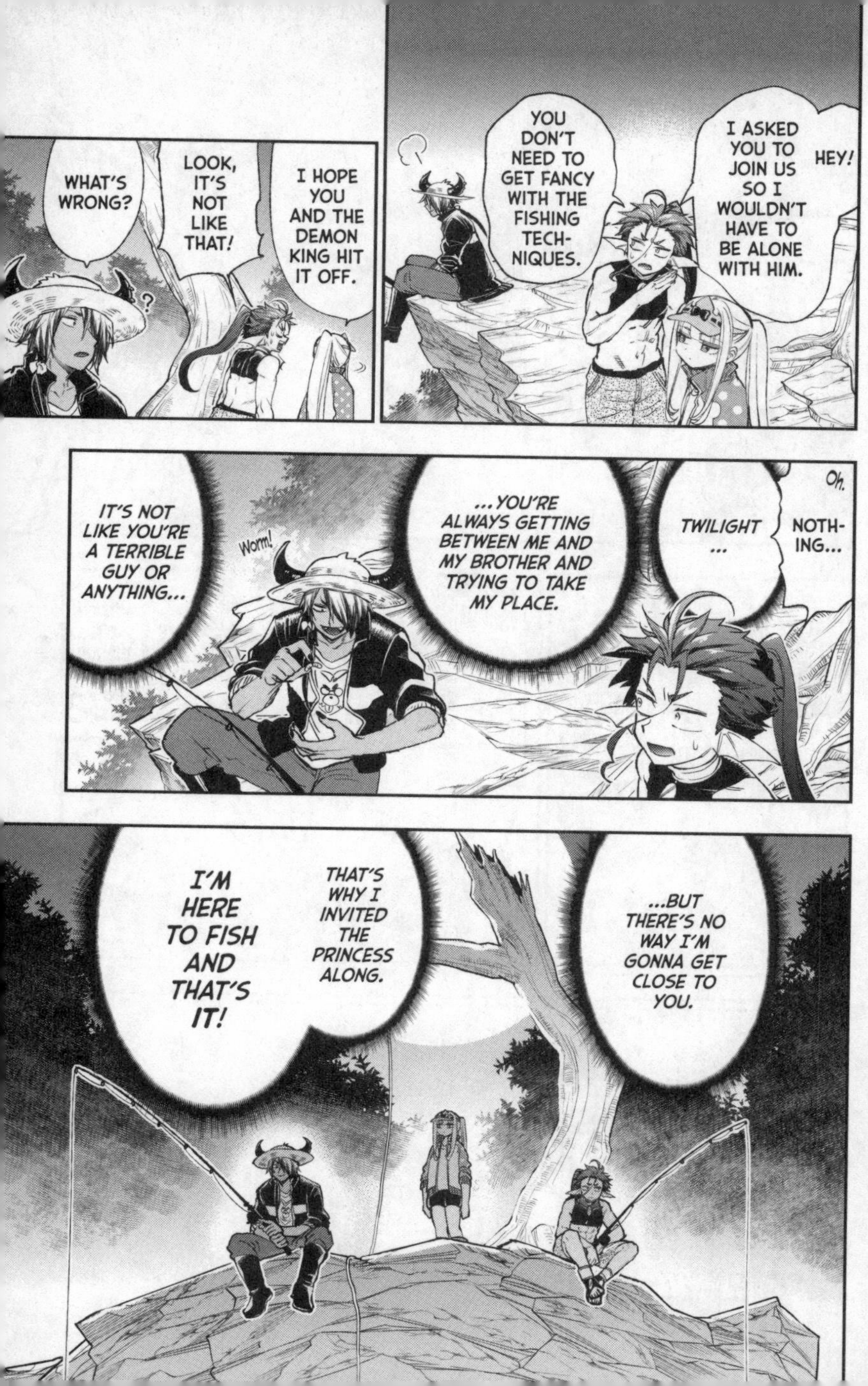
HEY!
I ASKED YOU TO JOIN US SO I WOULDN'T HAVE TO BE ALONE WITH HIM.
YOU DON'T NEED TO GET FANCY WITH THE FISHING TECH-NIQUES.
I HOPE YOU AND THE DEMON KING HIT IT OFF.
LOOK, IT'S NOT LIKE THAT!
WHAT'S WRONG?
?
Oh.
NOTH-ING...
TWILIGHT...
...YOU'RE ALWAYS GETTING BETWEEN ME AND MY BROTHER AND TRYING TO TAKE MY PLACE.
Worm!
IT'S NOT LIKE YOU'RE A TERRIBLE GUY OR ANYTHING...
...BUT THERE'S NO WAY I'M GONNA GET CLOSE TO YOU.
THAT'S WHY I INVITED THE PRINCESS ALONG.
I'M HERE TO FISH AND THAT'S IT!

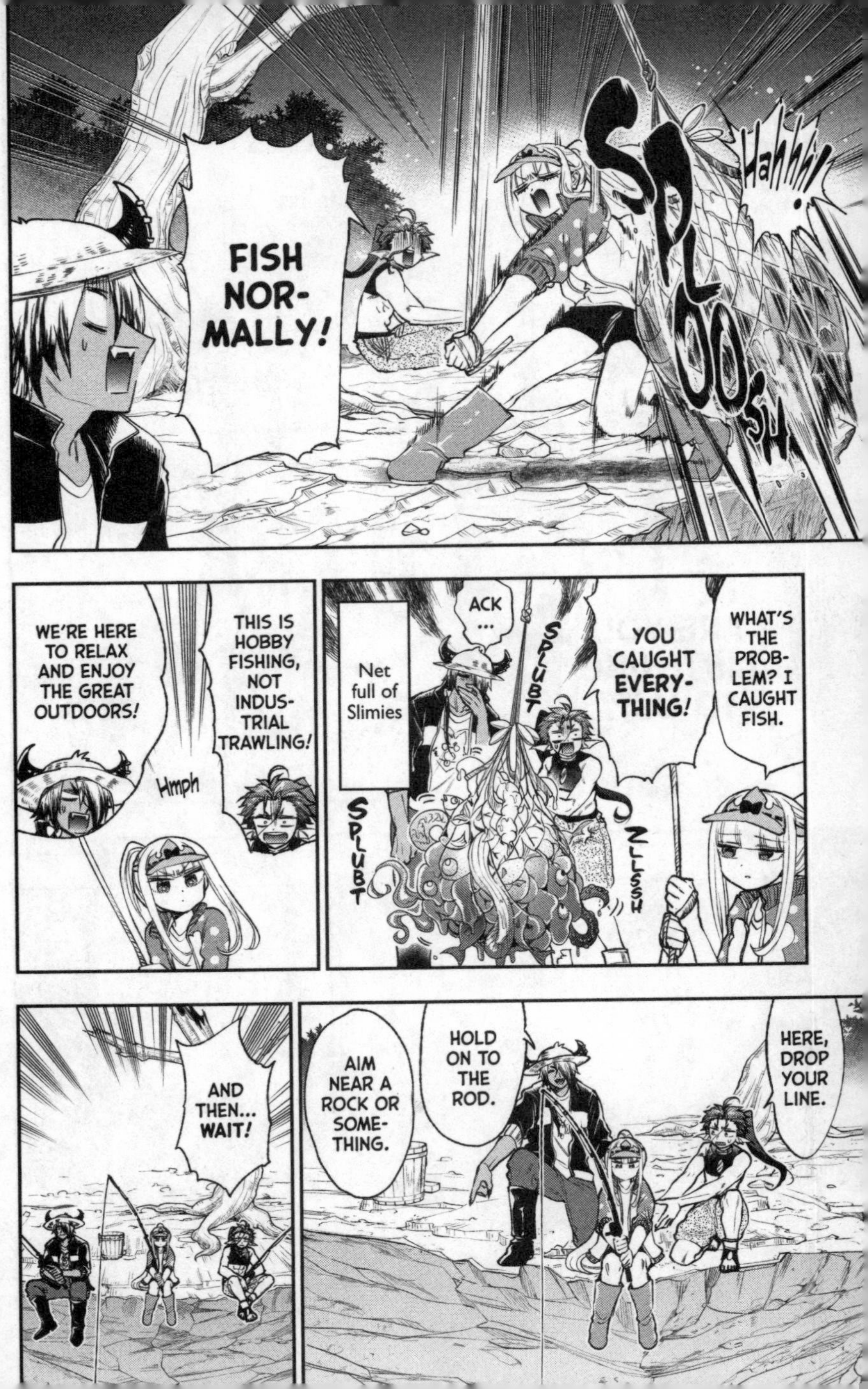

Hahhh!!
SPLOOSH
FISH NOR-MALLY!
WHAT'S THE PROB-LEM? I CAUGHT FISH.
YOU CAUGHT EVERY-THING!
ACK ...
SPLUBT
Net full of Slimies
ZLLSSH
SPLUBT
THIS IS HOBBY FISHING, NOT INDUS-TRIAL TRAWLING!
WE'RE HERE TO RELAX AND ENJOY THE GREAT OUTDOORS!
Hmph
HERE, DROP YOUR LINE.
HOLD ON TO THE ROD.
AIM NEAR A ROCK OR SOME-THING.
AND THEN... WAIT!

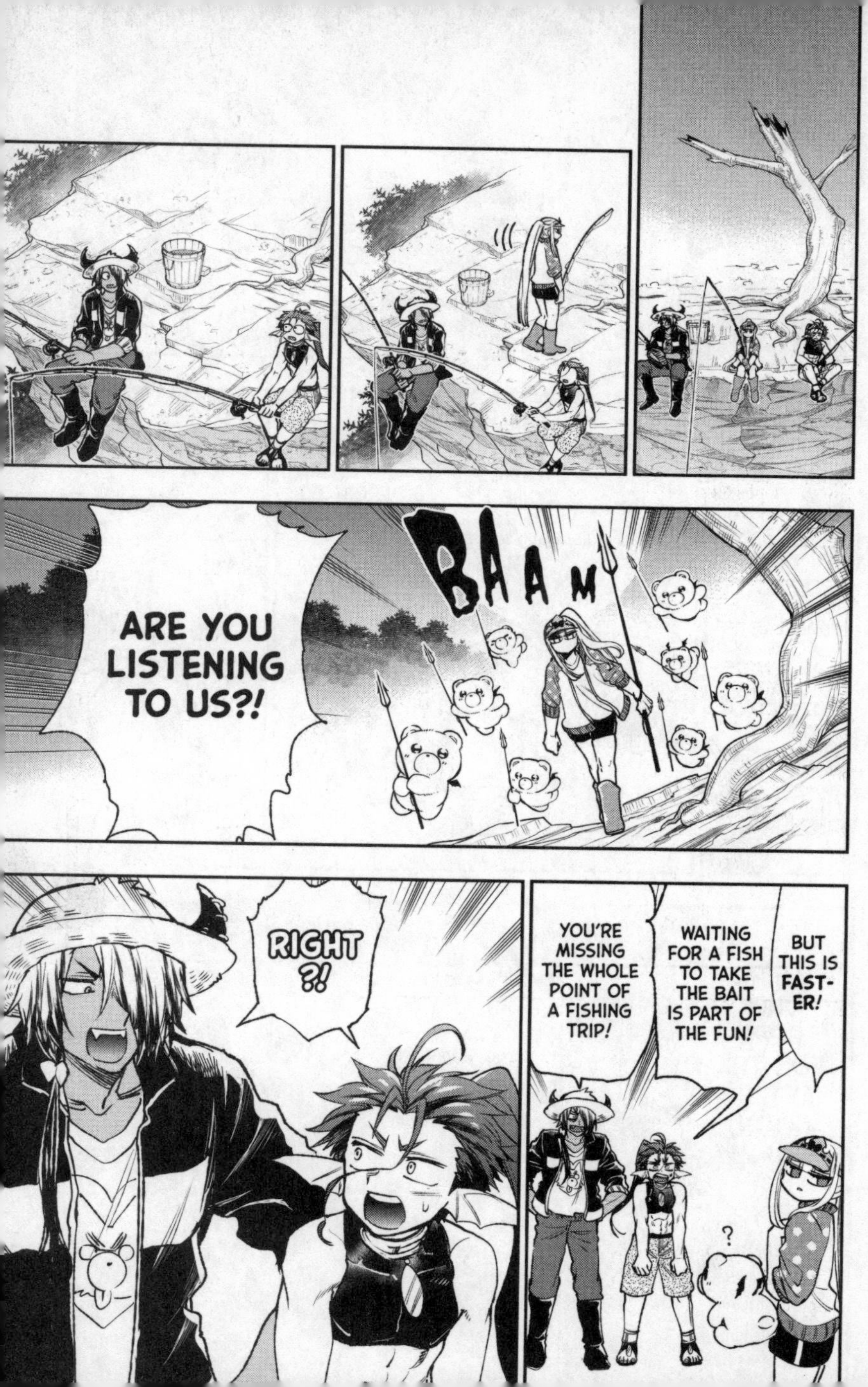
BAAM
ARE YOU LISTENING TO US?!
BUT THIS IS FASTER!
WAITING FOR A FISH TO TAKE THE BAIT IS PART OF THE FUN!
YOU'RE MISSING THE WHOLE POINT OF A FISHING TRIP!
?
RIGHT?!

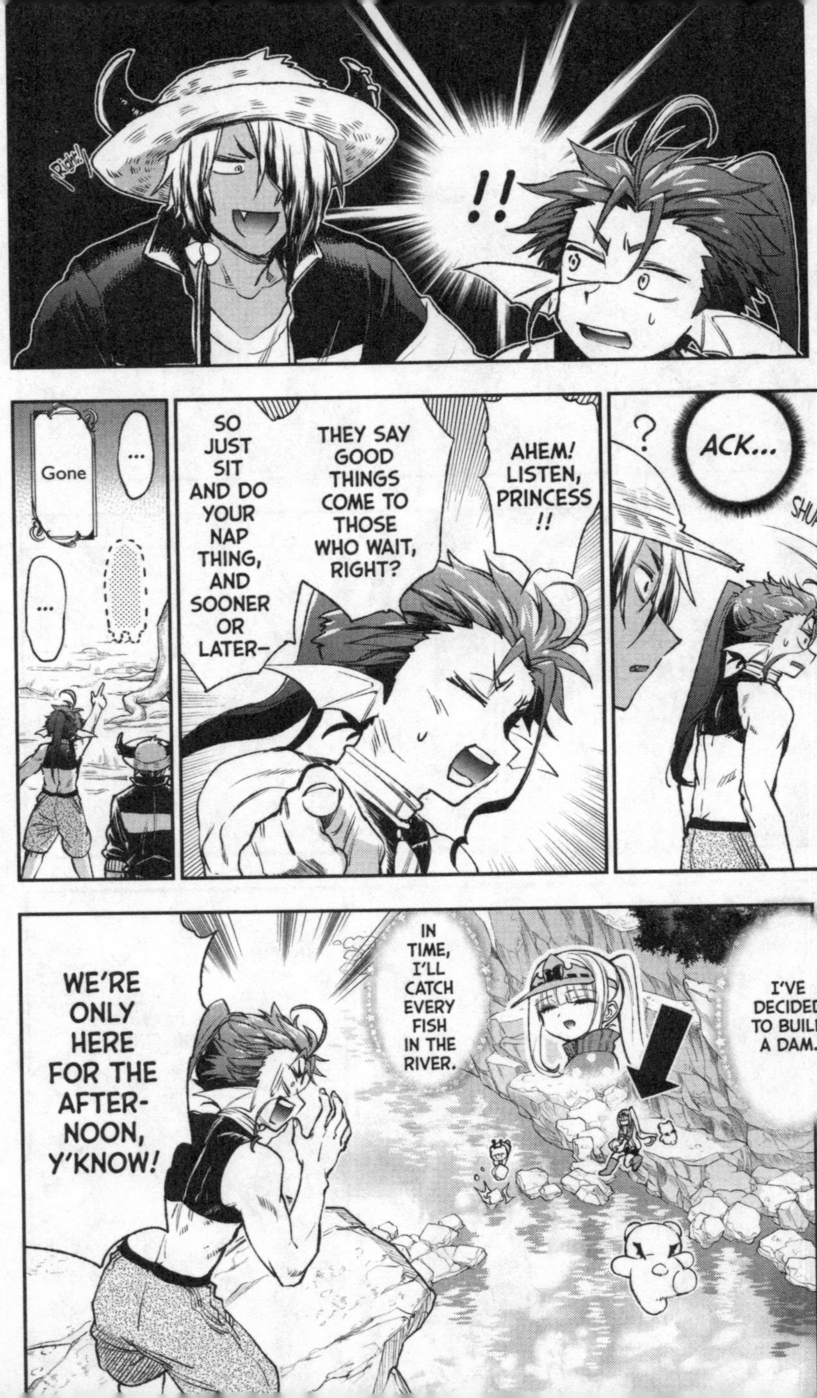
Right!
!!
?
ACK...
SHUP
AHEM! LISTEN, PRINCESS!!
THEY SAY GOOD THINGS COME TO THOSE WHO WAIT, RIGHT?
SO JUST SIT AND DO YOUR NAP THING, AND SOONER OR LATER—
...
Gone
...
I'VE DECIDED TO BUILD A DAM.
IN TIME, I'LL CATCH EVERY FISH IN THE RIVER.
WE'RE ONLY HERE FOR THE AFTER-NOON, Y'KNOW!

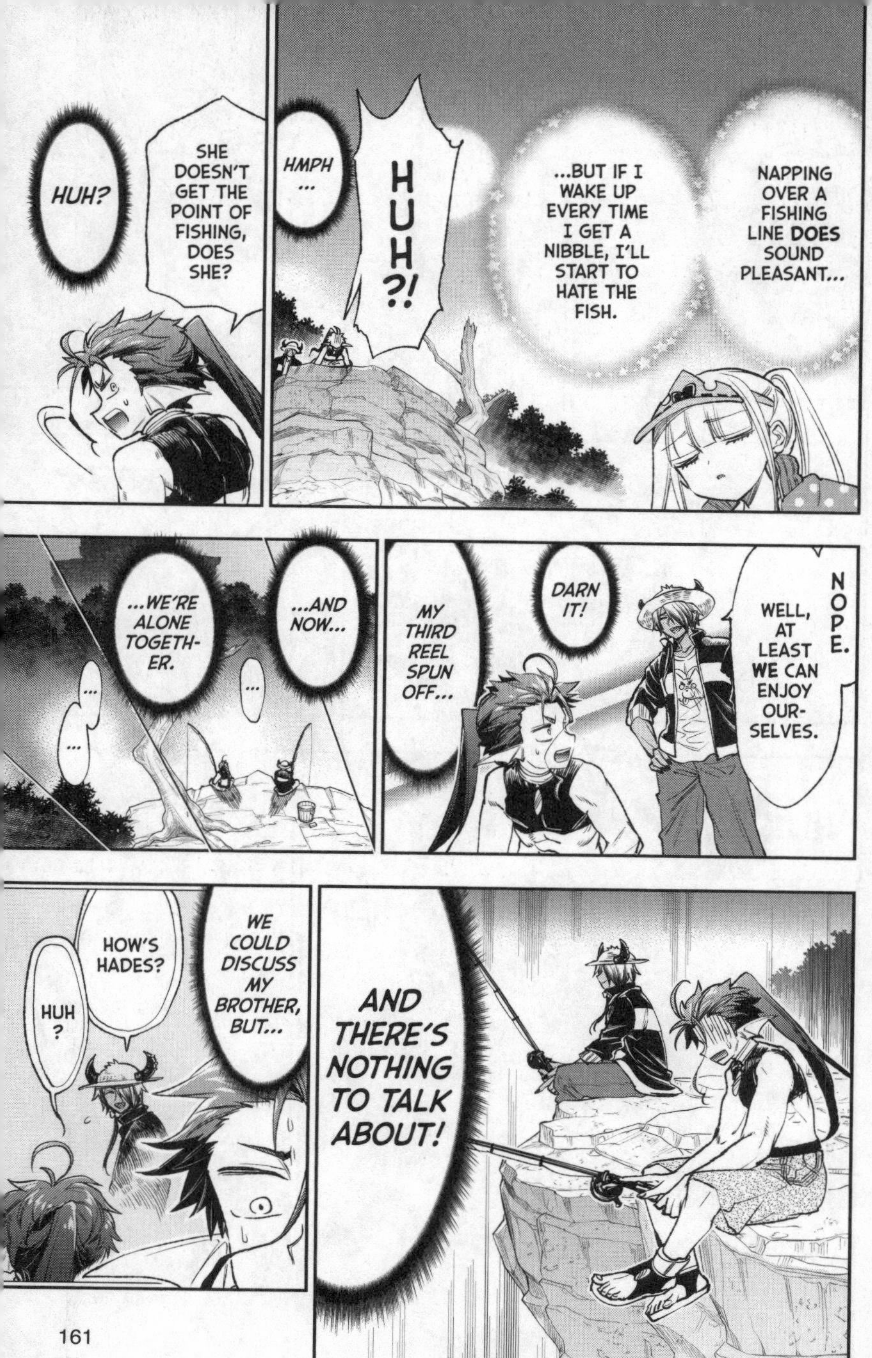
NAPPING OVER A FISHING LINE DOES SOUND PLEASANT...
...BUT IF I WAKE UP EVERY TIME I GET A NIBBLE, I'LL START TO HATE THE FISH.
HUH?!
HMPH ...
SHE DOESN'T GET THE POINT OF FISHING, DOES SHE?
HUH?
NOPE.
WELL, AT LEAST WE CAN ENJOY OURSELVES.
DARN IT!
MY THIRD REEL SPUN OFF...
...AND NOW...
...WE'RE ALONE TOGETH-ER.
...
...
AND THERE'S NOTHING TO TALK ABOUT!
WE COULD DISCUSS MY BROTHER, BUT...
HOW'S HADES?
HUH ?

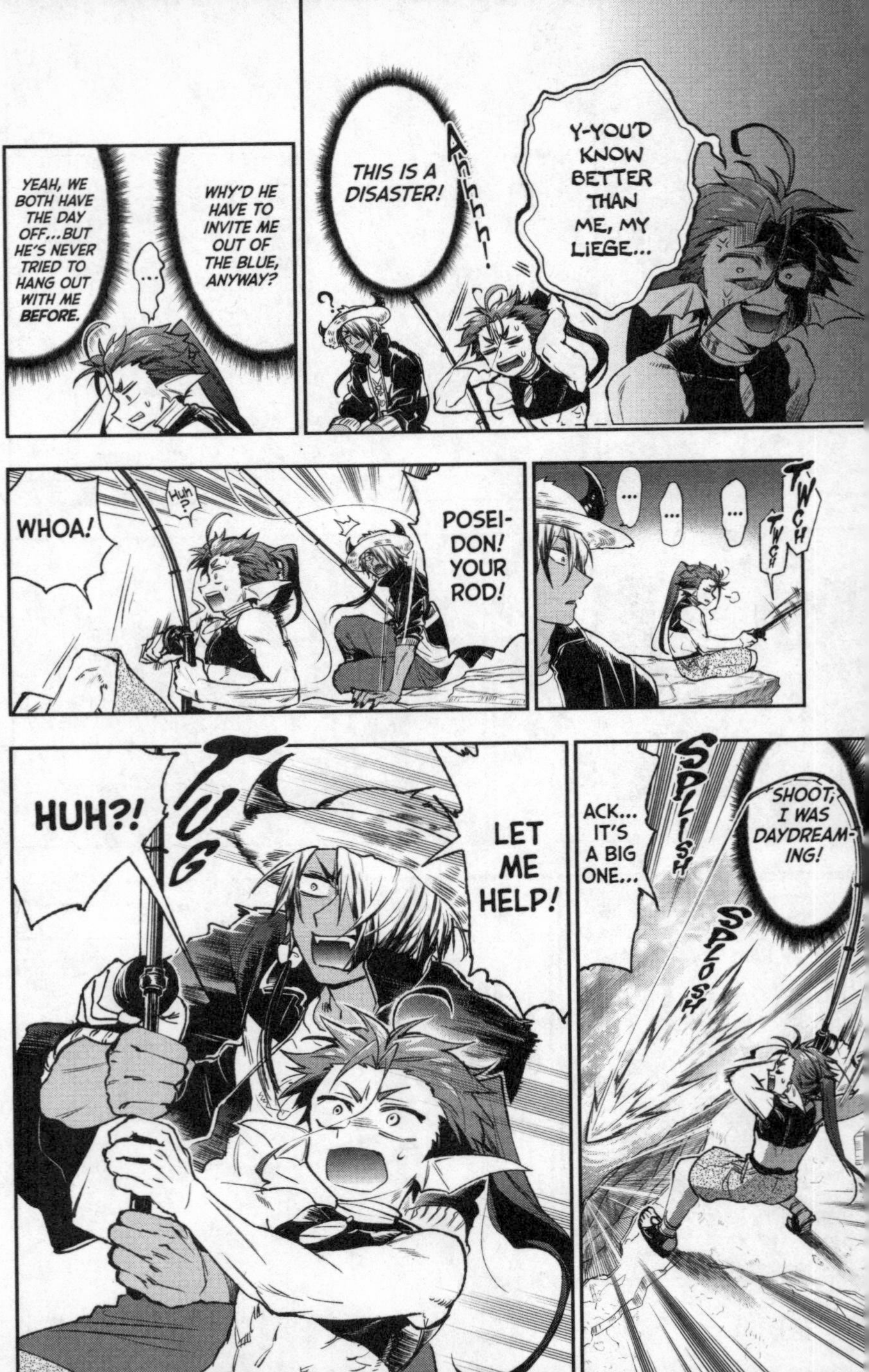
Y-YOU'D KNOW BETTER THAN ME, MY LIEGE...
Ahhhh!
THIS IS A DISASTER!
WHY'D HE HAVE TO INVITE ME OUT OF THE BLUE, ANYWAY?
YEAH, WE BOTH HAVE THE DAY OFF...BUT HE'S NEVER TRIED TO HANG OUT WITH ME BEFORE.
...
TWCH
TWCH
...
...
...
...
POSEIDON! YOUR ROD!
Huh?
WHOA!
SHOOT, I WAS DAYDREAMING!
SPLISH
SPLOSH
ACK... IT'S A BIG ONE...
LET ME HELP!
TUG
HUH?!

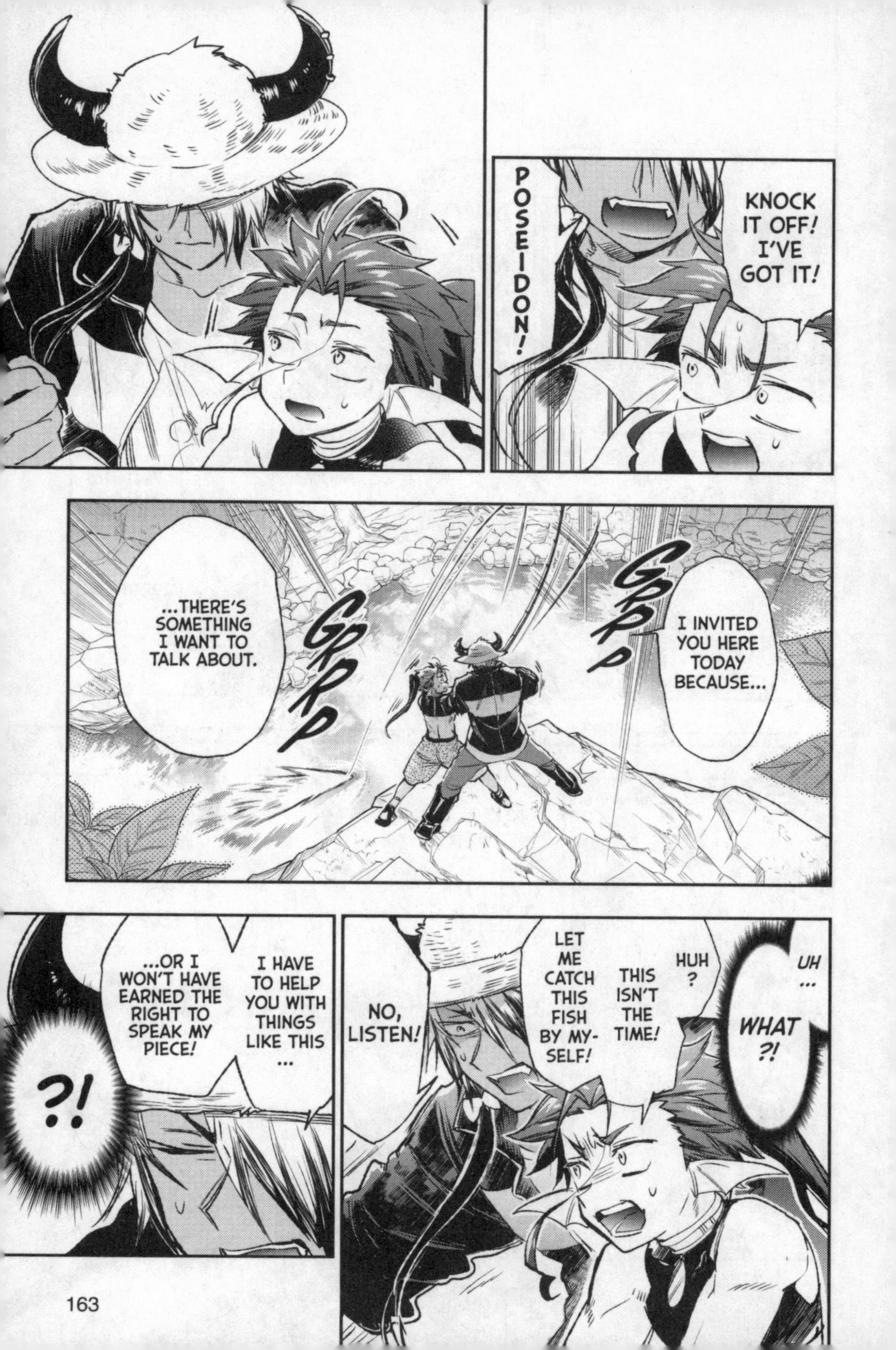
KNOCK IT OFF! I'VE GOT IT!
POSEIDON!
I INVITED YOU HERE TODAY BECAUSE...
GRRP
...THERE'S SOMETHING I WANT TO TALK ABOUT.
GRRP
UH... WHAT?!
HUH?
THIS ISN'T THE TIME!
LET ME CATCH THIS FISH BY MY-SELF!
NO, LISTEN!
I HAVE TO HELP YOU WITH THINGS LIKE THIS...
...OR I WON'T HAVE EARNED THE RIGHT TO SPEAK MY PIECE!
?!

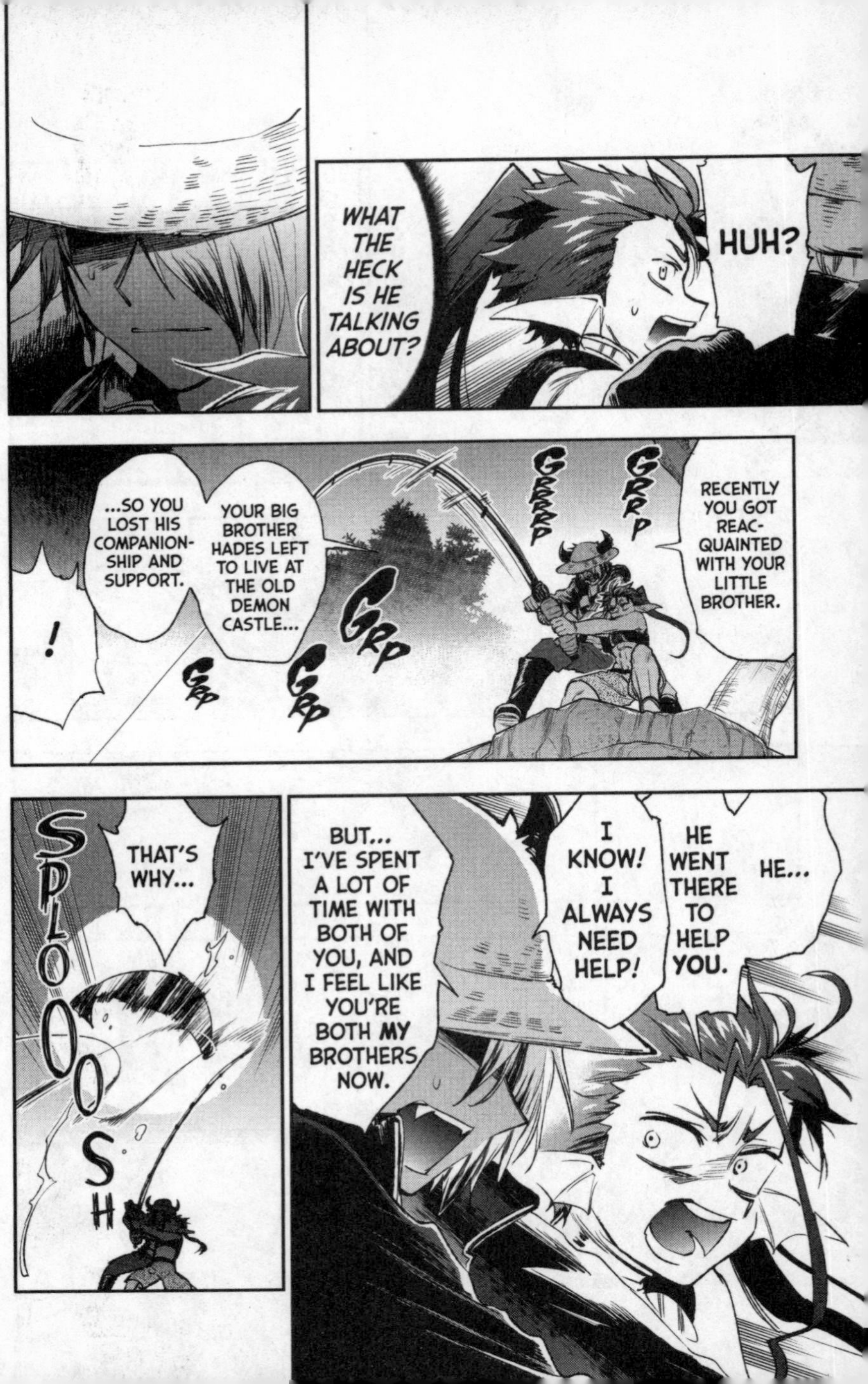
HUH?
WHAT THE HECK IS HE TALKING ABOUT?
RECENTLY YOU GOT REACQUAINTED WITH YOUR LITTLE BROTHER.
GRRP
GRRRRP
YOUR BIG BROTHER HADES LEFT TO LIVE AT THE OLD DEMON CASTLE...
...SO YOU LOST HIS COMPANIONSHIP AND SUPPORT.
GRP
GRP
GRP
!
HE...
HE WENT THERE TO HELP YOU.
I KNOW! I ALWAYS NEED HELP!
BUT... I'VE SPENT A LOT OF TIME WITH BOTH OF YOU, AND I FEEL LIKE YOU'RE BOTH MY BROTHERS NOW.
THAT'S WHY...
SPLOOOOSH

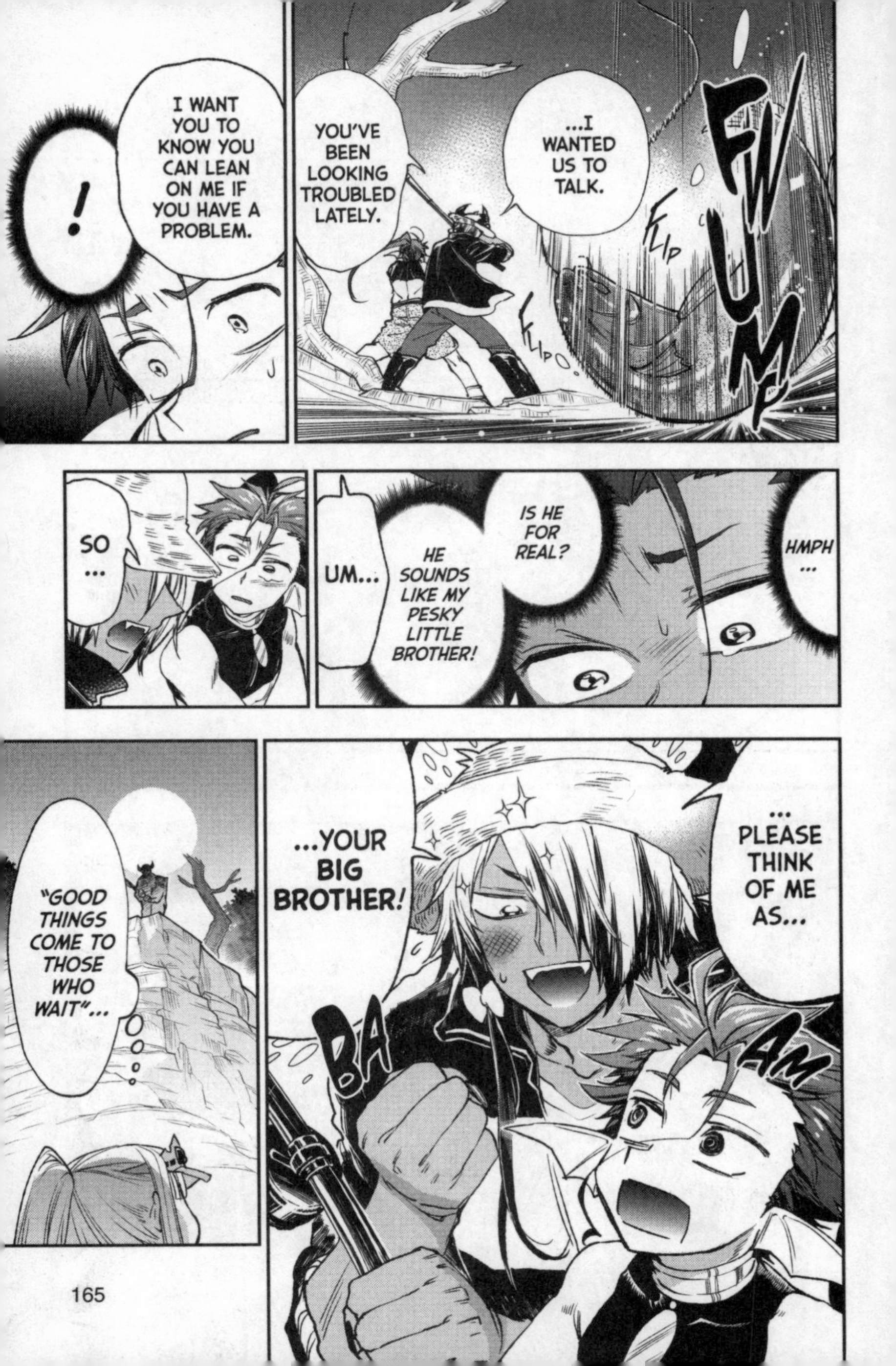
FWUMP
FLIP
FLIP
...I WANTED US TO TALK.
YOU'VE BEEN LOOKING TROUBLED LATELY.
I WANT YOU TO KNOW YOU CAN LEAN ON ME IF YOU HAVE A PROBLEM.
!
HMPH ...
IS HE FOR REAL?
HE SOUNDS LIKE MY PESKY LITTLE BROTHER!
UM...
SO ...
... PLEASE THINK OF ME AS...
...YOUR BIG BROTHER!
BAM
"GOOD THINGS COME TO THOSE WHO WAIT"...

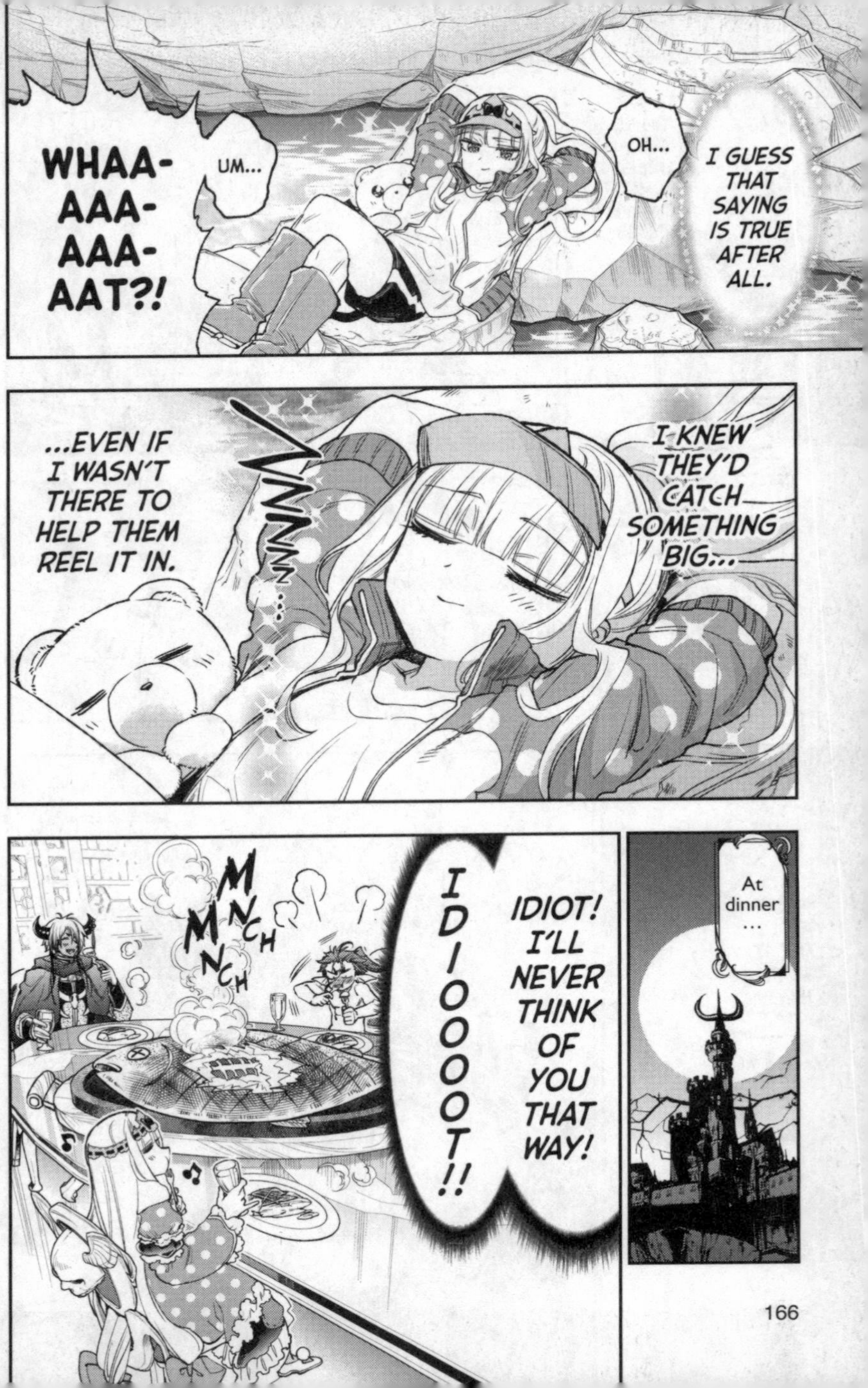
I GUESS THAT SAYING IS TRUE AFTER ALL.
OH...
UM...
WHAA-AAA-AAA-AAT?!
I KNEW THEY'D CATCH SOMETHING BIG...
...EVEN IF I WASN'T THERE TO HELP THEM REEL IT IN.
At dinner ...
IDIOT! I'LL NEVER THINK OF YOU THAT WAY!
IDIOOOOOT!!
MNCH
MNCH

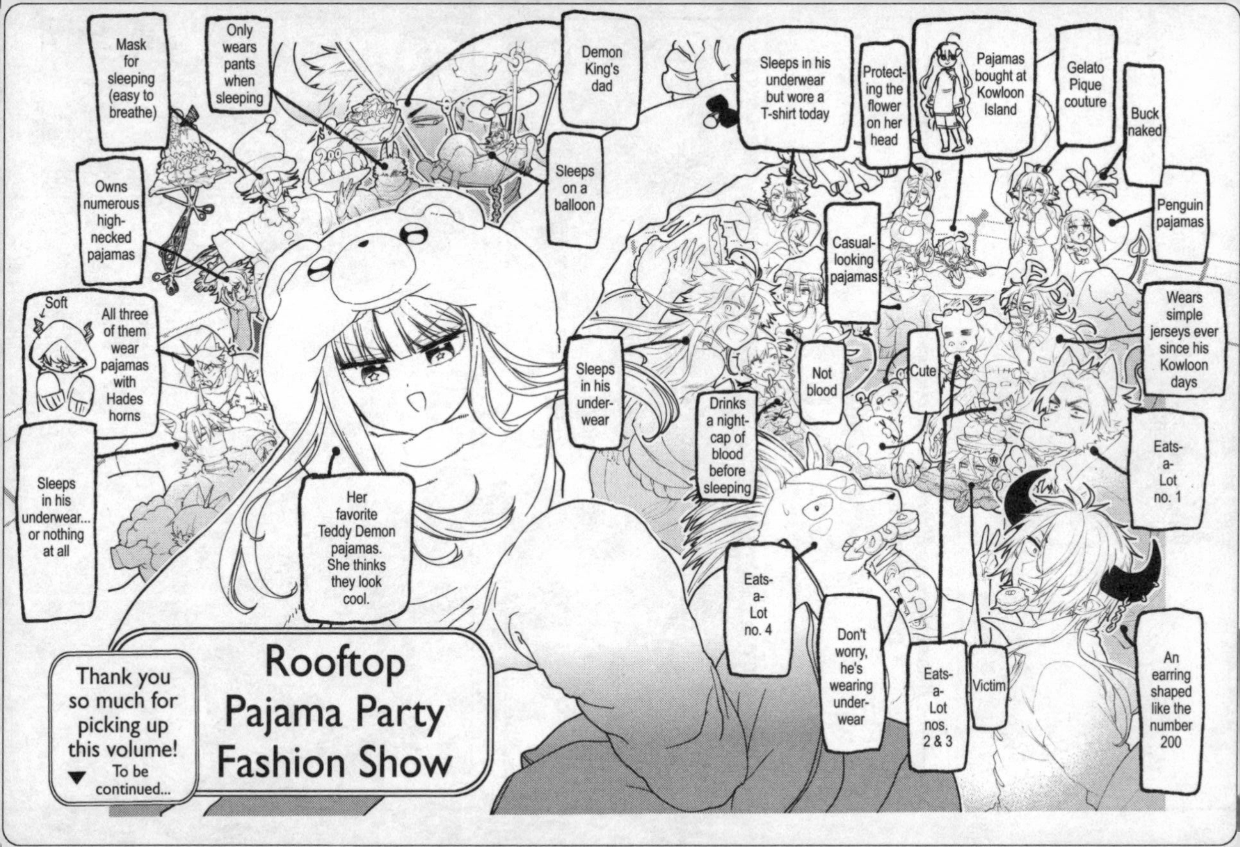
Buck naked
Gelato Pique couture
Pajamas bought at Kowloon Island
Protecting the flower on her head
Sleeps in his underwear but wore a T-shirt today
Demon King's dad
Only wears pants when sleeping
Mask for sleeping (easy to breathe)
Penguin pajamas
Casual-looking pajamas
Sleeps on a balloon
Owns numerous high-necked pajamas
Wears simple jerseys ever since his Kowloon days
Cute
Not blood
Sleeps in his underwear
Soft
All three of them wear pajamas with Hades horns
Eats-a-Lot no. 1
Drinks a nightcap of blood before sleeping
Her favorite Teddy Demon pajamas. She thinks they look cool.
Sleeps in his underwear... or nothing at all
An earring shaped like the number 200
Victim
Eats-a-Lot nos. 2 & 3
Don't worry, he's wearing underwear
Eats-a-Lot no. 4
Rooftop Pajama Party Fashion Show
Thank you so much for picking up this volume!
▼ To be continued...

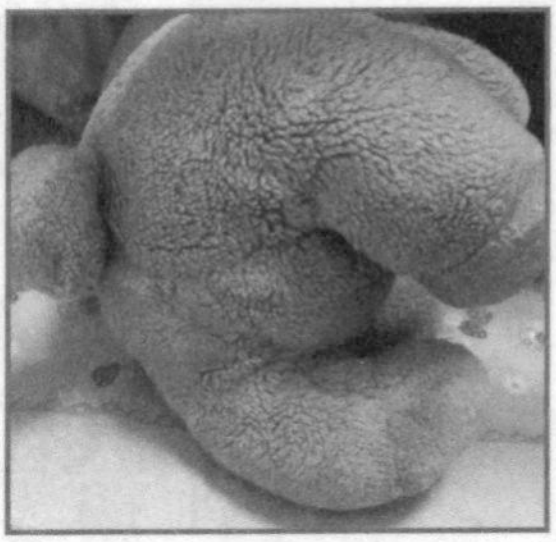

At long last *Sleepy Princess in the Demon Castle* is an anime.*
It's supercute, so please buy the Blu-ray.

— KAGIJI KUMANOMATA

*The creator's commentary refers to the 2020 release in Japan.

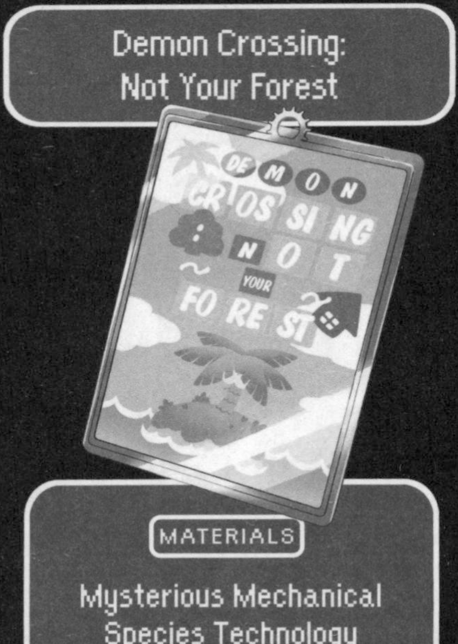

Demon Crossing:
Not Your Forest
MATERIALS
Mysterious Mechanical
Species Technology
Crave Gaming

Those who lurk beneath the cover...

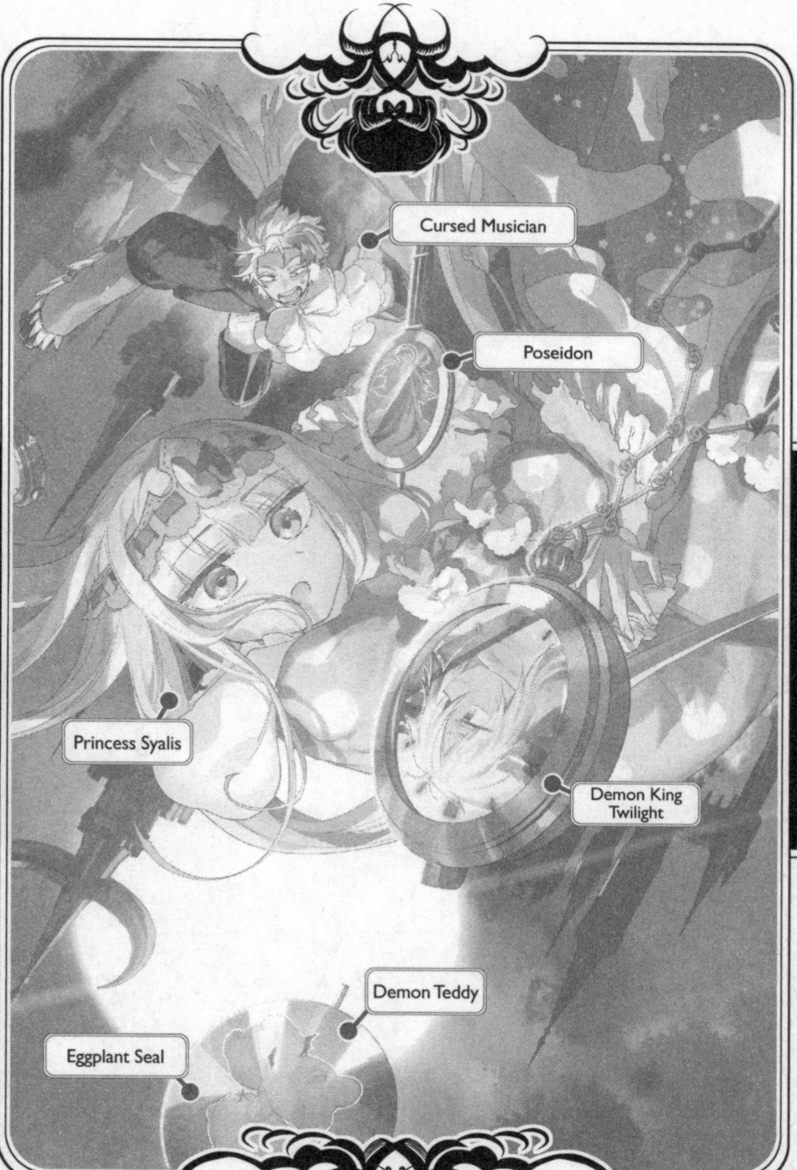
Cursed Musician
Poseidon
Princess Syalis
Demon King Twilight
Demon Teddy
Eggplant Seal

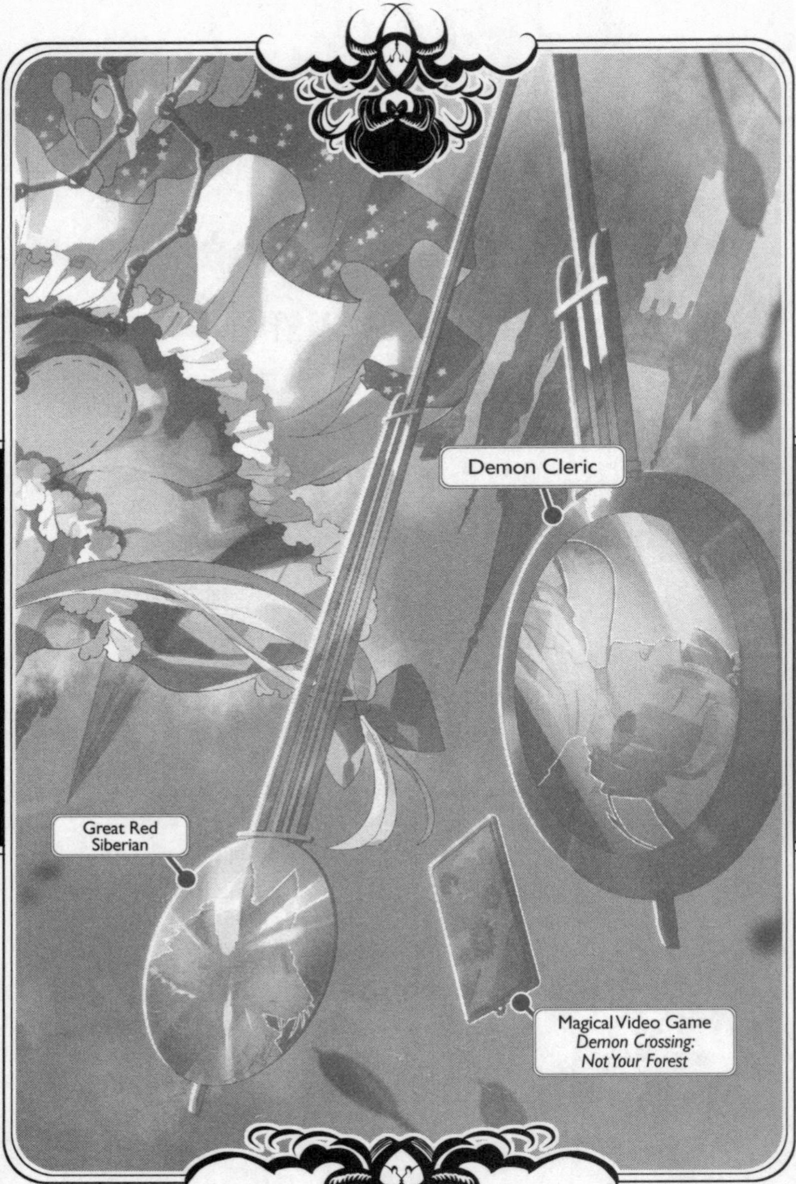
Demon Cleric
Great Red Siberian
Magical Video Game *Demon Crossing: Not Your Forest*

SLEEPY PRINCESS IN THE DEMON CASTLE

16

Shonen Sunday Edition

STORY AND ART BY

KAGIJI KUMANOMATA

MAOUJO DE OYASUMI Vol. 16
by Kagiji KUMANOMATA
© 2016 Kagiji KUMANOMATA
All rights reserved.
Original Japanese edition published by SHOGAKUKAN.
English translation rights in the United States of America, Canada,
the United Kingdom, Ireland, Australia and New Zealand arranged
with SHOGAKUKAN.

TRANSLATION **TETSUICHIRO MIYAKI**

ENGLISH ADAPTATION **ANNETTE ROMAN**

TOUCH-UP ART & LETTERING **JAMES GAUBATZ**

COVER & INTERIOR DESIGN **ALICE LEWIS**

EDITOR **ANNETTE ROMAN**

Printed in Canada

Published by VIZ Media, LLC
P.O. Box 77010
San Francisco, CA 94107

10 9 8 7 6 5 4 3 2 1
First printing, December 2021

VIZ MEDIA

viz.com

SHONEN SUNDAY

shonensunday.com

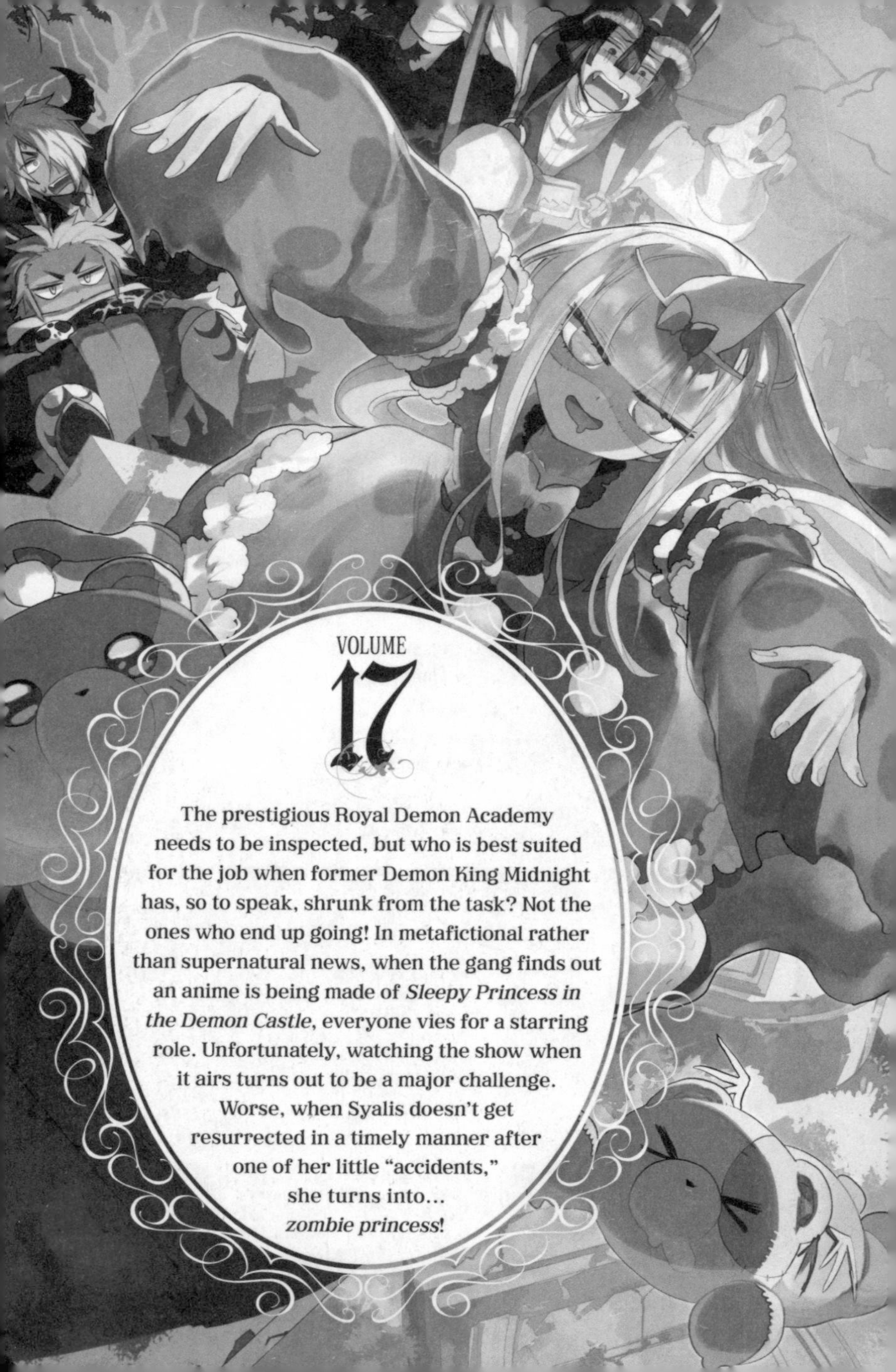

VOLUME

17

The prestigious Royal Demon Academy needs to be inspected, but who is best suited for the job when former Demon King Midnight has, so to speak, shrunk from the task? Not the ones who end up going! In metafictional rather than supernatural news, when the gang finds out an anime is being made of *Sleepy Princess in the Demon Castle*, everyone vies for a starring role. Unfortunately, watching the show when it airs turns out to be a major challenge. Worse, when Syalis doesn't get resurrected in a timely manner after one of her little "accidents," she turns into... *zombie princess*!

Komi Can't Communicate

Story & Art by Tomohito Oda

The journey to a hundred friends begins with a single conversation.

Socially anxious high school student Shoko Komi's greatest dream is to make some friends, but everyone at school mistakes her crippling social anxiety for cool reserve. With the whole student body keeping its distance and Komi unable to utter a single word, friendship might be forever beyond her reach.

SURPRISE!

You may be reading the wrong way!

It's true: In keeping with the original Japanese comic format, this book reads from right to left—so action, sound effects, and word balloons are completely reversed. This preserves the orientation of the original artwork—plus, it's fun! Check out the diagram shown here to get the hang of things, and then turn to the other side of the book to get started!

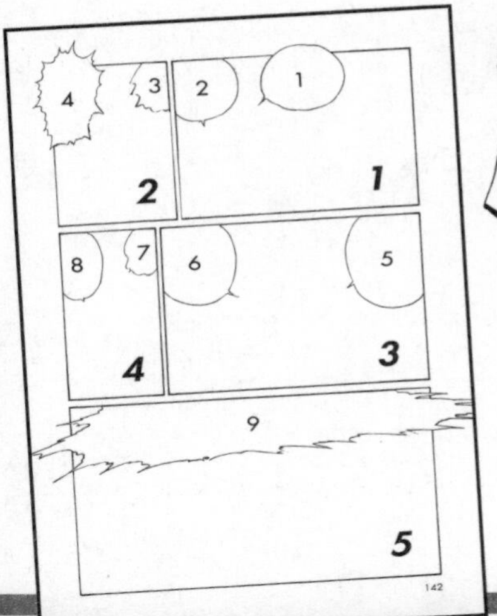

1
1
2
2
3
4
3
5
6
4
7
8
5
9
142

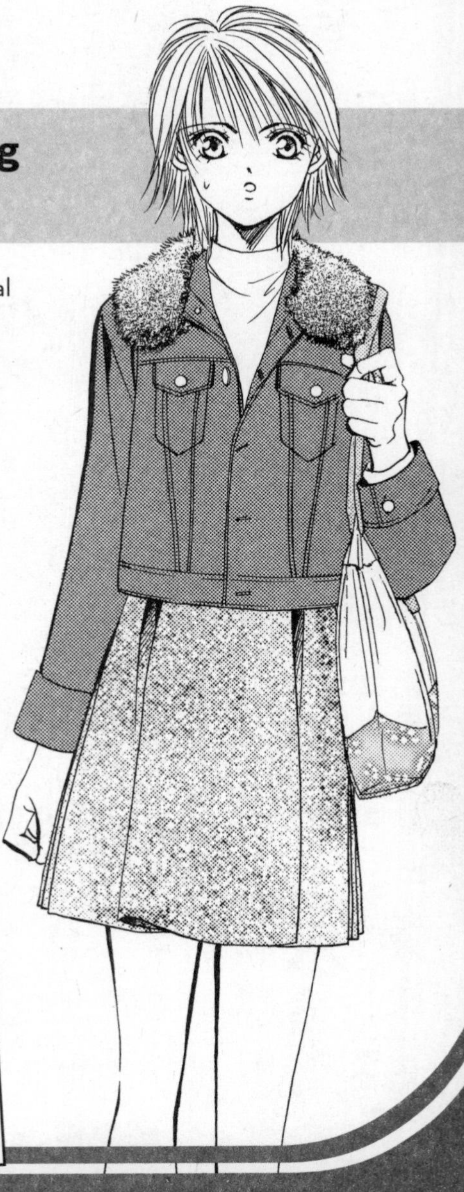

IDOL dreams

STORY & ART BY
ARINA TANEMURA

At age 31, office worker Chikage Deguchi feels she missed her chances at love and success. When word gets out that she's a virgin, Chikage is humiliated and wishes she could turn back time to when she was still young and popular. She takes an experimental drug that changes her appearance back to when she was 15. Now Chikage is determined to pursue everything she missed out on all those years ago—including becoming a star!

Thirty One Idream © Arina Tanemura 2014/HAKUSENSHA, Inc.